SEVENTH EDITION

iOS 14 Programming Fundamentals with Swift

Swift, Xcode, and Cocoa Basics

Matt Neuburg

Beijing · Boston · Farnham · Sebastopol · Tokyo

iOS 14 Programming Fundamentals with Swift, Seventh Edition

by Matt Neuburg

Copyright © 2021 Matt Neuburg. All rights reserved.

Printed in the United States of America.

Published by O'Reilly Media, Inc., 1005 Gravenstein Highway North, Sebastopol, CA 95472.

O'Reilly books may be purchased for educational, business, or sales promotional use. Online editions are also available for most titles (*http://oreilly.com*). For more information, contact our corporate/institutional sales department: 800-998-9938 or *corporate@oreilly.com*.

Editor: Rachel Roumeliotis	**Indexer:** Matt Neuburg
Production Editor: Kristen Brown	**Cover Designer:** Karen Montgomery
Proofreader: O'Reilly Production Services	**Interior Designer:** David Futato
Illustrator: Matt Neuburg	

April 2015:	First Edition
October 2015:	Second Edition
October 2016:	Third Edition
October 2017:	Fourth Edition
September 2018:	Fifth Edition
October 2019:	Sixth Edition
October 2020:	Seventh Edition

Revision History for the Seventh Edition

2020-09-23:   First Release

See *http://oreilly.com/catalog/errata.csp?isbn=9781492092094* for release details.

ISBN: 978-1-492-09209-4

[GP]

Table of Contents

Part I.   Language

Part II. IDE

Part III. Cocoa

Preface

Ten years ago, in July of 2010, Chris Lattner created a folder on his computer called *Shiny,* and a new computer language was born. Four years later, in 2014, that language, renamed Swift, was introduced to the public, and was greeted with a mixture of surprise and excitement — and skepticism.

Prior to that moment, Cocoa programming, on iOS and before that on Mac OS, had always been done chiefly in Objective-C. The Cocoa frameworks that give an iOS app its functionality are based on Objective-C; they expect to be spoken to in Objective-C. The tradition of using Objective-C was long and deeply ingrained. For all its faults, Objective-C was the language we had all learned to live with as the price of programming Cocoa. Could Cocoa be spoken to in a whole new language? Could this new language replace Objective-C as the iOS developer's language of choice?

No one knew. I certainly didn't know! So the first thing I did, as an experiment, was to try translating my own existing iOS apps into Swift. Not only was I able to do it, but I found the new Swift versions easier to understand and maintain than their Objective-C originals. From that moment, I was convinced that the vast majority of new iOS programmers would hitherto adopt Swift. I was right.

Swift is a superb language to learn, even (perhaps especially) if you've never programmed before, and is the easiest and clearest way to program iOS. It has these salient features:

Object-orientation

   Swift is a modern, object-oriented language. It is *purely* object-oriented: "Everything is an object."

Clarity

   Swift is easy to read and easy to write. Its syntax is clear, consistent, and explicit, with few hidden shortcuts and minimal syntactic trickery.

Safety

> Swift enforces strong typing to ensure that it knows, and that you know, what the type of every object reference is at every moment.

Economy

> Swift is a fairly small language, providing some basic types and functionalities and no more. The rest must be provided by your code, or by libraries of code that you use — such as Cocoa.

Memory management

> Swift manages memory automatically. You will rarely have to concern yourself with memory management.

Cocoa compatibility

> The Cocoa APIs are written primarily in C and Objective-C. Swift is explicitly designed to interface with most of the Cocoa APIs.

Earlier editions of this book, before 2014, taught the reader Objective-C. After 2014, they teach Swift. This edition is geared to Swift 5.3. The Swift language has reached a high state of maturity. It has achieved ABI stability, which means that the Swift language has become part of the system. Swift apps are smaller and faster than ever.

The Foundation and Cocoa APIs, however, are still written in C and Objective-C. To interact with them, you might have to know what those languages would expect. Therefore in this book I describe Objective-C in enough detail to allow you to read it when you encounter it in the documentation and on the internet, and I occasionally show some Objective-C code. Part III, on Cocoa, is largely about learning to think the way Objective-C thinks — because the structure and behavior of the Cocoa APIs are fundamentally based on Objective-C. And the book ends with an appendix that details how Swift and Objective-C communicate with one another, as well as explaining how your app can be written partly in Swift and partly in Objective-C.

The Scope of This Book

This book is intended to accompany and precede *Programming iOS 14*, which picks up where this book leaves off. If writing an iOS program is like building a house of bricks, this book teaches you what a brick is and how to handle it, while *Programming iOS 14* shows you some actual bricks and tells you how to assemble them.

When you have read this book, you'll know about Swift, Xcode, and the underpinnings of the Cocoa framework, and you will be ready to proceed directly to *Programming iOS 14*. Conversely, *Programming iOS 14* assumes a knowledge of this book; it begins, like Homer's *Iliad*, in the middle of the story, with the reader jumping with all four feet into views and view controllers, and with a knowledge of the language and the Xcode IDE already presupposed. If you started reading *Programming iOS 14* and wondered about such unexplained matters as Swift language basics, the UIApplicationMain function, the nib-loading mechanism, Cocoa patterns of delegation and notification, and retain cycles, wonder no longer — I didn't explain them there because I do explain them here.

This book doesn't show how to write any particularly interesting iOS apps, but it does constantly use my own real apps and real programming situations to illustrate and motivate its explanations, as it teaches you the underlying basis of iOS programming. It has three parts:

- Part I introduces the Swift language, from the ground up — I do not assume that you know any other programming languages. My way of teaching Swift is different from other treatments, such as Apple's; it is systematic and Euclidean, with pedagogical building blocks piled on one another in what I regard as the most helpful order. At the same time, I have tried to confine myself to the essentials. Swift is not a big language, but it has some subtle and unusual corners that you probably don't need to know about. Also, I never mention Swift playgrounds or the REPL. My focus here is real-life iOS programming, and my explanation of Swift concentrates on the practical aspects of the language that actually come into play in the course of programming iOS.

- Part II turns to Xcode, the world in which all iOS programming ultimately takes place. It explains what an Xcode project is and how it is transformed into an app, and how to work comfortably and nimbly with Xcode to consult the documentation and to write, navigate, and debug code, as well as how to bring your app through the subsequent stages of running on a device and submission to the App Store. There is also a chapter on nibs and the nib editor (Interface Builder), including outlets and actions as well as the mechanics of nib loading (but such specialized topics as autolayout constraints in the nib are postponed to the other book).

- Part III introduces the Cocoa Touch framework. The Foundation and UIKit frameworks, and other frameworks that they entail, constitute Cocoa, which provides the underlying functionality that any iOS app needs to have. To use a framework effectively, you have to think the way the framework thinks, put your code where the framework expects it, and fulfill many obligations imposed on you by the framework. Also, Cocoa uses Objective-C, so you need to know how your Swift code will interface with Cocoa's features and behaviors. Cocoa provides important foundational classes and adds linguistic and architectural devices such as categories, protocols, delegation, and notifications, as well as the pervasive responsibilities of memory management. Key–value coding and key–value observing are also discussed here.

The last chapter of Part III is about the general problem of how objects can refer to one another in an iOS program. In addition to the traditional Cocoa-based solutions, I also discuss the new Swift Combine framework. Also, in June of 2019, Apple introduced SwiftUI. It constitutes an alternative to UIKit and Cocoa, with a completely different programming paradigm for constructing apps. I do not teach SwiftUI in this book — that would require another entire book — but I do explain its chief linguistic features, and I talk about its solutions to the problem of communicating between objects within an iOS app and how they differ from Cocoa patterns.

From the Preface to the First Edition (Programming iOS 4)

The popularity of the iPhone, with its largely free or very inexpensive apps, and the subsequent popularity of the iPad, have brought and will continue to bring into the fold many new programmers who see programming for these devices as worthwhile and doable, even though they may not have felt the same way about OS X. Apple's own annual WWDC developer conventions have reflected this trend, with their emphasis shifted from OS X to iOS instruction.

The widespread eagerness to program iOS, however, though delightful on the one hand, has also fostered a certain tendency to try to run without first learning to walk. iOS gives the programmer mighty powers that can seem as limitless as imagination itself, but it also has fundamentals. I often see questions online from programmers who are evidently deep into the creation of some interesting app, but who are stymied in a way that reveals quite clearly that they are unfamiliar with the basics of the very world in which they are so happily cavorting.

It is this state of affairs that has motivated me to write this book, which is intended to ground the reader in the fundamentals of iOS. Here I have attempted to marshal and expound, in what I hope is a pedagogically helpful and instructive yet ruthlessly Euclidean and logical order, the principles and elements on which sound iOS programming rests. My hope, as with my previous books, is that you will both read this book cover to cover (learning something new often enough to keep you turning the pages) and keep it by you as a handy reference.

This book is not intended to disparage Apple's own documentation and example projects. They are wonderful resources and have become more wonderful as time goes on. I have depended heavily on them in the preparation of this book. But I also find that they don't fulfill the same function as a reasoned, ordered presentation of the facts. The online documentation must make assumptions as to how much you already know; it can't guarantee that you'll approach it in a given order. And online documentation is more suitable to reference than to instruction. A fully written example, no matter how well commented, is difficult to follow; it demonstrates, but it does not teach.

A book, on the other hand, has numbered chapters and sequential pages; I can assume you know views before you know view controllers for the simple reason that Part I precedes Part II. And along with facts, I also bring to the table a degree of experience, which I try to communicate to you. Throughout this book you'll find me referring to "common beginner mistakes"; in most cases, these are mistakes that I have made myself, in addition to seeing others make them. I try to tell you what the pitfalls are because I assume that, in the course of things, you will otherwise fall into them just as naturally as I did as I was learning. You'll also see me construct many examples piece by piece or extract and explain just one tiny portion of a larger app. It is not a massive finished program that teaches programming, but an exposition of the thought process that developed that program. It is this thought process, more than anything else, that I hope you will gain from reading this book.

Versions

This book is geared to Swift 5.3, iOS 14, and Xcode 12.

In general, only very minimal attention is given to earlier versions of iOS and Xcode. Earlier versions can be very different from the current version, and it would be impossible to go into detail about all that has changed over the years. Besides, that information is readily and compendiously available in my earlier books. Recent innovations are called out clearly. The book does contain some advice about backward compatibility (especially in Chapter 9).

I generally give method names in Swift, in the style of a function reference (as described in Chapter 2) — that is, the name plus parentheses containing the parameter labels followed by colon. Now and then, if a method is already under discussion and there is no ambiguity, I'll use the bare name. In a few places, such as Appendix A, where the Objective-C language is explicitly under discussion, I use Objective-C method names.

I have tried to keep my code up-to-date right up to the moment when the manuscript left my hands; but if, at some future time, a new version of Xcode is released along with a new version of Swift, some of the code in this book, and even some information about Swift itself, might be slightly incorrect. Please make allowances, and be prepared to compensate.

Screenshots of Xcode were taken using Xcode 12 under macOS 11 Big Sur. I have waited until the last moment before publication to take these screenshots; I don't expect the interface to have changed significantly by the time you read this, and if it does, the difference shouldn't cause any confusion.

Acknowledgments

This book was written with the aid of some wonderful software:

- Git (*http://git-scm.com*)
- Sourcetree (*http://www.sourcetreeapp.com*)
- TextMate (*http://macromates.com*)
- AsciiDoc (*http://www.methods.co.nz/asciidoc*)
- Asciidoctor (*http://asciidoctor.org*)
- BBEdit (*http://barebones.com/products/bbedit*)
- EasyFind (*https://www.devontechnologies.com/support/download*)
- Snapz Pro X (*http://www.ambrosiasw.com*)
- GraphicConverter (*http://www.lemkesoft.com*)
- OmniGraffle (*http://www.omnigroup.com*)

At O'Reilly Media, many people have made writing this book fun and easy; particular thanks go to Kristen Brown, Rachel Roumeliotis, Dan Fauxsmith, Adam Witwer, Nick Adams, Heather Scherer, Melanie Yarbrough, Sarah Schneider, and Sanders Kleinfeld. My first editor was Brian Jepson; his influence is present throughout.

Finally, a special thanks to my beloved wife, Charlotte Wilson, for her sharp eye, her critical ear, and her unflagging encouragement. This book could not have been written without her.

Conventions Used in This Book

The following typographical conventions are used in this book:

Italic

> Indicates new terms, URLs, email addresses, filenames, and file extensions.

`Constant width`

> Used for program listings, as well as within paragraphs to refer to program elements such as variable or function names, databases, data types, environment variables, statements, and keywords.

`Constant width bold`

> Shows commands or other text that should be typed literally by the user.

`Constant width italic`

> Shows text that should be replaced with user-supplied values or by values determined by context.

This element signifies a tip or suggestion.

 This element signifies a general note.

 This element indicates a warning or caution.

Using Code Examples

Supplemental material (code examples, exercises, etc.) is available for download at *http://github.com/mattneub/Programming-iOS-Book-Examples*.

This book is here to help you get your job done. In general, if example code is offered with this book, you may use it in your programs and documentation. You do not need to contact us for permission unless you're reproducing a significant portion of the code. For example, writing a program that uses several chunks of code from this book does not require permission. Selling or distributing a CD-ROM of examples from O'Reilly books does require permission. Answering a question by citing this book and quoting example code does not require permission. Incorporating a significant amount of example code from this book into your product's documentation does require permission.

We appreciate, but do not require, attribution. An attribution usually includes the title, author, publisher, and ISBN. For example: "*iOS 14 Programming Fundamentals with Swift* by Matt Neuburg (O'Reilly). Copyright 2021 Matt Neuburg, 978-1-492-09209-4."

If you feel your use of code examples falls outside fair use or the permission given above, feel free to contact us at *permissions@oreilly.com*.

O'Reilly Online Learning

 For almost 40 years, *O'Reilly Media* has provided technology and business training, knowledge, and insight to help companies succeed.

Our unique network of experts and innovators share their knowledge and expertise through books, articles, and our online learning platform. O'Reilly's online learning platform gives you on-demand access to live training courses, in-depth learning paths, interactive coding environments, and a vast collection of text and video from

O'Reilly and 200+ other publishers. For more information, please visit *http://oreilly.com*.

How to Contact Us

Please address comments and questions concerning this book to the publisher:

O'Reilly Media, Inc.
1005 Gravenstein Highway North
Sebastopol, CA 95472
800-998-9938 (in the United States or Canada)
707-829-0515 (international or local)
707-829-0104 (fax)

We have a web page for this book, where we list errata, examples, and any additional information. You can access this page at *https://oreil.ly/ios14-prog-fundamentals*.

To comment or ask technical questions about this book, send email to *bookquestions@oreilly.com*.

For news and more information about our books and courses, see our website at *http://www.oreilly.com*.

Find us on Facebook: *http://facebook.com/oreilly*

Follow us on Twitter: *http://twitter.com/oreillymedia*

Watch us on YouTube: *http://www.youtube.com/oreillymedia*

PART I

Language

This part of the book teaches the Swift language, from the ground up. The description is rigorous and orderly. Here you'll become sufficiently conversant with Swift to be comfortable with it, so that you can proceed to the practical business of actual programming.

- Chapter 1 surveys the structure of a Swift program, both physically and conceptually. You'll learn how Swift code files are organized, and you'll be introduced to the most important underlying concepts of the object-oriented Swift language: variables and functions, scopes and namespaces, object types and their instances.

- Chapter 2 explores Swift functions. We start with the basics of how functions are declared and called; then we discuss parameters — external parameter names, default parameters, and variadic parameters. Then we dive deep into the power of Swift functions, with an explanation of functions inside functions, functions as first-class values, anonymous functions, functions as closures, curried functions, and function references and selectors.

- Chapter 3 starts with Swift variables — their scope and lifetime, and how they are declared and initialized, along with features such as computed variables and setter observers. Then some important built-in Swift types are introduced, including Booleans, numbers, strings, ranges, tuples, and Optionals.

- Chapter 4 is all about Swift object types — classes, structs, and enums. It explains how these three object types work, and how you declare, instantiate, and use them. Then it proceeds to polymorphism and casting, protocols, generics, and extensions. The chapter concludes with a discussion of Swift's umbrella types, such as Any and AnyObject, and collection types — Array, Dictionary, and Set (including option sets).

- Chapter 5 is a miscellany. We start with Swift's flow control structures for branching, looping, and jumping, including error handling. Then I describe Swift access control (privacy), introspection (reflection), and how to create your own operators. Next I talk about Swift memory management. The chapter ends with a survey of some recently added Swift language features: synthesized protocol implementations, key paths, instances as functions, dynamic members, property wrappers, custom string interpolation, reverse generics, function builders, and Result.

CHAPTER 1

The Architecture of Swift

It will be useful at the outset for you to have a general sense of how the Swift language is constructed and what a Swift-based iOS program looks like. This chapter will survey the overall architecture and nature of the Swift language. Subsequent chapters will fill in the details.

Ground of Being

A complete Swift command is a *statement*. A Swift text file consists of multiple *lines* of text. Line breaks are meaningful. The typical layout of a program is one statement, one line:

```
print("hello")
print("world")
```

(The `print` command provides instant feedback in the Xcode console.)

You can combine more than one statement on a line, but then you need to put a semicolon between them:

```
print("hello"); print("world")
```

You are free to put a semicolon at the end of a statement that is last or alone on its line, but no one ever does (except out of habit, because C and Objective-C *require* the semicolon):

```
print("hello");
print("world");
```

Conversely, a single statement can be broken into multiple lines, to prevent long statements from becoming long lines. But you should try to do this at sensible places so as not to confuse Swift. After an opening parenthesis is a good place:

```
print(
    "world")
```

Comments are everything after two slashes in a line (so-called C++-style comments):

```
print("world") // this is a comment, so Swift ignores it
```

You can also enclose comments in /*...*/, as in C. Unlike C, C-style comments can be nested.

Many constructs in Swift use curly braces as delimiters:

```
class Dog {
    func bark() {
        print("woof")
    }
}
```

By convention, the contents of curly braces are preceded and followed by line breaks and are indented for clarity, as shown in the preceding code. Xcode will help impose this convention, but the truth is that Swift doesn't care, and layouts like this are legal (and are sometimes more convenient):

```
class Dog { func bark() { print("woof") }}
```

Swift is a *compiled* language. This means that your code must *build* — passing through the compiler and being turned from text into some lower-level form that a computer can understand — before it can *run* and actually do the things it says to do. The Swift compiler is very strict; in the course of writing a program, you will often try to build and run, only to discover that you can't even build in the first place, because the compiler will flag some *error*, which you will have to fix if you want the code to run. Less often, the compiler will let you off with a *warning*; the code can run, but in general you should take warnings seriously and fix whatever they are telling you about. The strictness of the compiler is one of Swift's greatest strengths, and provides your code with a large measure of audited correctness even before it ever runs.

The Swift compiler's error and warning messages range from the insightful to the obtuse to the downright misleading. You will sometimes know that *something* is wrong with a line of code, but the Swift compiler might not be telling you clearly exactly *what* is wrong or even *where* in the line to focus your attention (though Xcode 12 contains some significant improvements in this regard). My advice in these situations is to pull the line apart into several lines of simpler code until you reach a point where you can work out what the issue is. Try to love the compiler even when its messages seem mysterious; remember, it knows more than you do.

Everything Is an Object?

In Swift, "everything is an object." That's a boast common to various modern object-oriented languages, but what does it mean? Well, that depends on what you mean by "object" — and what you mean by "everything."

Let's start by stipulating that an object, roughly speaking, is something you can send a message to. A message, roughly speaking, is an imperative instruction. For example, you can give commands to a dog: "Bark!" "Sit!" In this analogy, those phrases are messages, and the dog is the object to which you are sending those messages.

In Swift, the syntax of message-sending is *dot-notation*. We start with the object; then there's a dot (a period); then there's the message. (Some messages are also followed by parentheses, but ignore them for now; the full syntax of message-sending is one of those details we'll be filling in later.) This is valid Swift syntax:

```
fido.bark()
rover.sit()
```

By the way, a dot is also another good place to break up a long line (*before* the dot):

```
fido
    .bark()
```

The idea of *everything* being an object is a way of suggesting that even "primitive" linguistic entities can be sent messages. Take, for example, 1. It appears to be a literal digit and no more. It will not surprise you, if you've ever used any programming language, that you can say things like this in Swift:

```
let sum = 1 + 2
```

But it *is* surprising to find that 1 can be followed by a dot and a message. This is legal and meaningful in Swift (don't worry about what it actually means):

```
let s = 1.description
```

But we can go further. Return to that innocent-looking 1 + 2 from our earlier code. It turns out that this is actually a kind of syntactic trickery, a convenient way of expressing and hiding what's really going on. Just as 1 is actually an object, + is actually a message; but it's a message with special syntax (*operator* syntax). In Swift, every noun is an object, and every verb is a message.

Perhaps the ultimate acid test for whether something is an object in Swift is whether you can modify it. An object type can be *extended* in Swift, meaning that you can define your own messages on that type. For example, you can't normally send the say-Hello message to a number, but you can change a number type so that you can:

```
extension Int {
    func sayHello() {
        print("Hello, I'm \(self)")
    }
}
1.sayHello() // outputs: "Hello, I'm 1"
```

In Swift, then, 1 is an object. In some languages, such as Objective-C, it clearly is not; it is a "primitive" or *scalar* built-in data type. So the distinction being drawn here is between object types on the one hand and scalars on the other. In Swift, there are no scalars; *all* types are ultimately object types. That's what "everything is an object" really means.

Three Flavors of Object Type

If you know Objective-C or some other object-oriented language, you may be surprised by Swift's notion of what *kind* of object 1 is. In many languages, such as Objective-C, an object is a *class* or an instance of a class (I'll explain later what an instance is). Swift has classes, but 1 in Swift is not a class or an instance of a class: the type of 1, namely Int, is a *struct*, and 1 is an instance of a struct. And Swift has yet another kind of thing you can send messages to, called an *enum*.

So Swift has three kinds of object type: classes, structs, and enums. I like to refer to these as the three *flavors* of object type. Exactly how they differ from one another will emerge in due course. But they are all very definitely object types, and their similarities to one another are far stronger than their differences. For now, just bear in mind that these three flavors exist.

(The fact that a struct or enum is an object type in Swift will surprise you particularly if you know Objective-C. Objective-C has structs and enums, but they are not objects. Swift structs, in particular, are much more important and pervasive than Objective-C structs. This difference between how Swift views structs and enums and how Objective-C views them can matter when you are talking to Cocoa.)

Variables

A variable is a *name* for an object. Technically, it *refers* to an object; it is an object *reference*. Nontechnically, you can think of it as a shoebox into which an object is placed. The object may undergo changes, or it may be replaced inside the shoebox by another object, but the name has an integrity all its own. The object to which the variable refers is the variable's *value*.

In Swift, no variable comes implicitly into existence; all variables must be *declared*. If you need a name for something, you must say "I'm creating a name." You do this with one of two keywords: let or var. In Swift, declaration is usually accompanied by *initialization* — you use an equal sign to give the variable a value immediately, as part of the declaration. These are both variable declarations (and initializations):

```
let one = 1
var two = 2
```

Once the name exists, you are free to use it. We can change the value of two to be the same as the value of one:

```
let one = 1
var two = 2
two = one
```

The last line of that code uses both the name one and the name two declared in the first two lines: the name one, on the right side of the equal sign, is used merely to *refer* to the value inside the shoebox one (namely 1); but the name two, on the left side of the equal sign, is used to *replace* the value inside the shoebox two. Before saying two = one, the value of two was 2; afterward, it is 1.

A statement with a variable name on the left side of an equal sign is called an *assignment*, and the equal sign is the *assignment operator*. The equal sign is not an assertion of equality, as it might be in an algebraic formula; it is a command. It means: "Get the value of what's on the right side of me, and use it to replace the value of what's on the left side of me."

The two kinds of variable declaration differ in that a name declared with let *cannot have its initial value replaced*. A variable declared with let is a *constant*; its value is assigned once and stays. This won't even compile:

```
let one = 1
var two = 2
one = two // compile error
```

It is always possible to declare a name with var to give yourself the most flexibility, but if you know you're never going to replace the initial value of a variable, it's better to use let, as this permits Swift to behave more efficiently — in fact, the Swift compiler will call your attention to any case of your using var where you could have used let, offering to change it for you.

Variables also have a *type*. This type is established when the variable is declared and *can never change*. This won't compile:

```
var two = 2
two = "hello" // compile error
```

Once two is declared and initialized as 2, it is a number (properly speaking, an Int) and it must always be so. You can replace its value with 1 because that's also an Int, but you can't replace its value with "hello" because that's a string (properly speaking, a String) — and a String is not an Int.

Variables literally have a life of their own — more accurately, a *lifetime* of their own. As long as a variable exists, it keeps its value alive. Thus, a variable can be not only a way of conveniently *naming* something, but also a way of *preserving* it. I'll have more to say about that later.

 By convention, type names such as String or Int (or Dog) start with a capital letter; variable names start with a small letter. *Do not violate this convention.* If you do, your code might still compile and run just fine, but I will personally send agents to your house to remove your kneecaps in the dead of night.

Functions

Executable code, like `fido.bark()` or `one = two` or `print("hello")`, cannot go just anywhere in your program. Failure to appreciate this fact is a common beginner mistake, and can result in a mysterious compile error message such as "Expected declaration."

In general, executable code must live inside the body of a *function*. A function is a batch of code that can be told, as a batch, to run. Its body is delimited by curly braces. Typically, a function has a name, and it gets that name through a function declaration. Function declaration syntax is another of those details that will be filled in later, but here's an example:

```
func go() {
    let one = 1
    var two = 2
    two = one
}
```

That describes a sequence of things to do — declare `one`, declare `two`, change the value of `two` to match the value of `one` — and it gives that sequence a *name*, `go`; but it doesn't *perform* the sequence. The sequence is performed when someone *calls* the function. Thus, we might say, elsewhere:

```
go()
```

That is a command to the `go` function that it should actually run. But again, that command is itself executable code, so it cannot live on its own either. It might live in the body of a different function:

```
func doGo() {
    go()
}
```

But wait! This is getting a little nutty. That, too, is just a function declaration; to run it, someone must call `doGo` by saying `doGo()` — and that's executable code too. This seems like some kind of infinite regression; it looks like none of our code will *ever* run. If all executable code has to live in a function, who will tell *any* function to run? The initial impetus must come from somewhere.

In real life, fortunately, this regression problem doesn't arise. Remember that your goal is ultimately to write an iOS app. Your app will be run on an iOS device (or the Simulator) by a runtime that already wants to call certain functions. So you start by writing special functions that you know the runtime itself will call. That gives your app a way to get started and gives you places to put functions that will be called by the runtime at key moments.

 Swift also has a special rule that a file called *main.swift*, exceptionally, *can* have executable code at its top level, outside any function body, and this is the code that actually runs when the program runs. You can construct your app with a *main.swift* file, but in general you won't need to. In the rest of this chapter I'll assume that we are not in a *main.swift* file.

The Structure of a Swift File

A Swift program can consist of one file or many files. In Swift, a file is a meaningful unit, and there are definite rules about the structure of the Swift code that can go inside it. Only certain things can go at the top level of a Swift file — chiefly the following:

Module `import` *statements*
> A module is an even higher-level unit than a file. A module can consist of multiple files, and these can all see each other automatically. Your app's files belong to a single module and can see each other. But a module can't see another module without an `import` statement. That is how you are able to talk to Cocoa in an iOS program: the first line of your file says `import UIKit`.

Variable declarations
> A variable declared at the top level of a file is a *global* variable: all code in any file will be able to see and access it, without explicitly sending a message to any object.

Function declarations
> A function declared at the top level of a file is a *global* function: all code in any file will be able to see and call it, without explicitly sending a message to any object.

Object type declarations
> The declaration for a class, a struct, or an enum.

This is a legal Swift file containing at its top level (just to demonstrate that it can be done) an `import` statement, a variable declaration, a function declaration, a class declaration, a struct declaration, and an enum declaration:

```
import UIKit
var one = 1
func changeOne() {
}
class Manny {
}
struct Moe {
}
enum Jack {
}
```

That's a very silly and mostly empty example, but remember, our goal is to survey the parts of the language and the structure of a file, and the example shows them.

So much for the top level of a file. But now let's talk about what can go inside the curly braces that we see in our example. It turns out that they, too, can all have variable declarations, function declarations, and object type declarations within them! Indeed, *any* structural curly braces can contain such declarations.

But what about executable code? You'll notice that I did *not* say that executable code can go at the top level of a file. That's because it can't! *Only a function body can contain executable code.* A statement like `one = two` or `print("hello")` is executable code, and can't go at the top level of a file. But in our previous example, `func change-One()` is a function declaration, so executable code *can* go inside its curly braces, because they constitute a function body:

```
var one = 1
// executable code can't go here!
func changeOne() {
    let two = 2 // executable code
    one = two    // executable code
}
```

Similarly, executable code can't go directly inside the curly braces that accompany the `class Manny` declaration; that's the top level of a class declaration, not a function body. But a class declaration can contain a function declaration, and that function declaration *can* contain executable code:

```
class Manny {
    let name = "manny"
    // executable code can't go here!
    func sayName() {
        print(name) // executable code
    }
}
```

To sum up, Example 1-1 is a legal Swift file, schematically illustrating the structural possibilities. (Ignore the hanky-panky with the `name` variable declaration inside the enum declaration for Jack; enum top-level variables have some special rules that I'll explain later.)

Example 1-1. Schematic structure of a legal Swift file

```
import UIKit
var one = 1
func changeOne() {
    let two = 2
    func sayTwo() {
        print(two)
    }
    class Klass {}
    struct Struct {}
    enum Enum {}
    one = two
}
class Manny {
    let name = "manny"
    func sayName() {
        print(name)
    }
    class Klass {}
    struct Struct {}
    enum Enum {}
}
struct Moe {
    let name = "moe"
    func sayName() {
        print(name)
    }
    class Klass {}
    struct Struct {}
    enum Enum {}
}
enum Jack {
    var name : String {
        return "jack"
    }
    func sayName() {
        print(name)
    }
    class Klass {}
    struct Struct {}
    enum Enum {}
}
```

Obviously, we can recurse down as far we like: we could have a class declaration containing a class declaration containing a class declaration, and so on. But I'm sure you have the idea by now, so there's no point illustrating further.

Scope and Lifetime

In a Swift program, things have a *scope*. This refers to their ability to be seen by other things. Things are nested inside of other things, making a nested hierarchy of things. The rule is that things can see things *at their own level and at a higher level containing them*. The levels are:

- A module is a scope.

- A file is a scope.

- Curly braces are a scope.

When something is declared, it is declared at some level within that hierarchy. Its place in the hierarchy — its scope — determines whether it can be seen by other things.

Look again at Example 1-1. Inside the declaration of Manny is a name variable declaration and a sayName function declaration; the code *inside* sayName's curly braces can see things *outside* those curly braces *at a higher containing level*, and can therefore see the name variable. Similarly, the code inside the body of the changeOne function can see the one variable declared at the top level of the file; indeed, *everything* throughout this file can see the one variable declared at the top level of the file.

Scope is thus a very important way of *sharing information*. Two different functions declared inside Manny would *both* be able to see the name declared at Manny's top level. Code inside Jack and code inside Moe can *both* see the one declared at the file's top level.

Things also have a *lifetime*, which is effectively equivalent to their scope. A thing lives as long as its surrounding scope lives. In Example 1-1, the variable one lives as long as the file lives — namely, as long the program runs. It is global *and persistent*. But the variable name declared at the top level of Manny exists only so long as a Manny instance exists (I'll talk in a moment about what that means).

Things declared at a deeper level live even shorter lifetimes. Consider this code:

```
func silly() {
    if true {
        class Cat {}
        var one = 1
        one = one + 1
    }
}
```

That code is silly, but it's legal: remember, I said that variable declarations, function declarations, and object type declarations can appear in *any* structural curly braces. In that code, the class Cat and the variable one will not even come into existence until someone calls the silly function, and even then they will exist only during the brief instant that the path of code execution passes through the if construct. Suppose the function silly is called; the path of execution then enters the if construct. Here, Cat is declared and comes into existence; then one is declared and comes into existence; then the executable line one = one + 1 is executed; and then the scope ends — and both Cat and one vanish in a puff of smoke. And throughout their brief lives, Cat and one were completely invisible to the rest of the program. (Do you see why?)

Object Members

Inside the three object types (class, struct, and enum), things declared at the top level have special names, mostly for historical reasons. Let's use the Manny class as an example:

```
class Manny {
    let name = "manny"
    func sayName() {
        print(name)
    }
}
```

In that code:

- name is a variable declared at the top level of an object declaration, so it is called a *property* of that object.

- sayName is a function declared at the top level of an object declaration, so it is called a *method* of that object.

Things declared at the top level of an object declaration — properties, methods, and any objects declared at that level — are collectively the *members* of that object. Members have a special significance, because they define the *messages* you are allowed to send to that object!

Namespaces

A *namespace* is a named region of a program. The names of things inside a namespace cannot be reached by things outside it without somehow first passing through the barrier of *saying* that region's name. This is a good thing because it allows the same name to be used in different places without a conflict. Clearly, namespaces and scopes are closely related notions.

Namespaces help to explain the significance of declaring an object at the top level of an object, like this:

```
class Manny {
    class Klass {}
}
```

This way of declaring Klass makes Klass a *nested type*. It effectively "hides" Klass inside Manny. Manny is a namespace! Code *inside* Manny can see (and say) Klass directly. But code outside Manny can't do that. It has to specify the namespace *explicitly* in order to pass through the barrier that the namespace represents. To do so, it must say Manny's name first, followed by a dot, followed by the term Klass. In short, it has to say `Manny.Klass`.

The namespace does not, of itself, provide secrecy or privacy; it's a convenience. In Example 1-1, I gave Manny a Klass class, and I also gave Moe a Klass class. But they don't conflict, because they are in different namespaces, and I can differentiate them, if necessary, as `Manny.Klass` and `Moe.Klass`.

It will not have escaped your attention that the syntax for diving explicitly into a namespace is the message-sending dot-notation syntax. They are, in fact, the same thing.

In effect, message-sending allows you to see into scopes you can't see into otherwise. Code inside Moe can't *automatically* see the Klass declared inside Manny, but it *can* see it by taking one easy extra step, namely by speaking of `Manny.Klass`. It can do *that* because it *can* see Manny (because Manny is declared at a level that code inside Moe can see).

Modules

The top-level namespaces are *modules*. Your app is a module and hence a namespace; that namespace's name is, by default, the name of the app. If my app is called MyApp, then if I declare a class Manny at the top level of a file, that class's *real* name is `MyApp.Manny`. But I don't usually need to use that real name, because my code is already inside the same namespace, and can see the name Manny directly.

When you import a module, all the top-level declarations of *that* module become visible to your code as well, without your having to use the module's namespace explicitly to refer to them. For example, Cocoa's Foundation framework, where NSString lives, is a module. When you program iOS, you will say `import Foundation` (or, more likely, you'll say `import UIKit`, which itself imports Foundation), allowing you to speak of NSString without saying `Foundation.NSString`.

Swift itself is defined in a module — the Swift module. But you don't have to import it, because your code *always implicitly imports the Swift module*. You could make this explicit by starting a file with the line `import Swift`; there is no need to do this, but it does no harm either.

That fact is important, because it solves a major mystery: where do things like `print` come from, and why is it possible to use them outside of any message to any object? `print` is in fact a function declared at the top level of the Swift module, and your code can see the Swift module's top-level declarations because it imports Swift. The `print` function becomes, as far as your code is concerned, an ordinary top-level function like any other; it is global to your code, and your code can speak of it without specifying its namespace. You *can* specify its namespace — it is perfectly legal to say things like `Swift.print("hello")` — but you probably never will, because you won't need to.

Your own app module, however, *overshadows* any modules you import. That means that if you declare a term identical to an imported term, you lose the magical ability to use the imported term without specifying the namespace. If you were to declare a `print` function of your own, it would effectively hide the Swift `print` function; you can still call the Swift `print` function, but now you *have* to use the namespaced `Swift.print` explicitly. Similarly, if you were to declare your own String type, all code that refers to Swift's String type would require you to say `Swift.String`. Nearly always, that sort of thing is accidental and you will prefer that your own terms not conflict with any imported terms.

 You can actually *see* the Swift top-level declarations and read and study them, and this can be a useful thing to do. For example, to see the declaration of `print`, Command-Control-click the term `print` in your code. Behold, there are some Swift top-level declarations! You won't see any executable Swift *code* here, but you will see the declarations for various available Swift terms, including `print`.

Instances

Object types — class, struct, and enum — have an important feature in common: they can be *instantiated*. In effect, when you declare an object type, you are only defining a *type*. To instantiate a type is to make a thing — an *instance* — of that type.

For example, I can declare a Dog class, and I can give my class a method:

```
class Dog {
    func bark() {
        print("woof")
    }
}
```

But I don't actually have any Dog objects in my program yet. I have merely described the *type* of thing a Dog *would* be if I had one. To get an actual Dog, I have to *make* one. The process of making an actual Dog object whose type is the Dog class is the process of instantiating Dog. The result is a new object — a Dog instance.

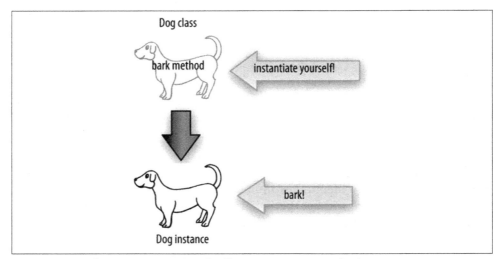

Figure 1-1. Making an instance and calling an instance method

In Swift, instances can be created by using the object type's name as a function name and calling the function. This involves using parentheses. When you append parentheses to the name of an object type, you are sending a very special kind of message to that object type: Instantiate yourself!

So now I'm going to make a Dog instance:

```
let fido = Dog()
```

There's a lot going on in that code! I did two things. I instantiated Dog, causing me to end up with a Dog instance. I also put that Dog instance into a shoebox called `fido` — I declared a variable and initialized the variable by assigning my new Dog instance to it. Now `fido` *is a Dog instance.* (Moreover, because I used `let`, `fido` will always be this same Dog instance. I could have used `var` instead, but even then, initializing `fido` as a Dog instance would mean `fido` could only be some Dog instance after that.)

Now that I have a Dog instance, I can send *instance messages* to it. And what do you suppose they are? They are Dog's properties and methods! For example:

```
let fido = Dog()
fido.bark()
```

That code is legal. Not only that, it is effective: it actually does cause "woof" to appear in the console. I made a Dog and I made it bark! (See Figure 1-1.)

There's an important lesson here, so let me pause to emphasize it. By default, properties and methods are *instance* properties and methods. You can't use them as messages to the object type itself; you have to have an *instance* to send those messages to. As things stand, this is illegal and won't compile:

```
Dog.bark() // compile error
```

It is possible to declare a function `bark` in such a way that saying `Dog.bark()` *is* legal, but that would be a different kind of function — a *class* function or a *static* function — and you would need to say so when you declare it.

The same thing is true of properties. To illustrate, let's give Dog a `name` property:

```
class Dog {
    var name = ""
}
```

That allows me to set a Dog's `name`, but it needs to be an *instance* of Dog:

```
let fido = Dog()
fido.name = "Fido"
```

It is possible to declare a property `name` in such a way that saying `Dog.name` is legal, but that would be a different kind of property — a *class* property or a *static* property — and you would need to say so when you declare it.

Why Instances?

Even if there were no such thing as an instance, an object type is itself an object. We know this because it is possible to send a message to an object type (the phrase `Manny.Klass` is a case in point). Why, then, do instances exist at all?

The answer has mostly to do with the nature of instance properties. The *value* of an instance property is defined with respect to *a particular instance*. This is where instances get their real usefulness and power.

Consider again our Dog class. I'll give it a `name` property and a `bark` method; remember, these are an instance property and an instance method:

```
class Dog {
    var name = ""
    func bark() {
        print("woof")
    }
}
```

A Dog instance comes into existence with a blank `name` (an empty string). But its `name` property is a `var`, so once we have any Dog instance, we can assign to its `name` a new String value:

```
let dog1 = Dog()
dog1.name = "Fido"
```

We can also ask for a Dog instance's `name`:

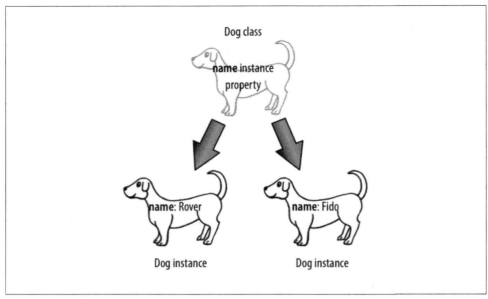

Dog class

name instance property

name: Rover

Dog instance

name: Fido

Dog instance

Figure 1-2. Two dogs with different property values

```
let dog1 = Dog()
dog1.name = "Fido"
print(dog1.name) // "Fido"
```

The important thing is that we can make more than one Dog instance, and that two different Dog instances can have two different name property values (Figure 1-2):

```
let dog1 = Dog()
dog1.name = "Fido"
let dog2 = Dog()
dog2.name = "Rover"
print(dog1.name) // "Fido"
print(dog2.name) // "Rover"
```

Note that a Dog instance's name property has nothing to do with the name of the variable to which a Dog instance is assigned. The variable is just a shoebox. You can pass an instance from one shoebox to another. But the instance itself maintains its own internal integrity:

```
let dog1 = Dog()
dog1.name = "Fido"
var dog2 = Dog()
dog2.name = "Rover"
print(dog1.name) // "Fido"
print(dog2.name) // "Rover"
dog2 = dog1
print(dog2.name) // "Fido"
```

That code didn't change Rover's `name`; it changed which dog was inside the `dog2` shoebox, replacing Rover with Fido.

The full power of object-based programming has now emerged. There is a Dog object type which defines *what it is to be a Dog*. Our declaration of Dog says that any and every Dog instance has a `name` property and a `bark` method. But each Dog instance can have its own `name` property *value*. So multiple instances of the same object type behave alike — both Fido and Rover can bark, and will do so when they are sent the `bark` message — but they are different instances and can have different property values: Fido's `name` is `"Fido"` while Rover's `name` is `"Rover"`.

An instance is responsible not only for the values but also for the *lifetimes* of its properties. Suppose we bring a Dog instance into existence and assign to its `name` property the value `"Fido"`. Then this Dog instance is keeping the string `"Fido"` alive just so long as we do not replace the value of its `name` with some other value — and just so long as this instance lives.

In short, an instance is both code and data. The code it gets from its type and in a sense is shared with all other instances of that type, but the data belong to it alone. The data can persist as long as the instance persists. The instance has, at every moment, a *state* — the complete collection of its own personal property values. An instance is a device for *maintaining state*. It's a box for storage of data.

The Keyword self

An instance is an object, and an object is the recipient of messages. Thus, an instance needs a way of sending a message to itself. This is made possible by the keyword `self`. This word can be used wherever an instance of the appropriate type is expected.

Let's say I want to keep the thing that a Dog says when it barks, such as `"woof"`, in a property. Then in my implementation of `bark` I need to refer to that property. I can do it like this:

```
class Dog {
    var name = ""
    var whatADogSays = "woof"
    func bark() {
        print(self.whatADogSays)
    }
}
```

Similarly, let's say I want to write an instance method `speak` which is merely a synonym for `bark`. My `speak` implementation can consist of simply calling my own `bark` method. I can do it like this:

```
class Dog {
    var name = ""
    var whatADogSays = "woof"
    func bark() {
        print(self.whatADogSays)
    }
    func speak() {
        self.bark()
    }
}
```

Observe that the term `self` in that example appears only in instance methods. When an instance's code says `self`, it is referring to *this* instance. If the expression `self.name` appears in a Dog instance method's code, it means the `name` of *this* Dog instance, the one whose code is running at that moment.

It turns out that every use of the word `self` I've just illustrated is optional. You can omit it and all the same things will happen:

```
class Dog {
    var name = ""
    var whatADogSays = "woof"
    func bark() {
        print(whatADogSays)
    }
    func speak() {
        bark()
    }
}
```

The reason is that if you omit the message recipient and the message you're sending can be sent to `self`, the compiler supplies `self` as the message's recipient under the hood. However, I never do that (except by mistake). As a matter of style, I like to be explicit in my use of `self`. I find code that omits `self` harder to read and understand. And there are situations where you *must* say `self`, so I prefer to use it whenever I'm allowed to.

Privacy

Earlier, I said that a namespace is not, of itself, an insuperable barrier to accessing the names inside it. But such a barrier is sometimes desirable. Not all data stored by an instance is intended for alteration by, or even visibility to, another instance. And not every instance method is intended to be called by other instances. Any decent object-based programming language needs a way to endow its object members with *privacy* — a way of making it harder for other objects to see those members if they are not supposed to be seen.

Consider, for example:

```
class Dog {
    var name = ""
    var whatADogSays = "woof"
    func bark() {
        print(self.whatADogSays)
    }
    func speak() {
        print(self.whatADogSays)
    }
}
```

Here, other objects can come along and change my property `whatADogSays`. Since that property is used by both `bark` and `speak`, we could easily end up with a Dog that, when told to `bark`, says `"meow"`. That seems somehow undesirable:

```
let dog1 = Dog()
dog1.whatADogSays = "meow"
dog1.bark() // meow
```

You might reply: Well, silly, why did you declare `whatADogSays` with `var`? Declare it with `let` instead. Make it a constant! Now no one can change it:

```
class Dog {
    var name = ""
    let whatADogSays = "woof"
    func bark() {
        print(self.whatADogSays)
    }
    func speak() {
        print(self.whatADogSays)
    }
}
```

That is a good answer, but it is not quite good enough. There are two problems. Suppose I want a Dog instance *itself* to be able to change *its own* `whatADogSays` — by assigning to `self.whatADogSays`. Then `whatADogSays` *has* to be a `var`; otherwise, even the instance itself can't change it. Also, suppose I don't want any other object to *know* what this Dog says, except by calling `bark` or `speak`. Even when declared with `let`, other objects can still *read* the value of `whatADogSays`. Maybe I don't like that.

To solve this problem, Swift provides the `private` keyword. I'll talk later about all the ramifications of this keyword, but for now it's enough to know that it exists:

```
class Dog {
    var name = ""
    private var whatADogSays = "woof"
    func bark() {
        print(self.whatADogSays)
    }
}
```

```
    func speak() {
        print(self.whatADogSays)
    }
}
```

Now `name` is a public property, but `whatADogSays` is a private property: it can't be seen by other types of object. A Dog instance can speak of `self.whatADogSays`, but a Cat instance with a reference to a Dog instance as `fido` cannot say `fido.whatADog-Says`. The important lesson here is that object members are public by default, and if you want privacy, you have to ask for it.

To sum up: A class declaration defines a namespace. This namespace requires that other objects use an extra level of dot-notation to refer to what's inside the namespace, but other objects *can* still refer to what's inside the namespace; the namespace does not, in and of itself, close any doors of visibility. The `private` keyword lets you close those doors.

Design

Instances do not come into being by magic. You have to instantiate a type in order to obtain an instance. Much of the action of your program, therefore, will consist of instantiating types. And of course you will want those instances to persist, so you will also assign each newly created instance to a variable as a shoebox to hold it, name it, and give it a lifetime. The instance will *persist* according to the lifetime of the variable that refers to it. And the instance will be *visible* to other instances according to the scope of the variable that refers to it.

Much of the art of object-based programming involves giving instances a sufficient lifetime and making them visible to one another. You will often put an instance into a particular shoebox — assigning it to a particular variable, declared at a certain scope — exactly so that, thanks to the rules of variable lifetime and scope, this instance will *persist* long enough to keep being useful to your program while it will still be needed, and so that other code can *get a reference* to this instance and talk to it later.

Planning how you're going to create instances, and working out the lifetimes and communication between those instances, may sound daunting. Fortunately, in real life, when you're programming iOS, the framework will provide scaffolding for you. Before you write a single line of code, the framework ensures that your app, as it launches, is given some instances that will persist for the lifetime of the app, providing the basis of your app's visible interface and giving you an initial place to put your own instances and give them sufficiently long lifetimes.

What about the question of what object types your program will need in the first place, and what methods and properties they should have? This is not as much of a worry as you might suppose. Swift itself supplies a library of powerful and useful object types. Moreover, much of your code when you're programming iOS will be focused on the details of real-world interface objects, such as labels and buttons that the user can see and tap, and the framework will make it clear what object types and facilities it offers for this purpose, and will provide ways to ensure the appropriate persistence and visibility of the associated instances.

What the framework cannot tell you is how to design the underlying business logic of whatever your app does behind the scenes. This is where you will have the most freedom — and the most difficulty arriving at an appropriate architecture of object types, functionalities, and relationships. These will not be easy decisions, and there are no clear-cut answers. Object-based programming is an art; and allowing your program (and your thinking) to evolve as you write code, discovering new needs and issues, is an art within that art, which I call *growing a program*. All individuals and teams develop their own way of meeting the long-term challenges involved.

CHAPTER 2

Functions

Nothing is so characteristic of Swift syntax as the way you declare and call functions. Probably nothing is so important, either! As I said in Chapter 1, all your executable code is going to be in functions; they are where the action is.

Function Parameters and Return Value

Remember those imaginary machines for processing miscellaneous stuff that you drew in your math textbook in elementary school? You know the ones I mean: with a funnel-like "hopper" at the top, and then a bunch of gears and cranks, and then a tube at the bottom where something is produced. A function works like that: you feed some stuff in, the stuff is processed in accordance with what this particular machine does, and something is produced. The stuff that goes in is the input; what comes out is the output. More technically, a function that expects input has *parameters*; a function that produces output has a *result*.

Here's the declaration for a silly but valid function that expects two Int values, adds them together, and produces that sum:

```
func sum (_ x:Int, _ y:Int) -> Int {
    let result = x + y
    return result
}
```

The syntax here is very strict and well-defined, and you can't use Swift unless you understand it perfectly. Let's pause to appreciate it in full detail. I'll break the first line into pieces so that I can call them out individually:

```
func sum                         ❶
    (_ x:Int, _ y:Int)           ❷❸
    -> Int {                     ❹❺
        let result = x + y       ❻
        return result            ❼
}
```

❶ The declaration starts with the keyword func, followed by the *name* of this function; here, it's sum. This is the name that must be used in order to *call* the function — that is, in order to run the code that the function contains.

❷ The name of the function is followed by its *parameter list*. It consists, minimally, of parentheses. If this function takes parameters (input), they are listed inside the parentheses, separated by a comma. Each parameter has a strict format: the *name* of the parameter, a colon, and the *type* of the parameter.

❸ This particular function declaration also has an underscore (_) and a space before each parameter name in the parameter list. I'm not going to explain that underscore yet, but I need it for the example, so just trust me for now.

❹ If the function is to return a value, then after the parentheses is an arrow operator (->) followed by the *type* of value that this function will return.

❺ Then we have curly braces enclosing the *body* of the function — its actual code.

❻ Within the curly braces, in the function body, the variables defined as the parameter names have sprung to life, with the types specified in the parameter list.

❼ If the function is to return a value, it must do so with the keyword return followed by that value. And, not surprisingly, the type of that value must match the type declared earlier for the return value (after the arrow operator).

Here are some further points to note about the parameters and return type of our function:

Parameters

Our sum function expects two parameters — an Int, to which it gives the name x, and another Int, to which it gives the name y. The function body code won't run unless code elsewhere calls this function and actually passes values of the specified types for its parameters. If I try to call this function *without* providing a value for each of these two parameters, or if either of the values I provide is *not* an Int, the compiler will stop me with an error.

In the body of the function, therefore, we can confidently use those values, referring to them by those names, certain that they will exist as specified by our parameter list. The parameter names x and y, indeed, are defined just so that the

---

parameter values *can* be referred to within the function body. The parameter declaration is thus a kind of variable declaration: we are declaring variables x and y for use inside this function. With regard to their scope, these variables are local (*internal*) to the function; *only* the function body can see them, and they are different from any other x and y that may be used in other functions or at a higher level of scope.

Return type

The last statement of our sum function's body returns the value of a variable called result; this variable was created by adding two Int values together, so it is an Int, which is what this function is supposed to produce. If I try to return a String (return "howdy"), or if I omit the return statement altogether, the compiler will stop me with an error.

The keyword return actually does *two* things. It *returns* the accompanying value, and it also *halts* execution of the function. It is permitted for more lines of code to follow a return statement, but the compiler will warn if this means that those lines can never be executed.

A function that returns a value must contain a return statement, so if its body consists of just a single statement, it must *be* the return statement. Starting in Swift 5.1, the keyword return can be omitted in that situation. This is mostly to facilitate the SwiftUI domain-specific language, and in general I like to say return explicitly, but in some situations it does feel more elegant to omit it.

You can view the function declaration before the curly braces as a *contract* about what kinds of values will be used as input and about what kind of output will be produced. According to this contract, the function *expects* a certain number of parameters, each of a certain type, and *yields* a certain type of result. Everything must correspond to this contract. The function body, inside the curly braces, can use the parameters as local variables. The returned value must match the declared return type.

The same contract applies to code elsewhere that *calls* this function. Here's some code that calls our sum function:

```
let z = sum(4,5)
```

Focus your attention on the right side of the equal sign — sum(4,5). That's the function call. How is it constructed? It uses the *name* of the function; that name is followed by *parentheses*; and inside those parentheses, separated by a comma, are the *values* to be passed to each of the function's parameters. Technically, these values are called *arguments*. Here, I'm using literal Int values, but I'm perfectly free to use Int variables instead; the only requirement is that I use things that have the correct type:

```
let x = 4
let y = 5
let z = sum(y,x)
```

In that code, I purposely used the names x and y for the variables whose values are passed as arguments, and I purposely reversed them in the call, to emphasize that these names have *nothing to do* with the names x and y inside the function parameter list and the function body. Argument names do not magically make their way to the function. Their *values* are all that matter; their values are the arguments.

What about the value returned by the function? That value is magically *substituted* for the function call, at the point where the function call is made. It happens that in the preceding code, the result is 9. So the last line is exactly as if I had said:

```
let z = 9
```

The programmer and the compiler both know what type of thing this function returns, so they also know where it is and isn't legal to call this function. It's fine to call this function as the initialization part of the declaration of the variable z, just as it would be to use 9 as the initialization part of that declaration: in both cases, we have an Int, and so z ends up being declared as an Int. But it would not be legal to write this:

```
let z = sum(4,5) + "howdy" // compile error
```

Because sum returns an Int, that's the same as trying to add an Int to a String — and by default, you can't do that in Swift.

Observe that it is legal to ignore the value returned from a function call:

```
sum(4,5)
```

That code is rather silly in this particular situation, because we have made our sum function go to all the trouble of adding 4 and 5 for us and we have then thrown away the answer without capturing or using it. The compiler knows this, and will warn that we are failing to use the result of our function call. Nevertheless, a warning is not an error; that code is legal. There are, in fact, lots of situations where it is perfectly reasonable to ignore the value returned from a function call; in particular, the function may do other things (technically called *side effects*) in addition to returning a value, and the purpose of your call to that function may be those other things.

 If you're ignoring a function call result deliberately, you can silence the compiler warning by assigning the function call to _ (a variable without a name) — for example, _ = sum(4,5). Alternatively, if the function being called is your own, you can prevent the warning by marking the function declaration with @discardableResult.

If you can call `sum` wherever you can use an Int, and if the parameters of `sum` have to be Int values, doesn't that mean you can call `sum` inside a call to `sum`? Of course it does! This is perfectly legal (and reasonable):

```
let z = sum(4,sum(5,6))
```

The only arguments against writing code like that are that you might confuse yourself and that it might make things harder to debug later. But technically it's legal and quite normal.

Void Return Type and Parameters

Let's return to our function declaration. With regard to a function's parameters and return type, there are two degenerate cases that allow us to express a function declaration more briefly:

A function without a return type

No law says that a function *must* return a value. A function may be declared to return *no* value. In that case, there are three ways to write the declaration: you can write it as returning Void; you can write it as returning ( ), an empty pair of parentheses; or you can omit the arrow operator and the return type entirely. These are all legal:

```
func say1(_ s:String) -> Void { print(s) }
func say2(_ s:String) -> () { print(s) }
func say3(_ s:String) { print(s) }
```

If a function returns no value, then its body need not contain a return statement. If it does contain a return statement, it will consist of the word `return` alone, and its purpose will be purely to end execution of the function at that point.

A call to a function that returns no value is made purely for the function's side effects; it has no useful return value that can be made part of a larger expression, so the statement that calls the function will usually consist of the function call and nothing else.

A function without any parameters

No law says that a function *must* take any parameters. If it doesn't, the parameter list in the function declaration can be completely empty. But you can't omit the parameter list parentheses themselves! They will be present in the function declaration, after the function's name:

```
func greet() -> String { return "howdy" }
```

Just as you cannot omit the parentheses (the parameter list) from a function *declaration*, you cannot omit the parentheses from a function *call*. Those parentheses will be empty if the function takes no parameters, but they must be present:

```
    let greeting = greet()
```
Notice the parentheses!

A function can lack both a return value and parameters; these are all ways of expressing the same thing:

```
func greet1() -> Void { print("howdy") }
func greet2() -> () { print("howdy") }
func greet3() { print("howdy") }
```

Function Signature

If we ignore the parameter names in the function declaration, we can completely characterize a function by the *types* of its inputs and its output. To do so, we write the parameter types in parentheses, followed by the arrow operator and the output type, like this:

```
(Int, Int) -> Int
```

That is a legal expression in Swift; it is the *signature* of a function. In this case, it's the signature of a function that takes two Int parameters and returns an Int. In fact, it's the signature of our sum function! Of course, there can be other functions that take two Int parameters and return an Int — and that's just the point. This signature characterizes *all* functions that have this number of parameters, of these types, and that return a result of this type. A function's signature is, in effect, *its* type — the type *of the function*. The fact that functions have types will be of great importance later on.

The signature of a function must include both the parameter list (without parameter names) and the return type, even if one or both of those is empty; the signature of a function that takes no parameters and returns no value may be written () -> Void or () -> ().

External Parameter Names

A function can *externalize* the names of its parameters. The external parameter names become part of the function's name, and must appear in a call to the function as *labels* to the arguments. There are several reasons why this is a good thing:

- It clarifies the purpose of each argument; an argument label can give a clue as to how that argument contributes to the behavior of the function.
- It distinguishes one function from another; two functions with the same name before the parentheses and the same signature, but with different external parameter names, are two distinct functions.
- It helps Swift to interface with Objective-C and Cocoa, where method parameters nearly always have external names.

It will be useful to have a term for the part of a function's name that precedes the parentheses, so I don't have to keep calling it "the name before the parentheses" to distinguish it from the external parameter names. Let's call it the function's *base name*.

External parameter names are so standard in Swift that there's a rule: by default, *all* parameter names are externalized *automatically*, using the internal name as the external name. If you want a parameter name to be externalized, and if you want the external name to be the same as the internal name, *do nothing* — that will happen all by itself.

If you want to depart from the default behavior, you can do either of the following in your function declaration:

Change the name of an external parameter
  If you want the external name of a parameter to be different from its internal name, precede the internal name with the external name and a space.

Suppress the externalization of a parameter
  To suppress a parameter's external name, precede the internal name with an underscore and a space.

That explains my declaration `func sum (_ x:Int, _ y:Int) -> Int` at the start of this chapter: I was suppressing the externalization of the parameter names, so as not to have to explain argument labels at the outset.

Here's the declaration for a function that concatenates a string with itself a given number of times:

```
func echoString(_ s:String, times:Int) -> String {
    var result = ""
    for _ in 1...times { result += s }
    return result
}
```

That function's first parameter has an internal name only, but its second parameter has an external name, which will be the same as its internal name, namely `times`. And here's how to call it:

```
let s = echoString("hi", times:3)
```

In the call, as you can see, the external name precedes the argument as a label, separated by a colon.

Now let's say that in our `echoString` function we prefer to use `times` purely as an external name for the second parameter, with a different name — say, n — as the internal name. And let's strip the `string` off the function's base name and make it the external name of the first parameter. Then the declaration would look like this:

```
func echo(string s:String, times n:Int) -> String {
    var result = ""
    for _ in 1...n { result += s }
    return result
}
```

In the body of that function, there is now no `times` variable available; `times` is purely an external name, for use as a label in the call. The internal name is `n`, and that's the name the code refers to. And here's how to call it:

```
let s = echo(string:"hi", times:3)
```

 The existence of external names doesn't mean that the call can use a different parameter order from the declaration. Our `echo(string:times:)` expects a String parameter and an Int parameter, *in that order*. The order can't be different in the call, even though the label might appear to disambiguate which argument goes with which parameter.

Overloading

In Swift, function *overloading* is legal (and common). This means that two functions with exactly the same name, *including* their external parameter names, can coexist as long as they have different signatures. (Two functions with the same base name but *different* external parameter names do *not* constitute a case of overloading; they are simply two different functions with two different names.) These two functions can coexist:

```
func say (_ what:String) {
}
func say (_ what:Int) {
}
```

The reason overloading works is that Swift has strict typing. A String parameter is not an Int parameter. Swift can tell them apart both in the declaration and in a function call. So Swift knows unambiguously that `say("what")` is different from `say(1)`, and it knows *which* `say` function each is calling.

Overloading works for the return type as well. Two functions with the same name and parameter types can have different return types. But the context of the call must disambiguate; that is, it must be clear what return type the caller is expecting.

For example, these two functions can coexist:

```
func say() -> String {
    return "one"
}
func say() -> Int {
    return 1
}
```

But now you can't call say like this:

```
let result = say() // compile error
```

The call is ambiguous, and the compiler tells you so. The call must be used in a context where the expected return type is clear. One solution, as I'll describe in Chapter 3, is to state the problematic type explicitly (rather than relying on type inference):

```
let result: String = say()
```

Alternatively, the context itself might disambiguate. Suppose we have another function that is not overloaded, and that expects a String parameter:

```
func giveMeAString(_ s:String) {
    print("thanks!")
}
```

Then giveMeAString(say()) is legal, because only a String can go in this spot, so we must be calling the say that returns a String. Similarly:

```
let result = say() + "two"
```

Only a String can be "added" to a String, so this must be the say that returns a String.

You can also disambiguate explicitly between overloads in a method call using the name of the method, the keyword as, and the signature of the desired method. The syntax is a little odd, because the entire expression must be enclosed in parentheses, followed immediately by the parentheses signifying that this is a method call:

```
let result = (say as () -> String)()
```

Default Parameter Values

A parameter can have a default value. This means that the caller can omit the parameter entirely, supplying no argument for it; the value will then be the default.

To specify a default value in a function declaration, append = and the default value after the parameter type:

```
class Dog {
    func say(_ s:String, times:Int = 1) {
        for _ in 1...times {
            print(s)
        }
    }
}
```

In effect, there are now *two* functions, one with a single unlabeled parameter, the other with an additional times: parameter. If you just want to say something once, you can call the say that takes a single unlabeled argument:

```
let d = Dog()
d.say("woof") // same as d.say("woof", times:1)
```

If you want repetition, call the say that takes a times: parameter:

```
let d = Dog()
d.say("woof", times:3)
```

Variadic Parameters

A parameter can be *variadic*. This means that the caller can supply as many values of this parameter's type as desired, separated by a comma; the function body will receive these values as an array.

To indicate in a function declaration that a parameter is variadic, follow it with three dots, like this:

```
func sayStrings(_ arrayOfStrings:String ...) {
    for s in arrayOfStrings { print(s) }
}
```

And here's how to call it:

```
sayStrings("hey", "ho", "nonny nonny no")
```

The global print function takes a variadic first parameter, so you can output multiple values with a single command:

```
print("Manny", 3, true) // Manny 3 true
```

The print function's default parameters dictate further details of the output. The default separator: (for when you provide multiple values) is a space, and the default terminator: is a newline; you can change either or both:

```
print("Manny", "Moe", separator:", ", terminator:", ")
print("Jack")
// output is "Manny, Moe, Jack" on one line
```

A function can declare a maximum of one variadic parameter (because otherwise it might be impossible to determine where the list of values ends).

 Unfortunately, there's a hole in the Swift language: there's no way to convert an array into a comma-separated list of arguments (comparable to splatting in Ruby). If what you're starting with is an array of some type, you can't use it where a variadic of that type is expected.

Ignored Parameters

A parameter whose local name is an underscore is ignored. The caller must supply an argument, but it has no name within the function body and cannot be referred to there. For example:

```
func say(_ s:String, times:Int, loudly _:Bool) {
```

No `loudly` parameter makes its way into the function body, but the caller must still provide it:

```
say("hi", times:3, loudly:true)
```

What's the purpose of this feature? It isn't to satisfy the compiler, because the compiler doesn't complain if a parameter is never referred to in the function body. I use it primarily as a kind of note to myself, a way of saying, "Yes, I know there is a parameter here, and I am deliberately not using it for anything."

Modifiable Parameters

In the body of a function, a parameter is essentially a local variable. By default, it's a variable implicitly declared with `let`. You can't assign to it:

```
func say(_ s:String, times:Int, loudly:Bool) {
    loudly = true // compile error
}
```

If your code needs to assign to a parameter name within the body of a function, declare a var local variable inside the function body and assign the parameter value to it; your local variable can even have the same name as the parameter:

```
func say(_ s:String, times:Int, loudly:Bool) {
    var loudly = loudly
    loudly = true // no problem
}
```

In that code, loudly is a local variable; assigning to it doesn't change the value of any variable outside the function body. However, it is also possible to configure a parameter in such a way that assigning to it *does* modify the value of a variable outside the function body! One typical use case is that you want your function to return more than one result. Here I'll write a rather advanced function that removes all occurrences of a given character from a given string and returns the number of occurrences that were removed:

```
func removeCharacter(_ c:Character, from s:String) -> Int {
    var s = s
    var howMany = 0
    while let ix = s.firstIndex(of:c) {
        s.remove(at:ix)
        howMany += 1
    }
    return howMany
}
```

And you call it like this:

```
let s = "hello"
let result = removeCharacter("l", from:s) // 2
```

That's nice, but the *original* string, s, is still "hello"! In the function body, we removed all occurrences of the character from the *local* copy of the String parameter.

If we want a function to alter the *original* value of an argument passed to it, we must do the following:

- The type of the parameter we intend to modify must be declared inout.
- When we call the function, the variable holding the value to be modified must be declared with var, not let.
- Instead of passing the variable as an argument, we must pass its *address*. This is done by preceding its name with an ampersand (&).

Our removeCharacter(_:from:) now looks like this:

```
func removeCharacter(_ c:Character, from s: inout String) -> Int {
    var howMany = 0
    while let ix = s.firstIndex(of:c) {
        s.remove(at:ix)
```

```
        howMany += 1
    }
    return howMany
}
```

And our call to removeCharacter(_:from:) now looks like this:

```
var s = "hello"
let result = removeCharacter("l", from:&s)
```

After the call, result is 2 *and* s is "heo". Notice the ampersand before the name s when we pass it as the from: argument. It is required; if you omit it, the compiler will stop you. I like this requirement, because it forces us to acknowledge explicitly to the compiler, and to ourselves, that we're about to do something potentially dangerous: we're letting this function, as a side effect, modify a value outside of itself.

 When a function with an inout parameter is called, the variable whose address was passed as argument to that parameter is *always* set, even if the function makes no changes to that parameter.

Calling Objective-C with Modifiable Parameters

You may encounter variations on this pattern when you're using Cocoa. The Cocoa APIs are written in C and Objective-C, so instead of the Swift term inout, you'll probably see some mysterious type such as UnsafeMutablePointer. From your point of view as the caller, however, it's the same thing: you'll prepare a var variable and pass its address.

For instance, consider the problem of learning a UIColor's RGBA components. There are four such components: the color's red, green, blue, and alpha values. A function that, given a UIColor, returned the components of that color, would need to return four values at once — and that is something that Objective-C cannot do. So a different strategy is used. The UIColor method getRed(_:green:blue:alpha:) returns only a Bool reporting whether the component extraction succeeded. Instead of returning the actual components, it says: "You hand me four CGFloats *as arguments*, and I will *modify* them for you so that they are the results of this operation." Here's roughly how the declaration for getRed(_:green:blue:alpha:) appears in Swift:

```
func getRed(_ red: UnsafeMutablePointer<CGFloat>,
    green: UnsafeMutablePointer<CGFloat>,
    blue: UnsafeMutablePointer<CGFloat>,
    alpha: UnsafeMutablePointer<CGFloat>) -> Bool
```

How would you call this function? The parameters are each an UnsafeMutable-Pointer to a CGFloat. You'll create four var CGFloat variables beforehand, giving them each some value even though that value will be replaced when you call get-Red(_:green:blue:alpha:). The arguments you'll pass will be the *addresses* of those variables. Those variables are where the component values will be after the call; and you'll probably be so sure that the component extraction will succeed, that you won't even bother to capture the call's actual result:

```
let c = UIColor.purple
var r : CGFloat = 0
var g : CGFloat = 0
var b : CGFloat = 0
var a : CGFloat = 0
c.getRed(&r, green: &g, blue: &b, alpha: &a)
// now r, g, b, a are 0.5, 0.0, 0.5, 1.0
```

Called by Objective-C with Modifiable Parameters

Sometimes, Cocoa will call *your* function with an UnsafeMutablePointer parameter, and *you* will want to change its value. To do this, you cannot assign directly to it, as we did earlier with the inout parameter s that we declared in our implementation of remove(from:character:). You're talking to Objective-C, not to Swift, and this is an UnsafeMutablePointer, not an inout parameter. The technique here is to assign to the UnsafeMutablePointer's pointee property. Here (without further explanation) is an example from my own code:

```
func popoverPresentationController(
    _ popoverPresentationController: UIPopoverPresentationController,
    willRepositionPopoverTo rect: UnsafeMutablePointer<CGRect>,
    in view: AutoreleasingUnsafeMutablePointer<UIView>) {
        view.pointee = self.button2
        rect.pointee = self.button2.bounds
}
```

Reference Type Modifiable Parameters

There is one very common situation where your function can modify a parameter *without* declaring it as inout — namely, when the parameter is an *instance of a class*. This is a special feature of classes, as opposed to the other two object type flavors, enum and struct. String isn't a class; it's a struct. That's why we had to use inout in order to modify a String parameter. So I'll illustrate by declaring a Dog class with a name property:

```
class Dog {
    var name = ""
}
```

Here's a function that takes a Dog instance parameter and a String, and sets that Dog instance's name to that String. Notice that no inout is involved:

```
func changeName(of d:Dog, to newName:String) {
    d.name = newName
}
```

Here's how to call it. We pass a Dog instance *directly*:

```
let d = Dog()
d.name = "Fido"
print(d.name) // "Fido"
changeName(of:d, to:"Rover")
print(d.name) // "Rover"
```

We were able to change a property of our Dog instance d, even though it wasn't passed as an inout parameter, and even though it was declared originally with let, not var. This appears to be an exception to the rules about modifying parameters — but it isn't. It's a feature of class instances, namely that they are themselves mutable. In changeName(of:to:), we didn't actually attempt to assign *a different Dog instance* to the parameter. To do that, the Dog parameter *would* need to be declared inout (and d would have to be declared with var and we would have to pass its address as argument).

Technically, we say that classes are *reference types*, whereas the other object type flavors are *value types*. When you pass an instance of a struct as an argument to a function, you effectively wind up with a *separate copy* of the struct instance. But when you pass an instance of a class as an argument to a function, you pass a reference to the class instance *itself*. I'll discuss this topic in more detail later ("Value Types and Reference Types" on page 153).

Function in Function

A function can be declared anywhere, including inside the body of a function. A function declared in the body of a function (also called a *local function*) is available to be called by later code within the same scope, but is completely invisible elsewhere.

This feature is an elegant architecture for functions whose sole purpose is to assist another function. If only function A ever needs to call function B, function B might as well be packaged inside function A.

Here's a typical example from one of my apps (I've omitted everything except the structure):

```
func checkPair(_ p1:Piece, and p2:Piece) -> Path? {
    // ...
    func addPathIfValid(_ midpt1:Point, _ midpt2:Point) {
        // ...
    }
    for y in -1..._yct {
        addPathIfValid((pt1.x,y),(pt2.x,y))
    }
    for x in -1..._xct {
```

```
                addPathIfValid((x,pt1.y),(x,pt2.y))
        }
        // ...
    }
```

What I'm doing in the first for loop (for y) and what I'm doing in the second for loop (for x) are the same — but with a different set of starting values. We could write out the functionality in full inside each for loop, but that would be an unnecessary and confusing repetition. (Such a repetition would violate the principle often referred to as *DRY*, for "Don't Repeat Yourself.") To prevent that repetition, we could refactor the repeated code into an instance method to be called by both for loops, but that exposes this functionality more broadly than we need, as it is called *only* by these two for loops inside checkPair. A local function is the perfect compromise.

 Local functions are really local variables with function values (a notion that I'll explain later in this chapter). Therefore, a local function can't have the same name as a local variable in the same scope, and two local functions can't have the same name as one another in the same scope.

Recursion

A function can call itself. This is called *recursion*. Recursion seems a little scary, rather like jumping off a cliff, because of the danger of creating an infinite loop; but if you write the function correctly, you will always have a "stopper" condition that handles the degenerate case and prevents the loop from being infinite:

```
func countDownFrom(_ ix:Int) {
    print(ix)
    if ix > 0 { // stopper
        countDownFrom(ix-1) // recurse!
    }
}
countDownFrom(5) // 5, 4, 3, 2, 1, 0
```

Function as Value

If you've never used a programming language where functions are first-class citizens, perhaps you'd better sit down now, because what I'm about to tell you might make you feel a little faint: In Swift, a function *is* a first-class citizen. This means that a function can be used wherever a value can be used. A function can be assigned to a variable; a function can be passed as an argument in a function call; a function can be returned as the result of a function.

Swift has strict typing. You can assign a value to a variable or pass a value into or out of a function only if it is the right *type* of value. In order for a function to be used as a

---

value, the function needs to *have* a type. And indeed it does: a function's *signature* is its type.

The chief purpose of using a function as a value is so that this function can later be called without a definite knowledge of *what* function it is. Here's the world's simplest (and silliest) example, just to show the syntax and structure:

```
func doThis(_ f:() -> ()) {
    f()
}
```

That is a function doThis that takes one parameter (and returns no value). The parameter, f, is itself a function! How do we know? Well, look at its type (after the colon): it is () -> (). That's a function signature; in particular, it is the signature of a function that takes no parameters and returns no value.

The function doThis, then, expects as its parameter a function, which it names f. Then, within its body, doThis *calls* the function f that it received as its parameter, by saying f(). So doThis is merely a function that trivially calls another function. But it does this without knowing in advance *what* function it is going to call. That's the power of functions being first-class citizens.

Having declared the function doThis, how would you call it? You'd need to pass it a function as argument. Here's one way to do that:

```
func doThis(_ f:() -> ()) {
    f()
}
func whatToDo() { ❶
    print("I did it")
}
doThis(whatToDo) ❷
```

❶ First, we declare a function (whatToDo) *of the proper type* — a function that takes no parameters and returns no value.

❷ Then, we call `doThis`, passing as argument a *function reference* — in effect, the bare name of the function. Notice that we are not *calling* `whatToDo` here; we are *passing* it.

Sure enough, this works: we pass `whatToDo` as argument to `doThis`; `doThis` calls the function that it receives as its parameter; and the string `"I did it"` appears in the console.

Obviously, that example, while demonstrating a remarkable ability of the Swift language, is far from compelling, because the outcome in practice is no different from what would have happened if we had simply called `whatToDo` directly. But in real life, encapsulating function-calling in a function can reduce repetition and opportunity for error. Moreover, a function may call its parameter function in some special way; it might call it after doing other things, or at some later time.

Here's a case from my own code. A common thing to do in Cocoa is to draw an image, directly, in code. One way of doing this involves four steps:

```
let size = CGSize(width:45, height:20)
UIGraphicsBeginImageContextWithOptions(size, false, 0) ❶
let p = UIBezierPath(
    roundedRect: CGRect(x:0, y:0, width:45, height:20), cornerRadius: 8)
p.stroke() ❷
let result = UIGraphicsGetImageFromCurrentImageContext()! ❸
UIGraphicsEndImageContext() ❹
```

❶ Open an image context.

❷ Draw into the context.

❸ Extract the image.

❹ Close the image context.

That works — in this case, it generates an image of a rounded rectangle — but it's ugly. The sole purpose of all that code is to obtain `result`, the image; but that purpose is buried in all the other code. At the same time, everything except for the two lines involving the UIBezierPath `p` (step 2) is boilerplate; every time I do this in any app, step 1, step 3, and step 4 are exactly the same. Moreover, I live in mortal fear of forgetting a step; if I were to omit step 4 by mistake, the universe would explode.

Since the only thing that's different every time I draw is step 2, step 2 is the only part I should have to write out! The entire problem is solved by writing a utility function expressing the boilerplate:

```
func imageOfSize(_ size:CGSize, _ whatToDraw:() -> ()) -> UIImage {
    UIGraphicsBeginImageContextWithOptions(size, false, 0)
    whatToDraw()
    let result = UIGraphicsGetImageFromCurrentImageContext()!
    UIGraphicsEndImageContext()
    return result
}
```

My `imageOfSize` utility is so useful that I declare it at the top level of a file, where all my files can see it. To make an image, I can perform step 2 (the actual drawing) in a function and pass that function as argument to the `imageOfSize` utility:

```
func drawing() {
    let p = UIBezierPath(
        roundedRect: CGRect(x:0, y:0, width:45, height:20),
        cornerRadius: 8)
    p.stroke()
}
let image = imageOfSize(CGSize(width:45, height:20), drawing)
```

Now *that* is a beautifully expressive and clear way to turn drawing instructions into an image.

 Evidently Apple agrees with my criticism of `UIGraphicsBeginImageContextWith-Options`, because in iOS 10 a new class was introduced, UIGraphicsImageRenderer, that expresses itself using syntax similar to my `imageOfSize`. Nevertheless, I'll continue using `imageOfSize` in this chapter, because it illustrates important aspects of Swift functions.

The Cocoa API is full of situations where you'll pass a function to be called by the runtime in some special way or at some later time. Some common Cocoa situations even involve passing *two* functions. For instance, when you perform view animation, you'll often pass one function prescribing the action to be animated and another function saying what to do afterward:

```
func whatToAnimate() { // self.myButton is a button in the interface
    self.myButton.frame.origin.y += 20
}
func whatToDoLater(finished:Bool) {
    print("finished: \(finished)")
}
UIView.animate(withDuration:0.4,
    animations: whatToAnimate, completion: whatToDoLater)
```

That means: Change the frame origin (that is, the position) of this button in the interface, but do it over time (four-tenths of a second); and then, when that's finished, print a log message in the console saying whether the animation was performed or not.

The Cocoa documentation will often describe a function to be passed in this way as a *handler*, and will refer it as a *block*, because that's the Objective-C syntactic construct needed here. In Swift, it's a function.

Anonymous Functions

Consider once again this example:

```
func whatToAnimate() { // self.myButton is a button in the interface
    self.myButton.frame.origin.y += 20
}
func whatToDoLater(finished:Bool) {
    print("finished: \(finished)")
}
UIView.animate(withDuration:0.4,
    animations: whatToAnimate, completion: whatToDoLater)
```

There's a slight bit of ugliness in that code. I'm declaring functions `whatToAnimate` and `whatToDoLater`, just because I want to pass those functions in the last line. But I don't really need the *names* `whatToAnimate` and `whatToDoLater` for anything, except to refer to them in the last line; neither the names nor the functions will ever be used again. In my call to `UIView.animate(withDuration:animations:completion:)`, it would be nice to be able to pass just the *body* of those functions *without* a declared name.

We can do that. A nameless function body is called an *anonymous* function, and is legal and common in Swift. To form an anonymous function, you do two things:

1. Create the function body itself, including the surrounding curly braces, but with no function declaration.

2. If necessary, express the function's parameter list and return type as the first thing *inside* the curly braces, followed by the keyword `in`.

Let's practice by transforming our named function declarations into anonymous functions. Here's the named function declaration for `whatToAnimate`:

```
func whatToAnimate() {
    self.myButton.frame.origin.y += 20
}
```

Here's an anonymous function that does the same thing. Notice how I've moved the parameter list and return type inside the curly braces:

```
{
    () -> () in
    self.myButton.frame.origin.y += 20
}
```

Here's the named function declaration for `whatToDoLater`:

```
func whatToDoLater(finished:Bool) {
    print("finished: \(finished)")
}
```

Here's an anonymous function that does the same thing:

```
{
    (finished:Bool) -> () in
    print("finished: \(finished)")
}
```

Using Anonymous Functions Inline

Now that we know how to make anonymous functions, let's use them. The point where we need the functions is the point where we're passing the second and third arguments to `animate(withDuration:animations:completion:)`. We can create and pass anonymous functions *right at that point*, like this:

```
UIView.animate(withDuration:0.4,
    animations: {
        () -> () in
        self.myButton.frame.origin.y += 20
    },
    completion: {
        (finished:Bool) -> () in
        print("finished: \(finished)")
    }
)
```

We can make the same improvement in the way we call the `imageOfSize` function from the preceding section. Earlier, we called that function like this:

```
func drawing() {
    let p = UIBezierPath(
        roundedRect: CGRect(x:0, y:0, width:45, height:20),
        cornerRadius: 8)
    p.stroke()
}
let image = imageOfSize(CGSize(width:45, height:20), drawing)
```

We now know, however, that we don't need to declare the `drawing` function separately. We can call `imageOfSize` with an anonymous function:

```
let image = imageOfSize(CGSize(width:45, height:20), {
    () -> () in
    let p = UIBezierPath(
        roundedRect: CGRect(x:0, y:0, width:45, height:20),
        cornerRadius: 8)
    p.stroke()
})
```

Anonymous functions are very commonly used in Swift, so make sure you can read and write that code!

Anonymous Function Abbreviated Syntax

Anonymous functions are so common and so important in Swift that some shortcuts for writing them are provided:

Omission of the return type

> If the anonymous function's return type is already known to the compiler, you can omit the arrow operator and the specification of the return type:

```
UIView.animate(withDuration:0.4,
    animations: {
        () in // *
        self.myButton.frame.origin.y += 20
    }, completion: {
        (finished:Bool) in // *
        print("finished: \(finished)")
})
```

(Occasionally the compiler will fail to infer the anonymous function's return type, even though you think it should be obvious, and will give a compile error. If that happens, just don't use this shortcut: supply an `in` expression with an explicit return type.)

Omission of the `in` expression when there are no parameters

> If the anonymous function takes no parameters, and if the return type can be omitted, the `in` expression itself can be omitted:

```
UIView.animate(withDuration:0.4,
    animations: { // *
        self.myButton.frame.origin.y += 20
    }, completion: {
        (finished:Bool) in
        print("finished: \(finished)")
})
```

Omission of the parameter types

> If the anonymous function takes parameters and their types are already known to the compiler, the types can be omitted:

```
UIView.animate(withDuration:0.4,
    animations: {
        self.myButton.frame.origin.y += 20
    }, completion: {
        (finished) in // *
        print("finished: \(finished)")
})
```

Omission of the parentheses

> If the parameter types are omitted, the parentheses around the parameter list can be omitted:

```
UIView.animate(withDuration:0.4,
    animations: {
        self.myButton.frame.origin.y += 20
    }, completion: {
        finished in // *
        print("finished: \(finished)")
})
```

Omission of the in *expression even when there are parameters*

If the return type can be omitted, and if the parameter types are already known to the compiler, you can omit the in expression and refer to the parameters directly within the body of the anonymous function by using the magic names $0, $1, and so on, in order:

```
UIView.animate(withDuration:0.4,
    animations: {
        self.myButton.frame.origin.y += 20
    }, completion: {
        print("finished: \($0)") // *
})
```

Omission of the parameter names

If the anonymous function body doesn't need to refer to a parameter, you can substitute an underscore for its name in the parameter list in the in expression:

```
UIView.animate(withDuration:0.4,
    animations: {
        self.myButton.frame.origin.y += 20
    }, completion: {
        _ in // *
        print("finished!")
})
```

 If an anonymous function takes parameters, you *must* acknowledge them somehow. You can omit the in expression and use the parameters by the magic names $0 and so on. Or you can keep the in expression and give the parameters names or ignore them with underscores. But you can't omit the in expression and *not* use the parameters' magic names! If you do, your code won't compile.

Omission of the function argument label

If your anonymous function is the last argument being passed in this function call — which will just about always be the case — you can close the function call with a right parenthesis *before* this last argument, and then put just the anonymous function body *without a label*. This is called *trailing closure syntax* (I'll explain in a moment what a closure is):

```
UIView.animate(withDuration:0.4,
    animations: {
        self.myButton.frame.origin.y += 20
    }) { // *
        _ in
        print("finished!")
}
```

In that code, the `completion:` parameter is last, so the call can pass the anonymous function argument outside the call's parentheses, using trailing closure syntax with no label.

But there's a curious asymmetry in that particular example, because this is a method that takes *two* function parameters. The `animations:` parameter is an anonymous function too, but it still sits inside the parentheses. New in Swift 5.3, that asymmetry is resolved; now, *multiple* anonymous function arguments can be expressed using trailing closure syntax. When you do that, the *first* anonymous function takes no label; the remaining functions *do* each have their labels, with *no comma:*

```
UIView.animate(withDuration:0.4) { // *
    self.myButton3.frame.origin.y += 20
} completion: { // *
    _ in
    print("finished")
}
```

Omission of the calling function parentheses

If you use a trailing closure, and if the function you are calling takes no parameters other than the function you are passing to it, you can omit the empty parentheses from the call. This is the *only* situation in which you can omit the parentheses from a function call! To illustrate, I'll declare and call a different function:

```
func doThis(_ f:() -> ()) {
    f()
}
doThis { // no parentheses!
    print("Howdy")
}
```

Omission of the keyword `return`

If the anonymous function body consists of exactly one statement consisting of returning a value with the keyword `return`, the keyword `return` can be omitted (and in this situation, I like to do so):

```
func greeting() -> String {
    return "Howdy"
}
func performAndPrint(_ f:()->String) {
    let s = f()
    print(s)
}
performAndPrint {
    greeting() // meaning: return greeting()
}
```

When writing anonymous functions, you will frequently find yourself taking advantage of all the omissions you are permitted. In addition, you'll sometimes shorten the *layout* of the code (though not the code itself) by putting the whole anonymous function together with the function call *on one line*. Thus, Swift code involving anonymous functions can be extremely compact.

Here's a typical example. We start with an array of Int values and generate a new array consisting of all those values multiplied by 2, by calling the map(_:) instance method. The map(_:) method of an array takes a function that takes one parameter of the same type as the array's elements, and returns a new value; here, our array is made of Int values, and we are passing to the map(_:) method a function that takes one Int parameter and returns an Int. We could write out the whole function, like this:

```
let arr = [2, 4, 6, 8]
func doubleMe(i:Int) -> Int {
    return i*2
}
let arr2 = arr.map(doubleMe) // [4, 8, 12, 16]
```

That, however, is not very Swifty. We don't need the name doubleMe for anything else, so this may as well be an anonymous function:

```
let arr = [2, 4, 6, 8]
let arr2 = arr.map ({
    (i:Int) -> Int in
    return i*2
})
```

Now let's abbreviate our anonymous function. Its parameter type is known in advance, so we don't need to specify that. Its return type is known by inspection of the function body, so we don't need to specify that. There's just one parameter and we are going to use it, so we don't need the in expression as long we refer to the parameter as $0. Our function body consists of just one statement, and it is a return statement, so we can omit return. And map(_:) doesn't take any other parameters, so we can omit the parentheses and follow the name directly with a trailing closure:

```
let arr = [2, 4, 6, 8]
let arr2 = arr.map {$0*2}
```

It doesn't get any Swiftier than that!

Define-and-Call

A pattern that's surprisingly common in Swift is to define an anonymous function and call it, all in one move:

```
{
    // ... code goes here
}()
```

Notice the parentheses after the curly braces! The curly braces *define* an anonymous function body; the parentheses *call* that anonymous function. I call this construct *define-and-call*.

Using define-and-call, an action can be taken at the point where it is needed, rather than in a series of preparatory steps. Here's a common Cocoa situation where we create and configure an NSMutableParagraphStyle and then use it as an argument in a call to the NSMutableAttributedString method `addAttribute(_:value:range:)`, like this:

```
let para = NSMutableParagraphStyle()
para.headIndent = 10
para.firstLineHeadIndent = 10
// ... more configuration of para ...
content.addAttribute( // content is an NSMutableAttributedString
    .paragraphStyle,
    value:para,
    range:NSRange(location:0, length:1))
```

I find that code ugly. We don't need `para` except to pass it as the `value:` argument within the call to `addAttribute(_:value:range:)`, so it would be much nicer to create and configure it right there within the call, as the `value:` argument itself. That sounds like an anonymous function — except that the `value:` parameter is not a function, but an NSMutableParagraphStyle object.

We can solve the problem by providing, as the `value:` argument, an anonymous function that *produces* an NSMutableParagraphStyle object *and calling it* so that it *does* produce an NSMutableParagraphStyle object:

```
content.addAttribute(
    .paragraphStyle,
    value: {
        let para = NSMutableParagraphStyle()
        para.headIndent = 10
        para.firstLineHeadIndent = 10
```

```
        // ... more configuration of para ...
        return para
    }(),
    range:NSRange(location:0, length:1))
```

I'll demonstrate some further uses of define-and-call in Chapter 3.

Closures

Swift functions are *closures*. This means they can *capture* references to external variables in scope within the body of the function. What do I mean by that? Well, recall from Chapter 1 that code in curly braces constitutes a scope, and this code can "see" variables and functions declared in a surrounding scope. For example:

```
class Dog {
    var whatThisDogSays = "woof"  ❶
    func bark() {
        print(self.whatThisDogSays)  ❷
    }
}
```

In that code:

❶ The variable whatThisDogSays is *external* to the function: it is *declared outside* the body of the function, and yet is *in scope* for the body of the function, so that the code inside the body of the function can see it.

❷ The code inside the body of the function *refers* to the external variable whatThis-DogSays — it says, explicitly, whatThisDogSays.

So far, so good; but we now know that the function bark can be passed as a value. In effect, it can travel from one environment to another. When it does, what happens to that reference to whatThisDogSays? Let's find out:

```
func doThis(_ f : () -> ()) {
    f()
}
let d = Dog()
d.whatThisDogSays = "arf"
let barkFunction = d.bark
doThis(barkFunction) // arf
```

We run that code, and "arf" appears in the console!

Perhaps that result doesn't seem very surprising to you. But think about it. We do not directly *call* d.bark(). We make a Dog instance and *pass* its bark function as a value into the function doThis. There, it is called. Now, whatThisDogSays is an instance property of a particular Dog. Inside the function doThis there is no whatThisDog-Says. Indeed, inside the function doThis there is no Dog instance! Nevertheless the call f() still works. The function d.bark, as it is passed around, evidently *carries* the variable whatThisDogSays along with itself.

But there's more. I'll change the example by moving the line where we set d.what-ThisDogSays to *after* we assign d.bark into our variable barkFunction:

```
func doThis(_ f : () -> ()) {
    f()
}
let d = Dog()
let barkFunction = d.bark        ❶
doThis(barkFunction) // woof      ❷
d.whatThisDogSays = "arf"         ❸
doThis(barkFunction) // arf       ❹
```

What just happened?

❶ We assigned d.bark to barkFunction, once and for all; after that, we never changed barkFunction.

❷ At that time, d.whatThisDogSays was "woof", so we passed barkFunction into doThis and got "woof".

❸ We then changed d.whatThisDogSays to "arf". We didn't change bark-Function.

❹ We passed barkFunction into doThis again, and this time we got "arf"!

After creating both d and barkFunction, changing a property of the Dog d changes the output of calling barkFunction! How can this be? Evidently, after step 1, when d.bark has been assigned to barkFunction, *both* our Dog variable d *and* the function barkFunction are holding references to the same Dog instance. This is because d.bark, which we assigned to barkFunction, refers to self, which *is* the Dog instance. That's what we mean when we say that a function is a closure and that it *captures* external variables referred to in its body.

How Closures Improve Code

You can use the fact that functions are closures to make your code more general, and hence more useful. To illustrate, here, once again, is my earlier example of a function that accepts drawing instructions and performs them to generate an image:

```
func imageOfSize(_ size:CGSize, _ whatToDraw:() -> ()) -> UIImage {
    UIGraphicsBeginImageContextWithOptions(size, false, 0)
    whatToDraw()
    let result = UIGraphicsGetImageFromCurrentImageContext()!
    UIGraphicsEndImageContext()
    return result
}
```

As you know, we can call `imageOfSize` with a trailing closure:

```
let image = imageOfSize(CGSize(width:45, height:20)) {
    let p = UIBezierPath(
        roundedRect: CGRect(x:0, y:0, width:45, height:20),
        cornerRadius: 8)
    p.stroke()
}
```

That code, however, contains an annoying repetition. This is a call to create an image of a given size consisting of a rounded rectangle of that size. We are repeating the size; the pair of numbers 45,20 appears twice. That's silly. Let's prevent the repetition by putting the size into a variable at the outset:

```
let sz = CGSize(width:45, height:20)
let image = imageOfSize(sz) {
    let p = UIBezierPath(
        roundedRect: CGRect(origin:CGPoint.zero, size:sz),
        cornerRadius: 8)
    p.stroke()
}
```

The variable `sz`, declared outside our anonymous function at a higher level, is visible inside it. Thus we can refer to it inside the anonymous function — and we do so. The anonymous function is just a function body; it won't be *executed* until `imageOfSize` calls it. Nevertheless, when we refer to `sz` from inside the function body in the expression `CGRect(origin:CGPoint.zero, size:sz)`, we capture its value *now*, because the function body is a closure. When `imageOfSize` calls `whatToDraw`, and `whatToDraw` turns out to be a function whose body refers to a variable `sz`, there's no problem, even though there is no `sz` anywhere in the neighborhood of `imageOfSize`.

Now let's go further. So far, we've been hard-coding the size of the desired rounded rectangle. Imagine, though, that creating images of rounded rectangles of various sizes is something we do often. It would make sense to package this code up as a function, where `sz` is not a fixed value but a parameter; the function will then return the image:

```
func makeRoundedRectangle(_ sz:CGSize) -> UIImage {
    let image = imageOfSize(sz) {
        let p = UIBezierPath(
            roundedRect: CGRect(origin:CGPoint.zero, size:sz),
            cornerRadius: 8)
```

```
            p.stroke()
        }
        return image
    }
```

Incredibly, that works! The parameter `sz` that arrives into `makeRoundedRectangle` is no longer a hard-coded value; we don't know what it will be. Nevertheless, when `make-RoundedRectangle` is called, `sz` *will* have a value, and the anonymous function captures `sz`, so when `imageOfSize` calls the anonymous function, `sz` inside that function will have the `sz` value that was passed to `makeRoundedRectangle`.

Our code is becoming beautifully compact. To call `makeRoundedRectangle`, supply a size; an image is returned. I can perform the call, obtain the image, and display that image, all in one move, like this (`self.iv` is a UIImageView in the interface):

```
self.iv.image = makeRoundedRectangle(CGSize(width:45, height:20))
```

Function Returning Function

But now let's go even further! Instead of returning an image, our function can return *a function* that makes rounded rectangles *of the specified size*. If you've never seen a function returned as a value from a function, you may now be gasping for breath. But a function, after all, can be used as a value. We have already passed a function *into* a function as an argument in the function call; now we are going to receive a function *from* a function call as its result:

```
func makeRoundedRectangleMaker(_ sz:CGSize) -> () -> UIImage {  ❶
    func f () -> UIImage {  ❷
        let im = imageOfSize(sz) {
            let p = UIBezierPath(
                roundedRect: CGRect(origin:CGPoint.zero, size:sz),
                cornerRadius: 8)
            p.stroke()
        }
        return im
    }
    return f  ❸
}
```

Let's analyze that code slowly:

❶ The declaration is the hardest part. What on earth is the type (signature) of this function `makeRoundedRectangleMaker`? It is `(CGSize) -> () -> UIImage`. That expression has *two* arrow operators. To understand it, keep in mind that everything after each arrow operator is the type of a returned value. So `makeRounded-RectangleMaker` is a function that takes a CGSize parameter and returns a `() -> UIImage`. Okay, and what's a `() -> UIImage`? We already know that: it's a function that takes no parameters and returns a UIImage. So `makeRounded-`

RectangleMaker is a function that takes a CGSize parameter and returns *a function* — a function that itself, when called with *no* parameters, will return a UIImage.

❷ Now here we are in the body of the function makeRoundedRectangleMaker, and our first step is to declare a function (a function-in-function, or local function) of precisely the type we intend to return, namely, one that takes no parameters and returns a UIImage. Here, we're naming this function f. The way this function works is simple and familiar: it calls imageOfSize, passing it an anonymous function that makes an image of a rounded rectangle (im) — and then it returns the image.

❸ Finally, we *return* the function we just made (f). We have fulfilled our contract: we said we would return a function that takes no parameters and returns a UIImage, and we do so.

But perhaps you are still gazing open-mouthed at makeRoundedRectangleMaker, wondering how you would ever call it and what you would get if you did. Let's try it:

```
let maker = makeRoundedRectangleMaker(CGSize(width:45, height:20))
```

What is the variable maker after that code runs? It's a *function* — a function that takes no parameters and that, when called, produces the image of a rounded rectangle of size 45,20. You don't believe me? I'll prove it — by *calling* the function that is now the value of maker:

```
let maker = makeRoundedRectangleMaker(CGSize(width:45, height:20))
self.iv.image = maker()
```

Now that you've gotten over your stunned surprise at the notion of a function that produces a function as its result, turn your attention once again to the implementation of makeRoundedRectangleMaker and let's analyze it again, a different way. Remember, I didn't write that function to show you that a function can produce a function. I wrote it to illustrate closures! Let's think about how the environment gets captured:

```
func makeRoundedRectangleMaker(_ sz:CGSize) -> () -> UIImage {
    func f () -> UIImage {
        let im = imageOfSize(sz) { // *
            let p = UIBezierPath(
                roundedRect: CGRect(origin:CGPoint.zero, size:sz), // *
                cornerRadius: 8)
            p.stroke()
        }
        return im
    }
    return f
}
```

The function f takes no parameters. Yet, twice within the function body of f (I've marked the places with asterisk comments), there are references to a size value sz. The body of the function f can see sz, the parameter of the surrounding function makeRoundedRectangleMaker, because it is in a surrounding scope. The function f *captures* the reference to sz at the time makeRoundedRectangleMaker is called, and *keeps* that reference when f is returned and assigned to maker:

```
let maker = makeRoundedRectangleMaker(CGSize(width:45, height:20))
```

That is why maker is now a function that, when it is called, creates and returns an image of the particular size 45,20 even though it itself will be called *with no parameters*. The knowledge of what size of image to produce has been *baked into* the function referred to by maker. Looking at it another way, makeRoundedRectangleMaker is a *factory* for creating a whole family of functions similar to maker, each of which produces an image of one particular size. That's a dramatic illustration of the power of closures.

Before I leave makeRoundedRectangleMaker, I'd like to rewrite it in a Swiftier fashion. Within f, there is no need to create im and then return it; we can return the result of calling imageOfSize directly:

```
func makeRoundedRectangleMaker(_ sz:CGSize) -> () -> UIImage {
    func f () -> UIImage {
        return imageOfSize(sz) {
            let p = UIBezierPath(
                roundedRect: CGRect(origin:CGPoint.zero, size:sz),
                cornerRadius: 8)
            p.stroke()
        }
    }
    return f
}
```

But there is no need to declare f and then return it either; it can be an anonymous function and we can return it directly:

```
func makeRoundedRectangleMaker(_ sz:CGSize) -> () -> UIImage {
    return {
        return imageOfSize(sz) {
            let p = UIBezierPath(
                roundedRect: CGRect(origin:CGPoint.zero, size:sz),
                cornerRadius: 8)
            p.stroke()
        }
    }
}
```

But our anonymous function consists of nothing but a return statement; the anonymous function parameter to imageOfSize consists of multiple statements, but the `imageOfSize` call itself is still just one Swift statement. We can omit the keyword `return` (and we could omit the remaining `return` too, but I prefer not to):

```
func makeRoundedRectangleMaker(_ sz:CGSize) -> () -> UIImage {
    return {
        imageOfSize(sz) {
            let p = UIBezierPath(
                roundedRect: CGRect(origin:CGPoint.zero, size:sz),
                cornerRadius: 8)
            p.stroke()
        }
    }
}
```

Closure Setting a Captured Variable

The power that a closure gets through its ability to capture its environment is even greater than I've shown so far. If a closure captures a reference to a variable outside itself, and if that variable is settable, then *the closure can set the variable*.

Let's say I've declared this simple function. All it does is to accept a function that takes an Int parameter, and to call that function with an argument of 100:

```
func pass100 (_ f:(Int) -> ()) {
    f(100)
}
```

Now, look closely at this code and try to guess what will happen when we run it:

```
var x = 0
print(x) // ?
func setX(newX:Int) {
    x = newX
}
pass100(setX)
print(x) // ?
```

The first `print(x)` call obviously produces 0. The second `print(x)` call produces 100! The `pass100` function has reached into my code and *changed* the value of my variable x. That's because the function `setX` that I passed to `pass100` contains a reference to x; not only does it contain it, but it captures it; not only does it capture it, but it sets its value. That x *is my x*. `pass100` was able to set my x just as readily as I would have set it by calling `setX` directly.

Closure Preserving Captured Environment

When a closure captures its environment, it *preserves* that environment *even if nothing else does*. Here's an example calculated to blow your mind — a function that modifies a function:

```
func countAdder(_ f: @escaping () -> ()) -> () -> () {
    var ct = 0
    return {
        ct = ct + 1
        print("count is \(ct)")
        f()
    }
}
```

The function countAdder accepts a function as its parameter and returns a function as its result. (I'll explain the @escaping attribute in the next section.) The function that it returns calls the function that it accepts, with a little bit added: it increments a variable and reports the result. So now try to guess what will happen when we run this code:

```
func greet () {
    print("howdy")
}
let countedGreet = countAdder(greet)
countedGreet() // ?
countedGreet() // ?
countedGreet() // ?
```

What we've done here is to take a function greet, which prints "howdy", and pass it through countAdder. What comes out the other side of countAdder is a new function, which we've named countedGreet. We then call countedGreet three times. Here's what appears in the console:

```
count is 1
howdy
count is 2
howdy
count is 3
howdy
```

Clearly, countAdder has added to the functionality of the function that was passed into it *the ability to report how many times it is called.* Now ask yourself: Where on earth is the variable that maintains this count? Inside countAdder, it was a local variable ct. But it isn't declared inside the anonymous function that countAdder returns. That's deliberate! If it *were* declared inside the anonymous function, we would be setting ct to 0 every time countedGreet is called — we wouldn't be counting. Instead, ct is initialized to 0 once *and then captured* by the anonymous function. This variable is preserved as part of the *environment* of countedGreet — it is *outside* countedGreet in some mysterious environment-preserving world, so that it can be incremented every time countedGreet is called.

Escaping Closures

If a function passed around as a value will be preserved for later execution, rather than being called directly, it is a closure that captures and preserves its environment *over time*. That's called an *escaping* closure. In some situations, the function's type must be explicitly marked `@escaping`. The compiler will detect violations of this rule, so if you find the rule confusing, don't worry about it; just let the compiler enforce it for you.

This function is legal because it receives a function and calls it directly:

```
func funcCaller(f:() -> ()) {
    f()
}
```

And this function is legal, even though it returns a function to be executed later, because it also *creates* that function internally. The function that it returns *is* an escaping closure, but the type of the function's returned value does not have to be marked as `@escaping`:

```
func funcMaker() -> () -> () {
    return { print("hello world") }
}
```

But this function is illegal. It receives a function as a parameter *and* returns that function to be executed later:

```
func funcPasser(f:() -> ()) -> () -> () { // compile error
    return f
}
```

The solution is to mark the type of the incoming parameter `f` as `@escaping`, and the compiler will prompt you to do so:

```
func funcPasser(f:@escaping () -> ()) -> () -> () {
    return f
}
```

A secondary feature of escaping closures is that, when you refer to a property or method of `self` within the function body, the compiler may insist that you say `self` explicitly. That's because such a reference *captures* `self`, and the compiler wants you to acknowledge this fact by *saying* `self`:

```
let f1 = funcPasser {
    print(view.bounds) // compile error, because self.view is implied
}
let f2 = funcPasser {
    print(self.view.bounds) // ok
}
```

I'll return to that point when I talk about memory management in Chapter 5.

Curried Functions

Return once more to `makeRoundedRectangleMaker`:

```
func makeRoundedRectangleMaker(_ sz:CGSize) -> () -> UIImage {
    return {
        imageOfSize(sz) {
            let p = UIBezierPath(
                roundedRect: CGRect(origin:CGPoint.zero, size:sz),
                cornerRadius: 8)
            p.stroke()
        }
    }
}
```

There's something I don't like about this method: the size of the rounded rectangle that it creates is a parameter (`sz`), but the `cornerRadius` of the rounded rectangle is hard-coded as 8. I'd like the ability to pass a value for the corner radius as part of the call. I can think of two ways to do that. One is to give `makeRoundedRectangleMaker` itself another parameter:

```
func makeRoundedRectangleMaker(_ sz:CGSize, _ r:CGFloat) -> () -> UIImage {
    return {
        imageOfSize(sz) {
            let p = UIBezierPath(
                roundedRect: CGRect(origin:CGPoint.zero, size:sz),
                cornerRadius: r)
            p.stroke()
        }
    }
}
```

And we would then call it like this:

```
let maker = makeRoundedRectangleMaker(CGSize(width:45, height:20), 8)
```

But there's another way. The function that we are returning from `makeRounded-RectangleMaker` takes no parameters. Instead, *it* could take the extra parameter:

```
func makeRoundedRectangleMaker(_ sz:CGSize) -> (CGFloat) -> UIImage {
    return { r in
        imageOfSize(sz) {
            let p = UIBezierPath(
                roundedRect: CGRect(origin:CGPoint.zero, size:sz),
                cornerRadius: r)
            p.stroke()
        }
    }
}
```

Now `makeRoundedRectangleMaker` returns a function that, itself, takes one parameter, so we must remember to supply that when we call it:

```
let maker = makeRoundedRectangleMaker(CGSize(width:45, height:20))
self.iv.image = maker(8)
```

If we don't need to conserve `maker` for anything, we can of course do all that in one line — a function call that yields a function which we immediately call to obtain our image:

```
self.iv.image = makeRoundedRectangleMaker(CGSize(width:45, height:20))(8)
```

When a function returns a function that takes a parameter in this way, it is called a *curried* function (after the computer scientist Haskell Curry).

Function References and Selectors

When you want to refer to a function by name — perhaps in order to pass it as argument to another function — you can often use its bare name. That's what I've been doing throughout this chapter, in examples like this:

```
func whatToAnimate() { // self.myButton is a button in the interface
    self.myButton.frame.origin.y += 20
}
func whatToDoLater(finished:Bool) {
    print("finished: \(finished)")
}
UIView.animate(withDuration:0.4,
    animations: whatToAnimate, completion: whatToDoLater) // *
```

A bare name like `whatToAnimate` or `whatToDoLater` is a *function reference*. It consists of the base name alone, the part of the function's name that precedes the parentheses. The lack of parentheses makes it clear that this is a reference, not a call. Use of the bare name as a function reference is legal when it's unambiguous: in this particular context, there's only one function called `whatToDoLater` in scope, and I'm using its name as argument in a function call where the parameter type is known (namely, `(Bool) -> ()`).

But now consider the following situation. Just as I can pass a function as an argument, I can assign a function as a value to a variable. And suppose I have *two* functions with the same name, one that takes a parameter, and one that doesn't:

```
class Dog {
    func bark() {
        print("woof")
    }
    func bark(_ loudly:Bool) {
        if loudly {
            print("WOOF")
        } else {
            self.bark()
        }
    }
}
```

```
        func test() {
            let barkFunction = bark // compile error
            // ...
        }
    }
```

That code won't compile, because the bare name bark is ambiguous in this context: which bark method does it refer to? To solve this problem, Swift provides a notation allowing you to refer to a function more precisely. This notation has two parts:

Full name

> The full name of a Swift function is the base name along with parentheses containing the external names of its parameters, each followed by colon (and no commas or spaces). If the external name of a parameter is suppressed, we represent its external name as an underscore.

Signature

> The signature of a Swift function may be appended to its bare name (or full name) with the keyword as.

So, for example:

```
    func say(_ s:String, times:Int) {
```

That method has full name say(_:times:) but may be referred to using a bare name and signature as say as (String, Int) -> ().

In our bark example, use of the full name solves the problem if the function to which we want a reference is the one that takes a parameter:

```
    class Dog {
        func bark() {
            // ... as before ...
        }
        func bark(_ loudly:Bool) {
            // ... as before ...
        }
        func test() {
            let barkFunction = bark(_:) // fine
        }
    }
```

But use of the full name *doesn't* solve the problem if the function to which we want a reference is the one that takes *no* parameters, because in that case the full name is the bare name, which is exactly what's ambiguous in this context. Use of the signature solves the problem:

```
    class Dog {
        func bark() {
            // ... as before ...
        }
```

```
func bark(_ loudly:Bool) {
    // ... as before ...
}
func test() {
    let barkFunction = bark as () -> () // fine
}
}
```

Obviously, an explicit signature is needed also when a function is *overloaded*:

```
class Dog {
    func bark() {
    }
    func bark(_ loudly:Bool) {
    }
    func bark(_ times:Int) {
    }
    func test() {
        let barkFunction = bark(_:) // compile error
    }
}
```

Here, we have said that we want the `bark` that takes one parameter, but there are *two* such `bark` functions, one whose parameter is a Bool, the other whose parameter is an Int. The signature disambiguates (and we can use the bare name):

```
let barkFunction = bark as (Int) -> () // "times", not "loudly"
```

Function Reference Scope

In the foregoing examples of function references, there was no need to tell the compiler *where* the function is defined. That's because the function is already in scope at the point where the function reference appears. If you can *call* the function without supplying further information, you can form the function *reference* without supplying further information.

However, a function reference *can* supply further information about where a function is defined; and sometimes it *must* do so. This is done by prefixing an instance or class to the function reference, using dot-notation. There are situations where the compiler would force you to use `self` to call a function; in those situations, you will have to use `self` to refer to the function as well:

```
class Dog {
    func bark() {
    }
    func bark(_ loudly:Bool) {
    }
    func test() {
        let f = {
```

```
            return self.bark(_:) // self required here
        }
    }
}
```

To form a function reference to an instance method of another type, you have two choices. If you have on hand an instance of that type, you can use dot-notation with a reference to that instance:

```
class Cat {
    func purr() {
    }
}
class Dog {
    let cat = Cat()
    func test() {
        let purrFunction = cat.purr
    }
}
```

The other possibility is to use *the type* with dot-notation (this works even if the function is an instance method):

```
class Cat {
    func purr() {
    }
}
class Dog {
    func bark() {
    }
    func test() {
        let barkFunction = Dog.bark // legal but not necessary
        let purrFunction = Cat.purr
    }
}
```

If you use the type with dot-notation and you need to disambiguate the function reference by giving its signature, the signature must describe the curried static/class version of the instance method (see "The Secret Life of Instance Methods" on page 134):

```
class Cat {
    func purr() {
    }
    func purr(_ loudly:Bool) {
    }
}
class Dog {
    func test() {
        let purrFunction = Cat.purr as (Cat) -> () -> Void
    }
}
```

Selectors

In Objective-C, a selector is a kind of method reference. In iOS programming, you might have to call a Cocoa method that wants a selector as one of its parameters; typically, this parameter will be named either `selector:` or `action:`. Usually, such a method also requires that you provide a *target* (an object reference); the idea is that the runtime can later call the method by turning the selector into a message and sending that message to that target.

Unfortunately, this architecture can be extremely risky. The reason is that to form the selector, it is necessary to construct a string representing a method's Objective-C name. If you construct that string incorrectly, then when the time comes to send the message to the target, the runtime will find that the target can't handle that message, because it has no such method, and the app comes to a violent and premature halt, dumping into the console the dreaded phrase "unrecognized selector." Here's a typical recipe for failure:

```
class ViewController : UIViewController {
    @IBOutlet var button : UIButton!
    func viewDidLoad() {
        super.viewDidLoad()
        self.button.addTarget( // prepare to crash!
            self, action: "buttonPressed", for: .touchUpInside)
    }
    @objc func buttonPressed(_ sender: Any) {
        // ...
    }
}
```

In that code, `self.button` is a button in the interface, and we are configuring it by calling `addTarget(action:for:)`, so that when the button is tapped, our `button-Pressed` method will be called. But we are configuring it incorrectly! Unfortunately, `"buttonPressed"` is *not* the Objective-C name of our `buttonPressed` method; the correct name would have been `"buttonPressed:"`, with a colon. (I'll explain why in Appendix A.) Therefore, our app will crash when the user taps that button.

The point is that if you don't know the rules for forming a selector string — or even if you do, but you make a typing mistake — an "unrecognized selector" crash is likely to result. Humans are fallible, and therefore "unrecognized selector" crashes have historically been extremely common among iOS programmers. The Swift compiler, however, is *not* fallible in this way. Therefore, Swift provides a way to let the compiler form the selector for you, by means of `#selector` syntax.

To ask the compiler to form an Objective-C selector for you, you use `#selector(...)` with a function reference inside the parentheses. We would rewrite our button action example like this:

```
class ViewController : UIViewController {
    @IBOutlet var button : UIButton!
    func viewDidLoad() {
        super.viewDidLoad()
        self.button.addTarget(
            self, action: #selector(buttonPressed), for: .touchUpInside)
    }
    @objc func buttonPressed(_ sender: Any) {
        // ...
    }
}
```

When you use that notation, two wonderful things happen:

The compiler validates the function reference
> If your function reference isn't valid, your code won't even compile. The compiler also checks that this function is exposed to Objective-C; there's no point forming a selector for a method that Objective-C can't see, as your app would crash if Objective-C were to try to call such a method. To ensure Objective-C visibility, the method may need to be marked with the `@objc` attribute; the compiler will enforce this requirement.

The compiler forms the Objective-C selector for you
> If your code compiles, the actual selector that will be passed into this parameter is guaranteed to be correct. *You* might form the selector incorrectly, but the compiler won't! It is impossible that the resulting selector should fail to match the method, and there is no chance of an "unrecognized selector" crash.

Very rarely, you still might need to create a selector manually. To do so, you can use a string, or you can instantiate Selector with the string as argument — for example, `Selector("woohoo:")`.

 You can still crash, even with `#selector` syntax, by sending an action message to the *wrong target*. In the preceding example, if you changed `self`, the first argument of the `addTarget` call, to `self.button`, you'd crash at runtime with "unrecognized selector" — because the `buttonPressed` method is declared in ViewController, not in UIButton. Unfortunately, the compiler won't help you with this kind of mistake.

CHAPTER 3

Variables and Simple Types

A variable is a named "shoebox" whose contained value must be of a single well-defined type. Every variable must be explicitly and formally declared. To put a value into the shoebox, causing the variable name to *refer* to that value, you *assign* the value to the variable. The variable name becomes a *reference* to that value.

This chapter goes into detail about declaration and initialization of variables. It then discusses all the primary built-in Swift simple types. (I mean "simple" as opposed to collections; the primary built-in collection types are discussed at the end of Chapter 4.)

Variable Scope and Lifetime

A variable not only gives its referent a name; it also, by virtue of *where* it is declared, endows its referent with a particular scope (visibility) and lifetime. (See "Scope and Lifetime" on page 12.) Assigning a value to a variable is a way of ensuring that this value can be *seen* by code that needs to see it and that it *persists* long enough to serve its purpose. There are three distinct levels of variable scope and lifetime:

Global variables

A global variable, or simply a *global*, is a variable declared at the top level of a Swift file. A global variable lives as long as the file lives, which is as long as the program runs. A global variable is visible everywhere (that's what "global" means). It is visible to all code within the *same* file, because it is at top level; any other code in the same file is therefore at the same level or at a lower contained level of scope. Moreover, it is visible (by default) to all code within any *other* file in the same module, because Swift files in the same module can automatically see one another, and hence can see one another's top levels:

```
// File1:
let globalVariable = "global"
class Dog {
    func printGlobal() {
        print(globalVariable) // *
    }
}
// File2:
class Cat {
    func printGlobal() {
        print(globalVariable) // *
    }
}
```

Properties

A *property* is a variable declared at the top level of an object type declaration (an enum, struct, or class). There are two kinds of properties: instance properties and static/class properties.

Instance properties

By default, a property is an *instance* property. Its value can differ for each instance of this object type, as I explained in Chapter 1. Its lifetime is the same as the lifetime of the instance. An instance comes into existence through deliberate instantiation of an object type; the subsequent lifetime of the instance, and hence of its instance properties, depends primarily on the lifetime of the variable to which the instance *itself* is assigned.

Static/class properties

A property is a static/class property if its declaration is preceded by the keyword `static` or `class`. (I'll go into detail about those terms in Chapter 4.) Its lifetime is the same as the lifetime of the object type. If the object type is declared at the top level of a file, the property lives as long as the program runs.

A property is visible only by way of the object. An object's methods can see that object's properties directly; such code can refer to the property using dot-notation with `self`, and I always do this as a matter of style, but `self` can usually be omitted except for purposes of disambiguation. An instance property is also visible (by default) to other code, provided the other code has a reference to this instance; in that case, the property can be referred to through dot-notation with the instance reference. A static/class property is visible (by default) to other code that can see the name of this object type; in that case, it can be referred to through dot-notation with the object type:

```
// File1:
class Dog {
    static let staticProperty = "staticProperty"
    let instanceProperty = "instanceProperty"
    func printInstanceProperty() {
        print(self.instanceProperty) // *
    }
}
// File2:
class Cat {
    func printDogStaticProperty() {
        print(Dog.staticProperty) // *
    }
    func printDogInstanceProperty() {
        let d = Dog()
        print(d.instanceProperty) // *
    }
}
```

Local variables

A local variable is a variable declared inside a function body. A local variable lives only as long as its surrounding curly-braces scope lives: it comes into existence when the path of execution passes into the scope and reaches the variable declaration, and it goes out of existence when the path of execution exits the scope. Local variables are sometimes called *automatic,* to signify that they come into and go out of existence automatically. A local variable can be seen only by subsequent code within the same scope (including a subsequent deeper scope within the same scope):

```
class Dog {
    func printLocalVariable() {
        let localVariable = "local"
        print(localVariable) // *
    }
}
```

Variable Declaration

A variable is declared with let or var:

- With let, the variable becomes a *constant* — its value can never be changed after the first assignment of a value.

- With var, the variable is a true variable, and its value can be changed by subsequent assignment.

A variable declaration is usually accompanied by *initialization* — you use an equal sign to assign the variable a value, as part of the declaration. That, however, is not a requirement; it is legal to declare a variable without immediately initializing it.

What is *not* legal is to declare a variable without giving it a *type*. A variable *must* have a type from the outset, and that type can *never be changed*. A variable declared with var can have its *value* changed by subsequent assignment, but the new value must conform to the variable's fixed type.

You can give a variable a type explicitly or implicitly:

Explicit variable type declaration
> After the variable's name in the declaration, add a colon and the name of the type:
>
> ```
> var x : Int
> ```

Implicit variable type by initialization
> If you initialize the variable as part of the declaration, and if you provide no explicit type, Swift will *infer* its type, based on the value with which it is initialized:
>
> ```
> var x = 1 // and now x is an Int
> ```

It is perfectly possible to declare a variable's type explicitly *and* assign it an initial value, all in one move:

```
var x : Int = 1
```

In that example, the explicit type declaration is superfluous, because the type (Int) would have been inferred from the initial value. Sometimes, however, providing an explicit type, even while also assigning an initial value, is *not* superfluous. Here are the main situations where that's the case:

Swift's inference would be wrong
> A very common case in my own code is when I want to provide the initial value as a numeric literal. Swift will infer either Int or Double, depending on whether the literal contains a decimal point. But there are a lot of other numeric types! When I mean one of those, I will provide the type explicitly, like this:
>
> ```
> let separator : CGFloat = 2.0
> ```

Swift can't infer the type
> Sometimes, the type of the initial value is completely unknown to the compiler unless you tell it. A very common case involves option sets (discussed in Chapter 4). This won't compile:
>
> ```
> var opts = [.autoreverse, .repeat] // compile error
> ```

The problem is that Swift doesn't know the type of .autoreverse and .repeat unless we tell it:

```
let opts : UIView.AnimationOptions = [.autoreverse, .repeat]
```

The programmer can't infer the type

I frequently include a superfluous explicit type declaration as a kind of note to myself. Here's an example from my own code:

```
let duration : CMTime = track.timeRange.duration
```

In that code, track is an AVAssetTrack. Swift knows perfectly well that the duration property of an AVAssetTrack's timeRange property is a CMTime. But I don't! In order to remind myself of that fact, I've shown the type explicitly.

 Even if the compiler can infer a variable's type correctly from its initial value, such inference takes time. You can reduce compilation times by providing your variable declarations with explicit types.

As I've already said, a variable doesn't have to be initialized when it is declared — even if the variable is a constant. It is legal to write this:

```
let x : Int
```

Now x is an empty shoebox — an Int variable without an initial value. You can assign this variable an initial value later. Since this particular variable is a constant, that initial value will be its only value from then on.

In the case of an instance property of an object (at the top level of an enum, struct, or class declaration), that sort of thing is quite normal, because the property can be initialized in the object's initializer function. (I'll have more to say about that in Chapter 4.) For a local variable, however, such behavior is unusual, and I strongly urge you to avoid it. It isn't a disaster — the Swift compiler will stop you from trying to use a variable that has never been assigned a value — but it's not a good habit. A local variable should generally be initialized as part of its declaration.

The exception that proves the rule is what we might call *conditional initialization*. Sometimes, we don't *know* a variable's initial value until we've performed some sort of conditional test. The variable itself, however, can be declared only once; so it must be declared in advance and conditionally initialized afterward. This sort of thing is not unreasonable:

```
let timed : Bool
if val == 1 {
    timed = true
} else {
    timed = false
}
```

That particular example can arguably be better expressed in other ways (which I'll come to in Chapter 5), but there are situations where conditional initialization is the cleanest approach.

When a variable's *address* is to be passed as argument to a function, the variable must be declared *and initialized* beforehand, even if the initial value is fake. Recall this example from Chapter 2:

```
var r : CGFloat = 0
var g : CGFloat = 0
var b : CGFloat = 0
var a : CGFloat = 0
c.getRed(&r, green: &g, blue: &b, alpha: &a)
```

After that code runs, our four CGFloat 0 values will have been replaced; they were just momentary placeholders, to satisfy the compiler.

On rare occasions, you'll want to call a Cocoa method that returns a value immediately and later uses that value in a function passed to that same method. For example, Cocoa has a UIApplication instance method declared like this:

```
func beginBackgroundTask(
    expirationHandler handler: (() -> Void)? = nil)
        -> UIBackgroundTaskIdentifier
```

beginBackgroundTask(expirationHandler:) returns an identifier object, and will later call the expirationHandler: function passed to it — a function in which you will want to *use* the identifier object that was returned at the outset. Swift's safety rules won't let you declare the variable that holds this identifier and use it in an anonymous function all in the same statement:

```
let bti = UIApplication.shared.beginBackgroundTask {
    UIApplication.shared.endBackgroundTask(bti)
} // error: variable used within its own initial value
```

Therefore, you need to declare the variable beforehand; but then Swift has another complaint:

```
var bti : UIBackgroundTaskIdentifier
bti = UIApplication.shared.beginBackgroundTask {
    UIApplication.shared.endBackgroundTask(bti)
} // error: variable captured by a closure before being initialized
```

One solution is to declare the variable beforehand with a fake initial value as a placeholder:

```
var bti : UIBackgroundTaskIdentifier = .invalid
bti = UIApplication.shared.beginBackgroundTask {
    UIApplication.shared.endBackgroundTask(bti)
}
```

Computed Variable Initialization

Sometimes, you'd like to run several lines of code in order to compute a variable's initial value. A simple and compact way to express this is with a define-and-call anonymous function (see "Define-and-Call" on page 50). I'll illustrate by rewriting an earlier example:

```
let timed : Bool = {
    if val == 1 {
        return true
    } else {
        return false
    }
}()
```

You can do the same thing when you're initializing an instance property. Here's a class with an image (a UIImage) that I'm going to need many times later on. It makes sense to create this image in advance as a constant instance property of the class. To create it means to draw it. That takes several lines of code. So I declare and initialize the property by defining and calling an anonymous function, like this (for my image-OfSize utility, see Chapter 2):

```
class RootViewController : UITableViewController {
    let cellBackgroundImage : UIImage = {
        return imageOfSize(CGSize(width:320, height:44)) {
            // ... drawing goes here ...
        }
    }()
    // ... rest of class goes here ...
}
```

You might ask: Instead of a define-and-call initializer, why don't I declare an instance method and initialize the instance property by calling that method? The reason is that that's illegal:

```
class RootViewController : UITableViewController {
    let cellBackgroundImage : UIImage = self.makeTheImage() // compile error
    func makeTheImage() -> UIImage {
        return imageOfSize(CGSize(width:320, height:44)) {
            // ... drawing goes here ...
        }
    }
}
```

The problem is that, at the time of initializing the instance property, there is no instance yet — the instance is what we are in the process of creating. Therefore you can't refer to self (implicitly or explicitly) in a property declaration's initializer. A define-and-call anonymous function, however, is legal. But the define-and-call anonymous function *still* can't refer to `self`! I'll provide a workaround a little later in this chapter.

Computed Variables

The variables I've been describing so far in this chapter have all been *stored* variables. The named shoebox analogy applies: a value can be put into the shoebox by assigning it to the variable, and it then sits there and can be retrieved later by referring to the variable, for as long the variable lives.

But a variable in Swift can work in a completely different way: it can be *computed*. This means that the variable, instead of having a value, has *functions*. One function, the *setter*, is called when the variable is assigned to. The other function, the *getter*, is called when the variable is referred to. Here's some code illustrating schematically the syntax for declaring a computed variable:

```
var now : String { ❶
    get { ❷
        return Date().description ❸
    }
    set { ❹
        print(newValue) ❺
    }
}
```

❶   The variable must be declared with `var` (not `let`). Its type must be declared explicitly. The type is followed immediately by curly braces.

❷   The getter function is called `get`. There is no formal function declaration; the word `get` is simply followed immediately by a function body in curly braces.

❸   The getter function must return a value of the same type as the variable. When the getter is a single statement, it is legal to omit the keyword `return` (starting in Swift 5.1).

❹   The setter function is called `set`. There is no formal function declaration; the word `set` is simply followed immediately by a function body in curly braces.

❺   The setter behaves like a function taking one parameter. By default, this parameter arrives into the setter function body with the local name `newValue`.

Here's some code that illustrates the use of our computed variable. You don't treat it any differently than any other variable! To assign to the variable, assign to it; to use the variable, use it. Behind the scenes, though, the setter and getter functions are called:

```
now = "Howdy" // Howdy ❶
print(now) // 2019-06-26 17:03:30 +0000 ❷
```

❶ Assigning to now calls its setter. The argument passed into this call is the assigned value; here, that's "Howdy". That value arrives in the set function as newValue. Our set function prints newValue to the console.

❷ Fetching now calls its getter. Our get function obtains the current date-time and translates it into a string, and returns the string. Our code then prints that string to the console.

There are a couple of variants on the basic syntax I've just illustrated:

- The name of the set function parameter doesn't have to be newValue. To specify a different name, put it in parentheses after the word set, like this:

  ```
  set (val) { // now you can use "val" inside the setter function body
  ```

- There doesn't have to be a setter. If the setter is omitted, this becomes a *read-only* variable. This is the computed variable equivalent of a let variable: attempting to assign to it is a compile error.

- There must always be a getter! However, if there is no setter, the word get and the curly braces that follow it can be omitted. This is a legal declaration of a read-only variable (omitting the return keyword):

  ```
  var now : String {
      Date().description
  }
  ```

Computed Properties

In real life, your main use of computed variables will nearly always be as instance properties. Here are some common ways in which computed properties are useful:

Façade for a longer expression
When a value can be readily calculated or obtained each time it is needed, it often makes for simpler syntax to express it as a read-only computed variable, which effectively acts as a shorthand for a longer expression. Here's an example from my own code:

```
var mp : MPMusicPlayerController {
    MPMusicPlayerController.systemMusicPlayer
}
var nowPlayingItem : MPMediaItem? {
    self.mp.nowPlayingItem
}
```

No work is saved by these computed variables; each time we ask for `self.now-PlayingItem`, we are fetching `MPMusicPlayerController.systemMusicPlayer.nowPlayingItem`. Still, the clarity and convenience of the resulting code justifies the use of computed variables here.

Façade for an elaborate calculation

A computed variable getter can encapsulate multiple lines of code, in effect turning a method into a property. Here's an example from my own code:

```
var authorOfItem : String? {
    guard let authorNodes =
        self.extensionElements(
            withXMLNamespace: "http://www.tidbits.com/dummy",
            elementName: "app_author_name")
        else {return nil}
    guard let authorNode = authorNodes.last as? FPExtensionNode
        else {return nil}
    return authorNode.stringValue
}
```

In that example, I'm diving into some parsed XML and extracting a value. I could have declared this as a method `func authorOfItem() -> String?`, but a method expresses a *process*, whereas a computed property characterizes it more intuitively as a *thing*.

Façade for storage

A computed variable can sit in front of one or more stored variables, acting as a gatekeeper on how those stored variables are set and fetched. This is comparable to an accessor method in Objective-C. Commonly, a public computed variable is backed by a private stored variable. The simplest possible storage façade would do no more than get and set the private stored variable directly:

```
private var _p : String = ""
var p : String {
    get {
        self._p
    }
    set {
        self._p = newValue
    }
}
```

That's legal but pointless. A storage façade becomes useful when it does *other* things while getting or setting the stored variable. Here's a more realistic example: a "clamped" setter. This is an Int property to which only values between 0 and 5 can be assigned; larger values are replaced by 5, and smaller values are replaced by 0:

```
private var _pp : Int = 0
var pp : Int {
    get {
        self._pp
    }
    set {
        self._pp = max(min(newValue,5),0)
    }
}
```

As the preceding examples demonstrate, a computed instance property getter or setter can refer to other instance members. That's important, because in general the initializer for a stored property can't do that. The reason it's legal for a computed property is that the getter and setter functions won't be called until the instance actually exists.

Property Wrappers

If we have several storage façade computed properties that effectively do the same thing, we're going to end up with a lot of repeated code. Imagine implementing more than one Int property with a clamped setter, as in the preceding section. It would be nice to move the common functionality off into a single location. Starting in Swift 5.1, we can do that, using a *property wrapper.*

A property wrapper is declared as a type marked with the @propertyWrapper attribute, and must have a wrappedValue computed property. Here's a property wrapper implementing the "clamped" pattern:

```
@propertyWrapper struct Clamped {
    private var _i : Int = 0
    var wrappedValue : Int {
        get {
            self._i
        }
        set {
            self._i = Swift.max(Swift.min(newValue,5),0)
        }
    }
}
```

The result is that we can declare a computed property marked with a custom attribute whose name is the same as that struct (@Clamped), with *no* getter or setter:

```
@Clamped var p
```

Our property p doesn't need to be initialized, because it's a computed property. And it doesn't need a getter or a setter — indeed, in this case it doesn't even need a type declaration — because the wrappedValue computed property of the Clamped struct supplies them!

Behind the scenes, an actual Clamped instance has been created for us. When we set self.p to some value through assignment, the assignment passes through the Clamped instance's wrappedValue setter, and the resulting clamped value is stored in the Clamped instance's _i property. When we fetch the value of self.p, what we get is the value returned from the Clamped instance's wrappedValue getter, which is the value stored in the Clamped instance's _i property.

Thanks to our property wrapper, we have *encapsulated* this computed property pattern, which means we can now declare *another* @Clamped property which will behave in just the same way. It's also nice that this pattern now has a *name:* the declaration @Clamped var tells us what the behavior of this computed property will be.

(Believe it or not, I created the Clamped example *before* discovering that the Swift language proposal for property wrappers uses the same example!)

There's considerably more to know about property wrappers, but I'll postpone further discussion to Chapter 5, after I've explained other language features that will help you appreciate their power and flexibility.

Setter Observers

Computed variables are not needed as a stored variable façade as often as you might suppose. That's because Swift has another feature, which lets you inject functionality into the setter of a *stored* variable — *setter observers.* These are functions that are called just before and just after other code sets a stored variable.

The syntax for declaring a variable with a setter observer is very similar to the syntax for declaring a computed variable; you can write a willSet function, a didSet function, or both:

```
var s = "whatever" { ❶
    willSet { ❷
        print(newValue) ❸
    }
    didSet { ❹
        print(oldValue) ❺
        // self.s = "something else"
    }
}
```

❶ The variable must be declared with var (not let). It can be assigned an initial value. It is then followed immediately by curly braces.

❷ The willSet function, if there is one, is the word willSet followed immediately by a function body in curly braces. It is called when other code sets this variable, just *before* the variable actually receives its new value.

❸ By default, the `willSet` function receives the incoming new value as `newValue`. You can change this name by writing a different name in parentheses after the word `willSet`. The old value is still sitting in the stored variable, and the `willSet` function can access it there.

❹ The `didSet` function, if there is one, is the word `didSet` followed immediately by a function body in curly braces. It is called when other code sets this variable, just *after* the variable actually receives its new value.

❺ By default, the `didSet` function receives the old value, which has already been replaced as the value of the variable, as `oldValue`. You can change this name by writing a different name in parentheses after the word `didSet`. The new value is already sitting in the stored variable, and the `didSet` function can access it there. Moreover, it is legal for the `didSet` function to set the stored variable to a different value.

 Setter observer functions are *not* called when the stored variable is initialized or when the `didSet` function changes the stored variable's value. That would be circular!

In real-life iOS programming, you'll want the visible interface to reflect the state of your objects. A setter observer is a simple but powerful way to synchronize the interface with a property. In this example, we have an instance property of a view class, determining how much the view should be rotated; every time this property changes, we change the interface to reflect it, setting `self.transform` so that the view *is* rotated by that amount:

```
var angle : CGFloat = 0 {
    didSet {
        // modify interface to match
        self.transform = CGAffineTransform(rotationAngle: self.angle)
    }
}
```

A computed variable can't have setter observers. But it doesn't need them! There's a setter function, so anything additional that needs to happen during setting can be programmed directly into that setter function. (But a property-wrapped computed variable *can* have setter observers.)

Lazy Initialization

The term *lazy* is not a pejorative puritanical judgment; it's a formal description of a useful behavior. If a stored variable is assigned an initial value as part of its declaration, and if it uses lazy initialization, then the initial value is not actually evaluated and assigned until running code accesses the variable's value.

There are three types of variable that can be initialized lazily in Swift:

Global variables

Global variables are *automatically lazy*. This makes sense if you ask yourself when they should be initialized. As the app launches, files and their top-level code are encountered. It would make no sense to initialize globals now, because the app isn't even running yet. Thus global initialization must be postponed to some moment that *does* make sense. Therefore, a global variable's initialization doesn't happen until other code first refers to that global. Under the hood, this behavior is implemented in such a way as to make initialization both singular (it can happen only once) and thread-safe.

Static properties

Static properties are *automatically lazy*. They behave exactly like global variables, and for basically the same reason. (There are no stored class properties in Swift, so class properties can't be initialized and thus can't have lazy initialization.)

Instance properties

An instance property is not lazy by default, but it may be made lazy by marking its declaration with the keyword `lazy`. This property must be declared with `var`, not `let`. The initializer for such a property might *never* be evaluated, namely if code assigns the property a value before any code fetches the property's value.

Singleton

Lazy initialization is often used to implement *singleton*. Singleton is a pattern where all code is able to get access to a single shared instance of a certain class:

```
class MyClass {
    static let shared = MyClass()
}
```

Now other code can obtain a reference to MyClass's singleton by saying `MyClass.shared`. The singleton instance is not created until the *first* time other code says `MyClass.shared`; subsequently, no matter how many times other code may say `MyClass.shared`, the instance returned is always *that same instance*. (That is *not* what would happen if this were a computed read-only property whose getter calls `MyClass()` and returns that instance; do you see why?)

Lazy Initialization of Instance Properties

Why might you want an instance property to be lazy? One reason is obvious: the initial value might be expensive to generate, so you'd like to avoid generating it unless it is actually needed. But there's another reason that turns out to be even more important: a lazy initializer can do things that a normal initializer can't.

In particular, a lazy initializer can *refer to the instance*. A normal initializer can't do that, because the instance doesn't yet exist at the time that a normal initializer would need to run (we're in the middle of creating the instance, so it isn't ready yet). A lazy initializer, by contrast, is guaranteed not to run until some time after the instance has fully come into existence, so referring to the instance is fine. This code would be illegal if the `arrow` property weren't declared `lazy`:

```
class MyView : UIView {
    lazy var arrow = self.arrowImage() // legal
    func arrowImage () -> UIImage {
        // ... big image-generating code goes here ...
    }
}
```

A very common idiom is to initialize a lazy instance property with a define-and-call anonymous function whose code can refer to `self`:

```
lazy var prog : UIProgressView = {
    let p = UIProgressView(progressViewStyle: .default)
    p.alpha = 0.7
    p.trackTintColor = UIColor.clear
    p.progressTintColor = UIColor.black
    p.frame =
        CGRect(x:0, y:0, width:self.view.bounds.size.width, height:20) // legal
    p.progress = 1.0
    return p
}()
```

There's no `lazy let` for instance properties, so you can't readily make a lazy instance property read-only. That's unfortunate, because there are some common situations that would benefit from such a feature.

Suppose we want to arm ourselves (`self`) with a `helper` property holding an instance of a Helper class that needs a reference back to `self`. We also want this one Helper instance to persist for the entire lifetime of `self`. We can enforce that rule by making `helper` a `let` property and initializing it in its declaration. But we can't pass `self` into the Helper instance at that point, because we can't refer to `self` in the property declaration.

We can solve the problem by declaring the `helper` property `lazy`, but then it has to be a `var` property, meaning that, in theory, other code can come along and replace this Helper with another. Of course, we'll try not to let that happen; but the point is that the expression `lazy var` fails to express and enforce this policy as an unbreakable contract. (It may be possible to work around the issue by making `helper` a computed property acting as a façade on storage — and we can even encapsulate that pattern as a property wrapper — but even then we can enforce our policy only at runtime, not at compile time the way `let` does.)

Unlike automatically lazy global and static variables, an instance property marked `lazy` does *not* initialize itself in a thread-safe way. When used in a multi-threaded context, `lazy` instance properties can cause multiple initialization and even crashes.

Built-In Simple Types

Every variable, and every value, must have a type. But what types are there? Up to this point, I've assumed the existence of some types, such as Int and String, without formally telling you about them. Here's a survey of the primary simple types provided by Swift, along with some instance methods, global functions, and operators that apply to them. (Collection types will be discussed at the end of Chapter 4.)

Bool

The Bool object type (a struct) has only two values, commonly regarded as true and false (or yes and no). You can represent these values using the literal keywords `true` and `false`, and it is natural to think of a Bool value as *being* either `true` or `false`:

```
var selected : Bool = false
```

In that code, `selected` is a Bool variable initialized to `false`; it can subsequently be set to `false` or `true`, and to no other values. Because of its simple yes-or-no state, a Bool variable of this kind is often referred to as a *flag*.

Cocoa methods very often expect a Bool parameter or return a Bool value. For example, when your app launches, Cocoa calls a method in your code declared like this:

```
func application(_ application: UIApplication,
    didFinishLaunchingWithOptions
    launchOptions: [UIApplication.LaunchOptionsKey : Any]?)
    -> Bool {
```

You can do anything you like in that method; often, you will do nothing. But you must return a Bool! And in real life, that Bool will probably be `true`. A minimal implementation looks like this:

```
func application(_ application: UIApplication,
    didFinishLaunchingWithOptions
    launchOptions: [UIApplication.LaunchOptionsKey : Any]?)
    -> Bool {
        return true
}
```

A Bool is useful in conditions; as I'll explain in Chapter 5, when you say `if` *something*, the *something* is the condition, and is a Bool or an expression that evaluates to a Bool. When you compare two values using the equality comparison operator `==`, the result is a Bool — `true` if they are equal to each other, `false` if they are not:

```
if meaningOfLife == 42 { // ...
```

(I'll talk more about equality comparison in a moment, when we come to discuss types that can be compared, such as Int and String.)

When preparing a condition, you will sometimes find that it enhances clarity to store the Bool value in a variable beforehand:

```
let comp = self.traitCollection.horizontalSizeClass == .compact
if comp { // ...
```

Observe that, when employing that idiom, we use the Bool variable comp *directly* as the condition. There is no need to test explicitly whether a Bool equals true or false; the conditional expression itself is already testing that. It is pointless to say if comp == true, because if comp already *means* "if comp is true."

Since a Bool can be used as a condition, a call to a function that returns a Bool can be used as a condition. Here's an example from my own code. I've declared a function that returns a Bool to say whether the cards the user has selected constitute a correct answer to the puzzle:

```
func isCorrect(_ cells:[CardCell]) -> Bool { // ...
```

I can then use a call to isCorrect as a condition:

```
if self.isCorrect(cellsToTest) { // ...
```

Unlike many computer languages, nothing else in Swift is implicitly coerced to or treated as a Bool. In C, for example, a boolean is actually a number, and 0 is false. But in Swift, nothing is false but false, and nothing is true but true.

The type name, Bool, comes from the English mathematician George Boole; Boolean algebra provides operations on logical values. Bool values are subject to these same operations:

! *(not)*

> The ! unary operator reverses the truth value of the Bool to which it is applied as a prefix. If ok is true, !ok is false — and *vice versa*.

&& *(logical-and)*

> Returns true only if both operands are true; otherwise, returns false. If the first operand is false, the second operand is not even evaluated (avoiding possible side effects).

|| *(logical-or)*

> Returns true if either operand is true; otherwise, returns false. If the first operand is true, the second operand is not even evaluated (avoiding possible side effects).

If a logical operation is complicated or elaborate, parentheses around subexpressions can help clarify both the logic and the order of operations.

A common situation is that we have a Bool stored in a `var` variable somewhere, and we want to reverse its value — that is, make it `true` if it is `false`, and `false` if it is `true`. The `!` operator solves the problem; we fetch the variable's value, reverse it with `!`, and assign the result back into the variable:

```
v.isUserInteractionEnabled = !v.isUserInteractionEnabled
```

That, however, is cumbersome and error-prone, so there's a simpler way — call the `toggle` method on the Bool variable:

```
v.isUserInteractionEnabled.toggle()
```

Numbers

The main numeric types are Int and Double — meaning that, left to your own devices, those are the types you'll generally use. Other numeric types exist mostly for compatibility with the C and Objective-C APIs that Swift needs to be able to talk to when you're programming iOS.

Int

The Int object type (a struct) represents an integer between `Int.min` and `Int.max` inclusive. The actual values of those limits might depend on the platform and architecture under which the app runs, so don't count on them to be absolute; in my testing at this moment, they are -2^{63} and $2^{63}-1$ respectively (64-bit words).

The easiest way to represent an Int value is as a numeric literal. A numeric literal without a decimal point is taken as an Int by default. Internal underscores are legal; this is useful for making long numbers readable. Leading zeroes are legal; this is useful for padding and aligning values in your code.

You can write an Int literal using binary, octal, or hexadecimal digits. To do so, start the literal with `0b`, `0o`, or `0x` respectively. For example, `0x10` is decimal 16.

 Negative numbers are stored in the two's complement format (consult Wikipedia if you're curious). You can write a binary literal that looks like the underlying storage, but to use it you must pass it through the `Int(bitPattern:)` initializer.

Double

The Double object type (a struct) represents a floating-point number to a precision of about 15 decimal places (64-bit storage).

The easiest way to represent a Double value is as a numeric literal. A numeric literal containing a decimal point is taken as a Double by default. Internal underscores and leading zeroes are legal.

A Double literal may *not* begin with a decimal point (unlike C and Objective-C). If the value to be represented is between 0 and 1, start the literal with a leading 0.

You can write a Double literal using scientific notation. Everything after the letter e is the exponent of 10. You can omit the decimal point if the fractional digits would be zero. For example, 3e2 is 3 times 10^2 (300).

You can write a Double literal using hexadecimal digits. To do so, start the literal with 0x. You can use exponentiation here too (and again, you can omit the decimal point); everything after the letter p is the exponent of 2. For example, 0x10p2 is decimal 64, because you are multiplying 16 by 2^2.

There are static properties Double.infinity and Double.pi, and an instance property isZero, among others.

Numeric coercion

Coercion is the conversion of a value from one type to another, and numeric coercion is the conversion of a value from one numeric type to another. Swift doesn't really have explicit coercion, but it has something that serves the same purpose — instantiation. Swift numeric types are supplied with initializers that take another numeric type as parameter. To convert an Int explicitly into a Double, instantiate Double with the Int in the parentheses. To convert a Double explicitly into an Int, instantiate Int with the Double in the parentheses; this will truncate the original value (everything after the decimal point will be thrown away):

```
let i = 10
let x = Double(i)
print(x) // 10.0, a Double
let y = 3.8
let j = Int(y)
print(j) // 3, an Int
```

When numeric values are assigned to variables or passed as arguments to a function, Swift can perform implicit coercion *of literals only*. This code is legal:

```
let d : Double = 10
```

But this code is not legal, because what you're assigning is a *variable* (not a literal) of a different type; the compiler will stop you:

```
let i = 10
let d : Double = i // compile error
```

The problem is that i is an Int and d is a Double, and never the twain shall meet. The solution is to *coerce explicitly* as you assign or pass the variable:

```
let i = 10
let d : Double = Double(i)
```

The same rule holds when numeric values are combined by an arithmetic operation. Swift will perform implicit coercion *of literals only*. The usual situation is an Int combined with a Double; the Int is treated as a Double:

```
let x = 10/3.0
print(x) // 3.33333333333333
```

But *variables* of different numeric types must be *coerced explicitly* so that they are the *same* type if you want to combine them in an arithmetic operation:

```
let i = 10
let n = 3.0
let x = i / n // compile error; you need to say Double(i)
```

These rules are evidently a consequence of Swift's strict typing; but (as far as I am aware) they constitute very unusual treatment of numeric values for a modern computer language, and will probably drive you mad in short order. The examples I've given so far were easily solved, but things can become more complicated if an arithmetic expression is longer, and the problem is compounded by the existence of other numeric types that are needed for compatibility with Cocoa, as I shall now proceed to explain.

Other numeric types

If you were using Swift in some isolated, abstract world, you could probably do all necessary arithmetic with Int and Double alone. But when you're programming iOS, you encounter Cocoa, which is full of other numeric types; and Swift has types that match every one of them. In addition to Int, there are signed integer types of various sizes — Int8, Int16, Int32, Int64 — plus the unsigned integer type UInt along with UInt8, UInt16, UInt32, and UInt64. In addition to Double, there is the lower-precision Float (32-bit storage, about 6 or 7 decimal places of precision), the even lower-precision Float16 (new in Swift 5.3), and the extended-precision Float80 — plus, in the Core Graphics framework, CGFloat (whose size can be that of Float or Double, depending on the bitness of the architecture).

You may also encounter a C numeric type when trying to interface with a C API. These types, as far as Swift is concerned, are just type aliases, meaning that they are alternate names for another type: a CDouble (corresponding to C's double) is just a Double by another name, a CLong (C's long) is an Int, and so on. Many other numeric type aliases will arise in various Cocoa frameworks; for example, Time-Interval (Objective-C NSTimeInterval) is merely a type alias for Double.

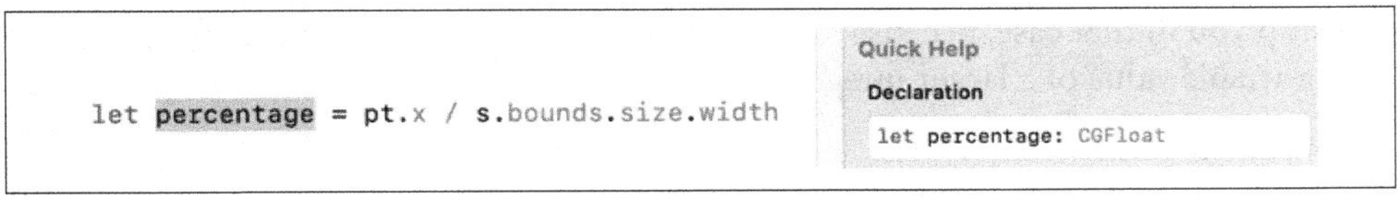

```
let percentage = pt.x / s.bounds.size.width
```

```
Quick Help
Declaration
let percentage: CGFloat
```

Figure 3-1. Quick Help displays a variable's type

Recall that you can't assign, pass, or combine values of different numeric types using variables; you have to coerce those values explicitly to the correct type. But now it turns out that you're being flooded by Cocoa with numeric values of many types! Cocoa will often hand you a numeric value that is neither an Int nor a Double — and you won't necessarily realize this, until the compiler stops you dead in your tracks for some sort of type mismatch. You must then figure out what you've done wrong and coerce everything to the same type.

Here's a typical example from one of my apps. A slider in the interface is a UISlider, whose `minimumValue` and `maximumValue` are Floats. In this code, `s` is a UISlider, `g` is a UIGestureRecognizer, and we're trying to use the gesture recognizer to move the slider's "thumb" to wherever the user tapped within the slider:

```
let pt = g.location(in:s) ❶
let percentage = pt.x / s.bounds.size.width ❷
let delta = percentage * (s.maximumValue - s.minimumValue) // compile error ❸
```

That won't compile. Here's why:

❶   `pt` is a CGPoint, and therefore `pt.x` is a CGFloat.

❷   Luckily, `s.bounds.size.width` is also a CGFloat, so the second line compiles; `percentage` is now inferred to be a CGFloat.

❸   We now try to combine `percentage` with `s.maximumValue` and `s.minimumValue` — and they are Floats, not CGFloats. That's a compile error.

This sort of thing is not an issue in C or Objective-C, where there is implicit coercion; but in Swift a CGFloat can't be combined with Floats. We must coerce explicitly:

```
let delta = Float(percentage) * (s.maximumValue - s.minimumValue)
```

The good news here is that if you can get enough of your code to compile, Xcode's Quick Help feature will tell you what type Swift has inferred for a selected variable (Figure 3-1). This can assist you in tracking down your issues with numeric types.

Another problem is that not every numeric value *can* be coerced to a numeric value of a different type. In particular, integers of various sizes can be out of range with respect to integer types of other sizes. For example, `Int8.max` is 127, so attempting to assign a literal `128` or larger to an Int8 variable is illegal. Fortunately, the compiler will stop you in that case, because it knows what the literal is. But now consider *coercing* a variable value of a larger integer type to an Int8:

```
let i : Int16 = 128
let ii = Int8(i)
```

That code is legal — and will crash at runtime. One solution is to call the numeric `exactly:` initializer; this is a *failable* initializer — meaning, as I'll explain in Chapter 4, that you won't crash, but you'll have to add code to test whether the coercion succeeded (and you'll understand what the test would be when you've read the discussion of Optionals later in this chapter):

```
let i : Int16 = 128
let ii = Int8(exactly:i)
if // ... test to learn whether ii holds a real Int8
```

Yet another solution is to call the `clamping:` initializer; it *always* succeeds, because an out of range value is forced to fall within range:

```
let i : Int16 = 128
let ii = Int8(clamping:i) // 127
```

(There is also a `truncatingIfNeeded:` initializer, but you probably won't need to know about it unless you are deliberately manipulating integers as binary, so I won't describe it here.)

When a floating-point type, such as a Double, is coerced to an integer type, the stuff after the decimal point is thrown away first and then the coercion is attempted. `Int8(127.9)` succeeds, because 127 is in bounds.

Arithmetic operations

Swift's arithmetic operators are as you would expect; they are familiar from other computer languages as well as from real arithmetic:

+ *(addition operator)*
    Add the second operand to the first and return the result.

- *(subtraction operator)*
    Subtract the second operand from the first and return the result. A different operator (unary minus), used as a prefix, looks the same; it returns the additive inverse of its single operand. (There is, in fact, also a unary plus operator, which returns its operand unchanged.)

* *(multiplication operator)*
    Multiply the first operand by the second and return the result.

/ *(division operator)*

Divide the first operand by the second and return the result. As in C, division of one Int by another Int yields an Int; any remaining fraction is stripped away. 10/3 is 3, not 3-and-one-third.

% *(remainder operator)*

Divide the first operand by the second and return the remainder. The result can be negative, if the first operand is negative; if the second operand is negative, it is treated as positive. For floating-point operands, use a method such as `remainder(dividingBy:)`.

Integers also have a `quotientAndRemainder(dividingBy:)` method, which returns a tuple of two integers labeled `quotient` and `remainder`. If the question is whether one integer evenly divides another, calling `isMultiple(of:)` may be clearer than checking for a zero remainder.

Integer types can be treated as binary bitfields and subjected to binary bitwise operations:

& *(bitwise-and)*

A bit in the result is 1 if and only if that bit is 1 in both operands.

| *(bitwise-or)*

A bit in the result is 0 if and only if that bit is 0 in both operands.

^ *(bitwise-or, exclusive)*

A bit in the result is 1 if and only if that bit is not identical in both operands.

~ *(bitwise-not)*

Precedes its single operand; inverts the value of each bit and returns the result.

<< *(shift left)*

Shift the bits of the first operand leftward the number of times indicated by the second operand.

>> *(shift right)*

Shift the bits of the first operand rightward the number of times indicated by the second operand.

 Technically, the shift operators perform a logical shift if the integer is unsigned, and an arithmetic shift if the integer is signed.

Integer overflow or underflow — for example, adding two Int values so as to exceed `Int.max` — is a runtime error (your app will crash). In simple cases the compiler will stop you, but you can get away with it easily enough:

```
let i = Int.max - 2
let j = i + 12/2 // crash
```

Under certain circumstances you might want to force such an operation to succeed, so special overflow/underflow methods are supplied. These methods return a tuple; I'll show you an example even though I haven't discussed tuples yet:

```
let i = Int.max - 2
let (j, over) = i.addingReportingOverflow(12/2)
```

Now j is Int.min + 3 (because the value has wrapped around from Int.max to Int.min) and over is an enum reporting that overflow occurred.

If you don't care to hear about whether or not there was an overflow/underflow, special arithmetic operators let you suppress the error: &+, &-, &*.

You will frequently want to combine the value of an existing variable arithmetically with another value and store the result in the same variable. To do so, you will need to have declared the variable as a var:

```
var i = 1
i = i + 7
```

As a shorthand, operators are provided that perform the arithmetic operation and the assignment all in one move:

```
var i = 1
i += 7
```

The shorthand (*compound*) assignment arithmetic operators are +=, -=, *=, /=, %=, &=, |=, ^=, <<=, >>=.

Operation precedence is largely intuitive: for example, * has a higher precedence than +, so x+y*z multiplies y by z first, and then adds the result to x. Use parentheses to dictate precedence explicitly: (x+y)*z performs the addition first.

Global functions from the Swift standard library include abs (absolute value), max, and min:

```
let i = -7
let j = 6
print(abs(i)) // 7
print(max(i,j)) // 6
```

Doubles are also stocked with mathematical methods. If d is a Double, you can say d.squareRoot() or d.rounded(); if dd is also a Double, you can say Double.maximum(d,dd). Other global mathematical functions, such as trigonometric sin and cos, come from the C standard libraries that are visible because you've imported UIKit. Also, a Swift package called Swift Numerics (*https://github.com/apple/swift-numerics*) unites all the floating-point types under the Real protocol and supplies most of the mathematical functions you could ever want.

Numeric types have a `random(in:)` static method allowing generation of a random number. The parameter is a range representing the bounds within which the random number should fall. (Ranges are discussed later in this chapter.) This method is much easier to use correctly than the C library methods such as `arc4random_uniform`, which should be avoided:

```
// pick a number from 1 to 10
let i = Int.random(in: 1...10)
```

Comparison

Numbers are compared using the comparison operators, which return a Bool. The expression `i==j` tests whether `i` and `j` are equal; when `i` and `j` are numbers, "equal" means numerically equal. So `i==j` is `true` only if `i` and `j` are "the same number," in exactly the sense you would expect.

The comparison operators are:

`==` *(equality operator)*
   Returns `true` if its operands are equal.

`!=` *(inequality operator)*
   Returns `false` if its operands are equal.

`<` *(less-than operator)*
   Returns `true` if the first operand is less than the second operand.

`<=` *(less-than-or-equal operator)*
   Returns `true` if the first operand is less than or equal to the second operand.

`>` *(greater-than operator)*
   Returns `true` if the first operand is greater than the second operand.

`>=` *(greater-than-or-equal operator)*
   Returns `true` if the first operand is greater than or equal to the second operand.

Curiously, you can compare values of different integer types, even though you can't combine them in an arithmetic operation:

```
let i:Int = 1
let i2:UInt8 = 2
let ok = i < i2 // true
let ok2 = i == i2 // false
let sum = i + i2 // error
```

Because of the way computers store numbers, equality comparison of Double values may not succeed where you would expect. To give a classic example, adding `0.1` to `0` ten times does not give the same result as multiplying `0.1` by ten:

```
let f = 0.1
var sum = 0.0
for _ in 0..<10 { sum += f }
let product = f * 10
let ok = sum == product // false
```

Working around this sort of thing is not easy. The usual approach is to check whether two values are sufficiently close to one another, but this begs the question of what constitutes sufficient closeness. A useful formula is:

```
let ok2 = sum >= product.nextDown && sum <= product.nextUp // true
```

String

The String object type (a struct) represents text. The simplest way to represent a String value is with a literal, delimited by double quotes:

```
let greeting = "hello"
```

A Swift string is thoroughly modern; under the hood, it's Unicode, and you can include any character (such as an emoji) directly in a string literal. If you don't want to bother typing a Unicode character whose codepoint you know, use the notation \u{...}, where what's between the curly braces is up to eight hex digits:

```
let leftTripleArrow = "\u{21DA}"
```

The backslash in that string representation is the *escape* character; it means, "I'm not really a backslash; I indicate that the next character gets special treatment." Various nonprintable and ambiguous characters are entered as escaped characters; the most important are:

\n

A Unix newline character

\t

A tab character

\"

A quotation mark (escaped to show that this is not the end of the string literal)

\\

A backslash (escaped because a lone backslash is the escape character)

Escaped quotation marks and backslashes can quickly make your string literals ugly and illegible. The issue arises particularly in contexts such as regular expression patterns. For example, the pattern \b\d\d\b (a word consisting of two digits) must be written "\\b\\d\\d\\b". But you can omit the escape character before quotes and backslashes by surrounding your literal with one or more hash characters (#); these are all identical strings:

```
let pattold = "\\b\\d\\d\\b"
let pattnew = #"\b\d\d\b"# // same thing
let pattnew2 = ##"\b\d\d\b"## // same thing
```

That's called a *raw* string literal. The downside is that if you *want* to use a backslash as an escape character in a raw string literal, you must follow it with the same number of # characters you are using to surround your literal. The string #"hello\nthere"# does not contain a newline character (\n), but #"hello\#nthere"# does.

A string literal containing newline characters can be entered as multiple lines (rather than a single-line expression containing \n characters). This is called a *multiline string literal*. The rules are:

- The multiline string literal must be delimited by a triple of double quotes (""") at start and end.
- No material may follow the opening delimiter on the same line.
- No material other than whitespace may appear on the same line as the closing delimiter.
- The last implicit newline character before the closing delimiter is ignored.
- The indentation of the closing delimiter dictates the indentation of the lines of text, which must be indented at least as far as the closing delimiter (except for completely empty lines).

For example:

```
func f() {
    let s = """
    Line 1
        Line 2
    Line 3
    """
    // ...
}
```

In that code, the string s consists of three lines of text; lines 1 and 3 start with no whitespace; line 2 starts with four spaces; and there are two newline characters, namely after lines 1 and 2. To add a newline after line 3, you could enter a blank line, or write it as an escaped \n.

Quotation marks do *not* have to be escaped. A line ending with a backslash is joined with the following line. In this code, the string s consists of just two lines of text; the second line consists of four spaces followed by "Line 2 and this is still line 2":

```
func f() {
    let s = """
    Line "1"
        Line 2 \
```

```
        and this is still Line 2
        """
        // ...
}
```

(You can surround a multiline string literal with # characters, making a raw multiline string literal; but you are unlikely to do so.)

String interpolation permits you to embed any value that can be output with `print` inside a string literal *as a string*, even if it is not itself a string. The notation is escaped parentheses: \(...):

```
let n = 5
let s = "You have \(n) widgets."
```

Now `s` is the string `"You have 5 widgets."` The example is not very compelling, because we know what `n` is and could have typed 5 directly into our string; but imagine that we *don't* know what `n` is! Moreover, the stuff in escaped parentheses doesn't have to be the name of a variable; it can be almost any expression that evaluates as legal Swift:

```
let m = 4
let n = 5
let s = "You have \(m + n) widgets."
```

String interpolation is legal inside a multiline string literal. It is also legal inside a raw string literal surrounded with # characters, but then the backslash must be followed by the same number of # characters, to indicate that it is the escape character.

String interpolation syntax can be customized to accept additional parameters, refining how the first parameter should be transformed. Expressions of this form can be legal:

```
let s = "You have \(n, roman:true) widgets"
```

(I'm imagining that if `n` is 5, this would yield `"You have V widgets"`.) I'll say more in Chapter 5 about how that is achieved. New in iOS 14, the Logger class takes advantage of that kind of syntax (Chapter 9).

To combine (concatenate) two strings, the simplest approach is to use the + operator:

```
let s = "hello"
let s2 = " world"
let greeting = s + s2
```

This convenient notation is possible because the + operator is *overloaded*: it does one thing when the operands are numbers (numeric addition) and another when the operands are strings (concatenation). As I'll explain in Chapter 5, *all* operators can be overloaded, and you can overload them to operate in some appropriate way on your own types.

The + operator comes with a += assignment shortcut; naturally, the variable on the left side must have been declared with `var`:

```
var s = "hello"
let s2 = " world"
s += s2
```

As an alternative to +=, you can call the `append(_:)` instance method:

```
var s = "hello"
let s2 = " world"
s.append(s2)
```

Another way of concatenating strings is with the `joined(separator:)` method. You start with an array of strings to be concatenated, and hand it the string that is to be inserted between all of them:

```
let s = "hello"
let s2 = "world"
let space = " "
let greeting = [s,s2].joined(separator:space)
```

The comparison operators are also overloaded so that they work with String operands. Two String values are equal (==) if they are, in the natural sense, the same text. A String is less than another if it is alphabetically prior.

Some additional convenient instance methods and properties are provided. `isEmpty` returns a Bool reporting whether this string is the empty string (""). `hasPrefix(_:)` and `hasSuffix(_:)` report whether this string starts or ends with another string; `"hello".hasPrefix("he")` is `true`. The `uppercased` and `lowercased` methods provide uppercase and lowercase versions of the original string.

Coercion between a String and an Int is possible. To make a string that represents an Int, it is sufficient to use string interpolation; alternatively, use a String initializer taking the Int:

```
let i = 7
let s = String(i) // "7"
```

Your string can also represent an Int in some other base; in the initializer, supply a `radix:` argument expressing the base:

```
let i = 31
let s = String(i, radix:16) // "1f"
```

A String that might represent a number can be coerced to a numeric type; an integer type will accept a `radix:` argument expressing the base. The coercion might fail, because the String might *not* represent a number of the specified type; so the result is not a number but an Optional wrapping a number (I haven't talked about Optionals yet, so you'll have to trust me for now; failable initializers are discussed in Chapter 4):

```
let s = "31"
let i = Int(s) // Optional(31)
let s2 = "1f"
let i2 = Int(s2, radix:16) // Optional(31)
```

Similarly, you can coerce a Bool to a String, which will be "true" or "false". Going the other way, you can coerce the string "true" to the Bool true and the string "false" to the Bool false; again, this is a failable initializer, and any other string will fail.

The length of a String, in characters, is given by its count property:

```
let s = "hello"
let length = s.count // 5
```

This property is called count rather then length because a String doesn't really have a simple length. The String comprises a sequence of Unicode codepoints, but multiple Unicode codepoints can combine to form a single character; so, in order to know how many characters are represented by such a sequence, we actually have to walk through the sequence and resolve it into the characters that it represents.

You, too, can walk through a String's characters. The simplest way is with the for...in construct (see Chapter 5). What you get when you do this are Character objects; I'll talk more about Character objects later:

```
let s = "hello"
for c in s {
    print(c) // print each Character on its own line
}
```

At an even deeper level, you can decompose a String into its UTF-8 codepoints or its UTF-16 codepoints, using the utf8 and utf16 properties:

```
let s = "\u{BF}Qui\u{E9}n?"
for i in s.utf8 {
    print(i) // 194, 191, 81, 117, 105, 195, 169, 110, 63
}
for i in s.utf16 {
    print(i) // 191, 81, 117, 105, 233, 110, 63
}
```

There is also a unicodeScalars property representing a collection (a String.Unicode-ScalarView) of the String's UTF-32 codepoints expressed as UnicodeScalar structs. To illustrate, here's a utility function that turns a two-letter country abbreviation into an emoji representation of its flag:

```
func flag(country:String) -> String {
    let base : UInt32 = 127397
    var s = ""
    for v in country.unicodeScalars {
        s.unicodeScalars.append(UnicodeScalar(base + v.value)!)
    }
```

```
        return String(s)
}
// and here's how to use it:
let s = flag(country:"DE")
```

The curious thing is that there aren't more methods for standard string manipulation. How do you capitalize a string, or find out whether a string contains a given substring? Most modern programming languages have a compact, convenient way of doing things like that; Swift doesn't. The reason appears to be that missing features are provided by the Foundation framework, to which you'll always be linked in real life (importing UIKit imports Foundation). A Swift String is bridged to a Foundation NSString. This means that, to a large extent, Foundation NSString properties and methods magically spring to life whenever you are using a Swift String:

```
let s = "hello world"
let s2 = s.capitalized // "Hello World"
```

The `capitalized` property comes from the Foundation framework; it's provided by Cocoa, not by Swift. It's an NSString property; it appears tacked onto String "for free." Similarly, here's how to locate a substring of a string:

```
let s = "hello"
let range = s.range(of:"ell") // Optional(Range(...)) [details omitted]
```

I haven't explained yet what an Optional is or what a Range is (I'll talk about them later in this chapter), but that innocent-looking code has made a remarkable round-trip from Swift to Cocoa and back again: the Swift String s becomes an NSString, an NSString method is called, a Foundation NSRange struct is returned, and the NSRange is converted to a Swift Range and wrapped up in an Optional.

Character and String Index

You are more likely to be interested in a string's characters than its codepoints. Codepoints are numbers, but what we naturally think of as characters are effectively minimal strings: a character is a single "letter" or "symbol" — formally, a *grapheme*. The equivalence between numeric codepoints and symbolic graphemes is provided, in Unicode, by the notion of a grapheme cluster. To embody this equivalence, Swift provides the Character object type (a struct), representing a single grapheme cluster.

A String (in Swift 4 and later) simply *is* a character sequence — quite literally, a Sequence of the Character objects that constitute it. That is why, as I mentioned earlier, you can walk through a string with `for...in` to obtain the String's Characters, one by one; when you do that, you're walking through the string *qua* character sequence:

```
let s = "hello"
for c in s {
    print(c) // print each Character on its own line
}
```

It isn't common to encounter Character objects outside of some character sequence of which they are a part. There isn't even a way to write a literal Character. To make a Character from scratch, initialize it from a single-character String:

```
let c = Character("h")
```

Similarly, you can pass a one-character String literal where a Character is expected, and many examples in this section will do so.

By the same token, you can initialize a String from a Character:

```
let c = Character("h")
let s = (String(c)).uppercased()
```

Characters can be compared for equality; "less than" means what you would expect it to mean.

Formally, a String is both a Sequence of Characters and a Collection of Characters. Sequence and Collection are protocols; I'll discuss protocols in Chapter 4, but what's important for now is that a String is endowed with methods and properties that it gets by virtue of being a Sequence and a Collection.

A String has a `first` and `last` property; the resulting Character is wrapped in an Optional because the string might be empty:

```
let s = "hello"
let c1 = s.first // Optional("h")
let c2 = s.last // Optional("o")
```

The `firstIndex(of:)` method locates the first occurrence of a given character within the sequence and returns its index. Again, this is an Optional, because the character might be absent:

```
let s = "hello"
let firstL = s.firstIndex(of:"l") // Optional(2)
```

All Swift indexes are numbered starting with 0, so 2 means the third character. The index value here, however, is not an Int; I'll explain in a moment what it is and what it's good for.

A related method, `firstIndex(where:)`, takes a function that takes a Character and returns a Bool. This code locates the first character smaller than `"f"`:

```
let s = "hello"
let firstSmall = s.firstIndex {$0 < "f"} // Optional(1)
```

Those methods are matched by `lastIndex(of:)` and `lastIndex(where:)`.

A String has a `contains(_:)` method that returns a Bool, reporting whether a certain character is present:

```
let s = "hello"
let ok = s.contains("o") // true
```

Alternatively, `contains(_:)` can take a function that takes a Character and returns a Bool. This code reports whether the target string contains a vowel:

```
let s = "hello"
let ok = s.contains {"aeiou".contains($0)} // true
```

The `filter(_:)` method, too, takes a function that takes a Character and returns a Bool, effectively eliminating those characters for which `false` is returned. Here, we delete all consonants from a string:

```
let s = "hello"
let s2 = s.filter {"aeiou".contains($0)} // "eo"
```

The `dropFirst` and `dropLast` methods return, in effect, a new string without the first or last character, respectively:

```
let s = "hello"
let s2 = s.dropFirst() // "ello"
```

I say "in effect" because a method that extracts a substring returns, in reality, a Substring instance. The Substring struct is an efficient way of pointing at part of some original String, rather than having to generate a new String. When we call `s.drop-First()` on the string `"hello"`, the resulting Substring points at the `"ello"` part of `"hello"`, which continues to exist; there is still only one string, and no new string storage memory is required.

In general, the difference between a String and a Substring will make little practical difference to you, because what you can do with a String, you can usually do also with a Substring. Nevertheless, they are different classes; this code won't compile:

```
var s = "hello"
let s2 = s.dropFirst()
s = s2 // compile error
```

To pass a Substring where a String is expected, coerce the Substring to a String explicitly:

```
var s = "hello"
let s2 = s.dropFirst()
s = String(s2)
```

You can coerce the other way, too, from a String to a Substring.

`prefix(_:)` and `suffix(_:)` extract a Substring of a given length from the start or end of the original string:

```
var s = "hello"
s = String(s.prefix(4)) // "hell"
```

`split(_:)` breaks a string up into an array, according to a function that takes a Character and returns a Bool. In this example, I obtain the words of a String, where a "word" is simplemindedly defined as a run of Characters other than a space:

```
let s = "hello world"
let arr = s.split {$0 == " "} // ["hello", "world"]
```

The result is actually an array of Substrings. If we needed to get String objects, we could apply the `map(_:)` function and coerce them all to Strings. I'll talk about `map(_:)` in Chapter 4, so you'll have to trust me for now:

```
let s = "hello world"
let arr = s.split {$0 == " "}.map {String($0)} // ["hello", "world"]
```

A String, *qua* character sequence, can also be manipulated similarly to an array. For example, you can use subscripting to obtain the character at a certain position. Unfortunately, this isn't as easy as it might be. What's the second character of `"hello"`? This doesn't compile:

```
let s = "hello"
let c = s[1] // compile error
```

The reason is that the indexes on a String are not Int values, but rather a nested type, String.Index (actually a type alias for String.CharacterView.Index). To make an object of this type is rather tricky. Start with a String's `startIndex` or `endIndex`, or with the return value from `firstIndex` or `lastIndex`; you can then call the `index(_:offsetBy:)` method to derive the index you want:

```
let s = "hello"
let ix = s.startIndex
let ix2 = s.index(ix, offsetBy:1)
let c = s[ix2] // "e"
```

The reason for this clumsy circumlocution is that Swift doesn't know where the characters of a character sequence are until it actually walks the sequence; calling `index(_:offsetBy:)` is how you make Swift do that.

To offset an index by a single position, you can obtain the next or preceding index value with the `index(after:)` and `index(before:)` methods. I could have written the preceding example like this:

```
let s = "hello"
let ix = s.startIndex
let c = s[s.index(after:ix)] // "e"
```

Another reason why it's necessary to think of a string index as an offset from the `startIndex` or `endIndex` is that those values may not be what you think they are — in particular, when you're dealing with a Substring. Consider, once again, the following:

```
let s = "hello"
let s2 = s.dropFirst()
```

Now s2 is "ello". What, then, is `s2.startIndex` (as an Int)? Not 0, but 1 — because s2 is a Substring pointing into the original "hello", where the index of the "e" is 1. Similarly, `s2.firstIndex(of:"o")` is not 3, but 4, because the index value is reckoned with respect to the original "hello".

Once you've obtained a desired character index value, you can use it to modify the String. The `insert(contentsOf:at:)` method inserts a string into a string:

```
var s = "hello"
let ix = s.index(s.startIndex, offsetBy:1)
s.insertContentsOf("ey, h", at: ix) // s is now "hey, hello"
```

Similarly, `remove(at:)` deletes a single character, and also returns that character. (Manipulations involving longer character stretches require use of a Range, which is the subject of the next section.)

On the other hand, a character sequence can be coerced directly to an Array of Character objects — `Array("hello")` creates an array of the characters "h", "e", and so on — and array indexes *are* Ints and are easy to work with. Once you've manipulated the array of Characters, you can coerce it directly to a String. I'll give an example in the next section (and I'll discuss arrays, and say more about collections and sequences, in Chapter 4).

Range

The Range object type (a struct) represents a pair of endpoints. There are two operators for forming a Range literal; you supply a start value and an end value, with one of the Range operators between them:

`...` *(closed range operator)*
> The notation `a...b` means "everything from `a` up to `b`, *including* `b`."

`..<` *(half-open range operator)*
> The notation `a..<b` means "everything from `a` up to but *not* including `b`."

Spaces around a Range operator are legal.

The types of a Range's endpoints will typically be some kind of number — most often, Ints:

```
let r = 1...3
```

If the end value is a negative literal, it has to be enclosed in parentheses or preceded by whitespace:

```
let r = -1000 ... -1
```

A very common use of a Range is to loop through numbers with `for...in`:

```
for ix in 1...3 {
    print(ix) // 1, then 2, then 3
}
```

There are no reverse Ranges: the start value of a Range can't be greater than the end value (the compiler won't stop you, but you'll crash at runtime). In practice, you can use Range's `reversed()` method to iterate from a higher value to a lower one:

```
for ix in (1...3).reversed() {
    print(ix) // 3, then 2, then 1
}
```

In Chapter 5 I'll show how to create a custom operator that effectively generates a reverse Range.

You can also use a Range's `contains(_:)` instance method to test whether a value falls within given limits:

```
let ix = // ... an Int ...
if (1...3).contains(ix) { // ...
```

For purposes of testing containment, a Range's endpoints can be Doubles:

```
let d = // ... a Double ...
if (0.1...0.9).contains(d) { // ...
```

There are also methods for learning whether two ranges overlap, and for clamping one range to another.

Another common use of a Range is to index into a sequence. Here's one way to get the second, third, and fourth characters of a String. As I suggested at the end of the preceding section, if we coerce the String to an Array of Character, we can then use an Int Range as an index into that array, and coerce back to a String:

```
let s = "hello"
let arr = Array(s)
let result = arr[1...3]
let s2 = String(result) // "ell"
```

A String is itself a sequence — a character sequence — so you can use a Range to index directly into a String; but then it has to be a Range of String.Index, which, as I've already pointed out, is rather tricky to obtain. By manipulating String.Index values, you can form a Range of the proper type and use it to extract a substring by subscripting:

```
let s = "hello"
let ix1 = s.index(s.startIndex, offsetBy:1)
let ix2 = s.index(ix1, offsetBy:2)
let s2 = s[ix1...ix2] // "ell"
```

The `replaceSubrange(_:with:)` method splices into a range, modifying the string:

```
var s = "hello"
let ix = s.startIndex
let r = s.index(ix, offsetBy:1)...s.index(ix, offsetBy:3)
s.replaceSubrange(r, with: "ipp") // s is now "hippo"
```

Similarly, you can delete a stretch of characters with the `removeSubrange(_:)` method:

```
var s = "hello"
let ix = s.startIndex
let r = s.index(ix, offsetBy:1)...s.index(ix, offsetBy:3)
s.removeSubrange(r) // s is now "ho"
```

It is possible to omit one of the endpoints from a Range literal, specifying a *partial range*. There are three kinds of partial range expression, corresponding to three types of Range-like struct. To illustrate, the following expressions are identical ways of specifying the range of an entire String s:

```
let range1 = s.startIndex..<s.endIndex       // Range
let range2 = ..<s.endIndex                   // PartialRangeUpTo
let range3 = ...s.index(before: s.endIndex)  // PartialRangeUpThrough
let range4 = s.startIndex...                 // PartialRangeFrom
```

If you need to convert a partial range to a range, call `relative(to:)`. In the preceding code, `range1` and `range2.relative(to:s)` are identical. But in general you won't need to do that, because a partial range literal can be used wherever you would use a range literal. For instance, a partial range is a legal String subscript value:

```
let s = "hello"
let ix2 = s.index(before: s.endIndex)
let s2 = s[..<ix2] // "hell"
```

I'll show further practical examples later on.

Tuple

A *tuple* is a lightweight custom ordered collection of multiple values. As a type, it is expressed by surrounding the types of the contained values with parentheses, separated by a comma. Here's a declaration for a variable whose type is a tuple of an Int and a String:

```
var pair : (Int, String)
```

The literal value of a tuple is expressed in the same way — the contained values, surrounded with parentheses and separated by a comma:

```
var pair : (Int, String) = (1, "Two")
```

Those types can be inferred, so there's no need for the explicit type in the declaration:

```
var pair = (1, "Two")
```

Tuples are a pure Swift language feature; they are not compatible with Cocoa and Objective-C, so you'll use them only for values that Cocoa never sees. Within Swift, however, they have many uses. For example, a tuple is an obvious solution to the problem that a function can return only one value; a tuple *is* one value, but it *contains* multiple values, so using a tuple as the return type of a function permits that function to return multiple values.

Tuples come with numerous linguistic conveniences. You can assign to a tuple of variable names as a way of assigning to multiple variables simultaneously:

```
let ix: Int
let s: String
(ix, s) = (1, "Two")
```

That's such a convenient thing to do that Swift lets you do it in one line, declaring and initializing multiple variables simultaneously:

```
let (ix, s) = (1, "Two")
```

To ignore one of the assigned values, use an underscore to represent it in the receiving tuple:

```
let pair = (1, "Two")
let (_, s) = pair // now s is "Two"
```

Assigning variable values to one another through a tuple swaps them safely:

```
var s1 = "hello"
var s2 = "world"
(s1, s2) = (s2, s1) // now s1 is "world" and s2 is "hello"
```

The `enumerated` method lets you walk a sequence with `for...in` and receive, on each iteration, each successive element's index number along with the element itself; this double result comes to you as — you guessed it — a tuple:

```
let s = "hello"
for (ix,c) in s.enumerated() {
    print("character \(ix) is \(c)")
}
```

I also pointed out earlier that numeric instance methods such as `addingReporting-Overflow` return a tuple.

You can refer to the individual elements of a tuple directly, in two ways. The first way is by index number, using a *literal number* (not a variable value) as the name of a message sent to the tuple with dot-notation:

```
let pair = (1, "Two")
let ix = pair.0 // now ix is 1
```

If you have a `var` reference to a tuple, you can assign into it by the same means:

```
var pair = (1, "Two")
pair.0 = 2 // now pair is (2, "Two")
```

The second way to access tuple elements is to give them labels. The notation is like that of function parameters, and must appear as part of the explicit or implicit type declaration. Here's one way to establish tuple element labels:

```
let pair : (first:Int, second:String) = (1, "Two")
```

And here's another way:

```
let pair = (first:1, second:"Two")
```

The labels are now part of the type of this value, and travel with it through subsequent assignments. You can then use them as literal messages, just like (and together with) the numeric literals:

```
var pair = (first:1, second:"Two")
let x = pair.first // 1
pair.first = 2
let y = pair.0 // 2
```

The tuple generated by the `enumerated` method has labels `offset` and `element`, so we can rewrite an earlier example like this:

```
let s = "hello"
for t in s.enumerated() {
    print("character \(t.offset) is \(t.element)")
}
```

You can assign from a tuple without labels into a corresponding tuple with labels (and *vice versa*):

```
let pair = (1, "Two")
let pairWithNames : (first:Int, second:String) = pair
let ix = pairWithNames.first // 1
```

You can also pass, or return from a function, a tuple without labels where a corresponding tuple with labels is expected:

```
func tupleMaker() -> (first:Int, second:String) {
    return (1, "Two") // no labels here
}
let ix = tupleMaker().first // 1
```

If you're going to be using a certain type of tuple consistently throughout your program, it might be useful to give it a type name. To do so, define a type alias. In my LinkSame app, I have a Board class describing and manipulating the game layout. The board is a grid of Piece objects. I need a way to describe positions of the grid. That's a pair of integers, so I define my own type as a tuple:

```
class Board {
    typealias Point = (x:Int, y:Int)
    // ...
}
```

The advantage of that notation is that it now becomes easy to use Points throughout my code. Given a Point, I can fetch the corresponding Piece:

```
func piece(at p:Point) -> Piece? {
    let (i,j) = p
    // ... error-checking goes here ...
    return self.grid[i][j]
}
```

Still, one should not overuse tuples. In a very real sense, they are not a full-fledged type. Keep your tuples small, light, and temporary.

 Void, the type of value returned by a function that doesn't return a value, is actually a type alias for an empty tuple. That's why it is also notated as ().

Optional

The Optional object type (an enum) wraps another object of any type. What makes an Optional optional is this: it *might* wrap another object, but then again it might not. Think of an Optional as being itself a kind of shoebox — a shoebox which can quite legally be empty.

Let's start by creating an Optional that does wrap an object. Suppose we want an Optional wrapping the String "howdy". One way to create it is with the Optional initializer:

```
var stringMaybe = Optional("howdy")
```

If we log `stringMaybe` to the console with `print`, we'll see an expression identical to the corresponding initializer: `Optional("howdy")`.

After that declaration and initialization, `stringMaybe` is typed, not as a String, nor as an Optional plain and simple, but as an Optional wrapping a String. This means that any other Optional wrapping a String can be assigned to it — but not an Optional wrapping some other type. This code is legal:

```
var stringMaybe = Optional("howdy")
stringMaybe = Optional("farewell")
```

This code, however, is not legal:

```
var stringMaybe = Optional("howdy")
stringMaybe = Optional(123) // compile error
```

`Optional(123)` is an Optional wrapping an Int, and you can't assign an Optional wrapping an Int where an Optional wrapping a String is expected.

Optionals are so important to Swift that special syntax for working with them is baked into the language. The usual way to make an Optional is not to use the Optional initializer (though you can certainly do that), but to assign or pass a value of some type to a reference that is already typed as an Optional wrapping that type. This seems as if it should not be legal — but it is. Once `stringMaybe` is typed as an Optional wrapping a String, it is legal to assign a String directly to it. The outcome is that the assigned String is wrapped in an Optional for us, automatically:

```
var stringMaybe = Optional("howdy")
stringMaybe = "farewell" // now stringMaybe is Optional("farewell")
```

We also need a way of typing something *explicitly* as an Optional wrapping a String. Otherwise, we cannot declare a variable or parameter with an Optional type. Formally, an Optional is a generic, so an Optional wrapping a String is an `Optional<String>`. (I'll explain that syntax in Chapter 4.) However, you don't have to write that. The Swift language supports syntactic sugar for expressing an Optional type: use the name of the wrapped type followed by a question mark:

```
var stringMaybe : String?
```

Thus I don't need to use the Optional initializer at all. I can type the variable as an Optional wrapping a String and assign a String into it for wrapping, all in one move:

```
var stringMaybe : String? = "howdy"
```

That, in fact, is the normal way to make an Optional in Swift.

Once you've got an Optional wrapping a particular type, you can use it wherever an Optional wrapping that type is expected — just like any other value. If a function expects an Optional wrapping a String as its parameter, you can pass `stringMaybe` as the argument:

```
func optionalExpecter(_ s:String?) {}
let stringMaybe : String? = "howdy"
optionalExpecter(stringMaybe)
```

Moreover, where an Optional wrapping a certain type of value is expected, you can pass a value of that wrapped type instead. That's because parameter passing is just like assignment: an unwrapped value will be wrapped implicitly for you. If a function expects an Optional wrapping a String, you can pass a String argument, which will be wrapped into an Optional in the received parameter:

```
func optionalExpecter(_ s:String?) {
    // ... here, s will be an Optional wrapping a String ...
    print(s)
}
optionalExpecter("howdy") // console prints: Optional("howdy")
```

But you cannot do the opposite — you cannot use an Optional wrapping a type where the wrapped type is expected. This won't compile:

```
func realStringExpecter(_ s:String) {}
let stringMaybe : String? = "howdy"
realStringExpecter(stringMaybe) // compile error
```

The error message reads: "Value of Optional type `String?` must be unwrapped." You're going to be seeing that sort of message a lot in Swift, so get used to it! If you want to use an Optional where the type of thing it wraps is expected, you must *unwrap* the Optional — that is, you must reach inside it and *retrieve* the actual thing that it wraps. Now I'm going to talk about how to do that.

Unwrapping an Optional

We have seen more than one way to wrap an object in an Optional. But what about the opposite procedure? How do we unwrap an Optional to get at the object wrapped inside it? One way is to use the *unwrap operator* (or *forced unwrap operator*), which is a postfixed exclamation mark:

```
func realStringExpecter(_ s:String) {}
let stringMaybe : String? = "howdy"
realStringExpecter(stringMaybe!)
```

In that code, the `stringMaybe!` syntax expresses the operation of reaching inside the Optional `stringMaybe`, grabbing the wrapped value, and substituting it at that point. Since `stringMaybe` is an Optional wrapping a String, the thing inside it is a String. That is exactly what the `realStringExpecter` function wants as its parameter!

stringMaybe is an Optional *wrapping* the String "howdy", but `stringMaybe!` *is* the String "howdy".

If an Optional wraps a certain type, you cannot send it a message expected by that type. You must unwrap it first. Let's try to get an uppercase version of `stringMaybe`:

```
let stringMaybe : String? = "howdy"
let upper = stringMaybe.uppercased() // compile error
```

The solution is to unwrap `stringMaybe` to get at the String inside it. We can do this directly, in place, using the unwrap operator:

```
let stringMaybe : String? = "howdy"
let upper = stringMaybe!.uppercased()
```

If an Optional is to be used several times where the unwrapped type is expected, and if you're going to be unwrapping it with the unwrap operator each time, your code can quickly start to look like the dialog from a 1960s Batman comic. For example, an app's window is an Optional UIWindow property (`self.window`):

```
// self.window is an Optional wrapping a UIWindow
self.window!.rootViewController = RootViewController()
self.window!.backgroundColor = UIColor.white
self.window!.makeKeyAndVisible()
```

That sort of thing soon gets old (or silly). One obvious alternative is to assign the unwrapped value *once* to a variable of the wrapped type and then use that variable:

```
// self.window is an Optional wrapping a UIWindow
let window = self.window!
// now window (not self.window) is a UIWindow, not an Optional
window.rootViewController = RootViewController()
window.backgroundColor = UIColor.white
window.makeKeyAndVisible()
```

Implicitly unwrapped Optional

Swift provides another way of using an Optional where the wrapped type is expected: you can declare the Optional *type* as being *implicitly unwrapped*. An implicitly unwrapped Optional is an Optional, but the compiler permits some special magic associated with it: its value can be used *directly* where the wrapped type is expected. You *can* unwrap an implicitly unwrapped Optional explicitly, but you don't have to, because it will be unwrapped for you, automatically, if you try to use it where the wrapped type is expected. Moreover, Swift provides syntactic sugar for expressing an implicitly unwrapped Optional type: use the name of the wrapped type followed by an exclamation mark:

```
func realStringExpecter(_ s:String) {}
var stringMaybe : String! = "howdy"
realStringExpecter(stringMaybe) // no problem
```

Bear in mind that *an implicitly unwrapped Optional is still an Optional.* It's just a convenience. By declaring something as an implicitly unwrapped Optional, you are asking the compiler, if you happen to use this value where the wrapped type is expected, to forgive you and to unwrap the value for you.

In reality, an implicitly unwrapped Optional type is not really a distinct type; it is merely an Optional marked in a special way that allows it to be used where the unwrapped type is expected. For this reason, implicit unwrapping does not propagate by assignment. Here's a case in point. If `self` is a UIViewController, then `self.view` is typed as `UIView!`. As a result, this expression is legal (assume v is a UIView):

```
self.view.addSubview(v)
```

But this is not legal:

```
let mainview = self.view
mainview.addSubview(v) // compile error
```

The problem is that, although `self.view` is an implicitly unwrapped Optional wrapping a UIView, `mainview` is a *normal* Optional wrapping a UIView, and so it would have to be unwrapped explicitly before you could send it the `addSubview` message. Alternatively, you could unwrap the implicitly unwrapped Optional explicitly at the outset:

```
let mainview = self.view!
mainview.addSubview(v)
```

In real life, the primary situation in which you're likely to declare an implicitly unwrapped Optional is when an instance property's initial value can't be provided until after the instance itself is created. I'll give some examples at the end of this chapter.

The keyword nil

I have talked so far about Optionals that contain a wrapped value. But what about an Optional that *doesn't* contain any wrapped value? Such an Optional is, as I've already said, a perfectly legal entity; that, indeed, is the whole point of Optionals.

You are going to need a way to *ask* whether an Optional contains a wrapped value, and a way to *specify* an Optional *without* a wrapped value. Swift makes both of those things easy, through the use of a special keyword, `nil`:

To learn whether an Optional contains a wrapped value
Test the Optional for equality against `nil`. If the test succeeds, the Optional is empty. An empty Optional is also reported in the console as `nil`.

To specify an Optional with no wrapped value
Assign or pass `nil` where the Optional type is expected. The result is an Optional of the expected type, containing no wrapped value.

To illustrate:

```
var stringMaybe : String? = "Howdy"
print(stringMaybe) // Optional("Howdy")
if stringMaybe == nil {
    print("it is empty") // does not print
}
stringMaybe = nil
print(stringMaybe) // nil
if stringMaybe == nil {
    print("it is empty") // prints
}
```

The keyword nil lets you express the concept, "an Optional wrapping the appropriate type, but not actually containing any object of that type." Clearly, that's very convenient magic; you'll want to take advantage of it. It is very important to understand, however, that it *is* magic: nil in Swift is *not* a thing and is *not* a value. *It is a shorthand.* It is natural to think and speak as if this shorthand were real. I will often say that something "is nil." But in reality, nothing "is nil"; nil isn't a thing. What I really mean is that this thing is equatable with nil, because it is an Optional not wrapping anything. (I'll explain in Chapter 4 how nil, and Optionals in general, really work.)

Because a variable typed as an Optional can be nil, Swift follows a special initialization rule: a variable (var) typed as an Optional *is* nil, automatically:

```
func optionalExpecter(_ s:String?) {}
var stringMaybe : String?
optionalExpecter(stringMaybe)
```

That code looks as if it should be illegal. We declared a variable stringMaybe, but we never assigned it a value. Nevertheless we are now passing it around as if it were an actual thing. That's because it *is* an actual thing. This variable has been *implicitly initialized* — to nil. A variable (var) typed as an Optional is the *only* sort of variable that gets implicit initialization in Swift.

We come now to perhaps the most important rule in all of Swift: You *cannot unwrap an Optional containing nothing* (an Optional equatable with nil). Such an Optional contains nothing; there's nothing to unwrap. Like Oakland, there's no there there. In fact, explicitly unwrapping an Optional containing nothing will *crash your program* at runtime:

```
var stringMaybe : String?
let s = stringMaybe! // crash
```

The crash message reads: "Fatal error: unexpectedly found nil while unwrapping an Optional value." Get used to it, because you're going to be seeing it a lot. This is an easy mistake to make. Unwrapping an Optional that contains no value is, in fact, probably the most common way to crash a Swift program. You should look upon this kind of crash as a blessing. Very often, in fact, you will *want* to crash if your Optional contains no value, because it *should* contain a value, and the fact that it doesn't indicates that you've made a mistake elsewhere.

In the long run, however, crashing is bad. To eliminate this kind of crash, you need to ensure that your Optional contains a value, and *don't* unwrap it if it doesn't! Ensuring that an Optional contains a value before attempting to unwrap it is clearly a very important thing to do. Accordingly, Swift provides several convenient ways of doing it. I'll describe some of them now, and I'll discuss others in Chapter 5.

One obvious approach is to test your Optional against `nil` explicitly before you unwrap it:

```
var stringMaybe : String?
// ... stringMaybe might be assigned a real value here ...
if stringMaybe != nil {
    let s = stringMaybe!
    // ...
}
```

But there's a more elegant way, as I shall now explain.

Optional chains

A common situation is that you want to send a message to the value wrapped inside an Optional. You *cannot* send such a message to the Optional *itself.* If you try to do so, you will get an error message from the compiler:

```
let stringMaybe : String? = "howdy"
let upper = stringMaybe.uppercased() // compile error
```

You must unwrap the Optional first, so that you can send that message to the *actual* thing wrapped inside. Conveniently, you can unwrap the Optional *in place.* I gave an example earlier:

```
let stringMaybe : String? = "howdy"
let upper = stringMaybe!.uppercased()
```

That form of code is called an *Optional chain.* In the middle of a chain of dot-notation, you have unwrapped an Optional.

However, if you unwrap an Optional that contains no wrapped object, you'll crash. So what if you're *not sure* whether this Optional contains a wrapped object? How can you send a message to the value inside an Optional in that situation?

Swift provides a special shorthand for exactly this purpose. To send a message *safely* to the value wrapped inside an Optional that might be empty, you can *unwrap the Optional optionally.* To do so, unwrap the Optional with the question mark postfix operator instead of the exclamation mark:

```
var stringMaybe : String?
// ... stringMaybe might be assigned a real value here ...
let upper = stringMaybe?.uppercased()
```

That's an Optional chain in which you used a question mark to unwrap the Optional. By using that notation, you have unwrapped the Optional optionally — meaning conditionally. The condition in question is one of safety; a test for `nil` is performed for us. Our code means: "If `stringMaybe` contains a String, unwrap it and send that String the `uppercased` message. If it doesn't (that is, if it equates to `nil`), *do not* unwrap it and *do not* send it any messages!"

Such code is a double-edged sword. On the one hand, if `stringMaybe` is `nil`, you won't crash at runtime. On the other hand, if `stringMaybe` is `nil`, that line of code won't do anything useful — you won't get any uppercase string.

But now there's a new question. In that code, we initialized a variable `upper` to an expression that involves sending the `uppercased` message. Now it turns out that the `uppercased` message might not even be sent. So what, exactly, is `upper` initialized *to*?

To handle this situation, Swift has a special rule. If an Optional chain contains an optionally unwrapped Optional, and if this Optional chain produces a value, that value is itself *wrapped in an Optional*. Thus, `upper` is typed as an Optional wrapping a String. This works brilliantly, because it covers both possible cases. Let's say, first, that `stringMaybe` contains a String:

```
var stringMaybe : String?
stringMaybe = "howdy"
let upper = stringMaybe?.uppercased()
```

After that code, `upper` is *not* a String; it is *not* `"HOWDY"`. It is an Optional wrapping `"HOWDY"`.

On the other hand, if the attempt to unwrap the Optional fails, the Optional chain can return `nil` instead:

```
var stringMaybe : String?
let upper = stringMaybe?.uppercased()
```

After that code, `upper` is typed as an Optional wrapping a String, but it wraps no string; its value is `nil`.

Unwrapping an Optional optionally in this way is elegant and safe; even if `string-Maybe` is `nil`, we won't crash at runtime. On the other hand, we've ended up with yet another Optional on our hands! `upper` is typed as an Optional wrapping a String, and in order to use that String, we're going to have to unwrap `upper`. And we don't know whether `upper` is `nil`, so we have exactly the same problem we had before — we need to make sure that we unwrap `upper` safely, and that we don't accidentally unwrap an empty Optional.

Longer Optional chains are legal. No matter how many Optionals are unwrapped in the course of the chain, if any of them is unwrapped optionally, the entire expression produces an Optional wrapping the type it would have produced if the Optionals were unwrapped normally, and is free to fail safely at any point along the way:

```
// self is a UIViewController
let f = self.view?.window?.rootViewController?.view?.frame
```

The `frame` property of a view is a CGRect. But after that code, f is *not* a CGRect. It's an Optional wrapping a CGRect. If *any* of the optional unwrapping along the chain fails (because the Optional we propose to unwrap is `nil`), f will be `nil` to indicate failure.

(Observe that the preceding code does *not* end up nesting Optionals; it doesn't produce a CGRect wrapped in an Optional wrapped in an Optional, and so on, merely because there are multiple Optionals being optionally unwrapped in the chain! However, it is possible, for other reasons, to end up with an Optional wrapped in an Optional, and I'll call out some examples as we proceed.)

If a function call returns an Optional, you can unwrap the result and use it. You don't necessarily have to capture the result in order to do that; you can unwrap it in place, by putting an exclamation mark or a question mark after the function call (that is, after the closing parenthesis). That's really no different from what we've been doing all along, except that instead of an Optional property or variable, this is a function call that returns an Optional:

```
class Dog {
    var noise : String?
    func speak() -> String? {
        return self.noise
    }
}
let d = Dog()
let bigname = d.speak()?.uppercased()
```

After that, don't forget, `bigname` is not a String — it's an Optional wrapping a String.

You can also assign safely into an Optional chain. If any of the optionally unwrapped Optionals in the chain turns out to be `nil`, nothing happens:

```
// self is a UIViewController
self.navigationController?.hidesBarsOnTap = true
```

A view controller might or might not have a navigation controller, so its `navigationController` property is an Optional. In that code, we are setting our navigation controller's `hidesBarsOnTap` property safely; if we happen to have no navigation controller, no harm is done — because nothing happens.

When assigning into an Optional chain, if you also want to know whether the assignment succeeded, you can capture the result of the assignment as an Optional wrapping a Void and test it for `nil`:

```
let ok : Void? = self.navigationController?.hidesBarsOnTap = true
```

Now, if `ok` is not `nil`, `self.navigationController` was safely unwrapped and the assignment succeeded.

 The ! and ? postfix operators, which are used to unwrap an Optional, have basically *nothing* to do with the ! and ? used with type names as syntactic sugar for expressing Optional types (such as `String?` and `String!`). The outward similarity has confused many a beginner.

Optional map and flatMap

When you want to do something to an Optional's wrapped value more elaborate than sending it a simple message, such as calling `uppercased()`, while keeping the advantages of Optional chaining, Swift provides a method that elegantly and safely permits you to do so: `map(_:)`. This is a method of Optional itself, so it's fine to send it to an Optional. The parameter is a function that you supply (usually an anonymous function) that takes whatever type is wrapped in the Optional; the *unwrapped* value is passed to this function, and now you can manipulate it in any desired manner. The result of the function is then wrapped as an Optional. If the original Optional was `nil`, the whole thing produces `nil`, safely:

```
let s : String? = "howdy"
let s2 = s.map {($0 + ", world").uppercased()}
```

In that example, we start with an Optional wrapping a String; we append a string to the string, and uppercase the result. You can't apply the + operator to an Optional string, but inside the `map` function, the string is *not* Optional. Afterward, `s2` is an Optional wrapping a String. If `s` had turned out to be `nil`, there would be no crash, and `s2` would be set to `nil` as well.

The output Optional type doesn't have to be the same as the input Optional type. To illustrate, I'll use a closely related Optional method, `flatMap(_:)`. Here's an elegant way to coerce an Optional String to an (Optional) Int:

```
let s : String? = // whatever
let i = s.flatMap {Int($0)}
```

In that code, we attempt to unwrap an Optional String and coerce it to an Int. The result is an Optional Int, which will be `nil` if `s` is `nil`, or if `s` isn't `nil` but the coercion fails because the string wrapped by `s` doesn't represent an integer.

That example also illustrates the difference between `map` and `flatMap`. If the map function itself produces an Optional — as coercing a String to an Int does — `flatMap` unwraps it before wrapping the result in an Optional. `map` doesn't do that, so if we had used `map` here, we would have ended up with a double-wrapped Optional (an `Int??`).

Comparison with Optional

In an equality comparison with something other than `nil`, an Optional gets special treatment: the wrapped value, not the Optional itself, is compared. This works:

```
let s : String? = "Howdy"
if s == "Howdy" { // ... they _are_ equal!
```

That shouldn't work — how can an Optional be the same as a String? — but it does. Instead of comparing the Optional itself with `"Howdy"`, Swift automagically (and safely) compares its wrapped value (if there is one) with `"Howdy"`. If the wrapped value is `"Howdy"`, the comparison succeeds. If the wrapped value is not `"Howdy"`, the comparison fails. If there is *no* wrapped value (`s` is `nil`), the comparison fails too — safely! You can compare `s` to `nil` or to a String, and the comparison works correctly in all cases.

(This feature depends upon the wrapped type itself being usable with `==`. This means that the wrapped type must adopt the Equatable protocol; otherwise, the compiler will stop you from using `==` with an Optional wrapping it. I'll talk about protocols and Equatable in Chapters 4 and 5.)

Direct comparison of Optionals does *not* work for an inequality comparison, using the greater-than and less-than operators:

```
let i : Int? = 2
if i < 3 { // compile error
```

To perform that sort of comparison, you can unwrap safely and perform the comparison directly on the unwrapped value:

```
if i != nil && i! < 3 { // ... it _is_ less
```

 Do not compare an implicitly unwrapped Optional with anything; you can crash at runtime.

Why Optionals?

Now that you know *how* to use an Optional, you are probably wondering *why* to use an Optional. Why does Swift have Optionals at all? What are they good for?

One important use of Optionals is to permit a value to be *marked as empty or erroneous*. Many built-in Swift functions use an Optional this way:

```
let arr = [1,2,3]
let ix = arr.firstIndex(of:4)
if ix == nil { // ...
```

Swift's `firstIndex(of:)` method returns an Optional because the object sought might not be present, in which case it has *no* index. The type returned cannot be an Int, because there is no Int value that can be taken to mean, "I didn't find this object at all." Returning an Optional solves the problem neatly: `nil` means "I didn't find the object," and otherwise the actual Int result is sitting there wrapped up in the Optional.

Another purpose of Optionals is to provide *interchange of object values with Objective-C*. In Objective-C, *any* object reference can be `nil`. You need a way to send `nil` to Objective-C and to receive `nil` from Objective-C. Swift Optionals provide your only way to do that.

Swift will typically assist you by a judicious use of appropriate types in the Cocoa APIs. Consider a UIView's `backgroundColor` property. It's a UIColor, but it can be `nil`, and you are allowed to set it to `nil`. Thus, it is typed as `UIColor?`. You don't need to work directly with Optionals in order to *set* such a value! Remember, assigning the wrapped type to an Optional is legal, as the assigned value will be wrapped for you. You can set `myView.backgroundColor` to a UIColor — or to `nil`. If you *get* a UIView's `backgroundColor`, you now have an Optional wrapping a UIColor, *and you must be conscious of that fact*, for all the reasons I've already discussed: if you're not, surprising things can happen:

```
let v = UIView()
let c = v.backgroundColor
let c2 = c.withAlphaComponent(0.5) // compile error
```

You're trying to send the `withAlphaComponent` message to `c`, as if it were a UIColor. It *isn't* a UIColor. It's an Optional wrapping a UIColor. Xcode will try to help you in this situation; if you use code completion (Chapter 9) to enter the name of the `withAlphaComponent` method, Xcode will insert a question mark after `c`, (optionally) unwrapping the Optional and giving you legal code:

```
let v = UIView()
let c = v.backgroundColor
let c2 = c?.withAlphaComponent(0.5)
```

In the vast majority of situations, however, a Cocoa object type will *not* be marked as an Optional. That's because, although in theory it *could* be `nil` (because any Objective-C object reference can be `nil`), in practice it won't be. Swift saves you a step by treating the value as the object type itself. This magic is performed by hand-tweaking the Cocoa APIs (also called *auditing*). In the very first public version of Swift (in June of 2014), *all* object values received from Cocoa were typed as Optionals (usually implicitly unwrapped Optionals); but then Apple embarked on the massive project of hand-tweaking the APIs to eliminate Optionals that didn't need to be Optionals, and that project is now essentially complete.

Finally, an important use of Optionals is to *defer initialization* of an instance property. If a variable (declared with `var`) is typed as an Optional, it has a value even if you don't initialize it — namely `nil`. That comes in very handy in situations where you know something *will* have a value, but not right away.

One way this can happen is that a property represents data that will take time to acquire. In my Albumen app, as we launch, I create an instance of my root view controller. I also want to gather a bunch of data about the user's music library and store that data in instance properties of the root view controller instance. But gathering that data will take time. Therefore I must instantiate the root view controller *first* and gather the data *later*, because if we pause to gather the data *before* instantiating the root view controller, the app will take too long to launch — the delay will be perceptible, and we might even crash (because iOS forbids long launch times). Therefore the data properties are all typed as Optionals; they are `nil` until the data are gathered, at which time they are assigned their "real" values:

```
class RootViewController : UITableViewController {
    var albums : [MPMediaItemCollection]? // initialized to nil
    // ...
}
```

This approach has a second advantage: as with `firstIndex`, the initial `nil` value of `albums` is a signal to the rest of my code that we don't yet have a real value. When my Albumen app launches, it displays a table listing all the user's music albums. At launch time, however, that data has not yet been gathered. My table-display code tests `albums` to see whether it's `nil` and, if it is, displays an empty table. After gathering the data, I tell my table to display its data *again*. This time, the table-display code finds that `albums` is *not* `nil`, but rather consists of actual data — and it now displays that data. The use of an Optional allows one and the same value, `albums`, to store the data or to state that there is no data.

Sometimes, a property's value isn't time-consuming to acquire, but it *still* won't be ready at initialization time. A common case in real life is an outlet, which is a reference to something in your interface such as a button:

```
class ViewController: UIViewController {
    @IBOutlet var myButton: UIButton! // initialized to nil
    // ...
}
```

Ignore, for now, the `@IBOutlet` designation, which is an internal hint to Xcode (as I'll explain in Chapter 7). The important thing is that this property, `myButton`, won't have a value when our ViewController instance first comes into existence, but shortly thereafter the view controller's view will be loaded and `myButton` will be set so that it points to an actual UIButton object in the interface. Therefore, the variable is typed as an implicitly unwrapped Optional:

- It's an Optional because we need a placeholder value (namely `nil`) for `myButton` when the ViewController instance first comes into existence.

- It's implicitly unwrapped so that in our code, once `self.myButton` has been assigned a UIButton value, we can treat it as a reference to an actual UIButton, passing through the Optional without noticing that it *is* an Optional. Moreover, most of this view controller's code will run after the view is loaded and the actual button is assigned to `myButton`, so the implicitly unwrapped Optional is generally safe: code can confidently refer to `myButton` as if it were a UIButton, without fear that it might be `nil`.

A shortcoming of this architecture is that our outlet property must be declared with `var`, meaning that, in theory, other code can come along later and replace this button reference with another. That is usually undesirable. This is similar to the lack of `lazy` `let` discussed earlier in this chapter — and you can work around the problem in a similar way, namely with a property wrapper that allows the outlet property's value, initialized to `nil`, to be set only once thereafter.

CHAPTER 4

Object Types

In the preceding chapter, I discussed some built-in object types. But I have not yet explained object types themselves. As I mentioned in Chapter 1, Swift object types come in three flavors: enum, struct, and class. What are the differences between them? And how would you create your own object type?

In this chapter, I'll describe first object types generally and then each of the three flavors. Then I'll explain three Swift ways of giving an object type greater flexibility: protocols, generics, and extensions. Finally, I'll complete the survey of Swift's main built-in types with three umbrella types and three collection types.

Object Type Declarations and Features

Object types are declared with the flavor of the object type (enum, struct, or class), the name of the object type (which should start with a capital letter), and curly braces:

```
class Manny {
}
struct Moe {
}
enum Jack {
}
```

The visibility of an object type to other code — its scope — depends upon where its declaration appears (compare "Variable Scope and Lifetime" on page 67):

Top level
    Object types declared at the top level of a file will, by default, be visible to all files in the same module. This is the usual place for object type declarations.

Inside another type declaration

Sometimes it's useful to declare a type inside the declaration of another type, giving it a namespace. This is called a *nested type*.

Function body

An object type declared within the body of a function will exist only inside the scope of the curly braces that surround it; such declarations are legal but rare.

Declarations for any object type may contain within their curly braces the following things:

Initializers

An object type is merely the *type* of an object. The purpose of declaring an object type will usually (though not always) be so that you can make an actual object — an *instance* — that *has* this type. An *initializer* is a function, declared and called in a special way, allowing you to do that.

Properties

A variable declared at the top level of an object type declaration is a *property*.

By default, a property is an *instance property*. An instance property is scoped to an instance: it is accessed through a particular instance of this type, and its value can be different for every instance of this type.

Alternatively, a property can be a *static/class property*. For an enum or struct, it is declared with the keyword `static`; for a class, it may instead be declared with the keyword `class`. It belongs to the object type itself: it is accessed through the type, and it has just one value, associated with the type.

Methods

A function declared at the top level of an object type declaration is a *method*.

By default, a method is an *instance method:* it is called by sending a message to a particular instance of this type. Inside an instance method, `self` is the instance.

Alternatively, a method can be a *static/class method*. For an enum or struct, it is declared with the keyword `static`; for a class, it may be declared instead with the keyword `class`. It is called by sending a message to the type. Inside a static/class method, `self` is the type.

Subscripts

A subscript is a special kind of method, called by appending square brackets to an instance reference or type name.

Object type declarations

An object type declaration can contain an object type declaration — a nested type. From inside the containing object type, the nested type is in scope; from outside the containing object type, the nested type must be referred to through the containing object type. The containing object type is a namespace for the nested type.

Initializers

An *initializer* is a function for producing an instance of an object type. Strictly speaking, it is a static/class method, because it is called by talking to the object type. It is usually called by means of special syntax: the name of the type is followed directly by parentheses, as if the type itself were a function. When an initializer is called, a new instance is created and returned as a result. You will usually do something with the returned instance, such as assigning it to a variable, in order to preserve it and work with it in subsequent code.

Suppose we have a Dog class:

```
class Dog {
}
```

Then we can make a Dog instance like this:

```
Dog()
```

That code, however, though legal, is silly — so silly that it warrants a warning from the compiler. We have created a Dog instance, but there is no reference to that instance. Without such a reference, the Dog instance comes into existence and then immediately vanishes in a puff of smoke. The usual sort of thing is more like this:

```
let fido = Dog()
```

Now our Dog instance will persist as long as the variable fido persists (see Chapter 3) — and the variable fido gives us a reference to our Dog instance, so that we can use it.

Observe that Dog() calls an initializer even though our Dog class doesn't declare any initializers! The reason is that object types may have *implicit initializers*. These are a convenience that save you the trouble of writing your own initializers. But you *can* write your own initializers, and you will often do so.

How to write an initializer

An initializer is a kind of function, but its declaration syntax doesn't involve the keyword func or a return type. Instead, you use the keyword init with a parameter list, followed by curly braces containing the code. An object type can have multiple initializers, distinguished by their parameters. A frequent use of the parameters is to set the values of instance properties.

Here's a Dog class with two instance properties, name (a String) and license (an Int). We give these instance properties default values that are effectively placeholders — an empty string and the number zero. Then we declare three initializers, so that the caller can create a Dog instance in three different ways: by supplying a name, by supplying a license number, or by supplying both. In each initializer, the parameters that are supplied are used to set the values of the corresponding properties:

```
class Dog {
    var name = ""
    var license = 0
    init(name:String) {
        self.name = name
    }
    init(license:Int) {
        self.license = license
    }
    init(name:String, license:Int) {
        self.name = name
        self.license = license
    }
}
```

In that code, in each initializer, I've given each parameter the same name as the property to which it corresponds. There's no reason to do that apart from stylistic clarity. In the initializer function body, I can distinguish the parameter from the property by using self explicitly to access the property.

The result of that declaration is that I can create a Dog in three different ways:

```
let fido = Dog(name:"Fido")
let rover = Dog(license:1234)
let spot = Dog(name:"Spot", license:1357)
```

But now I *can't* create a Dog with *no* initializer parameters. I wrote initializers, so my implicit initializer went away. This code is no longer legal:

```
let puff = Dog() // compile error
```

Of course, I could *make* that code legal by explicitly declaring an initializer with no parameters:

```
class Dog {
    var name = ""
    var license = 0
    init() {
    }
    init(name:String) {
        self.name = name
    }
    init(license:Int) {
        self.license = license
    }
    init(name:String, license:Int) {
```

```
            self.name = name
            self.license = license
        }
    }
```

Now, the truth is that we don't need those four initializers, because an initializer is a function, and a function's parameters can have default values. I can condense all that code into a single initializer, like this:

```
class Dog {
    var name = ""
    var license = 0
    init(name:String = "", license:Int = 0) {
        self.name = name
        self.license = license
    }
}
```

I can still make an actual Dog instance in four different ways:

```
let fido = Dog(name:"Fido")
let rover = Dog(license:1234)
let spot = Dog(name:"Spot", license:1357)
let puff = Dog()
```

Now comes the really interesting part. In my property declarations, I can *eliminate* the assignment of default initial values (as long as I declare explicitly the *type* of each property):

```
class Dog {
    var name : String // no default value!
    var license : Int // no default value!
    init(name:String = "", license:Int = 0) {
        self.name = name
        self.license = license
    }
}
```

That code is legal (and common) — because an initializer initializes! In other words, I don't have to give my properties initial values in their declarations, *provided I give them initial values in all initializers.* That way, I am guaranteed that all my instance properties have values when the instance comes into existence, which is what matters. Conversely, an instance property without an initial value when the instance comes into existence *is illegal.* A property *must* be initialized either as part of its declaration or by every initializer, and the compiler will stop you otherwise.

The Swift compiler's insistence that all instance properties be properly initialized is a valuable feature of Swift. (Contrast Objective-C, where instance properties can go uninitialized — and often do, leading to mysterious errors later.) Don't fight the compiler; work with it. The compiler will help you by giving you an error message

("Return from initializer without initializing all stored properties") until *all* your initializers initialize *all* your instance properties:

```
class Dog {
    var name : String
    var license : Int
    init(name:String = "") {
        self.name = name // compile error (do you see why?)
    }
}
```

Because setting an instance property in an initializer counts as initialization, it is legal even if the instance property is a constant declared with `let`:

```
class Dog {
    let name : String
    let license : Int
    init(name:String = "", license:Int = 0) {
        self.name = name
        self.license = license
    }
}
```

In our artificial examples, we have been very generous with our initializers: we are letting the caller instantiate a Dog without supplying a `name:` argument or a `license:` argument. Usually, however, the purpose of an initializer is just the opposite: we want to *force* the caller to supply *all* needed information at instantiation time. In real life, it is much more likely that our Dog class would look like this:

```
class Dog {
    let name : String
    let license : Int
    init(name:String, license:Int) {
        self.name = name
        self.license = license
    }
}
```

In that code, our Dog has a `name` property and a `license` property, and values for these *must* be supplied at instantiation time (there are no default values), and those values can never be changed thereafter (the properties are constants). In this way, we enforce a rule that every Dog must have a meaningful name and license. There is now only *one* way to make a Dog:

```
let spot = Dog(name:"Spot", license:1357)
```

Deferred initialization of properties

Sometimes there is no meaningful value that can be assigned to an instance property during initialization. Perhaps the initial value of this property will not be obtained until some time has elapsed *after* this instance has come into existence. This situation conflicts with the requirement that all instance properties be initialized either in their declaration or through an initializer. You could circumvent the problem by assigning a default initial value anyway; but this fails to communicate to your own code the fact that this isn't a "real" value.

A common solution, as I explained in Chapter 3, is to declare your instance property as a var having an Optional type. An Optional has a value, namely nil, signifying that no "real" value has been supplied; and an Optional var is initialized to nil automatically. Your code can test this instance property against nil and, if it is nil, it won't use the property. Later, the property will be given its "real" value. Of course, that value is now wrapped in an Optional; but if you declare this property as an implicitly unwrapped Optional, you can use the wrapped value directly, without explicitly unwrapping it — as if this weren't an Optional at all — once you're sure it is safe to do so:

```
// this property will be set automatically when the nib loads
@IBOutlet var myButton: UIButton!
// this property will be set after time-consuming gathering of data
var albums : [MPMediaItemCollection]?
```

Referring to self

An initializer may refer to an already initialized instance property, and may refer to an uninitialized instance property in order to initialize it. Otherwise, an initializer *may not refer to self*, explicitly or implicitly, until *all* instance properties have been initialized. This rule guarantees that the instance is fully formed before it is used. This code is illegal:

```
struct Cat {
    var name : String
    var license : Int
    init(name:String, license:Int) {
        self.name = name
        meow() // too soon - compile error
        self.license = license
    }
    func meow() {
        print("meow")
    }
}
```

The call to the instance method meow is implicitly a reference to self — it means self.meow(). The initializer can say that, but not until it has fulfilled its primary contract of initializing all uninitialized properties. The call to the instance method meow simply needs to be moved down one line, so that it comes *after* both name and license have been initialized.

Delegating initializers

Initializers within an object type can call one another by using the syntax `self.init(...)`. An initializer that calls another initializer is called a *delegating initializer*. When an initializer delegates, the other initializer — the one that it delegates to — must completely initialize the instance first, and then the delegating initializer can work with the fully initialized instance, possibly setting again a `var` property that was already set by the initializer that it delegated to.

A delegating initializer appears to be an exception to the rule against saying `self` too early. But it isn't, because it is saying `self` in order to delegate — and delegating will cause all instance properties to be initialized. In fact, the rules about a delegating initializer saying `self` are even more stringent: a delegating initializer *cannot refer to self at all*, not even to set a property, until *after* the call to the other initializer. For example:

```
struct Digit {
    var number : Int
    var meaningOfLife : Bool
    init(number:Int) {
        self.number = number
        self.meaningOfLife = false
    }
    init() { // this is a delegating initializer
        self.init(number:42)
        self.meaningOfLife = true
    }
}
```

A delegating initializer *cannot set a constant property* (a `let` variable). That is because it cannot refer to the property until after it has called the other initializer, and at that point the instance is fully formed — initialization proper is over, and the door for initialization of properties has closed. This property is a constant, it has been initialized, and that's that. The preceding code would be illegal if `meaningOfLife` were declared with `let`, because the second initializer is a delegating initializer and cannot set a constant property.

Be careful not to delegate recursively! If you tell an initializer to delegate to itself, or if you create a vicious circle of delegating initializers, the compiler won't stop you, but your running app will hang. Don't say this:

```
struct Digit { // do not do this!
    var number : Int = 100
    init(value:Int) {
        self.init(number:value)
    }
```

```
    init(number:Int) {
        self.init(value:number)
    }
}
```

Failable initializers

An initializer can return an Optional wrapping the new instance. In this way, `nil` can be returned to signal failure. An initializer that behaves this way is a *failable initializer*. To mark an initializer as failable when declaring it, put a question mark after the keyword `init`. If your failable initializer needs to return `nil`, explicitly write `return nil`. It is up to the caller to test the resulting Optional for equivalence with `nil`, unwrap it, and so forth, as with any Optional.

Here's a version of Dog with an initializer that returns an Optional, returning `nil` if the `name:` or `license:` arguments are invalid:

```
class Dog {
    let name : String
    let license : Int
    init?(name:String, license:Int) {
        if name.isEmpty {
            return nil
        }
        if license <= 0 {
            return nil
        }
        self.name = name
        self.license = license
    }
}
```

The resulting value is typed as an Optional wrapping a Dog, and the caller will need to unwrap that Optional (if isn't `nil`) before sending any messages to it.

Cocoa and Objective-C conventionally return `nil` from initializers to signal failure; the API for such initializers has been hand-tweaked as a Swift failable initializer if initialization really might fail. For example, the UIImage initializer `init?(named:)` is a failable initializer, because there might be no image with the given name. The resulting value is a `UIImage?`, and will typically have to be unwrapped before using it.

(Most Objective-C initializers, however, are *not* bridged as failable initializers, even though in theory *any* Objective-C initializer might return `nil`. This is essentially the same hand-tweaking policy I described in "Why Optionals?" on page 116.)

Properties

A *property* is a variable — one that happens to be declared at the top level of an object type declaration. This means that everything said about variables in Chapter 3 applies. A property has a fixed type; it can be declared with var or let; it can be stored or computed; it can have setter observers. An instance property can also be declared lazy.

A stored instance property must be given an initial value. As I explained a moment ago, this doesn't have to happen through assignment in the declaration; it can happen through initializer functions instead. Setter observers are not called during initialization of properties.

How properties are accessed

If a property is an instance property (the default), it can be accessed only through an instance, and its value is separate for each instance. To illustrate, let's start once again with a Dog class:

```
class Dog {
    let name : String
    let license : Int
    init(name:String, license:Int) {
        self.name = name
        self.license = license
    }
}
```

Our Dog class has a name instance property. Then we can make two different Dog instances with two different name values, and we can access each Dog instance's name through the instance:

```
let fido = Dog(name:"Fido", license:1234)
let spot = Dog(name:"Spot", license:1357)
let aName = fido.name // "Fido"
let anotherName = spot.name // "Spot"
```

A static/class property, on the other hand, is accessed through the type, and is scoped to the type, which usually means that it is global and unique. I'll use a struct as an example:

```
struct Greeting {
    static let friendly = "hello there"
    static let hostile = "go away"
}
```

Now code elsewhere can fetch the values of Greeting.friendly and Greeting.hostile. That example is neither artificial nor trivial; immutable static properties are a convenient and effective way to supply your code with nicely name-spaced constants.

Property initialization and self

A property declaration that assigns an initial value to the property *cannot fetch an instance property or call an instance method*. Such behavior would require a reference, explicit or implicit, to `self`; and during initialization, there is no `self` yet — `self` is exactly what we are in the process of initializing. Making this mistake can result in some of Swift's most perplexing compile error messages. This is illegal (and removing the explicit references to `self` doesn't make it legal):

```
class Moi {
    let first = "Matt"
    let last = "Neuburg"
    let whole = self.first + " " + self.last // compile error
}
```

There are two common solutions in that situation:

Make this a computed property

> A computed property can refer to `self` because the computation won't actually be performed until after `self` exists:

```
class Moi {
    let first = "Matt"
    let last = "Neuburg"
    var whole : String {
        self.first + " " + self.last
    }
}
```

Declare this property `lazy`

> Like a computed property, a `lazy` property can refer to `self` legally because that reference won't be accessed until after `self` exists:

```
class Moi {
    let first = "Matt"
    let last = "Neuburg"
    lazy var whole = self.first + " " + self.last
}
```

As I demonstrated in Chapter 3, a variable can be initialized as part of its declaration using multiple lines of code by means of a define-and-call anonymous function. If this variable is an instance property, and if the function code refers to `self`, the variable must also be declared `lazy`:

```
class Moi {
    let first = "Matt"
    let last = "Neuburg"
    lazy var whole : String = {
        var s = self.first
        s.append(" ")
        s.append(self.last)
        return s
    }()
}
```

Unlike instance properties, static properties *can* be initialized with reference to one another; the reason is that static property initializers *are* lazy:

```
struct Greeting {
    static let friendly = "hello there"
    static let hostile = "go away"
    static let ambivalent = friendly + " but " + hostile
}
```

Notice the lack of `self` in that code. In static/class code, `self` means the type itself. I like to use `self` explicitly wherever it would be implicit, but here I can't use it without arousing the ire of the compiler (I regard this as a bug). To clarify the status of the terms `friendly` and `hostile`, I can use the type name (or the term `Self`, as I'll explain later in this chapter):

```
struct Greeting {
    static let friendly = "hello there"
    static let hostile = "go away"
    static let ambivalent = Greeting.friendly + " but " + Greeting.hostile
}
```

On the other hand, if I write `ambivalent` as a computed property, I *can* use `self`:

```
struct Greeting {
    static let friendly = "hello there"
    static let hostile = "go away"
    static var ambivalent : String {
        self.friendly + " but " + self.hostile
    }
}
```

On the other other hand, I'm not allowed to use `self` when the initial value is set by a define-and-call anonymous function (again, I regard this as a bug):

```
struct Greeting {
    static let friendly = "hello there"
    static let hostile = "go away"
    static var ambivalent : String = {
        self.friendly + " but " + self.hostile // compile error
    }()
}
```

Methods

A *method* is a function — one that happens to be declared at the top level of an object type declaration. This means that everything said about functions in Chapter 2 applies.

By default, a method is an instance method. This means that it can be accessed only through an instance. Within the body of an instance method, `self` is the instance. To illustrate, let's continue to develop our Dog class:

```
class Dog {
    let name : String
    let license : Int
    let whatDogsSay = "woof"
    init(name:String, license:Int) {
        self.name = name
        self.license = license
    }
    func bark() {
        print(self.whatDogsSay)
    }
    func speak() {
        self.bark()
        print("I'm \(self.name)")
    }
}
```

Now I can make a Dog instance and tell it to speak:

```
let fido = Dog(name:"Fido", license:1234)
fido.speak() // woof I'm Fido
```

In my Dog class, the `speak` method calls the instance method `bark` by way of `self`, and obtains the value of the instance property `name` by way of `self`; and the `bark` instance method obtains the value of the instance property `whatDogsSay` by way of `self`. This is because instance code can use `self` to refer to this instance. Such code can omit `self` if the reference is unambiguous; I could have written this:

```
func speak() {
    bark()
    print("I'm \(name)")
}
```

But I never write code like that (except by accident). Omitting `self`, in my view, makes the code harder to read and maintain; the loose terms `bark` and `name` seem mysterious and confusing. Moreover, sometimes `self` cannot be omitted (for a case in point, see "Escaping Closures" on page 59), so it's more consistent to use it always.

A static/class method is accessed through the type. Within the body of a static/class method, `self` means the type:

```
struct Greeting {
    static let friendly = "hello there"
    static func beFriendly() {
        print(self.friendly)
    }
}
```

And here's how to call the static `beFriendly` method:

```
Greeting.beFriendly() // hello there
```

There is a kind of conceptual wall between static/class members, on the one hand, and instance members on the other; even though they may be declared within the same object type declaration, they inhabit different worlds. A static/class method can't refer to "the instance" because there is no instance; thus, a static/class method cannot directly refer to any instance properties or call any instance methods. An instance method, on the other hand, can refer to the type, and can thus access static/class properties and can call static/class methods.

Let's return to our Dog class and grapple with the question of what dogs say. Presume that all dogs say the same thing. We'd prefer, therefore, to express `whatDogsSay` not at instance level but at class level. This would be a good use of a static property. Here's a simplified Dog class that illustrates:

```
class Dog {
    static var whatDogsSay = "woof"
    func bark() {
        print(Dog.whatDogsSay)
    }
}
```

Now we can make a Dog instance and tell it to bark:

```
let fido = Dog()
fido.bark() // woof
```

(Instead of `Dog.whatDogsSay`, a Dog instance method can say `Self.whatDogsSay`, as I'll explain later in this chapter.)

Subscripts

A *subscript* is a method that is called by appending square brackets containing arguments directly to a reference. You can use this feature for whatever you like, but it is suitable particularly for situations where this is an object type with *elements* that can be appropriately accessed by key or by index number. I have already described (in Chapter 3) the use of this syntax with strings, and it is familiar also from dictionaries and arrays; you can use square brackets with strings and dictionaries and arrays exactly because Swift's String and Dictionary and Array types declare subscript methods.

The Secret Life of Instance Methods

Here's a secret: instance methods are actually static/class methods. This is legal (but strange):

```
class MyClass {
    var s = ""
    func store(_ s:String) {
        self.s = s
    }
}
let m = MyClass()
let f = MyClass.store(m) // what just happened!?
```

Even though `store` is an instance method, we are able to call it as a class method — with a parameter that is an instance of this class! The reason is that an instance method is actually a curried static/class method composed of two functions — one function that takes an instance, and another function that takes the parameters of the instance method. After that code, `f` is the *second* of those functions, and can be called as a way of passing a parameter to the `store` method *of the instance m*:

```
f("howdy")
print(m.s) // howdy
```

The syntax for declaring a subscript method is somewhat like a function declaration and somewhat like a computed property declaration. That's no coincidence. A subscript is like a function in that it can take parameters: arguments can appear in the square brackets when a subscript method is called. A subscript is like a computed property in that the call is used like a reference to a property: you can fetch its value or you can assign into it.

To illustrate the syntax, here's a struct that treats an integer as if it were a digit sequence, returning a digit that can be specified by an index number in square brackets; for simplicity, I'm deliberately omitting any error-checking:

```
struct Digit {
    var number : Int
    init(_ n:Int) {
        self.number = n
    }
    subscript(ix:Int) -> Int { ❶ ❷
        get { ❸
            let s = String(self.number)
            return Int(String(s[s.index(s.startIndex, offsetBy:ix)]))!
        }
    }
}
```

❶ After the keyword `subscript` we have a parameter list stating what parameters are to appear inside the square brackets. By default, *parameter names are not externalized*; if you want a parameter name to be externalized, your declaration must include an external name before the internal name, even if they are the same name — for example, `subscript(ix ix:Int)`. This is different from how external names work everywhere else in Swift (and therefore I regard it as a bug in the language).

❷ Then we have the type of value that is passed out (when the getter is called) or in (when the setter is called); this is parallel to the type declared for a computed property, except that (oddly) the type is preceded by the arrow operator instead of a colon.

❸ Finally, we have curly braces whose contents are exactly like those of a computed property. You can have `get` and curly braces for the getter, and `set` and curly braces for the setter. The setter can be omitted (as here); in that case, the word `get` and its curly braces can be omitted. If the getter consists of a single statement, the keyword `return` can be omitted. The setter receives the new value as `newValue`, but you can change that name by supplying a different name in parentheses after the word `set`.

Here's an example of calling the getter; the instance with appended square brackets containing the arguments is used just as if you were getting a property value:

```
var d = Digit(1234)
let aDigit = d[1] // 2
```

Now I'll expand my Digit struct so that its subscript method includes a setter (and again I'll omit error-checking):

```
struct Digit {
    var number : Int
    init(_ n:Int) {
        self.number = n
    }
    subscript(ix:Int) -> Int {
        get {
            let s = String(self.number)
            return Int(String(s[s.index(s.startIndex, offsetBy:ix)]))!
        }
        set {
            var s = String(self.number)
            let i = s.index(s.startIndex, offsetBy:ix)
            s.replaceSubrange(i...i, with: String(newValue))
            self.number = Int(s)!
        }
    }
}
```

And here's an example of calling the setter; the instance with appended square brackets containing the arguments is used just as if you were setting a property value:

```
var d = Digit(1234)
d[0] = 2 // now d.number is 2234
```

An object type can declare multiple subscript methods, distinguished by their parameters.

Starting in Swift 5.1, a subscript can be a static/class method. I'll demonstrate later, when we talk about enums.

Starting in Swift 5.2, a subscript can have default parameter values. I can declare my Digit subscript method like this (though I can't think why I'd want to):

```
subscript(ix:Int = 0) -> Int {
```

And then I can call it like this:

```
var d = Digit(1234)
let aDigit = d[] // 1
```

Nested Object Types

An object type may be declared inside an object type declaration, forming a nested type:

```
class Dog {
    struct Noise {
        static var noise = "woof"
    }
    func bark() {
        print(Dog.Noise.noise)
    }
}
```

A nested object type is no different from any other object type, but the rules for referring to it from the outside are changed; the surrounding object type acts as a namespace, and must be referred to explicitly in order to access the nested object type:

```
Dog.Noise.noise = "arf"
```

Here, the Noise struct is namespaced inside the Dog class. This namespacing provides clarity: the name Noise does not float free, but is explicitly associated with the Dog class to which it belongs. Namespacing also allows more than one Noise type to exist, without any clash of names. Swift built-in object types often take advantage of namespacing; for example, the String struct is one of several structs that contain an Index struct, with no clash of names.

A nested type can't refer directly to the surrounding type's instance members, but it can refer directly to the surrounding type's static/class members:

```
class Dog {
    static let sound = "ruff"
    struct Noise {
        static var noise = "woof"
        func barkTheDog() { bark() } // compile error
        var othernoise = sound // fine!
    }
    func bark() {
        print(Dog.Noise.noise)
    }
}
```

In that example, code inside Noise cannot refer directly to Dog's `bark` method, because it's an instance method, which can be referred to only by way of some specific instance of Dog. But code inside Noise *can* refer directly to Dog's `sound` static property. Moreover, it can do so *without explicit namespacing* — that is, it doesn't have to say `Dog.sound`. In effect, the term `sound` is global in scope to the nested type.

Enums

An *enum* is an object type whose instances represent *distinct predefined alternative values*. Think of it as a list of known possibilities. An enum is the Swift way to express a set of constants that are alternatives to one another. An enum declaration includes case statements. Each case is the name of one of the alternatives. An instance of an enum will represent exactly one alternative — one case.

In my Albumen app, different instances of the same view controller can list any of four different sorts of music library contents: albums, playlists, podcasts, or audiobooks. The view controller's behavior is slightly different in each case. So I need a sort of four-way switch that I can set once when the view controller is instantiated, saying which sort of contents this view controller is to display. That sounds like an enum!

Here's the basic declaration for that enum; I call it Filter, because each case represents a different way of filtering the contents of the music library:

```
enum Filter {
    case albums
    case playlists
    case podcasts
    case books
}
```

That enum doesn't have an initializer. You *can* write an initializer for an enum, as I'll demonstrate in a moment; but there is a default mode of initialization that you'll probably use most of the time — the name of the enum followed by dot-notation and one of the cases. Here's how to make an instance of Filter representing the `albums` case:

```
let type = Filter.albums
```

If the type is known in advance, you can omit the name of the enum; the bare case must still be preceded by a dot:

```
let type : Filter = .albums
```

You can't say `.albums` just anywhere out of the blue, because Swift doesn't know what enum it belongs to. But in that code, the variable is explicitly declared as a Filter, so Swift knows what `.albums` means. A similar thing happens when passing an enum instance as an argument in a function call:

```
func filterExpecter(_ type:Filter) {}
filterExpecter(.albums)
```

In the second line, I create an instance of Filter and pass it, all in one move, without having to include the name of the enum. That's because Swift knows from the function declaration that a Filter is expected here.

In real life, the space savings when omitting the enum name can be considerable — especially because, when talking to Cocoa, the enum type names are often long:

```
let v = UIView()
v.contentMode = .center
```

A UIView's `contentMode` property is typed as a UIView.ContentMode enum. Our code is neater and simpler because we don't have to include the type name explicitly here; `.center` is nicer than `UIView.ContentMode.center`. But either is legal.

Instances of an enum with the same case are regarded as equal. You can compare an enum instance for equality against a case. Again, the type of enum is known from the first term in the comparison, so the second term can omit the enum name:

```
func filterExpecter(_ type:Filter) {
    if type == .albums {
        print("it is albums")
    }
}
filterExpecter(.albums) // "it is albums"
```

Raw Values

Optionally, when you declare an enum, you can add a type declaration. The cases then all carry with them a fixed (constant) value of that type. The types attached to an enum in this way are limited to numbers and strings, and the values assigned must be literals.

If the type is an integer numeric type, the values can be implicitly assigned, and will start at zero by default:

```
enum PepBoy : Int {
    case manny
    case moe
    case jack
}
```

In that code, `.manny` carries a value of 0, `.moe` carries of a value of 1, and so on.

If the type is String, the implicitly assigned values are the string equivalents of the case names:

```
enum Filter : String {
    case albums
    case playlists
    case podcasts
    case books
}
```

In that code, `.albums` carries a value of `"albums"`, and so on.

Regardless of the type, you can assign values explicitly as part of the case declarations, like this:

```
enum Normal : Double {
    case fahrenheit = 98.6
    case centigrade = 37
}
enum PepBoy : Int {
    case manny = 1
    case moe // 2 implicitly
    case jack = 4
}
enum Filter : String {
    case albums = "Albums"
    case playlists = "Playlists"
    case podcasts = "Podcasts"
    case books = "Audiobooks"
}
```

The values carried by the cases are called their *raw values*. An enum with a type declaration implicitly adopts the RawRepresentable protocol, meaning that it implicitly has an `init(rawValue:)` initializer and a `rawValue` property. (I'll explain later what a protocol is.) So you can retrieve a case's assigned value as its `rawValue`:

```
let type = Filter.albums
print(type.rawValue) // Albums
```

Having each case carry a fixed raw value can be quite useful. In my Albumen app, the Filter cases really do have those String values, and `type` is a Filter instance property of the view controller; when the view controller wants to know what title string to put at the top of the screen, it simply retrieves `self.type.rawValue`.

The raw value associated with each case must be unique within this enum; the compiler will enforce this rule. Therefore, the mapping works the other way: given a raw value, you can derive the case; in particular, you can instantiate an enum that has raw values by using its `init(rawValue:)` initializer:

```
let type = Filter(rawValue:"Albums")
```

However, the attempt to instantiate the enum in this way still might fail, because you might supply a raw value corresponding to *no* case; therefore, this is a failable initializer, and the value returned is an Optional. In that code, `type` is not a Filter; it's an Optional wrapping a Filter. This might not be terribly important, however, because the thing you are most likely to want to do with an enum is to compare it for equality with a case of the enum; you can do that with an Optional without unwrapping it. This code is legal and works correctly:

```
let type = Filter(rawValue:"Albums")
if type == .albums { // ...
```

Associated Values

The raw values discussed in the preceding section are fixed in the enum's declaration: a given case carries with it a certain raw value, and that's that. But there's also a way to construct a case whose constant value can be set *when the instance is created*. The attached value here is called an *associated value*.

To write an enum with one or more cases taking an associated value, do not declare any raw value type for the enum as a whole; instead, you append to the name of the case an expression that looks very much like a tuple — that is, parentheses containing a list of possibly labeled types. Unlike a raw value, your choice of type is not limited. Most often, a single value will be attached to a case, so you'll write parentheses containing a single type name. Here's an example:

```
enum MyError {
    case number(Int)
    case message(String)
    case fatal
}
```

That code means that, at instantiation time, a MyError instance with the `.number` case must be assigned an Int value, a MyError instance with the `.message` case must be assigned a String value, and a MyError instance with the `.fatal` case can't be assigned any value. Instantiation with assignment of a value is really a way of calling an initialization function, so to supply the value, you pass it as an argument in parentheses:

```
let err : MyError = .number(4)
```

This is an ordinary function call, so the argument doesn't have to be a literal:

Inference of Type Name with Static/Class Members

Just as you can use a dot and the name of an enum case where an instance of that enum is expected, you can do the same thing when referring to a type's static/class member whose value is an instance of that type. For example, UIColor has many class properties that produce a UIColor instance, so you can omit UIColor where a UIColor is expected:

```
p.trackTintColor = .red // instead of UIColor.red
```

Similarly, suppose we have a struct Thing with static constants whose values are Thing instances:

```
struct Thing : RawRepresentable {
    let rawValue : Int
    static let one : Thing = Thing(rawValue:1)
    static let two : Thing = Thing(rawValue:2)
}
```

Then we can refer to Thing.one as .one where a Thing instance is expected:

```
let thing : Thing = .one
```

Many Objective-C enums are bridged to Swift as that kind of struct, as I'll explain later in the chapter.

In the same way, when a type has a static/class method that produces an instance of that type, the type name can be omitted when an instance of that type is expected. Moreover, an initializer is such a method! Suppose Dog has an initializer that expects a name: parameter, and dogExpecter is a function that takes a Dog as its parameter:

```
struct Dog {
    let name: String
}
func dogExpecter(_ dog: Dog) {
    print(dog.name)
}
```

Then we can create and pass a Dog to dogExpecter without using the term Dog:

```
dogExpecter(.init(name:"Fido"))
```

That sort of thing is regarded as good Swift style.

```
let num = 4
let err : MyError = .number(num)
```

 At the risk of sounding like a magician explaining his best trick, I can now reveal how an Optional works. An Optional is simply an enum with two cases: .none and .some. If it is .none, it carries no associated value, and it equates to nil. If it is .some, it carries the wrapped value as its associated value.

If a case's associated value type has a label, that label must be used at initialization time:

```
enum MyError2 {
    case number(Int)
    case message(String)
    case fatal(n:Int, s:String)
}
let err : MyError2 = .fatal(n:-12, s:"Oh the horror")
```

By default, the == operator cannot be used to compare cases of an enum if any case of that enum has an associated value:

```
if err == MyError.fatal { // compile error
```

But if you declare this enum explicitly as adopting the Equatable protocol (discussed later in this chapter and in Chapter 5), the == operator starts working:

```
enum MyError : Equatable { // *
    case number(Int)
    case message(String)
    case fatal
}
```

That code won't compile, however, unless all the associated types are themselves Equatable. That makes sense; if we declare case pet(Dog) and there is no way to know whether any two Dogs are equal, there is obviously no way to know whether any two pet cases are equal.

I'll explain in Chapter 5 how to *check the case* of an instance of an enum that has an associated value case, as well as how to *extract* the associated value from an enum instance that has one.

Enum Case Iteration

It is often useful to have a list — that is, an array — of all the cases of an enum. You could define this list manually as a static property of the enum:

```
enum Filter : String {
    case albums = "Albums"
    case playlists = "Playlists"
    case podcasts = "Podcasts"
    case books = "Audiobooks"
    static let cases : [Filter] = [.albums, .playlists, .podcasts, .books]
}
```

That, however, is error-prone and hard to maintain; if, as you develop your program, you modify the enum's cases, you must remember to modify the cases property to match. Instead, the list of cases can be generated for you *automatically*. Simply have your enum adopt the CaseIterable protocol (adoption of protocols is explained later

in this chapter); now the list of cases springs to life as a static property called all-
Cases:

```
enum Filter : String, CaseIterable {
    case albums = "Albums"
    case playlists = "Playlists"
    case podcasts = "Podcasts"
    case books = "Audiobooks"
    // static allCases is now [.albums, .playlists, .podcasts, .books]
}
```

I'll put this feature to use in the next section.

Automatic generation of allCases is impossible if any of the enum's cases has an
associated value, as it would then be unclear how that case should be defined in the
list.

Enum Initializers

An explicit enum initializer must do what default initialization does: it must return a
particular case of this enum. To do so, set self to the case. In this example, I'll
expand my Filter enum so that it can be initialized with a numeric argument:

```
enum Filter : String, CaseIterable {
    case albums = "Albums"
    case playlists = "Playlists"
    case podcasts = "Podcasts"
    case books = "Audiobooks"
    init(_ ix:Int) {
        self = Filter.allCases[ix]
    }
}
```

Now there are three ways to make a Filter instance:

```
let type1 = Filter.albums
let type2 = Filter(rawValue:"Playlists")!
let type3 = Filter(2) // .podcasts
```

In that example, we'll crash in the third line if the caller passes a number that's out of
range (less than 0 or greater than 3). If we want to avoid that, we can make this a
failable initializer and return nil if the number is out of range:

```
enum Filter : String, CaseIterable {
    case albums = "Albums"
    case playlists = "Playlists"
    case podcasts = "Podcasts"
    case books = "Audiobooks"
    init?(_ ix:Int) {
        if !Filter.allCases.indices.contains(ix) {
            return nil
```

```
        }
        self = Filter.allCases[ix]
    }
}
```

An enum can have multiple initializers. Enum initializers can delegate to one another by saying `self.init(...)`. The only requirement is that, at some point in the chain of calls, `self` must be set to a case; if that doesn't happen, your enum won't compile.

In this example, I improve my Filter enum so that it can be initialized with a String raw value without having to say `rawValue:` in the call. To do so, I declare a failable initializer with a string parameter that delegates to the built-in failable `rawValue:` initializer:

```
enum Filter : String, CaseIterable {
    case albums = "Albums"
    case playlists = "Playlists"
    case podcasts = "Podcasts"
    case books = "Audiobooks"
    init?(_ ix:Int) {
        if !Filter.allCases.indices.contains(ix) {
            return nil
        }
        self = Filter.allCases[ix]
    }
    init?(_ rawValue:String) {
        self.init(rawValue:rawValue)
    }
}
```

Now there are four ways to make a Filter instance:

```
let type1 = Filter.albums
let type2 = Filter(rawValue:"Playlists")!
let type3 = Filter(2)
let type4 = Filter("Audiobooks")!
```

Enum Properties

An enum can have instance properties and static properties, but there's a limitation: an enum instance property can't be a stored property. Computed instance properties are fine, however, and the value of the property can vary by rule in accordance with the case of `self`. In this example from my real code, I've associated an MPMedia-Query (obtained by calling an MPMediaQuery factory class method) with each case of my Filter enum, suitable for fetching the songs of that type from the music library:

```
enum Filter : String {
    case albums = "Albums"
    case playlists = "Playlists"
    case podcasts = "Podcasts"
    case books = "Audiobooks"
```

```
var query : MPMediaQuery {
    switch self {
    case .albums:
        return .albums()
    case .playlists:
        return .playlists()
    case .podcasts:
        return .podcasts()
    case .books:
        return .audiobooks()
    }
}
```

If an enum instance property is a computed variable with a setter, other code can assign to this property. However, that code's reference to the enum instance itself must be a variable (`var`), not a constant (`let`). If you try to assign to an enum instance property through a `let` reference to the enum, you'll get a compile error.

For example, here's a silly enum:

```
enum Silly {
    case one
    var sillyProperty : String {
        get { "Howdy" }
        set {} // do nothing
    }
}
```

It is then legal to say this:

```
var silly = Silly.one
silly.sillyProperty = "silly"
```

But if `silly` were declared with `let` instead of `var`, trying to set `silly.silly-Property` would cause a compile error.

An enum static property can have a property wrapper, but an enum instance property can't, because that would imply storage of an instance of the underlying `@propertyWrapper` type — and enums have no stored instance properties.

Enum Methods

An enum can have instance methods (including subscripts) and static methods. Writing an enum method is straightforward. Here's an example from my own code. In a card game, the cards draw themselves as rectangles, ellipses, or diamonds. I've abstracted the drawing code into an enum that draws itself as a rectangle, an ellipse, or a diamond, depending on its case:

```
enum Shape {
    case rectangle
    case ellipse
    case diamond
    func addShape (to p: CGMutablePath, in r: CGRect) -> () {
        switch self {
        case .rectangle:
            p.addRect(r)
        case .ellipse:
            p.addEllipse(in:r)
        case .diamond:
            p.move(to: CGPoint(x:r.minX, y:r.midY))
            p.addLine(to: CGPoint(x: r.midX, y: r.minY))
            p.addLine(to: CGPoint(x: r.maxX, y: r.midY))
            p.addLine(to: CGPoint(x: r.midX, y: r.maxY))
            p.closeSubpath()
        }
    }
}
```

Earlier, I mentioned that a subscript can be a static method. That gives me an idea for yet another way to make a Filter instance by number:

```
enum Filter : String, CaseIterable {
    case albums = "Albums"
    case playlists = "Playlists"
    case podcasts = "Podcasts"
    case books = "Audiobooks"
    static subscript(ix: Int) -> Filter {
        Filter.allCases[ix] // warning, no range checking
    }
}
```

And now we can say:

```
let type = Filter[2] // podcasts
```

An enum instance method that modifies the enum itself must be marked as mutating. For example, an enum instance method might assign to an instance property of self; even though this is a computed property, such assignment is illegal unless the method is marked as mutating. The caller of a mutating instance method must have a variable reference to the instance (var), not a constant reference (let).

A mutating enum instance method can replace this instance with another instance, by assigning another case to self. In this example, I add an advance method to my Filter enum. The idea is that the cases constitute a sequence, and the sequence can cycle. By calling advance, I transform a Filter instance into an instance of the next case in the sequence:

```
enum Filter : String, CaseIterable {
    case albums = "Albums"
    case playlists = "Playlists"
    case podcasts = "Podcasts"
    case books = "Audiobooks"
    mutating func advance() {
        let cases = Filter.allCases
        var ix = cases.firstIndex(of:self)!
        ix = (ix + 1) % cases.count
        self = cases[ix]
    }
}
```

And here's how to call it:

```
var type = Filter.books
type.advance() // type is now Filter.albums
```

Observe that `type` is declared with `var`; if it were declared with `let`, we'd get a compile error.

A subscript or computed property setter is considered mutating by default and does not have to be specially marked. However, if a getter sets another property as a side effect, it must be marked `mutating get`.

Why Enums?

An enum is a switch whose states have names. There are many situations where that's a desirable thing. You could implement a multistate value yourself; if there are five possible states, you could use an Int whose values can be 0 through 4. But then you would have to provide a lot of additional overhead, interpreting those numeric values correctly and making sure that no other values are used. A list of five named cases is much better!

Even when there are only *two* states, an enum is often better than, say, a mere Bool, because the enum's states have names. With a Bool, you have to know what `true` and `false` signify in a particular usage; with an enum, the name of the enum and the names of its cases *tell* you its significance.

Moreover, you can store extra information in an enum's associated value or raw value.

In my LinkSame app, the user can play a real game with a timer or a practice game without a timer. At various places in the code, I need to know which type of game this is. The game types are the cases of an enum:

```
enum InterfaceMode : Int {
    case timed = 0
    case practice = 1
}
```

The current game type is stored in an instance property `interfaceMode`, whose value is an InterfaceMode. It's easy to set the game type by case name:

```
// ... initialize new game ...
self.interfaceMode = .timed
```

And it's easy to examine the game type by case name:

```
// notify of high score only if user is not just practicing
if self.interfaceMode == .timed { // ...
```

And what are my InterfaceMode enum's raw value integers for? That's the really clever part. They correspond to the segment indexes of a UISegmentedControl in the interface! Whenever I change the `interfaceMode` property, a setter observer also selects the corresponding segment of the UISegmentedControl (`self.timed-Practice`), simply by fetching the `rawValue` of the current enum case:

```
var interfaceMode : InterfaceMode = .timed {
    willSet (mode) {
        self.timedPractice?.selectedSegmentIndex = mode.rawValue
    }
}
```

Structs

A *struct* is the Swift object type *par excellence*. An enum, with its fixed set of cases, is a reduced, specialized kind of object. A class, at the other extreme, will often turn out to be overkill; it has some features that a struct lacks (I'll talk later about what they are), but if you don't need those features, a struct may be preferable.

Of more than two hundred object types declared in the Swift header, maybe half a dozen are classes. A couple of dozen are enums. All the rest are structs. A String is a struct. An Int is a struct. A Range is a struct. An Array is a struct. And so on. That shows how powerful a struct can be.

Struct Initializers

A struct that doesn't have an explicit initializer and that doesn't *need* an explicit initializer — because it has no stored properties, or because all its stored properties are assigned default values as part of their declaration — automatically gets an implicit initializer with no parameters, `init()`. For example:

```
struct Digit {
    var number = 42
}
```

That struct can be initialized by saying `Digit()`. But if you add any explicit initializers of your own, you lose that implicit initializer:

```
struct Digit {
    var number = 42
    init(number:Int) {
        self.number = number
    }
}
```

Now you can say `Digit(number:42)`, but you can't say `Digit()` any longer. Of course, you can add an explicit initializer that does the same thing:

```
struct Digit {
    var number = 42
    init() {}
    init(number:Int) {
        self.number = number
    }
}
```

Now you can say `Digit()` once again, as well as `Digit(number:42)`.

A struct that has stored properties and that doesn't have an explicit initializer automatically gets an implicit initializer derived from its instance properties. This is called the *memberwise initializer*. For example:

```
struct Test {
    var number = 42
    var name : String
    let age : Int
    let greeting = "Hello"
}
```

That struct is legal, even though it seems we have not fulfilled the contract requiring us to initialize all stored properties in their declaration or in an initializer. The reason is that this struct automatically has a memberwise initializer which *does* initialize all its properties. Given that declaration, there are two ways to make a Test instance:

```
let t1 = Test(number: 42, name: "matt", age: 65)
let t2 = Test(name: "matt", age: 65)
```

The memberwise initializer includes `number`, `name`, and `age`, but not `greeting`, because `greeting` is a `let` property that has already been initialized before the initializer is called. `number` has been initialized too, but it is a `var` property, so the memberwise initializer includes it — but you can also omit it from your call to the memberwise initializer, because it has been initialized already and therefore has a default value.

(The ability to omit an initialized `var` property from a call to the memberwise initializer was introduced in Swift 5.1.)

But if you add any explicit initializers of your own, or if any of the properties involved are declared `private`, you lose the memberwise initializer (though of course you can write an explicit initializer that does the same thing).

All stored properties must be initialized either by direct initialization in the declaration or by all initializers. If a struct has multiple explicit initializers, they can delegate to one another by saying `self.init(...)`.

Struct Properties

A struct can have instance properties and static properties, which can be stored or computed variables. If other code wants to set a property of a struct instance, its reference to that instance must be a variable (`var`), not a constant (`let`).

Here's a Digit struct with a `var` `number` instance property:

```
struct Digit {
    var number : Int
    init(_ n:Int) {
        self.number = n
    }
}
```

Then this is legal:

```
var d = Digit(123)
d.number = 42
```

But if d were declared with `let`, trying to set `d.number` would cause a compile error.

Struct Methods

A struct can have instance methods and static methods, including subscripts. If an instance method sets a property, it must be marked as `mutating`, and the caller's reference to the struct instance must be a variable (`var`), not a constant (`let`).

Here's a new version of our Digit struct:

```
struct Digit {
    private var number : Int
    init(_ n:Int) {
        self.number = n
    }
    mutating func changeNumberTo(_ n:Int) {
        self.number = n
        // or: self = Digit(n)
    }
}
```

Here we have a private `number` property, along with a public method for setting it. We can then say this:

```
var d = Digit(123)
d.changeNumberTo(42)
```

The changeNumberTo method must be declared mutating, and if d were declared with let, trying to call d.changeNumberTo would cause a compile error.

A subscript or computed property setter is considered mutating by default and does not have to be specially marked. However, if a getter sets another property as a side effect, it must be marked mutating get.

A mutating instance method can replace this instance with another instance, by setting self to a different instance of the same struct.

Struct as Namespace

I often use a degenerate struct as a handy namespace for constants. I call such a struct "degenerate" because it consists entirely of static members; I don't intend to use this object type to make any instances.

Let's say I'm going to be storing user preference information in Cocoa's UserDefaults. UserDefaults is a kind of dictionary: each item is accessed through a key. The keys are typically strings. A common programmer mistake is to write out these string keys literally every time a key is used; if you then misspell a key name, there's no penalty at compile time, but your code will mysteriously fail to work correctly. A better approach is to embody those keys as constant strings and use the names of the strings; if you make a mistake typing a name, the compiler can catch you. A struct with static members is a great way to define constant strings and clump their names into a namespace:

```
struct Default {
    static let rows = "CardMatrixRows"
    static let columns = "CardMatrixColumns"
    static let hazyStripy = "HazyStripy"
}
```

That code means that I can now refer to a UserDefaults key with a name, such as Default.hazyStripy.

Classes

A *class* is similar to a struct, with the following key differences:

Reference type
    Classes are reference types. This means, among other things, that a class instance has two remarkable features that are not true of struct or enum instances:

Mutability
> A class instance is mutable in place. Even if your reference to an instance of a class is a constant (`let`), you can change the value of an instance property through that reference. An instance method of a class never has to be marked `mutating` (and cannot be).

Multiple references
> When a given instance of a class is assigned to multiple variables or passed as argument to a function, you get multiple references to *one and the same object*.

Inheritance
> A class can have a superclass. A class that has a superclass is a *subclass* of that superclass, and inherits its superclass's members. Class types can form a hierarchical tree.

In Objective-C, classes are the only object type. Some built-in Swift struct types are magically bridged to Objective-C class types, but your custom struct types don't have that magic. Thus, when programming iOS with Swift, one reason for declaring a class, rather than a struct, is as a form of interchange with Objective-C and Cocoa.

Value Types and Reference Types

A major difference between enums and structs, on the one hand, and classes, on the other, is that enums and structs are *value types*, whereas classes are *reference types*. I will now explain what that means.

Class instances are mutable

A value type is *not mutable in place*, even though it seems to be. Consider a struct. A struct is a value type:

```
struct Digit {
    var number : Int
    init(_ n:Int) {
        self.number = n
    }
}
```

Now, Swift's syntax of assignment would lead us to believe that changing a Digit's `number` is possible:

```
var d = Digit(123)
d.number = 42
```

But in reality, when you apparently mutate an instance of a value type, you are actually *replacing* that instance with a *different* instance. To see that this is true, add a setter observer:

```
var d : Digit = Digit(123) { // Digit is a struct
    didSet {
        print("d was set")
    }
}
d.number = 42 // "d was set"
```

That explains why it is impossible to mutate a value type instance if the reference to that instance is declared with `let`:

```
let d = Digit(123) // Digit is a struct
d.number = 42 // compile error
```

Under the hood, this change would require us to *replace* the Digit instance pointed to by d with another Digit instance — and we can't do that, because it would mean assigning into d, which is exactly what the `let` declaration forbids.

That also explains why an instance method of a struct or enum that sets a property of the instance must be marked explicitly with the `mutating` keyword. Such a method can potentially replace this object with another, so the reference to the object must be `var`, not `let`.

But classes are *not* value types. They are reference types. A reference to a class instance does *not* have to be declared with `var` in order to set a `var` property through that reference:

```
class Dog {
    var name : String = "Fido"
}
let rover = Dog()
rover.name = "Rover" // fine
```

In the last line of that code, the class instance pointed to by `rover` is being *mutated in place*. No implicit assignment to `rover` is involved, and so the `let` declaration is powerless to prevent the mutation. A setter observer on a Dog variable is *not* called when a property is set:

```
var rover : Dog = Dog() { // Dog is a class
    didSet {
        print("did set rover")
    }
}
rover.name = "Rover" // nothing in console
```

The setter observer would be called if we were to set `rover` explicitly (to another Dog instance), but it is not called merely because we change a property of the Dog instance already pointed to by `rover`.

Exactly the same difference between a value type and a reference type may be seen with a parameter of a function call. When we receive an instance of a value type as a

Mutating Captured Self

Here's a Digit struct with some mutating methods:

```
struct Digit {
    var number : Int
    init(_ n:Int) {
        self.number = n
    }
    mutating func changeNumberTo(_ n:Int) {
        self.number = n
    }
    func otherFunction(_ f: ()->()) {
    }
    mutating func callAnotherFunction() {
        otherFunction {
            self.changeNumberTo(345) // *
        }
    }
}
```

Whether that's legal depends on whether otherFunction declares its function parameter @escaping ("Escaping Closures" on page 59). If it does, the compiler will stop us:

```
func otherFunction(_ f: @escaping ()->()) {
}
```

That change causes a compile error at the starred line: "Escaping closure captures mutating self parameter." Now that otherFunction is escaping, we are threatening to mutate a persisting captured self *at some later time*. Digit is a struct, so that would involve *replacing* the captured self with a different Digit — and that's incoherent. No such problem arises if Digit is a class, because the persistent captured self can be mutated in place.

parameter into a function body, the compiler will stop us in our tracks if we try to assign to its instance property. This doesn't compile:

```
func digitChanger(_ d:Digit) { // Digit is a struct
    d.number = 42 // compile error
}
```

But this does compile:

```
func dogChanger(_ d:Dog) { // Dog is a class
    d.name = "Rover"
}
```

Class instance references are pointers

With a reference type, there is a concealed level of indirection between your reference to the instance and the instance itself; the reference actually holds a *pointer* to the instance. This means that when a class instance is assigned to a variable or passed as an argument to a function or as the result of a function, you can wind up with *multiple references to the same object*. That is not true of structs and enums:

Struct or enum instance (value type)
>   When an enum instance or a struct instance is assigned or passed, what is assigned or passed is essentially a *new copy* of that instance.

Class instance (reference type)
>   When a class instance is assigned or passed, what is assigned or passed is a reference to the *same* instance.

To prove it, I'll assign one reference to another, and then mutate the second reference — and then I'll examine what happened to the first reference. Let's start with the struct:

```
var d = Digit(123) // Digit is a struct
print(d.number) // 123
var d2 = d // assignment!
d2.number = 42
print(d.number) // 123
```

In that code, we changed the `number` property of d2, a struct instance; but nothing happened to the `number` property of d. Now let's try the class:

```
var fido = Dog() // Dog is a class
print(fido.name) // Fido
var rover = fido // assignment!
rover.name = "Rover"
print(fido.name) // Rover
```

In that code, we changed the `name` property of rover, a class instance — and the `name` property of fido was changed as well! That's because, after the assignment in the third line, fido and rover refer to *one and the same instance*.

The same thing is true of parameter passing. With a class instance, what is passed is a reference to the *same* instance:

```
func dogChanger(_ d:Dog) { // Dog is a class
    d.name = "Rover"
}
var fido = Dog()
print(fido.name) // "Fido"
dogChanger(fido)
print(fido.name) // "Rover"
```

The change made to d inside the function `dogChanger` affected *our* Dog instance `fido`! You can't do that with an enum or struct instance parameter — unless it's an `inout` parameter — because the instance is effectively *copied* as it is passed. But handing a class instance to a function does *not* copy that instance; it is more like *lending* that instance to the function.

Advantages of value types vs. reference types

The ability to generate multiple references to the same instance is significant particularly in a world of object-based programming, where objects persist and can have properties that persist along with them. If object A and object B are both long-lived, and if they both have a Dog property where Dog is a class, and if they have each been handed a reference to one and the same Dog instance, then either object A or object B can mutate its Dog, and this mutation will affect the other's Dog. You can be holding on to an object, only to discover that it has been mutated by someone else behind your back. If that happens unexpectedly, it can put your program into an invalid state.

Class instances are also more complicated behind the scenes. Swift has to manage their memory (as I'll explain in detail in Chapter 12), precisely because there can be multiple references to the same object; this management can involve quite a bit of overhead.

On the whole, therefore, you should prefer a value type (such as a struct) to a reference type (a class) wherever possible. Struct instances are not shared between references, and so you are relieved from any worry about such an instance being mutated behind your back; moreover, under the hood, storage and memory management are far simpler as well. Apple likes to say that value types are *easier to reason about*. The Swift language itself will help you by imposing value types in front of many Cocoa Foundation reference types. Objective-C NSDate and NSData are classes, but Swift will steer you toward using struct types Date and Data instead. (I'll talk about these types in detail in Chapter 10.)

But don't get the wrong idea. Classes are not bad; they're good! For one thing, a class instance is very efficient to pass around, because all you're passing is a pointer. No matter how big and complicated a class instance may be, no matter how many properties it may have containing vast amounts of data, passing the instance is incredibly fast and efficient.

And although a class may be a reference type, a *particular* class can be implemented in such a way as to exhibit value *semantics*. Simply put, a class's API can refuse to mutate that class in place. Cocoa NSString, NSArray, NSDictionary, NSDate, NSIndexSet, NSParagraphStyle, and many more behave like this; they are *immutable* by design. Two objects may hold a reference to the same NSArray without fear that it will be mutated behind their backs, not because it's a value type (it isn't) but because it's immutable. In effect, this architecture combines the ease of use of a value type with the pointer efficiency of a reference type.

Moreover, there are many situations where the independent identity of a class instance, no matter how many times it is referred to, is exactly what you want. The extended lifetime of a class instance, as it is passed around, can be crucial to its functionality and integrity. In particular, only a class instance can successfully represent an *independent reality*. A UIView needs to be a class, not a struct, because an individual UIView instance, no matter how it gets passed around, must continue to represent the same single real and persistent view in your running app's interface.

Still another reason for preferring a class over a struct or enum is when you need recursive references. A value type cannot be structurally recursive: a stored instance property of a value type cannot be an instance of the same type. This code won't compile:

```
struct Dog { // compile error
    var puppy : Dog?
}
```

More complex circular chains, such as a Dog with a Puppy property and a Puppy with a Dog property, are similarly illegal. But if Dog is a class instead of a struct, there's no error. This is a consequence of the nature of memory management of value types as opposed to reference types.

 An enum case's associated value *can* be an instance of that enum, provided the case (or the entire enum) is marked `indirect`:

```
enum Node {
    case none(Int)
    indirect case left(Int, Node)
    indirect case right(Int, Node)
    indirect case both(Int, Node, Node)
}
```

Subclass and Superclass

Two classes can be *subclass* and *superclass* of one another. For example, we might have a class Quadruped and a class Dog, with Quadruped as the superclass of Dog. A class may have many subclasses, but a class can have only one immediate superclass. I say "immediate" because that superclass might itself have a superclass, and so on until we get to the ultimate superclass, called the *base class*, or *root class*. Thus there is a hierarchical tree of subclasses, each group of subclasses branching from its superclass, and so on, with a single class, the base class, at the top.

As far as the Swift language itself is concerned, there is no requirement that a class should have any superclass, or, if it does have a superclass, that it should ultimately be descended from any particular base class. A Swift program can have many classes

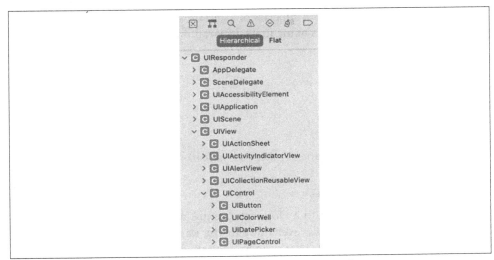

Figure 4-1. Part of the Cocoa class hierarchy as shown in Xcode

that have no superclass, and it can have many independent hierarchical subclass trees, each descended from a different base class.

Cocoa, however, doesn't work that way. In Cocoa, there is effectively just one base class — NSObject, which embodies all the functionality necessary for a class to *be* a class in the first place — and all other classes are subclasses, at some level, of that one base class. Cocoa thus consists of one huge tree of hierarchically arranged classes, even before you write a single line of code or create any classes of your own.

We can imagine diagramming this tree as an outline. And in fact Xcode will *show* you this outline (Figure 4-1): in an iOS project window, choose View → Navigators → Show Symbol Navigator and click Hierarchical, with the first and third icons in the filter bar selected (filled). Now locate NSObject in the list; the Cocoa classes are the part of the tree descending from it.

Inheritance

The reason for having a superclass–subclass relationship in the first place is to allow related classes to *share functionality*. Suppose we have a Dog class and a Cat class, and we are considering declaring a walk method for both of them. We might reason that both a dog and a cat walk in pretty much the same way, by virtue of both being quadrupeds. So it might make sense to declare walk as a method of the Quadruped class, and make both Dog and Cat subclasses of Quadruped. When we do that, both Dog and Cat can be sent the walk message, even if neither of them has a walk method, because each of them has a superclass that *does* have a walk method. We say that a subclass *inherits* the methods of its superclass.

To declare that a certain class is a subclass of a certain superclass, add a colon and the superclass name after the class's name in its declaration:

```
class Quadruped {
    func walk () {
        print("walk walk walk")
    }
}
class Dog : Quadruped {}
class Cat : Quadruped {}
```

Now let's prove that Dog has indeed inherited walk from Quadruped:

```
let fido = Dog()
fido.walk() // walk walk walk
```

The walk message can be sent to a Dog instance just as if the walk instance method were declared in the Dog class, even though the walk instance method is in fact declared in a superclass of Dog. That's inheritance at work.

 A class declaration can *prevent* the class from being subclassed by preceding the class declaration with the final keyword.

Additional functionality

The purpose of subclassing is not *merely* so that a class can inherit another class's methods; it's so that it can also declare methods *of its own*. Typically, a subclass consists of the methods inherited from its superclass *and then some*. For example, dogs can bark, but quadrupeds in general can't. If we declare bark in the Dog class, and walk in the Quadruped class, and make Dog a subclass of Quadruped, then Dog inherits the ability to walk from the Quadruped class *and also* knows how to bark:

```
class Quadruped {
    func walk () {
        print("walk walk walk")
    }
}
class Dog : Quadruped {
    func bark () {
        print("woof")
    }
}
```

Again, let's prove that it works:

```
let fido = Dog()
fido.walk() // walk walk walk
fido.bark() // woof
```

Within a class, it is a matter of indifference whether that class has an instance method because that method is declared in that class or because the method is declared in a superclass and inherited. A message to self works equally well either way. In this code, we have declared a barkAndWalk instance method that sends two messages to self, without regard to where the corresponding methods are declared (one is native to the subclass, one is inherited from the superclass):

```
class Quadruped {
    func walk () {
        print("walk walk walk")
    }
}
class Dog : Quadruped {
    func bark () {
        print("woof")
    }
    func barkAndWalk() {
        self.bark()
        self.walk()
    }
}
```

And here's proof that it works:

```
let fido = Dog()
fido.barkAndWalk() // woof walk walk walk
```

Overriding

It is also permitted for a subclass to *redefine* a method inherited from its superclass. For example, perhaps some dogs bark differently from other dogs. We might have a class NoisyDog, for instance, that is a subclass of Dog. Dog declares bark, but Noisy-Dog also declares bark, and defines it differently from how Dog defines it. This is called *overriding*. The very natural rule is that if a subclass overrides a method inherited from its superclass, then when the corresponding message is sent to an instance of that subclass, it is the subclass's version of that method that is called.

In Swift, when you override something inherited from a superclass, you must explicitly acknowledge this fact by preceding its declaration with the keyword override:

```
class Quadruped {
    func walk () {
        print("walk walk walk")
    }
}
class Dog : Quadruped {
    func bark () {
        print("woof")
    }
}
```

```
class NoisyDog : Dog {
    override func bark () {
        print("woof woof woof")
    }
}
```

And let's try it:

```
let fido = Dog()
fido.bark() // woof
let rover = NoisyDog()
rover.bark() // woof woof woof
```

Observe that a subclass method by the same *name* as a superclass's method is not necessarily, of itself, an override. Recall that Swift can distinguish two functions with the same name, provided they have different *signatures*. Those are different functions, and so an implementation of one in a subclass is not an override of the other in a superclass. An override situation exists only when the subclass redefines the *same* method that it inherits from a superclass — using the same name, including the external parameter names, and the same signature.

However, a method override need not have *exactly* the same signature as the overridden method. In particular, in a method override, the type of a parameter may be replaced with a superclass, or with an Optional wrapping the superclass. If we have a Cat class and its Kitten subclass, the following is legal:

```
class Dog {
    func barkAt(cat:Kitten) {}
}
class NoisyDog : Dog {
    override func barkAt(cat:Cat) {}
    // or barkAt(cat:Cat?)
}
```

Moreover, a parameter may be overridden with an Optional wrapping its own type, and an Optional parameter may be overridden with an Optional wrapping its wrapped type's superclass:

```
class Dog {
    func barkAt(cat:Cat) {}
    // or barkAt(cat:Kitten)
    // or barkAt(cat:Kitten?)
}
class NoisyDog : Dog {
    override func barkAt(cat:Cat?) {}
}
```

There are further rules along the same lines, but I won't try to list them all here; you probably won't need to take advantage of them, and in any case the compiler will tell you if your override is illegal.

Along with methods, a subclass also inherits its superclass's properties. Naturally, the subclass may also declare additional properties of its own. It is possible to override an inherited property (with some restrictions that I'll talk about later).

I'll have more to say about the implications of overriding when I talk about polymorphism, later in this chapter.

 A class declaration can *prevent* a class member from being overridden by a subclass by preceding the member's declaration with the `final` keyword.

The keyword super

It often happens that we want to override something in a subclass and yet access the thing overridden in the superclass. This is done by sending a message to the keyword `super`. Our `bark` implementation in NoisyDog is a case in point. What NoisyDog really does when it barks is the same thing Dog does when *it* barks, but more times. We'd like to express that relationship in our implementation of NoisyDog's `bark`. To do so, we have NoisyDog's `bark` implementation send the `bark` message, not to `self` (which would be circular), but to `super`; this causes the search for a `bark` instance method implementation to start in the superclass rather than in our own class:

```
class Dog : Quadruped {
    func bark () {
        print("woof")
    }
}
class NoisyDog : Dog {
    override func bark () {
        for _ in 1...3 {
            super.bark()
        }
    }
}
```

And it works:

```
let fido = Dog()
fido.bark() // woof
let rover = NoisyDog()
rover.bark() // woof woof woof
```

 A subscript function is a method. If a superclass declares a subscript, the subclass can declare a subscript with the same signature, provided it designates it with the `override` keyword. To call the superclass subscript implementation, the subclass can use square brackets after the keyword `super` (e.g. `super[3]`).

Class Initializers

Initialization of a class instance is considerably more complicated than initialization of a struct or enum instance, because of class inheritance. The chief task of an initializer is to ensure that all properties have an initial value, making the instance well-formed as it comes into existence; and an initializer may have other tasks to perform that are essential to the initial state and integrity of this instance. A class, however, may have a superclass, which may have properties and initializers of its own. Thus we must somehow ensure that when a subclass is initialized, its *superclass's* properties are initialized and the tasks of *its* initializers are performed in good order, in addition to those of the subclass itself.

Swift solves this problem coherently and reliably — and ingeniously — by enforcing some clear and well-defined rules about what a class initializer must do.

Kinds of class initializer

The rules begin with a distinction between the kinds of initializer that a class can have:

Designated initializer
> A class initializer, by default, is a *designated* initializer. A class can be instantiated only through a call to one of its designated initializers. A designated initializer must see to it that all stored properties are initialized. It may not delegate to another initializer in the same class; it is illegal for a designated initializer to use the phrase `self.init(...)`.
>
> A class with any stored properties that are not initialized as part of their declaration must have at least one explicit designated initializer. A class with no stored properties, or with stored properties all of which are initialized as part of their declaration, and that has *no* explicit designated initializers, has an *implicit* designated initializer `init()`.

Convenience initializer
> A *convenience* initializer is marked with the keyword `convenience`. A convenience initializer is not how a class is instantiated; it is merely a façade for a designated initializer. A convenience initializer is a delegating initializer; it *must* contain the phrase `self.init(...)`, which must call a *designated* initializer in the same class — or, if it calls another convenience initializer in the same class, the chain of convenience initializers must end by calling a designated initializer in the same class.

Here are some examples. This class has no stored properties, so it has an implicit `init()` designated initializer:

```
class Dog {
}
let d = Dog()
```

This class's stored properties have default values, so it has an implicit `init()` designated initializer too:

```
class Dog {
    var name = "Fido"
}
let d = Dog()
```

This class's stored properties have default values, but it has no implicit `init()` initializer because it has an explicit designated initializer:

```
class Dog {
    var name = "Fido"
    init(name:String) {self.name = name}
}
let d = Dog(name:"Rover") // ok
let d2 = Dog() // compile error
```

This class's stored properties have default values, and it has an explicit initializer, but it also has an implicit `init()` initializer because its explicit initializer is a convenience initializer. Moreover, the implicit `init()` initializer is a designated initializer, so the convenience initializer can delegate to it:

```
class Dog {
    var name = "Fido"
    convenience init(name:String) {
        self.init()
        self.name = name
    }
}
let d = Dog(name:"Rover")
let d2 = Dog()
```

This class has stored properties without default values; it has an explicit designated initializer, and all of those properties are initialized in that designated initializer:

```
class Dog {
    var name : String
    var license : Int
    init(name:String, license:Int) {
        self.name = name
        self.license = license
    }
}
let d = Dog(name:"Rover", license:42)
```

This class is similar to the previous example, but it also has convenience initializers forming a chain that ends with a designated initializer:

```
class Dog {
    var name : String
    var license : Int
    init(name:String, license:Int) {
        self.name = name
        self.license = license
    }
    convenience init(license:Int) {
        self.init(name:"Fido", license:license)
    }
    convenience init() {
        self.init(license:1)
    }
}
let d = Dog()
```

Note that the rules about what else an initializer can say and when it can say it, as I described them earlier in this chapter, are still in force:

- A designated initializer cannot, except in order to initialize a property (or to fetch the value of a property that is already initialized), say self, implicitly or explicitly, until *all* of this class's properties have been initialized.

- A convenience initializer is a delegating initializer, so it cannot say self for *any* purpose until after it has called, directly or indirectly, a designated initializer (and cannot set a constant property at all).

Subclass initializers

Having defined and distinguished between designated initializers and convenience initializers, we are ready for the rules about a subclass's initializers:

No declared initializers
    If a subclass doesn't have to have any initializers of its own, and if it declares no initializers of its own, then its initializers consist of the initializers inherited from its superclass. (A subclass thus has no implicit init() initializer unless it inherits it from its superclass.)

Convenience initializers only
    If a subclass doesn't have to have any initializers of its own, it is eligible to declare convenience initializers, and these work exactly as convenience initializers always do, because inheritance supplies the designated initializers that the convenience initializers must call by saying self.init(...).

Designated initializers
    If a subclass declares any designated initializers of its own, the entire game changes drastically. Now, *no initializers are inherited!* The existence of an explicit designated initializer *blocks initializer inheritance.* The only initializers the subclass now has are the initializers that you explicitly write (with one exception that

I'll mention later). This rule may seem surprising, but I'll justify it in an example later on.

Moreover, every designated initializer in the subclass now has an extra requirement: it must call one of the *superclass's designated initializers*, by saying `super.init(...)`. If it fails to do this, then `super.init()` is called implicitly if possible, but I disapprove of this feature (in my view, Swift should not indulge in secret behavior, even if that behavior might be considered "helpful").

At the same time, the rules about saying `self` continue to apply.

Thus, a subclass designated initializer must do these things *in this order*:

1. It must ensure that all properties of *this* class (the subclass) are initialized.

2. It must call `super.init(...)`, and the initializer that it calls must be a designated initializer.

3. Only then may this initializer say `self` for such purposes as to call an instance method or to access an inherited property.

Designated and convenience initializers

If a subclass declares both designated and convenience initializers, the convenience initializers in the subclass are still subject to the rules I've already outlined. They must call `self.init(...)`, calling a designated initializer directly or through a chain of convenience initializers. There are no inherited initializers, so the designated initializer must be explicitly declared in the subclass.

Override initializers

A subclass may override initializers from its superclass:

- An initializer whose parameters match a *convenience* initializer of the superclass can be a designated initializer or a convenience initializer, and is *not* marked `override`.

- An initializer whose parameters match a *designated* initializer of the superclass can be a designated initializer or a convenience initializer, and *must* be marked `override`. An `override` designated initializer must still call some superclass designated initializer (possibly even the one that it overrides) with `super.init(...)`.

If a subclass overrides *all* of its superclass's *designated* initializers, then the subclass inherits the superclass's *convenience* initializers. (This is the exception to the rule that if a subclass has any designated initializers, no initializers are inherited.)

Failable initializers

If an initializer called by a failable initializer is failable, the calling syntax does not change, and no additional test is needed — if a failable initializer fails, the whole initialization process will fail (and will be aborted) immediately.

There are some additional restrictions on failable initializers:

- `init` can override `init?`, but not *vice versa*.
- `init?` can call `init`.
- `init` can call `init?` by saying `init` and unwrapping the result with an exclamation mark (and if the `init?` fails, you'll crash).

At no time can a subclass initializer set a constant (`let`) property of a superclass. This is because, by the time the subclass is allowed to do anything other than initialize its own properties and call another initializer, the superclass has finished its own initialization and the door for initializing its constants has closed.

Subclass initializer examples

Your eyes may glaze over reading the subclass initializer rules, but the most important rules are very easy to understand with the help of some basic examples. We start with a subclass that has no explicit initializers of its own:

```
class Dog {
    var name : String
    var license : Int
    init(name:String, license:Int) {
        self.name = name
        self.license = license
    }
    convenience init(license:Int) {
        self.init(name:"Fido", license:license)
    }
}
class NoisyDog : Dog {
}
```

Given that code, you can make a NoisyDog like this:

```
let nd1 = NoisyDog(name:"Fido", license:1)
let nd2 = NoisyDog(license:2)
```

That code is legal, because NoisyDog inherits its superclass's initializers. However, you can't make a NoisyDog like this:

```
let nd3 = NoisyDog() // compile error
```

That code is illegal. Even though a NoisyDog has no properties of its own, it has no implicit `init()` initializer; its initializers are its inherited initializers, and its superclass, Dog, has no implicit `init()` initializer to inherit.

Now here is a subclass whose only explicit initializer is a convenience initializer:

```
class Dog {
    var name : String
    var license : Int
    init(name:String, license:Int) {
        self.name = name
        self.license = license
    }
    convenience init(license:Int) {
        self.init(name:"Fido", license:license)
    }
}
class NoisyDog : Dog {
    convenience init(name:String) {
        self.init(name:name, license:1)
    }
}
```

Observe how NoisyDog's convenience initializer fulfills its contract by calling self.init(...) to call a designated initializer — which it happens to have inherited. Given that code, there are three ways to make a NoisyDog, just as you would expect:

```
let nd1 = NoisyDog(name:"Fido", license:1)
let nd2 = NoisyDog(license:2)
let nd3 = NoisyDog(name:"Rover")
```

Next, here is a subclass that declares a designated initializer:

```
class Dog {
    var name : String
    var license : Int
    init(name:String, license:Int) {
        self.name = name
        self.license = license
    }
    convenience init(license:Int) {
        self.init(name:"Fido", license:license)
    }
}
class NoisyDog : Dog {
    init(name:String) {
        super.init(name:name, license:1)
    }
}
```

NoisyDog's explicit initializer is now a designated initializer. It fulfills its contract by calling a designated initializer in super. NoisyDog has now *cut off inheritance* of all initializers; the *only* way to make a NoisyDog is like this:

```
let nd1 = NoisyDog(name:"Rover")
```

Earlier, I promised to justify the rule that adding a designated initializer to a subclass cuts off initializer inheritance. That example is a case in point. It would be terrible if the caller could bypass NoisyDog's designated initializer by using an inherited Dog initializer instead. NoisyDog's initializer enforces a rule that a NoisyDog can only have a license value of 1; if you could say `NoisyDog(license:2)`, you'd bypass that rule. Here's another example that makes the same point a little more realistically:

```
class Dog {
    let name : String
    init(name:String) {
        self.name = name
    }
}
class RoverDog : Dog {
    init() {
        super.init(name:"Rover")
    }
}
let fido = RoverDog(name:"Fido") // compile error
```

Clearly that last line *needs* to be an error; otherwise, a RoverDog could be named Fido, undermining the point of the subclass.

Finally, here is a subclass that overrides its designated initializers:

```
class Dog {
    var name : String
    var license : Int
    init(name:String, license:Int) {
        self.name = name
        self.license = license
    }
    convenience init(license:Int) {
        self.init(name:"Fido", license:license)
    }
}
class NoisyDog : Dog {
    override init(name:String, license:Int) {
        super.init(name:name, license:license)
    }
}
```

NoisyDog has overridden *all* of its superclass's designated initializers, so it inherits its superclass's convenience initializers. There are thus two ways to make a NoisyDog:

```
let nd1 = NoisyDog(name:"Rover", license:1)
let nd2 = NoisyDog(license:2)
```

Those examples illustrate the main rules that you should keep in your head. You probably don't need to memorize the remaining rules, because the compiler will enforce them, and will keep slapping you down until you get them right.

Required initializers

There's one more thing to know about class initializers: a class initializer may be preceded by the keyword `required`. This means that a subclass may not lack this initializer. This, in turn, means that if a subclass implements designated initializers, thus blocking inheritance, it *must* override this initializer and mark the override `required`. Here's a (rather pointless) example:

```
class Dog {
    var name : String
    required init(name:String) {
        self.name = name
    }
}
class NoisyDog : Dog {
    var obedient = false
    init(obedient:Bool) {
        self.obedient = obedient
        super.init(name:"Fido")
    }
} // compile error
```

That code won't compile. Dog's `init(name:)` is marked `required`; our code won't compile unless we inherit or override `init(name:)` in NoisyDog. But we cannot inherit it, because, by implementing the NoisyDog designated initializer `init(obedient:)`, we have blocked inheritance. Therefore we must override it:

```
class Dog {
    var name : String
    required init(name:String) {
        self.name = name
    }
}
class NoisyDog : Dog {
    var obedient = false
    init(obedient:Bool) {
        self.obedient = obedient
        super.init(name:"Fido")
    }
    required init(name:String) {
        super.init(name:name)
    }
}
```

Observe that our overridden required initializer is not marked with `override`, but *is* marked with `required`, guaranteeing that the requirement continues drilling down to any further subclasses.

I have explained what declaring an initializer as `required` does, but I have not explained *why* you'd need to do it. That's another matter! I'll discuss it later in this chapter.

Class Deinitializer

A class can have a deinitializer. This is a function declared with the keyword `deinit` followed by curly braces containing the function body. You never call this function yourself; it is called by the runtime when an instance of this class goes out of existence. If a class has a superclass, the subclass's deinitializer (if any) is called before the superclass's deinitializer (if any).

A deinitializer is a class feature only; a struct or enum has no deinitializer. That's because a class is a reference type (as I explained earlier in this chapter). The idea is that you might want to perform some cleanup. Another good use of a class's `deinit` is to log to the console to prove to yourself that your instance is going out of existence in good order; I'll take advantage of that when I discuss memory management issues in Chapter 5.

Property observers are not called during `deinit`.

Class Properties

A subclass can override its inherited properties. The override must have the same name and type as the inherited property, and must be marked with `override`. (A property cannot have the same name as an inherited property but a different type, as there is no way to distinguish them.)

The chief restriction here is that an `override` property *cannot be a stored property*. More specifically:

- If the superclass property is writable (a stored property or a computed property with a setter), the subclass's override may consist of adding setter observers to this property.
- Alternatively, the subclass's override may be a computed property. In that case:
  - If the superclass property is stored, the subclass's computed property override must have both a getter and a setter.
  - If the superclass property is computed, the subclass's computed property override must have at least a getter, and:
    - If the superclass property has a setter, the override must have a setter.
    - If the superclass property has no setter, the override can add one.

The overriding property's functions may refer to — and may read from and write to — the inherited property, through the `super` keyword.

Static/Class Members

A class can have static members, marked `static`, just like a struct or an enum. It can also have class members, marked `class`. Both static and class members are inherited by subclasses.

Static methods vs. class methods

The chief difference between static and class *methods*, from the programmer's point of view, is that a static method *cannot be overridden*; it is as if `static` were a synonym for `class final`.

Here, I'll use a static method to express what dogs say:

```
class Dog {
    static func whatDogsSay() -> String {
        return "woof"
    }
    func bark() {
        print(Dog.whatDogsSay())
    }
}
```

A subclass now inherits `whatDogsSay`, but can't override it. No subclass of Dog may contain any implementation of a class method or a static method `whatDogsSay` with this same signature.

Now I'll use a class method to express what dogs say:

```
class Dog {
    class func whatDogsSay() -> String {
        return "woof"
    }
    func bark() {
        print(Dog.whatDogsSay())
    }
}
```

A subclass inherits `whatDogsSay`, and *can* override it, either as a class method or as a static method:

```
class NoisyDog : Dog {
    override class func whatDogsSay() -> String {
        return "WOOF"
    }
}
```

Static properties vs. class properties

The difference between static and class *properties* is similar to the difference between static and class methods, but with an additional, rather dramatic qualification: a static property can be stored, but a class property *must be a computed property*.

Here, I'll use a static class property to express what dogs say:

```
class Dog {
    static var whatDogsSay = "woof"
    func bark() {
        print(Dog.whatDogsSay)
    }
}
```

A subclass inherits whatDogsSay, but can't override it; no subclass of Dog can declare a class or static property whatDogsSay.

Now I'll use a class property to express what dogs say. It cannot be a stored property, so I'll have to use a computed property instead:

```
class Dog {
    class var whatDogsSay : String {
        return "woof"
    }
    func bark() {
        print(Dog.whatDogsSay)
    }
}
```

A subclass inherits whatDogsSay and can override it either as a class property or as a static property. But the rule about property overrides not being stored is still in force, even if the override is a static property:

```
class NoisyDog : Dog {
    override static var whatDogsSay : String {
        return "WOOF"
    }
}
```

Polymorphism

When a computer language has a hierarchy of types and subtypes, it must resolve the question of what such a hierarchy means for the relationship between the type of an *object* and the declared type of a *reference* to that object. Swift obeys the principles of *polymorphism*. In my view, it is polymorphism that turns an object-based language into a full-fledged object-oriented language. We may summarize Swift's polymorphism principles:

Substitution

Wherever a certain type of object is expected, the actual object may be a subtype of that type.

Internal identity

An object's real type is a matter of its internal nature, regardless of how that object is referred to.

To see what these principles mean in practice, imagine we have a Dog class, along with its subclass, NoisyDog:

```
class Dog {
}
class NoisyDog : Dog {
}
let d : Dog = NoisyDog()
```

In that code:

- The substitution rule says that the last line is legal: we can assign a NoisyDog instance to a reference, d, that is typed as Dog.

- The internal identity rule says that, under the hood, even though d is typed as Dog, the instance that it refers to is a NoisyDog.

You may be asking: How is the internal identity rule manifested? If a reference to a NoisyDog is typed as Dog, in what sense is this "really" a NoisyDog? To illustrate, let's examine what happens when a subclass overrides an inherited method. I'll redefine Dog and NoisyDog to demonstrate:

```
class Dog {
    func bark() {
        print("woof")
    }
}
class NoisyDog : Dog {
    override func bark() {
        for _ in 1...3 {
            super.bark()
        }
    }
}
```

Now consider the following code:

```
func tellToBark(_ d:Dog) {
    d.bark()
}
var nd = NoisyDog()
tellToBark(nd) // what will happen??????
```

That code is legal, because, by the substitution principle, we can pass nd, typed as NoisyDog, where a Dog is expected. Now, inside the `tellToBark` function, d is typed as Dog. How will it react to being told to `bark`? On the one hand, d is *typed* as Dog, and a Dog barks by saying "woof" once. On the other hand, in our code, when `tell-ToBark` is called, what is *really* passed is a NoisyDog instance, and a NoisyDog barks by saying "woof" three times. *What will happen?* Let's find out:

```
func tellToBark(_ d:Dog) {
    d.bark()
}
var nd = NoisyDog()
tellToBark(nd) // woof woof woof
```

The result is "woof woof woof". The internal identity rule says that what matters when a message is sent is not how the recipient of that message is *typed* through this or that *reference*, but what that recipient actually *is*. What arrives inside `tellToBark` is a NoisyDog, regardless of the type of variable that holds it; thus, the `bark` message causes this object to say "woof" three times.

Here's another important consequence of polymorphism — the meaning of the keyword `self`. Its meaning depends upon the type of the actual instance — even if the word `self` *appears* in a superclass's code. For example:

```
class Dog {
    func bark() {
        print("woof")
    }
    func speak() {
        self.bark()
    }
}
class NoisyDog : Dog {
    override func bark() {
        for _ in 1...3 {
            super.bark()
        }
    }
}
```

What happens when we tell a NoisyDog to `speak`? The `speak` method is declared in Dog, the superclass — not in NoisyDog. The `speak` method calls the `bark` method. It does this by way of the keyword `self`. (I could have omitted the explicit reference to `self` here, but `self` would still be involved implicitly, so I'm not cheating by making `self` explicit.) There's a `bark` method in Dog, and an override of the `bark` method in NoisyDog. *Which bark method will be called?* Let's find out:

```
let nd = NoisyDog()
nd.speak() // woof woof woof
```

The word self is encountered within the Dog class's implementation of speak. But what matters is not where the word self *appears* but what it *means*. It means *this instance*. And the internal identity principle tells us that this instance is a NoisyDog! Thus, it is NoisyDog's override of bark that is called when Dog's speak says self.bark().

Polymorphism applies to Optional types in the same way that it applies to the type of thing wrapped by the Optional. Suppose we have a reference typed as an Optional wrapping a Dog. You already know that you can assign a Dog to it. Well, you can also assign a NoisyDog, or an Optional wrapping a NoisyDog, and the underlying wrapped object will maintain its integrity:

```
var d : Dog?
d = Dog()
d = NoisyDog()
d = Optional(NoisyDog())
```

(The applicability of polymorphism to Optionals derives from a special dispensation of the Swift language: Optionals are *covariant*. I'll talk more about that later in this chapter.)

Thanks to polymorphism, you can take advantage of subclasses to add power and customization to existing classes. This is important particularly in the world of iOS programming, where most of the classes are defined by Cocoa and don't belong to you. The UIViewController class, for example, is defined by Cocoa; it has lots of built-in methods that Cocoa will call, and these methods perform various important tasks — but in a generic way. In real life, you'll make a UIViewController *subclass*, and you'll *override* those methods to do the tasks appropriate to your particular app. When you do that:

- It won't bother Cocoa in the slightest, because (substitution principle) wherever Cocoa expects to receive or to be talking to a UIViewController, it will accept without question an instance of your UIViewController subclass.

- The substituted UIViewController subclass will also work as expected, because (internal identity principle) whenever Cocoa calls one of those UIViewController methods on your subclass, it is your subclass's override that will be called, and wherever a UIViewController method refers to self, that will mean your subclass.

I'll talk more about subclassing Cocoa classes in Chapter 10.

Polymorphism is cool, but in the grand scheme of things it is also relatively slow. It requires *dynamic dispatch*, meaning that the compiler can't perform certain optimizations, and that the runtime has to think about what a message to a class instance means. You can reduce the need for dynamic dispatch by declaring a class or a class member `final` or `private`. Or use a struct, if appropriate; structs don't need dynamic dispatch.

Casting

Here's a conundrum. The Swift compiler, with its strict typing, imposes severe restrictions on what messages can be sent to an object reference. The messages that the compiler will permit to be sent to an object reference depend upon the reference's *declared* type. But the internal identity principle of polymorphism says that, under the hood, an object may have a *real* type that is different from its reference's declared type. Such an object may be *capable* of receiving certain messages, but the compiler *won't permit us* to send them.

To illustrate the problem, let's give NoisyDog a method that Dog doesn't have:

```
class Dog {
    func bark() {
        print("woof")
    }
}
class NoisyDog : Dog {
    override func bark() {
        super.bark(); super.bark()
    }
    func beQuiet() {
        self.bark()
    }
}
```

In that code, we configure a NoisyDog so that we can tell it to beQuiet. Now look at what happens when we try to tell an object typed as Dog to be quiet:

```
func tellToHush(_ d:Dog) {
    d.beQuiet() // compile error
}
let nd = NoisyDog()
tellToHush(nd)
```

Our code doesn't compile. We can't send the beQuiet message to the reference d inside the function body, because it is typed as Dog — and a Dog has no beQuiet method. But there is a certain irony here: for once, we happen to know more than the compiler does — namely, that this object is *in fact* a NoisyDog and *does* have a beQuiet method! Our code would run correctly — because d really is a NoisyDog — if only we could get our code to compile in the first place. We need a way to say to the compiler, "Look, compiler, just trust me: this thing is going to turn out to be a Noisy-Dog when the program actually runs, so let me send it this message."

There is in fact a way to do this — *casting*. To cast, you use a form of the keyword as followed by the name of the type you claim something really is.

Casting Down

Swift will not let you cast just any old type to any old other type — you can't cast a String to an Int — but it will let you cast a superclass to a subclass. This is called *casting down*. When you cast down, the form of the keyword as that you use is as! with an exclamation mark. The exclamation mark reminds you that you are *forcing* the compiler to do something it would rather not do:

```
func tellToHush(_ d:Dog) {
    (d as! NoisyDog).beQuiet()
}
let nd = NoisyDog()
tellToHush(nd)
```

That code compiles, and works. A useful way to rewrite the example is like this:

```
func tellToHush(_ d:Dog) {
    let d = d as! NoisyDog
    d.beQuiet()
    // ... other NoisyDog messages to d can go here ...
}
let nd = NoisyDog()
tellToHush(nd)
```

The reason that way of rewriting the code is useful is in case we have other NoisyDog messages to send to this object. Instead of casting every time we want to send a message to it, we cast the object once to its internal identity type, and assign it to a variable. Now that variable's type — inferred, in this case, from the cast — is the internal identity type, and we can send multiple messages to the variable.

Type Testing and Casting Down Safely

A moment ago, I said that the as! operator's exclamation mark reminds you that you are forcing the compiler's hand. It also serves as a warning: your code can now crash! The reason is that you might be lying to the compiler. Casting down is a way of telling the compiler to relax its strict type checking and to let you call the shots. If you use casting to make a false claim, the compiler may permit it, but you will crash when the app runs:

```
func tellToHush(_ d:Dog) {
    let d = d as! NoisyDog // crash
    d.beQuiet()
}
let d = Dog()
tellToHush(d)
```

In that code, we told the compiler that this object would turn out to be a NoisyDog, and the compiler obediently took its hands off and allowed us to send the beQuiet message to it. But in fact, this object was a Dog when our code ran, and so we ultimately crashed when the cast failed because this object was *not* a NoisyDog.

To prevent yourself from lying accidentally, you can *test* the type of an instance at runtime. One way to do that is with the keyword is. You can use is in a condition; if the condition passes, *then* cast, in the knowledge that your cast is safe:

```
func tellToHush(_ d:Dog) {
    if d is NoisyDog {
        let d = d as! NoisyDog
        d.beQuiet()
    }
}
```

The result is that we won't cast d to a NoisyDog unless it really *is* a NoisyDog.

An alternative way to solve the same problem is to use Swift's as? operator. This casts down, but with the option of failure; therefore what it casts to is (you guessed it) an Optional — and now we are on familiar ground, because we know how to deal safely with an Optional:

```
func tellToHush(_ d:Dog) {
    let d = d as? NoisyDog // an Optional wrapping a NoisyDog
    if d != nil {
        d!.beQuiet()
    }
}
```

That doesn't look much cleaner or shorter than our previous approach. But remember that we can safely send a message to an Optional by optionally unwrapping the Optional:

```
func tellToHush(_ d:Dog) {
    let d = d as? NoisyDog // an Optional wrapping a NoisyDog
    d?.beQuiet()
}
```

Or, as a one-liner:

```
func tellToHush(_ d:Dog) {
    (d as? NoisyDog)?.beQuiet()
}
```

First we use the `as?` operator to obtain an Optional wrapping a NoisyDog. Then we optionally unwrap that Optional and send a message to it. If the original d wasn't a NoisyDog, the Optional will be `nil` and it won't be unwrapped and no message will be sent.

Type Testing and Casting Optionals

The `is`, `as!`, and `as?` operators work with Optionals in the same way that the equality comparison operators do (Chapter 3): they are automatically applied to the object wrapped by the Optional.

Let's start with `is`. Consider an Optional d ostensibly wrapping a Dog (that is, d is a `Dog?` object). It might, in actual fact, be wrapping either a Dog or a NoisyDog. To find out which it is, you might be tempted to use `is`. But can you? After all, an Optional is neither a Dog nor a NoisyDog — it's an Optional! Nevertheless, Swift knows what you mean; when the thing on the left side of `is` is an Optional, Swift pretends that it's the value wrapped in the Optional. This works just as you would hope:

```
let d : Dog? = NoisyDog()
if d is NoisyDog { // it is!
```

When using `is` with an Optional, the test fails in good order if the Optional is `nil`. Our test really does *two* things: it checks whether the Optional is `nil`, and if it is not, it then checks whether the wrapped value is the type we specify.

What about casting? You can't really cast an Optional to anything. Nevertheless, Swift knows what you mean; you can use the `as!` operator with an Optional. When the thing on the left side of `as!` is an Optional, Swift treats it as the wrapped type. Moreover, the consequence of applying the `as!` operator is that two things happen: Swift unwraps first, and then casts. This code works, because d is unwrapped to give us d2, which is a NoisyDog:

```
let d : Dog? = NoisyDog()
let d2 = d as! NoisyDog
d2.beQuiet()
```

That code, however, is not safe. You shouldn't cast like that, without testing first, unless you are very sure of your ground. If d were nil, you'd crash in the second line because you're trying to unwrap a `nil` Optional. And if d were a Dog, not a Noisy-Dog, you'd *still* crash in the second line when the cast fails. That's why there's also an `as?` operator, which *is* safe — but yields an Optional:

```
let d : Dog? = NoisyDog()
let d2 = d as? NoisyDog
d2?.beQuiet()
```

In that code, we use `as?` to cast down from an Optional wrapping a Dog (d) to an Optional wrapping a NoisyDog (d2). The operation is safe, twice. If d is `nil`, d2 will be `nil`, safely. If d is not `nil` but wraps a Dog, not a NoisyDog, the cast will fail, and d2 will be `nil`, safely. If d wraps a NoisyDog, d2 wraps a NoisyDog. In the last line, we unwrap d2 and send it a NoisyDog message — safely.

Bridging to Objective-C

Another way you'll use casting is during a value interchange between Swift and Objective-C when two types are *equivalent*. For example, you can cast a Swift String to a Cocoa NSString, and *vice versa*. That's not because one is a subclass of the other, but because they are *bridged* to one another; in a very real sense, they are the same type. When you cast from String to NSString, you're not casting down, and what you're doing is not dangerous, so you use the `as` operator, with no exclamation mark or question mark.

In general, to cross the bridge from a Swift type to a bridged Objective-C type, you will need to cast explicitly (except in the case of a string literal):

```
let s : NSString = "howdy"         // string literal to NSString
let s2 = "howdy"
let s3 : NSString = s2 as NSString // String to NSString
let i : NSNumber = 1 as NSNumber   // Int to NSNumber
```

That sort of code, however, is rather artificial. In real life, you won't be casting all that often, because the Cocoa API will present itself to you in terms of Swift types. This is legal with no cast:

```
let name = "MyNib" // Swift String
let vc = ViewController(nibName:name, bundle:nil)
```

The UIViewController class comes from Cocoa, and its `nibName` property is an Objective-C NSString — not a Swift String. But you don't have to help the Swift String `name` across the bridge by casting, because, in the Swift world, `nibName:` is typed as a Swift String (actually, an Optional wrapping a String). The bridge, in effect, is crossed *later*.

Similarly, no cast is required here:

```
let ud = UserDefaults.standard
let s = "howdy"
ud.set(s, forKey:"greeting")
```

You don't have to help the Swift String s across the bridge by casting, because the first argument of `set(_:forKey:)` is typed as a Swift type, namely Any (actually, an Optional wrapping Any) — and any Swift type can be used, without casting, where an Any is expected. I'll talk more about Any later in this chapter.

Coming back the other way, it is possible that you'll receive from Objective-C a value about whose real underlying type Swift has no information. In that case, you'll probably want to cast explicitly to the underlying type — and now you *are* casting down, with all that that implies. Here's what happens when we go to retrieve the "howdy" that we put into UserDefaults in the previous example:

```
let ud = UserDefaults.standard
let test = ud.object(forKey:"greeting") as! String
```

When we call `ud.object(forKey:)`, Swift has no type information; the result is an Any (actually, an Optional wrapping Any). But we know that this particular call should yield a string — because that's what we put in to begin with. So we can force-cast this value down to a String — and it works. However, if `ud.object(forKey:"greeting")` were *not* a string (or if it were `nil`), we'd crash. If you're not sure of your ground, use `is` or `as?` to be safe.

Type References

This section talks about the ways in which Swift can refer to the type of an object, other than saying the bare type literally.

From Instance to Type

Sometimes, what you've got is an instance, and you want to know its type. This might be for no other reason than to log its type to the console, for the sake of information or debugging; or you might need to use the type as a value, as I'll explain later.

For this purpose, you can use the global `type(of:)` function:

```
let d : Dog = NoisyDog()
print(type(of:d)) // NoisyDog
```

As you would expect, the identity principle applies. We are not asking how d, the variable, is typed; we're asking what sort of object the instance referred to by d *really* is. It's typed as Dog, but it's a NoisyDog instance.

From self to Type

It is particularly important for an instance to be able to refer to its *own* type. Quite commonly, this is in order to send a message to that type. For instance, suppose an instance wants to send a class message to its class. In an earlier example, a Dog instance method fetched a Dog class property by sending a message to the Dog type, literally using the word Dog:

```
class Dog {
    class var whatDogsSay : String {
        return "woof"
    }
    func bark() {
        print(Dog.whatDogsSay) // woof
    }
}
```

The expression `Dog.whatDogsSay` seems clumsy and inflexible. Why should we hard-code into Dog a knowledge of what type it is? It *has* a type; it should just *know* what it is. We can refer to the current type — the type of `self` — using the keyword `Self` (with a capital letter):

```
class Dog {
    class var whatDogsSay : String {
        return "woof"
    }
    func bark() {
        print(Self.whatDogsSay) // woof
    }
}
```

Similarly, we wrote a Filter enum earlier in this chapter that accessed its static `all-Cases` by saying `Filter.allCases`. We can say `Self.allCases` instead, and I prefer to do so; it's prettier.

Saying `Self` instead of a type name isn't *just* prettier; it's more powerful, because `Self`, like `self`, obeys polymorphism. Here are Dog and its subclass, NoisyDog:

```
class Dog {
    class var whatDogsSay : String {
        return "woof"
    }
    func bark() {
        print(Self.whatDogsSay)
    }
}
class NoisyDog : Dog {
    override class var whatDogsSay : String {
        return "woof woof woof"
    }
}
```

Now watch what happens:

```
let nd = NoisyDog()
nd.bark() // woof woof woof
```

If we tell a NoisyDog instance to `bark`, it says `"woof woof woof"`. The reason is that `Self` means, "The type that this object actually is, right now." We send the `bark` message to a NoisyDog instance. The `bark` implementation refers to `Self`; even though the bark implementation is inherited from Dog, Self means the type of this instance, which is a NoisyDog, and so Self is the NoisyDog class, and it is NoisyDog's version of whatDogsSay that is fetched.

(This use of Self was introduced in Swift 5.1. Before that, you had to say type(of:self).)

Another important use of polymorphic Self is as a return type. To show why this is valuable, I'll introduce the notion of a *factory method*.

Suppose our Dog class has a name instance property, and its only initializer is init(name:). Let's give our Dog class a class method makeAndName. We want this class method to create and return a named Dog of whatever class we send the make-AndName message to. If we say Dog.makeAndName(), we should get a Dog. If we say NoisyDog.makeAndName(), we should get a NoisyDog. Well, we know how to do that; just initialize polymorphic Self. It works in a class method just as it works in an instance method:

```
class Dog {
    var name : String
    init(name:String) {
        self.name = name
    }
    class func makeAndName() -> Dog {
        let d = Self(name:"Fido") // compile error
        return d
    }
}
class NoisyDog : Dog {
}
```

However, there's a problem: that code doesn't compile. The reason is that the compiler is in doubt as to whether the init(name:) initializer is implemented by every possible subtype of Dog. To reassure it, we must declare that initializer with the required keyword:

```
class Dog {
    var name : String
    required init(name:String) { // *
        self.name = name
    }
    class func makeAndName() -> Dog {
        let d = Self(name:"Fido")
        return d
    }
}
class NoisyDog : Dog {
}
```

I promised earlier that I'd tell you why you might need to declare an initializer as `required`; now I'm fulfilling that promise! The `required` designation reassures the compiler; every subclass of Dog *must inherit or reimplement* `init(name:)`, so it's legal to call `init(name:)` message on a type reference that might refer to Dog or some subclass of Dog.

So now our code compiles, and we can call our function:

```
let d = Dog.makeAndName() // d is a Dog named Fido
let d2 = NoisyDog.makeAndName() // d2 is a NoisyDog named Fido
```

That code works as expected. But now there's *another* problem. Although d2 is in fact a NoisyDog, it is *typed* as a Dog. That's because our `makeAndName` class method is declared as returning a Dog. That isn't what we want to declare. We want to declare that this method returns an instance *of the same type* as the class to which the `makeAndName` message was originally sent. In other words, we need a polymorphic type declaration! That type is `Self` once again:

```
class Dog {
    var name : String
    required init(name:String) {
        self.name = name
    }
    class func makeAndName() -> Self { // *
        let d = Self(name:"Fido")
        return d
    }
}
class NoisyDog : Dog {
}
```

The `Self` type is used as a return type in a method declaration to mean "an instance of whatever type this is at runtime." So when we call `NoisyDog.makeAndName()` we get a NoisyDog typed as NoisyDog.

`Self` also works for instance method declarations. Therefore, we can write an instance method version of our factory method. Here, we start with a Dog or a NoisyDog and tell it to have a puppy of the same type as itself:

```
class Dog {
    var name : String
    required init(name:String) {
        self.name = name
    }
    func havePuppy(name:String) -> Self {
        return Self(name:name)
    }
}
class NoisyDog : Dog {
}
```

And here's some code to test it:

```
let d = Dog(name:"Fido")
let d2 = d.havePuppy(name:"Fido Junior")
let nd = NoisyDog(name:"Rover")
let nd2 = nd.havePuppy(name:"Rover Junior")
```

As expected, d2 is a Dog, but nd2 is a NoisyDog typed as NoisyDog.

Type as Value

In some situations, you may want to treat an object type *as a value*. That is legal. An object type is itself an object, of a sort; it's what Swift calls a *metatype*. So an object type can be assigned to a variable or passed as a parameter:

- To *declare* that an object type is acceptable — as when declaring the type of a variable or parameter — use dot-notation with the name of the type and the keyword Type.
- To *use* an object type as a value — as when assigning a type to a variable or passing it as a parameter — hand the object to type(of:), or use dot-notation with the name of the type and the keyword self. (In the latter case, the name of the type might be Self, in which case you'll be saying Self.self!)

Here's a function dogTypeExpecter that accepts a Dog type as its parameter:

```
func dogTypeExpecter(_ whattype:Dog.Type) {
}
```

And here's an example of calling that function:

```
dogTypeExpecter(Dog.self)
```

Or you could call it like this:

```
let d = Dog()
dogTypeExpecter(type(of:d))
```

The substitution principle applies, so you could call dogTypeExpecter like this:

```
dogTypeExpecter(NoisyDog.self)
```

Or like this:

```
let nd = NoisyDog()
dogTypeExpecter(type(of:nd))
```

To illustrate more practically, I'll rewrite our Dog factory method as a global factory function that will accept a Dog *type* as a parameter and will create an instance from that type. You can use a variable reference to a type (a metatype) to instantiate that type, but you can't just append parentheses to a variable reference:

```
func dogMakerAndNamer(_ whattype:Dog.Type) -> Dog {
    let d = whattype(name:"Fido") // compile error
    return d
}
```

Instead, you must explicitly send the reference an `init(...)` message:

```
func dogMakerAndNamer(_ whattype:Dog.Type) -> Dog {
    let d = whattype.init(name:"Fido")
    return d
}
```

And here's how to call our function:

```
let d = dogMakerAndNamer(Dog.self) // d is a Dog named Fido
let d2 = dogMakerAndNamer(NoisyDog.self) // d2 is a NoisyDog named Fido
```

Unfortunately, the global factory function `dogMakerAndNamer`, displays the same problem we had before — it returns an object typed as Dog, even if the underlying instance is in fact a NoisyDog. We can't return `Self` to solve the problem here, because there's no type for it to refer to. Swift does have a solution, however — generics. I'll discuss generic functions later in this chapter.

Summary of Type Terminology

All this terminology can get a bit confusing, so here's a quick summary:

`type(of:)`

> Applied to an object: the polymorphic (internal) type of the object, regardless of how a reference is typed.

`Self`

> In a method body, or in a method declaration when specifying the return type, this type or this instance's type, polymorphically.

`.Type`

> Appended to a type in a type declaration to specify that the type itself (or a subtype) is expected.

`.self`

> Sent to a type to generate a metatype, suitable for passing where a type (`.Type`) is expected.

Comparing Types

Type references can be compared to one another. On the right side of an `==` comparison, you can use the name of a type with `.self`; on the right side of an `is` comparison, you can use the name of a type with `.Type`. The difference, as you might expect, is that `==` tests for absolutely identical types, whereas `is` permits subtypes.

In this artificial example, if the parameter `whattype` is `Dog.self`, both `equality` and `typology` are `true`; if `whattype` is `NoisyDog.self`, `equality` is `false` but `typology` is still `true`:

```
func dogTypeExpecter(_ whattype:Dog.Type) {
    let equality = whattype == Dog.self
    let typology = whattype is Dog.Type
}
```

In that example, `whattype` might be replaced on the left side of the comparisons by the result of a call to `type(of:)` (or by a type name qualified by `.self`, though that would be pointless); and `Dog.self` might be replaced on the right side of the `==` comparison by `whattype` or the result of a call to `type(of:)`. But neither `whattype` nor `type(of:)` can appear on the right side of an `is` comparison; `is` requires a literal type as its second operand.

In real life, however, comparing type references is a *very* rare thing to do. Passing metatypes around is not Swifty, and comparing metatypes is *really* not Swifty. In general, if you find yourself talking like that, you should probably think of another way of doing whatever it is you're trying to do.

Protocols

A *protocol* is a way of expressing commonalities between otherwise unrelated types. For example, a Bee object and a Bird object might have features in common by virtue of the fact that both a bee and a bird can fly. Thus, it might be useful to define a Flier type. The question is: In what sense can both Bee and Bird be Fliers?

One possibility might be class inheritance. If Bee and Bird are both classes, Flier could be the superclass of both Bee and Bird. However, there may be other reasons why Flier *can't* be the superclass of both Bee and Bird. A Bee is an Insect; a Bird isn't. Yet they both have the power of flight — independently. We need a type that cuts across the class hierarchy somehow, tying remote classes together.

Moreover, what if Bee and Bird are *not* both classes? In Swift, that's a real possibility. Important and powerful objects can be structs instead of classes. But there is no hierarchy of superstructs and substructs! How can a Bee struct and a Bird struct both be Fliers?

Swift solves this problem through the use of protocols. Protocols are tremendously important in Swift; the Swift header defines over 60 protocols! Moreover, Objective-C has protocols as well, and Cocoa makes heavy use of protocols; Swift protocols correspond roughly to Objective-C protocols, and can interchange with them.

A protocol is an object *type*, but there are no protocol *objects* — you can't instantiate a protocol. A protocol declaration is just a lightweight list of properties and methods.

The properties have no values, and the methods have no code! The idea is that a "real" object type can formally declare that it belongs to a protocol type; this is called *adopting* the protocol. An object type that adopts a protocol is promising to implement the properties and methods listed by the protocol. And it must keep that promise! This is called *conforming to* the protocol.

Let's say that being a Flier consists of no more than implementing a `fly` method. Then a Flier protocol could specify that there must be a `fly` method; to do so, it lists the `fly` method *with no function body*, like this:

```
protocol Flier {
    func fly()
}
```

Any type — an enum, a struct, a class, or even another protocol — can then adopt this protocol. To do so, it lists the protocol after a colon after its name in its declaration. (If the adopter is a class with a superclass, the protocol comes after a comma after the superclass specification.)

Let's say Bird is a struct. Then it can adopt Flier like this:

```
struct Bird : Flier {
} // compile error
```

So far, so good. But that code won't compile. The Bird struct has promised to implement the features listed in the Flier protocol. Now it must keep that promise! The `fly` method is the only requirement of the Flier protocol. To satisfy that requirement, I'll just give Bird an empty `fly` method:

```
protocol Flier {
    func fly()
}
struct Bird : Flier {
    func fly() {
    }
}
```

That's all there is to it. We've defined a protocol, and we've made a struct adopt and conform to that protocol. Of course, in real life you'll probably want to make the adopter's implementation of the protocol's methods *do* something; but the protocol says nothing about that.

 A protocol can also declare a method *and provide its implementation*, thanks to protocol extensions, which I'll discuss later in this chapter.

Why Protocols?

Perhaps at this point you're wondering: So what? If we wanted a Bird to know how to fly, why didn't we just give Bird a `fly` method *without* adopting any protocol? What difference does the protocol make?

The answer has to do with types. A protocol, such as our Flier, is a type. Therefore, I can *use* Flier as a type when declaring the type of a variable or a function parameter:

```
func tellToFly(_ f:Flier) {
    f.fly()
}
```

Protocols thus give us another way of expressing the notion of type and subtype — and *polymorphism applies*. By the substitution principle, a Flier here could be an instance of *any* object type, *as long as it adopts the Flier protocol*. It might be a Bird, it might be something else; we don't care. If it adopts the Flier protocol, it can be passed where a Flier is expected; moreover, it must have a `fly` method, because that's exactly what it *means* to adopt the Flier protocol! Therefore we can confidently send the `fly` message to this object, and the compiler lets us do that.

The converse, however, is not true: an object with a `fly` method is *not* automatically a Flier. It isn't enough to *obey* the requirements of a protocol; the object type must formally *adopt* the protocol. This code won't compile:

```
func tellToFly(_ f:Flier) {
    f.fly()
}
struct Bee {
    func fly() {
    }
}
let b = Bee()
tellToFly(b) // compile error
```

A Bee *can* be sent the `fly` message, *qua* Bee. But `tellToFly` doesn't take a Bee parameter; it takes a Flier parameter. Formally, a Bee is *not* a Flier. To make a Bee a Flier, just declare formally that Bee adopts the Flier protocol! This code does compile:

```
func tellToFly(_ f:Flier) {
    f.fly()
}
struct Bee : Flier {
    func fly() {
    }
}
let b = Bee()
tellToFly(b)
```

Adopting a Library Protocol

Enough of birds and bees; we're ready for a real-life example! As I've already said, the Swift standard library is chock full of protocols already. Let's make one of our own object types adopt one and watch the powers of that protocol spring to life for us.

The CustomStringConvertible protocol requires that we implement a description String property. If we do that, a wonderful thing happens: when an instance of this type is used in string interpolation or with print (or the po command in the console, or in the String initializer init(describing:)), its description property value is used automatically to represent it.

Recall the Filter enum, from earlier in this chapter. I'll add a description property to it:

```
enum Filter : String {
    case albums = "Albums"
    case playlists = "Playlists"
    case podcasts = "Podcasts"
    case books = "Audiobooks"
    var description : String { return self.rawValue }
}
```

But that isn't enough, in and of itself, to give Filter the power of the CustomString-Convertible protocol; to do that, we also need to *adopt* the CustomStringConvertible protocol formally. There is already a colon and a type in the Filter declaration, so an adopted protocol comes after a comma:

```
enum Filter : String, CustomStringConvertible {
    case albums = "Albums"
    case playlists = "Playlists"
    case podcasts = "Podcasts"
    case books = "Audiobooks"
    var description : String { return self.rawValue }
}
```

We have now made Filter formally adopt the CustomStringConvertible protocol. The CustomStringConvertible protocol requires that we implement a description String property; we *do* implement a description String property, so our code compiles. Now we can interpolate a Filter into a string, or hand it over to print, or coerce it to a String, and its description will be used automatically:

```
let type = Filter.albums
print("It is \(type)") // It is Albums
print(type) // Albums
let s = String(describing:type) // Albums
```

Behold the power of protocols. You can give *any* object type the power of string conversion in exactly the same way.

Note that a type can adopt more than one protocol! The built-in Double type adopts CustomStringConvertible, Hashable, Strideable, and several other built-in protocols. To declare adoption of multiple protocols, list them separated by a comma after the protocol name and colon in the declaration (after the raw value type or superclass type if there is one):

```
struct MyType : CustomStringConvertible, TextOutputStreamable, Strideable {
    // ...
}
```

(Of course, that code won't compile unless I also declare, in MyType, any required properties and methods, so that MyType actually conforms to those protocols.)

Protocol Type Testing and Casting

The operators for mediating between an object's declared type and its real type work when the declared type is a protocol type. Given a protocol Flier that is adopted by both Bird and Bee, we can use the is operator to test whether a particular Flier is in fact a Bird:

```
func isBird(_ f:Flier) -> Bool {
    return f is Bird
}
```

Similarly, as! and as? can be used to cast an object declared as a protocol type down to its actual type. This is important to be able to do, because the adopting object will typically be able to receive messages that the protocol can't receive. Let's say that a Bird can get a worm:

```
struct Bird : Flier {
    func fly() {
    }
    func getWorm() {
    }
}
```

A Bird can fly *qua* Flier, but it can getWorm only *qua* Bird. You can't tell just any old Flier to get a worm:

```
func tellGetWorm(_ f:Flier) {
    f.getWorm() // compile error
}
```

But if this Flier is a Bird, clearly it *can* get a worm. That is exactly what casting is all about:

```
func tellGetWorm(f:Flier) {
    (f as? Bird)?.getWorm()
}
```

Declaring a Protocol

Protocol declaration can take place only at the top level of a file. To declare a protocol, use the keyword `protocol` followed by the name of the protocol (which should start with a capital letter, as this is a type). Then come curly braces which may contain declarations for any of the following:

Properties

A property declaration in a protocol consists of `var` (not `let`), the property name, a colon, its type, and curly braces containing the word `get` or the words `get set`. In the former case, the adopter's implementation of this property *can* be writable, while in the latter case, it *must* be: the adopter may not implement a `get set` property as a read-only computed property or as a constant (`let`) stored property.

To declare a static/class property, precede it with the keyword `static`. A class adopter is free to implement this as a `class` property.

Methods

A method declaration in a protocol is a function declaration without a function body; it has no curly braces and no code. Any object function type is legal, including `init` and `subscript`. (The syntax for declaring a subscript in a protocol is the same as the syntax for declaring a subscript in an object type, except that the curly braces will contain `get` or `get set`.)

To declare a static/class method, precede it with the keyword `static`. A class adopter is free to implement this as a `class` method.

To permit an enum or struct adopter to declare a method `mutating`, declare it `mutating` in the protocol. An adopter cannot add `mutating` if the protocol lacks it, but the adopter may omit `mutating` if the protocol has it.

A protocol can itself adopt one or more protocols; the syntax is just as you would expect — a colon after the protocol's name in the declaration, followed by a comma-separated list of the protocols it adopts. In effect, this gives you a way to create an entire secondary hierarchy of types! The Swift headers make heavy use of this.

A protocol that adopts another protocol may repeat the contents of the adopted protocol's curly braces, for clarity; but it doesn't have to, as this repetition is implicit. An object type that adopts a protocol must satisfy the requirements of this protocol and all protocols that the protocol adopts.

Protocol Composition

If the only purpose of a protocol is to combine other protocols by adopting all of them, without adding any new requirements, you can avoid formally declaring the protocol in the first place by specifying the protocol combination on the fly. To do so, join the protocol names with &. This is called *protocol composition*:

```
func f(_ x: CustomStringConvertible & CustomDebugStringConvertible) {
}
```

That is a function declaration with a parameter whose type is specified as being some object type that adopts both the CustomStringConvertible protocol and the Custom-DebugStringConvertible protocol.

A type can also be specified as a composite of a class type and one or more protocols. A case in point might look something like this:

```
protocol MyViewProtocol {
    func doSomethingReallyCool()
}
class ViewController: UIViewController {
    var v: (UIView & MyViewProtocol)?
    func test() {
        self.v?.doSomethingReallyCool() // a MyViewProtocol requirement
        self.v?.backgroundColor = .red // a UIView property
    }
}
```

To be assigned to ViewController's v property, an object would need to be an instance of a UIView subclass that is also an adopter of MyViewProtocol. In this way, we guarantee to the compiler that both UIView messages and MyViewProtocol messages can be sent to a ViewController's v; otherwise, we'd have to type v as a MyViewProtocol and then cast down to UIView in order to send it UIView messages, even if we knew that v would in fact always be a UIView.

There's another way to accomplish the same thing; we can declare MyViewProtocol itself in such a way that it can be adopted *only* by UIView, as I shall now explain.

Class Protocols

A protocol declaration may include the name of a class after the colon. This limits the types capable of adopting this protocol to that class or its subclasses:

```
protocol MyViewProtocol : UIView {
    func doSomethingReallyCool()
}
class ViewController: UIViewController {
    var v: MyViewProtocol? // and therefore a UIView
    func test() {
        self.v?.doSomethingReallyCool() // a MyViewProtocol requirement
        self.v?.backgroundColor = .red // a UIView property
    }
}
```

Here, MyViewProtocol can be adopted only by UIView or a UIView subclass. This means that an object typed as MyViewProtocol can be sent both MyViewProtocol messages and UIView messages, because *ex hypothesi* a MyViewProtocol adopter must *be* a UIView.

To specify that a protocol can be adopted only by *some* class (and not a struct or enum) without specifying *what* class it must be, use the protocol type AnyObject, which every class type adopts (as I'll explain later):

```
protocol MyClassProtocol : AnyObject {
    // ...
}
```

An alternative notation is a where clause before the curly braces. I have not yet talked about where clauses or the use of Self to signify the protocol's adopter, but I'll show you the notation now anyway:

```
protocol MyViewProtocol where Self:UIView {
    func doSomethingReallyCool()
}
protocol MyClassProtocol where Self:AnyObject {
    // ...
}
```

Instead of AnyObject after the colon following the name of the protocol, you can use the keyword class. That notation predates Swift 5 and may eventually be deprecated, but it is still legal as of this writing:

```
protocol MyClassProtocol : class {
    // ...
}
```

A valuable byproduct of declaring a class protocol is that the resulting type can take advantage of special memory management features that apply only to classes. I haven't discussed memory management yet, but I'll give an example anyway (and I'll repeat it when I talk about memory management in Chapter 5):

```
protocol SecondViewControllerDelegate : AnyObject {
    func accept(data:Any)
}
class SecondViewController : UIViewController {
    weak var delegate : SecondViewControllerDelegate?
    // ...
}
```

The keyword weak marks the delegate property as having special memory management that applies only to class instances. The delegate property is typed as a protocol, and a protocol might be adopted by a struct or an enum type. So to satisfy the compiler that this object *will* in fact be a class instance, and *not* a struct or enum instance, the protocol is declared as a class protocol.

An @objc protocol is a class protocol, as class protocols are the only kind of protocol Objective-C understands.

Optional Protocol Members

In Objective-C, a protocol member can be declared optional, meaning that this member doesn't have to be implemented by the adopter, but it may be. Swift allows optional protocol members, but this feature is solely for compatibility with Objective-C, and in fact is implemented *by* Objective-C; it isn't really a Swift feature at all. Therefore, everything about an optional protocol member must be explicitly exposed to Objective-C. The protocol declaration must be marked with the @objc attribute, and an optional member's declaration must be marked with the keywords @objc optional:

```
@objc protocol Flier {
    @objc optional var song : String {get}
    @objc optional func sing()
}
```

(I'll explain in Chapter 10 *how* Objective-C implements optional protocol members.)

Many Cocoa protocols have optional members. For example, your iOS app will have an app delegate class that adopts the UIApplicationDelegate protocol; this protocol has many methods, all of them optional. That fact, however, will have no effect on how you implement those methods; either you implement a method or you don't. (I'll talk more about Cocoa protocols in Chapter 10, and about delegate protocols in Chapter 11.)

An optional member is not guaranteed to be implemented by the adopter, so Swift doesn't know whether it's safe to send a Flier either the song message or the sing message. How Swift solves that problem depends on whether this is an optional property or an optional method.

Optional properties

In the case of an *optional property* like song, Swift solves the problem by wrapping its fetched value in an Optional. If the Flier adopter doesn't implement the property, the result is nil and no harm done:

```
@objc protocol Flier {
    @objc optional var song : String {get}
}
let f : Flier = Bird()
let s = f.song // s is an Optional wrapping a String
```

This is one of those rare situations where you can wind up with a double-wrapped Optional. If the value of the optional property song were itself a String?, then fetching its value from a Flier would yield a String??.

A curious limitation is that if a protocol declares an optional property {get set}, you can't set that property. If f is a Flier and song is declared {get set}, you can't set f.song:

```
@objc protocol Flier {
    @objc optional var song : String? {get set}
}
let f : Flier = Bird()
f.song = "tweet tweet" // compile error
```

The error message claims that f is immutable, which is blatantly false. This is evidently a bug in the language. A workaround (pointed out to me by Jordan Rose) is to use key path notation (which I'll explain in Chapter 5):

```
let f : Flier = Bird()
f[keyPath: \.song] = "tweet tweet"
```

Optional methods

In the case of an *optional method* like sing, things are more elaborate. If the method is not implemented, we must not be permitted to call it in the first place. To handle this situation, the method is typed as an Optional version of its declared type. To send the sing message to a Flier, therefore, you must unwrap it. What you are unwrapping is not the result of the method call; it's the method *itself.* In the method call, the unwrap operator must appear *before* the parentheses!

The safe approach is to unwrap an optional method optionally, with a question mark:

```
@objc protocol Flier {
    @objc optional func sing()
}
let f : Flier = Bird()
f.sing?()
```

The effect is to send the sing message to f only if this Flier adopter implements sing. If this Flier adopter *doesn't* implement sing, nothing happens. You could have force-unwrapped the call — f.sing!() — but then your app would crash if the adopter doesn't implement sing.

If an optional method returns a value, that value is wrapped in an Optional as well:

```
@objc protocol Flier {
    @objc optional func sing() -> String
}
```

If we now call sing?() on a Flier, the result is an Optional wrapping a String:

```
let f : Flier = Bird()
let s = f.sing?() // s is an Optional wrapping a String
```

If we force-unwrap the call — `f.sing!()` — the result is either a String (if the adopter implements `sing`) or a crash (if it doesn't).

Implicitly Required Initializers

Suppose that a protocol declares an initializer. And suppose that a class adopts this protocol. By the terms of this protocol, this class and any subclass it may ever have must implement this initializer. Therefore, the class not only must implement the initializer, but also must mark it as `required`. An initializer declared in a protocol is *implicitly required*, and the class is forced to make that requirement explicit.

Consider this simple example, which won't compile:

```
protocol Flier {
    init()
}
class Bird : Flier {
    init() {} // compile error
}
```

That code generates an elaborate but perfectly informative compile error message: "Initializer requirement `init()` can only be satisfied by a `required` initializer in non-final class Bird." To compile our code, we must designate our initializer as `required`:

```
protocol Flier {
    init()
}
class Bird : Flier {
    required init() {}
}
```

Alternatively, if Bird were marked `final`, there would be no need to mark its `init` as `required`, because this would mean that Bird *cannot have any subclasses* — guaranteeing that the problem will never arise in the first place.

In the above code, Bird is *not* marked as `final`, and its `init` *is* marked as `required`. This, as I've already explained, means that any subclass of Bird that implements any designated initializers — and thus loses initializer inheritance — must implement the required initializer and mark it `required` as well.

That fact is responsible for a strange and annoying feature of real-life iOS programming with Swift. Let's say you subclass the built-in Cocoa class UIViewController — something that you are extremely likely to do. And let's say you give your subclass an initializer — something that you are also extremely likely to do:

```
class ViewController: UIViewController {
    init() {
        super.init(nibName:"ViewController", bundle:nil) // compile error
    }
}
```

That code won't compile. The compile error says: "`required` initializer `init(coder:)` must be provided by subclass of UIViewController."

What's going on here? It turns out that UIViewController adopts a protocol called NSCoding. And this protocol requires an initializer `init(coder:)`. None of that is your doing; UIViewController and NSCoding are declared by Cocoa, not by you. But that doesn't matter! This is the same situation I was just describing. Your UIViewController subclass must either inherit `init(coder:)` or must explicitly implement it and mark it `required`. Well, your subclass has implemented a designated initializer of its own — thus *cutting off initializer inheritance*. Therefore it *must* implement `init(coder:)` and mark it `required`.

But that makes no sense if you are not expecting `init(coder:)` ever to be *called* on your UIViewController subclass. You are being forced to write an initializer for which you can provide no meaningful functionality! Fortunately, Xcode's Fix-it feature will offer to write the initializer for you, like this:

```
required init?(coder: NSCoder) {
    fatalError("init(coder:) has not been implemented")
}
```

That code satisfies the compiler. (I'll explain in Chapter 5 why it's a legal initializer even though it doesn't fulfill an initializer's contract.) It also deliberately crashes if it is ever called — which is fine, because *ex hypothesi* you don't expect it ever to be called.

If, on the other hand, you *do* have functionality for this initializer, you will delete the `fatalError` line and insert that functionality in its place. A minimum meaningful implementation would be to call `super.init(coder:coder)`, but of course if your class has properties that need initialization, you will need to initialize them first.

Not only UIViewController but *lots* of built-in Cocoa classes adopt NSCoding. You will encounter this problem if you subclass *any* of those classes and implement your own initializer. It's just something you'll have to get used to.

Expressible by Literal

One of the wonderful things about Swift is that so many of its features, rather than being built-in and accomplished by magic, are exposed in the Swift header. Literals are a case in point. The reason you can say 5 to express an Int whose value is 5, instead of formally initializing Int by saying `Int(5)`, is not because of magic (or at least, not entirely because of magic). It's because Int adopts a protocol, Expressible-ByIntegerLiteral. Not only Int literals, but *all* literals work this way. The following protocols are declared in the Swift header:

- ExpressibleByNilLiteral
- ExpressibleByBooleanLiteral
- ExpressibleByIntegerLiteral
- ExpressibleByFloatLiteral
- ExpressibleByStringLiteral
- ExpressibleByExtendedGraphemeClusterLiteral
- ExpressibleByUnicodeScalarLiteral
- ExpressibleByArrayLiteral
- ExpressibleByDictionaryLiteral

Your own object type can adopt an expressible by literal protocol as well. This means that a literal can appear where an instance of your object type is expected! Here we declare a Nest type that contains some number of eggs (its eggCount):

```
struct Nest : ExpressibleByIntegerLiteral {
    var eggCount : Int = 0
    init() {}
    init(integerLiteral val: Int) {
        self.eggCount = val
    }
}
```

Because Nest adopts ExpressibleByIntegerLiteral, we can pass an Int where a Nest is expected, and our init(integerLiteral:) will be called automatically, causing a new Nest object with the specified eggCount to come into existence at that moment:

```
func reportEggs(_ nest:Nest) {
    print("this nest contains \(nest.eggCount) eggs")
}
reportEggs(4) // this nest contains 4 eggs
```

Generics

A *generic* is a sort of placeholder for a type, into which an actual type will be slotted later. In particular, there are situations where you want to say that a certain *same* type is to be used in several places, without specifying precisely *what* type this is to be. Swift generics allow you to say that, without sacrificing or evading Swift's fundamental strict typing.

A motivating case in point arose earlier in this chapter, when we wrote a global factory function for dogs:

```
func dogMakerAndNamer(_ whattype:Dog.Type) -> Dog {
    let d = whattype.init(name:"Fido")
    return d
}
```

That works, but it isn't quite what we'd like to say. This function's declared return type is Dog. So if we are passed a Dog subclass such as NoisyDog as the parameter, we will instantiate that type (which is good) but then return that instance typed as Dog (which is bad). Instead, we'd like the type declared as the return type after the arrow operator to be the *same* type that we were passed as a parameter in the first line and that we instantiated in the second line — whatever that type may be. Generics permit us to say that:

```
func dogMakerAndNamer<WhatType:Dog>(_:WhatType.Type) -> WhatType { ❶ ❸
    let d = WhatType.init(name:"Fido") ❷
    return d
}
```

I haven't yet explained the syntax, but you can see the point. The angle brackets (`<WhatType:Dog>`) *declare* that the type WhatType is a generic type — a placeholder — and that it stands for Dog or for some subclass thereof. Then, WhatType is *used* in the course of the declaration, in three places:

❶   As the type passed in as parameter

❷   As the type instantiated in the function body

❸   As the declared type of the returned instance (after the arrow operator)

The generic function specifies that WhatType is the *same* type throughout, without having to specify exactly *what* type it is (beyond the fact that it is Dog or a Dog subclass).

However, Swift has strict typing, so in order to let us *call* this function, the compiler needs to know the *real* type that WhatType stands for. But in fact it knows this from looking at the call itself! For example:

```
let dog = dogMakerAndNamer(NoisyDog.self)
```

In that call, we pass `NoisyDog.self` as the parameter. That tells the compiler what WhatType is! It is NoisyDog. In effect, the compiler now *substitutes* NoisyDog for WhatType throughout the generic, like this (pseudocode):

```
func dogMakerAndNamer(_:NoisyDog.Type) -> NoisyDog {
    let d = NoisyDog.init(name:"Fido")
    return d
}
```

That process of substitution is called *resolving* (or *specializing*) the generic. The type in question is unambiguously clear *for this call* to our function, and the compiler is satisfied. And this resolution extends beyond the generic itself. Now that the compiler knows that this call to our function will return a NoisyDog instance, it can type the variable initialized to the result of the call as a NoisyDog by inference:

```
let dog = dogMakerAndNamer(NoisyDog.self) // dog is typed as NoisyDog
```

Let's consider another case in point: an Optional. Any type of value can be wrapped up in an Optional. Yet there is no doubt as to what type is wrapped up in a *particular* Optional. How can this be? It's because Optional is a generic! Here's how an Optional works.

I have already said that an Optional is an enum, with two cases: .none and .some. If an Optional's case is .some, it has an associated value — the value that is wrapped by this Optional. But what is the type of that associated value? On the one hand, one wants to say that it can be any type; that, after all, is why anything can be wrapped up in an Optional. On the other hand, any *particular* Optional can wrap a value only of some one *specific* known type. That sounds like a generic! The declaration for the Optional enum in the Swift header starts like this:

```
enum Optional<Wrapped> : ExpressibleByNilLiteral {
    case none
    case some(Wrapped)
    init(_ some: Wrapped)
    // ...
}
```

The angle-bracket syntax <Wrapped> *declares* that Wrapped is a placeholder. The rest of the enum declaration proceeds to *use* the placeholder. Besides the case .none, there's also a case .some, which has an associated value — of type Wrapped. And there's an initializer, which takes a parameter — of type Wrapped. Thus, the type with which we are initialized — whatever type that may be — *is* type Wrapped, and therefore is the type associated with the .some case.

And how will this placeholder be resolved? Well, when an Optional is created, it will be initialized with an actual value of some definite type:

```
let s = Optional("howdy")
```

We're calling init(_ some: Wrapped), so "howdy" is being supplied here as a Wrapped instance, resolving the generic as String. The compiler now knows that Wrapped is String *throughout* this particular Optional<Wrapped>; the declaration for this *particular* Optional looks, in the compiler's mind, like this (pseudocode):

```
enum Optional<String> {
    case none
    case some(String)
    init(_ some: String)
    // ...
}
```

That is the pseudocode declaration of an Optional whose Wrapped placeholder has been replaced everywhere with the String type. We can summarize this by saying that s is an `Optional<String>`. In fact, that is legal syntax! We can create the same Optional like this:

```
let s : Optional<String> = "howdy"
```

Generic Declarations

Here's a list of places where generics, in one form or another, can be declared in Swift:

Generic protocol with `Self`

In a protocol body, use of the keyword `Self` turns the protocol into a generic. `Self` here is a placeholder meaning *the type of the adopter*. Here's a Flier protocol that declares a method that takes a `Self` parameter:

```
protocol Flier {
    func flockTogetherWith(_ f:Self)
}
```

That means that if the Bird object type were to adopt the Flier protocol, its implementation of `flockTogetherWith` would need to declare its parameter as a Bird.

Generic protocol with associated type

A protocol can declare an *associated type* using an `associatedtype` statement. This turns the protocol into a generic; the associated type name is a placeholder:

```
protocol Flier {
    associatedtype Other
    func flockTogetherWith(_ f:Other)
    func mateWith(_ f:Other)
}
```

An adopter will declare a particular type at some point where the generic uses the associated type name, resolving the placeholder:

```
struct Bird : Flier {
    func flockTogetherWith(_ f:Bird) {}
    func mateWith(_ f:Bird) {}
}
```

The Bird struct adopts the Flier protocol and declares the parameter of `flock-TogetherWith` as a Bird. That declaration resolves Other to Bird for this particular adopter — and therefore Bird must declare the parameter for `mateWith` as a Bird as well.

Generic functions

A function declaration can use a generic placeholder type for any of its parameters, for its return type, and within its body. The placeholder name is declared in angle brackets after the function name:

```
func takeAndReturnSameThing<T> (_ t:T) -> T {
    print(T.self)
    return t
}
```

The caller will use a particular type at some point where the placeholder appears in the function declaration, resolving the placeholder:

```
let thing = takeAndReturnSameThing("howdy")
```

Here, the type of the argument "howdy" used in the call resolves T to String; therefore this call to takeAndReturnSameThing will also return a String, and the variable capturing the result, thing, is inferred to String as well.

Generic object types

An object type declaration can use a generic placeholder type anywhere within its curly braces. The placeholder name is declared in angle brackets after the object type name:

```
struct HolderOfTwoSameThings<T> {
    var firstThing : T
    var secondThing : T
    init(thingOne:T, thingTwo:T) {
        self.firstThing = thingOne
        self.secondThing = thingTwo
    }
}
```

A user of this object type will use a particular type at some point where the placeholder appears in the object type declaration, resolving the placeholder:

```
let holder = HolderOfTwoSameThings(thingOne:"howdy", thingTwo:"getLost")
```

Here, the type of the thingOne argument, "howdy", used in the initializer call, resolves T to String; therefore thingTwo must also be a String, and the properties firstThing and secondThing are Strings as well.

The angle brackets that declare a placeholder may declare multiple placeholders, separated by a comma:

```
func flockTwoTogether<T, U>(_ f1:T, _ f2:U) {}
```

The two parameters of flockTwoTogether can now be resolved to two different types (though they do not *have* to be different).

Inside a generic's code, the generic placeholder is a type reference standing for the resolved type, which can be interrogated using type reference comparison, as described earlier in this chapter:

```
func takeAndReturnSameThing<T> (_ t:T) -> T {
    if T.self is String.Type {
        // ...
    }
    return t
}
```

If we call `takeAndReturnSameThing("howdy")`, the condition will be true. That sort of thing, however, is unusual; a generic whose behavior depends on interrogation of the placeholder type may need to be rewritten in some other way.

Contradictory Resolution Is Impossible

Because the use of a generic resolves the generic, a resolution that would contradict itself is ruled out *at compile time*. This is one of the most important features of generics: contradictory resolution is impossible as a consequence of Swift's strict typing. A generic placeholder must be resolved consistently throughout the generic, or it cannot be resolved at all.

To illustrate, I'll return to an earlier example:

```
func dogMakerAndNamer<WhatType:Dog>(_:WhatType.Type) -> WhatType {
    let d = WhatType.init(name:"Fido")
    return d
}
```

Now consider this code:

```
let d : NoisyDog = dogMakerAndNamer(Dog.self)
```

That code makes no sense. On the one hand, the parameter `Dog.self` resolves What-Type to Dog. On the other hand, the explicit type of the result d resolves WhatType to NoisyDog. Those two resolutions contradict one another. The compiler knows this, and stops you in your tracks:

```
let d : NoisyDog = dogMakerAndNamer(Dog.self) // compile error
```

Similarly, recall this example:

```
protocol Flier {
    associatedtype Other
    func flockTogetherWith(_ f:Other)
    func mateWith(_ f:Other)
}
```

The placeholder Other may be resolved to any type, but it must be the *same* type. This is a legal adoption of Flier:

```
struct Bird : Flier {
    func flockTogetherWith(_ f: String) {}
    func mateWith(_ f:String) {}
}
```

But this is not:

```
struct Bird : Flier { // compile error
    func flockTogetherWith(_ f: String) {}
    func mateWith(_ f:Int) {}
}
```

The compiler stops you, complaining that Bird does not conform to Flier.

Type Constraints

A generic declaration can *limit* the types that are eligible to be used for resolving a particular placeholder. This is called a *type constraint*.

The simplest form of type constraint is to put a colon and a type name after the placeholder's name when it first appears. The type name after the colon can be a class name or a protocol name:

Class name
> A class name means that the type must be this class *or a subclass* of this class.

Protocol name
> A protocol name means that the type must be *an adopter* of this protocol.

For a protocol associated type, the type constraint appears as part of the associatedtype declaration:

```
protocol Flier {
    func fly()
}
protocol Flocker {
    associatedtype Other : Flier // *
    func flockTogetherWith(f:Other)
}
struct Bird : Flocker, Flier {
    func fly() {}
    func flockTogetherWith(f:Bird) {}
}
```

In that example, Flocker's associated type Other is constrained to be an adopter of Flier. Bird *is* an adopter of Flier; therefore it can also adopt Flocker while specifying that the parameter type in its flockTogetherWith implementation is Bird.

Observe that we could not have achieved the same effect without the associated type, by declaring Flocker like this:

```
protocol Flocker {
    func flockTogetherWith(f:Flier)
}
```

That's not the same thing! That requires that a Flocker adopter specify the parameter for flockTogetherWith *as Flier*. We would then have had to write Bird like this:

```
struct Bird : Flocker, Flier {
    func fly() {}
    func flockTogetherWith(f:Flier) {}
}
```

The constrained associated type, on the other hand, requires that a Flocker adopter specify the parameter for flockTogetherWith as *some Flier adopter* (such as Bird).

For a generic function or a generic object type, the type constraint appears in the angle brackets. The global function func dogMakerAndNamer<WhatType:Dog>, declared earlier in this chapter, is an example; Dog is a class, so the constraint says that WhatType must be Dog or a Dog subclass. Here's another example, using a protocol as a constraint:

```
func flockTwoTogether<T:Flier>(_ f1:T, _ f2:T) {}
```

In that example, Flier is a protocol, so the constraint says that T must be a Flier adopter. If Bird and Insect both adopt Flier, this flockTwoTogether function can be called with two Bird arguments or with two Insect arguments — but not with a Bird and an Insect, because T is just one placeholder, signifying one Flier adopter type. And you can't call flockTwoTogether with two String parameters, because a String is not a Flier.

A type constraint on a placeholder is often used to reassure the compiler that some message can be sent to an instance of the placeholder type. Let's say we want to implement a function myMin that returns the smallest from a list of the same type. Here's a promising implementation as a generic function, but there's one problem — it doesn't compile:

```
func myMin<T>(_ things:T...) -> T {
    var minimum = things.first!
    for item in things.dropFirst() {
        if item < minimum { // compile error
            minimum = item
        }
    }
    return minimum
}
```

The problem is the comparison item < minimum. How does the compiler know that the type T, the type of item and minimum, will be resolved to a type that can in fact be compared using the less-than operator in this way? It doesn't, and that's exactly why it rejects that code. The solution is to promise the compiler that the resolved type of T *will* in fact work with the less-than operator. The way to do that, it turns out, is to constrain T to Swift's built-in Comparable protocol:

```
func myMin<T:Comparable>(_ things:T...) -> T {
```

Now `myMin` compiles, because it cannot be called except by resolving T to an object type that adopts Comparable and hence can be compared with the less-than operator. Naturally, built-in object types that you think should be comparable, such as Int, Double, String, and Character, do in fact adopt the Comparable protocol! If you look in the Swift headers, you'll find that the built-in `min` global function is declared in just this way, and for just this reason.

 A generic protocol type can be used *only* as a type constraint. If you try to use it in any other way, you'll get a compile error. This restriction can be quite frustrating. The standard way of circumventing it is called *type erasure*; for an excellent discussion, see *http://robnapier.net/erasure*.

Explicit Specialization

In the generic examples so far, the placeholder's type has been resolved mostly through *inference*. But there's another way to perform resolution: we can resolve the type *manually*. This is called *explicit specialization*. In some situations, explicit specialization is mandatory — namely, if the placeholder type cannot be resolved through inference. There are two forms of explicit specialization:

Generic protocol with associated type
> The adopter of a protocol can resolve an associated type manually through a type alias defining the associated type as some explicit type:

```
protocol Flier {
    associatedtype Other
}
struct Bird : Flier {
    typealias Other = String
}
```

Generic object type
> The user of a generic object type can resolve a placeholder type manually using the same angle bracket syntax used to declare the generic in the first place, with the type name in the angle brackets:

```
class Dog<T> {
    var name : T?
}
let d = Dog<String>()
```

You cannot explicitly specialize a generic function. One solution is to make your generic function take a type parameter resolving the generic. That's what I did in my earlier dogMakerAndNamer example:

```
func dogMakerAndNamer<WhatType:Dog>(_:WhatType.Type) -> WhatType {
    let d = WhatType.init(name:"Fido")
    return d
}
```

The parameter to dogMakerAndNamer is never used within the function body, which is why it has no name (just an underscore). It does, however, serve to resolve the generic!

Another approach is not to use a generic function in the first place. Instead, declare a generic object type wrapping a nongeneric function that uses the generic type's placeholder. The generic type *can* be explicitly specialized, resolving the placeholder in the function:

```
protocol Flier {
    init()
}
struct Bird : Flier {
    init() {}
}
struct FlierMaker<T:Flier> {
    static func makeFlier() -> T {
        return T()
    }
}
let f = FlierMaker<Bird>.makeFlier() // returns a Bird
```

When a class is generic, you can subclass it, provided you resolve the generic. You can do this either through a matching generic subclass or by resolving the superclass generic explicitly. Here's a generic Dog:

```
class Dog<T> {
    func speak(_ what:T) {}
}
```

You can subclass it as a generic whose placeholder matches that of the superclass:

```
class NoisyDog<T> : Dog<T> {}
```

That's legal because the resolution of the NoisyDog placeholder T will resolve the Dog placeholder T. The alternative is to subclass an explicitly specialized Dog:

```
class NoisyDog : Dog<String> {}
```

In that case, a method override in the subclass can use the specialized type where the superclass uses the generic:

```
class NoisyDog : Dog<String> {
    override func speak(_ what:String) {}
}
```

Generic Invariance

In general, a generic type specialized to a subtype is *not polymorphic* with respect to
the same generic type specialized to a supertype. Suppose we have a simple generic
Wrapper struct along with a Cat class and its CalicoCat subclass:

```
struct Wrapper<T> {
}
class Cat {
}
class CalicoCat : Cat {
}
```

Then you can't assign a Wrapper specialized to CalicoCat where a Wrapper specialized to Cat is expected:

```
let w : Wrapper<Cat> = Wrapper<CalicoCat>() // compile error
```

It appears that polymorphism is failing here — but it isn't. The two generic types,
Wrapper<Cat> and Wrapper<CalicoCat>, are not superclass and subclass. Rather, if
this assignment were possible, we would say that the types are *covariant*, meaning
that the polymorphic relationship between the specializations of the placeholders is
applied to the generic types themselves. Certain Swift built-in generic types *are* covariant; Optional is a clear example! But, frustratingly, covariance is not a *general* language feature; there's no way for you to specify that *your* generic types should be
covariant.

One workaround is to have your generic placeholder constrained to a protocol, and
have your types adopt that protocol:

```
protocol Meower {
    func meow()
}
struct Wrapper<T:Meower> {
    let meower : T
}
class Cat : Meower {
    func meow() { print("meow") }
}
class CalicoCat : Cat {
}
```

Now it is legal to say:

```
let w : Wrapper<Cat> = Wrapper(meower:CalicoCat())
```

Associated Type Chains

When a generic placeholder is constrained to a generic protocol with an associated type, you can refer to the associated type using dot-notation: the placeholder name, a dot, and the associated type name.

Here's an example. Imagine that in a game program, soldiers and archers are enemies of one another. I'll express this by subsuming a Soldier struct and an Archer struct under a Fighter protocol that has an Enemy associated type, which is itself constrained to be a Fighter:

```
protocol Fighter {
    associatedtype Enemy : Fighter
}
```

I'll resolve that associated type manually for both the Soldier and the Archer structs:

```
struct Soldier : Fighter {
    typealias Enemy = Archer
}
struct Archer : Fighter {
    typealias Enemy = Soldier
}
```

Now I'll create a generic struct to express the opposing camps of these fighters:

```
struct Camp<T:Fighter> {
}
```

Now suppose that a camp may contain a spy from the opposing camp. What is the type of that spy? Well, if this is a Soldier camp, it's an Archer; and if it's an Archer camp, it's a Soldier. More generally, since T is a Fighter, it's the type of the Enemy of this adopter of Fighter. I can express that as T.Enemy:

```
struct Camp<T:Fighter> {
    var spy : T.Enemy?
}
```

The result is that if, for a particular Camp, T is resolved to Soldier, T.Enemy means Archer — and *vice versa*. We have created a correct and inviolable rule for the type that a Camp's spy must be. This won't compile:

```
var c = Camp<Soldier>()
c.spy = Soldier() // compile error
```

We've tried to assign an object of the wrong type to this Camp's spy property. But this does compile:

```
var c = Camp<Soldier>()
c.spy = Archer()
```

A generic protocol might have an associated type which is constrained to a generic protocol that *also* has an associated type. Therefore, longer chains of associated type names are possible. Let's give each type of Fighter a characteristic weapon: a soldier has a sword, while an archer has a bow. I'll make a Sword struct and a Bow struct, and I'll unite them under a Wieldable protocol:

```
protocol Wieldable {
}
struct Sword : Wieldable {
}
struct Bow : Wieldable {
}
```

I'll add a Weapon associated type to Fighter, which is constrained to be a Wieldable, and once again I'll resolve it manually for each type of Fighter:

```
protocol Fighter {
    associatedtype Enemy : Fighter
    associatedtype Weapon : Wieldable
}
struct Soldier : Fighter {
    typealias Weapon = Sword
    typealias Enemy = Archer
}
struct Archer : Fighter {
    typealias Weapon = Bow
    typealias Enemy = Soldier
}
```

Now let's say that every Fighter has the ability to steal his enemy's weapon. I'll give the Fighter generic protocol a steal(weapon:from:) method. How can the Fighter generic protocol express the parameter types in a way that causes its adopter to declare this method with the proper types?

The from: parameter type is this Fighter's Enemy. We already know how to express that: it's the placeholder plus dot-notation with the associated type name. Here, the placeholder is the adopter of this protocol — namely, Self. So the from: parameter type is Self.Enemy. And what about the weapon: parameter type? That's the Weapon of that Enemy! So the weapon: parameter type is Self.Enemy.Weapon:

```
protocol Fighter {
    associatedtype Enemy : Fighter
    associatedtype Weapon : Wieldable
    func steal(weapon:Self.Enemy.Weapon, from:Self.Enemy)
}
```

(We could omit Self from that code, and it would compile and would mean the same thing. But Self would still be the implicit start of the chain, and I think explicit Self makes the meaning of the code clearer.)

The result is that the following declarations for Soldier and Archer correctly adopt the Fighter protocol, and the compiler approves:

```
struct Soldier : Fighter {
    typealias Weapon = Sword
    typealias Enemy = Archer
    func steal(weapon:Bow, from:Archer) {
    }
}
struct Archer : Fighter {
    typealias Weapon = Bow
    typealias Enemy = Soldier
    func steal(weapon:Sword, from:Soldier) {
    }
}
```

Where Clauses

The most flexible way to express a type constraint is to add a where clause. Before I tell you what a where clause looks like, I'll tell you where it goes:

- For a generic function, a where clause may appear after the signature declaration (after the parameter list, following the arrow operator and return type if included).

- For a generic type, a where clause may appear after the type declaration, before the curly braces.

- For a generic protocol, a where clause may appear after the protocol declaration, before the curly braces.

- For an associated type in a generic protocol, a where clause may appear at the end of the associated type declaration.

Now let's talk about the syntax of a where clause. It starts with the keyword where. Then what? One possibility is a comma-separated list of additional constraints on an already declared placeholder. You already know that we can constrain a placeholder at the point of declaration, using a colon and a type (which might be a protocol composition):

```
func flyAndWalk<T: Flier> (_ f:T) {}
func flyAndWalk2<T: Flier & Walker> (_ f:T) {}
func flyAndWalk3<T: Flier & Dog> (_ f:T) {}
```

Using a where clause, we can move those constraints out of the angle brackets. No new functionality is gained, but the resulting notation is arguably neater:

```
func flyAndWalk<T> (_ f:T) where T: Flier {}
func flyAndWalk2<T> (_ f:T) where T: Flier & Walker {}
func flyAndWalk2a<T> (_ f:T) where T: Flier, T: Walker {}
func flyAndWalk3<T> (_ f:T) where T: Flier & Dog {}
func flyAndWalk3a<T> (_ f:T) where T: Flier, T: Dog {}
```

When a constraint on a placeholder is a generic protocol with an associated type, you can use an associated type chain to impose additional constraints *on the associated type.* This pseudocode shows what I mean (I've omitted the content of the where clause, to focus on what the where clause will be constraining):

```
protocol Flier {
    associatedtype Other
}
func flockTogether<T> (_ f:T) where T:Flier, T.Other /* ... */ {}
```

In that pseudocode, the placeholder T is constrained to be a Flier — and Flier is itself a generic protocol, with an associated type Other. Therefore, whatever type resolves T will resolve Other. We can proceed to constrain the types eligible to resolve T.Other — and this, in turn, will further constrain the types eligible to resolve T.

Let's fill in the blank in our pseudocode. What sort of restriction are we allowed to impose here? One possibility is a colon expression, as for any type constraint:

```
protocol Flier {
    associatedtype Other
}
struct Bird : Flier {
    typealias Other = String
}
struct Insect : Flier {
    typealias Other = Bird
}
func flockTogether<T> (_ f:T) where T:Flier, T.Other:Equatable {}
```

Both Bird and Insect adopt Flier. The flockTogether function can be called with a Bird argument, because a Bird's Other associated type is resolved to String, which adopts the built-in Equatable protocol. But flockTogether can't be called with an Insect argument, because an Insect's Other associated type is resolved to Bird, which *doesn't* adopt the Equatable protocol:

```
flockTogether(Bird()) // okay
flockTogether(Insect()) // compile error
```

The other possibility is the equality operator == followed by a type or an associated type chain, and the constrained type must then match it *exactly*:

```
protocol Flier {
    associatedtype Other
}
struct Bird : Flier {
    typealias Other = String
}
struct Insect : Flier {
    typealias Other = Int
}
func flockTwoTogether<T,U> (_ f1:T, _ f2:U)
    where T:Flier, U:Flier, T.Other == U.Other {}
```

The flockTwoTogether function can be called with a Bird and a Bird, and it can be called with an Insect and an Insect, but it can't be called with an Insect and a Bird, because they don't resolve the Other associated type to the same type.

The Swift header makes extensive use of where clauses with an == operator, especially as a way of restricting a sequence type. Take the String append(contentsOf:) method, declared like this:

```
mutating func append<S>(contentsOf newElements: S)
    where S:Sequence, S.Element == Character
```

The Sequence protocol has an Element associated type, representing the type of the sequence's elements. This where clause means that a sequence of characters — but *not* a sequence of something else, such as Int — can be concatenated to a String:

```
var s = "hello"
s.append(contentsOf: Array(" world")) // "hello world"
s.append(contentsOf: ["!" as Character, "?" as Character])
```

The Array append(contentsOf:) method is declared a little differently:

```
mutating func append<S>(contentsOf newElements: S)
    where S:Sequence, S.Element == Self.Element
```

An array is a sequence; its element type is its Element associated type. The where clause means that you can append to an Array the elements of any sort of Sequence, but only if they are the same kind of element as the elements of this array. If the array consists of String elements, you can add more String elements to it, but you can't add Int elements.

Actually, a sequence's Element associated type is just a kind of shorthand. In reality, a sequence has an Iterator associated type, which is constrained to be an adopter of the generic IteratorProtocol, which in turn has an associated type Element. So a sequence's element type is its Iterator.Element. But a generic protocol or its associated type can have a where clause, and this can be used to reduce the length of associated type chains:

```
protocol Sequence {
    associatedtype Iterator : IteratorProtocol
    associatedtype Element where Self.Element == Self.Iterator.Element
    // ...
}
```

As a result, wherever the Swift header would have to say Iterator.Element, it can say simply Element instead.

Extensions

An *extension* is a way of injecting your own code into an object type that has already been declared elsewhere; you are *extending* an existing object type. You can extend your own object types; you can also extend one of Swift's object types or one of Cocoa's object types, in which case you are *adding functionality* to a type that doesn't belong to you!

Extension declaration can take place only at the top level of a file. To declare an extension, put the keyword `extension` followed by the name of an existing object type, then optionally a colon plus the names of any protocols you want to add to the list of those adopted by this type, and finally curly braces containing the usual things that go inside an object type declaration — with some restrictions:

- An extension can't declare a stored property (but it can declare a computed property).
- An extension of a class can't declare a designated initializer or a deinitializer (but it can declare a convenience initializer).
- An extension can't override an existing member (but it can overload an existing method), and a method declared in an extension can't be overridden.

In my real programming life, I sometimes extend a built-in Swift or Cocoa type just to inject some missing functionality by expressing it as a property or method.

For example, Cocoa's Core Graphics framework has many useful functions associated with the CGRect struct, and Swift already extends CGRect to add some helpful properties and methods; but there's no shortcut for getting the center point (a CGPoint) of a CGRect, something that in practice is often needed. I extend CGRect to give it a `center` property:

```
extension CGRect {
    var center : CGPoint {
        return CGPoint(x:self.midX, y:self.midY)
    }
}
```

String ranges, as we've already seen, are hard to construct, because they are a range of String.Index rather than Int. We can extend String with methods that take an Int index and a count, yielding a Swift Range; while we're up, let's permit a negative index, as most modern languages do:

```
extension String {
    func range(_ start:Int, _ count:Int) -> Range<String.Index> {
        let i = self.index(start >= 0 ?
            self.startIndex :
            self.endIndex, offsetBy: start)
```

```
        let j = self.index(i, offsetBy: count)
        return i..<j
    }
}
```

An extension can declare a static or class member; this can be a good way to slot a global function into an appropriate namespace. In one of my apps, I find myself frequently using a certain color (a UIColor). Instead of creating that color repeatedly, it makes sense to encapsulate the instructions for generating it in a global function. But instead of making that function *completely* global, I make it — appropriately enough — a read-only static property of UIColor:

```
extension UIColor {
    static var myGolden : UIColor {
        return self.init(
            red:1.000, green:0.894, blue:0.541, alpha:0.900
        )
    }
}
```

Now I can use that color throughout my code as UIColor.myGolden, parallel to built-in class properties such as UIColor.red.

Extensions on one's own object types can help to organize code. A frequently used convention is to add an extension for each protocol the object type needs to adopt, like this:

```
class ViewController: UIViewController {
    // ... UIViewController method overrides go here ...
}
extension ViewController : UIPopoverPresentationControllerDelegate {
    // ... UIPopoverPresentationControllerDelegate methods go here ...
}
extension ViewController : UIToolbarDelegate {
    // ... UIToolbarDelegate methods go here ...
}
```

An extension on your own object type can also be a way to spread your definition of that object type over multiple files, if you feel that several shorter files are better than one long file.

When you extend a Swift struct, a curious thing happens with initializers: it becomes possible to declare an initializer and keep the implicit initializers:

```
struct Digit {
    var number : Int
}
extension Digit {
    init() {
        self.init(number:42)
    }
}
```

Class Extensions and Overrides

The rules about class extensions and overrides are more complicated than I've stated. A native Swift method in an extension can neither override nor be overridden, but then Objective-C comes along with its own rules and messes everything up. Let's say we have a class Dog and its subclass NoisyDog:

- If we have an extension on Dog that declares a method, NoisyDog *can* override it *if* the Dog extension method is exposed to Objective-C.
- If we have a method in Dog, an extension on NoisyDog *can* override it *if* Dog's method is exposed to Objective-C and marked `dynamic`.

Things are made even messier by the existence of modules; if there's a class with a method in a module, an extension on that class in another module can declare *the same method*, not overriding but effectively replacing it. No doubt Apple will eventually straighten all this out.

In that code, the explicit declaration of an initializer through an extension did not cause us to lose the implicit memberwise initializer, as would have happened if we had declared the same initializer inside the original struct declaration. Now we can instantiate a Digit by calling the explicitly declared initializer — `Digit()` — or by calling the implicit memberwise initializer — `Digit(number:7)`.

Extending Protocols

When you extend a protocol, you can add methods and properties to the protocol, just as for any object type. Unlike a protocol declaration, these methods and properties are not mere requirements, to be fulfilled by the adopter of the protocol; they are actual methods and properties, to be *inherited* by the adopter of the protocol:

```
protocol Flier {
}
extension Flier {
    func fly() {
        print("flap flap flap")
    }
}
struct Bird : Flier {
}
```

Observe that Bird can now adopt Flier without implementing the `fly` method. That's because the Flier protocol extension *supplies* the `fly` method! Bird *inherits* an implementation of `fly`:

```
let b = Bird()
b.fly() // flap flap flap
```

Of course, an adopter can still provide its own implementation of a method inherited from a protocol extension:

```
protocol Flier {
}
extension Flier {
    func fly() {
        print("flap flap flap")
    }
}
struct Insect : Flier {
    func fly() {
        print("whirr")
    }
}
let i = Insect()
i.fly() // whirr
```

But be warned: this kind of inheritance is *not polymorphic*. The adopter's implementation is not an override; it is merely another implementation. The internal identity rule does *not* apply; it matters how a reference is typed:

```
let f : Flier = Insect()
f.fly() // flap flap flap (!!)
```

Even though f is internally an Insect (as we can discover with the is operator), the fly message is being sent to an object reference typed as Flier, so it is Flier's implementation of the fly method that is called, not Insect's implementation.

To get something that looks like polymorphic inheritance, we must also declare fly as a requirement *in the original protocol*:

```
protocol Flier {
    func fly() // *
}
extension Flier {
    func fly() {
        print("flap flap flap")
    }
}
struct Insect : Flier {
    func fly() {
        print("whirr")
    }
}
```

Now an Insect maintains its internal integrity:

```
let f : Flier = Insect()
f.fly() // whirr
```

Extending Generics

When you extend a generic type, the placeholder type names are visible to your extension declaration. That's good, because you might need to use them; but it can make your code a little mystifying, because you seem to be using an undefined type name out of the blue. It might be a good idea to add a comment, to remind yourself what you're up to:

```
class Dog<T> {
    var name : T?
}
extension Dog {
    func sayYourName() -> T? { // T? is the type of self.name
        return self.name
    }
}
```

A generic type extension declaration can include a where clause. Similar to a generic constraint, this limits *which* resolvers of the generic can call the code injected by this extension, and assures the compiler that your code is legal for those resolvers.

For instance, recall this example from earlier in this chapter:

```
func myMin<T:Comparable>(_ things:T...) -> T {
    var minimum = things.first!
    for item in things.dropFirst() {
        if item < minimum {
            minimum = item
        }
    }
    return minimum
}
```

That's a global function. I'd prefer to inject it into Array as a method. I can do that with an extension. Array is a generic struct whose placeholder type is called Element. To make this work, I need somehow to bring along the Comparable type constraint that makes this code legal; without it, as you remember, my use of the < operator won't compile. I can do that with a where clause on the extension:

```
extension Array where Element:Comparable {
    func myMin() -> Element? {
        var minimum = self.first
        for item in self.dropFirst() {
            if item < minimum! {
                minimum = item
            }
        }
        return minimum
    }
}
```

The where clause is a constraint guaranteeing that this array's elements adopt Comparable, so the compiler permits the use of the < operator — and it doesn't permit the myMin method to be called on an array whose elements *don't* adopt Comparable. The Swift standard library makes heavy use of that sort of thing, and in fact Sequence has a min method declared like myMin.

New in Swift 5.3, the where clause can be applied to the method instead of the extension:

```
extension Array {
    func myMin() -> Element? where Element:Comparable {
        // ...
    }
}
```

The advantages are primarily organizational. In Swift 5.2 and before, the only way for a generic type to restrict a method to one or more constraints on the placeholder type was to put the method into an extension with all of the constraints in the extension declaration:

```
struct MyStruct<T> {
    // ...
}
extension MyStruct where T:Protocol1, T:Protocol2 {
    func f() {
        // ...
    }
}
```

In Swift 5.3, we can distribute the statement of the constraints in whatever way seems clearest. We could write this:

```
extension MyStruct where T:Protocol1 {
    func f() where T:Protocol2 {
        // ...
    }
}
```

We could even forego the extension altogether:

```
struct MyStruct<T> {
    // ...
    func f() where T:Protocol1, T:Protocol2 {
        // ...
    }
}
```

An extension with a where clause can also be used to express *conditional conformance* to a protocol. The idea is that a generic type should adopt a certain protocol only if something is true of its placeholder type — and the extension then contains whatever is needed to satisfy the protocol requirements when that's the case.

In the standard library, conditional conformance fills what used to be a serious hole in the Swift language. For example, an Array can consist of Equatable elements, and in that case it is possible to compare two arrays for equality:

```
let arr1 = [1,2,3]
let arr2 = [1,2,3]
if arr1 == arr2 { // ...
```

It's clear what array equality should consist of: the two arrays should consist of the same elements in the same order. The elements must be Equatable so as to guarantee the meaningfulness of the notion "same elements."

Ironically, however, there was, before Swift 4.1, no way to compare two arrays of arrays:

```
let arr1 = [[1], [2], [3]]
let arr2 = [[1], [2], [3]]
let arr1 == arr2 { // compile error before Swift 4.1
```

That's because there was no coherent way to make Array *itself* Equatable — because there was no way to assert that Array should be Equatable only just in case its elements are Equatable. That's conditional conformance! Now that conditional conformance exists, the standard library says:

```
extension Array : Equatable where Element : Equatable {
    // ...
}
```

And so comparing arrays of arrays becomes legal:

```
let arr1 = [[1], [2], [3]]
let arr2 = [[1], [2], [3]]
let arr1 == arr2 { // fine
```

Umbrella Types

Swift provides a few built-in types as general umbrella types, capable of embracing multiple real types under a single heading.

Any

The Any type is the universal Swift umbrella type. Where an Any object is expected, absolutely any object or function can be passed, without casting:

```
func anyExpecter(_ a:Any) {}
anyExpecter("howdy")      // a struct instance
anyExpecter(String.self)  // a struct type
anyExpecter(Dog())        // a class instance
anyExpecter(Dog.self)     // a class type
anyExpecter(anyExpecter)  // a function
```

Going the other way, if you want to type an Any object as a more specific type, you will generally have to cast down. Such a cast is legal for any specific object type or function type. A forced cast isn't safe, but you can easily make it safe, because you can also test an Any object against any specific object type or function type. Here, anything is typed as Any:

```
if anything is String {
    let s = anything as! String
    // ...
}
```

(In Chapter 5 I'll introduce a more elegant syntax for casting down safely.)

The Any umbrella type is the general medium of interchange between Swift and the Cocoa Objective-C APIs. When an Objective-C object type is nonspecific (id), it will appear to Swift as Any. Commonly encountered examples are UserDefaults and key-value coding (Chapter 10); these allow you to *pass* an object of indeterminate class along with a string key name, and they allow you to *retrieve* an object of indeterminate class by a string key name. That object is typed, in Swift, as Any (or as an Optional wrapping Any, so that it can be nil):

```
let ud = UserDefaults.standard
ud.set(Date(), forKey:"now") // Date to Any
```

The first parameter of UserDefaults set(_:forKey:) is typed as Any.

When a Swift object is assigned or passed to an Any that acts as a conduit to Objective-C, it crosses the bridge to Objective-C. If the object's type is not an Objective-C type (a class derived from NSObject), it will be transformed in order to cross the bridge. If this type is automatically bridged to an Objective-C class type, it becomes that type; other types are boxed up in a way that allows them to survive the journey into Objective-C's world, even though Objective-C can't deal with them directly. (For full details, see Appendix A.)

To illustrate, suppose we have an Objective-C class Thing with a method take1id:, declared like this:

```
- (void) take1id: (id) anid;
```

That appears to Swift as:

```
func take1id(_ anid: Any)
```

When we pass an object to take1Id(_:) as its parameter, it crosses the bridge:

```
let t = Thing()
t.take1id("howdy")   // String to NSString
t.take1id(1)         // Int to NSNumber
t.take1id(CGRect())  // CGRect to NSValue
t.take1id(Date())    // Date to NSDate
t.take1id(Bird())    // Bird (struct) to boxed type
```

Coming back the other way, if Objective-C hands you an Any object, you will need to cast it down to its underlying type in order to do anything useful with it:

```
let ud = UserDefaults.standard
let d = ud.object(forKey:"now")
if d is Date {
    let d = d as! Date
    // ...
}
```

The result returned from UserDefaults object(forKey:) is typed as Any — actually, as an Optional wrapping an Any, because UserDefaults might need to return nil to indicate that no object exists for that key. But you know that it's supposed to be a date, so you cast it down to Date.

AnyObject

AnyObject is an empty protocol with the special feature that *all class types* conform to it automatically. Although Objective-C APIs present Objective-C id as Any in Swift, Swift AnyObject *is* Objective-C id. AnyObject is useful primarily when you want to take advantage of the *behavior* of Objective-C id, as I'll demonstrate in a moment.

A class type can be assigned directly where an AnyObject is expected; to retrieve it as its original type, you'll need to cast down:

```
class Dog {
}
let d = Dog()
let anyo : AnyObject = d
let d2 = anyo as! Dog
```

Assigning a nonclass type to an AnyObject requires casting (with as). The bridge to Objective-C is then crossed immediately, as I described for Any in the preceding section:

```
let s = "howdy" as AnyObject   // String to NSString to AnyObject
let i = 1 as AnyObject         // Int to NSNumber to AnyObject
let r = CGRect() as AnyObject  // CGRect to NSValue to AnyObject
let d = Date() as AnyObject    // Date to NSDate to AnyObject
let b = Bird() as AnyObject    // Bird (struct) to boxed type to AnyObject
```

Suppressing type checking

Because AnyObject is Objective-C id, it can be used, like Objective-C id, to suspend the compiler's judgment as to whether a certain message can be sent to an object. Thus, you can send a message to an AnyObject without bothering to cast down to its real type.

You can't send just any old message to an AnyObject; this is an Objective-C feature, so the message must correspond to a class member that meets one of the following criteria:

- It is a member of an Objective-C class.
- It is a member of your own Swift subclass of an Objective-C class.
- It is a member of your own Swift extension of an Objective-C class.
- It is a member of a Swift class or protocol marked @objc.

This feature is fundamentally parallel to optional protocol members, which I discussed earlier in this chapter. Let's start with two classes:

```
class Dog {
    @objc var noise : String = "woof"
    @objc func bark() -> String {
        return "woof"
    }
}
class Cat {}
```

The Dog property `noise` and the Dog method `bark` are marked @objc, so they are visible as potential messages to be sent to an AnyObject. To prove it, I'll type a Cat as an AnyObject and send it one of those messages. Let's start with the `noise` property:

```
let c : AnyObject = Cat()
let s = c.noise
```

That code, amazingly, compiles. Moreover, it doesn't crash when the code runs! The `noise` property has been typed as an Optional wrapping its original type. Here, that's an Optional wrapping a String. If the object typed as AnyObject doesn't implement `noise`, the result is `nil` and no harm done.

Now let's try it with a method call:

```
let c : AnyObject = Cat()
let s = c.bark?()
```

Again, that code compiles and is safe. If the Object typed as AnyObject doesn't implement `bark`, no `bark()` call is performed; the method result type has been wrapped in an Optional, so s is typed as `String?` and has been set to `nil`. If the AnyObject turns out to have a `bark` method (because it's a Dog), the result is an Optional wrapping the returned String. If you call `bark!()` on the AnyObject instead, the result will be a String, but you'll crash if the AnyObject doesn't implement `bark`. Unlike an optional protocol member, you can even send the message *with no unwrapping*. This is legal:

```
let c : AnyObject = Cat()
let s = c.bark()
```

That's just like force-unwrapping the call: the result is a String, but it's possible to crash.

 Don't make a habit of sending messages to an AnyObject; because it involves dynamic lookup, it's expensive at build time and expensive at runtime.

Object identity

Sometimes, what you want to know is not what *type* an object is, but whether an object itself is the *particular object* you think it is. This problem can't arise with a value type, but it can arise with a reference type — in particular, with class instances.

Swift's solution is the identity operator (===). Its operands are typed as AnyObject?, meaning an object whose type is a class or an Optional whose wrapped type is a class; it compares one object reference with another. This is not a comparison of *values*, like the equality operator (==); you're asking whether two object *references* refer to *one and the same* object. There is also a negative version (!==) of the identity operator.

A typical use case is that a class instance arrives from Cocoa, and you need to know whether it is in fact a particular object to which you already have a reference. For example, a Notification has an object property that helps identify the notification (usually, it is the original sender of the notification). We can use === to test whether this object is a certain object to which we already have a reference. However, object is typed as Any (actually, as an Optional wrapping Any), so we must cast to Any-Object in order to take advantage of the identity operator:

```
@objc func changed(_ n:Notification) {
    let player = MPMusicPlayerController.applicationMusicPlayer
    if n.object as AnyObject === player {
        // ...
    }
}
```

AnyClass

AnyClass is the type of AnyObject. It corresponds to the Objective-C Class type. It arises typically in declarations where a Cocoa API wants to say that a class is expected. The UIView layerClass class property is declared, in its Swift translation, like this:

```
class var layerClass : AnyClass {get}
```

That means that if you override this class property, you'll implement your getter to return a class (which will presumably be a CALayer subclass):

```
override class var layerClass : AnyClass { CATiledLayer.self }
```

A reference to an AnyClass object behaves much like a reference to an AnyObject object. You can send it any Objective-C message that Swift knows about — any Objective-C *class* message. To demonstrate, once again I'll start with two classes:

```
class Dog {
    @objc static var whatADogSays : String = "woof"
}
class Cat {}
```

Objective-C can see `whatADogSays`, and it sees it as a class property. Therefore you can send `whatADogSays` to an AnyClass reference:

```
let c : AnyClass = Cat.self
let s = c.whatADogSays
```

Collection Types

Swift, in common with most modern computer languages, has built-in collection types Array and Dictionary, along with a third type, Set. Array and Dictionary are sufficiently important that the language accommodates them with some special syntax.

Array

An array (Array, a struct) is an ordered collection of object instances (the *elements* of the array) accessible by index number, where an index number is an Int numbered from 0. If an array contains four elements, the first has index 0 and the last has index 3. A Swift array cannot be sparse: if there is an element with index 3, there is also an element with index 2 and so on.

The salient feature of Swift arrays is their strict typing. Unlike some other computer languages, a Swift array's elements must be *uniform* — that is, the array must consist solely of elements of the same definite type. Even an empty array must have a definite element type, despite lacking elements at this moment. An array is itself typed in accordance with its element type. Two arrays whose elements are of different types are considered, themselves, to be of two different types: an array of Int elements has a different type from an array of String elements.

If all this reminds you of Optionals, it should. Like Optional, Array is a generic. It is declared as `Array<Element>`, where the placeholder Element is the type of a particular array's elements. And, like Optional types, Array types are covariant, meaning that they behave polymorphically in accordance with their element types: if Noisy-Dog is a subclass of Dog, then an array of NoisyDog can be used where an array of Dog is expected.

To state an Array type, then, you need to state its element type. You could explicitly resolve the generic placeholder; an array of Int elements would be an `Array<Int>`.

However, Swift offers syntactic sugar using square brackets around the name of the element type, like this: [Int]. That's the syntax you'll use most of the time.

A literal array is represented as square brackets containing a list of its elements separated by a comma (and optional spaces): [1,2,3]. The literal for an empty array is empty square brackets: [].

Array's default initializer init(), called by appending empty parentheses to the array's type, yields an empty array of that type. You can create an empty array of Int like this:

```
var arr = [Int]()
```

Alternatively, if a reference's type is known in advance, the empty array [] can be inferred to that type. So you can also create an empty array of Int like this:

```
var arr : [Int] = []
```

If you're starting with a literal array containing elements, you won't usually need to declare the array's type, because Swift will infer it by looking at the elements. Swift will infer that [1,2,3] is an array of Int. If the array element types consist of a class and its subclasses, like Dog and NoisyDog, Swift will infer the common superclass as the array's type. However, in some cases you will need to declare an array reference's type explicitly even while assigning a literal to that array:

```
let arr : [Any] = [1, "howdy"]        // mixed bag
let arr2 : [Flier] = [Insect(), Bird()] // protocol adopters
```

 If an array variable is declared and initialized to a literal with many elements, it's a good idea to declare the variable's type explicitly. This saves the compiler from having to examine the entire array to decide its type, and makes compilation faster.

Array also has an initializer whose parameter is a sequence. This means that if a type is a sequence, you can split an instance of it into the elements of an array. For example:

- Array(1...3) generates the array of Int [1,2,3].

- Array("hey") generates the array of Character ["h","e","y"].

- Array(d), where d is a Dictionary, generates an array of tuples of the key–value pairs of d.

Another Array initializer, init(repeating:count:), lets you populate an array with the same value. In this example, I create an array of 100 Optional strings initialized to nil:

```
let strings : [String?] = Array(repeating:nil, count:100)
```

That's the closest you can get in Swift to a sparse array; we have 100 slots, each of which might or might not contain a string (and to start with, none of them do).

Beware of using `init(repeating:count:)` with a reference type! If Dog is a class, and you say `let dogs = Array(repeating:Dog(), count:3)`, you don't have an array of three Dogs; you have an array consisting of three *references* to *one* Dog. I'll give a workaround later.

Array casting and type testing

When you assign, pass, or cast an array of a certain type to another array type, you are really operating on the individual elements of the array:

```
let arr : [Int?] = [1,2,3]
```

That code is actually syntactic sugar: assigning an array of Int where an array of Optionals wrapping Int is expected constitutes a request that each individual Int in the original array should be wrapped in an Optional. And that is exactly what happens:

```
let arr : [Int?] = [1,2,3]
print(arr) // [Optional(1), Optional(2), Optional(3)]
```

Similarly, suppose we have a Dog class and its NoisyDog subclass; then this code is legal:

```
let dog1 : Dog = NoisyDog()
let dog2 : Dog = NoisyDog()
let arr = [dog1, dog2]
let arr2 = arr as! [NoisyDog]
```

In the third line, we have an array of Dog. In the fourth line, we apparently cast this array down to an array of NoisyDog — which really means that we cast each individual Dog in the first array to a NoisyDog. We can crash when we do that, but we won't if each element of the first array really *is* a NoisyDog.

The `as?` operator will cast an array to an Optional wrapping an array, which will be `nil` if the requested cast cannot be performed for each element individually:

```
let dog1 : Dog = NoisyDog()
let dog2 : Dog = NoisyDog()
let dog3 : Dog = Dog()
let arr = [dog1, dog2]
let arr2 = arr as? [NoisyDog] // Optional wrapping an array of NoisyDog
let arr3 = [dog2, dog3]
let arr4 = arr3 as? [NoisyDog] // nil
```

You can test each element of an array with the `is` operator by testing the array itself. Given the array of Dog from the previous code, you can say:

```
if arr is [NoisyDog] { // ...
```

That will be `true` if each element of the array is in fact a NoisyDog.

Array comparison

Array equality works just as you would expect: two arrays are equal if they contain the same number of elements and all the elements are pairwise equal in order. Of course, this presupposes that the notion "equal" is meaningful for these elements:

```
let i1 = 1
let i2 = 2
let i3 = 3
let arr : [Int] = [1,2,3]
if arr == [i1,i2,i3] { // they are equal!
```

Two arrays don't have to be of the same type to be compared against one another for equality, but the test won't succeed unless they do in fact contain objects that are equal to one another. Here, I compare a Dog array against a NoisyDog array; this is legal if equatability is defined for two Dogs. (Dog might be an NSObject subclass; or you might make Dog adopt Equatable, as I'll explain in Chapter 5.) The two arrays are in fact equal, because the dogs they contain are the same dogs in the same order:

```
let nd1 = NoisyDog()
let d1 = nd1 as Dog
let nd2 = NoisyDog()
let d2 = nd2 as Dog
let arr1 = [d1,d2] // [Dog]
let arr2 = [nd1,nd2] // [NoisyDog]
if arr1 == arr2 { // they are equal!
```

Arrays are value types

Because an array is a struct, it is a value type, not a reference type. This means that every time an array is assigned to a variable or passed as argument to a function, it is effectively copied. I do not mean to imply, however, that merely assigning or passing an array is expensive, or that a lot of actual copying takes place every time. If the reference to an array is a constant, clearly no copying is necessary; and even operations that yield a new array derived from another array, or that mutate an array, may be quite efficient. You just have to trust that the designers of Swift have thought about these problems and have implemented arrays efficiently behind the scenes.

Although an array is *itself* a value type, its *elements* might not be. If an array of class instances is assigned to multiple variables, the result is multiple references to the same instances.

Array subscripting

The Array struct implements subscript methods to allow access to elements using square brackets after a reference to an array. You can use an Int inside the square brackets. If an array is referred to by a variable `arr`, then `arr[1]` accesses the second element.

You can also use a Range of Int inside the square brackets. If `arr` is an array, then `arr[1...2]` signifies the second and third elements. Technically, an expression like `arr[1...2]` yields something called an ArraySlice, which stands in relation to Array much as Substring stands in relation to String (Chapter 3). It's very similar to an array, and in general you will probably pretend that an ArraySlice *is* an array. You can subscript an ArraySlice in just the same ways you would subscript an array. Nevertheless, they are not the same thing. An ArraySlice is not a new array; it's just a way of pointing into a section of the original array. For this reason, its index numbers are those of the original array:

```
let arr = ["manny", "moe", "jack"]
let slice = arr[1...2] // ["moe", "jack"]
print(slice[1]) // moe
```

The ArraySlice `slice` consists of two elements, `"moe"` and `"jack"`, of which `"moe"` is the first element. But these are not merely `"moe"` and `"jack"` taken *from* the original array, but the `"moe"` and `"jack"` *in* the original array. For this reason, their index numbers are not 0 and 1, but rather 1 and 2, just as in the original array. If you need to extract a new array based on this slice, coerce the slice to an Array:

```
let arr2 = Array(slice) // ["moe", "jack"]
print(arr2[1]) // jack
```

If the reference to an array is mutable (`var`, not `let`), then it's possible to assign to a subscript expression. This alters what's in that slot. Of course, what is assigned must accord with the type of the array's elements:

```
var arr = [1,2,3]
arr[1] = 4 // arr is now [1,4,3]
```

If the subscript is a range, what is assigned must be a slice. You can assign a literal array, because it will be coerced for you to an ArraySlice; but if what you're starting with is an array reference, you'll have to coerce it to a slice yourself. Such assignment can change the length of the array being assigned to:

```
var arr = [1,2,3]
arr[1..<2] = [7,8] // arr is now [1,7,8,3]
arr[1..<2] = []    // arr is now [1,8,3]
arr[1..<1] = [10]  // arr is now [1,10,8,3] (no element was removed!)
let arr2 = [20,21]
// arr[1..<1] = arr2 // compile error! You have to say this:
arr[1..<1] = ArraySlice(arr2) // arr is now [1,20,21,10,8,3]
```

Subscripting an array with a Range is an opportunity to use partial range notation. The missing value is taken to be the array's first or last index. If `arr` is `[1,2,3]`, then arr[1...] is [2,3], and arr[...1] is [1,2]. Similarly, you can assign into a range specified as a partial range:

```
var arr = [1,2,3]
arr[1...] = [4,5] // arr is now [1,4,5]
```

 It is a runtime error to access an element by an index number larger than the largest element number or smaller than the smallest element number. If arr has three elements, speaking of arr[-1] or arr[3] is not illegal linguistically, but your program will crash.

Nested arrays

It is legal for the elements of an array to be arrays:

```
let arr = [[1,2,3], [4,5,6], [7,8,9]]
```

That's an array of arrays of Int. Its type declaration, therefore, is [[Int]]. (No law says that the contained arrays have to be the same length; that's just something I did for clarity.)

To access an individual Int inside those nested arrays, you can chain subscripts:

```
let arr = [[1,2,3], [4,5,6], [7,8,9]]
let i = arr[1][1] // 5
```

If the outer array reference is mutable, you can also write into a nested array:

```
var arr = [[1,2,3], [4,5,6], [7,8,9]]
arr[1][1] = 100
```

You can modify the inner arrays in other ways as well; for example, you can insert additional elements into them.

Thanks to conditional conformance (discussed earlier in this chapter), nested arrays can be compared with == as long as the inner array's elements are Equatable. If arr and arr2 are both [[Int]], you can compare them by saying arr == arr2.

Basic array properties and methods

An array is a Collection, which is itself a Sequence. If those terms have a familiar ring, they should: the same is true of a String's underlying character sequence, which I discussed in Chapter 3. For this reason, an array and a character sequence bear some striking similarities to one another.

As a collection, an array's count read-only property reports the number of elements it contains. If an array's count is 0, its isEmpty property is true.

An array's first and last read-only properties return its first and last elements, but they are wrapped in an Optional because the array might be empty and so these properties would need to be nil. (This is one of those rare situations in Swift where you can wind up with an Optional wrapping an Optional. Consider an array of Optionals wrapping Ints, and what happens when you get its last property.)

An array's largest accessible index is one less than its count. You may find yourself calculating index values with reference to the count; to refer to the last two elements of arr, you might say:

```
let arr = [1,2,3]
let slice = arr[arr.count-2...arr.count-1] // [2,3]
```

Swift doesn't adopt the modern convention of letting you use negative indexes as a shorthand for that calculation. On the other hand, for the common case where you want the last n elements of an array, you can use the suffix(_:) method:

```
let arr = [1,2,3]
let slice = arr.suffix(2) // [2,3]
```

Therefore, a neat way to obtain, say, the next-to-last element of an array is to combine suffix with first:

```
let arr = [1,2,3]
let nextToLast = arr.suffix(2).first // Optional(2)
```

Both suffix(_:) and its companion prefix(_:) yield ArraySlices, and have the remarkable feature that there is no penalty for going out of range:

```
let arr = [1,2,3]
let slice = arr.suffix(10) // [1,2,3] (and no crash)
```

Instead of describing the size of the suffix or prefix by its count, you can express the limit of the suffix or prefix by its index. And partial range notation may provide yet another useful alternative:

```
let arr = [1,2,3]
let slice = arr.suffix(from:1)    // [2,3]
let slice2 = arr[1...]            // [2,3]
let slice3 = arr.prefix(upTo:1)   // [1]
let slice4 = arr.prefix(through:1) // [1,2]
```

An array's startIndex property is 0, and its endIndex property is its count. An array's indices property is a half-open range whose endpoints are the array's startIndex and endIndex — that is, a range accessing the entire array. Moreover, these values are Ints, so you can use ordinary arithmetic operations on them:

```
let arr = [1,2,3]
let slice = arr[arr.endIndex-2..<arr.endIndex] // [2,3]
```

But the startIndex, endIndex, and indices of an ArraySlice are measured against the original array; after the previous code, slice.indices is 1..<3, and slice.startIndex is 1.

The `firstIndex(of:)` method reports the index of the first occurrence of an element in an array, but it is wrapped in an Optional so that `nil` can be returned if the element doesn't appear in the array. In general, the comparison uses `==` behind the scenes to identify the element being sought, and therefore the array elements must adopt Equatable (otherwise the compiler will stop you):

```
let arr = [1,2,3]
let ix = arr.firstIndex(of:2) // Optional wrapping 1
```

Alternatively, you can call `firstIndex(where:)`, supplying your own function that takes an element type and returns a Bool, and you'll get back the index of the first element for which that Bool is `true`. In this example, my Bird struct has a `name` String property:

```
let aviary = [Bird(name:"Tweety"), Bird(name:"Flappy"), Bird(name:"Lady")]
let ix = aviary.firstIndex {$0.name.count < 5} // Optional(2)
```

If what you want is not the index but the object itself, the `first(where:)` method returns it — wrapped, naturally, in an Optional. These methods are matched by `lastIndex(of:)`, `lastIndex(where:)`, and `last(where:)`.

As a sequence, an array's `contains(_:)` method reports whether it contains an element. Again, you can rely on the `==` operator if the elements are Equatable, or you can supply your own function that takes an element type and returns a Bool:

```
let arr = [1,2,3]
let ok = arr.contains(2) // true
let ok2 = arr.contains {$0 > 3} // false
```

The `starts(with:)` method reports whether an array's starting elements match the elements of a given sequence of the same type. Once more, you can rely on the `==` operator for Equatable elements, or you can supply a function that takes two values of the element type and returns a Bool stating whether they match:

```
let arr = [1,2,3]
let ok = arr.starts(with:[1,2]) // true
let ok2 = arr.starts(with:[1,-2]) {abs($0) == abs($1)} // true
```

The `min` and `max` methods return the smallest or largest element in an array, wrapped in an Optional in case the array is empty. If the array consists of Comparable elements, you can let the `<` operator do its work; alternatively, you can call `min(by:)` or `max(by:)`, supplying a function that returns a Bool stating whether the smaller of two given elements is the first:

```
let arr = [3,1,-2]
let min = arr.min() // Optional(-2)
let min2 = arr.min {abs($0)<abs($1)} // Optional(1)
```

If the reference to an array is mutable, the `append(_:)` and `append(contentsOf:)` instance methods add elements to the end of it. The difference between them is that `append(_:)` takes a single value of the element type, while `append(contentsOf:)` takes a sequence of the element type:

```
var arr = [1,2,3]
arr.append(4)
arr.append(contentsOf:[5,6])
arr.append(contentsOf:7...8) // arr is now [1,2,3,4,5,6,7,8]
```

The + operator is overloaded to behave like `append(contentsOf:)` (not `append(_:)`!) when the left-hand operand is an array, except that it generates a new array, so it works even if the reference to the array is a constant (`let`). If the reference to the array is mutable (`var`), you can append to it in place with the += operator:

```
let arr = [1,2,3]
let arr2 = arr + [4] // arr2 is now [1,2,3,4]
var arr3 = [1,2,3]
arr3 += [4] // arr3 is now [1,2,3,4]
```

If the reference to an array is mutable, the instance method `insert(at:)` inserts a single element at the given index. To insert multiple elements at once, call the `insert(contentsOf:at:)` method. Assignment into a range-subscripted array, which I described earlier, is even more flexible.

If the reference to an array is mutable, the instance method `remove(at:)` removes the element at that index; the instance method `removeLast` removes the last element. These methods also *return* the value that was removed from the array; you can ignore the returned value if you don't need it. These methods do not wrap the returned value in an Optional, and accessing an out-of-range index will crash your program. On the other hand, `popLast` does wrap the returned value in an Optional, and is safe even if the array is empty.

Similar to `removeLast` and `popLast` are `removeFirst` and `popFirst`. Alternate forms `removeFirst(_:)` and `removeLast(_:)` allow you to specify how many elements to remove, but return no value; they, too, can crash if there aren't as many elements as you specify. `popFirst`, remarkably, operates on a slice, not an array, presumably for the sake of efficiency: all it has to do is increase the slice's `startIndex`, whereas with an array, the whole array must be renumbered.

Even if the reference is not mutable, you can use the `dropFirst` and `dropLast` methods to return a slice with the end element removed. Again, you can supply a parameter stating how many elements to drop. And again, there is no penalty for dropping too many elements; you simply end up with an empty slice.

The `joined(separator:)` instance method starts with an array of arrays. It extracts their individual elements, and interposes between each sequence of extracted elements the elements of the `separator:`. The result is an intermediate sequence called a

---

JoinSequence, which might have to be coerced further to an Array if that's what you were after:

```
let arr = [[1,2], [3,4], [5,6]]
let joined = Array(arr.joined(separator:[10,11]))
// [1, 2, 10, 11, 3, 4, 10, 11, 5, 6]
```

Calling `joined()` with no `separator:` is a way to flatten an array of arrays. Again, it returns an intermediate sequence (or collection), so you might want to coerce to an Array:

```
let arr = [[1,2], [3,4], [5,6]]
let arr2 = Array(arr.joined())
// [1, 2, 3, 4, 5, 6]
```

The `split` instance method breaks an array into an array of slices at elements matching the parameter, if you call `split(separator:)`, or at elements that pass a specified test, if you call `split(isSeparator:)`; in the latter, the parameter is a function that takes a value of the element type and returns a Bool. The separator elements themselves are eliminated:

```
let arr = [1,2,3,4,5,6]
let arr2 = arr.split {$0.isMultiple(of:2)} // split at evens: [[1], [3], [5]]
```

The `reversed` instance method yields a new array whose elements are in the opposite order from the original.

The `sort` and `sorted` instance methods respectively sort the original array (if the reference to it is mutable) and yield a new sorted array based on the original. Once again, you get two choices. If this is an array of Comparable elements, you can let the `<` operator dictate the new order. Alternatively, you can call `sort(by:)` or `sorted(by:)`; you supply a function that takes two parameters of the element type and returns a Bool stating whether the first parameter should be ordered before the second (just like `min` and `max`):

```
var arr = [4,3,5,2,6,1]
arr.sort() // [1, 2, 3, 4, 5, 6]
arr.sort {$0 > $1} // [6, 5, 4, 3, 2, 1]
```

In that last line, I provided an anonymous function. Alternatively, of course, you can pass as argument the name of a declared function. In Swift, comparison operators *are* the names of functions! Therefore, I can do the same thing like this:

```
var arr = [4,3,5,2,6,1]
arr.sort(by: >) // [6, 5, 4, 3, 2, 1]
```

An interesting problem is *subsorting* an array. Suppose we have a Person struct with a `firstName` and a `lastName`, and we have an array of Persons:

```
var arr = [
    Person(firstName: "Manny", lastName: "Pep"),
    Person(firstName: "Harpo", lastName: "Marx"),
    Person(firstName: "Jack", lastName: "Pep"),
    Person(firstName: "Groucho", lastName: "Marx")
]
```

We wish to sort this array by last name, but if two Persons have the *same* last name, they should be sorted by first name. In other words, all Marx brothers should precede all Pep boys, and within those groups, Groucho should precede Harpo, and Jack should precede Manny.

Cocoa provides an elegant solution, NSSortDescriptor; but Swift has no native equivalent (though there are proposals to introduce one). We could write out an elaborate comparison function; but that's an invitation to make a mistake, and won't scale if we're subsorting on many properties.

In a simple case like this one, where the comparison operator is the same for all properties, there's a trick: use *tuples*. It turns out that tuples, by default, are comparable if their element types are comparable, by a rule that a given element is compared only if all preceding elements are equal. That's exactly how we want to sort this array! So we can sort the array in accordance with the corresponding tuple:

```
arr.sort {
    ($0.lastName, $0.firstName) < ($1.lastName, $1.firstName)
}
```

The swapAt method accepts two Int index numbers and interchanges those elements of a mutable array:

```
var arr = [1,2,3]
arr.swapAt(0,2) // [3,2,1]
```

The shuffle and shuffled methods sort an array in random order, while the random-Element method generates a valid index at random and hands you the element at that index (wrapped in an Optional, in case the array is empty).

Array enumeration and transformation

An array is a sequence, and so you can enumerate it, inspecting or operating with each element in turn. The simplest way is by means of a for...in loop; I'll have more to say about this construct in Chapter 5:

```
let pepboys = ["Manny", "Moe", "Jack"]
for pepboy in pepboys {
    print(pepboy) // prints Manny, then Moe, then Jack
}
```

Alternatively, you can use the forEach(_:) instance method. Its parameter is a function that takes an element and returns no value. Think of it as the functional equivalent of the imperative for...in loop:

```
let pepboys = ["Manny", "Moe", "Jack"]
pepboys.forEach {print($0)} // prints Manny, then Moe, then Jack
```

If you need the index numbers as well as the elements, call the enumerated instance method and loop on the result; what you get on each iteration is a tuple with labels offset and element:

```
let pepboys = ["Manny", "Moe", "Jack"]
for (ix,pepboy) in pepboys.enumerated() {
    print("Pep boy \(ix) is \(pepboy)") // Pep boy 0 is Manny, etc.
}
// or:
pepboys.enumerated().forEach {
    print("Pep boy \($0.offset) is \($0.element)")
}
```

The allSatisfy(_:) method tells you whether all elements pass some test; you supply a function that takes an element and returns a Bool:

```
let pepboys = ["Manny", "Moe", "Jack"]
let ok = pepboys.allSatisfy {$0.hasPrefix("M")} // false
let ok2 = pepboys.allSatisfy {$0.hasPrefix("M") || $0.hasPrefix("J")} // true
```

Swift also provides some powerful array transformation instance methods. Like forEach(_:) and allSatisfy(_:), these methods enumerate the array for you, so that the loop is buried implicitly inside the method call, making your code tighter and cleaner.

The filter(_:) instance method yields a new array, each element of which is an element of the old array, in the same order; but some of the elements of the old array may be omitted — they were filtered out. What filters them out is a function that you supply; it accepts a parameter of the element type and returns a Bool stating whether this element should go into the new array:

```
let pepboys = ["Manny", "Moe", "Jack"]
let pepboys2 = pepboys.filter {$0.hasPrefix("M")} // ["Manny", "Moe"]
```

If the function is effectively negative, and if the reference to the collection is mutable, you should call removeAll(where:) rather whan filter(_:):

```
var pepboys = ["Manny", "Jack", "Moe"]
pepboys.removeAll {$0.hasPrefix("M")} // pepboys is now ["Jack"]
```

That's better in general than saying pepboys.filter {!$0.hasPrefix("M")} because of efficiencies achieved under the hood.

Similar to `filter(_:)` is `prefix(while:)`. The difference is that `prefix(while:)` stops looping as soon as it encounters an element for which the supplied function returns `false`; it returns the start of the original array as a slice. The complement of `prefix(while:)` is `drop(while:)`; it stops where `prefix(while:)` stops, but it returns the *rest* of the original array as a slice:

```
let pepboys = ["Manny", "Jack", "Moe"]
let arr1 = pepboys.filter {$0.hasPrefix("M")} // ["Manny", "Moe"]
let arr2 = pepboys.prefix {$0.hasPrefix("M")} // ["Manny"]
let arr3 = pepboys.drop {$0.hasPrefix("M")} // ["Jack", "Moe"]
```

The `map(_:)` instance method yields a new array, each element of which is the result of passing the corresponding element of the old array through a function that you supply. This function accepts a parameter of the element type and returns a result which may be of some other type; Swift can usually infer the type of the resulting array elements by looking at the type returned by the function.

Here's how to multiply every element of an array by 2:

```
let arr = [1,2,3]
let arr2 = arr.map {$0 * 2} // [2,4,6]
```

Here's another example, to illustrate the fact that `map(_:)` can yield an array with a different element type:

```
let arr = [1,2,3]
let arr2 = arr.map {Double($0)} // [1.0, 2.0, 3.0]
```

Here's a real-life example showing how neat and compact your code can be when you use `map(_:)`. In order to remove all the table cells in a section of a UITableView, I have to specify the cells as an array of IndexPath objects. If `sec` is the section number, I can form those IndexPath objects individually like this:

```
let path0 = IndexPath(row:0, section:sec)
let path1 = IndexPath(row:1, section:sec)
// ...
```

Hmmm, I think I see a pattern here! I could generate my array of IndexPath objects by looping through the row values using `for...in`. But with `map(_:)`, there's a much tighter way to express the same loop — namely, to loop through the range `0..<ct` (where `ct` is the number of rows in the section). Since `map(_:)` is a Collection instance method, and a Range is itself a Collection, I can call `map(_:)` directly on the range:

```
let paths = (0..<ct).map {IndexPath(row:$0, section:sec)}
```

The `map(_:)` method provides a neat alternative to `init(repeating:count:)` with a reference type:

```
let dogs = Array(repeating:Dog(), count:3) // probably a mistake
```

You probably wanted an array of three Dogs. But if Dog is a class, the array consists of three references to *one and the same* Dog instance! Instead, generate the array using map(_:), like this:

```
let dogs = (0..<3).map {_ in Dog()}
```

The map(_:) method has a specialized companion, flatMap(_:). Applied to an array, flatMap(_:) first calls map(_:), and then, if the map function produces an array of arrays, flattens it. For instance, [[1],[2]].flatMap {$0} is [1,2]. Here's a more interesting example:

```
let arr = [[1, 2], [3, 4]]
let arr2 = arr.flatMap {$0.map {String($0)}} // ["1", "2", "3", "4"]
```

First our map function calls map(_:) to coerce the individual elements of each inner array to a string, yielding an array of arrays of String: [["1", "2"], ["3", "4"]]. Then flatMap(_:) flattens the array of arrays, and we end up with a simple array of String.

Another specialized map(_:) companion is compactMap(_:). (Before Swift 4.1, this was another form of flatMap(_:).) Given a map function that produces an array of Optionals, compactMap(_:) safely unwraps them by first eliminating any nil elements. This neatly solves a type of problem that arises quite often. In particular, we can coerce or cast an array safely by eliminating those elements that *can't* be coerced or cast.

Suppose I have a mixed bag of strings, some of which represent integers. I'd like to coerce to Int those that *can* be coerced to Int, and eliminate the others. Int coercion of a String yields an Optional, so the compactMap(_:) lightbulb should go on in our heads:

```
let arr = ["1", "hey", "2", "ho"]
let arr2 = arr.compactMap {Int($0)} // [1, 2]
```

First we map the original array to an array of Optionals wrapping Int, by coercing: [Optional(1), nil, Optional(2), nil]. Then compactMap(_:) removes the nil elements and unwraps the remaining elements, resulting in an array of Int.

The reduce instance method is a way of *combining* all the elements of an array (actually, a sequence) into a single value. This value's type — the result type — doesn't have to be the same as the array's element type. reduce takes two parameters:

- You supply, as the *second* parameter, a function that takes two parameters; the first is of the result type, the second is of the element type, and the function's result is your combination of those two parameters, as the result type. That result, on each iteration, becomes the function's *first* parameter in the *next* iteration, along with the next element of the array as the *second* parameter. In this way, the output of combining pairs accumulates, and the final accumulated value is the final output of the function.

- However, that doesn't explain where the first parameter for the *first* iteration comes from. The answer is that you have to supply it as the *first* parameter of the reduce call.

That will all be easier to understand with a simple example. Let's assume we've got an array of Int. Then we can use reduce to sum the elements of the array. Here's some pseudocode where I've left out the first argument of the call, so that you can think about what it needs to be:

```
let sum = arr.reduce(/* ... */) {$0 + $1}
```

Each pair of parameters will be added together to get the first parameter ($0) on the next iteration. The second parameter on every iteration ($1) is a successive element of the array. Clearly we are just summing the elements, adding each element one by one to the accumulated total. So the remaining question is: What should the *first* element of the array be added to? We want the actual sum of all the elements, no more and no less; so the first element of the array should be added to 0:

```
let arr = [1, 4, 9, 13, 112]
let sum = arr.reduce(0) {$0 + $1} // 139
```

The + operator is the name of a function of the required type, so here's another way to write the same thing:

```
let sum = arr.reduce(0, +)
```

There is also reduce(into:), which greatly improves efficiency when the goal is to build a collection such as an array or a dictionary. The into: argument is passed into your function as an inout parameter, and persists through each iteration; instead of returning a value, your function modifies it, and the final result is its final value.

Suppose we have an array of integers, and our goal is to "deal" them into two piles consisting of the even elements and the odd elements respectively. You can't do that with a single call to map; you'd have to cycle through the original array *twice*. With reduce(into:), both target arrays are constructed while cycling through the original array *once*:

```
let nums = [1,3,2,4,5]
let result = nums.reduce(into: [[],[]]) { temp, i in
    temp[i%2].append(i)
}
// result is now [[2, 4], [1, 3, 5]]
```

Swift's array transformation methods are very powerful and very useful. In real life, your code is likely to depend heavily on all of these methods, especially filter, map, and reduce, alone or in combination, nested or chained together.

Swift Array and Objective-C NSArray

When you're programming iOS, you import the Foundation framework (or UIKit, which imports Foundation) and the Objective-C NSArray type. Swift Array is bridged to Objective-C NSArray. The most general medium of array interchange is [Any]; if an Objective-C API specifies an NSArray, with no further type information, Swift will see this as an array of Any. This reflects the fact that Objective-C's rules for what can be an element of an NSArray are looser than Swift's: the elements of an NSArray do not all have to be of the same type. On the other hand, the elements of an Objective-C NSArray must be Objective-C *objects* — that is, they must be class types.

Passing a Swift array to Objective-C is usually easy. Typically, you'll just pass the array, either by assignment or as an argument in a function call:

```
let arr = [UIBarButtonItem(), UIBarButtonItem()]
self.navigationItem.leftBarButtonItems = arr
```

The objects that you pass as elements of the array will cross the bridge to Objective-C in the usual way:

```
let lay = CAGradientLayer()
lay.locations = [0.25, 0.5, 0.75] // bridged to NSArray of NSNumber
```

CAGradientLayer's locations property needs to be an array of NSNumber. But we can pass an array of Double, because Double is bridged to NSNumber, and so Objective-C receives an NSArray of NSNumber.

To call an NSArray method on a Swift array, you may have to cast to NSArray:

```
let arr = ["Manny", "Moe", "Jack"]
let s = (arr as NSArray).componentsJoined(by:", ")
// s is "Manny, Moe, Jack"
```

A Swift Array seen through a var reference is mutable, but an NSArray isn't mutable ever. For mutability in Objective-C, you need an NSMutableArray, a subclass of NSArray. You can't cast, assign, or pass a Swift array as an NSMutableArray; you have to coerce. The best way is to call the NSMutableArray initializer init(array:), to which you can pass a Swift array directly. To convert back from an NSMutable-Array to a Swift array, you can cast:

```
var arr = ["Manny", "Moe", "Jack"]
let arr2 = NSMutableArray(array:arr)
arr2.remove("Moe")
arr = arr2 as! [String]
```

Now let's talk about what happens when an NSArray arrives from Objective-C into Swift. There won't be any problem crossing the bridge: the NSArray will arrive safely as a Swift Array. But a Swift Array *of what?*

Of itself, an NSArray carries no information about what type of element it contains. Starting in Xcode 7, however, the Objective-C language was modified so that the declaration of an NSArray, NSDictionary, or NSSet — the three collection types that are bridged to Swift — can include element type information. (Objective-C calls this a *lightweight generic*.) Thus, for the most part, the arrays you receive from Cocoa will be correctly typed.

For example, this elegant code was impossible in the bad old days before Xcode 7:

```
let arr = UIFont.familyNames.map {
    UIFont.fontNamesForFamilyName($0)
}
```

The result is an array of arrays of String, listing all available fonts grouped by family. That code is possible because both of those UIFont class methods are seen by Swift as returning an array of String. Before Xcode 7, however, those arrays were untyped, and casting down to an array of String was up to you.

Nevertheless, lightweight generics are not omnipresent. You might read an array from a *.plist* file stored on disk with NSArray's initializer `init(contentsOf:)`; you might retrieve an array from UserDefaults; you might even be dealing with an Objective-C API that hasn't been updated to use lightweight generics. In such a situation, you're going to end up with a plain vanilla NSArray or a Swift array of Any. If that happens, you will usually want to cast down or otherwise transform this array into an array of some specific Swift type. Here's an Objective-C class containing a method whose return type of NSArray hasn't been marked up with an element type:

```
@implementation Pep
- (NSArray*) boys {
    return @[@"Manny", @"Moe", @"Jack"];
}
@end
```

To call that method and do anything useful with the result, it will be necessary to cast that result down to an array of String. If I'm sure of my ground, I can force the cast:

```
let p = Pep()
let boys = p.boys() as! [String]
```

As with any cast, though, be sure you don't lie! An Objective-C array can contain more than one type of object. Don't force such an array to be cast down to a type to which not all the elements can be cast, or you'll crash when the cast fails; you'll need a more deliberate strategy (possibly involving `compactMap`) for eliminating or otherwise transforming the problematic elements.

Dictionary

A dictionary (Dictionary, a struct) is an unordered collection of object pairs. In each pair, the first object is the *key*; the second object is the *value*. The idea is that you use a key to access a value. Keys are usually strings, but they don't have to be; the formal requirement is that they be types that conform to the Hashable protocol.

For a type to be Hashable requires three things:

- The type must be Equatable.

- The type must implement an Int `hashValue` property.

- The type's implementation of equality and `hashValue` must be such that *equal keys have equal hash values*. The protocol itself cannot formally insist upon this rule, but that is what is needed for hashability to be useful and well-behaved.

The hash values can then be used behind the scenes for rapid key access. Most Swift standard types are Hashable; I'll talk in Chapter 5 about how to make your own object types Hashable.

Do not use mutable objects as keys. Mutating a key while it is in use will break the dictionary (lookup will no longer work correctly).

As with arrays, a given dictionary's types must be uniform. The key type and the value type don't have to be the same as one another, and they often will not be. But within any dictionary, all keys must be of the same type, and all values must be of the same type. Formally, a dictionary is a generic, and its placeholder types are its key type and its value type: `Dictionary<Key,Value>`. As with arrays, Swift provides syntactic sugar for expressing a dictionary's type, and that is what you'll usually use: `[Key: Value]`. That's square brackets containing a colon (and optional spaces) separating the key type from the value type. This code creates an empty dictionary whose keys (when they exist) will be Strings and whose values (when they exist) will be Strings:

```
var d = [String:String]()
```

The colon is used also between each key and value in the literal syntax for expressing a dictionary. The key–value pairs appear between square brackets, separated by a comma, just like an array. This code creates a dictionary by describing it literally (and the dictionary's type of `[String:String]` is inferred):

```
var d = ["CA": "California", "NY": "New York"]
```

If a dictionary variable is declared and initialized to a literal with many elements, it's a good idea to declare the variable's type explicitly. This saves the compiler from having to examine the entire dictionary to decide its type, and makes compilation faster.

The literal for an empty dictionary is square brackets containing just a colon: `[:]`. That notation can be used provided the dictionary's type is known in some other way. This is another way to create an empty `[String:String]` dictionary:

```
var d : [String:String] = [:]
```

You can also initialize a dictionary from a sequence of key–value tuples. This is useful particularly if you're starting with two sequences. Suppose we happen to have state abbreviations in one array and state names in another:

```
let abbrevs = ["CA", "NY"]
let names = ["California", "New York"]
```

We can combine those two arrays into a single array of tuples and call `init(unique-KeysWithValues:)` to generate a dictionary:

```
let tuples = (abbrevs.indices).map {(abbrevs[$0],names[$0])}
let d = Dictionary(uniqueKeysWithValues: tuples)
// ["NY": "New York", "CA": "California"]
```

There is actually a simpler way to form those tuples — the global `zip` function, which takes two sequences and yields a sequence of tuples:

```
let tuples = zip(abbrevs, names)
let d = Dictionary(uniqueKeysWithValues: tuples)
```

A nice feature of `zip` is that if one sequence is longer than the other, the extra elements of the longer sequence are ignored — tuple formation simply stops when the end of the shorter sequence is reached. For example, one of the zipped sequences can be a partial range; in theory the range is infinite, but in fact the end of the other sequence ends the range as well:

```
let r = 1...
let names = ["California", "New York"]
let d = Dictionary(uniqueKeysWithValues: zip(r,names))
// [2: "New York", 1: "California"]
```

If the keys in the tuple sequence are not unique, you'll crash at runtime when `init(uniqueKeysWithValues:)` is called. To work around that, you can use `init(_:uniquingKeysWith:)` instead. The second parameter is a function taking two values — the existing value for this key, and the new incoming value for the same key — and returning the value that should actually be used for this key. I'll give an example later.

Another way to form a dictionary is `init(grouping:by:)`. This is useful for forming a dictionary whose values are *arrays*. You start with a sequence of the *elements* of the arrays, and the initializer clumps them into arrays for you, in accordance with a function that generates the corresponding key from each value.

Suppose we have a list (`states`) of the 50 U.S. states in alphabetical order as an array of strings, and we want to group them by the letter they start with. Here's a verbose strategy. We loop through the list to construct two arrays (an array of String and an array of arrays of String); we then zip those arrays together to form the dictionary:

```
var sectionNames = [String]()
var cellData = [[String]]()
var previous = ""
for aState in states {
    // get the first letter
    let c = String(aState.prefix(1))
    // only add a letter to sectionNames when it's a different letter
    if c != previous {
        previous = c
        sectionNames.append(c.uppercased())
        // and in that case also add new subarray to our array of subarrays
        cellData.append([String]())
    }
    cellData[cellData.count-1].append(aState)
}
let d = Dictionary(uniqueKeysWithValues: zip(sectionNames,cellData))
// ["H": ["Hawaii"], "V": ["Vermont", "Virginia"], ...
```

With `init(grouping:by:)`, however, that becomes effectively a one-liner:

```
let d = Dictionary(grouping: states) {$0.prefix(1).uppercased()}
```

Dictionary subscripting

Access to a dictionary's contents is usually by subscripting. To fetch a value by key, use the key as a subscript:

```
let d = ["CA": "California", "NY": "New York"]
let state = d["CA"]
```

If you try to fetch a value through a nonexistent key, there is no error, but Swift needs a way to report failure; to do so, by default, it returns `nil`. This, in turn, implies that the value returned when you successfully access a value through a key must be an Optional wrapping the real value. After that code, therefore, `state` is not a String — it's an Optional wrapping a String! Forgetting this is a common beginner mistake.

You can change that behavior by supplying your own `default` value as part of the subscript. If the key isn't found in the dictionary, the `default` value is returned, and so there is no need for the returned value to be wrapped in an Optional:

```
let d = ["CA": "California", "NY": "New York"]
let state = d["MD", default:"N/A"] // state is a String (not an Optional)
```

If the reference to a dictionary is mutable, you can also assign into a key subscript expression. If the key already exists, its value is replaced. If the key doesn't already exist, it is created and the value is attached to it:

```
var d = ["CA": "California", "NY": "New York"]
d["CA"] = "Casablanca"
d["MD"] = "Maryland"
// d is now ["MD": "Maryland", "NY": "New York", "CA": "Casablanca"]
```

Instead of assigning into a subscript expression, you can call `updateValue(_:for-Key:)`; it has the advantage that it returns the old value.

As with fetching a value by key, you can supply a `default` value when assigning into a key subscript expression. This can be a source of great economy of expression. Consider the common task of collecting a histogram: we want to know how many times each element appears in a sequence:

```
let sentence = "how much wood would a wood chuck chuck"
let words = sentence.split(separator: " ").map {String($0)}
```

Our goal is now to make a dictionary pairing each word with the number of times it appears. A manual approach would be rather laborious, along these lines:

```
var d = [String:Int]()
for word in words {
    let ct = d[word]
    if ct != nil {
        d[word]! += 1
    } else {
        d[word] = 1
    }
}
// d is now ["how": 1, "wood": 2, "a": 1, "chuck": 2, "would": 1, "much": 1]
```

With a default value, it's effectively a one-liner:

```
var d = [String:Int]()
words.forEach {d[$0, default:0] += 1}
```

Earlier, I promised to give an example of `init(_:uniquingKeysWith:)`, so here it is, forming the same histogram in a silly but interesting way; I start with a values array of ones, and sum the values whenever a duplicate key is encountered:

```
let ones = Array(repeating: 1, count: words.count)
let d = Dictionary(zip(words,ones)) {$0+$1}
```

By a kind of shorthand, assigning `nil` into a key subscript expression removes that key–value pair if it exists:

```
var d = ["CA": "California", "NY": "New York"]
d["NY"] = nil // d is now ["CA": "California"]
```

Alternatively, call `removeValue(forKey:)`; it has the advantage that it returns the removed value before it removes the key–value pair.

Dictionaries have no order

Dictionaries are *unordered*. Whenever you probe a dictionary's entire contents — when you `print` them, when you cycle through them with `for...in`, and so forth — each entry arrives in a completely unpredictable order. If you run the same code as I do (indeed, even if you run the same code as yourself on two different occasions), your results may be ordered differently. This makes no difference to the actual contents of the dictionary, which consists of particular keys, each associated with a particular value. `[2: "New York", 1: "California"]` is actually the same dictionary as `[1: "California", 2: "New York"]`.

If you needed order to be meaningful, you were thinking of an array, not a dictionary. To put it another way, you can have rapid access by key or meaningful order with rapid access by index number, but not both. For an ordered array of key-value pairs — with no subscripting by key, no hashability requirement, and no guaranteed uniqueness of keys — you can use a KeyValuePairs object, which is essentially an array of tuples with labels `key` and `value`; it can be initialized from a dictionary literal:

```
let pairs : KeyValuePairs = ["CA": "California", "NY": "New York"]
print(pairs.count) // 2
print(pairs[0]) // (key: "CA", value: "California")
// to access by key, cycle through the array
if let pair = pairs.first(where: {$0.key == "NY"}) {
    let val = pair.value // New York
}
```

Dictionary casting and comparison

As with arrays, a dictionary type is legal for casting down, meaning that the individual elements will be cast down. Typically, only the value types will differ:

```
let dog1 : Dog = NoisyDog()
let dog2 : Dog = NoisyDog()
let d = ["fido": dog1, "rover": dog2]
let d2 = d as! [String : NoisyDog]
```

As with arrays, `is` can be used to test the actual types in the dictionary, and `as?` can be used to test and cast safely.

Dictionary equality is like array equality. Key types are necessarily Equatable, because they are Hashable. Value types are not necessarily Equatable, but if they are, the `==` and `!=` operators work as you would expect.

Basic dictionary properties and enumeration

A dictionary has a `count` property reporting the number of key–value pairs it contains, and an `isEmpty` property reporting whether that number is 0.

A dictionary has a `keys` property reporting all its keys, and a `values` property reporting all its values. These are effectively opaque structs providing a specialized view of the dictionary itself. You can't assign one to a variable, or print it out, but you can work with them as collections. For example, you can enumerate them with `for...in` (though you should not expect them to arrive in any particular order, as a dictionary is unordered):

```
var d = ["CA": "California", "NY": "New York"]
for s in d.keys {
    print(s) // NY, then CA (or vice versa)
}
```

You can coerce them to an array:

```
var d = ["CA": "California", "NY": "New York"]
var keys = Array(d.keys) // ["NY", "CA"] or ["CA", "NY"]
```

You can sort them, filter them, or map them (yielding an array); you can take their min or max; you can reduce them; you can compare keys of different dictionaries for equality:

```
let d : [String:Int] = ["one":1, "two":2, "three":3]
let keysSorted = d.keys.sorted() // ["one", "three", "two"]
let arr = d.values.filter {$0 < 2} // [1]
let min = d.values.min() // Optional(1)
let sum = d.values.reduce(0, +) // 6
let ok = d.keys == ["one":1, "three":3, "two":2].keys // true
```

You can also enumerate a dictionary itself. Each iteration provides a key–value tuple (arriving in no particular order, because a dictionary is unordered):

```
var d = ["CA": "California", "NY": "New York"]
for (abbrev, state) in d {
    print("\(abbrev) stands for \(state)")
}
```

The tuple members have labels key and value, so the preceding example can be rewritten like this:

```
var d = ["CA": "California", "NY": "New York"]
for pair in d {
    print("\(pair.key) stands for \(pair.value)")
}
```

You can extract a dictionary's entire contents at once as an array of key–value tuples (in an unpredictable order) by coercing the dictionary to an array:

```
var d = ["CA": "California", "NY": "New York"]
let arr = Array(d)
// [(key: "NY", value: "New York"), (key: "CA", value: "California")]
```

When you apply filter to a dictionary, what you get is a dictionary. In addition, there's a mapValues method that yields a dictionary with its values changed according to your map function:

```
let d = ["CA": "California", "NY": "New York"]
let d2 = d.filter {$0.value > "New Jersey"}.mapValues {$0.uppercased()}
// ["NY": "NEW YORK"]
```

There's also a compactMapValues method that applies a map function yielding an Optional and filters out any keys for which the resulting value is nil.

You can combine two dictionaries with the merging(_:uniquingKeysWith:) method — or, if your reference to the first dictionary is mutable, you can call merge to modify it directly. The second parameter is like the second parameter of init(_:uniquing-KeysWith:), saying what the value should be in case the second dictionary has a key matching an existing key in the first dictionary:

```
let d1 = ["CA": "California", "NY": "New York"]
let d2 = ["MD": "Maryland", "NY": "New York"]
let d3 = d1.merging(d2) {orig, _ in orig}
// ["MD": "Maryland", "NY": "New York", "CA": "California"]
```

Swift Dictionary and Objective-C NSDictionary

The Foundation framework dictionary type is NSDictionary, and Swift Dictionary is bridged to it. The untyped API characterization of an NSDictionary will be [Any-Hashable:Any]. (AnyHashable is a *type eraser* struct, to cope with the possibility, legal in Objective-C, that the keys may be of different Hashable types.)

Like NSArray element types, NSDictionary key and value types can be marked in Objective-C using a lightweight generic. The most common key type in a real-life Cocoa NSDictionary is NSString, so you might well receive an NSDictionary typed as [String:Any]. Specific typing of an NSDictionary's *values* is rare, because dictionaries that you pass to and receive from Cocoa will often have values of multiple types; it is not surprising to have a dictionary whose keys are strings but whose values include a string, a number, a color, and an array. For this reason, you will usually *not* cast down the entire dictionary's type; instead, you'll work with the dictionary as having Any values, and cast when fetching an *individual value* from the dictionary. Since the value returned from subscripting a key is itself an Optional, you will typically unwrap and cast the value as a standard single move.

Here's an example. A Cocoa Notification object comes with a userInfo property. It is an NSDictionary that might itself be nil, so the Swift API characterizes it as [Any-Hashable:Any]?. Let's say I'm expecting this dictionary to be present and to contain a "progress" key whose value is an NSNumber containing a Double. My goal is to extract that NSNumber and assign the Double that it contains to a property, self.progress. Here's one way to do that safely, using optional unwrapping and optional casting (n is the Notification object):

```
let prog = n.userInfo?["progress"] as? Double
if prog != nil {
    self.progress = prog!
}
```

The variable prog is implicitly typed as an Optional wrapping a Double. The code is safe, because if there is no userInfo dictionary, or if it doesn't contain a "progress" key, or if that key's value isn't a Double, nothing happens, and prog will be nil.

I then test prog to see whether it *is* nil; if it isn't, I know that it's safe to force-unwrap it, and that the unwrapped value is the Double I'm after.

(In Chapter 5 I'll describe another syntax for accomplishing the same goal, using conditional binding.)

Conversely, here's a typical example of creating a dictionary and handing it off to Cocoa. This dictionary is a mixed bag: its values are a UIFont, a UIColor, and an NSShadow. Its keys are all strings, which I obtain as constants from Cocoa. I form the dictionary as a literal and pass it, all in one move, with no need to cast anything:

```
UINavigationBar.appearance().titleTextAttributes = [
    .font: UIFont(name: "ChalkboardSE-Bold", size: 20)!,
    .foregroundColor: UIColor.darkText,
    .shadow.: {
        let shad = NSShadow()
        shad.shadowOffset = CGSize(width:1.5,height:1.5)
        return shad
    }()
]
```

As with NSArray and NSMutableArray, if you want Cocoa to mutate a dictionary, you must coerce to NSDictionary's subclass NSMutableDictionary:

```
var d1 = ["NY":"New York", "CA":"California"]
let d2 = ["MD":"Maryland"]
let mutd1 = NSMutableDictionary(dictionary:d1)
mutd1.addEntries(from:d2)
d1 = mutd1 as! [String:String]
// d1 is now ["MD": "Maryland", "NY": "New York", "CA": "California"]
```

Set

A set (Set, a struct) is an *unordered* collection of *unique* objects. Its elements must be all of one type; it has a count and an isEmpty property; it can be initialized from any sequence; you can cycle through its elements with for...in (where the order of elements is unpredictable).

The uniqueness of set elements is implemented by constraining their type to be Hashable (and hence Equatable), just like the keys of a dictionary, so that the hash values can be used behind the scenes for rapid access. Checking whether a set contains a given element, which you can do with the contains(_:) instance method, is *very* efficient — far more efficient than doing the same thing with an array. Therefore, if element uniqueness is acceptable (or desirable) and you don't need indexing or a guaranteed order, a set can be a much better choice of collection than an array.

 The warnings in the preceding section apply: don't store a mutable value in a Set, and don't expect Set values to be reported to you in any particular order. I'll talk in Chapter 5 about how to make your own types Hashable.

There are no set literals in Swift, but you won't need them because you can pass an array literal where a set is expected. There is no syntactic sugar for expressing a set type, but the Set struct is a generic, so you can express the type by explicitly specializing the generic:

```
let set : Set<Int> = [1, 2, 3, 4, 5]
```

In that particular example there was no real need to specialize the generic, as the Int type can be inferred from the array. However, when setting a Set variable from a literal, it is more efficient to specialize the generic. This saves the compiler the trouble of reading the whole literal.

It sometimes happens (more often than you might suppose) that you want to examine one element of a set as a kind of sample. Order is meaningless, so it's sufficient to obtain *any* element, such as the first element. For this purpose, use the `first` instance property; it returns an Optional, just in case the set is empty.

The distinctive feature of a set is the uniqueness of its objects. If an object is added to a set and that object is already present, it isn't added a second time. Conversion from an array to a set and back to an array is a quick and reliable way of *uniquing* the array — though of course order is not preserved:

```
let arr = [1,2,1,3,2,4,3,5]
let set = Set(arr)
let arr2 = Array(set) // [5, 2, 3, 1, 4], perhaps
```

A set is a Collection and a Sequence. Like Array, Set has a `map(_:)` instance method; it returns an array, but of course you can turn that right back into a set if you need to:

```
let set : Set = [1,2,3,4,5]
let set2 = Set(set.map {$0+1}) // Set containing 2, 3, 4, 5, 6
```

On the other hand, applying `filter` to a Set yields a Set directly:

```
let set : Set = [1,2,3,4,5]
let set2 = set.filter {$0>3} // Set containing 4, 5
```

If the reference to a set is mutable, you can add an object to it with `insert(_:)`; there is no penalty for trying to add an object that's already in the set, but the object won't be added. `insert(_:)` also returns a result, a tuple whose `inserted` element will be `false` if an equivalent object was already present in the set. This result is usually disregarded, but it can sometimes be useful; here, we use it to unique an array while preserving its order:

```
var arr = ["Manny", "Manny", "Moe", "Jack", "Jack", "Moe", "Manny"]
var temp = Set<String>()
arr = arr.filter { temp.insert($0).inserted }
```

The other element of the tuple returned by `insert(_:)` is `memberAfterInsert`. If `inserted` is `true`, this is simply the parameter of `insert(_:)`. If `inserted` is `false`, however, it is the existing member of the set that caused the insertion to fail because it is regarded as equal to the parameter of insert(_:); this may be of interest because it tells you *why* the insertion was rejected.

Instead of insert(_:), you can call update(with:); the difference is that if you're trying to add an object that already has an equivalent in the set, the former doesn't insert the new object, but the latter *always* inserts, replacing the old object (if there is one) with the new one.

You can remove an object and return it by specifying an equivalent object with the remove(_:) method; it returns the object from the set, wrapped in an Optional, or nil if the object was not present. You can remove and return an arbitrary object from the set with removeFirst; it crashes if the set is empty, so take precautions — or use popFirst, which is safe.

Equality comparison (==) is defined for sets as you would expect; two sets are equal if every element of each is equal to an element of the other.

If the notion of a set evokes visions of Venn diagrams from elementary school, that's good, because sets have instance methods giving you all those set operations you remember so fondly. The parameter can be a set, or it can be any sequence, which will be converted to a set; it might be an array, a range, or even a character sequence:

intersection(_:), formIntersection(_:)
> Yields the elements of this set that also appear in the parameter. The first forms a new Set; the second is mutating.

union(_:), formUnion(_:)
> Yields the elements of this set along with the (unique) elements of the parameter. The first forms a new Set; the second is mutating.

symmetricDifference(_:), formSymmetricDifference(_:)
> Yields the elements of this set that don't appear in the parameter, plus the (unique) elements of the parameter that don't appear in this set. The first forms a new Set; the second is mutating.

subtracting(_:), subtract(_:)
> Yields the elements of this set except for those that appear in the parameter. The first forms a new Set; the second is mutating.

isSubset(of:), isStrictSubset(of:)
isSuperset(of:), isStrictSuperset(of:)
> Returns a Bool reporting whether the elements of this set are respectively embraced by or embrace the elements of the parameter. The "strict" variant yields false if the two sets consist of the same elements.

```
isDisjoint(with:)
```
   Returns a Bool reporting whether this set and the parameter have no elements in common.

Here's a real-life example of Set usage from one of my apps. I have a lot of numbered pictures, of which we are to choose one randomly. But I don't want to choose a picture that has recently been chosen. Therefore, I keep a list of the numbers of all recently chosen pictures. When it's time to choose a new picture, I convert the list of all possible numbers to a Set, convert the list of recently chosen picture numbers to a Set, and call subtracting(_:) to get a list of unused picture numbers! Now I choose a picture number at random and add it to the list of recently chosen picture numbers:

```
let ud = UserDefaults.standard
let recents = ud.object(forKey: Defaults.recents) as? [Int] ?? []
var forbiddenNumbers = Set(recents)
let legalNumbers = Set(1...PIXCOUNT).subtracting(forbiddenNumbers)
let newNumber = legalNumbers.randomElement()!
forbiddenNumbers.insert(newNumber)
ud.set(Array(forbiddenNumbers), forKey:Defaults.recents)
```

Option sets

An *option set* (OptionSet struct) is Swift's way of treating a certain type of Cocoa enumeration as a Swift struct. It is not, strictly speaking, a Set; but it is deliberately set-like, sharing common features with Set through the SetAlgebra protocol. An option set has contains(_:), insert(_:), and remove(_:) methods, along with all the various set operation methods.

The purpose of option sets is to help you grapple with Objective-C *bitmasks*. A bitmask is an integer whose bits are used as switches when multiple options are to be specified simultaneously. Bitmasks are very common in Cocoa. In Objective-C, bitmasks are manipulated through the arithmetic bitwise-or and bitwise-and operators. Such manipulation can be mysterious and error-prone. But in Swift, thanks to option sets, bitmasks can be manipulated easily through set operations instead.

For example, when specifying how a UIView is to be animated, you are allowed to pass an options: argument whose value comes from the UIView.AnimationOptions enumeration, whose definition (in Objective-C) begins:

```
typedef NS_OPTIONS(NSUInteger, UIViewAnimationOptions) {
    UIViewAnimationOptionLayoutSubviews          = 1 << 0,
    UIViewAnimationOptionAllowUserInteraction    = 1 << 1,
    UIViewAnimationOptionBeginFromCurrentState   = 1 << 2,
    UIViewAnimationOptionRepeat                  = 1 << 3,
    UIViewAnimationOptionAutoreverse             = 1 << 4,
    // ...
};
```

Pretend that an NSUInteger is 8 bits (it isn't, but let's keep things simple and short). Then this enumeration means that (in Swift) the following name–value pairs are defined:

```
UIView.AnimationOptions.layoutSubviews          0b00000001
UIView.AnimationOptions.allowUserInteraction    0b00000010
UIView.AnimationOptions.beginFromCurrentState   0b00000100
UIView.AnimationOptions.repeat                  0b00001000
UIView.AnimationOptions.autoreverse             0b00010000
```

These values can be combined into a single value — a *bitmask* — that you pass as the `options:` argument for your animation. All Cocoa has to do to understand your intentions is to look to see which bits in the value that you pass are set to 1. So, for example, `0b00011000` would mean that `UIView.AnimationOptions.repeat` and `UIView.AnimationOptions.autoreverse` are both true (and that the others are all false).

The question is how to *form* the value `0b00011000` in order to pass it. You could form it directly as a literal and set the `options:` argument to `UIView.Animation-Options(rawValue:0b00011000)`; but that's not a very good idea, because it's error-prone and makes your code incomprehensible. In Objective-C, you'd use the arithmetic bitwise-or operator, analogous to this Swift code:

```
let val =
    UIView.AnimationOptions.autoreverse.rawValue |
    UIView.AnimationOptions.repeat.rawValue
let opts = UIView.AnimationOptions(rawValue: val)
```

That's rather ugly! However, help is on the way: The UIView.AnimationOptions type is an option set struct in Swift (because it is marked as `NS_OPTIONS` in Objective-C), and therefore can be treated much like a Set. Given a UIView.AnimationOptions value, you can add an option to it using `insert(_:)`:

```
var opts = UIView.AnimationOptions.autoreverse
opts.insert(.repeat)
```

Alternatively, you can start with an array literal, just as if you were initializing a Set:

```
let opts : UIView.AnimationOptions = [.autoreverse, .repeat]
```

 To indicate that no options are to be set, pass an empty option set (`[]`) or, where permitted, omit the `options:` parameter altogether.

Sometimes Cocoa hands *you* a bitmask, and you want to know whether a certain bit is set. In this example from a UITableViewCell subclass, the cell's `state` comes to us as a bitmask; we want to know about the bit indicating that the cell is showing its edit control. The Objective-C way is to extract the raw values and use the bitwise-and operator:

```
override func didTransition(to state: UITableViewCell.StateMask) {
    let editing = UITableViewCell.StateMask.showingEditControl.rawValue
    if state.rawValue & editing != 0 {
        // ... the ShowingEditControl bit is set ...
    }
}
```

That's a tricky formula, all too easy to get wrong. But in Swift this is an option set, so the contains(_:) method tells you the answer:

```
override func didTransition(to state: UITableViewCell.StateMask) {
    if state.contains(.showingEditControl) {
        // ... the ShowingEditControl bit is set ...
    }
}
```

Swift Set and Objective-C NSSet

Swift's Set type is bridged to Objective-C NSSet. The untyped medium of interchange is Set<AnyHashable>. Coming back from Objective-C, if Objective-C doesn't know what this is a set of, you would probably cast down as needed. As with NSArray, however, NSSet can be marked up using lightweight generics to indicate its element type, in which case no casting will be necessary:

```
override func touchesBegan(_ touches: Set<UITouch>, with event: UIEvent?) {
    let t = touches.first // an Optional wrapping a UITouch
    // ...
}
```

CHAPTER 5

Flow Control and More

This chapter is a miscellany. I'll start by describing Swift's flow control constructs for branching, looping, and jumping. Then, I'll summarize Swift's privacy and introspection features, and talk about how to override operators and how to create your own operators. Next, I'll explain some specialized aspects of Swift memory management. Finally, I'll survey some recently added Swift language features: synthesized protocol implementations, key paths, instance as function, dynamic members, property wrappers, custom string interpolation, reverse generics, function builders, and Result.

Flow Control

A computer program has a *path of execution* through its code statements. Normally, this path follows a simple rule: execute each statement in succession. But there is another possibility. *Flow control* can be used to make the path of execution skip some statements, or go back and repeat some statements.

Flow control is what makes a computer program "intelligent." By testing in real time the truth value of a *condition* — an expression that evaluates to a Bool and is thus `true` or `false` — the program decides *at that moment* how to proceed. Flow control based on testing a condition may be divided into two general types:

Branching
> The code is divided into alternative chunks, like roads that diverge in a wood, and the program is presented with a choice of possible ways to go; the truth of a condition is used to determine which chunk will actually be executed.

Looping
> A chunk of code is marked off for possible repetition; the truth of a condition is used to determine whether the chunk should be executed, and then whether it should be executed again. Each repetition is called an *iteration*.

The chunks of code in flow control, which I refer to as *blocks*, are demarcated by curly braces. These curly braces constitute a scope (Chapter 1). New local variables can be declared here, and go out of existence automatically when the path of execution exits the curly braces (Chapter 3). For a loop, this means that local variables come into existence and go out of existence on each iteration. As with any scope, code inside the curly braces can see the surrounding higher scope.

Swift flow control is fairly simple, and by and large is similar to flow control in C and related languages. There are two fundamental syntactic differences between Swift and C, both of which make Swift simpler and clearer:

- A condition *does not have to be wrapped in parentheses* in Swift.
- The curly braces *can never be omitted* in Swift.

Moreover, Swift adds some specialized flow control features to help you grapple more conveniently with Optionals, and boasts a particularly powerful form of switch statement.

Branching

Swift has two forms of branching: the if construct, and the switch statement. I'll also discuss conditional evaluation, a compact form of if construct.

If construct

The Swift branching construct with `if` is similar to C. Many examples of if constructs have appeared already in this book. The construct may be formally summarized as shown in Example 5-1.

Example 5-1. The Swift if construct

```
if condition {
    statements
}

if condition {
    statements
} else {
    statements
}

if condition {
    statements
} else if condition {
    statements
} else {
    statements
}
```

The third form, containing else if, can have as many else if blocks as needed, and the final else block may be omitted.

Here's a real-life if construct that lies at the heart of one of my apps:

```
// okay, we've tapped a tile; there are three cases
if self.selectedTile == nil { // no selected tile: select and play this tile
    self.select(tile:tile)
    self.play(tile:tile)
} else if self.selectedTile == tile { // selected tile tapped: deselect it
    self.deselectAll()
    self.player?.pause()
} else { // there was a selected tile, another tile was tapped: swap them
    self.swap(self.selectedTile, with:tile, check:true, fence:true)
}
```

Conditional binding

In Swift, if can be followed immediately by a variable declaration and assignment — that is, by let or var and a new local variable name, possibly followed by a colon and a type declaration, then an equal sign and a value:

```
if let var = val {
    // the block
}
```

This syntax, called a *conditional binding*, is actually a shorthand for *conditionally unwrapping an Optional*. The assigned value (*val*) is expected to be an Optional — the compiler will stop you if it isn't — and this is what happens:

- If the Optional (*val*) is nil, the condition fails and the block is skipped, with execution resuming after the block.

- If the Optional is *not* nil, then:

    1. The Optional is unwrapped.

    2. The unwrapped value is assigned to the declared local variable (*var*).

    3. The block is executed with the local variable in scope. The local variable is *not* in scope outside the block.

So a conditional binding safely passes an unwrapped Optional into a block. The Optional is unwrapped, and the block is executed, only if the Optional *can* be unwrapped.

It is perfectly reasonable for the local variable in a conditional binding to have the same name as an existing variable in the surrounding scope. It can even have the same name as the Optional being unwrapped! There is then no need to make up a new name, and inside the block the unwrapped value of the Optional neatly overshadows the original Optional so that the latter can't be accessed accidentally.

Recall this code from Chapter 4, where I optionally unwrap a Notification's `userInfo` dictionary, attempt to fetch a value from the dictionary using the `"progress"` key, and proceed only if that value turns out to be an NSNumber that can be cast down to a Double:

```
let prog = n.userInfo?["progress"] as? Double
if prog != nil {
    self.progress = prog!
}
```

We can rewrite that code more elegantly and compactly as a conditional binding:

```
if let prog = n.userInfo?["progress"] as? Double {
    self.progress = prog
}
```

It is also possible to nest conditional bindings. To illustrate, I'll rewrite the previous example to use a separate conditional binding for each Optional in the chain:

```
if let ui = n.userInfo {
    if let prog = ui["progress"] as? Double {
        self.progress = prog
    }
}
```

The result, if the chain involves many optional unwrappings, can be somewhat verbose and the nest can become deeply indented — Swift programmers like to call this the "pyramid of doom." To help avoid the indentation, successive conditional bindings can be combined into a *condition list*, with each condition separated by a comma:

```
if let ui = n.userInfo, let prog = ui["progress"] as? Double {
    self.progress = prog
}
```

In that code, the assignment to `prog` won't even be attempted if `n.userInfo` is `nil`; the assignment to `ui` fails and that's the end.

Condition lists do not have to consist solely of conditional bindings. They can include ordinary conditions. The important thing is the left-to-right order of evaluation, which allows each condition to depend upon the previous one. It would be possible (though not as elegant) to rewrite the previous example like this:

```
if let ui = n.userInfo, let prog = ui["progress"], prog is Double {
    self.progress = prog as! Double
}
```

Nevertheless, I am not fond of this kind of extended condition list. I actually prefer the pyramid of doom, where the structure reflects perfectly the successive stages of testing. If I want to avoid the pyramid of doom, I can usually use a sequence of `guard` statements ("Guard" on page 292):

```
guard let ui = n.userInfo else {return}
guard let prog = ui["progress"] as? Double else {return}
self.progress = prog
```

Switch statement

A switch statement is a neater way of writing an extended if...else if...else construct. In C (and Objective-C), a switch statement contains hidden traps; Swift eliminates those traps, and adds power and flexibility. As a result, switch statements are commonly used in Swift (whereas they are relatively rare in my Objective-C code).

In a switch statement, the condition involves the comparison of different possible values, called *cases*, against a single value, called the *tag*. The case comparisons are performed *successively in order*. As soon as a case comparison succeeds, that case's code is executed and the entire switch statement is exited. The schema is shown in Example 5-2; there can be as many cases as needed, and the default case can be omitted (subject to restrictions that I'll explain in a moment).

Example 5-2. The Swift switch statement

```
switch tag {
case pattern1:
    statements
case pattern2:
    statements
default:
    statements
}
```

Here's an actual example:

```
switch i {
case 1:
    print("You have 1 thingy!")
case 2:
    print("You have 2 thingies!")
default:
    print("You have \(i) thingies!")
}
```

In that code, an Int variable i functions as the tag. The value of i is first compared to the value 1. If it *is* 1, that case's code is executed and that's all. If it is *not* 1, it is compared to the value 2. If it *is* 2, *that* case's code is executed and that's all. If the value of i matches neither of those, the default case's code is executed.

In Swift, a switch statement must be *exhaustive*. This means that *every* possible value of the tag must be covered by a case. The compiler will stop you if you try to violate this rule. If you don't want to write every case explicitly, you must add a "mop-up" case that covers all other cases; a common way to do that is to add a `default` case. It's easy to write an exhaustive switch when the tag is an enum with a small number of cases, but when the tag is an Int, there is an infinite number of possible cases, so a "mop-up" case *must* appear.

Each case's code can consist of multiple statements; it doesn't have to be a single statement, like the cases in the preceding example. However, it must consist of *at least* a single statement; it is illegal for a Swift switch case to be empty. It is legal for the first (or only) statement of a case's code to appear on the same line as the case, after the colon; I could have written the preceding example like this:

```
switch i {
case 1: print("You have 1 thingy!")
case 2: print("You have 2 thingies!")
default: print("You have \(i) thingies!")
}
```

The minimum single statement of case code is the keyword `break`; used in this way, `break` acts as a placeholder meaning, "Do nothing." It is very common for a switch statement to include a `default` (or other "mop-up" case) consisting of nothing but the keyword `break`; in this way, you exhaust all possible values of the tag, but if the value is one that no case explicitly covers, you do nothing.

Now let's focus on the comparison between the tag value and the case value. In the preceding example, it works like an equality comparison (==); but that isn't the only possibility. In Swift, a case value is actually a special expression called a *pattern*, and the pattern is compared to the tag value using a "secret" pattern-matching operator, ~=. The more you know about the syntax for constructing a pattern, the more powerful your case values and your switch statements will be.

A pattern can include an underscore (_) to absorb all values without using them. An underscore case is thus an alternative form of "mop-up" case:

```
switch i {
case 1:
    print("You have 1 thingy!")
case _:
    print("You have many thingies!")
}
```

A pattern can include a declaration of a local variable name (an unconditional binding) to absorb all values and use the actual value. This is yet another alternative form of "mop-up" case:

```
switch i {
case 1:
    print("You have 1 thingy!")
case let n:
    print("You have \(n) thingies!")
}
```

When the tag is a Comparable, a case can include a Range; the test involves sending the Range the contains message:

```
switch i {
case 1:
    print("You have 1 thingy!")
case 2...10:
    print("You have \(i) thingies!")
default:
    print("You have more thingies than I can count!")
}
```

A Range pattern can be an opportunity to use partial range syntax:

```
switch i {
case ..<0:
    print("i is negative, namely \(i)")
case 1...:
    print("i is positive, namely \(i)")
case 0:
    print("i is 0")
default:break
}
```

When the tag is an Optional, a case can test it against nil. Moreover, appending ? to a case pattern safely unwraps an Optional tag. Presume that i is an Optional wrapping an Int:

```
switch i {
case 1?:
    print("You have 1 thingy!")
case let n?:
    print("You have \(n) thingies!")
case nil: break
}
```

When the tag is a Bool, a case can test it against a condition. Thus, by a clever perversion, you can use the cases to test *any* conditions you like by using true as the tag; a switch statement becomes a genuine substitute for an extended if...else if construct. In this example from my own code, I could have used if...else if, but a switch statement seems cleaner:

```
func position(for bar: UIBarPositioning) -> UIBarPosition {
    switch true {
    case bar === self.navbar:  return .topAttached
    case bar === self.toolbar: return .bottom
    default:                   return .any
    }
}
```

A pattern can include a where clause adding a condition to limit the truth value of the case. This is often, though not necessarily, used in combination with a binding; the condition can refer to the variable declared in the binding:

```
switch i {
case let j where j < 0:
    print("i is negative, namely \(j)")
case let j where j > 0:
    print("i is positive, namely \(j)")
case 0:
    print("i is 0")
default:break
}
```

A pattern can include the is operator to test the tag's type. In this example, we have a Dog class and its NoisyDog subclass, and d is typed as Dog:

```
switch d {
case is NoisyDog:
    print("You have a noisy dog!")
case _:
    print("You have a dog")
}
```

A pattern can include a cast with the as (not as?) operator. Typically, you'll combine this with a binding that declares a local variable; despite the use of unconditional as, the value is conditionally cast and, if the cast succeeds, the local variable carries the cast value into the case code. Again, d is typed as Dog, which has a NoisyDog subclass; assume that Dog implements bark and that NoisyDog implements beQuiet:

```
switch d {
case let nd as NoisyDog:
    nd.beQuiet()
case let d:
    d.bark()
}
```

You can also use as (not as?) to cast down the tag (and possibly unwrap it) conditionally as part of a test against a specific match. In this example, i might be an Any or an Optional wrapping an Any:

```
switch i {
case 0 as Int:
    print("It is 0")
default:break
}
```

You can perform multiple tests at once by expressing the tag as a tuple and wrapping the corresponding tests in a tuple. The case passes only if every test in the case tuple succeeds against the corresponding member of the tag tuple. In this example, we start with a dictionary d typed as [String:Any]. Using a tuple, we can safely attempt to fetch and cast two values at once:

```
switch (d["size"], d["desc"]) {
case let (size as Int, desc as String):
    print("You have size \(size) and it is \(desc)")
default:break
}
```

When a tag is an enum, the cases can be cases of the enum. A switch statement is thus an excellent way to handle an enum. Here's the Filter enum from Chapter 4:

```
enum Filter {
    case albums
    case playlists
    case podcasts
    case books
}
```

And here's a switch statement, where the tag, type, is a Filter; no mop-up is needed, because I've exhausted the cases:

```
switch type {
case .albums:
    print("Albums")
case .playlists:
    print("Playlists")
case .podcasts:
    print("Podcasts")
case .books:
    print("Books")
}
```

 If an enum comes from Objective-C (or C) or the Swift standard library, an exhaustive switch over it might get you a warning from the compiler that the enum "may have additional unknown values." I'll explain what that means, and what to do about it, in Appendix A.

A switch statement provides a way to extract an associated value from an enum case. Recall this enum from Chapter 4:

```
enum MyError {
    case number(Int)
    case message(String)
    case fatal
}
```

If a case of the enum has an associated value, a tuple of patterns after the matched case name is applied to the associated value. If a pattern is a binding variable, it captures the associated value. The let (or var) can appear inside the parentheses or after the case keyword; this code illustrates both alternatives:

```
switch err {
case .number(let theNumber):
    print("It is a number: \(theNumber)")
case let .message(theMessage):
    print("It is a message: \(theMessage)")
case .fatal:
    print("It is fatal")
}
```

If the let (or var) appears after the case keyword, I can add a where clause:

```
switch err {
case let .number(n) where n > 0:
    print("It's a positive error number \(n)")
case let .number(n) where n < 0:
    print("It's a negative error number \(n)")
case .number(0):
    print("It's a zero error number")
default:break
}
```

If I don't want to extract the error number but just want to match against it, I can use some other pattern inside the parentheses:

```
switch err {
case .number(1...):
    print("It's a positive error number")
case .number(..<0):
    print("It's a negative error number")
case .number(0):
    print("It's a zero error number")
default:break
}
```

This same pattern also gives us yet another way to deal with an Optional tag. An Optional, as I explained in Chapter 4, is in fact an enum. It has two cases, .none and .some, where the wrapped value is the .some case's associated value. But now we know how to extract the associated value! We can rewrite yet again the earlier example where i is an Optional wrapping an Int:

```
switch i {
case .none: break
case .some(1):
    print("You have 1 thingy!")
case .some(let n):
    print("You have \(n) thingies!")
}
```

To combine switch case tests (with an implicit logical-or), separate them with a comma:

```
switch i {
case 1,3,5,7,9:
    print("You have a small odd number of thingies")
case 2,4,6,8,10:
    print("You have a small even number of thingies")
default:
    print("You have too many thingies for me to count")
}
```

In this example, i is declared as an Any:

```
switch i {
case is Int, is Double:
    print("It's some kind of number")
default:
    print("I don't know what it is")
}
```

A comma can even combine patterns that declare binding variables, provided they declare the same variable of the same type (err is our MyError once again):

```
switch err {
case let .number(n) where n > 0, let .number(n) where n < 0:
    print("It's a nonzero error number \(n)")
case .number(0):
    print("It's a zero error number")
default:break
}
```

Another way of combining cases is to jump from one case to the next by using a fallthrough statement. When a fallthrough statement is encountered, the current case code is aborted immediately and the next case code runs *unconditionally*. The test of the next case is not performed, so the next case can't declare any binding variables, because they would never be set. It is not uncommon for a case to consist entirely of a fallthrough statement:

```
switch pep {
case "Manny": fallthrough
case "Moe": fallthrough
case "Jack":
```

```
        print("\(pep) is a Pep boy")
    default:
        print("I don't know who \(pep) is")
    }
```

If case

When all you want to do is extract an associated value from one enum case, a full switch statement may seem a bit heavy-handed. The lightweight if case construct lets you use in a condition the same sort of pattern syntax you'd use in a case of a switch statement. The structural difference is that, whereas a switch case pattern is compared against a previously stated tag, an if case pattern is followed by an equal sign and then the tag. In this code, err is our MyError enum once again:

```
if case let .number(n) = err {
    print("The error number is \(n)")
}
```

The condition starting with case can be part of a longer comma-separated condition list:

```
if case let .number(n) = err, n < 0 {
    print("The negative error number is \(n)")
}
```

Conditional evaluation

An interesting problem arises when you'd like to decide on the fly what value to use — for example, what value to assign to a variable. This seems like a good use of a branching construct. You can, of course, declare the variable first without initializing it, and then set it from within a subsequent branching construct. It would be nice, however, to use a branching construct *as* the variable's value. Here, I try (and fail) to write a variable assignment where the equal sign is followed directly by a branching construct:

```
let title = switch type { // compile error
case .albums:
    "Albums"
case .playlists:
    "Playlists"
case .podcasts:
    "Podcasts"
case .books:
    "Books"
}
```

There are languages that let you talk that way, but Swift is not one of them. However, an easy workaround does exist — use a define-and-call anonymous function, as I suggested in Chapter 2:

```
let title : String = {
    switch type {
    case .albums:
        return "Albums"
    case .playlists:
        return "Playlists"
    case .podcasts:
        return "Podcasts"
    case .books:
        return "Books"
    }
}()
```

In the special case where a value can be decided by a two-pronged condition, Swift provides the C ternary operator (?:). Its scheme is:

```
condition ? exp1 : exp2
```

If the condition is true, the expression *exp1* is evaluated and the result is used; otherwise, the expression *exp2* is evaluated and the result is used. You can use the ternary operator while performing an assignment, using this schema:

```
let myVariable = condition ? exp1 : exp2
```

What myVariable gets initialized to depends on the truth value of the condition.

I use the ternary operator heavily in my own code. Here's an example:

```
cell.accessoryType =
    ix.row == self.currow ? .checkmark : .disclosureIndicator
```

The context needn't be an assignment; here, we're deciding what value to pass as a function argument:

```
context.setFillColor(self.hilite ? purple.cgColor : beige.cgColor)
```

The ternary operator can also be used to determine the receiver of a message. In this example, one of two UIViews will have its background color set:

```
(self.firstRed ? v1 : v2).backgroundColor = .red
```

In Objective-C, there's a collapsed form of the ternary operator that allows you to test a value against nil. If it is nil, you get to supply a substitute value. If it *isn't* nil, the tested value itself is used. In Swift, the analogous operation would involve testing an Optional: if the tested Optional is nil, use the substitute value; if it *isn't* nil, *unwrap* the Optional and use the unwrapped value. Swift has such an operator — the ?? operator (called the *nil-coalescing* operator).

Here's a real-life example from my own code:

```
func tableView(_ tv: UITableView, numberOfRowsInSection sec: Int) -> Int {
    return self.titles?.count ?? 0
}
```

In that example, `self.titles` is of type `[String]?`. If it's not `nil`, I want to unwrap the array and return its `count`. But if it *is* `nil`, there is no data and no table to display — but I *must* return *some* number, so clearly I want to return zero. The nil-coalescing operator lets me express all that very neatly.

The nil-coalescing operator together with the Optional `map(_:)` method neatly solves a class of problem where your goal is to *process* the wrapped value of an Optional or, if it is `nil`, to assign some default value. Suppose our goal is to produce a string expressing the index of `target` within `arr` if it is present, or `"NOT FOUND"` if it is not. This works, but it's ugly:

```
let arr = ["Manny", "Moe", "Jack"]
let target = // some string
let pos = arr.firstIndex(of:target)
let s = pos != nil ? String(pos!) : "NOT FOUND"
```

Here's a more elegant way:

```
let arr = ["Manny", "Moe", "Jack"]
let target = // some string
let s = arr.firstIndex(of:target).map {String($0)} ?? "NOT FOUND"
```

Expressions using `??` can be chained:

```
let someNumber = i1 as? Int ?? i2 as? Int ?? 0
```

That code tries to cast `i1` to an Int and use that Int. If that fails, it tries to cast `i2` to an Int and use *that* Int. If *that* fails, it gives up and uses `0`.

Loops

The usual purpose of a loop is to repeat a block of code with some simple difference on each iteration. This difference will typically serve also as a signal for when to stop the loop. Swift provides two basic loop structures: while loops and for loops.

While loops

A while loop comes in two forms, schematized in Example 5-3.

Example 5-3. The Swift while loop

```
while condition {
    statements
}

repeat {
    statements
} while condition
```

The chief difference between the two forms is the timing of the test. In the second form, the condition is tested after the block has executed — meaning that the block will be executed at least once.

Usually, the code inside the block will change something that alters the environment and hence the value of the condition, eventually bringing the loop to an end. Here's a typical example from my own code (movenda is an array):

```
while self.movenda.count > 0 {
    let p = self.movenda.removeLast()
    // ...
}
```

Each iteration removes an element from movenda, so eventually its count, evaluated in the condition, falls to 0 and the loop is no longer executed; execution then proceeds to the next line after the closing curly braces.

In its first form, a while loop's condition can involve a conditional binding of an Optional. This provides a compact way of safely unwrapping an Optional and looping until the Optional is nil; the local variable containing the unwrapped Optional is in scope inside the curly braces. My previous code can be rewritten more compactly:

```
while let p = self.movenda.popLast() {
    // ...
}
```

Here's an example of repeat...while from my own code. In my LinkSame app, if there are no legal moves, we pick up all the cards, shuffle them, and redeal them into the same positions. It's possible that when we do that, there will *still* be no legal moves. So we do it again until there *is* a legal move:

```
repeat {
    var deck = self.gatherUpCards()
    deck.shuffle()
    self.redeal(deck)
} while self.legalPath() == nil
```

Similar to the if case construct, while case lets you use a switch case pattern. In this rather artificial example, we have an array of various MyError enums:

```
let arr : [MyError] = [
    .message("ouch"), .message("yipes"), .number(10), .number(-1), .fatal
]
```

We can extract the .message associated string values from the start of the array, like this:

```
var i = 0
while case let .message(message) = arr[i] {
    print(message) // "ouch", then "yipes"; then the loop stops
    i += 1
}
```

oops

Swift for loop is schematized in Example 5-4.

Example 5-4. The Swift for loop

```
for variable in sequence {
    statements
}
```

With a for loop, you cycle through (*enumerate*) a sequence. The sequence must be an instance of a type that adopts the Sequence protocol. An Array is a Sequence. A Dictionary is a Sequence. A Set is a Sequence. A String is a Sequence. A Range is a Sequence (as long as it is a range of something that comes in discrete steps, like Int). Those, and sequences derived from them, are the things to which you will regularly apply for...in.

On each iteration, a successive element of the sequence is used to initialize the variable. The variable is local to the block; it is in scope inside the curly braces, and is not visible outside them. The variable is implicitly declared with let; it is immutable by default. If you need to assign to or mutate the variable within the block, write for var.

A common use of for loops is to iterate through successive numbers. This is easy in Swift, because you can readily create a sequence of numbers on the fly — a Range:

```
for i in 1...5 {
    print(i) // 1, 2, 3, 4, 5
}
```

A Sequence has a makeIterator method that yields an iterator object adopting IteratorProtocol. According to this protocol, the iterator has a mutating next method that returns the next object in the sequence wrapped in an Optional, or nil if there is no next object. Under the hood, for...in is repeatedly calling the next method in a while loop. The previous code actually works like this:

```
var iterator = (1...5).makeIterator()
while let i = iterator.next() {
    print(i) // 1, 2, 3, 4, 5
}
```

Sometimes you may find that writing out the while loop explicitly in that way makes the loop easier to control and to customize.

When you cycle through a sequence with for...in, what you're actually cycling through is a *copy* of the sequence. That means it's safe to mutate the sequence while you're cycling through it:

```
var s : Set = [1,2,3,4,5]
for i in s {
    if i.isMultiple(of:2) {
        s.remove(i)
    }
} // s is now [1,3,5]
```

That may not be the most elegant way to remove all even numbers from the Set s, but it's not illegal or dangerous.

Not only is the *sequence* a copy; if the variable type is a value type ("Value Types and Reference Types" on page 153), the *variable* is a copy. So even if you mutate the variable (which is legal if you say for var), the original sequence's elements are unaffected. Here's a Dog that's a struct, not a class:

```
struct Dog {
    var name : String
    init(_ n:String) {
        self.name = n
    }
}
```

We cycle through an array of Dogs, uppercasing their names:

```
var dogs : [Dog] = [Dog("rover"), Dog("fido")]
for var dog in dogs {
    dog.name = dog.name.uppercased()
}
```

But nothing useful happens; dogs still consists of Dogs named "rover" and "fido". If the Sequence is also a Collection, one workaround is to cycle through its indices instead, so that you can assign back into the original array:

```
var dogs : [Dog] = [Dog("rover"), Dog("fido")]
for ix in dogs.indices {
    dogs[ix].name = dogs[ix].name.uppercased()
}
```

Now dogs consists of Dogs named "ROVER" and "FIDO".

As I explained in Chapter 4, you may encounter an array coming from Objective-C whose elements will need to be cast down from Any. If your goal is to iterate through that array, you can cast down as part of the sequence specification:

```
let p = Pep() // p.boys() is an array of Any
for boy in p.boys() as! [String] {
    // ...
}
```

The sequence enumerated method yields a succession of tuples in which each element of the original sequence (labeled element) is preceded by its index number (labeled offset). In this example from my real code, `tiles` is an array of UIViews and `centers` is an array of CGPoints saying where those views are to be positioned:

```
for (i,v) in self.tiles.enumerated() {
    v.center = self.centers[i]
}
```

A `for...in` construct can take a where clause, allowing you to skip some values of the sequence:

```
for i in 0...10 where i.isMultiple(of:2) {
    print(i) // 0, 2, 4, 6, 8, 10
}
```

Like `if case` and `while case`, there's also `for case`, permitting a switch case pattern to be used in a for loop. The tag is each successive value of the sequence, so no assignment operator is used. To illustrate, let's start again with an array of MyError enums:

```
let arr : [MyError] = [
    .message("ouch"), .message("yipes"), .number(10), .number(-1), .fatal
]
```

Here we cycle through the whole array, extracting only the `.number` associated values:

```
for case let .number(i) in arr {
    print(i) // 10, -1
}
```

Another common use of `for case` is to cast down conditionally, picking out only those members of the sequence that can be cast down safely. Let's say I want to hide all subviews that happen to be buttons:

```
for case let b as UIButton in self.boardView.subviews {
    b.isHidden = true
}
```

A sequence also has instance methods, such as `map(_:)`, `filter(_:)`, and `reversed`; you can apply these to hone the sequence through which we will cycle. In this example, I count backward by even numbers:

```
let range = (0...10).reversed().filter {$0.isMultiple(of:2)}
for i in range {
    print(i) // 10, 8, 6, 4, 2, 0
}
```

Yet another approach is to generate the sequence by calling global functions such as `stride(from:through:by)` or `stride(from:to:by:)`. These are applicable to adopters of the Strideable protocol, such as numeric types and anything else that can be incremented and decremented. Which form you use depends on whether you want the sequence to include the final value. The `by:` argument can be negative:

```
for i in stride(from: 10, through: 0, by: -2) {
    print(i) // 10, 8, 6, 4, 2, 0
}
```

For maximum flexibility, you can use the global `sequence` function to generate your sequence by rule. It takes two parameters — an initial value, and a generation function that returns the next value based on what has gone before. In theory, the sequence generated by the `sequence` function can be infinite in length — though this is not a problem, because the resulting sequence is "lazy," meaning that an element isn't generated until you ask for it. In reality, you'll use one of two techniques to limit the result:

Return `nil`

The generation function can limit the sequence by returning `nil` to signal that the end has been reached:

```
let seq = sequence(first:1) {$0 >= 10 ? nil : $0 + 1}
for i in seq {
    print(i) // 1,2,3,4,5,6,7,8,9,10
}
```

Stop requesting elements

You can request just a piece of the infinite sequence — for example, by cycling through the sequence for a while and then stopping, or by taking a finite `prefix`:

```
let seq = sequence(first:1) {$0 + 1}
for i in seq.prefix(5) {
    print(i) // 1,2,3,4,5
}
```

The `sequence` function comes in two forms:

`sequence(first:next:)`

Initially hands `first` into the `next:` function and subsequently hands the previous result of the `next:` function into the `next:` function, as illustrated in the preceding examples.

`sequence(state:next:)`

This form is more general: it repeatedly hands `state` into the `next:` function as an `inout` parameter; the `next:` function is expected to set that parameter, using it as a scratchpad, in addition to returning the next value in the sequence.

An obvious illustration of the second form is the Fibonacci series:

```
let fib = sequence(state:(0,1)) { (pair: inout (Int,Int)) -> Int in
    let n = pair.0 + pair.1
    pair = (pair.1,n)
    return n
```

Trailing closures do not play well with subsequent flow control blocks; therefore parentheses are sometimes needed where generally they would not be. The closing curly brace of the trailing closure, followed by the opening curly brace of the block, upsets the compiler:

```
for i in arr.map {$0*2} { // warning
    print(i)
}
```

To silence the warning, wrap the trailing closure in parentheses:

```
for i in arr.map ({$0*2}) {
    print(i)
}
```

In this example, the curly braces are not adjacent, but you get the warning anyway:

```
if arr.map {$0*2}.first == 4 { // warning
```

Again, parentheses are the simplest solution:

```
if arr.map ({$0*2}).first == 4 {
```

```
}
for i in fib.prefix(10) {
    print(i) // 1, 2, 3, 5, 8, 13, 21, 34, 55, 89
}
```

 Any sequence can be made "lazy" by asking for its `lazy` property. This can be a source of efficiency if you're going to be looping through the sequence (explicitly or implicitly) and potentially short-circuiting the loop; there's no point generating more elements of the sequence than the loop will actually process, and that is what `lazy` prevents. Importantly, laziness propagates through a chain of sequence operations. I'll give an example in the next section.

Jumping

Although branching and looping constitute the bulk of the decision-making flow of code execution, sometimes they are insufficient to express the logic of what needs to happen next. It can be useful to interrupt your code's progress completely and *jump* to a different place within it. In this section, I'll list Swift's modes of jumping. These are all controlled forms of *early exit* from the current flow of code.

Return

You already know one form of early exit: the return statement. One function calls another, which may call another, and so on, forming a call stack. When a return statement is encountered, execution of this function is aborted and the path of execution jumps to the point where the call was made in the function one level up the call stack.

Short-circuiting and labels

Swift has several ways of short-circuiting the flow of branch and loop constructs:

`fallthrough`
> A `fallthrough` statement in a switch case aborts execution of the current case code and immediately begins executing the code of the next case. There must *be* a next case or the compiler will stop you.

`continue`
> A `continue` statement in a loop construct aborts execution of the current iteration and proceeds to the next iteration:
>
> - In a while loop, `continue` means to perform immediately the conditional test.
> - In a for loop, `continue` means to proceed immediately to the next iteration if there is one.

`break`
> A `break` statement aborts the current construct and proceeds after the end of the construct:
>
> - In a loop, `break` aborts the loop.
> - In a switch case, `break` aborts the entire switch construct.

When constructs are nested, you may need to specify *which* construct you mean when you say `continue` or `break`. Therefore, Swift permits you to put a *label* before the start of an if construct, a switch statement, a while loop, or a for loop (or a do block, which I'll describe later). The label is an arbitrary name followed by a colon. You can then use that label name in a continue statement or a break statement within the labeled construct at any depth, to specify that this is the construct you are referring to.

To illustrate, here's a simple struct for generating prime numbers:

```
struct Primes {
    static var primes = [2]
    static func appendNextPrime() {
        next: for i in (primes.last!+1)... {
            let sqrt = Int(Double(i).squareRoot())
            for prime in primes.lazy.prefix(while: {$0 <= sqrt}) {
                if i.isMultiple(of: prime) {
                    continue next
```

```
                }
            }
            primes.append(i)
            return
        }
    }
}
```

The algorithm is crude — it could be optimized further — but it's effective and straightforward. The struct maintains a list of the primes we've found so far, and appendNextPrime basically just looks at each successive larger integer i to see whether any of the primes we've already found (prime) divides it. If so, i is not a prime, so we want to go on to the next i. But if we merely say continue, we'll jump to the next prime, not to the next i. The label solves the problem.

(That example also demonstrates lazy. We want to keep prefix(while:_) from working harder than it has to; there's no point extracting *all* the primes less than the square root of i in advance, because the loop might be short-circuited. So we make primes lazy, which makes prefix(while:_) lazy, and so a prime is tested as a divisor of i only if it has to be.)

Throwing and catching errors

Sometimes a situation arises where further coherent progress is impossible: the entire operation in which we are engaged has failed. It can then be desirable to abort the current scope, and possibly the current function, and possibly even the function that called that function, and so on, exiting to some point where we can acknowledge this failure and proceed in good order in some other way.

For this purpose, Swift provides a mechanism for *throwing and catching errors*. In keeping with its usual insistence on safety and clarity, Swift imposes strict conditions on the use of this mechanism, and the compiler will ensure that you adhere to them.

An *error*, in this sense, is a kind of message, presumably indicating what went wrong. This message is passed up the nest of scopes and function calls as part of the error-handling process, and the code that recovers from the failure can read it. In Swift, an error must be an object of a type that adopts the Error protocol, which has just two requirements: a String _domain property and an Int _code property. The purpose of those properties is to help errors cross the bridge between Swift and Objective-C; in real life, they are hidden and you will be unaware of them. The Error object will be one of the following:

A Swift type that adopts Error
> As soon as a Swift type formally declares adoption of the Error protocol, it is ready to be used as an error object; the protocol requirements are magically fulfilled for you behind the scenes. Typically, this type will be an enum, with

---

different cases distinguishing different kinds of possible failure, perhaps with raw values or associated types to carry further information.

NSError

NSError is Cocoa's class for communicating the nature of a problem; Swift extends NSError to adopt Error and bridges them to one another. If your call to a Cocoa method generates a failure, Cocoa will send you an NSError instance typed as an Error.

There are two stages of the error mechanism to consider:

Throwing an error

Throwing an error aborts the current path of execution and hands an error object to the error mechanism.

Catching an error

Catching an error receives that error object from the error mechanism and responds in good order, with the path of execution resuming after the point of catching. In effect, we have *jumped* from the throwing point to the catching point.

To *throw an error*, use the keyword `throw` followed by an error object. That's all it takes! The current block of code is immediately aborted, and the error mechanism takes over. However, to ensure that the `throw` command is used coherently, Swift imposes a rule that you can say `throw` *only in a context where the error will be caught*. What is such a context?

The primary context for throwing and catching an error is the `do...catch` construct. This consists of a do block and one or more catch blocks. It is legal to throw in the do block; an accompanying catch block can then be fed any errors thrown from within the do block. The `do...catch` construct's schema looks like Example 5-5.

Example 5-5. The Swift `do...catch` construct

```
do {
    statements // a throw can happen here
} catch errortype {
    statements
} catch {
    statements
}
```

A single do block can be accompanied by multiple catch blocks. Catch blocks are like the cases of a switch statement, and will usually have the same logic: first, you might have specialized catch blocks, each of which is designed to handle some limited set of possible errors; finally, you might (and usually will) have a general catch block that acts as the default, mopping up any errors that were not caught by any of the specialized catch blocks.

In fact, the *syntax* used by a catch block to specify what sorts of error it catches *is* the pattern syntax used by a case in a switch statement! Imagine that this *is* a switch statement, and that the tag is the error object. Then the matching of that error object to a particular catch block is performed just as if you had written `case` instead of `catch`. Typically, when the Error is an enum, a specialized catch block will state at least the enum that it catches, and possibly also the case of that enum; it can have a binding, to capture the enum or its associated type; and it can have a where clause to limit the possibilities still further.

To illustrate, I'll start by defining a couple of errors:

```
enum MyFirstError : Error {
    case firstMinorMistake
    case firstMajorMistake
    case firstFatalMistake
}
enum MySecondError : Error {
    case secondMinorMistake(i:Int)
    case secondMajorMistake(s:String)
    case secondFatalMistake
}
```

And here's a `do...catch` construct designed to demonstrate some of the different ways we can catch different errors in different catch blocks:

```
do {
    // throw can happen here
} catch MyFirstError.firstMinorMistake, MyFirstError.firstMajorMistake {
    // catches MyFirstError.firstMinorMistake
    // also catches MyFirstError.firstMajorMistake
} catch let err as MyFirstError {
    // catches other case(s) of MyFirstError
} catch MySecondError.secondMinorMistake(let i) where i < 0 {
    // catches e.g. MySecondError.secondMinorMistake(i:-3)
} catch {
    // catches everything else
}
```

Now let's talk about how the error object makes its way into each of the catch blocks:

Catch block with pattern
   In a catch block with an accompanying pattern, it is up to you to capture in the pattern any desired information about the error. If you want the error itself to travel as a variable into the catch block, you'll need a binding in the pattern.

Catch block with "mop-up" binding

A catch block whose pattern is *only* a binding catches *any* error under that name; `catch let mistake` is a "mop-up" catch block that catches any error as a variable called `mistake`.

Bare catch block

In a "mop-up" catch block with *no* accompanying pattern (that is, the bare word `catch` and no more), the error arrives into the block *automatically* as a variable called `error`.

Let's look again at the previous example, but this time we'll note whether and how the error object arrives into each catch block:

```
do {
    // throw can happen here
} catch MyFirstError.firstMinorMistake {
    // no error object
    // but we know it's either MyFirstError.firstMinorMistake
    // or MyFirstError.firstMajorMistake
} catch let err as MyFirstError {
    // MyFirstError arrives as err
} catch MySecondError.secondMinorMistake(let i) where i < 0 {
    // only i arrives, but we know it's MySecondError.secondMinorMistake
} catch {
    // error object arrives as error
}
```

So much for the `do...catch` construct. But there's something else that can happen to a thrown error; instead of being caught directly, it can percolate up the call stack, leaving the current function and arriving at the point where this function was called. In this situation, the error won't be caught here, at the point of throwing; it needs to be caught further up the call stack. This can happen in one of two ways:

Throw without a corresponding catch

A `do...catch` construct might lack a "mop-up" catch block. Then a throw inside the do block might *not* be caught here.

Throw outside a do block

A `throw` might occur outside of any immediate `do...catch` construct.

However, a thrown error *must* be caught *somehow*. We therefore need a way to say to the compiler: "Look, I understand that it looks like this throw is not happening in a context where it will be caught, but that's only because you're not looking far enough up the call stack. If you do look up far enough, you'll see that a throw at this point *is* eventually caught." And there is a way to say that! Use the `throws` keyword in a function declaration.

If you mark a function with the `throws` keyword, then its *entire body* becomes a legal place for throwing. The syntax for declaring a `throws` function is that the keyword `throws` appears immediately after the parameter list (and before the arrow operator, if there is one):

```
enum NotLongEnough : Error {
    case iSaidLongIMeantLong
}
func giveMeALongString(_ s:String) throws {
    if s.count < 5 {
        throw NotLongEnough.iSaidLongIMeantLong
    }
    print("thanks for the string")
}
```

The addition of `throws` to a function declaration creates a distinct function type. The type of `giveMeALongString` is not `(String) -> ()`, but rather `(String) throws -> ()`. If a function receives as parameter a function that can throw, that parameter's type needs to be specified accordingly:

```
func receiveThrower(_ f:(String) throws -> ()) {
    // ...
}
```

That function can now be called with `giveMeALongString` as argument:

```
func callReceiveThrower() {
    receiveThrower(giveMeALongString)
}
```

An anonymous function, if necessary, can include the keyword `throws` in its `in` expression, in the same place where it would appear in a normal function declaration. But this is not necessary if, as is usually the case, the anonymous function's type is known by inference:

```
func receiveThrower(_ f:(String) throws -> ()) {
    // ...
}
func callReceiveThrower() {
    receiveThrower {
        s in // can say "s throws in", but not required
        if s.count < 5 {
            throw NotLongEnough.iSaidLongIMeantLong
        }
        print("thanks for the string")
    }
}
```

So now we know that `throws` functions exist. But there's more. Swift imposes some requirements on the *caller* of a `throws` function:

- The caller of a `throws` function must precede the function call with the keyword `try`. This keyword acknowledges, to the programmer and to the compiler, that this function can throw.

- The function call must be made in a place where throwing is legal! A function called with `try` can throw, so saying `try` is just like saying `throw`: you must say it either in the do block of a `do...catch` construct or in the body of a `throws` function.

Swift also provides two variants of `try` that you will often use as a shorthand:

`try!`

> If you are very sure that a `throws` function will in fact *not* throw, then you can call it with the keyword `try!` instead of `try`. This relieves you of all further responsibility: you can say `try!` *anywhere*, without catching the possible throw. But be warned: if you're wrong, and this function *does* throw when your program runs, your program can crash at that moment, because you have allowed an error to percolate, uncaught, all the way up to the top of the call stack.

`try?`

> Like `try!`, you can use `try?` anywhere; but, like a `do...catch` construct, `try?` catches the throw if there is one, without crashing. If there's a throw, you don't receive any error information, as you would with a `do...catch` construct; but `try?` tells you if there *was* a throw, by returning `nil`. Thus, `try?` is useful particularly in situations where you're calling a `throws` function that returns a value. If there's a throw, `try?` returns `nil`. If there's no throw, `try?` wraps the returned value in an Optional. Commonly, you'll unwrap that Optional safely in the same line with a conditional binding.

To illustrate, here's an artificial test method that can either throw or return a String:

```
func canThrowOrReturnString(shouldThrow:Bool) throws -> String {
    enum Whoops : Error {
        case oops
    }
    if shouldThrow {
        throw Whoops.oops
    }
    return "Howdy"
}
```

We can call that method with `try` inside a `do...catch` construct:

```
do {
    let s = try self.canThrowOrReturnString(shouldThrow: true)
    print(s)
} catch {
    print(error)
}
```

Rethrows

A function that receives a `throws` function parameter, and that calls that function (with `try`), and that doesn't throw for any *other* reason, may itself be marked as `rethrows` instead of `throws`. The difference is that when a `rethrows` function is called, the caller can pass as argument a function that does *not* throw, and in that case the call doesn't have to be marked with `try` (and the calling function doesn't have to be marked with `throws`):

```
func receiveThrower(_ f:(String) throws -> ()) rethrows {
    try f("ok?")
}
func callReceiveThrower() { // no throws needed
    receiveThrower { s in // no try needed
        print("thanks for the string!")
    }
}
```

At the other extreme, we can call that method with `try!` anywhere, but if the method throws, we'll crash:

```
let s = try! self.canThrowOrReturnString(shouldThrow: false)
print(s)
```

In between, we can call our method with `try?` anywhere. If the method doesn't throw, we'll receive a String wrapped in an Optional; if it does throw, we won't crash and we'll receive `nil` (but no error information):

```
if let s = try? self.canThrowOrReturnString(shouldThrow: true) {
    print(s)
} else {
    print("failed")
}
```

Just as with an Optional chain, if a `throws` function returns no value, the return type from `try?` is `Void?` — and you can capture that and compare it against `nil` to learn whether there was an error. In this example, `canThrowButReturnsNoValue` throws but returns no value:

```
let ok : Void? = try? self.canThrowButReturnsNoValue()
```

Now, if ok is not `nil`, no error was thrown.

An initializer can throw — that is, the initializer's declaration is marked `throws`. So in designing an initializer, when should you prefer a failable initializer (`init?`) and when should you prefer a throwing initializer (`init...throws`)? No hard and fast rule can be given; it depends on your overall design goals. In general, `init?` implies simple failure to create an instance, whereas throws implies that there is useful information to be gleaned by studying the error.

Even if your own code never uses the keyword throw explicitly, you're still very likely, in real life, to call Cocoa methods that are marked with throws. (For the details of how the error mechanism works in Objective-C and how this is bridged to the Swift throws mechanism, see Appendix A.) Objective-C will be supplying an NSError; this class is bridged to Swift Error. Swift helps you cross the bridge by giving Error a localizedDescription property, allowing you to read NSError's localized-Description. Moreover, you can catch a specific NSError by its name. The name you'll use is the NSError domain, and optionally (with dot-notation) the Cocoa name of its code.

For example, NSString initWithContentsOfFile:encoding:error: appears to Swift as:

```
init(contentsOfFile path: String, encoding enc: String.Encoding) throws
```

So let's say we call that initializer, and we want specifically to catch the error thrown when there is no such file. This NSError's domain, according to Cocoa, is "NSCocoa-ErrorDomain". Its code is 260, for which Cocoa provides the name NSFileReadNo-SuchFileError (I found that out by looking in the *FoundationErrors.h* header file in Objective-C). The Swift Foundation overlay translates those into CocoaError and .fileReadNoSuchFile respectively, so we can catch the error like this:

```
do {
    let f = // path to some file, maybe
    let s = try String(contentsOfFile: f)
    // ... if successful, do something with s ...
} catch CocoaError.fileReadNoSuchFile {
    print("no such file")
} catch {
    print(error)
}
```

Objective-C sees a Swift error coherently as well. By default, it receives a Swift error as an NSError whose domain is the name of the Swift object type. If the Swift object type is an enum, the NSError's code is the index number of its case; otherwise, the code is 1. When you want to provide Objective-C with a fuller complement of information, make your error type adopt one or both of these protocols:

LocalizedError

Adopts Error, adding three optional properties: errorDescription (NSError localizedDescription), failureReason (NSError localizedFailureReason), and recoverySuggestion (NSError localizedRecoverySuggestion). Observe that these are String? properties; declaring them as simple String rather than

Optional fails to communicate the information to Objective-C, and is a common mistake.

CustomNSError

Adopts Error, adding three properties with default implementations: `error-Domain`, `errorCode`, and `errorUserInfo`, which Objective-C will see as the NSError's `domain`, `code`, and `userInfo`.

 Later in this chapter, I'll talk about a new Swift 5 feature, the Result enum, that lets you deal elegantly with errors in an asynchronous context.

Nested scopes

When a local variable needs to exist only for a few lines of code, you might like to define an artificial scope — a custom nested scope, at the start of which you can introduce your local variable, and at the end of which that variable will be permitted to go out of scope, destroying its value automatically. Swift does not permit you to use bare curly braces to do this. Instead, use a bare do block without a `catch`.

Here's a rewrite of our earlier code (Chapter 4) for uniquing an array while keeping its order:

```
var arr = ["Manny", "Manny", "Moe", "Jack", "Jack", "Moe", "Manny"]
do {
    var temp = Set<String>()
    arr = arr.filter { temp.insert($0).inserted }
}
```

The only purpose of `temp` is to act as a "helper" for this one `filter` call. So we embed its declaration and the `filter` call in a bare do block; that way, `temp` is in a lower scope that doesn't clutter up our local namespace, and as soon as the `filter` call is over, we exit the block and `temp` is destroyed.

Another use of a bare do block is to implement the simplest form of early exit. The do block gives you a scope to jump out of; now you can label the do block and break to that label:

```
out: do {
    // ...
    if somethingBadHappened {
        break out
    }
    // we won't get here if somethingBadHappened
}
```

Defer statement

A defer statement applies to the scope in which it appears, such as a function body, a while block, an if construct, a do block, and so on. Wherever you say defer, curly braces surround it somehow; the defer block will be executed *when the path of execution leaves those curly braces*. Leaving the curly braces can involve reaching the last line of code within the curly braces, or any of the forms of early exit described earlier in this section.

To see one reason why this is useful, consider the following pair of commands:

`self.view.window?.isUserInteractionEnabled = false`
> Stops all user touches from reaching any view of the application.

`self.view.window?.isUserInteractionEnabled = true`
> Restores the ability of user touches to reach views of the application.

It can be valuable to turn off user interactions at the start of some slightly time-consuming operation and then turn them back on after that operation, especially when, during the operation, the interface or the app's logic will be in some state where the user's tapping a button, say, could cause things to go awry. It is not uncommon for a method to be constructed like this:

```
func doSomethingTimeConsuming() {
    self.view.window?.isUserInteractionEnabled = false
    // ... do stuff ...
    self.view.window?.isUserInteractionEnabled = true
}
```

All well and good — *if* we can guarantee that the only path of execution out of this function will be by way of that last line. But what if we need to return early from this function? Our code now looks like this:

```
func doSomethingTimeConsuming() {
    self.view.window?.isUserInteractionEnabled = false
    // ... do stuff ...
    if somethingHappened {
        return
    }
    // ... do more stuff ...
    self.view.window?.isUserInteractionEnabled = true
}
```

Oops! We've just made a terrible mistake. By providing an additional path out of our doSomethingTimeConsuming function, we've created the possibility that our code might never encounter the call to set isUserInteractionEnabled to true. We might leave our function by way of the return statement — and the user will then be left unable to interact with the interface. Obviously, we need to add another isUser-InteractionEnabled = true call inside the if construct, just before the return statement. But as we continue to develop our code, we must remember, if we add *further* ways out of this function, to add *yet another* isUserInteractionEnabled = true call for *each* of them. This is madness!

The defer statement solves the problem. It lets us specify *once* what should happen when we leave this scope, *no matter how*. Our code now looks like this:

```
func doSomethingTimeConsuming() {
    defer {
        self.view.window?.isUserInteractionEnabled = true
    }
    self.view.window?.isUserInteractionEnabled = false
    // ... do stuff ...
    if somethingHappened {
        return
    }
    // ... do more stuff ...
}
```

The isUserInteractionEnabled = true call in the defer block will be executed, not where it appears, but before the return statement, or before the last line of the method — whichever path of execution ends up leaving the function. The defer statement says: "Eventually, and as late as possible, be sure to execute this code." We have *ensured* the necessary balance between turning off user interactions and turning them back on again. Most uses of the defer statement will probably come under this same rubric: you'll use it to balance a command or restore a disturbed state.

Observe that in the preceding code, I placed the defer statement very early in its surrounding scope. This placement is important because a defer statement is itself a command. If a defer statement is not actually *encountered* by the path of execution before we exit from the surrounding scope, *its block won't be executed.* For this reason, always place your defer statement as close to the start of its surrounding block as you can, to ensure that it will in fact be encountered.

When a defer statement changes a value that is returned by a return statement, the return happens first and the defer statement happens second. In other words, defer effectively lets you return a value *and then change it.* This example comes from Apple's own code (in the documentation, demonstrating how to write a struct that can adopt the Sequence protocol):

```
struct Countdown: Sequence, IteratorProtocol {
    var count: Int
    mutating func next() -> Int? {
        if count == 0 {
            return nil
        } else {
            defer { count -= 1 }
```

```
            return count
        }
    }
}
```

That code returns the current value of count and *then* decrements count, ready for the next call to the next method. Without defer, we'd decrement count and then return the decremented value, which is not what's wanted.

If the current scope has multiple defer blocks pending, they will be called in the reverse of the order in which they were originally encountered. In effect, there is a defer *stack*; each successive defer statement, as it is encountered, pushes its code onto the top of the stack, and exiting the scope in which a defer statement appeared pops that code and executes it.

Aborting the whole program

Aborting the whole program is an extreme form of flow control; the program stops dead in its tracks. In effect, you have deliberately crashed your own program. This is an unusual thing to do, but it can be useful as a way of raising a very red flag: you don't really *want* to abort, so if you *do* abort, things must be so bad that you've no choice.

One way to abort is by calling the global function fatalError. It takes a String parameter permitting you to provide a message to appear in the console. I've already given this example:

```
required init?(coder: NSCoder) {
    fatalError("init(coder:) has not been implemented")
}
```

That code says, in effect, that execution should *never* reach this point. We have declared init(coder:) just because it is required, and we need to satisfy the compiler; but we have no real implementation of init(coder:), and we do not expect to be initialized this way. If we *are* initialized this way, something has gone very wrong, and we *want* to crash, because our program has a serious bug.

An initializer containing a fatalError call does not have to initialize any properties. This is because fatalError is declared as returning the special Never enum type, which causes the compiler to abandon any contextual requirements. Similarly, a function that returns a value does not have to return any value if a fatalError call is encountered.

You can abort conditionally by calling the assert function. Its first parameter is a condition — something that evaluates as a Bool. If the condition is false, we will abort; the second parameter is a String message to appear in the console if we *do* abort. The idea here is that you are making a bet (an *assertion*) that the condition is true — a bet that you feel so strongly about that if the condition is `false`, there's a serious bug in your program and you want to crash so you can learn of this bug and fix it.

By default, `assert` works only when you're developing your program. When your program is to be finalized and made public, you throw a different build switch, telling the compiler that `assert` should be ignored. In effect, the conditions in your `assert` calls are then disregarded; they are all seen as `true`. This means that you can safely leave `assert` calls in your code. By the time your program ships, of course, none of your assertions should be failing; any bugs that caused them to fail should already have been ironed out.

The disabling of assertions in shipping code is performed in an interesting way. The condition parameter is given an extra layer of indirection by declaring it as an `@autoclosure` function. This means that, even though the parameter is *not* in fact a function, the compiler will wrap it in a function; the runtime won't call that function unless it has to. In shipping code, the runtime will *not* call that function. This mechanism averts expensive and unnecessary evaluation: an `assert` condition test may involve side effects, but the test won't even be performed when assertions are turned off in your shipping program.

In addition, Swift provides the `assertionFailure` function. It's like an `assert` that always fails — and, like an `assert`, it *doesn't* fail in your shipping program where assertions are turned off. It's a convenient synonym for `assert(false)`, as a way of assuring yourself that your code never goes where it's never supposed to go.

`precondition` and `preconditionFailure` are similar to `assert` and `assertionFailure`, except that they *do* fail even in a shipping program.

Guard

When your code needs to decide whether to exit early, Swift provides a special syntax — the guard construct. In effect, a guard construct is an if construct where you exit early if the condition fails. Its form is shown in Example 5-6.

Example 5-6. The Swift guard construct

```
guard condition else {
    statements
    exit
}
```

A guard construct consists solely of a condition and an `else` block. The `else` block *must* jump out of the current scope, by any of the means that Swift provides, such as `return`, `break`, `continue`, `throw`, or `fatalError` — anything that guarantees to the compiler that, in case of failure of the condition, execution absolutely will not proceed within the block that contains the guard construct.

Because the guard construct guarantees an exit on failure of the condition, the compiler knows that the condition has succeeded after the guard construct if we do *not* exit. An elegant consequence is that a conditional binding in the condition is in scope *after* the guard construct, without introducing a further nested scope:

```
guard let s = optionalString else {return}
// s is now a String (not an Optional)
```

For the same reason, a guard construct's conditional binding can't use, on the left side of the equal sign, a name already declared in the same scope. This is illegal:

```
let s = // ... some Optional
guard let s = s else {return} // compile error
```

The reason is that `guard let`, unlike `if let` and `while let`, doesn't declare the bound variable for a *nested* scope; it declares it for *this* scope. We can't declare s here because s has already been declared in the same scope.

In my own code, it's not uncommon to have a series of guard constructs, one after another. This may seem a rather clunky and imperative mode of expression, but I'm fond of it nevertheless. It's a nice alternative to a single elaborate if construct, or to the "pyramid of doom" that I discussed earlier; and it looks like exactly what it is, a sequence of gates through which the code must pass in order to proceed further. Here's an actual example from my real-life code:

```
@objc func tapField(_ g: Any) {
    // g must be a gesture recognizer
    guard let g = g as? UIGestureRecognizer else {return}
    // and the gesture recognizer must have a view
    guard g.view != nil else {return}
    // okay, now we can proceed...
}
```

It's often possible to combine multiple guard statement conditions into a single condition list:

```
@objc func tapField(_ g: Any) {
    // g must be a gesture recognizer
    // and the gesture recognizer must have a view
    guard let g = g as? UIGestureRecognizer, g.view != nil
        else {return}
    // okay, now we can proceed...
}
```

A guard construct will also come in handy in conjunction with `try?`. Let's presume we can't proceed unless `String(contentsOfFile:)` succeeds. Then we can call it like this:

```
let f = // path to some file, maybe
guard let s = try? String(contentsOfFile: f) else {return}
// s is now a String (not an Optional)
```

There is also a guard case construct, forming the logical inverse of if case. To illustrate, we'll use our MyError enum once again:

```
guard case let .number(n) = err else {return}
// n is now the extracted number
```

guard case helps to solve an interesting problem. Suppose we have a function whose returned value we want to check in a guard statement:

```
guard howMany() > 10 else {return}
```

All well and good; but suppose also that in the *next* line we want to *use* the value returned from that function. We don't want to call the function *again*; it might be time-consuming and it might have side effects. We want to *capture* the result of calling the function and pass that captured result on into the subsequent code. But we can't do that with guard let, because that requires an Optional, and our function howMany doesn't return an Optional.

What should we do? guard case to the rescue:

```
guard case let output = howMany(), output > 10 else {return}
// now output is in scope
```

Privacy

Privacy (also known as *access control*) refers to the explicit modification of the normal scope rules. I gave an example in Chapter 1:

```
class Dog {
    var name = ""
    private var whatADogSays = "woof"
    func bark() {
        print(self.whatADogSays)
    }
}
```

The intention here is to limit how other objects can see the Dog property whatADog-Says. It is a private property, intended primarily for the Dog class's own internal use: a Dog can speak of self.whatADogSays, but other objects should not be aware that it even exists.

Swift has five levels of privacy:

`internal`

The default rule is that declarations are *internal*, meaning that they are globally visible *within the containing module*. That is why Swift files within the same module can see one another's top-level contents automatically, with no effort on your part. (That's different from C and Objective-C, where files can't see each other at all unless you explicitly show them to one another through `include` or `import` statements.)

`fileprivate` *(narrower than* `internal`*)*

A thing declared `fileprivate` is visible *only within its containing file*. Two object types declared in the same file can see one another's members declared `fileprivate`, but code in other files cannot see those members.

`private` *(even narrower than* `fileprivate`*)*

A thing declared `private` is visible *only within its containing curly braces*. In effect, the visibility of an object type's member declared `private` is limited to code within this type declaration. (A `private` declaration at the top level of a file is equivalent to `fileprivate`.)

`public` *(wider than* `internal`*)*

A thing declared `public` is visible *even outside its containing module*. Another module must first import this module before it can see anything at all. But even when another module *has* imported this module, it *still* won't be able to see anything in this module that hasn't been explicitly declared `public`. If you don't write any modules, you might never need to declare anything `public`. If you do write a module, you *must* declare *something* `public`, or your module is useless.

`open` *(even wider than* `public`*)*

If a class is declared `open`, code in another module can subclass it; it can't do that if the class is declared merely `public`. If an open class member is declared `open`, code in another module that subclasses this class can override this member; it can't do that if the member is declared merely `public`.

Private and Fileprivate

Declaring something `private` restricts its visibility. In this way, you specify by inversion what the public API of this object is. Here's an example from my own code:

```
class CancelableTimer: NSObject {
    private var q = DispatchQueue(label: "timer")
    private var timer : DispatchSourceTimer!
    private var firsttime = true
    private var once : Bool
    private var handler : () -> ()
    init(once:Bool, handler:@escaping () -> ()) {
```

```
        // ...
    }
    func start(withInterval interval:Double) {
        // ...
    }
    func cancel() {
        // ...
    }
}
```

The initializer `init(once:handler:)` and the `start(withInterval:)` and `cancel` methods, which are *not* marked `private`, are this class's public API. They say, "Please feel free to call me!" The properties, however, are all private; no other code can see them, either to get them or to set them. They are purely for the internal use of the methods of this class. They maintain state, but it is not a state that any other code needs to know about.

Privacy is not magically violated by the existence of a special object relationship. Even a subclass cannot see its superclass's private members. (This comes as a surprise to those coming from a language with a `protected` privacy level.) You can work around this by declaring the class and its subclass in the same file and declaring those members `fileprivate` instead of `private`.

A nested type can see the private members of the type in which it is nested. This makes sense, because the outer type is a surrounding scope; the nested type sees what everything else inside this type sees.

An extension can see the private members of the type it extends, provided the type and the extension are in the same file:

```
class Dog {
    private var whatADogSays = "woof"
}
extension Dog {
    func speak() {
        print(self.whatADogSays) // ok
    }
}
```

In effect, an extension sees its type's `private` as meaning `fileprivate`. This lets you break up a type into extensions without being forced to raise the type's private members to `fileprivate` just so the extensions can see them.

It may be that on some occasions you will want to draw a distinction between the privacy of a variable regarding setting and its privacy regarding getting. To draw this distinction, place the word `set` in parentheses after its own privacy declaration. `private(set) var myVar` means that the *setting* of this variable is restricted, but says nothing about the *getting* of this variable, which is left at the default. Similarly, you

---

can say `public private(set) var myVar` to make getting this variable public, while setting this variable is kept private.

The existence of Objective-C adds complications. Things marked `@objc` can be marked `private` without harm; Objective-C can still see them. (That includes things marked `@IBAction` and `@IBOutlet`, which imply `@objc`.) But your implementation of a member defined by an Objective-C protocol cannot be marked `private` without hiding it from Objective-C. In particular, optional methods defined by a Cocoa protocol must be at least `internal` (the default), or Cocoa won't be able to find them and won't call them. You are forced to expose these methods to other files in your module, as if they were part of this class's public API, even though you would probably prefer not to.

Public and Open

If you write a module, you'll need to specify at least some object type declaration as `public`; otherwise, code that imports your module won't be able to see that type. Other declarations that are not declared `public` are internal, meaning that they are private to the module. Judicious use of `public` declarations configures the public API of your module.

The members of a public object type are not, themselves, automatically public. If you want a method to be public, you have to declare it `public`. This is an excellent default behavior, because it means that these members are not shared outside the module unless you want them to be. (As Apple puts it, you must "opt in to publishing" object members.)

In my Zotz app, which is a card game, the files declaring object types for creating and portraying cards and for combining them into a deck are bundled into a framework called ZotzDeck. A framework is a module. The idea is for these files to be able to see one another freely while limiting access from the rest of my app. Many of the Zotz-Deck types, such as Card and Deck, are declared `public`. Many utility object types, however, are not; the classes within the ZotzDeck module can see and use them, but code outside the module doesn't need to be aware of them. Moreover, the Card class is declared `public` but its initializer is not, because the public way to get cards is by initializing a Deck; the initializer for Deck *is* declared `public`, so you can do that.

 If the only initializer for a public type is implicit, code in another module can't see it and cannot create an instance of this type. If you want other code to be able to create an instance of this type, you must declare the initializer explicitly and make it public.

The open access level draws a further distinction. It is applicable only to classes and to members of open classes. A public class can't be subclassed in another module that can see this class; an open class can. A public member of an open class that has been subclassed in another module can't be overridden in that subclass; an open member can.

Privacy Rules

There is an extensive set of rules for ensuring that the privacy level of related things is coherent. Here are some of them:

- A variable can't be public if its type is private, because other code wouldn't be able to use such a variable.
- A subclass can't be public unless the superclass is public.
- A subclass can change an overridden member's access level, but it cannot even *see* its superclass's private members unless they are declared in the same file together.

And so on. I could proceed to list all the rules, but I won't. There is no need for me to enunciate them formally. They are spelled out in great detail in the Swift manual, which you can consult if you need to. In general, you probably won't need to; the privacy rules make intuitive sense, and you can rely on the compiler to help you with useful error messages if you violate one.

Introspection

Swift provides limited ability to *introspect* an object, letting an object display the names and values of its properties. This feature is intended for debugging, not for use in your program's logic. For example, you can use it to modify the way your object is displayed in the Xcode Debug pane.

To introspect an object, use it as the `reflecting:` parameter when you instantiate a Mirror. The Mirror's `children` will then be name–value tuples describing the original object's properties. Here's a Dog class with a `description` property that takes advantage of introspection. Instead of hard-coding a list of the class's instance properties, we introspect the instance to obtain the names and values of the properties. This means that we can later add more properties without having to modify our `description` implementation:

```
struct Dog : CustomStringConvertible {
    var name = "Fido"
    var license = 1
    var description : String {
        var desc = "Dog ("
        let mirror = Mirror(reflecting:self)
        for (k,v) in mirror.children {
            desc.append("\(k!): \(v), ")
```

```
        }
        return desc.dropLast(2) + ")"
    }
}
```

If we now instantiate Dog and `print` that instance, this is what we see in the console:

```
Dog (name: Fido, license: 1)
```

The main use of Mirror is to generate the console output for the Swift `dump` function (or the po command when debugging). By adopting the CustomReflectable protocol, we can take charge of what a Mirror's `children` are. To do so, we implement the `customMirror` property to return our own custom Mirror object whose `children` property we have configured as a collection of name–value tuples.

In this (silly) example, we implement `customMirror` to supply altered names for our properties:

```
struct Dog : CustomReflectable {
    var name = "Fido"
    var license = 1
    var customMirror: Mirror {
        let children : [Mirror.Child] = [
            ("ineffable name", self.name),
            ("license to kill", self.license)
        ]
        let m = Mirror(self, children:children)
        return m
    }
}
```

The outcome is that when our code says `dump(Dog())`, our custom property names are displayed:

```
* Dog
  - ineffable name : "Fido"
  - license to kill : 1
```

Operators

Swift operators such as + and > are not magically baked into the language. They are, in fact, functions; they are explicitly declared and implemented just like any other function. That is why, as I pointed out in Chapter 4, the term + can be passed as the second parameter in a `reduce` call; reduce expects a function taking two parameters and returning a value whose type matches that of the first parameter, and + *is* in fact the name of such a function. It also explains how Swift operators can be overloaded for different types of operand. You can use + with numbers, strings, or arrays — with a different meaning in each case — because Swift functions can be overloaded; there are multiple declarations of the + function, and Swift is able to determine from the parameter types *which* + function you are calling.

These facts are not merely an intriguing behind-the-scenes implementation detail. They have practical implications for you and your code. You are free to overload existing operators to apply to *your* object types. You can even invent *new* operators! In this section, we'll do both.

First we'll talk about how operators are declared. Clearly there is some sort of syntactical hanky-panky (a technical computer science term), because you don't *call* an operator function in the same way as a normal function. You don't say +(1,2); you say 1+2. Even so, 1 and 2 in that second expression *are* the parameters to a + function call. How does Swift know that the + function uses this special syntax?

To see the answer, look in the Swift header:

```
infix operator + : AdditionPrecedence
```

That is an operator declaration. An operator declaration announces that this symbol *is* an operator, and specifies how many parameters it has and what the usage syntax will be in relation to those parameters. The really important part is the stuff before the colon: the keyword `operator`, preceded by an operator *type* — here, `infix` — and followed by the name of the operator. The types are:

`infix`
> This operator takes two parameters and appears between them.

`prefix`
> This operator takes one parameter and appears before it.

`postfix`
> This operator takes one parameter and appears after it.

The term after the colon in an operator declaration is the name of a precedence group. Precedence groups dictate the order of operations when an expression contains multiple operators. I'm not going to go into the details of how precedence groups are defined. The Swift header declares about a dozen precedence groups, and you can easily see how those declarations work. You will probably have no need to declare a new precedence group; you'll just look for an operator similar to yours and copy its precedence group (or omit the colon and the precedence group from your declaration).

An operator is also a function, so you also need a function declaration stating the type of the parameters and the result type of the function. Again, the Swift header shows us an example:

```
func +(lhs: Int, rhs: Int) -> Int
```

That is one of many declarations for the + function in the Swift header. In particular, it is the declaration for when the parameters are both Int. In that situation, the result is itself an Int. (The local parameter names `lhs` and `rhs`, which don't affect the special calling syntax, presumably stand for "left-hand side" and "right-hand side.")

An operator declaration must appear at the top level of a file. The corresponding function declaration may appear either at the top level of a file or at the top level of a type declaration; in the latter case, it must be marked `static`. If the operator is a `prefix` or `postfix` operator, the function declaration must start with the word `prefix` or `postfix`; the default is `infix` and can be omitted.

We now know enough to override an operator to work with an object type of our own! As a simple example, imagine a Vial full of bacteria:

```
struct Vial {
    var numberOfBacteria : Int
    init(_ n:Int) {
        self.numberOfBacteria = n
    }
}
```

When two Vials are combined, you get a Vial with all the bacteria from both of them. So the way to add two Vials is to add their bacteria:

```
extension Vial {
    static func +(lhs:Vial, rhs:Vial) -> Vial {
        let total = lhs.numberOfBacteria + rhs.numberOfBacteria
        return Vial(total)
    }
}
```

And here's code to test our new + operator override:

```
let v1 = Vial(500_000)
let v2 = Vial(400_000)
let v3 = v1 + v2
print(v3.numberOfBacteria) // 900000
```

In the case of a compound assignment operator, the first parameter is the thing being assigned to. Therefore, to implement such an operator, the first parameter must be declared `inout`. Let's do that for our Vial class:

```
extension Vial {
    static func +=(lhs:inout Vial, rhs:Vial) {
        let total = lhs.numberOfBacteria + rhs.numberOfBacteria
        lhs.numberOfBacteria = total
    }
}
```

Here's code to test our += override:

```
var v1 = Vial(500_000)
let v2 = Vial(400_000)
v1 += v2
print(v1.numberOfBacteria) // 900000
```

Next, let's invent a completely new operator. As an example, I'll inject an operator into Int that raises one number to the power of another. As my operator symbol, I'll use ^^ (I'd like to use ^ but it's already in use for something else). For simplicity, I have omitted error-checking for edge cases (such as exponents less than 1):

```
infix operator ^^
extension Int {
    static func ^^(lhs:Int, rhs:Int) -> Int {
        var result = lhs
        for _ in 1..<rhs {result *= lhs}
        return result
    }
}
```

That's all it takes! Here's some code to test it:

```
print(2^^2) // 4
print(2^^3) // 8
print(3^^3) // 27
```

Here's another example. I've already illustrated the use of Range's `reversed` method to allow iteration from a higher value to a lower one. That works, but I find the notation unpleasant. There's an asymmetry with how you iterate up; the endpoints are in the wrong order, and you have to remember to surround a literal range with parentheses:

```
let r1 = 1..<10
let r2 = (1..<10).reversed()
```

Let's define a custom operator that calls `reversed()` for us:

```
infix operator >>> : RangeFormationPrecedence
func >>><Bound>(maximum: Bound, minimum: Bound)
    -> ReversedCollection<Range<Bound>>
    where Bound : Strideable {
        return (minimum..<maximum).reversed()
}
```

Now our expressions can be more symmetrical and compact:

```
let r1 = 1..<10
let r2 = 10>>>1
```

The Swift manual lists the special characters that can be used as part of a custom operator name:

```
/ = - + ! * % < > & | ^ ? ~
```

An operator name can also contain many other symbol characters (that is, characters that can't be mistaken for some sort of alphanumeric) that are harder to type; see the manual for a formal list.

Memory Management

Swift memory management is handled automatically, and you will usually be unaware of it. Objects come into existence when they are instantiated and go out of existence as soon as they are no longer needed. Nevertheless, there are some memory management issues of which you must be conscious.

Memory Management of Reference Types

Memory management of reference type objects ("Value Types and Reference Types" on page 153) is quite tricky under the hood; I'll devote Chapter 12 to a discussion of the underlying mechanism. Swift normally does all the work for you, but trouble can arise when two class instances have references to one another. When that's the case, you can have a *retain cycle* which will result in a *memory leak*, meaning that the two instances *never* go out of existence. Some computer languages solve this sort of problem with a periodic "garbage collection" phase that detects retain cycles and cleans them up, but Swift doesn't do that; you have to fend off retain cycles manually.

One way to test for and observe a memory leak is to implement a class's `deinit`. This method is called when the instance goes out of existence. If the instance never goes out of existence, `deinit` is never called. That's a bad sign, if you were expecting that the instance *should* go out of existence.

Here's an example. First, I'll make two class instances and watch them go out of existence:

```
func testRetainCycle() {
    class Dog {
        deinit {
            print("farewell from Dog")
        }
    }
    class Cat {
        deinit {
            print("farewell from Cat")
        }
    }
    let d = Dog()
    let c = Cat()
}
testRetainCycle() // farewell from Cat, farewell from Dog
```

When we run that code, both "farewell" messages appear in the console. We created a Dog instance and a Cat instance, but the only references to them are automatic (local) variables inside the `testRetainCycle` function. When execution of that function's body comes to an end, all automatic variables are destroyed; that is what it means to be an automatic variable. There are no other references to our Dog and Cat instances that might make them persist, and so they are destroyed in good order.

Now I'll change that code by giving the Dog and Cat objects references to each other:

```
func testRetainCycle() {
    class Dog {
        var cat : Cat?
        deinit {
            print("farewell from Dog")
        }
    }
    class Cat {
        var dog : Dog?
        deinit {
            print("farewell from Cat")
        }
    }
    let d = Dog()
    let c = Cat()
    d.cat = c // create a...
    c.dog = d // ...retain cycle
}
testRetainCycle() // nothing in console
```

When we run that code, *neither* "farewell" message appears in the console. The Dog and Cat objects have references to one another. Those are *strong* references (also called *persisting* references). A strong reference sees to it that as long as our Dog has a reference to a particular Cat, that Cat will not be destroyed, and *vice versa*. That's a good thing, and is a fundamental principle of sensible memory management. The bad thing is that the Dog and the Cat have strong references *to one another*. That's a retain cycle! Neither the Dog instance nor the Cat instance can be destroyed, because neither of them can "go first" — it's like Alphonse and Gaston who can never get through the door because each requires the other to precede him. The Dog can't be destroyed first because the Cat has a strong reference to it, and the Cat can't be destroyed first because the Dog has a strong reference to it.

These objects are now *leaking*. Our code is over; both d and c are gone. There are *no* further references to either of these objects; neither object can ever be referred to again. No code can mention them; no code can reach them. But they live on, floating, useless, and taking up memory.

The term "retain cycle" is based on the `retain` command, which is used in Objective-C to form a strong reference. You can't say `retain` in Swift, so Apple often refers to this kind of cycle as a *strong reference cycle*. But a strong reference cycle *is* a retain cycle — the compiler is in fact inserting `retain` commands under the hood — and I'll continue calling it a retain cycle.

Weak references

One solution to a retain cycle is to mark the problematic reference as `weak`. This means that the reference is *not* a strong reference. It is a *weak reference*. The object referred to can now go out of existence even while the referrer continues to exist. Of course, this might present a danger, because now the object referred to may be destroyed behind the referrer's back. But Swift has a solution for that, too: only an Optional reference can be marked as `weak`. That way, if the object referred to *is* destroyed behind the referrer's back, the referrer will see something coherent, namely `nil`. Also, the reference must be a `var` reference, precisely because it can change spontaneously to `nil`.

This code breaks the retain cycle and prevents the memory leak:

```
func testRetainCycle() {
    class Dog {
        weak var cat : Cat?
        deinit {
            print("farewell from Dog")
        }
    }
    class Cat {
        weak var dog : Dog?
        deinit {
            print("farewell from Cat")
        }
    }
    let d = Dog()
    let c = Cat()
    d.cat = c
    c.dog = d
}
testRetainCycle() // farewell from Cat, farewell from Dog
```

I've gone overboard in that code. To break the retain cycle, there's no need to make *both* Dog's `cat` and Cat's `dog` weak references; making just *one* of the two a weak reference is sufficient to break the cycle. That, in fact, is the usual solution when a retain cycle threatens. One of the pair will typically be more of an "owner" than the other; the one that is *not* the "owner" will have a weak reference to its "owner."

Value types are not subject to the same memory management issues as reference types, but a value type can still be *involved* in a retain cycle with a class instance. In my retain cycle example, if Dog is a class and Cat is a struct, we still get a retain cycle. The solution is the same: make Cat's dog a weak reference. (You can't make Dog's cat a weak reference if Cat is a struct; only a reference to a class type can be declared weak.)

Do *not* use weak references unless you have to! Memory management is not to be toyed with lightly. Nevertheless, there are real-life situations in which weak references are the right thing to do, even when no retain cycle appears to threaten. The delegation pattern (Chapter 11) is a typical case in point; an object typically has no business owning (retaining) its delegate. And a view controller @IBOutlet property is usually weak, because it refers to a subview already owned by its own superview.

Unowned references

There's another Swift solution for retain cycles. Instead of marking a reference as weak, you can mark it as unowned. This approach is useful in special cases where one object absolutely cannot exist without a reference to another, but where this reference need not be a strong reference.

Let's pretend that a Boy may or may not have a Dog, but every Dog must have a Boy — and so I'll give Dog an init(boy:) initializer. The Dog needs a reference to its Boy, and the Boy needs a reference to his Dog if he has one; that's potentially a retain cycle:

```
func testUnowned() {
    class Boy {
        var dog : Dog?
        deinit {
            print("farewell from Boy")
        }
    }
    class Dog {
        let boy : Boy
        init(boy:Boy) { self.boy = boy }
        deinit {
            print("farewell from Dog")
        }
    }
    let b = Boy()
    let d = Dog(boy: b)
    b.dog = d
}
testUnowned() // nothing in console
```

We can solve this by declaring Dog's boy property unowned:

```
func testUnowned() {
    class Boy {
        var dog : Dog?
        deinit {
```

```
            print("farewell from Boy")
        }
    }
    class Dog {
        unowned let boy : Boy // *
        init(boy:Boy) { self.boy = boy }
        deinit {
            print("farewell from Dog")
        }
    }
    let b = Boy()
    let d = Dog(boy: b)
    b.dog = d
}
testUnowned() // farewell from Boy, farewell from Dog
```

An advantage of an unowned reference is that it doesn't have to be an Optional and it can be a constant (let). But an unowned reference is also *genuinely* dangerous, because the object referred to can go out of existence behind the referrer's back, and an attempt to use that reference will cause a crash, as I can demonstrate by this rather forced code:

```
var b = Optional(Boy())
let d = Dog(boy: b!)
b = nil // destroy the Boy behind the Dog's back
print(d.boy) // crash
```

Clearly you should use unowned only if you are absolutely certain that the object referred to will outlive the referrer.

Stored anonymous functions

A particularly insidious kind of retain cycle arises when an instance property holds a function referring to the instance:

```
class FunctionHolder {
    var function : (() -> ())?
    deinit {
        print("farewell from FunctionHolder")
    }
}
func testFunctionHolder() {
    let fh = FunctionHolder()
    fh.function = {
        print(fh)
    }
}
testFunctionHolder() // nothing in console
```

Oops! I've created a retain cycle, by referring, inside the anonymous function, to the object that is holding a reference to it. Because functions are closures, the Function-

Holder instance fh, declared outside the anonymous function, is captured by the anonymous function as a strong reference when the anonymous function says print(fh). But the anonymous function has also been assigned to the function property of the FunctionHolder instance fh, and that's a strong reference too. So that's a retain cycle: the FunctionHolder persistently refers to the function, which persistently refers to the FunctionHolder.

In this situation, I *cannot* break the retain cycle by declaring the function property as weak or unowned. Only a reference to a class type can be declared weak or unowned, and a function is not a class. I must declare the captured value fh *inside the anonymous function* as weak or unowned instead.

Swift provides an ingenious syntax for doing that. At the very start of the anonymous function body, you put square brackets containing a comma-separated list of any problematic references that will be captured from the surrounding environment, each preceded by weak or unowned. This is called a *capture list*. If you have a capture list, you must follow it with the keyword in if there's no in expression already:

```
class FunctionHolder {
    var function : (() -> ())?
    deinit {
        print("farewell from FunctionHolder")
    }
}
func testFunctionHolder() {
    let fh = FunctionHolder()
    fh.function = {
        [weak fh] in // *
        print(fh)
    }
}
testFunctionHolder() // farewell from FunctionHolder
```

This syntax solves the problem. But marking a reference as weak in a capture list has a mild side effect that you will need to be aware of: the reference passes into the anonymous function as an Optional. This is good, because it means that if the object referred to goes out of existence behind our back, the value of the Optional is nil. But of course you must also adjust your code accordingly, unwrapping the Optional as needed in order to use it. The usual technique is to perform the *weak–strong dance*: you unwrap the Optional once, right at the start of the function, in a conditional binding:

```
fh.function = {
    [weak fh] in  // weak
    guard let fh = fh else { return }
    print(fh)     // strong (and not Optional)
}
```

The conditional binding `let fh = fh` elegantly accomplishes three goals:

- It unwraps the Optional version of `fh` that arrived into the anonymous function.

- It declares another `fh` that is a normal (strong) reference. So if the unwrapping succeeds, this new `fh` will persist for the rest of this scope.

- It causes the second `fh` to overshadow the first `fh` (because they have the same name). So it is impossible after the `guard` statement to refer accidentally to the weak Optional `fh`.

Now, it happens that, in this particular example, there is no way the FunctionHolder instance `fh` can go out of existence while the anonymous function lives on. There are no other references to the anonymous function; it persists only as a property of `fh`. Therefore I can avoid some behind-the-scenes bookkeeping overhead, as well as the weak–strong dance, by declaring `fh` as `unowned` in my capture list instead of `weak`. In real life, my own most frequent use of `unowned` is precisely in this context. Very often, the reference marked as `unowned` in the capture list will be `self`.

There's another way to write a capture list: you can capture a value and assign it to a constant name. Here's an example from my own code (without explanation of the context):

```
self.undoer.registerUndo(withTarget: self) {
    [oldCenter = self.center] myself in
    myself.setCenterUndoably(oldCenter)
}
```

That code declares a constant `oldCenter` and sets its value to `self.center`. This avoids capturing `self`, because `self` never appears in the anonymous function, explicitly or implicitly; instead, the value of a property of `self` is captured *directly*, and that *value* is what passes into the anonymous function. Not only does this prevent a retain cycle, but also it avoids closure semantics; the value of `self.center` is evaluated *now*, when `registerUndo` is called, rather than later, when the anonymous function is called (at which time the value of `self.center` may have changed).

Recall, from Chapter 2, that the compiler forces you to say `self` explicitly when you refer to a property or method of `self` within the function body of an escaping closure. Now we can see why: you are threatening to form a retain cycle involving `self`, and the compiler wants to make sure you realize that. Of course, you're probably *not* going to form a retain cycle! But the compiler can't check for that; once the closure is escaping, anything could happen:

```
let f1 = funcPasser {
    print(view.bounds) // compile error, because self.view is implied
}
let f2 = funcPasser {
    print(self.view.bounds) // ok
}
```

Many people don't like saying self, though; and if this anonymous function implies self many times, it may be objectionable to have to say self explicitly many times. New in Swift 5.3, there's a stylistic alternative: if you put [self] in the capture list, that satisfies the compiler, and you don't have to write self as the implicit target in the function body:

```
let f3 = funcPasser { [self] in
    print(view.bounds) // ok in Swift 5.3
}
```

Above all, don't panic. Beginners may be tempted to backstop *all* their anonymous functions with [weak self]. That's wrong. Only a *stored* function can raise even the possibility of a retain cycle. Merely passing a function does *not* introduce such a possibility, especially if the function being passed will be called immediately. And even if a function *is* stored, if it is stored *elsewhere*, it might not imply a retain cycle. Always confirm that you actually *have* a retain cycle before concerning yourself with how to prevent it.

Consider the standard expression of an animation, which I discussed in Chapter 2:

```
UIView.animate(withDuration:0.4) {
    self.myButton3.frame.origin.y += 20
} completion: { _ in
    self.someMethod()
}
```

No one should be using [weak self] in these anonymous functions. There's no retain cycle, because the anonymous functions are not being retained by self (the view controller). Moreover, the view controller is *not* going to go out of existence while the animation is proceeding. In fact, capturing the view controller as self in the body of the anonymous function actually *prevents* it from going out of existence while the animation is proceeding — and that's *good!* Extending the lifetime of an object, such as self, long enough for an anonymous function to be called at some future time, is a *useful* thing to do. (In fact, it's so useful that Swift provides a way to do it *without* explicitly capturing the object in the anonymous function: there's a global function, withExtendedLifetime, for precisely that purpose.)

Memory management of protocol-typed references

Only a reference to an instance of a class type can be declared weak or unowned. A reference to an instance of a struct or enum type cannot be so declared, because its

---

memory management doesn't work the same way (and is not subject to retain cycles). A reference that is declared as a protocol type, therefore, has a problem. A reference typed as a protocol that might be adopted by a struct or an enum cannot be declared weak or unowned. You can only declare a protocol-typed reference weak or unowned if the compiler knows that only a class can adopt it. You can assure the compiler of that by making the protocol a class protocol.

In this code, SecondViewControllerDelegate is a protocol that I've declared. This code won't compile unless SecondViewControllerDelegate is declared as a class protocol:

```
class SecondViewController : UIViewController {
    weak var delegate : SecondViewControllerDelegate?
    // ...
}
```

Here's the actual declaration of SecondViewControllerDelegate; it *is* declared as a class protocol, and that's why the preceding code is legal:

```
protocol SecondViewControllerDelegate : AnyObject {
    func accept(data:Any)
}
```

A protocol declared in Objective-C is implicitly marked as @objc and is a class protocol. This declaration from my real-life code is legal:

```
weak var delegate : WKScriptMessageHandler?
```

WKScriptMessageHandler is a protocol declared by Cocoa (in particular, by the Web Kit framework), so only a class can adopt WKScriptMessageHandler, and the compiler is satisfied that the delegate variable will be an instance of a class — and the reference can be treated as weak.

Exclusive Access to Value Types

Even value types can have memory management issues. In particular, a struct and its members might be directly accessed simultaneously, which could lead to unpredictable results. Fortunately, the compiler will usually stop you before such an issue can arise.

To illustrate, imagine that we have a Person struct with a firstName string property. Now let's write a function that takes both a Person and a string as inout parameters:

```
func change(_ p:inout Person, _ s:inout String) {}
```

So far so good; but now imagine calling that function with both a Person and that same Person's firstName as the parameters:

```
var p = Person(firstName: "Matt")
change(&p, &p.firstName) // compile error
```

The compiler will stop you from doing that, with this message: "Overlapping accesses to p, but modification requires exclusive access." The problem is that the single function change is being given direct access to the memory of both the struct and a member of that struct, simultaneously. We are threatening to alter the struct in some unpredictable way. This dangerous situation is forbidden; the compiler enforces *exclusive access* when a struct is being modified.

You may encounter that error message from the compiler under surprising circumstances:

```
let c = UIColor.purple
var components = Array(repeating: CGFloat(0), count: 4)
c.getRed(&components[0], green: &components[1],
    blue: &components[2], alpha: &components[3]) // compile error
```

That code was legal in Swift 3 and before; in Swift 4 and later, it isn't. No exclusive access problem is evident to the untrained eye; you just have to take the compiler's word for it. One workaround is to take control of memory access yourself, silencing the compiler:

```
components.withUnsafeMutableBufferPointer { ptr -> () in
    c.getRed(&ptr[0], green: &ptr[1], blue: &ptr[2], alpha: &ptr[3])
}
```

It might be better to write a UIColor extension that assembles the array without any simultaneous memory access to multiple elements of the array:

```
extension UIColor {
    func getRedGreenBlueAlpha() -> [CGFloat] {
        var (r,g,b,a) = (CGFloat(0),CGFloat(0),CGFloat(0),CGFloat(0))
        self.getRed(&r, green: &g, blue: &b, alpha: &a)
        return [r,g,b,a]
    }
}
```

Sometimes the compiler can't see the issue coming, and you'll crash at runtime instead:

```
var i = 0
func tweak(_ ii:inout Int) {
    print(i) // legal, but crash
}
tweak(&i)
```

In that code, tweak is accessing i in two ways simultaneously. On the one hand, i is being passed into tweak as an inout parameter. On the other hand, tweak is reaching out directly to i (which is in scope). Even though tweak never actually modifies i and never mentions its own inout parameter ii, that's a simultaneous access, and is forbidden.

Miscellaneous Swift Language Features

This chapter is a miscellany, and this section is a miscellany within a miscellany. It surveys some "advanced" Swift language features that have been added relatively recently. The reason for postponing the discussion to this point is in part to avoid cluttering up the earlier exposition and in part to ensure that you know enough to understand the subject matter.

Synthesized Protocol Implementations

A few protocols built into the Swift standard library have the ability to synthesize implementations of their own requirements. Such a protocol can supply code behind the scenes so that an object that adopts the protocol will satisfy the protocol's requirements *automatically*.

Equatable

Equatable is one such protocol. That's good, because making your custom type adopt Equatable is often a really useful thing to do. Equatable adoption means that the == operator can be used to check whether two instances of this type are equal. The only requirement of the Equatable protocol is that you do, in fact, define == for your type. Using our Vial struct from earlier in this chapter, let's first do that manually:

```
struct Vial {
    var numberOfBacteria : Int
    init(_ n:Int) {
        self.numberOfBacteria = n
    }
}
extension Vial : Equatable {
    static func ==(lhs:Vial, rhs:Vial) -> Bool {
        return lhs.numberOfBacteria == rhs.numberOfBacteria
    }
}
```

Now that Vial is an Equatable, not only can it be compared with ==, but also lots of methods that need an Equatable parameter spring to life. For example, Vial becomes a candidate for use with methods such as firstIndex(of:):

```
let v1 = Vial(500_000)
let v2 = Vial(400_000)
let arr = [v1,v2]
let ix = arr.firstIndex(of:v1) // Optional wrapping 0
```

What's more, the complementary inequality operator != has sprung to life for Vial automatically! That's because it's already defined for *any* Equatable in terms of the == operator.

Our implementation of == for Vial was easy to write, but that's mostly because this struct has just one property. As soon as you have multiple properties, implementing == manually, though theoretically trivial, becomes tedious and possibly hard to maintain. This is just the kind of task computers are good at! You're likely going to want to define == in terms of the equality of all your type's properties simultaneously; well, Swift will implement == *automatically* in exactly that way. All we have to do is declare adoption of Equatable, like this:

```
struct Vial : Equatable {
    var numberOfBacteria : Int
    init(_ n:Int) {
        self.numberOfBacteria = n
    }
}
```

That code compiles, even though we now have no implementation of ==. That's because the implementation has been synthesized for us. Behind the scenes, two Vial objects are now equal just in case their numberOfBacteria are equal — which is exactly the implementation we supplied when we wrote the code explicitly.

For Equatable synthesis to operate, the following requirements must be met:

- Our object type is a struct or an enum.
- We have adopted Equatable, *not* in an extension.
- We have *not* supplied an implementation of the == operator.
- All of our struct's stored property types are themselves Equatable.

For an enum, the requirement here is that, if the enum has associated values, the types of those associated values must be Equatable. The synthesized == implementation will then say that two instances of our enum are equal if they are the same case and, if that case has an associated value, the associated values are equal for both instances. Recall that our MyError enum in Chapter 4 couldn't be used with the == operator until we explicitly declared it Equatable:

```
enum MyError : Equatable {
    case number(Int)
    case message(String)
    case fatal
}
```

(If an enum has *no* associated values, then it is already effectively Equatable and there is no need to adopt Equatable explicitly.)

If you don't like the synthesized implementation of == (perhaps because there is a property that you don't want involved in the definition of equality), all you have to do is write your own, explicitly. You lose the convenience of automatic synthesis, but you're no worse off than you were before automatic synthesis existed.

Let's say we have a Dog struct with a `name` property and a `license` property and a `color` property. And let's say we think two Dogs are equal just in case they have the same name and license; we don't care whether the colors are the same. Then we just have to write the implementation of `==` ourselves, omitting `color` from the calculation:

```
struct Dog : Equatable {
    let name : String
    let license : Int
    let color : UIColor
    static func ==(lhs:Dog,rhs:Dog) -> Bool {
        return lhs.name == rhs.name && lhs.license == rhs.license
    }
}
```

Hashable

Another protocol that performs synthesis of its own implementation is Hashable. Recall that a type must be Hashable to be used in a Set or as the key type of a Dictionary. A struct whose properties are all Hashable, or an enum whose associated values are all Hashable, can conform to Hashable merely by declaring that it adopts Hashable.

Hashable requires that its adopter, in addition to being Equatable, have a `hashValue` Int property; the idea is that two equal objects should have equal hash values. The implicit implementation combines the `hashValue` of the Hashable members to produce a `hashValue` for the object itself. That's good, because *you* would surely have no idea how to do that for yourself. Writing your own hash function is a very tricky business! Thanks to this feature, you don't have to.

But suppose you don't like the synthesized implementation of `hashValue`. Then you *will* have to calculate the `hashValue` yourself. Luckily, Swift 4.2 introduced a way to do that. You ignore `hashValue`, and instead implement the `hash(into:)` method. There is then no need to implement `hashValue`, because it is autogenerated based on the result of `hash(into:)`. In this method, you are handed a Hasher object; you call `hash(into:)` with that object on every property that you want included in the hash calculation — and omit the ones you don't. For hashability to work properly in a Dictionary or Set, these should be the very same properties you've included in the Equatable calculation of `==`.

So, for our Dog struct, we could write:

```
struct Dog : Hashable { // and therefore Equatable
    let name : String
    let license : Int
    let color : UIColor
    static func ==(lhs:Dog,rhs:Dog) -> Bool {
        return lhs.name == rhs.name && lhs.license == rhs.license
```

```
    }
    func hash(into hasher: inout Hasher) {
        name.hash(into:&hasher)
        license.hash(into:&hasher)
    }
}
```

Other protocols, alas, do not provide the same convenience. If we want our Vial struct to be Comparable, we must implement < explicitly. (And when we do, the other three comparison operators spring to life automatically as well.)

Comparable

New in Swift 5.3, the Comparable protocol *does* provide a synthesized implementation — but only for an enum, and only if the enum has no raw value. The order of the cases is the order in which they are declared; if a case has an associated value, it must be of a Comparable type, so that if two instances of the enum have the same case, they can be ordered by their associated value:

```
enum Planet : Comparable {
    case mercury
    case venus
    case earth
    case mars
    case asteroid(String)
    case jupiter
}
// let's test it!
let test1 = Planet.mercury < Planet.venus // true
let test2 = Planet.jupiter > Planet.asteroid("Ceres") // true
let test3 = Planet.asteroid("Ceres") < Planet.asteroid("Vesta") // true
```

Key Paths

Key paths, a language feature introduced in Swift 4, effectively stand in relation to properties the way function references stand in relation to function calls — they are a way of storing a reference to a property without actually accessing the property.

Suppose we have a Person struct with a `firstName` String property and a `lastName` String property, and that we want to access one of these properties on a Person p, without knowing until runtime *which* property we are to access. We might write something like this:

```
var getFirstName : Bool = // ...
let name : String = {
    if getFirstName {
        return p.firstName
```

```
        } else {
            return p.lastName
        }
    }()
```

That's not altogether atrocious, but it's hardly elegant. If we do the same sort of thing in several places, the same choice must somehow be repeated in each of those places — and the more choices there are, the more elaborate our code must be each time.

Key paths solve the problem by permitting us to encapsulate the *notion* of accessing a particular property of a type, such as Person's `firstName` or `lastName`, without actually *performing* the access. That notion is expressed as an instance; therefore, we can store it as a variable, or pass it as a function parameter. That instance then acts as a token that we can use to access the actual property on an actual instance of that type at some future time.

The literal notation for constructing a key path is:

```
\Type.property.property...
```

We start with a backslash. Then we have the name of a type, which may be omitted if the type can be inferred from the context. Then we have a dot followed by a property name — and this may be repeated if that property's type itself has a property that we will want to access, and so on.

In our simple case, we might store the notion of accessing a particular property as a key path variable, like this:

```
var prop = \Person.firstName
```

To perform the actual access, start with a reference to a particular instance and fetch its `keyPath:` subscript:

```
let whatname = p[keyPath:prop]
```

If p is a Person with a `firstName` of "Matt" and a `lastName` of "Neuburg", then `whatname` is now "Matt". Moreover, `whatname` is inferred to be a String, because the key path carries within itself information about the type of the property that it refers to (it is a generic).

Now imagine substituting a different key path for the value of `prop`:

```
var prop = \Person.firstName
// ... time passes ...
prop = \.lastName // inferred as \Person.lastName
```

That substitution is legal, because both `firstName` and `lastName` are Strings. Instantly, throughout our program, all occurrences of the Person [`keyPath:prop`] subscript take on a new meaning!

If the property referenced by a key path is writable and you have a writable object reference, then you can also set *into* the keyPath: subscript on that object, changing the value of the property:

```
p[keyPath:prop] = "Ethan"
```

Here's a practical example where my own code takes advantage of key paths. One of my apps is a version of a well-known game involving a deck of 81 cards, where every card has four attributes (color, number, shape, and fill), each of which can have three possible values. (81 is 3^4.) The player's job is to spot three cards obeying the following rule: each attribute has either the *same* value for *all* three cards or a *different* value for *each* of the three cards. The problem is to express that rule succinctly.

For the four card attributes, I use enums with Int raw values. This allows me to represent any attribute as a common type (Int). I express those raw values as computed properties, and I vend a list of all four computed properties as an array of key paths (attributes):

```
struct Card {
    let itsColor : Color
    let itsNumber : Number
    let itsShape : Shape
    let itsFill : Fill
    var itsColorRaw : Int { return itsColor.rawValue }
    var itsNumberRaw : Int { return itsNumber.rawValue }
    var itsShapeRaw : Int { return itsShape.rawValue }
    var itsFillRaw : Int { return itsFill.rawValue }
    static let attributes : [KeyPath<Card, Int>] = [
        \.itsColorRaw, \.itsNumberRaw, \.itsShapeRaw, \.itsFillRaw
    ]
    // ...
}
```

Now I can express the rule clearly and elegantly:

```
func isValidTriple(_ cards:[Card]) -> Bool {
    func evaluateOneAttribute(_ n:[Int]) -> Bool {
        let allSame = (n[0] == n[1]) && (n[1] == n[2])
        let allDiff = (n[0] != n[1]) && (n[1] != n[2]) && (n[2] != n[0])
        return allSame || allDiff
    }
    return Card.attributes.allSatisfy {attribute in
        evaluateOneAttribute(cards.map {$0[keyPath:attribute]}) // wow!
    }
}
```

Starting in Swift 5.2, a keypath literal can be used wherever a function is expected that takes that object's type as its sole parameter and produces that property's type as its result. That sentence is enough to make one's head swim, but the idea is quite simple. Consider our Person with a firstName and a lastName String property. If you have an array of Person, you can extract a list of first names using map, like this:

```
let names = arrayOfPersons.map {$0.firstName}
```

Well, now you can use a keypath literal instead:

```
let names = arrayOfPersons.map (\.firstName)
```

That's more than mere syntactic sugar; the point is that `\.firstName` acts as *the name of a function*. Here's a more surprising case in point:

```
let f : (Person) -> String = \Person.firstName
```

Instance as Function

Sometimes a type's primary job is to contain or represent a function. In those situations, it makes for cleaner code if we can treat an instance of that type *as* a function. The ability to do that was introduced in Swift 5.2.

Before I explain, I'll give an example. (This particular example comes more or less directly from Apple.) Imagine I have a struct Adder, whose job is to store a base value and add it to any addend we care to supply:

```
let add3 = Adder(3)
let sum = add3(4)
print(sum) // 7
```

That code, and indeed the entire concept of Adder, should remind you of the notion of a function as a factory for other functions (see "Function Returning Function" on page 54). In the second line, we treat add3 as a function that takes an Int and returns another Int, namely the first Int with 3 added to it. But here's the thing: add3 is *not* a function! It is an instance of a struct. We are treating an instance as a function.

The implementation, behind the scenes, is simple. If a type declares an instance method named callAsFunction, you can "call" an instance of that type as if it *were* a function: the "call" is routed to the callAsFunction method. Here's Adder:

```
struct Adder {
    let base: Int
    init(_ base:Int) {
        self.base = base
    }
    func callAsFunction(_ addend:Int) -> Int {
        return self.base + addend
    }
}
```

So when we create an Adder instance named add3 and then say add3(4), it is *exactly* the same as if we had said add3.callAsFunction(4).

The function notation in add3(4) is mere syntactic sugar. But it's very nice syntactic sugar, because it reflects the truth more compactly. To be sure, we could have given

Adder an `add` method that performs the addition, or a `makeAdder` method that produces a function that performs the addition:

```
struct Adder {
    let base: Int
    init(_ base:Int) {
        self.base = base
    }
    func add(_ addend:Int) -> Int {
        return self.base + addend
    }
    // or:
    func makeAdder() -> (Int) -> Int {
        return { addend in self.base + addend }
    }
}
```

Either of those would have been just fine. But the job of Adder is to act like a function, so rather than having it contain or produce that function, we can use `callAsFunction` to let an Adder effectively *be* that function.

You can give your type multiple `callAsFunction` overloads, distinguished in the usual way by parameter types, parameter labels, or both. In this way, a single instance can behave as if it were itself an overloaded function.

Dynamic Membership

Dynamic membership was introduced in Swift 4.2, with additional features in Swift 5. It allows you to do two things:

- Access a nonexistent property (a *dynamic* property) of an instance or type.
- Treat a reference to an instance as the name of a nonexistent function (a *dynamic function*).

Before I explain, I'll give an example. Imagine I have a class Flock that acts as a gatekeeper to a dictionary. I proceed to talk to a Flock instance like this:

```
let flock = Flock()
flock.chicken = "peep"
flock.partridge = "covey"
// flock's dictionary is now ["chicken": "peep", "partridge": "covey"]
if let s = flock.partridge {
    print(s) // covey
}
flock(remove:"partridge")
// flock's dictionary is now ["chicken": "peep"]
```

That's surprising, because Flock has no `chicken` property and no `partridge` property, and it is not the name of a function with a `remove:` parameter. So why am I able to talk that way?

Here's how the implementation works:

Dynamic properties

The type must be marked @dynamicMemberLookup, and must declare a subscript taking a single parameter that is either a string or a key path and has an external name dynamicMember. The subscript return type is up to you, and you can have multiple overloads distinguished by the return type. When other code accesses a nonexistent property of this type, the corresponding subscript function — the getter or, if there is one, the setter — is called with the name of the property as parameter.

Dynamic functions

The type must be marked @dynamicCallable, and must declare either or both of these methods, where the type T is up to you:

dynamicallyCall(withArguments:[T])

Other code uses an instance as a function name and calls it with a variadic parameter of type T. The variadic becomes an array. If T is Int, and the caller says myObject(1,2), then this method is called with parameter [1,2].

dynamicallyCall(withKeywordArguments:KeyValuePairs<String, T>)

Other code uses an instance as a function name and calls it with labeled arguments of type T. The label–value pairs become string–T pairs; if a label is missing, it becomes an empty string. If T is String, and the caller says myObject(label:"one", "two"), then this method is called with parameter ["label":"one", "":"two"].

So here's the implementation of Flock. Its dynamic properties are turned into dictionary keys, and it can be called as a function with a "remove" label to remove a key:

```
@dynamicMemberLookup
@dynamicCallable
class Flock {
    var d = [String:String]()
    subscript(dynamicMember s:String) -> String? {
        get { d[s] }
        set { d[s] = newValue }
    }
    func dynamicallyCall(withKeywordArguments kvs:KeyValuePairs<String, String>) {
        if kvs.count == 1 {
            if let (key,val) = kvs.first {
                if key == "remove" {
                    d[val] = nil
                }
            }
        }
    }
}
```

As originally conceived, dynamic membership is not intended for general use; its primary purpose is to prepare Swift for future interoperability with languages like Ruby, and perhaps to permit domain-specific languages. It is, after all, constitutionally opposed to the spirit of Swift: dynamism means that the compiler's validity checking is thrown away.

On the other hand, `@dynamicMemberLookup` with a subscript that takes a key path *is* Swift-like, because the validity of a given key path is checked at compile time. This feature is good particularly for forwarding messages to a wrapped value. Here's a Kennel struct that wraps a Dog:

```
struct Dog {
    let name : String
    func bark() { print("woof") }
}
@dynamicMemberLookup
struct Kennel {
    let dog : Dog
    subscript(dynamicMember kp:KeyPath<Dog,String>) -> String {
        self.dog[keyPath:kp]
    }
}
```

If `k` is a Kennel instance, we can now fetch `k.name` as a way of fetching `k.dog.name`. An attempt to say `k.nickname`, however, won't even compile; key paths maintain validity checking.

Property Wrappers

The idea of property wrappers, as you'll recall from Chapter 3, is that commonly used computed property getter and setter patterns can be encapsulated into a type with a `wrappedValue` computed property:

```
@propertyWrapper struct MyWrapper {
    // ...
    var wrappedValue : SomeType {
        get { /*...*/ }
        set { /*...*/ }
    }
}
```

You can then declare your computed property using the property wrapper type name as a custom attribute:

```
@MyWrapper var myProperty
```

The result is that, behind the scenes, a MyWrapper instance is created for you, and when your code gets or sets the value of `myProperty`, it is the getter or setter of this MyWrapper instance that is called.

In real life, your property wrapper's purpose will almost certainly be to act as a façade for access to a stored instance property, declared inside the property wrapper's type. This alone makes the property wrapper worth the price of admission, because now your main code is not cluttered with private stored properties acting as the backing store for computed properties; the stored properties are hidden in the property wrapper instances.

To introduce the syntax, I'll start with a property wrapper that acts as a façade for storage, and no more:

```
@propertyWrapper struct Facade<T> {
    private var _p : T
    init(wrappedValue:T) {
        self._p = wrappedValue
    }
    var wrappedValue : T {
        get {
            return self._p
        }
        set {
            self._p = newValue
        }
    }
}
```

That's a fairly normal-looking struct. It's a generic so that our property declaration can be of any type. The only special feature here is the initializer. The rule is that if you declare an `init(wrappedValue:)` initializer, it will be called automatically with the value to which the property is initialized:

```
@Facade var p = "test"
```

Here, the property wrapper's generic is resolved to String, and its `init(wrappedValue:)` initializer is called with parameter `"test"`. You can call other initializers instead, by treating the custom attribute name as a type name (which, of course, is just what it is) and putting parentheses after it. Suppose our property wrapper declares an initializer with no external parameter name:

```
init(_ val:T) {
    self._p = val
}
```

Then we can call that initializer by declaring our property like this:

```
@Facade("test") var p
```

More practically, here's a generalized version of the Clamped property wrapper from Chapter 3; we accept any Comparable type (so that min and max are available), and we accept (and require) initialization with a minimum and maximum to clamp to:

```
@propertyWrapper struct Clamped<T:Comparable> {
    private var _i : T
    private let min : T
    private let max : T
    init(wrappedValue: T, min:T, max:T) {
        self._i = wrappedValue
        self.min = min
        self.max = max
    }
    var wrappedValue : T {
        get {
            self._i
        }
        set {
            self._i = Swift.max(Swift.min(newValue,self.max),self.min)
        }
    }
}
```

And here's how to use it:

```
@Clamped(min:-7, max:7) var i = 0
@Clamped(wrappedValue:0, min:-7, max:7) var ii
```

Those declarations are equivalent, but the first is more natural; behind the scenes, the value with which we initialize the property is routed to the wrappedValue: parameter of the property wrapper initializer.

As I've said, when you declare a property with a property wrapper attribute, an actual property wrapper instance is generated. That instance is accessible to our code under the same name as the computed property with underscore (_) prefixed to it. In the case of our @Facade property p, if we set p to "howdy" and then say print(_p), the console says Facade<String>(_p: "howdy"). You might use this feature for debugging, or to expose additional public members of the struct. This underscore-prefixed variable is declared with var, so you can even assign to it a property wrapper instance that you've initialized manually.

The property wrapper may also vend a value that can be referred to elsewhere by prefixing a dollar sign ($) to the property name. It does this by declaring a projected-Value property (this will usually be a computed property). You might use this to expose some useful secondary object. That's how the SwiftUI @State attribute works. It is a property wrapper (one of several that are commonly used in SwiftUI). The State property wrapper struct has a projectedValue computed property whose getter returns the State struct's binding property. That property is a Binding, so when you use your @State property's $ name, you get a Binding (see Chapter 13).

Be careful not to cause a name clash! If you declare a @Facade property p, you can't declare a property _p in the same scope, because that's the name of the synthesized property wrapper instance. (The same issue does not arise for the $ name, because a variable name can't start with $.)

Property wrappers are a brilliant addition to Swift, and can be of practical value immediately. For instance, I've pointed out already that deferred initialization of an instance property using an Optional ("Deferred initialization of properties" on page 126) entails an architectural flaw: the property must be declared with var. Property wrappers can't change that, but they can prevent further assignment at runtime:

```
@propertyWrapper struct DeferredConstant<T> {
    private var _value: T? = nil
    var wrappedValue: T {
        get {
            if _value == nil {
                fatalError("not yet initialized")
            }
            return _value!
        }
        set {
            if _value == nil {
                _value = newValue
            }
        }
    }
}
```

Suppose we now declare an outlet as a DeferredConstant:

```
@IBOutlet @DeferredConstant var myButton: UIButton!
```

The result is that after a real button from the interface is assigned to myButton, subsequent code that tries to assign a different value to myButton will fail silently.

Despite the name, property wrappers can be applied to global variables. They cannot be applied to local variables, but that may become possible in the future.

Custom String Interpolation

Starting in Swift 5, string interpolation syntax can be customized. The example I imagined in Chapter 3 is an expression such as "You have \(n, roman:true) widgets", where n is an Int; the idea is that, if n is 5, this would yield "You have V widgets", expressing the Int in Roman numerals instead of Arabic notation. This would be an odd goal to accomplish through string interpolation, but it demonstrates the syntax; so let's implement that example.

To implement string interpolation, you need an adopter of the ExpressibleByString-Literal protocol that also adopts the ExpressibleByStringInterpolation protocol. This might be some custom type of your own, but in most situations you'll just use the built-in type that already adopts both of these protocols — String. "You have \(n, roman:true) widgets" is a String, and it already implements string interpolation.

That makes our job easy: all we have to do is customize String's already existing implementation of string interpolation. That implementation hinges on two methods, appendInterpolation and appendLiteral. The overall string is broken into segments, the interpolations (appendInterpolation) and the other parts (append-Literal), and those methods are called; our job is to assemble them into a single object. String is already doing that job, and we don't need to modify the way it implements appendLiteral; we just need to modify the way it implements append-Interpolation.

To help us do that, there's another protocol, DefaultStringInterpolation. We extend this protocol to inject a version of appendInterpolation that takes our interpolated type — in this case, Int — along with any additional parameters. Our implementation should perform any necessary transformations to get a String, and then call the default appendInterpolation(_:).

Here's an Int method toRoman() that yields an Optional String (Int values of 0 or less will return nil, to indicate that they can't be expressed in Roman numerals):

```
extension Int {
    func toRoman() -> String? {
        guard self > 0 else { return nil }
        let rom = ["M","CM","D","CD","C","XC","L","XL","X","IX","V","IV","I"]
        let ar = [1000,900,500,400,100,90,50,40,10,9,5,4,1]
        var result = ""
        var cur = self
        for (c, num) in zip(rom, ar) {
            let div = cur / num
            if (div > 0) {
                for _ in 0..<div { result += c }
                cur -= num * div
            }
        }
        return result
    }
}
```

Our interpolated type is Int, and we want to add one parameter, roman:, a Bool. So our extension of DefaultStringInterpolation will inject an implementation of append-Interpolation like this:

```
extension DefaultStringInterpolation {
    mutating func appendInterpolation(_ i: Int, roman: Bool) {
        if roman {
            if let r = i.toRoman() {
                self.appendInterpolation(r)
                return
            }
        }
        self.appendInterpolation(i)
    }
}
```

For a practical example of custom string interpolation in action, take a look at the Logger struct, introduced in Swift 5.3 as a Swifty wrapper for OSLog (Chapter 9). Its methods take string literals, but the parameter here is not a String; it is a special OSLogMessage struct that adopts ExpressibleByStringLiteral and ExpressibleByString-Interpolation and performs the interpolation at runtime, with custom interpolation parameters, by way of an OSLogInterpolation struct that adopts StringInterpolation-Protocol.

Reverse Generics

Starting in Swift 5.1 and iOS 13, a function return type can be specified as a subtype of some supertype without stating *what* subtype it is. The syntax is the keyword some followed by the supertype. Suppose we have a protocol P and a struct S that adopts it:

```
protocol P {}
struct S : P {}
```

Then we can declare a function that returns a P adopter without specifying what adopter it is, by saying some P:

```
func f() -> some P {
    return S()
}
```

A computed property getter (or a subscript getter) is a function, so a computed property can also be declared a some P:

```
var p : some P { S() }
```

A stored variable cannot be declared a some P explicitly, but it can be a some P by inference:

```
var p2 = f() // now p2 is typed as some P
```

In those examples, the type *actually* being returned is S — and the compiler knows this by inference. But users of f and p know only that the type is an unspecified adopter of P. For this reason, this is sometimes called a *reverse generic* (or an *opaque type*). Instead of you declaring a placeholder and helping the compiler resolve it, the compiler has already resolved it and hides that resolution behind the placeholder.

A reverse generic `some` P is different from declaring the returned type as P. For one thing, in some situations you *can't* declare the returned type as P — as when P is a generic protocol. (A generic protocol, you remember, can be used only as a type constraint.) But more important, if f declared its return type as P, then it could return *any* P adopter on any occasion. That's not the case with `some` P; f returns an S and can return *only* an S. The compiler uses strict typing to enforce this — but the external declaration hides what exactly the compiler is enforcing. If there are two P adopters, S and S2, then a `some` P resolved to S has the same underlying type as another `some` P resolved to S, but it does not have the same type as a `some` P resolved to S2. This should remind you of a regular generic: an `Optional<String>` is a different type from an `Optional<Int>`.

As a result, a `some` type plays well with a generic in a way that an ordinary supertype would not. Suppose we have a Named protocol and an adopter of that protocol:

```
protocol Named {
    var name : String {get set}
}
struct Person : Named {
    var name : String
}
```

And suppose we have a generic function that uses this protocol as a type constraint:

```
func haveSameName<T:Named>(_ named1:T, _ named2:T) -> Bool {
    return named1.name == named2.name
}
```

Obviously, you can hand two Person objects to this generic function, because they resolve the generic placeholder T the same way:

```
let matt = Person(name: "Matt")
let ethan = Person(name: "Ethan")
let ok = haveSameName(matt,ethan) // fine
```

But you couldn't do that with two Named objects, because they might or might not represent the same adopting type:

```
let named1 : Named = Person(name: "Matt")
let named2 : Named = Person(name: "Ethan")
let ok = haveSameName(named1, named2) // compile error
```

Now suppose we have a function `namedMaker` that makes a `some` Named out of a String:

```
func namedMaker(_ name: String) -> some Named {
    return Person(name:name)
}
```

You, the user of `namedMaker`, do not necessarily know what Named adopter is produced by `namedMaker`. But you *do* know that every call to `namedMaker` produces the *same* type of Named adopter! The compiler knows this too, and it also knows *what* type of Named adopter `namedMaker` produces. Therefore you might write this, and the compiler will allow it:

```
let named1 = namedMaker("Matt")
let named2 = namedMaker("Ethan")
let ok = haveSameName(named1, named2) // fine
```

The main place you are likely to encounter `some` is when using SwiftUI or some other domain-specific language or library that wants to vend specific types while masking them under some common identity. (You are less likely to use `some` in your own code, though I suppose it could be useful for masking types in one area of your code from visibility in another area.)

For example, in SwiftUI a View's `body` is typed as `some View`. You are shielded from the underlying complexities of compound view types, such as:

```
VStack<TupleView<(Text, HStack<TupleView<(Image, Image)>>)>>
```

At the same time, the compiler knows that that *is* the type of this View's body, and therefore behind the scenes SwiftUI can reason coherently about this view.

Function Builders

Swift 5.1 introduced the ability to intercept a function passed to another function, capture its parameters and content, and transform them by way of a *function builder* to get a different function that is actually passed. This complex and highly specialized feature is aimed at enabling Swift to embrace domain-specific languages — the chief such language, at the moment, being SwiftUI. You can say this in SwiftUI:

```
VStack {
    Text("Hello")
    Text("World")
}
```

That doesn't look like legal Swift, so what's going on? Well, VStack is a type, and we are creating an instance of that type. We call an initializer to instantiate VStack. This particular initializer takes a function as its `content:` parameter. We could write this as `VStack(content:f)`, but instead we use trailing closure syntax; the curly braces embrace the body of an anonymous function. This body is now handed off to a function builder, which detects its structure and transforms it into something that *is* legal Swift (and that creates a VStack instance consisting of two Texts). The entire look and feel of SwiftUI code rests on this mechanism.

Result

A frustrating problem arises when you want to throw an error in a context where this is forbidden. To see what I mean, consider a function that does some networking:

```
func doSomeNetworking(completion:@escaping (Data) -> ()) {
    URLSession.shared.dataTask(with: myURL) { data, _, err in
        if let data = data {
            completion(data)
        }
        if let err = err {
            throw err // compile error
        }
    }.resume()
}
```

In doSomeNetworking, we get some data from across the internet by calling resume on a URLSession's dataTask, supplying an anonymous function to be called when either data arrives or we get an error. These are handed to us as separate Optional parameters: an Optional wrapping a Data (data), and an Optional wrapping an Error (err). If the data arrives, data won't be nil, and we hand it back to whoever called doSome-Networking by calling a completion function that takes a Data object. If there's an error, data will be nil and err won't be. The question is: now what? We're not allowed to throw err; we're not in a throwing context, and there's no place for the thrown error to percolate up to; the dataTask anonymous function isn't a throws function, and even if it were, we'd be talking to the URLSession, not to the caller of doSomeNetworking.

One option is to respond to the error somehow right here in the anonymous function. Often, though, what we'd really like to do is to hand the error back to the caller of doSomeNetworking. One way to do that is to give the completion function another parameter, perpetuating the separate Optional parameters that were foisted upon us by Objective-C:

```
func doSomeNetworking(completion:@escaping (Data?, Error?) -> ()) {
    URLSession.shared.dataTask(with: myURL) { data, _, err in
        completion(data, err)
    }.resume()
}
```

But here's a cleaner solution — a type that expresses the notion of data-or-error in a single object. It's a generic enum called Result, with a success case and a failure case, each of them carrying an associated value which is the data or error, respectively:

```
func doSomeNetworking(completion:@escaping (Result<Data,Error>) -> ()) {
    URLSession.shared.dataTask(with: myURL) { data, _, err in
        if let data = data {
            completion(.success(data))
        }
        if let err = err {
```

```
            completion(.failure(err))
        }
    }.resume()
}
```

The really cool part is that Result provides an initializer that lets us express ourselves in a much more Swifty way: we can return the data or throw the error, just as we would if we weren't in this asynchronous situation:

```
func doSomeNetworking(completion:@escaping (Result<Data,Error>) -> ()) {
    URLSession.shared.dataTask(with: myURL) { data, _, err in
        let result = Result<Data,Error> {
            if let err = err {
                throw err
            }
            return data!
        }
        completion(result)
    }.resume()
}
```

And things work the same way at the caller's end. We call the Result object's get method, which is a throws function. Either this gives us the data or else it throws:

```
self.doSomeNetworking { result in
    do {
        let data = try result.get()
        // do something with the data
    } catch {
        // respond to the error
    }
}
```

That summarizes the most important aspects of the Result enum; there's more to know, but you can explore further on your own if you need to.

PART II

IDE

By now, you're doubtless anxious to jump in and start writing an app. To do that, you need a solid grounding in the tools you'll be using. The heart and soul of those tools can be summed up in one word: Xcode. In this part of the book we explore Xcode, the *IDE* (integrated development environment) in which you'll be programming iOS. Xcode is a big program, and writing an app involves coordinating a lot of pieces; this part of the book will help you become comfortable with Xcode. Along the way, we'll generate a simple working app through some hands-on tutorials.

- Chapter 6 tours Xcode and explains the architecture of the *project*, the collection of files from which an app is generated.

- Chapter 7 is about nibs. A *nib* is a file containing a drawing of your interface. Understanding nibs — how they work and how they relate to your code — is crucial to your use of Xcode and to development of just about any Cocoa app.

- Chapter 8 pauses to discuss the Xcode documentation and other sources of information on the API.

- Chapter 9 explains editing your code, testing and debugging your code, and the various steps you'll take on the way to submitting your app to the App Store. You'll probably want to skim this chapter quickly at first, returning to it as a detailed reference later while developing and submitting an actual app.

CHAPTER 6

Anatomy of an Xcode Project

Xcode is the application used to develop an iOS app. An Xcode *project* is the source for an app; it's the entire collection of files and settings used to construct the app. To create, develop, and maintain an app, it helps to know how to manipulate and navigate an Xcode project. You'll want to be familiar with Xcode, and you'll need to know about the nature and structure of Xcode projects and how Xcode shows them to you. That's the subject of this chapter.

Xcode is a powerful, complex, and very large program. Our survey will chart a safe, restricted, and essential path, focusing on aspects of Xcode that you most need to understand immediately, and resolutely ignoring everything else.

 The term "Xcode" is used in two ways. It's the name of the application in which you edit and build your app, and it's the name of an entire suite of utilities that accompanies it; in the latter sense, Instruments and the Simulator are part of Xcode. This ambiguity should generally present little difficulty.

New Project

Even before you've written any code, an Xcode project is quite elaborate. To see this, let's make a new, essentially "empty" project; you'll find that it isn't empty at all.

1. Start up Xcode and choose File → New → Project.

2. The "Choose a template" dialog appears. The *template* is your project's initial set of files and settings. When you pick a template, you're really picking an existing folder full of files; this folder is hidden deep inside the Xcode bundle, and will essentially be copied, with a few values filled in, to create your project.

   In this case, select iOS; under Application, select the App template. Click Next.

3. You are now asked to provide a name for your project (Product Name). Let's call our new project *Empty Window*.

   As Xcode copies the template folder, it's going to insert the project's name in several places, including using it as the name of the app. Whatever you type at this moment is something you'll be seeing throughout your project. You are not locked into the name of your project forever, though, and there's a separate setting allowing you to change the name of the app that your project produces. (I'll talk later about name changes; see "Renaming Parts of a Project" on page 373.)

   Spaces are legal in the project name, the app name, and the various names of files and folders that Xcode will generate automatically; and in the few places where spaces are problematic (such as the bundle identifier, which I'll discuss in a moment), the name you type as the Product Name will have its spaces converted to hyphens. But do *not* use any other punctuation in your project name! Such punctuation can cause Xcode features to break in subtle ways.

4. Ignore the Team pop-up menu for now; I'll discuss its significance in Chapter 9. Ignore the Organization Name as well; it is used only in some automatically generated code comments.

5. Note the Organization Identifier field. The first time you create a project, this field will be blank, and you should fill it in. The goal here is to create a unique string identifying you or your organization. The convention is to start the organization identifier with com. and to follow it with a string (possibly with multiple dot-components) that no one else is likely to use. Every app on a device or submitted to the App Store needs a unique bundle identifier. Your app's bundle identifier, which is shown in gray below the organization identifier, will consist by default of the organization identifier plus a version of the project's name; if you choose a unique organization identifier and give every project a unique name within your personal world, the bundle identifier will uniquely identify this project and the app that it produces. (You will be able to change the bundle identifier manually later if necessary.)

6. The Interface pop-up menu should say Storyboard, not SwiftUI. (The Life Cycle pop-up menu will then automatically be set to UIKit App Delegate.)

7. The Language pop-up menu lets you choose between Swift and Objective-C. This choice is not positively binding; it dictates the initial structure and code of the project template, but you are free to add Swift files to an Objective-C project, or Objective-C files to a Swift project. You can even start with an Objective-C project and decide later to convert it completely to Swift. (See "Bilingual Targets" on page 658.) For now, choose Swift.

8. For this example project, make sure Use Core Data and Include Tests are *not* checked. Click Next.

---

9. You've now told Xcode how to construct your project. Basically, it's going to copy a template folder from somewhere deep within the Xcode application bundle. But you need to tell it where to copy this template folder *to*. That's why Xcode is now presenting a Save dialog with a Create button. You are to specify the location of a folder that is about to be created — the *project folder* for this project. The project folder can go just about anywhere, and you can move it after creating it. I usually create new projects on the Desktop.

10. Xcode also offers, through a checkbox, to create a Git repository for your project. (You might need to click Options to see the checkbox.) In real life, this can be a great convenience (see Chapter 9), but for now, uncheck that checkbox. (If you see an Add To pop-up menu, leave it at the default, "Don't add to any project or workspace.") Click Create.

The *Empty Window* project folder is created on disk (on the Desktop, if that's the location you just specified), and the project window for the Empty Window project opens in Xcode.

The project we've just created is a working project; it really does build an iOS app called Empty Window. To see this, you can actually build the app — and run it! The scheme and destination in the project window's toolbar will be listed as Empty Window and some model of iPhone. (The scheme and destination are actually pop-up menus, so you can click them to change their values if needed.) Choose Product → Run. After some delay, the Simulator application opens and displays your app running — an empty white screen.

To *build* a project is to compile its code and assemble the compiled code, together with various resources, into the actual app. Typically, if you want to know whether your code compiles and your project is consistently and correctly constructed, you'll build the project (Product → Build). To *run* a project is to launch the built app, in the Simulator or on a connected device; if you want to know whether your code works as expected, you'll run the project (Product → Run), which automatically builds first if necessary.

The Project Window

An Xcode project embodies a lot of information about what files constitute the project and how they are to be used when building the app, such as:

- The source files (your code) that are to be compiled

- Any *.storyboard* or *.xib* files, graphically expressing interface objects to be instantiated as your app runs

- Any resources, such as icons, images, or sound files, that are to be part of the app

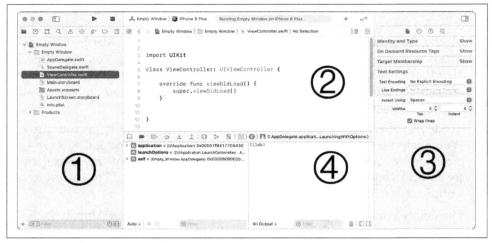

Figure 6-1. The project window

- All settings (instructions to the compiler, to the linker, and so on) that are to be obeyed as the app is built
- Any frameworks that the code will need when it runs

A single Xcode project window presents all of this information, lets you access, edit, and navigate your code, and reports the progress and results of such procedures as building or debugging an app and more. This window displays a lot of information and embodies a lot of functionality! A project window is powerful and elaborate; learning to navigate and understand it takes time. Let's pause to explore this window and see how it is constructed.

A project window has four main parts (Figure 6-1):

1. On the left is the Navigator pane. Show and hide it with View → Navigators → Show/Hide Navigator (Command-0) or with the button at the left end of the toolbar.

2. In the middle is the Editor pane (or simply "editor"). This is the main area of a project window. A project window nearly always displays an Editor pane.

3. On the right is the Inspectors pane. Show and hide it with View → Inspectors → Show/Hide Inspectors (Command-Option-0) or with the button at the right end of the toolbar.

4. At the bottom is the Debug pane. Show and hide it with View → Debug Area → Show/Hide Debug Area (Command-Shift-Y).

 All Xcode keyboard shortcuts can be customized; see the Key Bindings pane of the Preferences window. Keyboard shortcuts that I cite are the defaults.

The Navigator Pane

The Navigator pane is the column of information at the left of the project window. Among other things, it's your primary mechanism for controlling what you see in the main area of the project window (the editor). An important use pattern for Xcode is: you select something in the Navigator pane, and that thing is displayed in the editor.

It is possible to toggle the visibility of the Navigator pane (View → Navigators → Hide/Show Navigator, or Command-0); you might hide the Navigator pane temporarily to maximize your screen real estate (especially on a smaller monitor). You can change the Navigator pane's width by dragging the vertical line at its right edge. New in Xcode 12, if the project window is being displayed fullscreen with the Navigator pane hidden, you can display the Navigator pane by hovering the mouse at the left side of the screen.

The Navigator pane can display nine different sets of information; there are actually nine navigators. These are represented by the nine icons across its top; to switch among them, use these icons or their keyboard shortcuts (Command-1, Command-2, and so on). If the Navigator pane is hidden, pressing a navigator's keyboard shortcut both shows the Navigator pane and switches to that navigator.

Depending on your settings in the Behaviors pane of Xcode's preferences, a navigator might show itself automatically when you perform a certain action. For example, when you build your project, if warning messages or error messages are generated, the Issue navigator may appear. This automatic behavior will not prove troublesome, because it is usually the behavior you want, and if it isn't, you can change it; plus you can easily switch to a different navigator at any time.

Let's begin experimenting immediately with the various navigators:

Project navigator (Command-1)

Click here for basic navigation through the files that constitute your project (Figure 6-2). For example, in the Empty Window folder (the folder-like things in the Project navigator are actually called *groups*), click *AppDelegate.swift* to view its code in the editor.

At the top of the Project navigator, with a blue Xcode icon, is the Empty Window project itself; click it to view the settings associated with your project and its targets. Don't change anything here without knowing what you're doing!

The filter bar at the bottom of the Project navigator lets you limit what files are shown; when there are many files, this is great for quickly reaching a file with a known name. For example, try typing "delegate" in the filter bar search field. Don't forget to remove your filter when you're done experimenting.

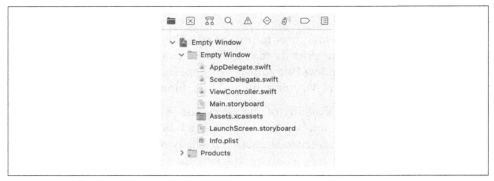

Figure 6-2. The Project navigator

Once you've filtered a navigator, it stays filtered until you remove the filter — even if you close the project! A common mistake is to filter a navigator, forget that you've done so, fail to notice the filter (because you're looking at the navigator itself, not down at the bottom where the filter bar is), and wonder, "Hey, where did all my files go?"

Source Control navigator (Command-2)

The Source Control navigator helps you manipulate how your project's files are handled through version control. I'll discuss version control in Chapter 9.

Symbol navigator (Command-3)

A *symbol* is a name, typically the name of a class or method. The Symbol navigator lists symbols available to your code. Among other things, this can be useful for navigating. For example, highlight the first two icons in the filter bar (so that they are filled), twist open the class listings, and see how quickly you can reach your code's implementation of SceneDelegate's `sceneDidBecomeActive(_:)` method.

Try highlighting the filter bar icons in various ways to see how the contents of the Symbol navigator change. Type in the search field in the filter bar to limit what appears in the Symbol navigator; for example, try typing "active" in the search field, and see what happens.

Find navigator (Command-4)

This is a powerful search facility for finding text globally in your project. You can also summon the Find navigator with Find → Find in Project (Command-Shift-F). The words above the search field show what options are currently in force; they are pop-up menus, so click one to change the options. This is a powerful intelligent search that can filter on how a term is used. Try searching for "delegate" among References; then change it to search among Definitions (Figure 6-3). Click a search result to jump to it in your code.

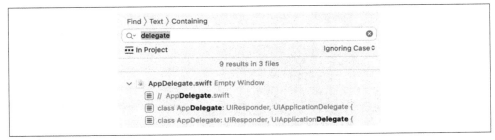

Figure 6-3. The Find navigator

Below the search field, at the left, is the current *search scope*. This limits what files will be searched. Click it to reveal the search scopes. You can create or edit a "smart" scope (for example, search only *.swift* files), and you can limit the search to one or more groups (folders).

You can type in the other search field, the one in the filter bar at the bottom, to limit further which search results are displayed. (I'm going to stop calling your attention to the filter bar now; every navigator has it in some form.)

Issue navigator (Command-5)

You'll need this navigator primarily when your code has issues. This doesn't refer to emotional instability; it's Xcode's term for warning and error messages emitted when you build your project. The Issue navigator can also display certain runtime issues (such as leaks, as I'll explain in Chapter 9).

To see the Issue navigator in action, let's give your code a buildtime issue. Navigate to the file *AppDelegate.swift*, and in the blank line after the last comment at the top of the file's contents, above the `import` line, type `howdy`. Build the project (Command-B). Switch to the Issue navigator if it doesn't appear automatically; in its Buildtime pane, it displays some error messages, showing that the compiler is unable to cope with this illegal word appearing in an illegal place. Click an issue to see it within its file. In your code, issue banners appear to the right of lines containing issues; the compiler can even underline the troublesome spot within a line. But it's always a good idea to look at the Issue navigator as well, because it may contain additional useful information.

Now that you've made Xcode miserable, select "howdy" and delete it; save and build again, and your issues will be gone. If only real life were this easy!

You can create a custom buildtime issue, either a compile error or a warning, by starting a line with `#error` or `#warning` respectively followed by a string literal in parentheses, like this: `#warning("Fix this!")`. This can be a dramatic way to leave a note to whoever subsequently tries to compile this code — possibly your future self.

Figure 6-4. The Debug layout

Test navigator (Command-6)

This navigator lists test files and individual test methods and permits you to run your tests and see whether they succeeded. A test is code that isn't part of your app; rather, it calls a bit of your app's code, or exercises your app's interface, to see whether things behave as expected. I'll talk more about tests in Chapter 9.

Debug navigator (Command-7)

By default, this navigator will appear when your code is paused while you're debugging it. There is not a strong distinction in Xcode between running and debugging; the milieu is the same. The difference is mostly a matter of whether breakpoints are obeyed (more about that, and about debugging in general, in Chapter 9).

To see the Debug navigator in action, you'll need to give your code a breakpoint. Navigate once more to the file *AppDelegate.swift*, select in the line that says return true, and choose Debug → Breakpoints → Add Breakpoint at Current Line to make a breakpoint arrow appear on that line. Run the project. By default, as the breakpoint is encountered, the Navigator pane switches to the Debug navigator, and the Debug pane appears at the bottom of the window. This overall layout (Figure 6-4) will rapidly become familiar as you debug your projects.

The Debug navigator starts with several numeric and graphical displays of profiling information (at a minimum, you'll see CPU, Memory, Disk, and Network); click one to see extensive graphical information in the editor. This information allows you to track possible misbehavior of your app as you run it, without the added complexity of running the Instruments utility (discussed in Chapter 9). To toggle the visibility of the profiling information at the top of the Debug navigator, click the "gauge" icon (to the right of the process's name).

The Debug navigator also displays the call stack, with the names of the nested methods in which a pause occurs; as you would expect, you can click a method name to navigate to it. You can shorten or lengthen the list with the first button in the filter bar at the bottom of the navigator.

The Debug pane, which can be shown or hidden at will (View → Debug Area → Hide/Show Debug Area, or Command-Shift-Y), has at its top the *debug bar* containing various buttons, and consists of two subpanes:

The variables list (on the left)
> The variables in scope for the selected method in the call stack at the point where we are paused, along with their values.

The console (on the right)
> Here the debugger displays text messages; that's how you learn of exceptions thrown by your running app, plus you can have your code deliberately send you log messages describing your app's progress and behavior. Such messages are important, so keep an eye on the console as your app runs. You can also use the console to enter commands to the debugger. This can often be a better way to explore values during a pause than the variables list.

Either the variables list or the console can be hidden using the two buttons at the bottom right of the pane. The console can also be summoned by choosing View → Debug Area → Activate Console.

Breakpoint navigator (Command-8)
> This navigator lists all your breakpoints. At the moment you have only one, but when you're actively debugging a large project with many breakpoints, you'll be glad of this navigator. Also, this is where you create special breakpoints (such as symbolic breakpoints), and in general it's your center for managing existing breakpoints. We'll return to this topic in Chapter 9.

Report navigator (Command-9)
> This navigator lists your recent major actions, such as building or running (debugging) your project. Click a listing to see (in the editor) the report generated when you performed that action. The report might contain information that isn't displayed in any other way, and also it lets you dredge up console messages from the recent past ("What was that exception I got while debugging a moment ago?").

By clicking on the listing for a successful build, we can see the steps by which a build takes place (Figure 6-5). To reveal the full text of a step, click that step and

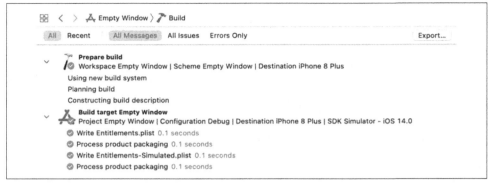

Figure 6-5. The start of a build report

then click the Expand Transcript button that appears at the far right (and see also the menu items in the Editor menu).

The Inspectors Pane

The Inspectors pane is the column at the right of the project window. It contains inspectors that provide information about the current selection or its settings; if those settings can be changed, this is where you change them. The Inspectors pane's importance emerges mostly when you're editing a *.storyboard* or *.xib* file (Chapter 7). But it can be useful also while editing code, mostly because Quick Help, a form of documentation (Chapter 8), is displayed here as well. To toggle the visibility of the Inspectors pane, choose View → Inspectors → Hide/Show Inspectors (Command-Option-0). You can change the Inspectors pane's width by dragging the vertical line at its left edge. New in Xcode 12, if the project window is being displayed fullscreen with the Inspectors pane hidden, you can display the Inspectors pane by hovering the mouse at the right side of the screen.

What appears in the Inspectors pane depends on what's selected in the current editor:

A code file is being edited

The Inspectors pane shows the File inspector, the History inspector, or the Quick Help inspector. Toggle between them with the icons at the top of the Inspectors pane, or with their keyboard shortcuts (Command-Option-1, Command-Option-2, Command-Option-3). The File inspector consists of multiple sections, each of which can be expanded or collapsed by clicking its header; I'll give an example of using it in Chapter 9 when I talk about localization. History is about version control (Chapter 9 as well). Quick Help can be useful because it displays documentation (Chapter 8).

A .storyboard or .xib file is being edited

The Inspectors pane adds the Identity inspector (Command-Option-4), the Attributes inspector (Command-Option-5), the Size inspector (Command-Option-6), and the Connections inspector (Command-Option-7). These inspectors can consist of multiple sections, each of which can be expanded or collapsed by clicking its header. I'll talk more about them in Chapter 7.

Other forms of editing may cause other inspector combinations to appear here.

The Editor

In the middle of the project window is the *editor*. This is where you get actual work done, reading and writing your code (Chapter 9) or designing your interface in a *.storyboard* or *.xib* file (Chapter 7). The editor is the core of the project window. You can hide the Navigator pane, the Inspectors pane, and the Debug pane, but there is basically no such thing as a project window without an editor.

The *jump bar* across the top shows you hierarchically what file is currently being edited. It also allows you to switch to a different file. Each path component in the jump bar is a pop-up menu. These pop-up menus can be summoned by clicking on a path component, or by using keyboard shortcuts (shown in the View → Editor submenu). Control-4 summons a hierarchical pop-up menu, which can be navigated entirely with the keyboard, allowing you to choose a different file in your project to edit. Each pop-up menu in the jump bar also has a filter field; to see it, summon a pop-up menu from the jump bar and start typing. Thus you can navigate your project even if the Project navigator isn't showing.

Command-click a jump bar component to summon a menu showing the corresponding file in the Finder and its hierarchy of enclosing folders.

The symbol at the left end of the jump bar (Control-1) summons the Related Items menu. This helps you navigate to files conceptually related to the current one. Its contents depend on both the current file and the current selection within it. You can navigate to files declaring related types (Superclasses, Subclasses, Siblings, and adopted Protocols) and to methods that call or are called by the currently selected method. The Generated Interface menu displays a file's public interface as seen by Swift or Objective-C (see Appendix A).

The editor remembers the history of what it has displayed, and you can return to previously viewed content with the Back button in the jump bar, which is also a pop-up menu (Control-2). Alternatively, choose Navigate → Go Back (Command-Control-Left).

Editor panes

It is likely, as you develop a project, that you'll want to edit more than one file simultaneously, or obtain multiple views of a single file so that you can edit different areas of it simultaneously. For this purpose, the Editor pane area of the project window can be subdivided into smaller editor panes. Each pane can display a different file, or a different area of the same file.

To summon a new editor pane, choose File → New → Editor (Command-Control-T) or click the Add Editor button at the top right of an editor. Alternatively, if there is only one editor pane, Option-click a file listing in the Project navigator to open it in a new editor pane.

The new pane appears to the right of the current editor or below it; choose View → Change Editor Orientation to reverse this default or to move a pane from the right to below (or *vice versa*). To summon a new editor pane in the other orientation, choose File → New → Editor Below / On Right, or Option-click the Add Editor button.

To close an editor pane, choose File → Close Editor, or click the X button at the top left of an editor pane.

To zoom an editor pane temporarily, so that it takes over the whole editor area without closing any other panes, choose View → Editor → Focus, or click the outward double-arrow button at the top left of the pane. To unzoom, do the same thing again: choose View → Editor → Hide Focus, or click the inward double-arrow button. While a pane is zoomed, Close Editor and the X button are disabled; you have to unzoom the pane before you can close it.

 Zooming a pane, deliberately or accidentally, and then wondering why you can't make additional editor panes, is a common beginner mistake.

When there are multiple editor panes, what happens when you click a file listing in the Project navigator? By default, its destination is current editor pane. But you can Option-click a file listing to specify a different destination; the exact details depend on your settings in the Navigation pane of Xcode's preferences. For maximum flexibility, Option-Shift-click a file listing to enter *destination chooser* mode; you can then navigate with arrow keys to specify where you want this file to open — in an existing pane or as a new additional pane, to the right or below — and hit Return to open it there.

I like the destination chooser so much that I have made it the default: in the Navigation preference pane, under Optional Navigation, I've selected Uses Destination Chooser. The outcome is that the Option-click and Option-Shift-click shortcuts are swapped: the destination chooser appears when I hold the Option key while navigating.

If the Project navigator selection gets out of sync with the file displayed in the current editor pane, you can bring it back in sync by choosing Navigate → Reveal in Project Navigator (Command-Shift-J).

Assistant panes

An assistant pane is a special kind of editor pane tied to some primary editor pane, in the following way: when you cause the primary pane to display a different file, its assistant pane *automatically* displays a different file to match. To summon an assistant pane, choose Editor → Assistant (or choose Assistant from the Editor Options pop-up menu at the top right of the editor pane). You'll know you've entered editor-and-assistant mode because both panes will display an icon showing two linked rings. To configure whether the assistant pane divides the editor vertically or horizontally, choose Editor → Layout → Assistant On Right/Bottom (or use the Editor Options pop-up menu).

Exactly what category of file the assistant pane automatically displays depends upon what you've specified as its relationship to the primary pane. You do that with the first pop-up menu in the assistant pane's jump bar, containing the linked rings icon (Control-4). Your choices here are much like the menu items in the Related Items menu.

If more than one file falls into the category in question — for example, you've set the assistant to show Callers and in the primary pane you've selected a method with more than one caller — then a pair of arrow buttons appears at the right end of the assistant's jump bar, with which you can navigate between them, or use the second jump bar component (Control-5).

Tabs and windows

New in Xcode 12, there are two kinds of tab. This is rather confusing, because menu commands don't always distinguish them. There are *document tabs* and *window tabs*:

Document tabs
> A document tab (new in Xcode 12) is an alternative way of populating an editor pane with multiple files. Instead of *splitting* the editor pane into two or more smaller panes, the editor pane displays different files as different tabs that you see *one at a time*, occupying the *entire* editor pane — and then you can readily switch between them.
>
> To make a document tab, choose File → Open In Tab (Command-Option-O), or Control-click on a file listing in the Project navigator and choose Open In Tab. Or, if the document tab bar is already showing, you can drag file listings into it from the Project navigator to open them as tabs. (To show the document tab bar all the time, choose View → Always Show Tab Bar so that it is checked.) Additionally, in the Navigation preference pane, you can set Optional Navigation or

Double-click Navigation to Uses Tab. I like the latter; that way, I double-click a listing in the Project navigator to open it as a document tab.

A file opened as a document tab is "pinned" as a tab in the editor pane. By "pinned," I mean that if you click a different file listing in the Project navigator, it opens as a separate tab rather than replacing this file. So "pinned" files have a degree of permanence. They mean: These are the particular files I want to work on right now. (Tabs that open *without* being pinned *are* replaceable; they display their filenames in italics.) You can "pin" as many files as you like, making it easy to switch between them and ensure that none of them will be replaced accidentally.

Window tabs (and windows)

A window tab (which Xcode 11 and before calls simply a tab) doesn't just display a file, like an editor pane or a document tab; it displays the *whole project window interface*, and can display it differently from another window tab. Thus one window tab might show the Project navigator, while another might have the Project navigator hidden, or display a different navigator. In other words, a window tab is like a second window on the same project, except that it doesn't occupy any independent screen real estate: rather, it shares the space with an existing project window.

To make a new window tab, choose File → New → Window Tab (Command-T), revealing the window's tab bar (just below the toolbar) if it wasn't showing already. Or, instead of a window tab, you can display a second independent window on the same project. To make a new window, choose File → New → Window (Command-Shift-T), or promote a window tab to be a window by dragging it right out of its current window.

In the Navigation preference pane, you can set Optional Navigation or Double-click Navigation to Uses Separate Window Tab or Uses Separate Window.

Project File and Dependents

The first item in the Project navigator represents the project itself. (In the Empty Window project that we created earlier in this chapter, it is called Empty Window.) Hierarchically dependent upon it are items that contribute to the building of the project. Many of the listings in the Project navigator correspond to items on disk in the project folder.

To survey this correspondence, let's view our Empty Window project in two ways simultaneously — in the Project navigator in the Xcode project window, and in the project folder in a Finder window. Select the project listing in the Project navigator and choose File → Show in Finder. The Finder displays the contents of your project folder (Figure 6-6).

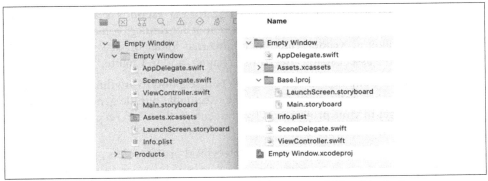

Figure 6-6. The Project navigator (Xcode) and the project folder (Finder)

Contents of the Project Folder

The most important file in the project folder is *Empty Window.xcodeproj*. This is the *project file*, corresponding to the project listed first in the Project navigator. All Xcode's knowledge about your project — what files it consists of and how to build the project — is stored in this file. To open a project from the Finder, double-click the project file. (Alternatively, you can drag the project folder onto Xcode's icon in the Finder, the Dock, or the application switcher; Xcode will locate the project file and open it for you.)

The Project navigator displays groups (folder-like things) and files hierarchically from the project. Let's consider how these correspond to reality on disk as portrayed in the Finder (Figure 6-6):

- The Empty Window group corresponds directly to the *Empty Window* folder on disk. Groups in the Project navigator don't necessarily correspond to folders on disk in the Finder, and folders on disk in the Finder don't necessarily correspond to groups in the Project navigator. But in this case, they do correspond (this is a *folder-linked group*, as I'll explain later).

- Files within the Empty Window group, such as *AppDelegate.swift*, correspond to real files on disk that are inside the *Empty Window* folder. If you were to create additional code files (which, in real life, you would almost certainly do in the course of developing your project), you would likely put them in the Empty Window group in the Project navigator, and they, too, would then be in the *Empty Window* folder on disk. (However, your files can live anywhere and your project will still work fine.)

- Two files in the Empty Window group, *Main.storyboard* and *LaunchScreen.storyboard*, appear in the Finder inside a folder that doesn't visibly correspond to anything in the Project navigator, called *Base.lproj*. This arrangement has to do with *localization*, which I'll discuss in Chapter 9.

- The item *Assets.xcassets* in the Project navigator corresponds to a specially structured folder *Assets.xcassets* on disk. This is an *asset catalog*; you add resources to the asset catalog in Xcode, which maintains that folder on disk for you. I'll talk more about the asset catalog later in this chapter, and in Chapter 9.

- The Products group and its contents don't correspond to anything in the project folder. Xcode generates a reference to the executable bundle generated by building each target in your project, and by convention these references appear in the Products group.

Now that you have inspected the contents of a typical project folder, you should have little need to open a project folder ever again, except in order to double-click the project file to open the project. Generally speaking, you should not manipulate the contents of a project folder by way of the Finder; manipulate the project *in the project window*. The project expects things in the project folder to be a certain way; if you make any alterations to the project folder directly in the Finder, behind the project's back, you can upset those expectations and break the project. When you work in the project window, it is Xcode itself that makes any necessary changes in the project folder, and all will be well.

Groups

The purpose of groups in the Project navigator is to make the Project navigator work conveniently for you. So feel free to add further groups! If some of your code files have to do with a login screen that your app sometimes presents, you might clump them together in a Login group. If your app is to contain some sound files, you might put them into a Sounds group. And so on.

A group might or might not correspond to a folder on disk in the project folder. There's a visual distinction: a group that corresponds to a folder on disk is a *folder-linked group*, and has a solid folder icon, like the Empty Window group in Figure 6-6; a group plain and simple exists purely within the Project navigator, and has a marked folder icon, like the Products group in Figure 6-6. You'll encounter this distinction at various times:

Creating a group
> When you make a new group, there's a choice of menu items: in the contextual menu, you might see New Group and New Group Without Folder. (Confusingly, the choice might sometimes be New Group and New Group *With* Folder.) The one without a folder creates a group plain and simple; the other creates a folder-linked group.

Using a group
> When you place a file into a folder-linked group, it goes into the corresponding folder on disk (like the contents of the *Empty Window* folder in Figure 6-6).

When you place a file into a group plain and simple, the group is effectively ignored in determining where the file will go; it generally will go into the same place as files at the same level as the group.

Renaming a group

To rename a group, select it in the Project navigator and press Return to make the name editable. When you rename a folder-linked group, the folder on disk is renamed as well.

The Target

A *target* is a collection of parts along with rules and settings for how to build a product from those parts. Whenever you build, what you're building is a target (possibly more than one target).

Select the Empty Window project at the top of the Project navigator, and you'll see the project itself along with its targets listed on the left side of the editor (Figure 6-7). Our Empty Window project comes with one target — the *app target*, called Empty Window (like the project itself). The app target is the target that you use to build and run your app. Its settings are the settings that tell Xcode how your app is to be built; its product is the app itself.

Under certain circumstances, you might add further targets to a project:

- You might want to add unit tests or interface tests to your project. A test bundle is a target.
- You might write an application extension, such as a photo editing extension (custom photo editing interface to appear in the Photos app). An extension is a target.
- You might write a library, such as a custom framework, as part of your iOS app. A custom framework is a target.

The project name and the list of targets can appear in two ways (Figure 6-7): either as a column on the left side of the editor, or, if that column is collapsed to save space, as a pop-up menu at the top left of the editor. If, in the column or pop-up menu, you select the *project*, you *edit the project*; if you select a *target*, you *edit the target*.

Build Phases

Edit the app target and click Build Phases at the top of the editor (Figure 6-8). These are the stages by which your app is built. The *build phases* are both a report to you on how the target will be built and a set of instructions to Xcode on how to build the target; if you change the build phases, you change the build process. Click each build phase to see a list of the files in your target to which that build phase will apply.

Figure 6-7. Two ways of showing the project and targets

Two of the build phases have contents. The meanings of these build phases are pretty straightforward:

Compile Sources

Certain files (your code) are compiled, and the resulting compiled code is copied into the app. This build phase typically applies to all of the target's *.swift* files. Sure enough, it currently contains all three Swift files supplied by the app template when we created the project.

Copy Bundle Resources

Certain files are copied into the app, so that your code or the system can find them there when the app runs. This build phase currently applies to the asset catalog; any resources you add to the asset catalog will be copied into your app as part of the catalog. It also applies to your launch storyboard file, *LaunchScreen.storyboard*, and your app's interface storyboard file, *Main.storyboard*.

Copying doesn't necessarily mean making an identical copy. Certain types of file are automatically treated in special ways as they are copied into the app bundle. Copying the asset catalog means that icons in the catalog are written out to the top level of the app bundle, while the asset catalog itself is transformed into a *.car* file; copying a *.storyboard* file means that it is transformed into a *.storyboardc* file, which is itself a bundle containing nib files.

You can alter these lists manually, and sometimes you may need to do so. For instance:

- If something in your project, such as a sound file, is not in Copy Bundle Resources and you want it copied into the app during the build process, drag it from the Project navigator into the Copy Bundle Resources list, or (easier) click the Plus button beneath the Copy Bundle Resources list to get a helpful dialog listing everything in your project.

- Conversely, if something in your project is in the Copy Bundle Resources list and you *don't* want it copied into the app, delete it from the list; this will not delete it

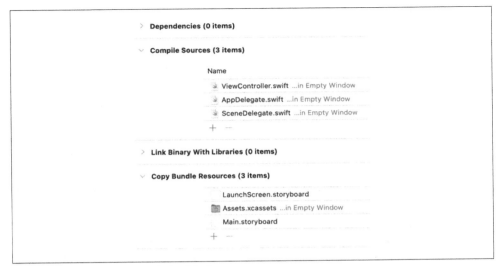

Figure 6-8. The app target's build phases

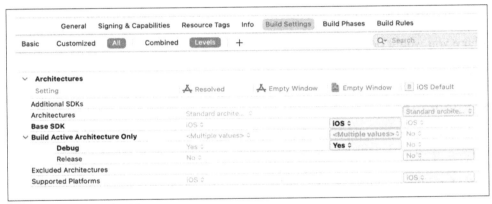

Figure 6-9. Target build settings

from your project, from the Project navigator, or from the Finder, but only from the list of things to be copied into your app.

Build Settings

Build phases are only one aspect of how a target knows how to build the app. The other aspect is *build settings*. To see them, edit the target and click Build Settings at the top of the editor (Figure 6-9). Here you'll find a long list of settings, most of which you'll never touch. Xcode examines this list in order to know what to do at various stages of the build process. Build settings are the reason your project compiles and builds the way it does.

You can determine what build settings are displayed by clicking Basic or All. The settings are combined into categories, and you can close or open each category heading to save room. To locate a setting quickly based on something you already know about it, such as its name, use the search field at the top right to filter what settings are shown.

You can determine how build settings are displayed by clicking Combined or Levels; in Figure 6-9, I've clicked Levels, in order to discuss what levels are. It turns out that not only does a *target* contain values for the build settings, but the *project* also contains values for the same build settings; furthermore, Xcode has certain built-in default build setting values. The Levels display shows all of these levels at once, so you can trace the derivation of the actual values used for every build setting.

To understand the chart, read from right to left. For example, the iOS default for the Build Active Architecture Only setting's Debug configuration (far right) is No. But then the project comes along (second column from the right) and sets it to Yes. The target (third column from the right) doesn't change that setting, so the result (fourth column from the right) is that the setting resolves to Yes.

You will rarely have occasion to manipulate build settings directly, as the defaults are usually acceptable. Nevertheless, you *can* change build setting values, and this is where you would do so. You can change a value at the project level or at the target level. You can select a build setting and show Quick Help in the Inspectors pane to learn more about it.

Configurations

There are actually multiple lists of build setting values — though only one such list applies when a particular build is performed. Each such list is called a *configuration*. Multiple configurations are needed because you build in different ways at different times for different purposes, and you'll want certain build settings to take on different values under different circumstances.

By default, there are two configurations:

Debug
    This configuration is used throughout the development process, as you write and run your app.

Release
    This configuration is used for late-stage testing, when you want to check performance on a device, and for archiving the app to be submitted to the App Store.

Configurations exist at all because the project says so. To see where the project says so, edit the project and click Info at the top of the editor (Figure 6-10). Note that these configurations are just names. You can create additional configurations, and

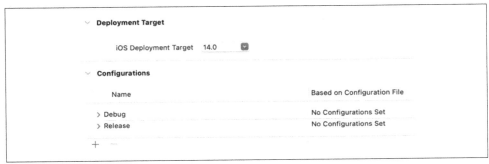

Figure 6-10. Configurations

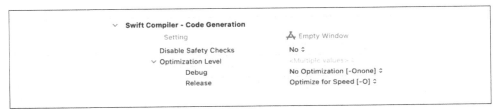

Figure 6-11. How configurations affect build settings

when you do, you're just adding to the list of names. The importance of configurations emerges only when those names are coupled with build setting values. Configurations can affect build setting values both at the project level and at the target level.

For example, return to the target build settings (Figure 6-9) and type "optim" into the search field. Now you can look at the Optimization Level build setting for Swift, at the very bottom of the window (Figure 6-11):

- The Debug configuration value for Optimization Level is No Optimization: while you're developing your app, you build with the Debug configuration, so your code is just compiled line by line in a straightforward way.

- The Release configuration value for Optimization Level is Optimize for Speed. When your app is ready to ship, you build it with the Release configuration, so the resulting binary is optimized for speed, which is great for your users running the app on a device, but would be no good while you're developing the app because breakpoints and stepping in the debugger wouldn't work properly. Compilation may take longer when the compiler must optimize for speed, but you won't mind the delay, because you won't do a Release build very often.

Schemes and Destinations

So far, I have not said how Xcode knows *which* configuration to use during a particular build. This is determined by a scheme.

Figure 6-12. The scheme editor

A *scheme* unites a target (or multiple targets) with a build configuration, with respect to the purpose for which you're building. A new project comes by default with a single scheme, named after the project. The Empty Window project's single scheme is currently called Empty Window. To see it, choose Product → Scheme → Edit Scheme. The scheme editor dialog opens (Figure 6-12).

On the left side of the scheme editor are listed various actions you might perform from the Product menu. Click an action to see its corresponding settings in this scheme.

The first action, the Build action, is different from the other actions, because it is common to all of them — the other actions all implicitly involve building. The Build action merely determines what target(s) will be built when each of the other actions is performed. For our project this means that the app target is always to be built, regardless of the action you perform.

The second action, the Run action, determines the settings that will be used when you build and run. The Build Configuration pop-up menu (in the Info pane) is set to Debug. That explains where the current build configuration comes from: whenever you build and run (Product → Run, or click the Run button in the toolbar), you're using the Debug build configuration and the build setting values that correspond to it, because you're using this scheme, and that's what this scheme says to do when you build and run.

You can edit an existing scheme, and this can be useful especially as a temporary measure for doing certain kinds of specialized debugging. For example, the Run action's Diagnostics tab contains checkboxes that let you turn on the Address Sanitizer or the Thread Sanitizer, useful for tracking down certain types of obscure

Figure 6-13. The Scheme pop-up menu

runtime error. You'd check the checkbox, build and run, work on the error, and then uncheck the checkbox again.

Alternatively, you can add a scheme. A typical approach is to duplicate an existing scheme and then modify the duplicate. Instead of changing your main scheme to turn on the Address Sanitizer temporarily, you might have a second scheme where the Address Sanitizer is always turned on; you would then use the Address Sanitizer by switching schemes.

Handy access to schemes and their management is through the Scheme pop-up menu in the project window toolbar (Figure 6-13).

The Scheme pop-up menu is something you're going to be using a lot. Your schemes are listed here; hierarchically appended to each scheme are the destinations. A *destination* is effectively a machine that can run your app. On any given occasion, you might want to run the app on a physical device or in the Simulator — and, if in the Simulator, you might want to specify that a particular type of device should be simulated. To make that choice, pick a destination in the Scheme pop-up menu.

Destinations and schemes have nothing to do with one another. The presence of destinations in the Scheme pop-up menu is just a convenience, letting you choose a scheme or a destination or both in a single move. To switch easily among destinations without changing schemes, click the destination name in the Scheme pop-up menu. To switch among schemes, possibly also determining the destination (as shown in Figure 6-13), click the scheme name in the Scheme pop-up menu. You can open the Scheme pop-up menu with Control-0 (zero), and the Destination pop-up menu with Control-Shift-0; the menu can then be navigated with the keyboard, and is also filterable in the same way as the jump bar (discussed earlier in this chapter).

Each simulated device has a system version that is installed on that device. At the moment, all our simulated devices are running iOS 14; there is no distinction to be drawn, and the system version is not shown. But you can download earlier SDKs (systems) in Xcode's Components preference pane. If you do, and if your app can run

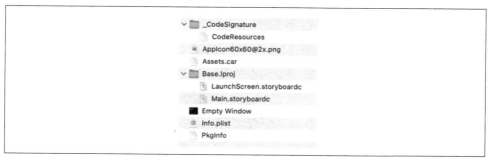

Figure 6-14. Contents of the app package

under more than one system version, you might also see a system version listed in the Scheme pop-up menu as part of a Simulator destination name.

To manage destinations, choose Window → Devices and Simulators. Switch to the Simulators pane if necessary. This is where you govern what simulated devices exist. Here you can create, delete, and rename simulated devices, and specify whether a simulated device actually appears as a destination in the Scheme pop-up menu.

From Project to Built App

Now that you know what's in a project, I'm going to summarize how Xcode builds that project into an app. Let's first jump ahead and examine the end product — the app itself.

What *is* an app anyway? It's actually a special kind of folder called a *package* (and a special kind of package called a *bundle*). The Finder normally disguises a package as a file and does not dive into it to reveal its contents to the user, but you can bypass this protection and investigate an app bundle with the Show Package Contents command. By doing so, you can study the internal structure of your built app bundle.

We'll use the Empty Window app that we built earlier as a sample minimal app to investigate. Open the Products group in the Project navigator, Control-click the app listing, and choose Show in Finder. In the Finder, Control-click the Empty Window app, and choose Show Package Contents. Here you can see the results of the build process (Figure 6-14).

Think of the app bundle as a transformation of the project folder. Here are some of the things it contains, and how they relate to what's in the project folder:

Empty Window
> Our app's compiled code. The build process has compiled all our Swift files into this single file, our app's binary. This is the heart of the app, its actual executable material.

Main.storyboardc

Our app's interface storyboard file. The project's *Main.storyboard* is currently where our app's interface comes from — in this case, an empty white view occupying the entire window. The build process has compiled *Main.storyboard* into a tighter format, resulting in a *.storyboardc* file, which is actually a bundle of nib files to be loaded as required while the app runs. One of these nib files, loaded as our app launches, will be the source of the hitherto empty view displayed in the interface. *Main.storyboardc* sits in the same *Base.lproj* subfolder as *Main.storyboard* does in the project folder; as I said earlier, this folder structure has to do with localization (to be discussed in Chapter 9).

LaunchScreen.storyboardc

This is the compiled version of *LaunchScreen.storyboard*, containing the interface that will be displayed briefly during the time it takes for our app to launch (the *launch screen*).

Assets.car, AppIcon60x60@2x.png

An asset catalog and an icon file. In preparation for this build, I added an icon image to the original asset catalog, *Assets.xcassets*. The build process has compiled this file, resulting in a compiled asset catalog file (*.car*) containing any resources that have been added to the catalog; at the same time, the icon file has been written out to the top level of the app bundle.

Info.plist

A configuration file in a strict text format (a *property list* file). It is derived from, but is not identical to, the project's *Info.plist*. It contains instructions to the system about how to treat and launch the app. For example, the project's *Info.plist* has a calculated bundle name derived from the product name, $(PRODUCT_NAME); in the built app's *Info.plist*, this calculation has been performed, and the value reads Empty Window, which is why our app is labeled "Empty Window" on the device. Also, in conjunction with the asset catalog writing out our icon file to the app bundle's top level, a setting has been added to the built app's *Info.plist* telling the system the name of that icon file, so that the system can find it and display it as our app's icon.

Frameworks

The built app contains no frameworks. That was a major innovation of Swift 5, standing in sharp contrast to what used to happen; previously, several megabytes of framework files were added to the app, containing the entirety of the Swift language! One of the great overarching achievements of Swift 5 was the introduction of *ABI stability,* which means, in practical terms, that the Swift frameworks could be moved off into the system, reducing the size and overhead of your built apps. However, that's only on iOS 13 and later. If you were to build this app for an

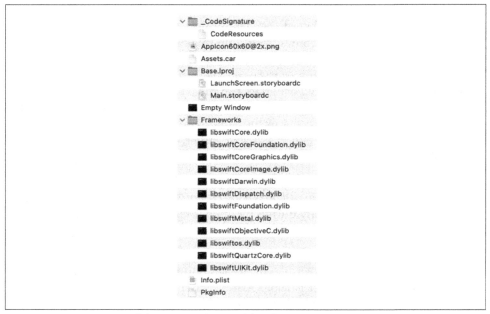

Figure 6-15. Contents of the app package, old style

earlier system, those framework files would return, and the app package would look more like Figure 6-15.

In real life, an app bundle may contain more files, but the difference will be mostly one of degree, not kind. Our project might have additional *.storyboard* or *.xib* files, additional frameworks, or additional resources such as sound files. All of these would make their way into the app bundle. Also, an app bundle built to run on a device will contain some security-related files.

You are now in a position to appreciate, in a general sense, how the components of a project are treated and assembled into an app, and what responsibilities accrue to you, the programmer, in order to ensure that the app is built correctly. The rest of this section outlines what goes into the building of an app from a project.

Build Settings

We have already talked about how build settings are determined. Xcode itself, the project, and the target all contribute to the resolved build setting values, some of which may differ depending on the build configuration. You, the programmer, will have specified a scheme before building; the scheme determines the build configuration, meaning the specific set of build setting values that will apply as this build proceeds.

Property List Settings

Your project contains a property list file that will be used to generate the built app's *Info.plist* file. The file in the project does not have to be named *Info.plist*! The app target knows what file it is because it is specified in the Info.plist File build setting. In our project, the value of the app target's Info.plist File build setting is *Empty Window/Info.plist*.

The property list file is a collection of key–value pairs. You can edit it, and you may need to do so. There are three main ways to edit your project's *Info.plist*:

- Edit the target, and switch to the General pane. Some of the settings here are effectively ways of editing the *Info.plist*. For example, when you click a Device Orientation checkbox here, you are changing the value of the "Supported interface orientations" key in the *Info.plist*.

- Edit the *Info.plist* file manually by selecting it in the Project navigator. The editor displays a special *.plist* editor interface. By default, most of the key names (and some of the values) are displayed descriptively, in terms of their functionality; for example, it says "Bundle name" instead of the actual key, which is CFBundleName. To view the actual keys, choose Editor → Raw Keys & Values, or use the contextual menu.

    If you like, you can see the file in its true XML text form: Control-click the *Info.plist* file in the Project navigator and choose Open As → Source Code from the contextual menu. (But editing an *Info.plist* as raw XML is risky, because if you make a mistake you can invalidate the XML, causing things to break with no warning.)

- Edit the target, and switch to the Info pane. The Custom iOS Target Properties section shows effectively the same information as editing the *Info.plist* in the editor.

Some values in the project's *Info.plist* are processed at build time to transform them into their final values in the built app's *Info.plist*. For example, the "Executable file" key's value in the project's *Info.plist* is $(EXECUTABLE_NAME); for this will be substituted the value of the EXECUTABLE_NAME build environment variable, supplied by Xcode at build time. Also, some additional key–value pairs will be injected into the *Info.plist* during processing.

For a complete list of the possible keys and their meanings, consult Apple's *Information Property List Key Reference* in the documentation archive (see Chapter 8). I'll talk more in Chapter 9 about some *Info.plist* settings that you're particularly likely to edit.

Nib Files

A nib file is a file with the extension *.nib* containing a description of a piece of user interface in a compiled format. You edit a *.xib* or *.storyboard* file graphically, as in a drawing program. Your *.xib* and *.storyboard* files are then transformed into nib files by compilation during the build process. This compilation takes place by virtue of the *.storyboard* or *.xib* file being listed in the app target's Copy Bundle Resources build phase. A *.xib* file results in a single nib file; a *.storyboard* file results in a *.storyboardc* bundle containing multiple nib files.

Our Empty Window project generated from the iOS App template contains an interface *.storyboard* file called *Main.storyboard*. This is our app's *main storyboard* — not because of its name, but because the *Info.plist* file says so, under the key "Main storyboard file base name" (`UIMainStoryboardFile`). I'll talk more about the main storyboard later in this chapter; in Chapter 7 I'll explain how nib files create instances when your code runs.

Resources

Resources are ancillary files embedded in your app bundle to be extracted as needed while the app runs. At some point during your app's lifetime you might want to display some images, or play some sound files; to do so, you can include these files in your app bundle. In effect, your app bundle is being treated as a folder full of extra stuff.

There are two different places to add resources to your project in Xcode:

The Project navigator
> If you add a resource to the Project navigator, it is copied by the build process to the top level of your app bundle (assuming that it is also listed in the Copy Bundle Resources build phase).

An asset catalog
> If you add a resource to an asset catalog, then when the asset catalog is copied and compiled by the build process to the top level of your app bundle, the resource's data will be embedded inside it.

Resources in the Project navigator

To add a resource to your project through the Project navigator, choose File → Add Files to [Project], or drag the resource from the Finder into the Project navigator. A dialog appears (Figure 6-16):

Copy items if needed
> Check this checkbox so that the resource is copied into the project folder. Otherwise, your project will depend on a file that's outside the project folder, where

Figure 6-16. Options when adding a resource to a project

you might delete or change it unintentionally; keeping all of your project's contents inside the project folder is far safer.

Added folders

If what you're adding to the project is a folder, these choices determine how the project references the folder contents:

Create groups

The folder's name becomes the name of a folder-linked group within the Project navigator, and its contents appear in this group; but the folder contents are listed individually in the Copy Bundle Resources build phase and are copied individually to the top level of the app bundle.

Create folder references

The folder becomes a *folder reference*. It is shown in blue in the Project navigator, and the folder itself is listed in the Copy Bundle Resources build phase. The build process will copy *the folder itself*, along with its contents, into the app bundle; the resources won't be at the top level of the app bundle, but rather in a subfolder within the app bundle. Your code for accessing a resource will have to specify the subfolder.

Add to targets

This checkbox determines whether the resource is added to a target's Copy Bundle Resources build phase. If your purpose is to make this resource available to the app when it runs, the app target checkbox should be checked. If your purpose is merely to use the project folder as convenient storage for something that isn't part of your app, the checkbox should *not* be checked. If you get this wrong, you can change this setting later by editing the target's Copy Bundle Resources build phase.

Resources in an asset catalog

Asset catalogs were invented originally to accommodate image files; they can now contain any kind of data file. Keeping your resources in an asset catalog provides certain advantages over keeping them at the top level of the app bundle.

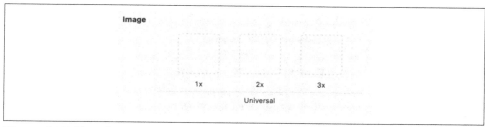

Figure 6-17. Slots for an image set in the asset catalog

For example, you might need two or three versions of an image file, corresponding to the single-, double-, and triple-resolution screens of target devices; the asset catalog provides resolution slots to make that easy (Figure 6-17). The asset catalog can perform certain transformations on an image as it is loaded. And asset catalog images load more efficiently, because they are stored in a special format.

Asset catalogs can also hold named colors, Sprite Kit textures, and general data objects. Different versions of the same asset can load in response to device type, light or dark mode, and localization. An asset catalog can contain "folders" that subdivide the assets between namespaces, and multiple asset catalogs can be distinguished by putting them in different bundles (such as frameworks).

Code Files

The build process compiles a code file into the app's binary if it is listed in the app target's Compile Sources build phase. The Swift files provided by the app template are listed under Compile Sources already. As you develop a real app, you'll create new Swift files by choosing File → New → File; a Save dialog will appear, offering to make this file part of the app target, and if you accept, the file will be added to the app target's Compile Sources build phase. If you get this wrong, your code probably won't compile, because the compiler won't see the newly added Swift file; you can fix this by editing the Compile Sources build phase.

When you create a new file using the Cocoa Touch Class template, you get some boilerplate code for free. A file template might import the UIKit framework and write the initial class declaration for you, and in the case of some commonly subclassed superclasses, such as UIViewController and UITableViewController, it even provides stub declarations of some of that class's methods.

Frameworks, SDKs, and Packages

A *framework* is a library of compiled code used by your code. Most of the frameworks you are likely to use when programming iOS will be Apple's built-in frameworks. These frameworks are the locus of all the stuff that every app might need to do; they are Cocoa. That's a lot of stuff, and a lot of compiled code. Your app gets to share in the goodness and power of the frameworks because it is hooked up to them. Your code works as if the framework code were incorporated into it. Yet your app is relatively tiny; it's the frameworks that are huge.

The Cocoa frameworks are already part of the system on the device where your app will run; they live in */System/Library/Frameworks* on the device, though you can't tell that because there's no way (normally) to inspect a device's file hierarchy directly.

Your compiled code also needs to be connected to those frameworks when the project is being built and run on your computer. To make this possible, the iOS device's */System/Library/Frameworks* is duplicated on your computer, inside Xcode itself. This duplicated subset of the device's system is called an *SDK* (for "software development kit"). Which SDK is used depends upon what destination you're building for.

The process of hooking up your compiled code with the frameworks that it needs, whether on your computer or on an actual device, is called *linking*. Linking takes care of connecting your compiled code to any needed frameworks, but your code also needs to be able to compile in the first place. The frameworks are full of classes and methods that your code will call. To satisfy the compiler, the frameworks publish their API in header files, which your code can import. For instance, your code can speak of NSString and can call range(of:) because it imports the NSString header. (Actually, what your code imports is the UIKit header, which in turn imports the Foundation header, which in turn imports the NSString header, which declares the range(of:) method.)

Using a framework is therefore a two-stage process. Your code must import the framework's header in order to compile, and it must link to the framework's binary so that your code can communicate with the framework's code at runtime. Luckily, Swift's use of modules simplifies the importing and linking process (as well as improving compilation times). A Swift import statement takes care of everything. The import UIKit statement at the top of our project's code files imports the UIKit framework's header files and allows your code to compile; then, at build time, it also enables linkage with the UIKit framework.

A custom framework can be a useful way to subdivide your code into modules, allowing your code to be compartmentalized and shared between other modules. Also, a framework is a bundle, so it can include resources that are referenced by specifying that bundle. Here's how to create a framework in your project:

1. Edit the target and choose Editor → Add Target.

2. Select iOS. Under Framework & Library, select Framework. Click Next.

3. Give your framework a name; let's call it *MyCoolFramework*. You can pick a language, but I'm not sure this makes any difference, as no code files will be created.

Figure 6-18. Adding a local package to the app target

> The Project and Embed in Application pop-up menus should be correctly set by default. Click Finish.

A new MyCoolFramework target is created in your project. If you now add a Swift file to the MyCoolFramework target, and inside it define an object type and declare it `public`, then, back in one of your main app target's files, such as *AppDelegate.swift*, your code can `import MyCoolFramework` and will then be able to see that object type and its public members. In the built app, the app bundle contains a *Frameworks* folder which, in turn, contains a *MyCoolFramework.framework* package containing your framework's code and resources — a secondary bundle embedded in your app.

Sharing frameworks between apps, however, is not simple; it can be rather tricky to use a framework in more than one app of your own, and it's even harder to distribute your code to others as a framework, and for others to embed your framework in their own app. Starting in Xcode 11, a far more convenient mechanism is available: *Swift packages*. The primary purpose of a Swift package is to share your code as open source. A package is simpler and more efficient than a framework, because it is basically just a collection of source code, which doesn't need linking.

Here's how to create a package:

1. In your project (such as our Empty Window project), choose File → New → Swift Package.

2. Give the package a name, such as *MyCoolPackage*. At the bottom of the Save dialog, specify that you want to add this package to the existing project (Empty Window), and make sure you're adding it at the top level of the project, not inside any group. Observe that this is a folder and will not necessarily be placed inside your project folder, though you can specify that if you want to. Click Create.

3. The initial package files appear in the Project navigator, but this module is not yet available to the app target. Edit the app target; in the General pane, under Frameworks, Libraries, and Embedded Content, click Plus and choose the package library in the dialog (Figure 6-18). Click Add.

In your app target's code, you can now `import MyCoolPackage` to access public types declared in the package. There is already one source file, *MyCoolPackage.swift*, ready for you to play with.

A package is not a framework, and it's not a full-fledged target. There are no build settings or build phases; instead, at the top level of the package is a configuration file, *Package.swift,* consisting primarily of a single call to the Package class initializer. This call is the *package manifest.* In effect, it does in code for a package what you would have done with build settings and phases for a full-fledged target. This call declares a target called "MyCoolPackage"; this name corresponds to the MyCoolPackage group inside Sources, so that whatever is inside that group, such as the *MyCoolPackage.swift* file, goes into that target. If you add code files to the package, add them inside this same MyCoolPackage group, so that they too are compiled as part of the target.

Here's the interesting part. When your app uses a Swift package consisting of code files, then when you build the app, nothing new is visibly added to the built app. There is no Frameworks folder. There is no additional bundle. So where did the package code go? It has been compiled together with your app target's code, and is part of your app's binary. There is no need for linking! In effect, the package has been incorporated directly into the app target.

When packages were introduced in Xcode 11, there was a severe limitation: they had to consist *only* of code. You couldn't include images, a storyboard, or anything else that wasn't code.

New in Xcode 12, however, you *can* add bundle resources, as well as localizations, to your Swift package. For instance, suppose we want to add an asset catalog. Select the existing source file, *MyCoolPackage.swift,* and choose File → New → File. In the template chooser, choose iOS → Resource → Asset Catalog. We have now added the asset catalog to the package's target, simply by virtue of its place within the MyCoolPackage group.

The result is that now the built app *will* contain an actual bundle, called *MyCoolPackage_MyCoolPackage.bundle,* created at top level, containing this asset catalog. To access an image in the asset catalog, code in the package must specify the bundle; the easiest way to do that is with the convenience variable Bundle.module, which is implemented for you by the build process. (Your app's own code can also specify the bundle, but not so easily; the expectation is that resources in a package are for direct use by the package, not the surrounding app.)

You can also include individual files or folders as resources in your package, but in that case the package build mechanism needs to be told what to do with them. You do that by editing the .target value in the package manifest:

- A file that you *don't* want to add to the target would be added to the target's excludes: array.
- A file that you *do* want to add to the target would be added to the target's resources: array as a .process Resource object; for an entire folder (similar to a folder reference, discussed earlier), it would be a .copy Resource object.

(For more details, there's a good WWDC 2020 video on this topic.)

What we've created is a *local* package. But one of the key features of packages is that they can readily be made public. You place your package folder under Git control (see Chapter 9) and upload it to an online remote Git repository, such as GitHub. That's easy for *you* to do. Now other programmers can incorporate it into their projects. That's easy for *them* to do.

To demonstrate, let's turn the tables and see how easy it is for you to incorporate other programmers' public packages into your own projects. For example, to add to your project the Swift Numerics package that I mentioned in Chapter 3:

1. Choose File → Swift Packages → Add Package Dependency.

2. Enter the URL *https://github.com/apple/swift-numerics* into the field in the dialog.

3. Click Next (twice).

4. Check the checkbox next to Numerics in the final dialog, and click Finish.

The package is downloaded and made available to your project, and now you can `import Numerics` in your project's code files and use the package code.

Interestingly, the package code is shown in your project, but the package is *not* stored in your project folder. It's stored in Xcode's *DerivedData* folder, where Xcode can incorporate it into your project's build process without polluting your project. From now on, whenever you open your project, Xcode will check to see whether it has the package code, and if it doesn't, it will download it there and then.

In addition, Xcode checks the *version* of the package code. This is one of the most important features of Swift packages. Xcode can ascertain online whether you've got the latest official version of a package, and will update the package source if you don't. Choose File → Swift Packages → Update to Latest Package Versions to make Xcode go online and check for updates. Moreover, a package can declare a *dependency*, meaning that it relies on some other package — and Xcode will also download *that* package and make sure that *it* stays up to date. The package version numbering system and the rules for determining whether a dependency needs updating are quite sophisticated.

When you upload your own package, or when you update your package, you need to declare its version number. You do this by attaching a Git tag, in the form of a version string, to the most recent commit:

```
% git tag "0.0.1"
% git push --tags
```

Xcode's package management mechanism works fine with private repositories, so you can share your code without making it public; you can upload your package and share it *with yourself.* This is a great way to factor out common code and use it in different projects.

The App Launch Process

When the user launches your app, or when you launch it by building and running it in Xcode, a lot needs to happen. Your app needs some initial instances and an initial interface, and at least some of your code needs an opportunity to run.

The Entry Point

When the app launches, the system knows where to find the compiled binary inside the app's bundle, because the app bundle's *Info.plist* file has an "Executable file" key (`CFBundleExecutable`) whose value is the name of the binary; by default, the binary's name comes from the `EXECUTABLE_NAME` environment variable (such as "Empty Window").

The system locates and loads the binary and links any needed frameworks. Now it must call into the binary's code to start it running. But where?

If this app were an Objective-C program, the answer would be clear. Objective-C is C, so the entry point is the `main` function. Our project would typically have a *main.m* file containing the `main` function, like this:

```
int main(int argc, char *argv[]) {
    @autoreleasepool {
        return UIApplicationMain(argc, argv, nil,
            NSStringFromClass([AppDelegate class]));
    }
}
```

The `main` function does two things:

- It sets up a memory management environment — the `@autoreleasepool` and the curly braces that follow it.
- It calls the `UIApplicationMain` function, which helps your app pull itself up by its bootstraps and get running.

Our app, however, is a Swift program. It has no `main` function! Instead, Swift has a special attribute: `@main`. You can see it in the *AppDelegate.swift* file, attached to the declaration of the AppDelegate class:

```
@main
class AppDelegate: UIResponder, UIApplicationDelegate {
```

This attribute essentially does everything that the Objective-C *main.m* file was doing: it creates an entry point that calls `UIApplicationMain` to get the app started.

The term @main is new in Swift 5.3; formerly, this attribute was called @UIApplicationMain.

It would be very unusual for you to give your Swift app project a *main* file. But you are free to do so. Delete the @main attribute and instead create a *main.swift* file, making sure it is added to the app target. The name is crucial, because a file called *main.swift* gets a special dispensation: it is allowed to put executable code at the top level of the file (Chapter 1)! The file should contain essentially the Swift equivalent of the Objective-C call to UIApplicationMain, like this:

```
import UIKit
UIApplicationMain(
    CommandLine.argc, CommandLine.unsafeArgv, nil,
        NSStringFromClass(AppDelegate.self)
)
```

New in Swift 5.3 and Xcode 12, there's another way. Instead of writing a *main.swift* file, you can designate one of your own types as @main and give it a static main function, where you do whatever you would have done in the *main.swift* file. Behind the scenes, the *main.swift* file is synthesized for you. Here's a minimal implementation:

```
@main
struct MyMain {
    static func main() -> Void {
        UIApplicationMain(
            CommandLine.argc, CommandLine.unsafeArgv, nil,
                NSStringFromClass(AppDelegate.self)
        )
    }
}
```

(This use of the @main attribute is key to the new SwiftUI app architecture, where your code doesn't need to refer to any UIKit classes in order to bootstrap the app.)

Regardless of whether you rely on the Swift @main attribute or write your own *main.swift* file, in a Cocoa app you are calling the UIApplicationMain function. This one function call is the primary thing your app does. Your entire app is really nothing but a single gigantic call to UIApplicationMain! Moreover, UIApplicationMain is responsible for solving some tricky problems as your app gets going. Where will your app get its initial instances? What instance methods will initially be called on those instances? Where will your app's initial interface come from? UIApplicationMain to the rescue!

How an App Gets Going

Let's trace the sequence of events as your app launches and UIApplicationMain is called. The opening sequence varies somewhat, depending on the circumstances. So let's focus on what happens for a new project created in Xcode 12, such as the Empty Window project we created earlier in this chapter, which has these key features:

- The app supports scenes: the *Info.plist* contains an "Application Scene Manifest" dictionary (Figure 6-19), and the code mentions classes and protocols whose names begin with UIScene.
- The app has a main storyboard.

When an app with that structure launches in iOS 13 or later, here's what happens:

1. `UIApplicationMain` creates the shared application instance, subsequently accessible to your code as `UIApplication.shared`. The default class is UIApplication; it is possible to specify a different class, but it is unlikely that you'd need to do so.

2. `UIApplicationMain` creates the application instance's *delegate*. With an explicit call to `UIApplicationMain`, the fourth argument specifies, as a string, what the class of the app delegate instance should be; in the *main.swift* file I described earlier, that specification is `NSStringFromClass(AppDelegate.self)`. When we use the `@main` attribute in the AppDelegate class declaration in *AppDelegate.swift*, it means: "*This* is the app delegate class!"

3. If this app supports scenes, `UIApplicationMain` turns to the app delegate and, for the first time, runs some of your code: it calls `application(_:didFinish-LaunchingWithOptions:)`. This is a place for you to perform certain initializations.

4. `UIApplicationMain` creates a UISceneSession, a UIWindowScene, and your app's window scene *delegate*. The *Info.plist* typically specifies, as a string, what the class of the window scene delegate instance should be. In the app template, it is the SceneDelegate class, which is declared in *SceneDelegate.swift*; in the "Application Scene Manifest" entry in the *Info.plist,* this value is written as `$(PRODUCT_MODULE_NAME).SceneDelegate` to take account of Swift "name mangling" (Figure 6-19).

5. If there is a storyboard associated with this scene, as specified by the *Info.plist*, `UIApplicationMain` loads it and looks inside it to find the view controller designated as this storyboard's *initial view controller* (or *storyboard entry point*); it instantiates this view controller, a UIViewController subclass. In our app template, the app's main storyboard, *Main.storyboard*, is the initial scene's storyboard; in that storyboard, the initial view controller is an instance of the ViewController class, which is declared in *ViewController.swift*.

6. `UIApplicationMain` creates your app's *window*. This window is assigned to the scene delegate's `window` property. `UIApplicationMain` then assigns the initial view controller instance to the window instance's `rootViewController` property. This view controller is now the app's *root view controller*.

7. More of your code now has a chance to run: `UIApplicationMain` calls the scene delegate's `scene(_:willConnectTo:options:)` method.

8. `UIApplicationMain` causes your app's interface to appear, by calling the UIWindow instance method `makeKeyAndVisible`.

9. The window is about to appear. This causes the window to turn to the root view controller and tell it to obtain its main view. If this view controller gets its view from a nib file, that nib is loaded and its objects are instantiated and initialized (as I'll describe in Chapter 7). The view controller's `viewDidLoad` is then called — another early opportunity for your code to run. Finally, the root view controller's main view is placed into the window, where it and its subviews are visible to the user.

More of your code can run at this time (some further app delegate and scene delegate methods are called if they are implemented), but basically the app is now up and running, with an initial set of instances and a visible interface. `UIApplicationMain` is *still* running (like Charlie on the M.T.A., `UIApplicationMain` never returns), and is just sitting there, watching for the user to do something, maintaining the *event loop*, which will respond to user actions as they occur. Henceforth, your app's code will be called only in response to Cocoa events (as I'll explain in Chapter 11).

App Without a Storyboard

In the preceding description of the app launch process, I assume that the app has a main storyboard. It is possible, however, *not* to have a main storyboard. Without a main storyboard, things like creating a window instance, assigning it to the `window` property, creating an initial view controller, assigning that view controller to the window's `rootViewController` property, and calling `makeKeyAndVisible` on the window to show the interface, must be done by your code. This architecture is useful when your intention is to create the entire interface in code.

Let's try it. Make a new project starting with the iOS App template; call it Truly Empty. Now follow these steps:

1. Edit the target. In the General pane, select "Main" in the Main Interface field and delete it (and press Tab to set this change).

2. In the *Info.plist*, select the "Storyboard Name" entry in the "Application Scene Configuration" dictionary (Figure 6-19) and press Delete (and save).

3. Optionally, in the Project navigator, delete *Main.storyboard* from the project. You don't have to do this, because even if *Main.storyboard* remains, it will now be ignored.

4. In *SceneDelegate.swift*, edit `scene(_:willConnectTo:options:)` to look like Example 6-1.

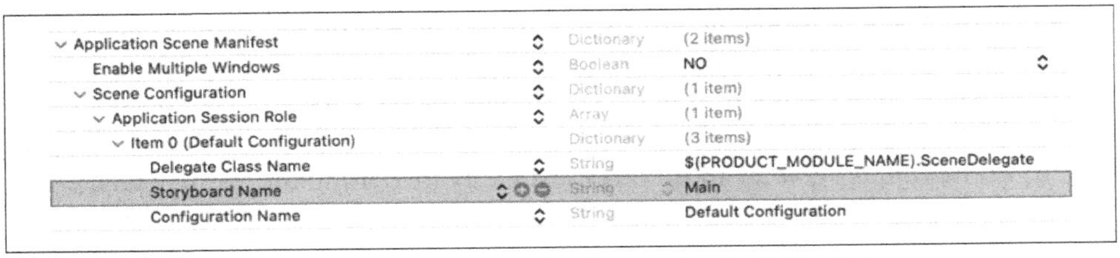

Figure 6-19. The "Application Scene Manifest" entry in the Info.plist

Example 6-1. A scene delegate with no storyboard

```
func scene(_ scene: UIScene,
           willConnectTo session: UISceneSession,
           options connectionOptions: UIScene.ConnectionOptions) {
    if let windowScene = scene as? UIWindowScene {
        let window = UIWindow(windowScene: windowScene)
        window.backgroundColor = .white
        window.rootViewController = ViewController()
        self.window = window
        window.makeKeyAndVisible()
    }
}
```

The result is a minimal working app with an empty white window. You can prove to yourself that the app is working normally by editing *ViewController.swift* so that its `viewDidLoad` method changes the main view's background color:

```
override func viewDidLoad() {
    super.viewDidLoad()
    self.view.backgroundColor = .red
}
```

Run the app again; sure enough, the background is now red.

In between an app with a main storyboard and an app without a main storyboard, there is a hybrid architecture where there's a main storyboard (you omit steps 1, 2, and 3 in the earlier example) but you sometimes ignore it at launch time (step 4). A common use case would be an app with a sign-in screen that should appear when the user first launches the app (you create the sign-in view controller manually), but once the user has signed in, that screen shouldn't appear on any future launch (you let the main storyboard construct the interface).

Renaming Parts of a Project

The name you give your project at creation time is used in many places throughout the project. Beginners may worry that they can never rename a project without breaking something. But in fact it's not a problem.

In the first place, you probably don't *need* to rename the project. The project name isn't something the user will ever see, so what does it matter? Typically, what you want to change is the name of the *app* — the name that the user sees on the device, associated with this app's icon. To do so, change (or create) the "Bundle Display Name" in the *Info.plist*; you can do this most easily by editing the Display Name text field at the top of the General pane when you edit the target (see "Property List Settings" on page 497).

If you really *do* want to rename the project, select the project listing at the top of the Project navigator, press Return to make its name editable, type the new name, and press Return again. Xcode presents a dialog proposing to change some other names to match, including the app target and the built app and, by implication, various relevant build settings.

Everything that needs to change changes coherently when you rename the project in this way. The only thing that isn't changed is the scheme name; there is no particular need to change it, but you can do so: choose Product → Manage Schemes and click the scheme name to make it editable.

You can change the name of the project folder in the Finder at any time, and you can move the project folder in the Finder at will, because all build setting references to file and folder items in the project folder are relative.

 When you change the name of a folder-linked group, Xcode automatically changes the name of the corresponding folder on disk, but does *not* change build settings that depend upon the name of that folder, such as the Info.plist File build setting. I regard this as a bug, because it means that changing a group's name can prevent your project from building. However, it usually isn't hard to fix the problem by changing manually any build settings that have broken.

CHAPTER 7

Nib Files

A *view* (UIView) is an interface object, which draws itself into a rectangular area. Your app's visible interface consists of views. When your app launches, some view controller is made the root view controller of your app's window ("How an App Gets Going" on page 370). That view controller has a main view. That view and its subviews now occupy the window. Whatever that view and its subviews look like when they draw themselves, that is what the user will see.

Where do these interface views come from? Well, UIView is a class; an individual UIView is an instance of that class. And you know how to make an instance of a class — you call that class's initializer:

```
let v = UIView()
```

So you could create all your interface views in code, one by one. For each view, you would *instantiate* it; then you would *configure* it. You'd say where it should go on the screen, what size it should have, what color it should be. If the view is a button or a label, you'd say what text it should display. And so on.

But that could be a lot of code. Wouldn't it be nice if, instead, you could *draw* your desired interface, just as in a drawing application, and have the runtime build the interface for you, based on your drawing? Well, you can — using a nib.

A *nib* is a file, in a special format, consisting of instructions for creating and configuring instances — primarily UIView instances. You "write" those instructions graphically, by drawing. You design your app's interface visually. Under the hood, Xcode encodes that design. When the app runs and it's time for those UIView instances to appear visibly to the user, the runtime *loads* the nib. It decodes the instructions and obeys them: it actually creates and configures the view instances that the nib describes.

Xcode includes a graphical design environment so that you can draw your interface into a nib file. I call this the *nib editor*. Long ago, the files on which the nib editor operated were literally nib files — that is, they had a *.nib* file extension. Nowadays, you'll use the nib editor to edit a *.storyboard* file or a *.xib* file. However, they *will* be turned into actual *.nib* files when you build your project ("Nib Files" on page 362), so I still refer to them loosely as nibs or nib files.

 The name *nib* has nothing to do with fountain pens or bits of chocolate. The nib editor used to be a separate application called Interface Builder. The operating system for which it was originally developed was called NeXTStep. The files created by Interface Builder were given the *.nib* file extension as an acronym for "NeXTStep Interface Builder."

You don't *have* to use nibs to create your interface objects. The loading of a nib does nothing that you could not have done directly, in code. A nib is just a device for making the creation of interface views convenient and compact; one nib file can generate many views, and the nib editor's visual representation of those views can be more intuitive than a code description. But you still have the alternative of using code: you can programmatically instantiate a UIView, you can configure it, you can place that view into your interface — manually, step by step, one line of code at a time. You are free to mix and match; you can generate some views in code and design other views in the nib editor, or design a view in the nib editor but complete its configuration in code. Clearly, nibs can be a powerful and convenient way to create your app's interface, in whole or in part.

Beginners often use nibs, to take advantage of that power and convenience, without knowing what they really are, how they really work, or how to manipulate them in code — as if nibs were some kind of impenetrable magic. But nibs are *not* magic, and they are not hard to understand. Failure to understand nibs and nib loading opens the door to some elementary, confusing mistakes that can be avoided or corrected merely by grasping the basic facts outlined in this chapter.

 One of the salient features of SwiftUI is that it avoids nibs completely. By condensing the code needed to create views programmatically, it lets you describe your interface clearly and compactly in Swift. Part of the goal is multiplatform reusability: the same code can construct an interface destined for an Apple Watch, an iPhone, an Apple TV, or a desktop Mac.

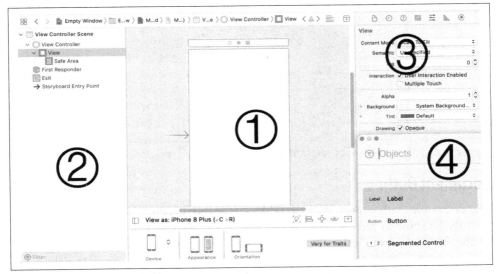

Figure 7-1. Editing a nib file

The Nib Editor Interface

Let's explore Xcode's nib editor. This is where you'll draw your app's interface graphically. In Chapter 6, we created a simple project, Empty Window, directly from the iOS App template; it contains a storyboard file, so we'll use that. In Xcode, open the Empty Window project, locate *Main.storyboard* in the Project navigator, and click to edit it.

Figure 7-1 shows part of the project window after selecting *Main.storyboard* in the Project navigator. The interface may be considered in four pieces:

1. The bulk of the editor is devoted to the *canvas*, where you physically design your app's interface. The canvas portrays views graphically. View controllers are also represented in the canvas; a view controller isn't a view, so it isn't drawn in your app's interface, but it *has* a view, which *is* drawn.

2. At the left of the editor is the *document outline*, listing the storyboard's contents hierarchically by name.

3. To the right of the editor, the inspectors in the Inspectors pane let you edit details of the currently selected object.

4. The Objects Library, available as a floating window (View → Show Library, Command-Shift-L), is your source of interface objects to be added to the canvas or the document outline.

(If your nib editor's canvas is displaying more panes to the right, choose Editor → Show Editor Only to remove them.)

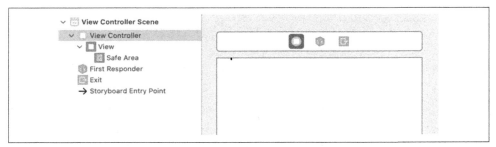

Figure 7-2. A view controller selected in a storyboard

Document Outline

The document outline portrays hierarchically the relationships between the objects in the nib. To show or hide the document outline, choose Editor → Document Outline, or choose Document Outline from the Editor Options pop-up menu at the top right of the canvas. The document outline can also be hidden by dragging its right edge, and it can be shown or hidden by clicking the button at the bottom left corner below the canvas.

The structure of what's displayed in the document outline differs slightly depending on whether you're editing a *.storyboard* file or a *.xib* file.

In a storyboard file, the primary constituents are *scenes*. A scene is, roughly speaking, a single view controller, along with some ancillary material; every scene has a single view controller at its top level.

A view controller isn't an interface object, but it manages an interface object, a view that serves as its *main view*. A scene's view controller is displayed in the canvas with its main view inside it. In Figure 7-1, the large rectangle in the canvas is a view controller's main view, and is actually inside a view controller. The view controller itself can be seen and selected in the document outline. When anything in this scene is selected, the view controller is also represented as an icon in the *scene dock*, which appears above the view controller in the canvas (Figure 7-2).

In the document outline, all the scenes are listed. Each scene is the top level of a hierarchical list. Hierarchically down from each scene are the objects that also appear in the view controller's scene dock: the view controller itself, along with two *proxy objects*, the First Responder token and the Exit token. They are the scene's *top-level objects*. Then, hierarchically down from the view controller, we have the view controller's main view, along with the main view's subviews (if any) appearing hierarchically down from that, reflecting the interface hierarchy of superviews and subviews.

Objects listed in the document outline are of two kinds:

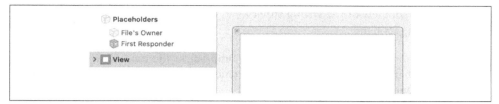

Figure 7-3. A .xib file containing a view

Nib objects

> The view controller, along with its main view and its subviews, will be turned into actual instances when the nib is loaded by the running app. They are called *nib objects.*

Proxy objects

> The First Responder and Exit tokens will *not* be turned into instances when the nib is loaded. They are *proxy objects.* They represent objects that *already* exist. They are displayed in the nib in order to facilitate communication between nib objects and those already existing objects; I'll give examples later in this chapter.

The document outline also contains the Storyboard Entry Point. This isn't an object of any kind. It's an indicator that this view controller is the storyboard's initial view controller (because Is Initial View Controller is checked in the view controller's Attributes inspector); it corresponds to the right-pointing arrow seen at the left of this view controller in the canvas in Figure 7-1.

In a *.xib* file, there are no scenes. What would be, in a *.storyboard* file, the top-level objects of a scene become, in a *.xib* file, the top-level objects of the nib itself; and the top-level interface object of a *.xib* file is usually a view. (A *.xib* file *can* contain a view controller, but it usually doesn't.) A *.xib* file's top-level view might well be a view that is to serve as a view controller's main view, but that's not a requirement. Figure 7-3 shows a *.xib* file with a structure parallel to the single scene of Figure 7-2.

The document outline in Figure 7-3 lists three top-level objects. Two of them are proxy objects, termed Placeholders in the document outline: the File's Owner, and the First Responder. The third is a nib object, a view; it will be turned into a UIView instance when the nib is loaded as the app runs.

At present, the document outline may seem unnecessary, because there is very little hierarchy; all objects in Figures 7-2 and 7-3 are readily accessible in the canvas. But when a storyboard contains many scenes, and when a view contains many levels of hierarchically arranged objects, some of which are difficult to see or select in the canvas, you're going to be very glad of the document outline, which lets you survey the contents of the nib in a nice hierarchical structure, and where you can locate and select the object you're after. You can also rearrange the hierarchy here; if you've made a view a subview of the wrong superview, you can reposition it within this outline by dragging its name.

 You can also select objects using the jump bar at the top of the editor: the last jump bar path component is a hierarchical pop-up menu similar to the document outline.

If the names of nib objects in the document outline seem generic and uninformative, you can change them. The name is technically a *label*, and has no special meaning, so feel free to assign nib objects labels that are useful to you. Select a nib object's label in the document outline and press Return to make it editable, or select the object and edit the Label field in the Document section of the Identity inspector.

Canvas

The canvas provides a graphical representation of a view and its subviews, similar to what you're probably accustomed to in any drawing program. The canvas is scrollable and automatically accommodates however many graphical representations it contains, and can also be zoomed (Option-scroll, or choose Editor → Zoom, or use the contextual menu or the zoom buttons at the bottom of the canvas). New in Xcode 12, you can also display the *minimap,* which shows you the whole content of the canvas in miniature and lets you scroll around it by dragging; choose Editor → Canvas → Minimap or choose Minimap from the Editor Options pop-up menu at the top right of the canvas.

Our simple Empty Window project's *Main.storyboard* contains just one scene, so the only thing it represents in the canvas is that scene's view controller with its main view inside it. When the app runs, this view controller will become the window's rootView-Controller; therefore its view will occupy the entire window, and will effectively be our app's initial interface. That gives us an excellent opportunity to experiment: any visible changes we make within this view should be visible when we subsequently build and run the app! To prove it, let's add a subview:

1. Start with the nib editor looking more or less like Figure 7-1.

2. Summon the Objects Library (Command-Shift-L, or click the Library button in the project window toolbar). Make sure it's displaying objects (not images or colors). If it's in icon view (a grid of icons without text), switch to list view. Click in the search field and type "button" so that only button objects are shown in the list. The Button object we're after is listed first.

3. Drag the Button object from the Library into the view controller's main view in the canvas (Figure 7-4), and let go of the mouse.

A button is now present in the view in the canvas. The move we've just performed — dragging from the Library into the canvas — is extremely characteristic; you'll do it often as you design your interface.

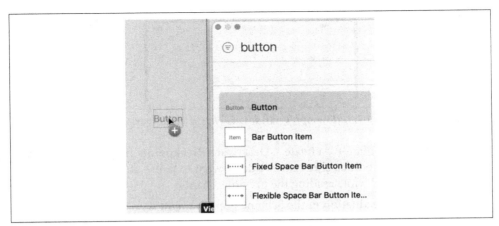

Figure 7-4. Dragging a button into a view

 By default, the Library floating window is temporary; it vanishes as soon as you drag something out of it. To make it remain onscreen after the drag, hold Option when summoning the Library or when dragging out of it; the Library window's toolbar then contains a close button, and the window will remain open until you click that button.

Much as in a drawing program, the nib editor provides features to aid you in designing your interface. Here are some things to try:

- Select the button: resizing handles appear.

- Using the resizing handles, resize the button to make it wider: dimension information appears.

- Drag the button near an edge of the view: a guideline appears, showing standard spacing. Similarly, drag the button near the center of the view: a guideline shows you when the button is centered.

- With the button selected, hold Option (but *not* the mouse button) and hover the mouse outside the button: arrows and numbers appear showing the distance between the button and the edges of the view.

- Control-Shift-click the button: a menu appears, letting you select the button or whatever is behind it or up the hierarchy from it. This is useful particularly when views overlap.

- Double-click the button's title. The title becomes editable. Give it a new title, such as "Hello." Press Return to set the new title.

To prove that we really are designing our app's interface, we'll run the app:

1. Drag the button to a position near the *top left* corner of the canvas. (If you don't do this, the button could be off the screen when the app runs.)

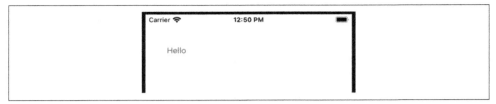

Figure 7-5. The Empty Window app's window is empty no longer

2. Examine the Debug → Activate / Deactivate Breakpoints menu item. If it says Deactivate Breakpoints, choose it; we don't want to pause at any breakpoints you may have created while reading the previous chapter.

3. Make sure the destination in the Scheme pop-up menu is an iPhone simulator.

4. Choose Product → Run (or click the Run button in the toolbar).

After a heart-stopping pause, the Simulator opens, and presto, our empty window is empty no longer (Figure 7-5); it contains a button! You can tap this button with the mouse, emulating what the user would do with a finger; the button highlights as you tap it.

Inspectors

In addition to the File, History, and Quick Help inspectors, four inspectors appear in conjunction with the nib editor, and apply to whatever object is selected in the document outline, dock, or canvas:

Identity inspector (Command-Option-4)
The first section of this inspector, Custom Class, is the most important. Here you can learn — and can change — the selected object's class.

Attributes inspector (Command-Option-5)
Settings here correspond to properties and methods that you might use to configure the object in code. For instance, selecting our view and choosing from the Background pop-up menu in the Attributes inspector corresponds to setting the view's backgroundColor property in code.

The Attributes inspector has sections corresponding to the selected object's class inheritance. The UIButton Attributes inspector has three sections: in addition to a Button section, there's a Control section (because a UIButton is also a UIControl) and a View section (because a UIControl is also a UIView).

Size inspector (Command-Option-6)
The X, Y, Width, and Height fields determine the object's position and size within its superview, corresponding to its frame property in code; you can

---

equally set these values in the canvas by dragging and resizing, but numeric precision can be desirable.

Connections inspector (Command-Option-7)
    I'll demonstrate use of the Connections inspector later in this chapter.

Loading a Nib

A nib file is a collection of *potential* instances — its nib objects. They become *actual* instances only if, while your app is running, the nib is *loaded*. At that moment, the nib objects described in the nib are effectively transformed into instances that are available to your app. I call this process — the loading of a nib and the resulting creation of instances — the *nib-loading mechanism*. We may speak as if a nib contains literal object instances; we may speak of "loading" or "instantiating" a view controller or a view from a nib. But in fact the nib contains nothing but *instructions* for creating a view controller or view instance, and the nib-loading mechanism fulfills those instructions.

Using nibs as a source of instances is efficient. Interface is relatively heavyweight stuff, but a nib is small. Moreover, a nib isn't loaded until it is needed; indeed, it might never be loaded. So this heavyweight stuff won't come into existence until and unless it is about to be displayed.

There's no such thing as "unloading" a nib. A nib is loaded, its nib objects are turned into instances, those instances are handed over to the running app, and that's all; the nib has done its job. It is then up to the running app to decide what to do with the instances that just sprang to life. It must hang on to them for as long as it needs them, and will let them go out of existence when they are no longer needed. Typically, it will do this by adding them to the interface, where they will persist until that interface as a whole is removed.

The same nib file can be loaded multiple times, generating a new set of instances each time. A nib is thus a mechanism for reproducing a view controller or a view hierarchy as many times as necessary. A single nib file might represent interface that you intend to use in several places in your app — possibly several places simultaneously — by loading the nib repeatedly. A case in point is the repeated cells in a table view.

Loading a View Controller Nib

A nib containing a view controller will almost certainly come from a storyboard. (A *.xib* file can contain a view controller, but it usually won't.) A storyboard is a collection of scenes. Each scene starts with a view controller. When the app is built and the storyboard is compiled, each view controller in the storyboard ends up in its own individual nib. When the app runs, if that view controller is needed, that nib is loaded.

A view controller may be loaded from a storyboard automatically (by the runtime) or manually (by your code):

Automatic creation of a view controller
There are two main occasions when a view controller is loaded automatically from a nib:

At app launch time
As your app launches, if it has a main storyboard, the runtime looks for that storyboard's *initial view controller* (entry point) and loads its nib, turning it into a view controller instance to serve as the app's root view controller ("How an App Gets Going" on page 370).

When a segue is performed
A storyboard typically contains several scenes connected by segues; when a segue is performed, the destination scene's view controller nib is loaded and turned into an instance.

Manual instantiation of a view controller
In code, to turn a view controller in a storyboard into a view controller instance, you start with a UIStoryboard instance, and call one of these methods:

`instantiateInitialViewController`
Loads the storyboard's initial view controller nib and turns it into a view controller instance.

`instantiateViewController(withIdentifier:)`
Loads the nib of a view controller within the storyboard whose scene is named by an identifier string, and turns it into a view controller instance.

Loading a Main View Nib

A view controller has a main view. But for reasons of efficiency, a view controller, when it is instantiated, *lacks its main view*. It obtains its main view *later*, when that view is needed because it is to be placed into the interface. We say that a view controller loads its view *lazily*. A view controller can obtain its main view in several ways; one way is to load it from a nib. There are two main cases to consider:

View controller in a storyboard
When a view controller and its view belong to a scene in a storyboard, then when the app is built and the storyboard is compiled, we end up with *two* nibs: the nib containing the view controller, and the nib containing the view. The app runs, and let's say the nib containing the view controller is loaded in order to instantiate the view controller, as I just described; later, when the view controller instance needs its main view, it *automatically* loads that nib and generates its main view from it.

View controller instantiated in code

Another fairly common configuration is a view controller instantiated entirely in code, whose main view has been designed in a *.xib* file in your project. When you call the view controller's designated initializer `init(nibName:bundle:)`, the `nib-Name:` parameter tells this view controller instance the name of the nib file generated from that *.xib* file. Alternatively, you might override the view controller's `nibName` property. Subsequently, when the view controller needs its main view, it *automatically* loads that nib and generates its main view from it.

Those two ways of getting the view controller's main view are actually the same. In each case, there is a view controller and an associated nib. The view controller's `nib-Name` property is the key; it tells the view controller what nib to load in order to generate its main view when it needs it.

Loading a View Nib Manually

A view can be designed in a *.xib* file. When the app is built, this file is turned into a nib. Assume that this is *not* a view controller's main view. In the running app, to load that nib and create the view instance requires a call to one of these methods:

`loadNibNamed(_:owner:options:)`
A Bundle instance method. Usually, you'll direct it to `Bundle.main`.

`instantiate(withOwner:options:)`
A UINib instance method. The nib in question was specified when UINib was instantiated and initialized with `init(nibName:bundle:)`.

Sometimes the runtime will make those calls for you. Alternatively, you can make those calls yourself to load a nib view directly. That's the best way to explore and exercise the nib-loading mechanism. Let's try it!

First we'll create and configure a *.xib* file in our Empty Window project:

1. In the Empty Window project, choose File → New → File and specify iOS → User Interface → View. This will be a *.xib* file containing a UIView instance. Click Next.

2. In the Save dialog, accept the default name, View, for the new *.xib* file. Click Create.

3. We are now back in the Project navigator; our *View.xib* file has been created and selected, and we're looking at its contents in the editor. Those contents consist of a single UIView.

4. Our view is too large for purposes of this demonstration, so select it and, in the Attributes inspector, change the Size pop-up menu, under Simulated Metrics, to

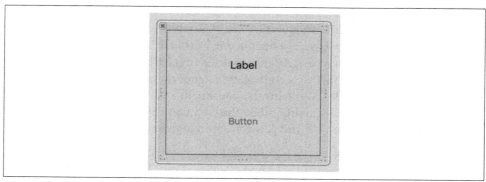

Figure 7-6. Designing a view in a .xib file

Freeform. Handles appear around the view in the canvas; drag them to make the view smaller. About 240×200 would be a good size.

5. Populate the view with some arbitrary subviews by dragging them into it from the Library. You can also configure the view itself; for example, in the Attributes inspector, change its background color (Figure 7-6).

Our goal now is to *load* this nib file, manually, in code, when the app runs. There are three tasks you have to perform when you load a nib:

1. Load the nib.

2. Obtain the instances that it creates as it loads.

3. Do something with those instances.

I've already said that to load the nib we can call `loadNibNamed(_:owner:)`. This would be the complete code for loading our nib:

```
Bundle.main.loadNibNamed("View", owner: nil)
```

That's the first task. But if that's *all* we do, we will load the nib *to no effect*. The instances will be created and will then vanish in a puff of smoke. In order to prevent that, we need to *capture* those instances. Here's one way to do that. The call to `load-NibNamed(_:owner:)` returns an array of instances created from the nib's top-level nib objects through the loading of that nib. Our nib contains just one top-level nib object — the UIView — so it is sufficient to capture the first (and only) element of this array:

```
let arr = Bundle.main.loadNibNamed("View", owner: nil)!
let v = arr[0] as! UIView
```

We have now performed the second task: we've captured an instance that we created by loading the nib. The variable v now refers to a brand-new UIView instance.

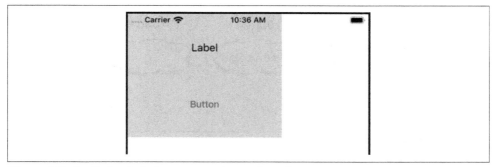

Figure 7-7. A nib-loaded view appears in our interface

Now let's perform the third task — doing something with the view we've just instantiated. A useful and dramatic thing to do with it, and probably the reason you'd load a nib in the first place, is to put that view into your interface. Let's do that! Edit *View-Controller.swift* and put these lines of code into its `viewDidLoad` method:

```
let arr = Bundle.main.loadNibNamed("View", owner: nil)!
let v = arr[0] as! UIView
self.view.addSubview(v)
```

Build and run the app. There's our view, visible in the running app's interface! This proves that our loading of the nib worked (Figure 7-7).

Connections

A *connection* is a directional linkage in the nib editor running from one object to another. I'll call the two objects the *source* and the *destination* of the connection. There are two kinds of connection: outlet connections and action connections. The rest of this section describes them, explains how to create and configure them, and discusses the nature of the problems that they are intended to solve.

Outlets

When a nib loads and its instances come into existence, those instances are useless unless you can get a reference to them. In the preceding section, we solved that problem by capturing the array of instances returned from the loading of the nib. But there's another way: use an outlet. This approach is more complicated — it requires some advance configuration, which can easily go wrong. But it is also more common, especially when nibs are loaded automatically.

An *outlet* is a connection that has a *name*, which is effectively just a string. When the nib loads, something unbelievably clever happens. The source object and the destination object are no longer just potential objects in a nib; they are now real, full-fledged instances. The runtime looks in the outlet's source object for an *instance property*

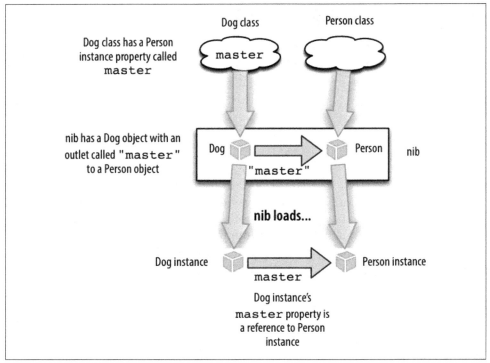

Figure 7-8. How an outlet provides a reference to a nib-instantiated object

with the same name as the outlet, and *assigns the destination object to that property.* The source object now has a reference to the destination object!

To illustrate, suppose that the following three things are true:

1. As defined in code, a Dog has a master instance property which is typed as Person.

2. There's a Dog object and a Person object in a nib.

3. We make an outlet from the Dog object to the Person object in the nib, and we name that outlet "master".

In that case, when the nib loads and the Dog instance and the Person instance are created, that Person instance will be assigned as the value of that Dog instance's master property (Figure 7-8), just as if we had said dog.master = person in code.

As you can see, for an outlet to work, preparation must be performed in *two different places*: in the class of the source object, where the instance property is declared, and in the nib, where the outlet is created and configured. This is a bit tricky; Xcode does try to help you get it right, but it is still possible to mess it up. (I will discuss ways of messing it up, in detail, later in this chapter.)

The Nib Owner

Consider once again the view-loading example that we implemented earlier (illustrated in Figure 7-7). Let's implement that example again; this time, instead of assigning the nib-loaded view to a variable in code, we'll use an outlet connection to capture the nib-loaded view into a property.

Now, there is an important difference between the Dog-and-Person example I just outlined and the view-loading example. In our view-loading example, who is the Dog, and who is the Person? The Person is the view in the nib. But the Dog is the view controller (a ViewController instance) — and the view controller is *not in the nib*.

For our view controller to use an outlet to capture a reference to a view instance created from a nib, therefore, we need an outlet that runs from an object *outside* the nib (the view controller) to an object *inside* the nib (the view). That seems metaphysically impossible — but it isn't. The nib editor cleverly permits such an outlet to be created, using the *nib owner object*.

Before I explain what the nib owner is, I'll tell you where to find the nib owner object in the nib editor:

In a storyboard scene
> In a storyboard scene, the nib owner is the view controller. It is the first object listed for that scene in the document outline, and the first object shown in the scene dock.

In a .xib file
> In a .xib file, the nib owner is a proxy object. It is the first object shown in the document outline, listed under Placeholders as the File's Owner.

So what *is* the nib owner object? It's a proxy representing an instance that *already* exists *outside* the nib at the time that the nib is loaded. When the nib is loaded, the nib-loading mechanism *doesn't* instantiate that object; the nib owner is *already* an instance. Instead, the nib-loading mechanism *substitutes* the real, already existing instance for the nib owner object, using the real instance to fulfill any connections that involve the nib owner.

But wait! How does the nib-loading mechanism *know* what real, already existing instance to substitute for the nib owner object in the nib? It knows because it is told, in one of two ways, at nib-loading time:

Your code loads the nib

If your code loads a nib manually, either by calling `loadNib-Named(_:owner:options:)` or by calling `instantiate(withOwner:options:)`, you specify an owner object as the `owner:` argument.

A view controller loads the nib

If a view controller instance loads a nib automatically in order to obtain its main view, the view controller instance specifies *itself* as the owner object.

Let's do a thought-experiment with our Dog and Person objects. This time, suppose the following four things are true:

1. As defined in code, a Dog has a `master` instance property which is typed as Person.

2. There is a Person nib object in our nib, but no Dog nib object.

3. We configure an outlet in the nib from the nib owner object to the Person object, and we name that outlet `"master"`. We can't do that unless the nib owner object's class is Dog, so we'll set its class first if necessary (using the Identity inspector).

4. When we load the nib, we specify an existing Dog instance as owner.

The nib-loading mechanism will then match the Dog nib owner object with the already existing actual Dog instance that we specified as owner, and will assign the newly instantiated Person instance as that Dog instance's `master` (Figure 7-9).

Back in the real world, let's reconfigure our Empty View nib-loading project to demonstrate this mechanism. In *ViewController.swift*, we're already loading the View nib in code. This code is running inside a ViewController instance. We want to use that instance as the nib owner. This will be a little tedious to configure, but bear with me, because understanding how it works is crucial:

1. We need an instance property in ViewController. At the start of the body of the ViewController class declaration, insert the property declaration, like this:

```
class ViewController: UIViewController {
    @IBOutlet var coolview : UIView!
```

The `var` declaration you already understand; we're making an instance property called `coolview`. It is declared as an Optional because it won't have a "real" value when the ViewController instance is created; it's going to get that value later through the loading of the nib ("Deferred initialization of properties" on page 126). The `@IBOutlet` attribute is a hint to Xcode to allow us to create the outlet in the nib editor.

2. Edit *View.xib*. We'd like to make the outlet, but in order to do that, we must ensure that the nib owner object is designated as a ViewController instance. Select the File's Owner proxy object and switch to the Identity inspector. In the

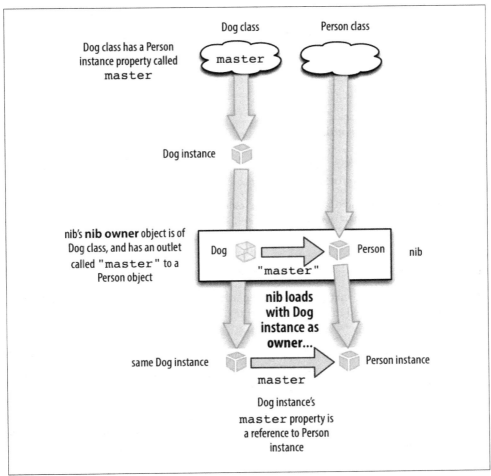

Dog class has a Person
instance property called
`master`

Dog class

Person class

`master`

Dog instance

nib's **nib owner** object is of
Dog class, and has an outlet
called "`master`" to a
Person object

Dog Person nib
"`master`"

**nib loads
with Dog
instance as
owner...**

same Dog instance Person instance

`master`

Dog instance's
`master` property is
a reference to Person
instance

Figure 7-9. An outlet from the nib owner object

first text field, under Custom Class, set the Class value as `ViewController`. Tab
out of the text field and save.

3. Now we're ready to make the outlet! In the document outline, hold Control and
Control-drag from the File's Owner object to the View; a little line follows the
mouse as you drag. Release the mouse when the View is highlighted. A little
HUD (heads-up display) appears, listing possible outlets we are allowed to create
(Figure 7-10). There are two of them: `coolview` and `view`. Click `coolview` (*not*
`view`!).

4. Finally, we need to modify our nib-loading code. We no longer need to capture
the result of our call to `loadNibNamed(_:owner:)`. That's the whole point of this

Figure 7-10. Creating an outlet

exercise! Instead, we're going to load the nib *with ourself as owner*. This will cause our `coolview` instance property to be set automatically:

```
Bundle.main.loadNibNamed("View", owner: self)
self.view.addSubview(self.coolview)
```

Build and run. It works! The first line loaded the nib, instantiated the view, *and set our `coolview` instance property* to that view. The second line can display `self.coolview` in the interface, because `self.coolview` now *is* that view.

Let's sum up what we just did. Our preparatory configuration was a little tricky, because it was performed in two places — in code, and in the nib:

In code

There must be an *instance property* in the class whose instance will act as owner when the nib loads. It must be marked as `@IBOutlet`; otherwise, Xcode won't permit us to create the outlet in the nib editor.

In the nib editor

The *class of the nib owner object* must be set to the class whose instance will act as owner when the nib loads; otherwise, Xcode *still* won't permit us to create the outlet. We must then *create the outlet*, with the same name as the property, from the nib owner to some nib object.

If all those things are true, then, when the nib loads, *if* it is loaded with an owner of the correct class, that owner's instance property will be set to the outlet destination.

 When you configure an outlet to an object in the nib, that object's name as listed in the document outline ceases to be generic (e.g. "View") and takes on the name of the outlet (e.g. "coolview"). This name is still just a label — it has no effect on the operation of the outlet — and you can change it in the Identity inspector.

Automatically Configured Nibs

Now that we've created a nib owner outlet *manually* and loaded a nib *manually*, we have demystified the nib-loading mechanism. When a view controller gets its main view from a nib *automatically*, everything works exactly like what we just did!

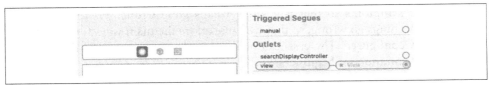

Figure 7-11. A view controller's view outlet connection

Consider our Empty Window project's *Main.storyboard*, with its single scene consisting of a ViewController and its main view:

- In our manual example, we started with an instance property in our nib owner class. Well, ViewController is a UIViewController, and UIViewController has an instance property — its `view` property! This is the property that needs to be set in order for the view controller to obtain its main view.

- In our manual example, in the nib editor, we made sure that the nib owner object's class would be the class of the owner when the nib loads. Well, in our *Main.storyboard* scene, the View Controller object *is* the nib owner, and it *is* of the correct class, namely ViewController (the class declared in the *View-Controller.swift* file). Look and see: select the ViewController object in the storyboard and examine its class in the Identity inspector.

- In our manual example, in the nib editor, we created an outlet with the same name as the owner instance property, leading from the owner to the nib object. Well, in our *Main.storyboard* scene, the ViewController object *is* the view nib owner, and it *has* an outlet named `view` which *is* connected to the main view. Look and see: select the view controller object in the storyboard and examine its Connections inspector (Figure 7-11).

So the storyboard has *already* been configured in a manner exactly parallel to how we configured *View.xib* in the preceding section. And the result is exactly the same! When the view controller needs its view, it loads the view nib with itself as owner, the nib-loading mechanism sees the connected `view` outlet, the view at the destination of that outlet is assigned to the view controller's `view` property, and voilà! The view controller has its main view.

Moreover, the view controller's main view is then placed into the interface. And *that* is why whatever we design in this view in the storyboard, such as putting into it a button whose title is "Hello," actually appears in the interface when the app runs.

Misconfigured Outlets

Setting up an outlet to work correctly involves several things being true at the same time. You should expect that at some point in the future you will fail to get this right, and your outlet won't work properly — and your app will probably crash. So be prepared! And don't worry; this happens to everyone. The important thing is to recognize the symptoms so that you know what's gone wrong. We're deliberately going to make things go wrong, so that we can explore the main ways for an outlet to be incorrectly configured. The crashes I'm about to describe, especially the first two, are extremely common for beginners.

Outlet–property name mismatch

Start with our working Empty Window example. Run the project to prove that all is well. Now, in *ViewController.swift*, change the property name to `badview`:

```
@IBOutlet var badview : UIView!
```

In order to get the code to compile, you'll also have to change the reference to this property in `viewDidLoad`:

```
self.view.addSubview(self.badview)
```

The code compiles just fine. But when you run it, the app crashes with this message in the console: "This class is not key value coding-compliant for the key `coolview`."

I'll explain that message in Chapter 10. For now, just think of it as a technical way of saying that the name of the outlet in the nib (which is still `coolview`) doesn't match the name of any property of the nib's owner when the nib loads — because we changed the name of that property to `badview` and wrecked the configuration. In effect, we had everything set up correctly, but then we went behind the nib editor's back and removed the corresponding instance property from the outlet source's class. When the nib loads, the runtime can't match the outlet's name with any property in the outlet's source — the ViewController instance — and we crash.

There are other ways to bring about this same misconfiguration. You could change things so that the nib owner is an instance of *the wrong class*. You might do that in the nib editor, by selecting the nib owner and changing its class in the Identity inspector. Alternatively, you might do it in code:

```
Bundle.main.loadNibNamed("View", owner: NSObject())
```

We made the `owner` a plain vanilla NSObject instance. The NSObject class has no property with the same name as the outlet, so the app crashes when the nib loads, complaining about the owner not being "key value coding-compliant."

 To change an outlet property's name *without* breaking the connection from the nib, select the property name in code and choose Editor → Refactor → Rename.

No outlet in the nib

Fix the problem from the previous example by changing both references to the property name from `badview` back to `coolview` in *ViewController.swift*. Run the project to prove that all is well. Now we're going to mess things up at the other end! Edit *View.xib*. Select the File's Owner and switch to the Connections inspector, and disconnect the `coolview` outlet by clicking the X at the left end of the second cartouche. Run the project. We crash with this error message in the console: "Fatal error: unexpectedly found `nil` while unwrapping an Optional value."

We removed the outlet from the nib. So when the nib loaded, our ViewController instance property `coolview`, which is typed as an implicitly unwrapped Optional wrapping a UIView, was *never set to anything*. It kept its initial value, which is `nil`. We then tried to *use* the implicitly unwrapped Optional by putting it into the interface:

```
self.view.addSubview(self.coolview)
```

Swift tries to obey by unwrapping the Optional, but you can't unwrap `nil`, so we crash.

No view outlet

I can't demonstrate this problem using a *.storyboard* file. What we'd like to do is *disconnect* the `view` outlet in *Main.storyboard*, but the storyboard editor guards against this. But if you *could* make this mistake, then trying to run the project would result in a crash at launch time, with a console message complaining that "the view outlet was not set."

A nib that is to serve as the source of a view controller's main view *must* have a connected `view` outlet from the view controller (the nib owner object) to the view. In a *.xib* file whose view is to function as a view controller's main view, you *can* make this mistake — usually by forgetting to connect the File's Owner `view` outlet to the view in the first place.

Deleting an Outlet

Deleting an outlet coherently — that is, without causing one of the problems described in the previous section — involves working in several places at once, just as creating an outlet does. I recommend proceeding in this order:

1. Disconnect the outlet in the nib.
2. Remove the outlet declaration from the code.
3. Attempt compilation and let the compiler catch any remaining issues for you.

Let's suppose that you decide to delete the `coolview` outlet from the Empty Window project. You would follow the same three-step procedure that I just outlined:

1. Disconnect the outlet in the nib. To do so, edit *View.xib*, select the source object (the File's Owner proxy object), and disconnect the `coolview` outlet in the Connections inspector by clicking the X.

2. Remove the outlet declaration from the code. To do so, edit *ViewController.swift* and delete or comment out the `@IBOutlet` declaration line.

3. Now attempt to build the project; the compiler issues an error on the line referring to `self.coolview` in *ViewController.swift*, because there is now no such property. Delete or comment out that line, and build again to prove that all is well.

More Ways to Create Outlets

Earlier, we created an outlet by control-dragging from the source to the destination in the document outline. Xcode provides many other ways to create outlets — too many to list here. I'll survey some of the most interesting. We'll continue to use the Empty Window project and the *View.xib* file. All of this works exactly the same way for a *.storyboard* file.

To prepare, delete the outlet in *View.xib* as I described in the previous section (if you haven't already done so). In *ViewController.swift*, create (or uncomment) the property declaration, and save:

```
@IBOutlet var coolview : UIView!
```

Now we're ready to experiment:

Drag from source Connections inspector
You can drag from a circle in the Connections inspector in the nib editor to connect the outlet. In *View.xib*, select the File's Owner and switch to the Connections inspector. The `coolview` outlet is listed here, but it isn't connected: the circle at its right is open. Drag from the circle next to `coolview` to the UIView object in the nib. You can drag to the view in the canvas or in the document outline. You don't need to hold Control as you drag from the circle, and there's no HUD because you're dragging from a specific outlet, so Xcode knows which one you mean.

Drag from destination Connections inspector
Now let's make that same move the other way round. Delete the outlet in the nib. Select the View and look at the Connections inspector. We want an outlet that has this view as its destination: that's a "referencing outlet." Drag from the circle next to New Referencing Outlet to the File's Owner object. The HUD appears: click `coolview` to make the outlet connection.

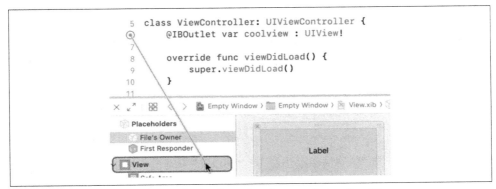

```
5  class ViewController: UIViewController {
       @IBOutlet var coolview : UIView!
7
8      override func viewDidLoad() {
9          super.viewDidLoad()
10     }
11
```

Figure 7-12. Connecting an outlet by dragging from code to nib editor

Drag from source HUD

Instead of starting by dragging, we can start by Control-clicking to summon a HUD and then drag from that HUD. Again delete the outlet in the Connections inspector. Control-click the File's Owner. A HUD appears, looking a lot like the Connections inspector. Drag from the circle at the right of coolview to the UIView.

Drag from destination HUD

Again, let's make that same move the other way round. Delete the outlet in the Connections inspector. Either in the canvas or in the document outline, Control-click the view. There's the HUD showing its Connections inspector. Drag from the New Referencing Outlet circle to the File's Owner. A second HUD appears, listing possible outlets; click coolview.

Again, delete the outlet. Now we're going to create the outlet by dragging *between the code and the nib editor*. This will require that you work in two places at once: you're going to need two editor panes (see Chapter 6). In one editor pane, show *View-Controller.swift*. In the other editor pane, show *View.xib*, in such a way that the view is visible.

Drag from property declaration to nib

Next to the property declaration in the code, in the gutter, is an empty circle. Drag from that circle *right across the barrier* to the View in the nib editor (Figure 7-12). You've done it! The outlet connection has been formed in the nib; you can see this by looking at the Connections inspector, and also because, back in the code, the circle in the gutter is now filled in.

You can hover over the filled circle, or click it, to learn what the outlet in the nib is connected to. You can click the little menu that appears when you click in the filled circle to navigate to the destination object.

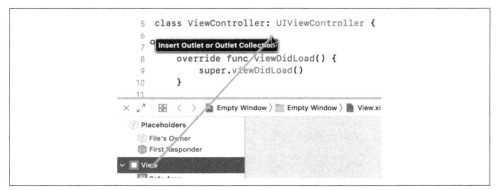

Figure 7-13. Creating an outlet by dragging from nib editor to code

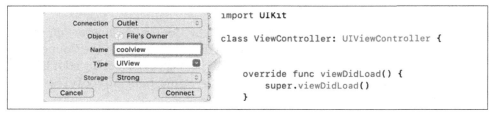

Figure 7-14. Configuring an outlet property declaration

Here's one more way — the most amazing of all. Keep the two-pane arrangement from the preceding example. Again, delete the outlet (you will probably need to use the Connections inspector or HUD in the nib editor pane to do this). Also delete the @IBOutlet line from the code! We're going to create the property declaration and connect the outlet, *in a single move!*

Drag from nib to code

Control-drag from the view in the nib editor across the pane barrier to just inside the body of the class ViewController declaration. A HUD offers to Insert Outlet or Outlet Collection (Figure 7-13). Release the mouse. A popover appears, where you can configure the declaration to be inserted into your code. Configure it as shown in Figure 7-14: you want an outlet, and this property should be named coolview. Click Connect. The property declaration is inserted into your code, and the outlet is connected in the nib.

Making an outlet by connecting directly between code and the nib editor is cool and convenient, but don't be fooled: there's no such direct connection. There are *two distinct and separate things* — an instance property in a class, and an outlet in the nib *with the same name* and *coming from an instance of that class*. It is the identity of the names and classes that allows the two to be matched at runtime when the nib loads. Xcode tries to help you get everything set up correctly, but it is *not* in fact magically connecting the code to the nib, and it is still possible to mess up the configuration later, as I've already described.

Outlet Collections

An *outlet collection* is an *array* instance property (in code) matched (in a nib) by *multiple* connections to objects of the same type.

Suppose a class contains this property declaration:

```
@IBOutlet var coollabels: [UILabel]!
```

The outcome is that, in the nib editor, with an instance of this class selected, the Connections inspector lists `coollabels` — not under Outlets, but under Outlet Collections. This means that you can form multiple `coollabels` outlets, each one connected to a different UILabel object in the nib. When the nib loads, those UILabel instances become the elements of the array `coollabels`; the order of elements in the array is the order in which the outlets were formed. Your code can then refer to the labels by number (the index into the array). This can be cleaner than having a separate instance property for each label.

Action Connections

An action connection, like an outlet connection, is a way of giving one object in a nib a reference to another. But, unlike an outlet connection, it's not a property reference; it's a *message-sending* reference.

An *action* is a message emitted automatically by a Cocoa UIControl interface object (a *control*), sent to another object when the user does something to it, such as tapping the control. The various user behaviors that will cause a control to emit an action message are called *events*. To see a list of possible events, look at the UIControl.Event documentation. For example, in the case of a UIButton, the user tapping the button corresponds to the `.touchUpInside` control event.

For this architecture to work, the control object must know three things:

Control event
    What control event to respond to

Action
    What message to send (that is, what method to call) when that control event occurs

Target
    What object to send that message to

An action connection in a nib builds the knowledge of those three things into itself. It has the control object as its source; its destination is the target; and you tell the action connection, as you form it, what the control event and action message should be. To form the action connection, you need to configure the class of the *destination* object so that it has an instance method suitable as an action message.

To experiment with action connections, we'll need a UIControl object in a nib, such as a button. You may already have such a button in the Empty Window project's *Main.storyboard* file. However, it's probable that, when the app runs, we've been covering the button with the view that we're loading from *View.xib*. So first clear out the ViewController class declaration body in *ViewController.swift*, so that there is no outlet property and no manual nib-loading code; this should be all that's left:

```
class ViewController: UIViewController {
}
```

Now let's arrange to use the view controller in our Empty Window project as a target for an action message emitted by the button's .touchUpInside event (meaning that the button was tapped). We'll need a method in the view controller that will be called by the button when the button is tapped. To make this method dramatic and obvious, we'll have the view controller put up an alert window. Insert this method into the ViewController declaration body:

```
@IBAction func buttonPressed(_ sender: Any) {
    let alert = UIAlertController(
        title: "Howdy!", message: "You tapped me!", preferredStyle: .alert)
    alert.addAction(
        UIAlertAction(title: "OK", style: .cancel))
    self.present(alert, animated: true)
}
```

The @IBAction attribute is like @IBOutlet: it's a hint to Xcode itself, asking Xcode to make this method available in the nib editor. And indeed, if we look in the nib editor, we find that it *is* now available: edit *Main.storyboard*, select the View Controller object and switch to the Connections inspector, and you'll find that buttonPressed:, which is the Objective-C name of our action method, is now listed under Received Actions.

In *Main.storyboard*, in the single scene that it contains, the top-level View Controller's View should contain a button. (We created it earlier in this chapter: see Figure 7-4.) If it doesn't, add one, and position it in the upper left corner of the view. Our goal now is to connect that button's Touch Up Inside event, as an action, to the buttonPressed(_:) method in ViewController.

As with an outlet connection, there is a source and a destination. The source here is the button in the storyboard; the destination is the ViewController instance acting as owner of the nib containing the button. There are many ways to form this action connection, all of them completely parallel to the formation of an outlet connection. The difference is that we must configure *both* ends of the connection. At the button

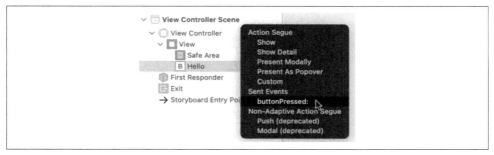

Figure 7-15. A HUD showing an action method

(source) end, we must specify that the control event we want to use is Touch Up Inside; fortunately, this is the default for a UIButton, so we might be able to skip this step. At the view controller (destination) end, we must specify that the action method to be called is our `buttonPressed(_:)` method.

Let's form the action connection by Control-dragging from the button to the view controller in the nib editor:

1. Control-drag from the button (in the canvas or in the document outline) to the View Controller listing in the document outline (or to the view controller icon in the scene dock above the view in the canvas).

2. A HUD listing possible connections appears (Figure 7-15); it lists mostly segues, but it also lists Sent Events, and in particular it lists `buttonPressed:`.

3. Click the `buttonPressed:` listing in the HUD.

The action connection has now been formed. This means that when the app runs, any time the button gets a Touch Up Inside event — meaning that it was tapped — it will call the `buttonPressed(_:)` method in the target, which is the view controller instance. We know what that method should do: it should put up an alert. Try it! Build and run the app, and when the app appears in the Simulator, tap the button. It works!

More Ways to Create Actions

Other ways to form the action connection in the nib, having created the action method in *ViewController.swift*, include the following:

Drag from source Connections inspector
   Select the button and use the Connections inspector. Drag from the Touch Up Inside circle to the view controller. A HUD appears, listing the known action methods in the view controller; click `buttonPressed:`.

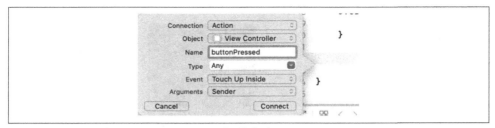

Figure 7-16. Configuring an action method declaration

Drag from source HUD

Control-click the button. A HUD appears, similar to the Connections inspector. Proceed as in the previous case.

Drag from destination HUD

Control-click the view controller. A HUD appears, similar to the Connections inspector. Drag from buttonPressed: (under Received Actions) to the button. Another HUD appears, listing possible control events. Click Touch Up Inside.

Drag from action method to nib

Make two editor panes. Arrange to see *ViewController.swift* in one pane and the storyboard in the other. The buttonPressed(_:) declaration in *View-Controller.swift* has a circle to its left, in the gutter. Drag from that circle across the pane barrier to the button in the nib.

As with an outlet connection, the most impressive way to make an action connection is to drag from the nib editor to your code, inserting the action method and forming the action connection in the nib *in a single move*. To try this, first delete the button-Pressed(_:) method in your code and delete the action connection in the nib. Make two editor panes. Arrange to see *ViewController.swift* in one pane and the storyboard in the other. Now:

1. Control-drag from the button in the nib editor to an empty area in the View-Controller class declaration's body. A HUD offering to create an outlet *or an action* appears in the code. Release the mouse.

2. The popover view appears:

   a. Always look first at the Connection pop-up menu. It *might* be offering to create an outlet connection. That isn't what you want; you want an action connection! If it says Outlet, *change* it to Action.

   b. Enter the name of the action method (here, buttonPressed) and configure the rest of the declaration. The defaults are probably good enough: see Figure 7-16.

Xcode forms the action connection in the nib, and inserts a stub method into your code:

```
@IBAction func buttonPressed(_ sender: Any) {
}
```

The method is just a stub (Xcode can't read your mind and guess what you want the method to do), so in real life, at this point, you'd insert some functionality between those curly braces. As with an outlet connection, the filled circle next to the code in an action method tells you that Xcode believes that this connection is correctly configured, and you can click the filled circle to learn, and navigate to, the object at the source of the connection.

Misconfigured Actions

As with an outlet connection, configuring an action connection involves setting things up correctly at both ends (the nib and the code) so that they match. So of course you can wreck an action connection's configuration and crash your app. So be prepared! The typical misconfiguration, commonly encountered by beginners, is that the name of the action method as embedded in the action connection in the nib no longer matches the name of the action method in the code.

To see this, change the name of the action method in the code from `buttonPressed` to something else, like `buttonPushed`. Now run the app and tap the button. Your app crashes, displaying in the console this dreaded error message: "Unrecognized selector sent to instance." A selector is a message — the name of a method (Chapter 2). The runtime tried to send a message to an object, but that object turned out to have no corresponding method (because we renamed it). If you look a little earlier in the error message, it even tells you the name of this method:

```
-[Empty_Window.ViewController buttonPressed:]
```

The runtime is telling you (using Objective-C notation) that it tried to call the `button-Pressed(_:)` method in your Empty Window module's ViewController class, but the ViewController class has no such method.

 To change an action method's name *without* breaking the connection from the nib, select the method name in code and choose Editor → Refactor → Rename.

Connections Between Nibs — Not!

You cannot draw an outlet connection or an action connection between an object in a nib and an object in a *different* nib:

- You cannot open nib editors on two different *.xib* files and Control-drag a connection from one to the other.
- In a *.storyboard* file, you cannot Control-drag a connection between an object in one scene and an object in another scene.

The reason is obvious when you consider what a nib *is*. Objects in a nib together will become instances together, at the moment when the nib loads, so it makes sense to connect them in that nib, because we know what instances we'll be talking about when the nib loads. The two objects may both be instantiated by loading the nib, or one of them may be a proxy object (the nib owner), but they must both be represented *in the same nib*, so that the actual instances can be configured in relation to one another on each particular occasion when this nib loads.

If an outlet connection or an action connection were drawn from an object in one nib to an object in another nib, there would be no way to understand what actual future instances the connection is supposed to connect, because they are different nibs and will be loaded at different times (if ever). The problem of communicating between an instance generated from one nib and an instance generated from another nib is a special case of the more general problem of how to communicate between instances in a program, discussed in Chapter 13.

Additional Configuration of Nib-Based Instances

After a nib finishes loading, the instances that it describes have been initialized and configured with all the attributes dictated through the Attributes and Size inspectors, and their outlets have been used to set the values of the corresponding instance properties. Nevertheless, you might want to append your own code to the initialization process as an object is instantiated by loading a nib. This section describes some ways you can do that.

A common situation is that a view controller, functioning as the owner when a nib containing its main view loads (and therefore represented in the nib by the nib owner object), has an outlet to an interface object instantiated by the loading of the nib. In this architecture, the view controller can perform further configuration on that interface object, because it has a reference to it after the nib loads — the corresponding instance property. The earliest place where it can perform such configuration is its viewDidLoad method. At the time viewDidLoad is called, the view controller's view has been instantiated and assigned to its view property, and all its outlets have been connected; but the view is not yet in the visible interface.

Another possibility is that you'd like the nib object to configure itself, over and above whatever configuration has been performed in the nib. Often, this will be because you've got a custom subclass of a built-in interface object class; in fact, you might want to *create* a subclass precisely so as to have a place to put this self-configuring code. The problem you're trying to solve might be that the nib editor doesn't let you perform the configuration you're after, or that you have many objects that need to be configured similarly, so that it makes more sense for them to configure themselves by virtue of sharing a common class than to configure each one individually.

One approach is to implement awakeFromNib in your custom class. The awakeFrom-Nib message is sent to all nib-instantiated objects just after they are instantiated by the loading of the nib: the object has been initialized and configured and its connections are operational.

Let's make a button whose background color is always red, regardless of how it's configured in the nib. (This is a nutty example, but it's dramatically effective.) In the Empty Window project, we'll create a button subclass, RedButton:

1. In the Project navigator, choose File → New → File. Specify iOS → Source → Cocoa Touch Class. Click Next.

2. Call the new class RedButton. Make it a subclass of UIButton. Click Next.

3. Make sure you're saving into the project folder, in the Empty Window group, and that the Empty Window app target is checked. Click Create. Xcode creates *RedButton.swift*.

4. In *RedButton.swift*, inside the body of the RedButton class declaration, implement awakeFromNib:

```
override func awakeFromNib() {
    super.awakeFromNib()
    self.backgroundColor = .red
}
```

We now have a UIButton subclass that turns itself red when it's instantiated from a nib. But we have no instance of this subclass in any nib. Let's fix that. Edit the storyboard, select the button that's already in the main view, and use the Identity inspector

Custom Class		Hide
Class	RedButton	
Module	Empty_Window	
	☑ Inherit Module From Target	

Identity		Show

User Defined Runtime Attributes

Key Path	Type	Value
layer.cornerRadius	Number	◇ 10

+ −

Figure 7-17. Rounding a button's corners with a runtime attribute

to change this button's class to RedButton. Now build and run the project. Sure enough, the button is red!

A further possibility is to take advantage of the User Defined Runtime Attributes in the nib object's Identity inspector. This can allow you to configure, in the nib editor, aspects of a nib object for which the nib editor itself provides no built-in interface. What you're actually doing here is sending the nib object, at nib-loading time, a `set-Value(_:forKeyPath:)` message; Cocoa key paths are discussed in Chapter 10. Naturally, the object needs to be prepared to respond to the given key path, or your app will crash when the nib loads.

One of the disadvantages of the nib editor is that it provides no way to configure layer attributes. Let's say we'd like to use the nib editor to round the corners of our red button. In code, we would do that by setting the button's `layer.cornerRadius` property. The nib editor gives no access to this property. Instead, we can select the button in the nib editor and use the User Defined Runtime Attributes in the Identity inspector. We set the Key Path to `layer.cornerRadius`, the Type to Number, and the Value to whatever value we want — let's say 10 (Figure 7-17). Now build and run; sure enough, the button's corners are now rounded.

 If you define your own property, your User Defined Runtime Attributes setting for that property will fail silently unless you mark the property `@objc`.

You can also configure a custom property of a nib object by making that property *inspectable*. To do so, add the `@IBInspectable` attribute to the property's declaration in your code. This causes the property to be listed in the nib object's Attributes inspector. (It also implicitly marks it `@objc`.)

Let's make it possible to configure our button's border in the nib editor. At the start of the RedButton class declaration body, add this code:

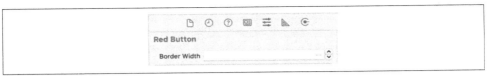

Figure 7-18. An inspectable property in the nib editor

```
@IBInspectable var borderWidth : CGFloat {
    get {
        return self.layer.borderWidth
    }
    set {
        self.layer.borderWidth = newValue
    }
}
```

That code declares a RedButton property, borderWidth, and makes it a façade in front of the layer's borderWidth property. It also causes the nib editor to display that property in the Attributes inspector for any button that is an instance of the Red-Button class (Figure 7-18). The result is that when we give this property a value in the nib editor, that value is sent to the setter for this property at nib-loading time, and the button border appears with that width.

To intervene with a nib object's initialization even earlier, if the object is a UIView (or a UIView subclass), you can override init(coder:). A minimal implementation would look like this:

```
required init?(coder: NSCoder) {
    super.init(coder:coder)
    // your code here
}
```

CHAPTER 8

Documentation

Knowledge is of two kinds. We know a subject ourselves,
or we know where we can find information upon it.
—Samuel Johnson,
Boswell's Life of Johnson

No aspect of iOS programming is more important than a fluid and nimble relationship with the documentation. In addition to Swift's own types, there are hundreds of built-in Cocoa classes along with their numerous methods and properties and other details. Apple's documentation, whatever its flaws, is the definitive official word on how you can expect Cocoa to behave, and on the contractual rules incumbent upon you in working with this massive framework whose inner workings you cannot see directly.

Your primary access to the documentation is in Xcode, through the documentation window. But there are other forms of documentation and assistance. Quick Help popovers and the Quick Help inspector provide documentation without leaving the code editor. You can examine the code headers, which provide a useful overview and often contain valuable comments, and you can jump quickly to a symbol declaration. Apple provides sample code, and there are lots of additional online resources.

The Documentation Window

There are two main categories of documentation provided by Apple:

Primary documentation
The primary documentation (*reference* documentation) for Cocoa classes and other symbols is included entirely within Xcode, and is displayed in the documentation window (Window → Developer Documentation or Help → Developer

Documentation, Command-Shift-0). You can also view the same documentation online, at *https://developer.apple.com/documentation*.

Secondary documentation

Secondary documentation consisting of older guides, sample code, and technical notes and Q&As is available only online, at *https://developer.apple.com/library/ archive/navigation*. Apple refers to this material as the *documentation archive*.

Within the documentation window, the primary pathway is a search; press Command-Shift-0 (or Command-L or Command-Shift-F if you're already in the documentation window) and type a search term, typically a class name such as "NSString" or "UIButton." As you type, you're shown the top search results pertinent to the language of your choice (such as Swift or Objective-C). You can choose a result with the mouse, or you can navigate the results with arrow keys and press Return to select the desired hit.

You can also perform a documentation window search starting from within your code. You'll very often want to do this: you're looking directly at a symbol (a type name, a function name, a property name, and so on) at its point of use in your code, and you want to know more about it. Select text in your code (or anywhere else) and choose Help → Search Documentation for Selected Text (Command-Option-Control-/). This is like typing that text into the search field in the documentation window.

The documentation window behaves basically as a sort of web browser. Terms shown in a documentation page are links; click one to navigate to the documentation page about that term. You can then navigate between pages you've already loaded, using Navigate → Go Back and Navigate → Go Forward (or the back and forward buttons in the documentation window). To split your view of the documentation into multiple tabs, choose File → New → Window Tab (Command-T); to open a link in a new tab, hold Command when you click the link.

A hierarchical table of contents for the whole documentation appears in the navigator pane at the left of the documentation window; to see it if it isn't showing, choose View → Navigators → Show Navigator (Command-0), or click the Navigator button in the window toolbar. The table of contents can display any of three panes: Swift, Objective-C, or Other. You can switch between them with the pop-up menu at the top of the table of contents, or use the keyboard shortcuts (Command-1 and so on). To select in the table of contents the page you're currently viewing, choose Editor → Reveal in Navigator (or use the contextual menu).

To search for text *within* the current documentation page, use the Find menu commands. Find → Find (Command-F) summons a find bar, as in Safari.

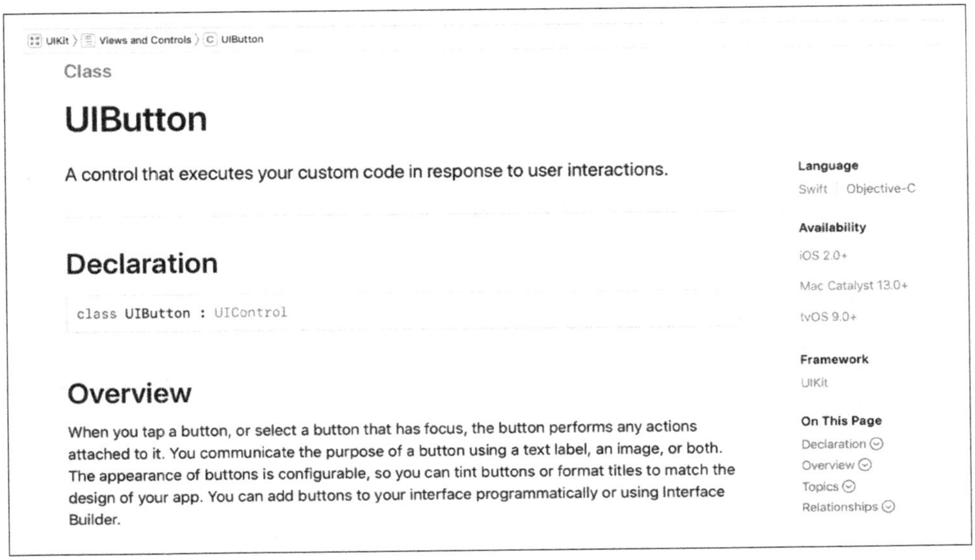

Figure 8-1. The start of the UIButton class documentation page

Class Documentation Pages

When dealing with Cocoa, your target documentation page will most likely be the documentation for a class, such as the page shown in Figure 8-1. Here are some typical features of a class documentation page:

Jump bar
At the top of the page is the jump bar. This has two main purposes:

Breadcrumbs
The jump bar functions as a kind of "breadcrumbs" display of where you are. The UIButton class documentation page is in the Views and Controls section of the UIKit division of the documentation. This is the same hierarchy in which the page is displayed in the navigator table of contents.

Navigation
Each item in the jump bar is a hierarchical menu, displaying the same hierarchy as in the navigator table of contents. Choose a menu item to navigate there. As with the Xcode project window editor's jump bar, you can type to filter the items of the currently selected menu.

Language
Links let you choose between Swift and Objective-C as the language for display of symbol names.

Availability

This list tells you two important things:

- What sort of *hardware* you're programming for when you use this class. That's important because searches are not filtered by hardware type. If you were to stumble accidentally into the NSViewController class documentation page, you might be confused about how this class fits into the rest of iOS programming, unless you notice that iOS is not even listed in this class's Availability; this is a macOS class (AppKit).

- The lowest *version number* in which this class became available. For example, the UIGraphicsImageRenderer page tells you that this class is available in iOS 10.0 and later. So you wouldn't be able to use it in code intended to run on iOS 9.

Framework

The framework that vends this class.

On This Page

The class reference page is divided into sections, and these are links to them, in order:

Declaration

The formal declaration for this class, showing its superclass.

Overview

If a page has an Overview section, read it! It explains what this class is for and how to use it. It may also contain valuable links to guides that provide related information.

Topics

These are primarily the class's members — its properties and methods — grouped by their purpose. Each member is accompanied by a short description; click the member itself to see further details. (I'll talk more about that in a moment.) There may also be listings for enums used by this class's properties and methods, and notifications if this class emits any; the UIApplication class documentation page is a case in point.

Relationships

There are two chief kinds of relationship that a class can have, and you'll want to keep an eye on both of them; a common beginner mistake is failing to follow the documentation links in this section:

Inherits from

This class's superclass. A class inherits from its superclasses, so the functionality or information you're looking for may be in a superclass. You won't find `addTarget(_:action:for:)` listed in the UIButton class page; it's in the UIControl class page (UIButton's superclass). You won't find out that a UIButton has a `frame` property from the UIButton class page; that information is in the UIView class page (UIControl's superclass).

Conforms to

Protocols adopted by this class. Again, the functionality or information you're looking for might be documented for a protocol rather than in this class's own page. For instance, you won't discover the `viewWill-Transition(to:with:)` method on the UIViewController class page; you have to look in the documentation for the UIContentContainer protocol, which UIViewController adopts.

When you click the name of a property or method in a class documentation page, you're taken to a separate page that describes it in detail. This page is laid out similarly to a class documentation page:

Jump bar

The jump bar provides breadcrumb navigation leading back to the class documentation page.

Language

The page gives you a choice of languages.

Availability

The availability for a property or method need not be the same as its class's availability, because a class can acquire (and lose) members over time. The UINavigationBar class is as old as iOS itself and is available starting in iOS 2.0, but its `prefersLargeTitles` property didn't appear until iOS 11.0.

On This Page

There is no separate Overview section, but there is always an initial summary of purpose (the same summary that appears on the class documentation page). The other sections of a method's page are:

Declaration

The formal declaration for this method, showing its parameters and return type.

Parameters

Separate explanations for each parameter.

Return Value

An explicit description of what this method returns.

Figure 8-2. Filtering the jump bar for the UIButton topics

> Discussion
> > Often contains extremely important further details about how this method behaves. Always pay attention to this section!

> See Also
> > Links to related methods and properties. Helpful for getting a larger perspective on how this method fits into the overall behavior of this class.

The Topics section of a class documentation page may list many class members, and these can rapidly threaten to become overwhelming. If you know the name of a class member that you're interested in, or you want to get to a particular topic quickly, how are you going to reach it without the tedium of scrolling? *Don't forget the jump bar!* The jump bar lists all the class members listed on the page, grouped by topic. And that list can be filtered by typing. Let's say I know that the class member I'm interested in contains the term "background." I summon the rightmost level of the jump bar, type "back," and am shown a shortened list of just those terms (Figure 8-2). Now it's easy to navigate to the detail page for any of those items.

In addition to the class documentation, the built-in primary documentation includes explanatory guides on overall topics. The existence of these guides is not always obvious. The UIButton class documentation is inside the Views and Controls section; that page, the section page, is an introductory guide to views and controls. Sometimes there are extensive explanatory pages, effectively constituting the chapters of a virtual booklet. The Table of Contents can be a big help in spotting these; such pages are marked with a document icon. The discussion of Swift Packages is a case in point.

Quick Help

Quick Help is a condensed rendering of the documentation for a particular symbol such as a type, function, or property name. It appears with regard to the current selection or insertion point automatically in the Quick Help inspector (Command-Option-3) if the inspector is showing. For instance, if you're editing code and the insertion point or selection is within the term viewDidLoad, documentation for the viewDidLoad method automatically appears in the Quick Help inspector if it is visible. Quick Help is also available in the Quick Help inspector for interface objects selected in the nib editor.

Quick Help documentation can also be displayed as a popover window. Select a term in the code editor and choose Help → Show Quick Help for Selected Item (Command-Control-Shift-?). Alternatively, hold Option and hover the mouse over a term until the cursor becomes a question mark; then Option-click the term.

 When you're developing Swift code, Quick Help is of increased importance. If you click in the name of a Swift variable whose type is inferred, Quick Help shows the inferred type (see Figure 3-1). This can help you understand compile errors and other surprises.

The Quick Help documentation contains links. Click the Open in Developer Reference link to see the full documentation in the documentation window.

You can inject documentation for your own code into Quick Help. To do so, precede a declaration with a comment enclosed in /**...*/ or a sequence of single-line comments starting with ///. Within the comment, Markdown formatting can be used (*http://daringfireball.net/projects/markdown/syntax*). The first paragraph of the comment becomes the Summary field for Quick Help; remaining paragraphs become the Description field, except that certain list items (paragraphs beginning with * or - followed by space) are treated in a special way, such as:

- List paragraphs beginning with `Parameter` *paramname*: are incorporated into the Parameters field.
- A list paragraph beginning with `Throws:` becomes the Throws field.
- A list paragraph beginning with `Returns:` becomes the Returns field.
- A list paragraph beginning with `Note:` becomes a Note field.

Here's a function declaration with a preceding comment:

```
/**
Many people would like to dog their cats. So it is *perfectly*
reasonable to supply a convenience method to do so:

* Because it's cool.
* Because it's there.

* Parameter cats: A string containing cats

* Returns: A string containing dogs
*/

func dogMyCats(_ cats:String) -> String {
    return "Dogs"
}
```

Figure 8-3. Custom documentation injected into Quick Help

The double asterisk in the opening comment delimiter denotes that this is documentation, which is automatically associated with the `dogMyCats` method declaration that follows it. The outcome is that when `dogMyCats` is selected anywhere in my code, its documentation is displayed in Quick Help (Figure 8-3). The first paragraph of the comment becomes the Summary, and is also displayed as part of code completion (see Chapter 9). The word surrounded by asterisks is formatted as italics; the asterisked paragraphs become bulleted paragraphs; and the last two paragraphs become special fields.

You can also generate a documentation comment automatically. Select within the declaration line and choose Editor → Structure → Add Documentation. The comment is inserted before the declaration. The description, plus (if this is a function declaration) the Parameters, Returns, and Throws fields, as applicable, are provided as placeholders.

There are additional special documentation fields. For more information about these, see the "Markup Functionality" page of Apple's *Markup Formatting Reference*.

Symbol Declarations

A *symbol* is a declared term, such as the name of a function, variable, or object type. If you can see the name of a symbol in the code editor, you can jump quickly to the declaration of that symbol. Select the term and choose Navigate → Jump to

Definition (Command-Control-J); alternatively, hold Command-Control and hover the mouse over a prospective term, until the cursor becomes a pointing finger, and then Command-Control-click the term:

- If the symbol is declared in your code, you jump to its declaration in your code; this can be helpful not only for understanding your code but also for navigation.
- If the symbol is declared in the Swift library or a Cocoa framework, you jump to its declaration in the header file. (I'll talk more about header files in the next section.)

 Command-Control-click is the default for jumping to a symbol's declaration, but it can be changed. In the Navigation pane of Xcode's preferences, under Command-click on Code, switch the pop-up menu to Jumps to Definition. Now you can jump to a symbol declaration with a simple Command-click.

To jump to the declaration of a symbol whose name you know, even if you don't see the name in the code before you, choose File → Open Quickly (Command-Shift-O). A search field appears. In it, type key letters from the name, which will be interpreted intelligently; to search for `application(_:didFinishLaunchingWithOptions:)`, you might type "appdidf." Possible matches are shown in a scrolling list below the search field; you can navigate this list with the mouse or by keyboard alone. Besides declarations from the framework headers, declarations in your own code are listed as well, so this, too, can be a rapid way of navigating your code.

In addition, a list of available symbols appears in the Symbol navigator (Chapter 6). If the second icon in the filter bar is highlighted, these are symbols declared in your project; if not, symbols from imported frameworks are listed as well. Click to navigate to a symbol declaration.

Header Files

A header file can be a useful form of documentation. The header is necessarily accurate, up-to-date, and complete, and it may contain comments telling you things that the documentation doesn't. Also, a single header file can contain declarations for multiple classes and protocols. So it can be an excellent quick reference.

The previous section describes various ways of jumping to a symbol declaration; since most symbols are declared in header files, these are ways of reaching header files. To reach *NSString.h*, select the term `NSString` wherever it may appear in your code and jump to its declaration, or choose File → Open Quickly (Command-Shift-O) and type "NSString." Once you're in a header file, you can navigate it conveniently through the jump bar at the top of the editor.

When you jump to a header file from your code, the header file, if it is written in Objective-C, can appear in Objective-C or Swift:

- To switch from an Objective-C original to its Swift translation, choose Generated Interface from the Related Items menu (at the left end of the jump bar, Control-1).
- To switch from a Swift translated (generated) header to the Objective-C original, choose Navigate → Jump to Original Source, or choose Original Source from the Related Items menu.

You can learn a lot about the Swift language and the built-in library functions by examining the Swift header file. The special Swift header files for Core Graphics and Foundation are also likely to prove useful. A neat trick is to write an `import` statement just so that you can reach the corresponding header. If you `import Swift` at the top of a Swift file, the word `Swift` itself is a symbol that you can use to jump to the Swift header.

Sample Code

The documentation archive includes plenty of sample code projects. You can view the code in a browser, but you can see only one file at a time, so it's difficult to get an overview. Instead, click the Download Sample Code button and open the downloaded project in Xcode; with the sample code project open in a project window, you can read the code, navigate it, edit it, and of course run the project.

Some of the primary documentation guides contain links to downloadable sample code as well. This sample code can be difficult to discover. In a few cases, the documentation archive links to it. In other cases, you just have to stumble across it. Again, the table of contents in the documentation window can be a big help here; sample code pages are marked with a curly braces icon.

As a form of documentation, sample code is both good and bad. It can be a superb source of working code that you can often copy and paste and use with very little alteration in your own projects. It is usually heavily commented, because the Apple folks are aware, as they write the code, that it is intended for instructional purposes. Sample code also illustrates concepts that users have difficulty extracting from the documentation. But the logic of a project is often spread over multiple files, and nothing is more difficult to understand than someone else's code (except, perhaps, your own code). Moreover, what learners most need is not the *fait accompli* of a fully written project but the reasoning process that constructed the project, which no amount of commentary can provide.

Apple's sample code is generally thoughtful and instructive, and is definitely a major component of the documentation; it deserves more appreciation and usage than it seems to get. But it is most useful, I think, after you've reached a certain level of competence and comfort. Also, while some of the sample code is astoundingly well-written, some of it is a bit careless or even downright faulty.

Internet Resources

Programming has become a lot easier since the internet came along and Google started indexing it. It's amazing what you can learn with a Google search. Your problem is very likely one that someone else has faced, solved, and written about on the internet. Often you'll find sample code that you can paste into your project and adapt.

Apple's own online resources go beyond the formal documentation. There are WWDC videos (*https://developer.apple.com/videos*) from the current and previous years. Apple also hosts developer forums (*https://developer.apple.com/forums*); some interesting discussions take place in these forums, and they are patrolled by helpful Apple employees.

Other online resources have sprung up spontaneously as iOS programming has become more popular, and lots of iOS and Cocoa programmers post tutorials or blog about their experiences. Stack Overflow (*http://www.stackoverflow.com*) is a site that I'm particularly fond of; it's a general programming question-and-answer site, not devoted exclusively to iOS programming, but with lots of iOS programmers hanging out there; questions are answered succinctly and correctly, and the interface lets you focus on the right answer quickly and easily.

CHAPTER 9

Life Cycle of a Project

This chapter surveys some of the main stages in the life cycle of an Xcode project, from inception to submission at the App Store. The survey will provide an opportunity to discuss some additional features of the Xcode development environment as well as various tasks you'll typically perform as you work on your app, including editing, debugging, and testing your code, running your app on a device, profiling, localization, and releasing to the public.

Environmental Dependencies

It may be useful to have your app behave differently depending on the environment in which it finds itself when compiling or running:

Buildtime dependencies

These are choices made at build time. They affect the build process, including what the compiler does. Typical dependencies are:

- The version of Swift under which we're compiling.
- The type of destination for which we're compiling — a simulator or a real device.
- A custom compilation condition defined for the current build configuration in the build settings.
- The action that causes the build — for instance, whether we're building to run or to archive.

Runtime dependencies

These are choices made depending on what the app discovers its environment to be when it runs. Typical dependencies are the type of device we turn out to be running on (iPad vs. iPhone) and the system version installed on this device:

- Should the app be permitted to run under this environment?

- Should the app do different things, or load different resources, depending on the environment?

- Should the app respond to the presence of an argument or environment variable injected by Xcode?

Conditional Compilation

Stretches of code that might or might not be compiled into your built app depending on the compile-time environment are fenced off by `#if...#endif` directives, as shown in Example 9-1.

Example 9-1. Swift conditional compilation

```
#if condition
    statements
#elseif condition
    statements
#else
    statements
#endif
```

The `#elseif` and `#else` sections can be omitted, and there can be multiple `#elseif` sections. There are *no curly braces*, and the `statements` will not in fact be indented by the code editor.

The conditions are treated as Bools, so they can be combined with the usual Boolean logic operators. However, they are not Swift code expressions! They must come from a limited predefined set of reserved words. The ones you are most likely to use are:

`swift(>=5.3)`, `compiler(>=5.3)` *(or some other version number)*
:   The version of the Swift language or compiler under which we're building. The only legal operators are `<` and `>=`. The `swift` version depends on the Swift Language Version build setting, but the compiler version depends on the Xcode version. Under Xcode 12, if the Swift Language Version is `Swift 4.2`, then `swift` is less than 5, but `compiler` is not.

`targetEnvironment(simulator)`
:   Whether we're building for a simulator or device destination. This can allow an app to run coherently on the simulator even though the simulator lacks certain capabilities, such as the camera.

`canImport(UIKit)` *(or some other module name)*
:   Whether the module in question is available on the platform for which we're building.

Figure 9-1. Compilation conditions in the build settings

Custom compilation condition

A name that you enter in the Active Compilation Conditions build setting will yield `true` for purposes of conditional compilation.

The *statements* enclosed in each block will not be compiled at all unless the appropriate condition is met, as this (very silly) example demonstrates:

```
#if swift(>=5.3)
print("howdy")
#else
Hey! Ba-Ba-Re-Bop
#endif
```

That code compiles without complaint in a plain vanilla project built from the iOS App template in Xcode 12. The statement `Hey! Ba-Ba-Re-Bop` is not a legal Swift expression, but the compiler doesn't care, because our Swift version *is* Swift 5.3, so the compiler never even examines the `#else` block.

An `#if` condition can distinguish between build configurations by way of the Active Compilation Conditions build setting. In fact, your project already comes with one such condition by default: the `DEBUG` condition is defined for the Debug configuration but not for the Release configuration (Figure 9-1). This means that for a Debug build, but not for a Release build, the test `#if DEBUG` will succeed.

A useful technique is to define a configuration, define an Active Compilation Conditions setting for that configuration, and make a scheme that builds using that configuration, or have different actions of one scheme use different configurations.

For instance, if the Run action uses the Debug build configuration but the Test action uses your custom Testing build configuration, you can define Active Compilation Conditions for the Testing configuration that will be present only when testing; in this way, you can use conditional compilation to apply to testing only. I often make a private method public during testing only, just so that method can be tested. (I'll talk more about testing later in this chapter.)

Build Action

The Development Assets build setting (introduced in Xcode 11) lets you specify one or more paths for resources that won't be included in an archive build — meaning a build to be distributed to other users, as I'll explain later in this chapter. In this way your app can include resources such as default data during development and testing, while guaranteeing that those resources won't pollute the ultimately released built app.

The paths that you specify can designate individual resources, entire asset catalogs, or even folders. A neat approach is a folder-linked group in the Project navigator: put your development-only resources into that group, and specify the path to the corresponding folder in Development Assets.

If you combine the Development Assets build setting with the `target-Environment(simulator)` compilation condition, you have the makings of a simulator-only test bed — code that is present only on the simulator, along with ancillary files that won't be present when you ultimately distribute the app to others.

For example, my Albumen app is all about displaying the contents of the user's music library. The Simulator doesn't really have a music library, so I use conditional compilation with `#if targetEnvironment(simulator)`; on the simulator, I have the app load some preconfigured data from a text file, and the app displays that data instead. But I don't want that text file to be present in the App Store release, so I list it in the Development Assets.

Permissible Runtime Environment

Under what environments should this app be permitted to run? The choices are determined by build settings, but you can configure them through a more convenient interface:

Device Type
> The device type(s) on which your app will run natively. This is the app target's Targeted Device Family build setting; to set, edit the app target, switch to the General pane, and use the Device checkboxes (under Deployment Info):

> *iPhone*
>> The app will run on an iPhone or iPod touch. It can also run on an iPad, but not as a native iPad app; it runs in a reduced enlargeable window (Apple sometimes refers to this as "compatibility mode").

> *iPad*
>> The app will run only on an iPad.

> *Both*
>> The app will run natively on both kinds of device; it is a *universal* app (and the Targeted Device Family setting will be Universal).

iOS Deployment Target

The *earliest* system your app can run on: in Xcode 12, this can be any major iOS system as far back as iOS 9.0. To set, edit the app target, switch to the General pane, and choose from the Target pop-up menu (under Deployment Info). There is also a drop-down list when you edit the project, in the Info pane.

Backward Compatibility

Writing an app whose iOS Deployment Target system version is lower than the current system version — that is, an app that is *backward compatible* to an earlier system — can be challenging. With each new system, Apple adds new features. You'll want to take advantage of these. But your app will *crash* if execution encounters features not supported by the system on which it is actually running!

Fortunately, when the compiler knows that a feature is unsupported by an earlier system, it will prevent you from accidentally using that feature on that system. Here's a line of code where we prepare to draw a small image:

```
let r = UIGraphicsImageRenderer(size:CGSize(width:10,height:10))
```

The UIGraphicsImageRenderer class exists only in iOS 10.0 and later. If your deployment target is iOS 9, the compiler will stop you with an error: "UIGraphicsImageRenderer is only available on iOS 10.0 or newer."

How does the compiler know we've got a potential problem here? It's because a term (a type or a member) states its availability in its declaration. The UIGraphicsImageRenderer class declaration is preceded (in Swift) with this annotation:

```
@available(iOS 10.0, *)
```

The details of the notation are not very important (if you're interested, consult the Attributes chapter of Apple's *Swift Reference Manual*). The important thing is that the annotation tells the compiler — and you — that this class isn't present until iOS 10 and later.

When you encounter this kind of issue, you cannot proceed until you guarantee to the compiler that this code will run only on a system that supports it. Luckily, Xcode's Fix-it feature (discussed later in this chapter) will help you do exactly that. Here, it offers to surround that line with an *availability check*:

```
if #available(iOS 10.0, *) {
    let r = UIGraphicsImageRenderer(size:CGSize(width:10,height:10))
} else {
    // Fallback on earlier versions
}
```

The `if #available` condition tests the current system at runtime. It needs to match the `@available` annotation, and Xcode's Fix-it will make sure that it does. You can use `#available` in an if construct or a guard construct.

You can also annotate your own type and member declarations with an `@available` attribute. If you do, your own code will then have to use an availability check in order to refer to that type or that member. If your method is declared `@available(iOS 14.0, *)`, then when the deployment target is earlier than iOS 14, you can't call that method without an availability check that matches it: `if #available(iOS 14.0, *)`. Within such a method, you don't need the availability check, because you've already guaranteed that this method won't run on a system earlier than iOS 14.

A case in point is the built-in iOS App template. This template is not very backward compatible, because it uses a scene delegate (Chapter 6). Scene delegates and the related classes were introduced in iOS 13; they don't exist in iOS 12 and before, and the launch process is different without them. To make a project generated from the template backward compatible, you need to mark the entire SceneDelegate class, and any methods in the AppDelegate class that refer to UISceneSession, with an availability annotation: `@available(iOS 13.0, *)`.

Your code now compiles, and it runs on iOS 12. But it doesn't actually *work* on iOS 12. To fix that, you also need to declare a `window` property in the AppDelegate class:

```
var window : UIWindow?
```

The result is that when this app runs in iOS 13 or later, the scene delegate has the `window`, but when it runs in iOS 12 or before, the app delegate has the `window` — and your other code may then need to take account of *that* in order to be backward compatible.

A more insidious problem arises when the very same method or property *does* exist on different systems, but behaves differently. Often this is because Apple introduces a bug, or fixes a bug, or both. For example, setting UIProgressView's `progressImage` property worked in iOS 7.0, didn't work at all from iOS 7.1 through iOS 8.4, and then started working again in iOS 9 and later. When that sort of thing happens, the compiler can't help you, and you usually have no way of knowing about it other than trial and error (and working around the problem coherently can be tricky).

To *test* your app on an earlier system, you'll need a destination that *runs* that earlier system. You can download an earlier Simulator SDK going back as far as iOS 10.3.1 through Xcode's Components preference pane (see Chapter 6). To test on an earlier system than that, you'll need an older version of Xcode, and probably an older device. This can be difficult to configure, and may not be worth the trouble.

Device Type

An app might need to respond differently depending on the hardware on which it finds itself running. A universal app might need to behave differently depending on whether it is running on an iPad or an iPhone, different devices have different screen resolutions that might call for using different images, and so on.

You can learn in code whether we're running on an iPhone or an iPad. The current UIDevice (`UIDevice.current`), or the `traitCollection` of any UIViewController or UIView in the hierarchy, will tell you the current device's type as its `userInterfaceIdiom`, which will be a UIUserInterfaceIdiom, either `.phone` or `.pad`.

When it comes to loading resources, there are some built-in shortcuts. Image files to be loaded from the top level of the app bundle can be distinguished automatically by using the same name but different suffixes, such as `@2x` and `@3x` to indicate the screen resolution, or `~iphone` and `~ipad` to indicate the device type. Or you can use an asset catalog (see "Resources in an asset catalog" on page 363), which allows you to specify different images for different runtime environments just by putting them in the correct slot. Either way, the runtime will automatically choose the image variant appropriate to the current environment.

Certain *Info.plist* settings come with name suffixes as well. For example, it is usual for a universal app to adopt one set of possible orientations on iPhone and another set on iPad: typically, the iPhone version permits a limited set of orientations while the iPad version permits all orientations. You configure this using two groups of "Supported interface orientations" settings in the *Info.plist*:

`UISupportedInterfaceOrientations`
    A general set of orientations.

`UISupportedInterfaceOrientations~ipad`
    An iPad-only set that overrides the general set when the app runs on an iPad.

The clearest and most reliable way to make these configurations is to edit the *Info.plist* directly. Alternatively, there are some checkboxes you can use, in the General pane when you edit the target, under Deployment Info:

1. Uncheck iPad, check iPhone, and check the desired Device Orientation checkboxes for the iPhone.

2. Uncheck iPhone, check iPad, and check the desired Device Orientation checkboxes for the iPad.

3. Check both iPad and iPhone. Even though you're now seeing just one set of orientations, both sets are remembered.

(That is surely one of Xcode's least intuitive bits of interface!)

Similarly, your app can load different nib files and display different interfaces depending on the device type. If the nib comes from a *.xib* file, use the image file naming convention: a nib file by the same name with `~ipad` appended will load automatically if we are running on an iPad. If you want to have two different main storyboards, use the *Info.plist* naming convention: configure two "Main storyboard file base name" keys, `UIMainStoryboardFile` and `UIMainStoryboardFile~ipad` — or,

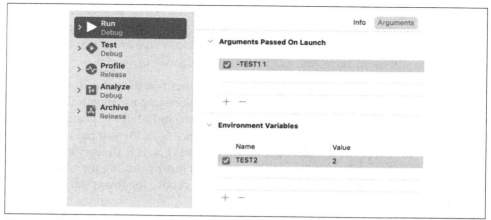

Figure 9-2. The Arguments tab of the scheme's Run action

with window scenes under iOS 13 and later, configure two "Application Scene Manifest" keys, `UIApplicationSceneManifest` and `UIApplicationSceneManifest~ipad`, that specify different `UISceneStoryboardFile` values.

Arguments and Environment Variables

You can inject key–value pairs into the environment, making them available to your code, when running the app from Xcode. Edit the scheme and go to the Arguments tab of the Run action. There are two categories (Figure 9-2); to add a key–value pair, click the Plus button under the desired category and enter a name and value:

Arguments Passed On Launch
> The name of the argument must be preceded by a hyphen, and followed with a space and the value. This allows you to inject key–value pairs into user defaults. If an argument is `-TEST1 1`, then you can say:
>
> ```
> if UserDefaults.standard.integer(forKey: "TEST1") == 1 {
> ```

Environment Variables
> There's a Name column and a Value column (which is always a string). To retrieve an environment variable, use the ProcessInfo class. If the name is `TEST2` and the value is 2, then you can say:
>
> ```
> if let t = ProcessInfo.processInfo.environment["TEST2"], t == "2" {
> ```

A configured pair can be toggled on or off for subsequent builds by clicking the checkbox to its left. So you don't have to delete a configured pair just because you don't want to use it at the moment.

Arguments and environment variables configured for the Run action are present when you build and run, but not when you are testing. But the Test action has its own arguments and environment variables, which are present *only* when you are testing. That gives your code a way to detect that it is under test. For example, you might conditionally substitute a "mock" version of a class or struct during testing.

These arguments and environment variables are present only when you build and run *from Xcode*; a user who launches your app on a device will be unaffected by them. So you can take advantage of this feature during development without worrying that its effects will leak out into the real world.

Version Control

Sooner rather than later in the life of any real app, you should consider putting your project under version control. Version control is a way of taking periodic snapshots (technically called *commits*) of your project. Its purpose might be:

Security
Version control can store your commits in a repository offsite, so that your code isn't lost in case of a local computer glitch or some equivalent "hit by a bus" scenario.

Publication
You might want to make your project's source publicly available through an online site such as GitHub.

Collaboration
Version control affords multiple developers ready, rational access to the same code.

Confidence
Progress on your code may require changes in many files, possibly over many days, before a new feature can be tested. Version control tracks and lists those changes, and if things go badly, helps to pinpoint what's gone wrong, and lets you withdraw the changes altogether if necessary. You can confidently embark on a programmatic experiment whose result may not be apparent until much later.

Xcode's version control facilities are geared primarily to Git (*http://git-scm.com*). You can use a different version control system with your projects, but not in an integrated fashion from inside Xcode. Even with Git, it is possible to ignore Xcode's integrated version control and rely on the Terminal command line or a specialized third-party GUI front end such as Sourcetree (*http://www.sourcetreeapp.com*). In that case, you might turn off Xcode's version control integration by unchecking Enable Source Control in the Source Control preference pane. If you check Enable Source Control, additional checkboxes spring to life so that you can configure what automatic behaviors you want. In this discussion, I'll assume that Enable Source Control is checked.

When you create a new project, the Save dialog includes a checkbox that offers to place a Git repository into your project folder from the outset. If you have no reason to decide otherwise, I suggest that you check that checkbox! If you don't, and if you change your mind later and want to add a Git repository to an existing project, open the project and choose Source Control → New Git Repositories. Conversely, to download a working copy of an existing project from a remote server, choose Source Control → Clone and enter the required information.

When you open an existing project, if that project is already managed with Git, Xcode detects this and displays version control information in its interface. Files in the Project navigator are marked with their status. You can distinguish modified files (M), new untracked files (?), and new files added to the index (A).

Version control management commands are available in these places:

- The Source Control menu
- The file's contextual menu, in the Source Control submenu (Control-click the file's listing in the Project navigator)
- The change bars in a source editor pane
- The Source Control navigator (Command-2) and Source Control inspector (Command-Option-4)
- The Code Review editor
- The History inspector (Command-Option-2)

To commit changes for a *single* file, choose Source Control → Commit [Filename] in the contextual menu for that file; to commit changes for *all* files, choose Source Control → Commit from the menu bar. These commands summon a comparison view of the changes; each change can be excluded from this commit (or reverted entirely), so related file hunks can be grouped into meaningful commits. You can discard changes, push, and pull using the Source Control menu. Cherry-pick and stashing commands are also present.

Branches, stashes, tags, and remotes are handled in the Source Control navigator. Selecting an item here causes relevant information to be displayed in the Source Control inspector; selecting a branch displays its corresponding remote, and selecting a remote displays its URL. Selecting a branch also shows the log of its commits in the editor. The list of commits is filterable through a search field at the top of the editor. Selecting a commit in this list displays in the inspector its branches, its commit message, and its involved files. Double-click a commit to see its involved files and their differences from the previous commit in a comparison view.

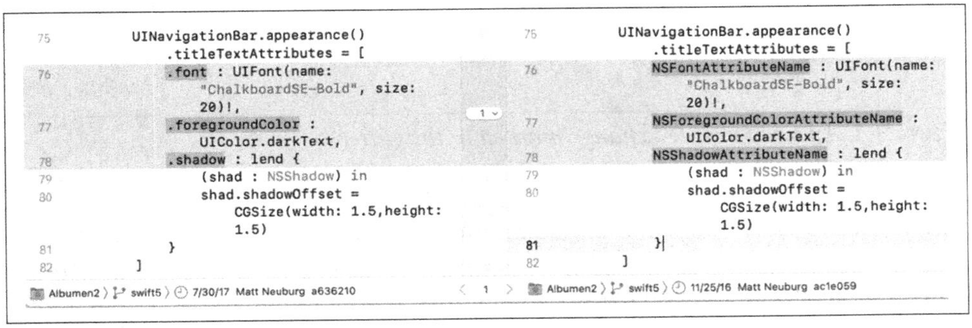

Figure 9-3. Version comparison

Other relevant commands appear in the contextual menu for items in the Source Control navigator. To add a remote, Control-click the Remotes listing. To make a new branch, check out a branch, tag a branch, delete a branch, or merge a branch, Control-click the branch listing.

To see a comparison view for the file currently being edited, display the Code Review editor: choose View → Show Code Review (Command-Option-Shift-Return), or click the Code Review button in the project window toolbar. This editor fills the entire editor area, covering all individual editor panes. You can switch target files using the Project navigator or jump bar while the Code Review editor is showing.

In Figure 9-3, I'm using a comparison view to see that in the more recent version of this file (on the left) I've changed my `titleTextAttributes` dictionary (because the Swift language changed). The jump bar at the bottom permits me to view any commit's version of the current file. In the contextual menu I can choose Copy Source Changes to capture the corresponding diff text (a patch file) on the clipboard.

The History inspector (Command-Option-2) lists the commit log from the current branch for any file, without having to show the comparison view. Click a commit to summon a popover containing the full commit message along with buttons to show the commit and its files, switch to the Code Review editor, or address an email to the commit's author.

For similar information in a source editor pane, choose Editor → Authors, or choose Authors from the Editor Options pop-up menu at the top right of the pane. The file is divided into hunks corresponding to the individual commits, with the commit author and date listed at the right (a Git "blame" view). Click a commit to summon the popover. Or, to get information on just a given line of code, select it and choose Editor → Show Last Change For Line (or the contextual menu).

If you've checked Show Source Control Changes in the Source Control preferences pane, change bars appear in the source editor pane, in the gutter at the left, showing what you've changed since the last commit (Figure 9-4). In my opinion, this is

Figure 9-4. An uncommitted change marked in the gutter

Xcode's most valuable Git integration feature. By Command-clicking on a change bar, you can display both the old committed text and the new uncommitted text simultaneously. You can also click a change bar to see a menu that lets you discard an individual change (be careful not to do that by mistake).

If you have an account with any of three popular online sites that allow ready management of code submitted through version control — GitHub (*https://github.com*), Bitbucket (*https://bitbucket.org*), and GitLab (*https://gitlab.com*) — you can enter your authentication information into Xcode's Accounts preference pane. Once you've done that:

Create a remote repository
  If your project is already under Git control locally, switch to the Source Control navigator, Control-click Remotes, and choose Create [Project Name] Remote. A dialog lets you choose a remote site and upload to it.

Clone a remote repository
  When you choose Source Control → Clone, your repositories on those sites are listed in a dialog and you can clone one of them directly. Also, when you're in a web browser looking at a GitHub repository consisting of an Xcode project, if you click the Code button, there's an option to Open with Xcode; the repository is cloned and the project is opened, in a single move.

Editing and Navigating Your Code

Many aspects of Xcode's editing environment can be modified to suit your tastes.

Your first step should be to go to Xcode's Themes preference pane and choose a theme and a Source Editor font face and size. Nothing is so important as being able to read and write code comfortably! I like a pleasant monospaced font. SF Mono is included and is the default; I think it's very nice. Other possibilities might be Menlo or Consolas, or the freeware Inconsolata (*http://levien.com/type/myfonts*) or Source Code Pro (*https://github.com/adobe-fonts/source-code-pro*). I also like a largish size (13, 14, or even 16).

You also get a choice of line spacing (leading) and cursor. You can change the theme and font size on the fly with the Editor → Font Size and Editor → Theme hierarchical menus.

Text Editing Preferences

The exact look and behavior of the source code editor depends upon your settings in the three tabs of Xcode's Text Editing preference pane — Display, Editing, and Indentation. I like to check just about everything here. Here are some particularly interesting Text Editing settings.

Display

With "Line numbers" checked, line numbers appear in the gutter to the left of source code text. Visible line numbers are useful when debugging.

Code folding lets you collapse the text between matching curly braces. With "Code folding ribbon" checked, code folding bars appear to the left of your code (at the right of the gutter), displaying your code's hierarchical structure and allowing you to collapse and expand just by clicking the bars. I'm not fond of code folding, and I don't want to trigger it accidentally, so I leave that checkbox unchecked. If I need code folding, it remains available through the Editor → Code Folding hierarchical menu.

A divider line for a MARK: comment (discussed later in this chapter) can appear in your code, above the comment; check "Mark separators."

With Editor Overscroll turned on, Xcode pretends that your file ends with some extra whitespace, so that when you scroll to the end, the last line appears in the middle of the editor pane rather than at the bottom. Since the bottom of the editor pane is usually the bottom of your screen, this let you keep your eyes focused more or less straight ahead as you work; also, you can append lines without the editor constantly scrolling to accommodate them.

Editing

The first two checkboxes under Editing have to do with autocompletion; I'll discuss them separately in a moment.

With "Enable type-over completions" checked, Xcode helps balance delimiters. Let's say I intend to make a UIView by calling its initializer init(frame:). I type as far as this:

```
let v = UIView(fr
```

Xcode automatically appends the closing right parenthesis, with the insertion point still positioned before it:

```
let v = UIView(fr)
// I have typed ^
```

When I finish typing the parameter and then type a right parenthesis, I don't end up with two adjacent right parentheses; instead, Xcode moves the insertion point through the existing right parenthesis:

```
let v = UIView(frame:r)
//        I have typed ^
```

With "Enclose selection in matching delimiters" checked, if you select some text and type a left delimiter (such as a quotation mark or a left parenthesis), the selected text is not replaced; rather, it is surrounded with left and right delimiters. I find this natural and convenient.

Indentation

I like to have just about everything checked under Indentation; I find the way Xcode lays out code to be excellent with these settings. If a line of code isn't indenting itself correctly, select the problematic area and choose Editor → Structure → Re-Indent (Control-I). Pasted code is not indented automatically unless you've checked "Re-Indent on paste."

 Whether to indent case labels in a switch statement in Swift is a subject of semi-religious warfare. I'm not about to get involved.

Multiple Selection

You probably know from experience how to use the mouse and keyboard to select text. In addition to the familiar forms of selection, Xcode lets you set *multiple simultaneous selections* in your code. With a multiple selection, your edits, including typing and keyboard navigation, are performed at each selection site simultaneously, which is useful when you have many parallel changes to make. Some ways to get a multiple selection are:

- Option-click and drag to create a rectangular selection.
- Control-Shift-click (and perhaps drag, double-click, and so on) to add a selection to the existing selection.
- Select a symbol and choose Editor → Selection → Select All Symbols; each occurrence of that symbol is selected simultaneously. (Alternatively, Editor → Edit All In Scope selects all occurrences of the currently selected term within the same scope.)
- Select any text and choose Find → Select Next Occurrence.
- Press Command-F to bring up the search field at the top of the editor, enter a search term, and choose Find → Find and Select Next, or Find → Select All Find Matches.
- Select a stretch of code consisting of multiple lines, and choose Editor → Selection → Split Selection By Lines.

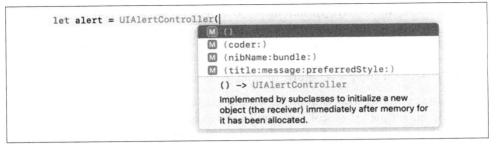

Figure 9-5. The autocompletion menu

Autocompletion and Placeholders

As you write code, you'll want to take advantage of Xcode's autocompletion feature. Type names and member names can be astonishingly verbose, and whatever reduces your time and effort typing will be a relief. Autocompletion behavior is governed by two checkboxes in the Editing pane of the Text Editing preferences:

Suggest completions while typing
  If this is checked, autocompletion is basically on all the time.

Use Escape key to show completion suggestions
  If this is checked, you can ask for autocompletion manually by pressing Esc.

I like to have the first checkbox unchecked and the second checkbox checked. That way, I get autocompletion on demand.

Suppose I want my code to create an alert. I type as far as `let alert = UIAl` and press Esc. A menu pops up, listing completions, including `UIAlertController`. You can navigate this menu, dismiss it, or accept the selection, using the mouse or the keyboard alone. I like to use the keyboard. I arrow down to `UIAlertController` and hit Return, and `UIAlertController` is entered in my code.

Now I type a left parenthesis, so that I've got `UIAlertController(`, and again I press Esc. Now the menu pops up listing the initializers appropriate to a UIAlertController (Figure 9-5). The last one is the one I want, so I arrow down to it and hit Return.

At this point, the template for the method call is entered in my code (I've broken it into multiple lines here):

```
let alert = UIAlertController(
    title: <#T##String?#>,
    message: <#T##String?#>,
    preferredStyle: <#T##UIAlertController.Style#>)
```

The expressions in `<#...#>` are *placeholders*, showing the type of each parameter. They appear in Xcode as cartouche-like "text tokens" to prevent them from being edited accidentally. To navigate among placeholders, press Tab or choose Navigate → Jump to Next Placeholder (Control-/). In this way, you can select each placeholder in turn, typing to replace it with the actual argument you wish to pass and then tabbing to the next placeholder. To convert a placeholder to a normal string without the delimiters, select it and press Return, or double-click it.

When you're entering a declaration for a method that's inherited from a superclass or defined in an adopted protocol, you don't need to type the initial `func`; just type the first few letters of the method's name. In my app delegate class I might type:

```
app
```

If I then press Esc, I see a list of methods such as `application(_:didFinish-LaunchingWithOptions:)`; these are methods that might be sent to my app delegate (by virtue of its being the app delegate, as discussed in Chapter 11). When I choose one, the entire declaration is filled in for me, including the curly braces:

```
func application(_ application: UIApplication,
    didFinishLaunchingWithOptions
    launchOptions: [UIApplication.LaunchOptionsKey : Any]?) -> Bool {
        <#code#>
}
```

A placeholder for the code appears between the curly braces, and it is selected, ready for me to start entering the body of the function. If a function needs an `override` designation, Xcode's code completion provides it.

What you type in connection with autocompletion doesn't have to be the literal start of a symbol. In the preceding example, I can get `application(_:didFinish-LaunchingWithOptions:)` to be the *only* thing in the code completion menu if I start by typing `launch`.

Snippets

Autocompletion is supplemented by code snippets. A code snippet is a bit of text with an abbreviation. Code snippets are kept in the Snippets library, which appears when you summon the Library floating window (Command-Shift-L) while editing code. With the Library showing, you can double-click or drag to insert a snippet into your code. But the real point is that a code snippet's abbreviation is available to code completion, which means you can insert a snippet *without* showing the library: you type the abbreviation and the snippet's name is included among the completions.

For example, to enter a `class` declaration at the top level of a file, I would type `class` and press Esc to get autocompletion, and choose Class — Subclass. The template for a class declaration appears in my code: the class name and superclass name are place-holders, the curly braces are provided, and the body of the declaration (between the curly braces) is another placeholder.

In the Library, single-click on a snippet to see its details: its expansion, its language, its platform(s), its code completion abbreviation (labeled Completion), and the scope where it applies (labeled Availability). If the details don't appear, click the Details button at the top right of the Library floating window.

You can add your own snippets to the Snippets library. These will be categorized as user snippets and will appear first. Unlike built-in snippets, user snippets can be edited and deleted.

To create a user snippet, select some text and choose Editor → Create Code Snippet. The Library floating window will appear, with the new snippet's details ready for editing. Provide a name, a description, and an abbreviation; the Availability pop-up menu lets you narrow the scope in which the snippet will be available through code completion. In the text of the snippet, use the `<#...#>` construct to form any desired placeholders.

I've created an `outlet` snippet (Chapter 7), with an availability scope of Class Implementation, defined like this:

```
@IBOutlet private var <#name#> : <#type#>!
```

And I've created an `action` snippet, defined like this:

```
@IBAction private func <#name#> (_ sender: Any) {
    <#code#>
}
```

My other snippets constitute a personal library of utility functions that I've developed. My `delay` snippet inserts my `DispatchQueue.main.asyncAfter` wrapper function (see Chapter 11), and has an availability scope of Top Level.

Refactoring and Structure Editing

Refactoring is an intelligent form of code reorganization. To use it, select within your code and then choose from the Editor → Refactor hierarchical menu, or Control-click and choose from the Refactor hierarchical menu in the contextual menu. Here are some of the refactoring commands you're most likely to use:

Rename
> The selected symbol's declaration and all references to it are changed, throughout your code. This also allows you to change the name of an outlet property or action method without breaking the connection from the nib (Chapter 7).

Extract to Method
> Creates a new method and moves the selected lines of code into the body of that method, replacing the original lines with a call to that method. The method name and the new call to it are then selected, ready for you to supply a meaningful name.

Extract to Variable

Creates a new variable and assigns the selected code expression to that variable, replacing the original expression with a reference to the variable. If the same expression appears multiple times and you choose Extract All Occurrences, they are all replaced with a reference to the variable. The variable name and the new reference(s) to it are then selected, ready for you to supply a meaningful name.

Add Missing Protocol Requirements

In a type declaration, when the type name is selected, if the type declares adoption of a protocol and does not in fact conform to the protocol's requirements, inserts stubs declaring the missing required members.

Generate Memberwise Initializer

In a type declaration, when the type name is selected, synthesizes an initializer based on the instance property names. This is a great convenience for classes, because they, unlike structs, have no implicit memberwise initializer. It can also be useful for structs, because if you add an initializer to a struct, you lose the implicit memberwise initializer — so this is a way to regain it.

Expand Switch Cases

In a switch statement where the tag is an enum, when the keyword `switch` is selected, adds any missing cases.

Wrap in NSLocalizedString

When the selection is inside a literal string, replaces the literal string with a call to NSLocalizedString where the literal string is the key. This is useful when localizing your app, as I'll explain later in this chapter.

Another way to refactor is to Command-click (or, depending on your Navigation preferences, Command-Control click) in a keyword that introduces curly braces. A popover appears containing menu items that let you edit the structure of your code. Some of the popover menu commands are like the refactoring commands I've just listed. Others let you insert templates for standard structural components associated with that keyword:

A class or struct declaration (click `class` or `struct`)
Add Method and Add Property

A method declaration (click `func`)
Add Parameter and Add Return Type

An if construct (click `if`)
Add "else" Statement and Add "else if" Statement

A switch statement (click `switch`)
Add "case" Statement and Add "default" Statement

```
let transform2 : CGAffineTransform = transform1.inverted  ⊗  Function produc...

let transform2 : CGAffineTransform = transform1.inverted
                      ⊘  Function produces expected type 'CGAffineTransform'; did you   ⊗
                         mean to call it with '()'?
                      Insert '()'                                                  Fix
```

Figure 9-6. A compile error with a Fix-it suggestion

Fix-it and Live Syntax Checking

Xcode's Fix-it feature allows the compiler to make *and implement* positive suggestions on how to avert a problem that has arisen as a warning or compile error. In effect, you're getting the compiler to edit your code for you.

Here's an example. Figure 9-6, at the top, shows that I've accidentally forgotten the parentheses after a method call. This causes a compile error. But the stop-sign icon next to the error tells me that Fix-it has a suggestion. I click the stop-sign icon, and Figure 9-6, at the bottom, shows what happens: a dialog pops up, not only showing the full error message but also telling me how Fix-it proposes to fix the problem — by inserting the parentheses. If I click the Fix button in the dialog, Xcode does insert the parentheses — and the error vanishes, because the problem is solved.

The intelligence of Fix-it is sometimes the same as the intelligence of refactoring. If a switch statement's tag is an enum and you omit cases, Fix-it will add them. If a type adopts a protocol and fails to implement required members, Fix-it will insert stubs for those members.

 If you're confident that Fix-it will do the right thing, you can have it implement *all* suggestions simultaneously: choose Editor → Fix All Issues.

Live syntax checking is like continual compilation, emitting a warning or error even if you don't actually compile. This feature can be toggled on or off using the "Show live issues" checkbox in Xcode's General preference pane. I keep it turned off, because I find it intrusive. My code is almost never valid while I'm in the middle of typing, because things are always half-finished; that's what it means to be typing! Merely typing `let` and pausing will likely cause the live syntax checker to complain.

Navigation

Developing an Xcode project involves editing code in many files. You'll need to leap nimbly from file to file; you might want to see multiple files simultaneously. Fortunately, Xcode provides numerous ways to navigate your code, some of which have been mentioned already in Chapters 6 and 8:

The Project navigator

Lists all your project's files by name. If you know something about the name of a file, you can find it quickly in the Project navigator by typing into the search field in the filter bar at the bottom of the navigator (Edit → Filter → Filter in Navigator, Command-Option-J). For example, type story to see just your *.storyboard* files.

The Symbol navigator

If you highlight the first two icons in the filter bar (so that they are filled), the Symbol navigator lists your project's object types and their members. Click a symbol to navigate to its declaration in the editor. As with the Project navigator, the filter bar's search field can help get you where you want to go.

The jump bar

Every path component of an editor pane's jump bar is a menu:

The bottom level

At the jump bar's bottom level (the rightmost menu, Control-6) is a list of your file's object and member declarations, in the order in which they appear. Hold Command while choosing the menu to see them in alphabetical order instead. To filter what the menu displays, start typing while the menu is open.

Another useful trick is to inject section titles into this menu; to do so, put a comment in your code whose first word is MARK:, TODO:, or FIXME:, followed by the section title. To make a divider line in the menu, put a hyphen:

```
// MARK: - View lifecycle
```

Higher levels

Higher-level path components are hierarchical menus; you can use any of them to work your way down the file hierarchy and reach any file without using the project navigator. These menus can also be filtered.

History

Each editor pane remembers the names of files you've edited in it. The Back and Forward indicators are buttons as well as pop-up menus (or choose Navigate → Go Back and Navigate → Go Forward, Command-Control-Left and Command-Control-Right).

Related items

The leftmost button in the jump bar summons the Related Items menu, a hierarchical menu of files related to the current file, such as superclasses and adopted protocols. This list even includes functions that call or are called by the currently selected function.

Editor panes

Using multiple editor panes allows you to work in two places at once.

Assistant pane

The assistant pane lets you walk through all places that relate to your code in a specific way, such as all callers of a selected method.

Document tabs

Using document tabs allows a single editor pane to be switched between specific places where you want to work.

Window tabs and windows

You can work in two places at once by opening a window tab or a separate window.

Jump to definition

Navigate → Jump to Definition (Command-Control-J, Command-Control-click) lets you jump from a selected or clicked symbol in your code to its declaration.

Open quickly

File → Open Quickly (Command-Shift-O) opens a dialog where you can search for a symbol in your code and in the framework headers.

Breakpoints

The Breakpoint navigator lists all breakpoints in your code. Xcode lacks code bookmarks, but you can misuse a breakpoint as a bookmark. Breakpoints are discussed later in this chapter.

Minimap

The minimap helps you navigate a single large source code file. To see it, choose Editor → Minimap, or use the Editor Options pop-up menu at the top right of the editor pane. The minimap displays the entire file in miniature — too small to read, but indicating the structure of the code, including MARK: comments, along with transients such as warnings and errors, change bars, breakpoints, and Find results. Drag the shaded area to scroll. Hover the mouse to display structure and symbols; hold Command while hovering to display *all* symbols (Figure 9-7). Click a symbol to navigate to it.

Finding

Finding is a form of navigation. Xcode has both an editor level find and a global find. You'll want to configure your search with find options:

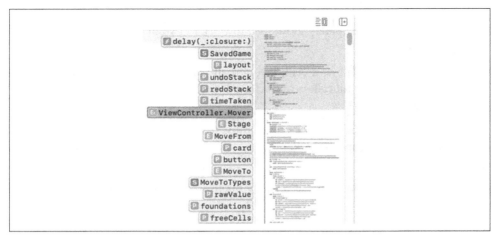

Figure 9-7. The minimap

Editor level find (Find → Find, Command-F)
    Appears in a bar at the top of the editor pane. A button at the right end of the search field toggles case-sensitive search; a pop-up menu lets you specify containment, word exact match, word start, word end, or regular expression search.

Global find (Find → Find in Project, Command-Shift-F)
    Appears in the Find navigator. The options appear above and below the search field. Above the search field, you can choose between Text, References (where a symbol is used), Definitions (where a symbol is defined), Regular Expression, and Call Hierarchy (tracing call stacks backward); you can search by word contents, word exact match, word start, or word end. Below the search field, you can toggle case sensitivity, and you can specify a scope determining which files will be searched: click the current scope to see the Search Scopes panel, where you can select a different scope or create a custom scope.

 Globally finding the Call Hierarchy is one of Xcode's best, yet least-known, features. It displays hierarchically the complete call stack, tracing all the paths by which the search target is accessed. When you're struggling to understand how your code works (or doesn't), this display is magic. There's even a shortcut: select a term and choose Find → Find Call Hierarchy.

To find and replace:

Editor level find and replace
    Next to the magnifying glass icon, click Find and choose Replace to toggle the visibility of the With field. You can perform a Find and then click Replace to replace that instance, or click All to replace all occurrences (hold Option to change it to All in Selection).

Global find and replace

Above the left end of the search bar, click Find and choose Replace. You can replace all occurrences (Replace All), or select particular find results in the Find navigator and replace only those (Replace); conversely, you can press Delete to remove a find result from the Find navigator, to protect it from being affected by Replace All.

Running in the Simulator

When you build and run with a simulator as the destination, you run in the Simulator application. A Simulator window represents a specific type of device. Depending on your app target's Deployment Target and Targeted Device Family build settings, and on what SDKs you have installed, you may have choices about the device type and system as you specify your destination before running (see Chapter 6).

The Simulator can display multiple windows, representing different devices. You can run different projects simultaneously, in the same Simulator window or different Simulator windows. When you choose from the Simulator's File → Open Simulator hierarchical menu, you switch to the window representing the chosen device, launching that device's simulator if needed.

A Simulator window can display the bezel surrounding the device's screen. Choose Window → Show Device Bezels to toggle this feature (for all windows). Displaying the bezel allows you to press hardware buttons (Home button, volume buttons, screen lock button) by clicking the mouse; also, certain gestures, such as swiping from the screen edge, become easier to perform. On the other hand, hiding the bezel is arguably neater, and all those hardware buttons are still available through menu commands.

A Simulator window can be resized by dragging an edge or corner. You also have a choice of three standard sizes (you might have to uncheck Show Device Bezels to enable them all):

Window → Physical Size

The device screen displayed on your computer monitor is the size of the screen of the physical device. If you hold up the physical device next to the Simulator window on the monitor, the screen dimensions will match perfectly.

Window → Point Accurate

One point on the device screen is one point on the computer monitor. An iPhone 6s screen is 375 points wide, so it occupies 375 points of computer screen width.

Window → Pixel Accurate
One pixel on the device screen is one pixel on the computer monitor. My computer monitor is single-resolution, but an iPhone 6s is double-resolution, so it occupies 750 pixels of computer screen width. If your computer monitor resolution matches the resolution of the device, Pixel Accurate and Point Accurate are the same.

New in Xcode 12, you can also maximize the Simulator window with Window → Fit Screen; you can float the Simulator window in front of all other applications, including Xcode; and you can tile it into fullscreen mode, which is useful for splitting the screen between just the Simulator and Xcode.

You can interact with the Simulator in some of the same basic ways as you would a device. Using the mouse, you can tap on the device's screen; hold Option to make the mouse represent two fingers moving symmetrically around their common center, and Option-Shift to represent two fingers moving in parallel.

For an iPad, you can also capture the keyboard or (new in Xcode 12) the keyboard and pointer; buttons for toggling this appear above the Simulator window. That means you're simulating a hardware keyboard or mouse being connected; a captured pointer belongs entirely to the Simulator, so now you can't use your mouse to do anything else until you end capture mode by pressing Esc (or whichever keyboard shortcut you've specified in the Simulator preferences).

Items in the Device menu let you perform hardware gestures such as rotating the device, shaking it, locking its screen, and clicking the Home button; starting in Xcode 11.4, buttons for clicking Home and rotating the device are visible above the simulator window as well.

Items in the Features menu let you test your app by simulating special situations such the arrival of a phone call or the user switching between light and dark mode (Toggle Appearance).

The Debug menu in the Simulator is useful for detecting problems with animations and drawing. Slow Animations, if checked, makes animations unfold in slow motion so that you can see in detail what's happening. The four menu items whose names begin with Color reveal possible sources of inefficiency in screen drawing. Simulate Memory Warning lets you pretend your app is running low on memory.

The Simulator application supports "side-loading" of apps. This means you can get an app onto a simulator without launching it from Xcode. To do so, drag a built *.app* file from the Finder onto an open simulator window. Various other types of resource, such as images and push notification payloads, can be side-loaded as well.

While running your app from Xcode in the Simulator, you can change certain user settings on the simulated device without passing through the Settings app. In the debug bar, click the Environment Overrides button to summon a popover where you can switch between light and dark modes, change the dynamic text size, and alter various accessibility settings.

Another powerful way to control a simulator is from the command line. In the Terminal, type `xcrun simctl` to see a list of things you can do. Among other things, in addition to side-loading files, you can change your app's privacy permissions, manipulate its keychain, and send it an external URL (such as a universal link).

In Xcode 11 and before, closing a Simulator window stops the corresponding simulator; to use that simulator again later, it must be rebooted. New in Xcode 12, the Preferences let you elect to keep simulators running when closed and even when the Simulator app isn't running.

Debugging

Debugging is the art of figuring out what's wrong with the behavior of your app as it runs. I divide this art into two main techniques: caveman debugging and pausing your running app.

Caveman Debugging

Caveman debugging consists of altering your code, usually temporarily. Typically, you'll add code to produce informative messages that you'll read in the Xcode console in the project window's Debug pane as your app runs.

The simplest Swift command for sending a message to the Xcode console is the `print` function. You might print a string saying where the path of execution is:

```
print("view did load")
```

You might output a value:

```
print("i is", i)
```

When you print an object, the output comes from that object's `description` property. Cocoa objects generally have a useful built-in `description` property implementation:

```
print(self.view)
```

The output in the console reads something like this (I've formatted it for clarity here):

```
<UIView: 0x79121d40;
   frame = (0 0; 320 480);
   autoresize = RM+BM;
   layer = <CALayer: 0x79121eb0>>
```

We learn the object's class, its address in memory (useful for confirming whether two instances are in fact the same instance), and the values of some additional properties.

In your own object types, you can adopt CustomStringConvertible and implement the `description` property as desired (Chapter 4).

Instead of `print`, you might like to use `dump`. Its console output describes an object along with its class inheritance and its instance properties, by way of a Mirror object:

```
dump(self)
```

If `self` is a view controller of class ViewController with a `didInitialSetup` instance property, the console output looks like this:

```
* ViewController
  - super: UIViewController
    - super: UIResponder
      - super: NSObject
  - didInitialSetup: true
```

In your own object types, you can adopt CustomReflectable and implement the `customMirror` property as desired (Chapter 5).

An important feature of `print` and `dump` is that they are effectively suppressed when the app is launched independently of Xcode. That's good, because it means you're free to pepper your code with `print` statements and they'll have no effect on your app in the real world. But what if you want to send yourself messages when you're running the app independently of Xcode?

The traditional solution is to import Foundation (which, in real-life iOS programming, you're already doing) and call the `NSLog` C function. It takes an NSString which operates as a format string, followed by the format arguments. A *format string* is a string containing symbols called *format specifiers*, for which values (the format arguments) will be substituted at runtime. See "String Format Specifiers" in Apple's *String Programming Guide* in the documentation archive. All format specifiers begin with a percent sign (%), so the only way to enter a literal percent sign in a format string is as a double percent sign (%%). The character(s) following the percent sign specify the type of value that will be supplied at runtime. The most common format specifiers are `%@` (an object reference), `%d` (an int), `%ld` (a long), and `%f` (a double):

```
NSLog("the view: %@", self.view)
```

In that example, `self.view` is the first (and only) format argument, so its value will be substituted for the first (and only) format specifier, `%@`, when the format string is printed in the console:

```
2015-01-26 10:43:35.314 Empty Window[23702:809945]
  the view: <UIView: 0x7c233b90;
    frame = (0 0; 320 480);
    autoresize = RM+BM;
    layer = <CALayer: 0x7c233d00>>
```

Over the past several years, `NSLog` has gradually been superseded by a new unified logging system, OSLog. It still uses format specifiers, but it adds some specialized efficiencies and lifts some limits on the length of a message. New in iOS 14 and Swift 5.3, a Swift native type, Logger, acts as a comfortable façade for OSLog. To use Logger, `import os` and create a Logger object, typically as an instance property or global:

```
import os
let mylog = Logger(subsystem: "com.neuburg.matt", category: "testing")
```

The `subsystem` and `category` strings are arbitrary but useful, because you can refer to them to focus on the particular log messages that interest you. To send a log message, call a method of your Logger instance; to start with, you can use `log`:

```
mylog.log("this is a test")
```

The argument has to be a literal string, but it can include string interpolations. Behind the scenes, your interpolations are turned into `NSLog` format specifiers and arguments, and are evaluated efficiently at runtime outside of your app's process, so that they don't slow down the app itself:

```
mylog.log("this is a test of \(self)")
```

When you run the app from Xcode, log messages from NSLog, OSLog, and Logger appear in the Xcode console, and are tagged with the current time and date, along with the process name, process ID, and thread ID (useful for determining whether two logging statements are called on the same thread). With Logger, the category from your Logger configuration is also present, in square brackets; this gives you something to filter on so that only the desired messages appear.

Even more important, these log messages appear *even when the app is running outside of Xcode.* To view them, use the Console application. In the Sources pane at the left, under Devices, are shown all running simulators and any devices currently visible to the computer. Select the desired device and exercise the app, while watching the Console output. To eliminate unwanted output, set up a filter in the toolbar search field. You can filter by the name of the process (that is, the name of your app); even better, you can filter by the subsystem and category you configured when creating your Logger object. You can specify what information to show by choosing the columns that appear, such as the Time, Process, Thread ID, Category, Subsystem, and Type columns.

But perhaps you didn't have the Console application configured and ready at the time you ran your app? Then there's another option: you can read your log messages after the fact. To do so, use the `log` command-line tool. Suppose I say this in the Terminal:

```
% sudo log collect --device-name "TheMattPhone" --last 1h
```

The result is that my home directory now contains a file called *system_logs.logarchive*. I can open this file with the Console application and explore it with filtering in exactly the same way as I've just described for a live logging stream. Alternatively, I can filter in the Terminal with another `log` command:

```
% log show --predicate 'category == "testing"' system_logs.logarchive
```

Bear in mind that what you can do, the user can do. The user can see your logging messages just as well as you can. For this reason, string interpolations are *redacted* by default when your app is running independently of Xcode. If you want an interpolation to be always legible in the Console or the system log, you have to specify that it is public, using a Swift 5 string interpolation parameter:

```
mylog.log("this is a test of \(self, privacy: .public)")
```

You can also use string interpolation parameters to perform various sorts of string formatting that you would otherwise have had to perform using `NSLog` format specifiers, such as dictating the number of digits after the decimal point and other sorts of padding and alignment:

```
mylog.log("the number is \(i, format: .decimal(minDigits: 5))") // e.g. 00001
```

Another way to mediate between public and private logging is by specifying the logging *level* at which messages are to be sent. To do so, call a Logger instance method that specifies the level: the methods are `debug`, `info`, `notice` (same as `log`), `error`, and `fault`. The significance of logging levels is:

Noisiness

What you're categorizing is how bad the situation is. `fault` means that, if we log this at all, there is an unexpected bug in the program.

Persistence

A `debug` message is not written into the log file and doesn't propagate to the Console application. So it works more like `print`: only you can see it, and only while running the app from Xcode. The others are written into the log file, and the level reflects how hard the message will resist being expunged as time elapses and further data is accumulated.

Lagginess

A `debug` message has the least overhead, because there is no need to talk to the file-writing mechanism, and on the user's device the format specifier arguments won't even be evaluated, so the expense is effectively zero.

Interface

The levels correspond to markings in the Console application. A `fault` message calls attention to itself with a red filled dot.

Another useful form of caveman debugging is deliberately aborting your app because something has gone seriously wrong. See the discussion of `assert`, `precondition`, and `fatalError` in Chapter 5. `precondition` and `fatalError` work even in a Release build. By default, `assert` is inoperative in a Release build, so it is safe to leave it in your code when your app is ready to ship; by that time, of course, you should be confident that the bad situation your `assert` was intended to detect has been debugged and will never actually occur.

Purists may scoff at caveman debugging, but I use it heavily: it's easy, informative, and lightweight. And sometimes it's the only way. Unlike the debugger, console logging works with any build configuration (Debug or Release) and wherever your app runs (in the Simulator or on a device). It works when pausing is impossible (because of threading issues, for instance). It even works on someone else's device, such as a tester to whom you've distributed your app.

 Swift defines four special literals, particularly useful when logging because they describe their own location within the source code: `#file`, `#line`, `#column`, and `#function`.

The Xcode Debugger

When Xcode is running your app, you can pause in the debugger and use Xcode's debugging facilities. The important thing, if you want to use the debugger, is that the app should be built with the Debug build configuration (the default for a scheme's Run action). The debugger is not very helpful against an app built with the Release build configuration, not least because compiler optimizations can destroy the correspondence between steps in the compiled code and lines in your source code.

Breakpoints

There isn't a strong difference between running and debugging in Xcode; the main distinction is whether breakpoints are effective or ignored. The effectiveness of breakpoints can be toggled at two levels:

Globally (active vs. inactive)
Breakpoints as a whole are either *active or inactive*. If breakpoints are inactive, we won't pause at any breakpoints.

Individually (enabled vs. disabled)
A given breakpoint is either *enabled or disabled*. Even if breakpoints are active, we won't pause at this one if it is disabled. Disabling a breakpoint allows you to leave in place a breakpoint that you might need later without pausing at it every time it's encountered.

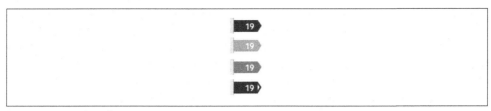

Figure 9-8. A breakpoint

To create a breakpoint, select in the editor the line where you want to pause, and choose Debug → Breakpoints → Add/Remove Breakpoint at Current Line (Command-\). This menu item toggles between adding and removing a breakpoint for the current line. Alternatively, a simple click in the gutter adds a breakpoint. The breakpoint is symbolized by an arrow in the gutter (Figure 9-8, first). To remove a breakpoint gesturally, drag the arrow out of the gutter.

To disable a breakpoint at the current line, click the breakpoint in the gutter to toggle its enabled status. Alternatively, select in the line and choose Debug → Breakpoints → Enable/Disable Breakpoint at Current Line; or Control-click the breakpoint and choose Enable/Disable Breakpoint in the contextual menu. A dark breakpoint is enabled; a light breakpoint is disabled (Figure 9-8, second).

To toggle the active status of breakpoints as a whole, click the Breakpoints button in the debug bar, or choose Debug → Activate/Deactivate Breakpoints (Command-Y). If breakpoints are inactive, they are simply ignored *en masse*, and no pausing at breakpoints takes place. Breakpoint arrows are a solid color if breakpoints are active, gray if they are inactive (Figure 9-8, third). The active status of breakpoints as a whole doesn't affect the enabled or disabled status of any breakpoints.

Once you have some breakpoints in your code, you'll want to survey and manage them. That's what the Breakpoint navigator is for. Here you can navigate to a breakpoint, enable or disable a breakpoint by clicking on its arrow in the navigator, and delete a breakpoint.

You can also configure a breakpoint's behavior. Control-click the breakpoint, in the gutter or in the Breakpoint navigator, and choose Edit Breakpoint; or double-click the breakpoint. You can have a breakpoint pause only under a certain condition or after it has been encountered a certain number of times, and you can have a breakpoint perform one or more actions when it is encountered, such as issuing a debugger command, logging, playing a sound, speaking text, or running a script. A breakpoint whose behavior has been configured is badged (Figure 9-8, fourth).

A breakpoint can be configured to continue automatically after performing its action when it is encountered. A breakpoint that logs and continues can be an excellent alternative to caveman debugging. By definition, such a breakpoint operates only when you're actively debugging the project; it won't dump any messages into the console when the app runs independently, because breakpoints exist only in Xcode.

Certain special kinds of breakpoint (*event* breakpoints) can be created in the Breakpoint navigator — click the Plus button at the bottom of the navigator and choose from its pop-up menu — or by choosing from the Debug → Breakpoints hierarchical menu. Here are the ones you're most likely to use:

Swift error breakpoint
Pauses when your code says `throw`.

Exception breakpoint
Pauses when an Objective-C exception is thrown or caught, without regard to whether the exception would crash your app later. An exception breakpoint that pauses on all exceptions when they are thrown gives the best view of the call stack and variable values at the moment of the exception.

(Sometimes Apple's code will throw an exception and catch it, deliberately. This isn't a crash, and nothing has gone wrong; but if you've created an exception breakpoint, your app will pause at it, which can be confusing. If this happens to you, choose Debug → Continue to resume your app; if it keeps happening, you might need to disable the exception breakpoint.)

Symbolic breakpoint
Pauses when a certain method or function is called, regardless of what object called it. The method doesn't have to be your method! A symbolic breakpoint can help you probe Cocoa's behavior. A method may be specified in one of two ways:

Using Objective-C method notation
The instance method or class method symbol (- or +) followed by square brackets containing the class name and the method name:

```
-[UIApplication beginReceivingRemoteControlEvents]
```

By Objective-C method name
The Objective-C method name alone. The debugger will resolve this for you into all possible class–method pairs, as if you had entered them using the Objective-C notation that I just described:

```
beginReceivingRemoteControlEvents
```

If you enter the method specification incorrectly, the symbolic breakpoint won't do anything; however, you might be assisted by code completion, and in general you'll know if you got things right, because you'll see the resolved breakpoint(s) listed hierarchically below yours (though resolution may not take place until you actually run the project).

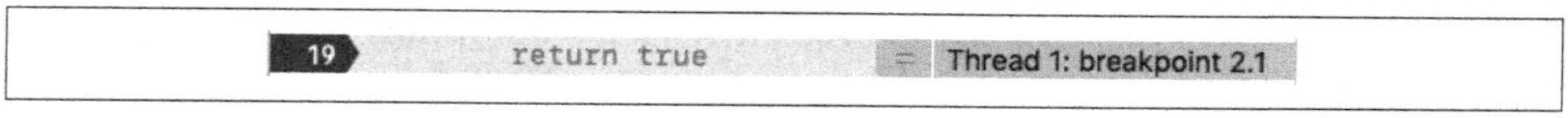

| 19 | `return true` | ☰ Thread 1: breakpoint 2.1 |

Figure 9-9. Paused at a breakpoint

Breakpoints come in three levels of exposure:

Local to you and a project
> The default. The breakpoint appears in this project on this machine.

Global to you
> Use the contextual menu to say Move Breakpoint To → User. The breakpoint now appears in all your projects on this machine. Symbolic and exception breakpoints are particularly good candidates for this level.

Shared with others
> Use the contextual menu to say Share Breakpoint. The breakpoint is now visible in this project to others with whom you share the project.

Paused at a breakpoint

When the app runs with breakpoints active and an enabled breakpoint is encountered (and assuming its conditions are met, and so on), the app pauses. In the active project window, the editor shows the file containing the point of execution, which will usually be the file containing the breakpoint. We are paused at the line that is *about* to be executed, which is shown by the *instruction pointer* (Figure 9-9). Depending on the settings for Running → Pauses in the Behaviors preference pane, the Debug navigator and the Debug pane may also appear.

Here are some things you might like to do while paused at a breakpoint:

See where you are
> One common reason for setting a breakpoint is to make sure that the path of execution is passing through a certain line. Functions listed in the call stack in the Debug navigator with a User icon are yours; click one to see where you are paused in that function. (Other listings are functions and methods for which you have no source code, so there would be little point clicking one unless you know something about assembly language.) You can also view and navigate the call stack using the jump bar in the debug bar.

Study variable values
> In the Debug pane, variable values for the current scope (corresponding to what's selected in the call stack) are visible in the variables list. You can see additional object features, such as collection elements, properties, and even some private information, by opening disclosure indicators.

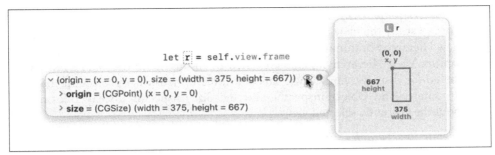

Figure 9-10. A data tip

You can use the search field to filter variables by name or value. If a formatted summary isn't sufficiently helpful, you can send `description` (or, if this object adopts CustomDebugStringConvertible, `debugDescription`) to an object variable and view the output in the console: choose Print Description of [Variable] from the contextual menu, or select the variable and click the Info button below the variables list.

You can also view a variable's value graphically: select the variable and click the Quick Look button (an eye icon) below the variables list, or press the space bar. For example, in the case of a CGRect, the graphical representation is a correctly proportioned rectangle. You can make instances of your own custom class viewable in the same way; declare the following method and return an instance of one of the permitted types (see Apple's *Quick Look for Custom Types in the Xcode Debugger* in the documentation archive):

```
@objc func debugQuickLookObject() -> Any {
    // ... create and return your graphical object here ...
}
```

You can also inspect a variable's value in place in your code, by examining its data tip. To see a data tip, hover the mouse over the name of a variable in your code. The data tip is much like the display of this value in the variables list: there's a disclosure indicator that you can open to see more information, plus an Info button that displays the value description here and in the console, and a Quick Look button for showing a value graphically (Figure 9-10).

Set a watchpoint

A watchpoint is like a breakpoint, but instead of depending on a certain line of code it depends on a variable's value: the debugger pauses whenever the variable's value changes. You can set a watchpoint only while paused in the debugger. Control-click the variable in the variables list and choose Watch [Variable]. Watchpoints, once created, are listed and managed in the Breakpoint navigator.

Inspect your view hierarchy

You can study the view hierarchy while paused in the debugger. Click the Debug View Hierarchy button in the debug bar, or choose Debug → View Debugging → Capture View Hierarchy. Views are listed in an outline in the Debug navigator. The editor displays your views; this is a three-dimensional projection that you can rotate. The Object inspector and the Size inspector display information about the currently selected view.

Inspect your object graph

Using the Memory Debugger, you can study the object graph (what objects you've created and how they refer to one another) while paused in the debugger. I'll talk more about that later in this chapter.

Manage expressions

An expression is code to be added to the variables list and evaluated every time we pause. Choose Add Expression from the contextual menu in the variables list. The expression is evaluated within the current context in your code, so be careful of side effects.

Talk to the debugger

You can communicate directly with the debugger through the console. Xcode's debugger interface is a front end to the *real* debugger, LLDB (*http:// lldb.llvm.org*); by talking directly to LLDB, you can do everything that you can do through the Xcode debugger interface, and more. Common commands are:

ty loo (*short for* type lookup)
Followed by a type name, dumps a full declaration for the type, listing all its members (properties and methods). For Cocoa classes, you might get better information by performing the lookup in Objective-C:

```
(lldb) ty loo -l objc -- ClassName
```

v (*or* fr v, *short for* frame variable)
Alone, prints out all variables locally in scope, similar to the display in the variables list. Alternatively, can be followed by the name of a variable you want to examine. Fast and lightweight because it reaches right into the stack and grabs the value, but it has some limitations; for obvious reasons, it doesn't work for computed properties.

p (*or* expression, expr, *or simply* e)
Compiles and executes, in the current context, any expression in the current language. Be careful of your expression's side effects! This is more heavy-weight than v.

po *(meaning "print object")*

Like p, but displays the value of the executed expression in accordance with its description or debugDescription (similar to Print Description). It is actually an alias for expr -O, meaning "object description." Twice as expensive as p because it has to be compiled and executed *twice.*

Fiddle with breakpoints

You are free to create, destroy, edit, enable and disable, and otherwise manage breakpoints even while your app is running, which is useful because where you'd like to pause next might depend on what you learn while you're paused here. Indeed, this is one of the main advantages of breakpoints over caveman debugging. To change your caveman debugging, you have to stop the app, edit it, rebuild it, and start running the app all over again. But to fiddle with breakpoints, you don't have to be stopped; you don't even have to be paused! An operation that went wrong, if it doesn't crash your app, can probably be repeated in real time, so you can just add a breakpoint and try again. If tapping a button produces the wrong results, you can add a breakpoint to the action method and tap the button again; you pass through the same code, and this time you pause and can work out what the trouble is.

Continue or step

To proceed with your paused app, you can either resume running or take one step and pause again. The commands are in the Debug menu, or you can click the convenient buttons in the debug bar:

Continue

Resume running (until a breakpoint is encountered).

Step Over

Pause at the next line.

Step Into

Pause in your function that the current line calls, if there is one; otherwise, pause at the next line.

Step Out

Pause when we return from the current function.

Start over, or abort

To kill the running app, click Stop in the toolbar (Product → Stop, Command-Period). Clicking the Home button in the Simulator (Hardware → Home) or on the device does *not* stop the running app.

You can make changes to your code while the app is running or paused in the Simulator or on a device, but those changes are not magically communicated to the running app. To see your changes in action, you must stop the running app, build, run, and launch the app all over again.

However, you can inject changes into your code by means of an `expr` command, given either at the LLDB console or through a custom-configured breakpoint. Moreover, you can skip a line of code by dragging the instruction pointer down; if you combine that with `expr`, you've effectively replaced one line of code with another. So it may be possible to modify your app's logic and test a proposed change to your code *without* rebuilding and relaunching.

 Local variable values can exist even if, at the point where you are paused, those variables have not yet been initialized; but *such values are meaningless*, so ignore them. This applies to the variables list, data tips, and so forth. Forgetting this is a common beginner mistake.

Testing

A *test* is code that isn't part of your app target; its purpose is to exercise your app and make sure that it works as expected. Tests can be broadly of two kinds:

Unit tests
> A unit test exercises your app *internally*, from the point of view of its *code*. A unit test might call some method in your code, handing it various parameters and looking to see if the expected result is returned each time, not just under normal conditions but also when incorrect or extreme inputs are supplied.

Interface (UI) tests
> An interface test exercises your app *externally*, from the point of view of a *user*. Such a test guides your app through use case scenarios by effectively tapping buttons with a ghost finger, watching to make sure that the interface behaves as expected.

(You may sometimes hear a third type of test distinguished, an *integration* test. In Xcode, an integration test is a higher-level form of unit test.)

Tests — especially unit tests — should ideally be written and run constantly as you develop your app. It can even be useful to write unit tests *before* writing the real code, as a way of developing a working algorithm. Having initially ascertained that your code passes your tests, you continue to run those tests to detect whether a bug has been introduced during the course of development (when that happens, it's called a *regression*).

Tests are bundled in a separate target (see Chapter 6). The app templates give you an opportunity to add test targets at the time you create your project. Alternatively, you can easily create a new test target at any time: make a new target and specify iOS → Test → Unit Testing Bundle or UI Testing Bundle.

A test class is a subclass of XCTestCase, which is itself a subclass of XCTest. A test method is an instance method of a test class, returning no value and taking no parameters, whose name starts with test. A test method does not run — indeed, it is not even compiled — until you explicitly ask it to do so. The test target has a dependency upon the main target that it tests (usually, your app target); this means that when a test class is to be compiled and built, the main target will be compiled and built automatically first. But building the main target (with Product → Build, Command-B, or Product → Run, Command-R) does *not* build the test target! To build a test target so as to learn whether its code compiles successfully, but without running a test method, choose Product → Build For → Testing (Command-Shift-U).

Each test method that runs may succeed or fail; more precisely, it succeeds if it *doesn't* fail. A test method can fail in two ways:

Assertions
> A test method may call one or more assertions. These are global functions whose names begin with XCTAssert; for a list, see the XCTest class documentation. If any assertion fails, the test method fails.
>
> By default, a test method continues running after an assertion fails. That might not be what you want; arguably, failure puts the test method in a bad state. To prevent it, set the continueAfterFailure property of your XCTestCase to false beforehand.

Throws
> A test method can be declared with throws. In that case, throwing an error in the body of the method counts as the test failing. Throwing aborts the test method immediately.

Alternatively, rather than succeeding or failing, a test method declared with throws may be *skipped*. The idea is that you skip a test based on conditions discovered at runtime (for instance, perhaps this test makes sense only on a certain kind of device). To test those conditions, you can call a global function, either XCTSkipIf or XCTSkip-Unless; these are throwing functions, so the call is preceded by try, and what they throw is an XCTSkip instance. Or you can test the conditions yourself, and construct and throw your own XCTSkip instance. When an XCTSkip instance is thrown, the test method is aborted and neither succeeds nor fails.

A test class may contain utility methods that are called by the test methods; their names do *not* begin with test. New in Xcode 12, a utility method can behave like a test method — that is, it can fail through an assertion or by throwing — and the call stack is traced to point the finger at the right spot.

To accompany your test methods, you can override any of these special methods inherited from XCTestCase:

setUp *class method*
Called once before *all* test methods in the class.

setUp *instance method*
Called before *each* test method. Starting in Swift 5.2, there's a throwing alternative: setUpWithError. If you implement both setUp and setUpWithError, the error method is executed *first*.

tearDown *instance method*
Called after *each* test method. Starting in Swift 5.2, there's a throwing alternative: tearDownWithError. If you implement both tearDown and tearDownWithError, the error method is executed *last*.

tearDown *class method*
Called once after *all* test methods in the class.

 Each test method runs in its own separate XCTestCase instance. So if your XCTestCase has instance properties, there is no need to use setUp or tearDown just to reinitialize them; they are automatically initialized before each test method is called.

As an alternative to the tearDown instance method, you can use a teardown *block*. To do so, call self.addTeardownBlock(_:) with a function (typically an anonymous function) to be called at teardown time; self here is the XCTestCase instance. When the teardown block is called depends on where it is added; if you call addTeardown-Block within a test method, the block is called only on exit from that method, but if you call it in the setUp instance method, the block is called after every test method, because the block was added freshly before every test method.

Running a test also runs the app. The test target's product is a bundle; a unit test bundle is loaded into the app as it launches, whereas an interface test bundle is loaded into a special test runner app generated for you by Xcode. Resources, such as test data, can be included in the bundle. You might use setUp to load such resources; you can get a reference to the bundle by way of the test class, by saying Bundle(for:Self.self).

Unit Tests

Unit tests need to see into the target to be tested, so the test target must import the target to be tested, as a module. To overcome privacy restrictions, the import statement should be preceded by the @testable attribute; this attribute temporarily changes internal (explicit or implicit) to public throughout the imported module. A private or fileprivate method is not directly testable, but you can work around that by providing an `internal` trampoline method that exists only during testing thanks to conditional compilation (as I described earlier).

As an example of writing and running a unit test method, we can use our Empty Window project. Let's give the ViewController class a (nonsensical) instance method `dogMyCats`:

```
func dogMyCats(_ s:String) -> String {
    return ""
}
```

The method `dogMyCats` is supposed to receive any string and return the string `"dogs"`. At the moment, though, it doesn't; it returns an empty string instead. That's a bug. Now we'll write a test method to ferret out this bug.

First, we'll need a unit test target:

1. In the Empty Window project, choose File → New → Target and specify iOS → Test → Unit Testing Bundle.
2. Call the product *EmptyWindowTests*; observe that the target to be tested is the app target.
3. Click Finish.

In the Project navigator, a new group has been created, EmptyWindowTests, containing a single test file, *EmptyWindowTests.swift*. It contains a test class Empty-WindowTests, including stubs for two test methods, `testExample` and `testPerformanceExample`. Comment out those two methods. We're going to replace them with a test method that calls `dogMyCats` and makes an assertion about the result:

1. At the top of *EmptyWindowTests.swift*, where we are importing XCTest, we must also import the target to be tested, which is the app target:

   ```
   @testable import Empty_Window
   ```

2. Prepare an instance property in the declaration of the EmptyWindowTests class to store our ViewController instance:

   ```
   var viewController = ViewController()
   ```

3. Write the test method. Its name must start with `test`! Let's call it `testDogMyCats`. It has access to the ViewController instance as `self.viewController`:

   ```
   func testDogMyCats() {
       let input = "cats"
       let output = "dogs"
       XCTAssertEqual(output,
           self.viewController.dogMyCats(input),
           "Failed to produce \(output) from \(input)")
   }
   ```

Figure 9-11. The Report navigator reports a test failure

We are now ready to run our test. There are many ways to do this. Switch to the Test navigator, and you'll see that it lists our test target, our test class, and our test method. You can run a test method, or the whole class suite, using the contextual menu or with Run buttons that appear when you hover the mouse over a listing. In addition, in *EmptyWindowTests.swift* itself, there are diamond-shaped indicators in the gutter to the left of the class declaration and the test method name; when you hover the mouse over one of them, it changes to a Run button. You can click that button to run, respectively, all tests in this class or an individual test. Or, to run all tests in all test classes, you can choose Product → Test.

 After running a test, to run just that test again, choose Product → Perform Action → Run [Test] Again. To run multiple individual tests, Command-click in the Test navigator to select just those tests; then choose Product → Perform Action → Run [n] Test Methods (or use the contextual menu).

So now let's run `testDogMyCats`. The app target is compiled and built; the test target is compiled and built. (If any of those steps fails, we can't test, and we'll be back on familiar ground with a compile error or a build error.) The app launches in the Simulator, and the test runs.

The test fails! (Well, we knew that was going to happen, didn't we?) The error is described in a banner next to the assertion that failed in our code; moreover, red X marks appear everywhere — at the top of the project window, in the Test navigator next to `testDogMyCats`, and in *EmptyWindowTests.swift* next to the first line of `test-DogMyCats`.

The best place to survey what went wrong is the Report navigator. Typically, what you'll want to look at is the summary report; this is what you see in the editor when you select the line that says Test in the Report navigator (Figure 9-11).

The failure is automatically tied to the place in your code where it took place. Hover the mouse over the failure line in the report; a button with an arrow appears at the right. Click it to jump to your code. Alternatively, a button with two linked rings also appears at the right (new in Xcode 12); click it to open your code in an assistant pane, so that you can view the report and the code simultaneously. Select any failure in the report pane to see the corresponding code in the code pane.

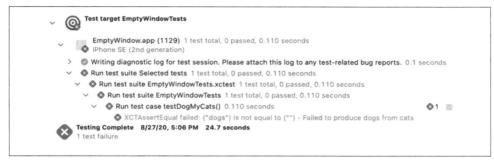

Figure 9-12. The Report navigator details a test failure

Occasionally you might need to view further details. To do so, choose Test → Log from the jump bar at the top of the editor (Figure 9-12); by expanding transcripts, you can see the full console output from the test run, including any caveman debugging messages that you may have sent from your test code (to show them, click the little horizontal lines icon at the far right).

Now let's fix our code. In *ViewController.swift*, modify `dogMyCats` to return `"dogs"` instead of an empty string. Now run the test again. It passes!

When a test failure occurs, you might like to pause at the point where the assertion is about to fail. To do so, in the Breakpoint navigator, click the Plus button at the bottom and choose Test Failure Breakpoint. This is like an Exception breakpoint, pausing on the assertion line in your test method just before it reports failure. You could then switch to the method being tested and debug it, examining its variables and so forth, to work out the reason for the impending failure. Don't forget to continue running afterward, so that the test can finish and generate the report.

Xcode's code coverage feature lets you assess how much of your app target's code is being exercised by your unit tests. To switch it on, edit the Test action in your scheme and check Code Coverage in the Options pane. Run your tests. Afterward, the Report navigator has a Coverage section displaying statistics (Figure 9-13); you can also choose Editor → Code Coverage (or use the Editor Options pop-up menu at the top right of the editor pane) to reveal a gutter at the right of your code calling attention to stretches of code that didn't run during the tests.

Here are two further features of unit tests worth knowing about:

Asynchronous testing
> Asynchronous testing allows a test method to wait for a time-consuming operation to finish. Asynchronous code *must* use asynchronous testing if you want to make an assertion there. Here's a typical pattern of usage:

Name		Coverage
∨ ▦ EmptyWindow.app	▬▬▬▬▬▬▬▬▬▬	61.1%
∨ ▦ AppDelegate.swift	▬▬▬▬▬▬▬▬▬▬	100.0%
▣ AppDelegate.application(_:didFinishLaunchingWithOptions:)	▬▬▬▬▬▬▬▬▬	100.0%
∨ ▦ ViewController.swift	▬▬▬▬▬▬	50.0%
▣ ViewController.dogMyCats(_:)	▬▬▬▬▬▬▬▬	100.0%
▣ ViewController.buttonPressed(_:)	▬▬▬▬▬▬▬▬	0.0%
▣ ViewController.viewDidAppear(_:)	▬▬▬▬▬▬▬▬	100.0%

Figure 9-13. The Report navigator displays code coverage statistics

```
let expect = XCTestExpectation()
doSomethingAsynchronous { ok in
    XCTAssert(ok, "got wrong asynchronous result")
    expect.fulfill()
}
let result = XCTWaiter().wait(for: [expect], timeout: 0.5)
XCTAssert(result == .completed, "did not complete properly")
```

We begin by forming an expectation — in effect, something to wait for. The first assert checks the asynchronous result; we then call fulfill so that the code can proceed after XCTWaiter().wait. The second assert checks that the expectation was fulfilled within the time limit.

Performance testing

Performance testing lets you check that the speed of an operation has not fallen off by running that operation repeatedly and timing the result. Call the XCTest-Case instance method measure; it takes a function whose execution time will be recorded. The first time you run a performance test, you establish a baseline measurement, and on subsequent runs, it fails if the standard deviation of the times is too far from the baseline, or if the average time has grown too much.

Starting in Xcode 11, in addition to measuring elapsed time, your performance tests can measure things like CPU and memory usage. Call measure(metrics:) with an array of XCTMetric objects, such as XCTCPUMetric. A performance test can also exercise launching your app and report whether it launches as quickly as it should.

For realistic performance testing you should run a release build without the debugger attached and with all sanitizers and diagnostics turned off. You can manage that with a custom scheme (and possibly a test plan, as I'll explain a bit later).

Interface Tests

Now let's experiment with interface testing. I'm going to assume that you still have (from Chapter 7) a button in the Empty Window interface with an action connection to a ViewController method that summons an alert. We'll write a test that taps that button and makes sure that the alert is summoned. Add a UI Testing Bundle to the project; call it *EmptyWindowUITests*.

Interface test code is based on *accessibility*, a feature that allows the screen interface to be described verbally and to be manipulated programmatically. It revolves around three classes: XCUIElement, XCUIApplication (an XCUIElement subclass), and XCUIElementQuery. In the long run, it's best to learn about these classes and write your own UI test code; but to help you get started, accessibility actions are *recordable*, meaning that you can generate code automatically by performing the actual actions that constitute the test. Let's try it:

1. In the `testExample` stub method, create a new empty line and leave the insertion point within it.

2. Choose Editor → Start Recording UI Test. (Alternatively, there's a Record button in the debug bar.) The app launches in the Simulator.

3. In the Simulator, tap the button in the interface. When the alert appears, tap OK to dismiss it.

4. Return to Xcode and choose Editor → Stop Recording UI Test. Also choose Product → Stop to stop running in the Simulator.

The following code, or something similar, has been generated:

```
let app = XCUIApplication()
app.staticTexts["Hello"].tap()
app.alerts["Howdy!"].scrollViews.otherElements.buttons["OK"].tap()
```

The `app` object, obviously, is an XCUIApplication instance. Properties such as `static-Texts` and `alerts` return XCUIElementQuery objects. Subscripting such an object returns an XCUIElement, which can then be sent action methods such as `tap`.

Now run the test by clicking in the diamond in the gutter at the left of the `test-Example` declaration. The app launches in the Simulator, and a ghost finger performs the same actions we performed, tapping first the button in the interface and then, when the alert appears, the OK button that dismisses it. The test ends and the app stops running in the simulator. The test passes!

More important, if the interface stops looking and behaving as it does now, the test will *not* pass. To see this, in *Main.storyboard*, select the button and, under Control in the Attributes inspector, uncheck Enabled. The button is still there, but it can't be tapped; we've broken the interface. Run the test. The test fails, and the Report

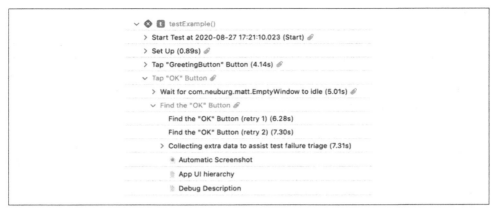

Figure 9-14. The Report navigator displays a failed UI test

navigator explains why (Figure 9-14): when we came to the Tap "OK" Button step, we first had to Find the "OK" Button, and we failed because there was no alert.

Ingeniously, the report also supplies lots of information about the view hierarchy, along with a screenshot, so that we can inspect the state of the interface during the test. Under Find the "OK" Button, you can double-click Automatic Screenshot to learn what the screen looked like at that moment: it's easy to see the disabled interface button (and no alert).

Persisting screenshots

Screenshots such as those taken automatically during the UI test I just described can be useful for other purposes. You might like to retain a more permanent record of how your interface looks under various circumstances — as marketing materials, for submission to the App Store, to help with localization, and so on. In fact, you might construct some of your UI tests for no other purpose than to take screenshots!

To this end, you can have your UI test *deliberately* take a screenshot and make it persist. To do so, call the XCUIElement (or XCUIScreen) screenshot method, turn the resulting XCUIScreenshot object into an XCTAttachment, and call the XCTestCase add method to retain the actual screenshot. Along the way, be sure to extend the lifetime of the attachment so that it persists even if the test succeeds; you can also give the screenshot a convenient name:

```
let screenshot = XCUIApplication().screenshot()
let attachment = XCTAttachment(screenshot: screenshot)
attachment.lifetime = .keepAlways
attachment.name = "OpeningScreen"
self.add(attachment)
```

Figure 9-15. The Report navigator displays a persisting screenshot

In the Report navigator, our screenshot is displayed under the name we assigned to it (Figure 9-15).

Interface testing and accessibility

During interface testing, your app is in effect being viewed from the outside, as a human being would view it. As I've already said, that depends upon accessibility. Standard interface objects are accessible, but other interface that you create might not be. Select an interface element in the nib editor to view its accessibility characteristics in the Identity inspector. Run the app in the Simulator and choose Xcode → Open Developer Tool → Accessibility Inspector to explore in real time the accessibility characteristics of whatever is under the cursor.

Another useful trick is to put a breakpoint in a UI test method, run the test, pause, and tell the debugger to `po XCUIApplication()` to see the full view hierarchy as accessibility sees it. To see fewer results, form a query specifying the type of entity you're interested in, such as `po XCUIApplication().buttons`.

Referring to an interface object by its visible title, as in our code `app.static-Texts["Hello"]`, is poor practice. If the title changes, or if the app is localized for another language (discussed later in this chapter), the reference breaks. Instead, we should give our button a fixed accessibility identifier, either in code or in the Identity inspector in the nib editor. If the Hello button's accessibility identifier is `Greeting-Button`, we can refer to it as `app.buttons["GreetingButton"]` instead.

For more about adding useful accessibility to your interface objects, see Apple's *Accessibility Programming Guide for iOS* in the documentation archive.

Test Plans

When you've built up several suites of tests, you'll want a way to configure what tests should be run under what conditions on a given occasion. Before Xcode 11, such configuration was confined to a *scheme*. By editing a scheme's Test action, you could determine the complete set of tests that would run when you chose Product → Test. If you wanted more than one set of tests, you needed multiple schemes.

Starting in Xcode 11, this scheme-based architecture has been superseded by *test plans*. A test plan is a text file (in JSON format), but you won't have to deal with it as text; you edit it in a dedicated editor, similar to how an *Info.plist* is treated. To create a test plan, choose Product → Test Plan → New Test Plan. The test plan should not be part of any target, and you'll probably put it at the top level of your project. Edit the new test plan. Click the Plus button and select the targets containing the tests you want to use.

In the Tests pane of the test plan, you can specify individual test classes and test methods to be run. In the Configurations pane, you can specify the behavior of your tests, including various choices you would previously have made in the scheme editor and elsewhere: arguments and environment variables, system language, simulated location, screenshot policy, diagnostics, whether to use code coverage, and whether tests should run in random order (which can help unmask hidden dependencies between tests).

You can make configuration choices on two levels, a set of shared settings and individual named configurations that inherit the shared settings and can override them. It's important to give each named configuration a meaningful name, because this name is the identifier that will be displayed in the test report.

Having created one or more test plans, you still can't *use* them for anything until you convert your scheme to use test plans. To do so, choose Product → Scheme → Convert Scheme to Use Test Plans. (I presume that some day test plans will be the default and this step will no longer be needed.) The Test action of your scheme will now point to the test plans you've added to it. These should include *every* test plan you might ever want to use with this scheme.

Your scheme may now have multiple test plans, but only one test plan is current at any given moment. When you choose Product → Test, it is the current test plan that runs. Here's how the current test plan is determined:

In the Test navigator
   At the top, the Test navigator has a pop-up menu letting you pick a test plan from among those attached to the current scheme. Whatever test plan is currently displayed here is the current test plan. If the current test plan doesn't include a test, that test is dimmed and you can't run it from the Test navigator (though of course you can select it and run it from the test source).

In the Product menu
   The Product → Test Plan hierarchical menu lists the test plans attached to the current scheme. Whatever test plan is checked here is the current test plan.

Figure 9-16. A test report with an activity

 If the current test plan has more than one configuration, then whenever you run a test method, it runs by default under *all* configurations successively. That can come as a surprise. If it isn't what you want, Control-click to summon the contextual menu; it lets you specify a configuration for this run.

Massaging the Report

Nothing is more important after running your tests than understanding what happened. Your key source of information is the report. XCTest includes powerful features that give you a lot of control over what goes into the report.

One simple but effective trick is to group the report output into meaningful activities. To do so, in your test method call XCTContext.runActivity(named:). In addition to the name, which should be some explanatory string, it takes a function; that function is where you'll do your testing and call your assertions. The outcome is that, in the test report summary, the activity name appears as a line in the report, and the test results are grouped hierarchically under that line (Figure 9-16).

Another useful device is attachments. We've already seen that you can attach a screen shot to your report. But an attachment can be *any* kind of data. XCTAttachment has initializers for attaching a string, an image, the contents of a file or a directory, a Data object, and more. As we've seen, you can call self.add (where self is the XCTest) to get your attachment into the test report. A call to XCTContext.runActivity is also a great place to add an attachment: the function parameter hands you an XCTActivity object, and you call add with your attachment.

It's possible that a test will hang — perhaps there's a threading deadlock — or just take too long. You don't want to come back from running your tests overnight and discover that they're still incomplete because of a hang. New in Xcode 12, an XCTest-Case or a test plan can declare an *execution time allowance*. If a test takes longer than that, it fails, and a spindump file is attached to the test report.

Finally, new in Xcode 12, the entire report mechanism relies upon an XCTIssue object that is passed into the XCTestCase record method to contribute to the report. You can intervene in this mechanism! Instead of throwing or calling a built-in assert, you can create your own XCTIssue, populate it, and record it, like this:

```
let loc = XCTSourceCodeLocation(filePath: #file, lineNumber: #line)
var issue = XCTIssue(type: .assertionFailure, compactDescription: "oh darn")
issue.add(XCTAttachment(string:"yipes"))
issue.sourceCodeContext = XCTSourceCodeContext(location: loc)
self.record(issue)
```

At an even deeper level, you can override `record` and modify the incoming XCTIssue before calling `super` — or *don't* call `super` and thus suppress the failure entirely.

Clean

From time to time, during repeated testing and debugging, and before making a different sort of build (switching from Debug to Release, or running on a device instead of the Simulator), it's a good idea to *clean* your target. This means that existing builds will be removed and caches will be cleared, so that all code will be considered to be in need of compilation and you can build your app from scratch.

Cleaning removes the cruft, quite literally. Suppose you have been including a certain resource in your app, and you decide it is no longer needed. You can remove it from the Copy Bundle Resources build phase (or from your project as a whole), but that doesn't necessarily remove it from your built app. This sort of leftover resource can cause all kinds of mysterious trouble. The wrong version of a nib may seem to appear in your interface. Code that you've edited may seem to behave as it did before the edit. Cleaning removes the built app and all the intermediate build products that Xcode caches in order to construct it, and very often solves the problem.

You can choose Product → Clean Build Folder, which removes the entire build folder for this project. For an even more extensive cleaning, quit Xcode, open your user *~/Library/Developer/Xcode/DerivedData* folder, and move all its contents to the trash. This is a complete clean for every project you've opened recently — plus the module cache. Removing the module cache can reset Swift itself, causing occasional mysterious compilation, code completion, or syntax coloring issues to go away.

In addition to cleaning your project, you should also remove your app from the Simulator. This is for the same reason as cleaning the project: when a new build of the app is copied to the Simulator, existing resources inside the old build may not be removed (in order to save time), and this may cause the app to behave oddly. To clean out the current simulator while running the Simulator, choose Hardware → Erase All Content and Settings. To clean out *all* simulators, quit the Simulator and then say, in the Terminal:

```
% xcrun simctl erase all
```

Running on a Device

Eventually, you'll want to progress from running and testing and debugging in the Simulator to running and testing and debugging on a real device. The Simulator is nice, but it's only a simulation; there are many differences between the Simulator and a real device. The Simulator is really your computer, which is fast and has lots of memory, so problems with memory management and speed won't be exposed until you run on a device. User interaction with the Simulator is limited to what can be done with a mouse: you can click, you can drag, you can hold Option to simulate use of two fingers, but more elaborate gestures can be performed only on an actual device. And many iOS facilities, such as the accelerometer and access to the music library, are not present on the Simulator at all, so that testing an app that uses them is possible *only* on a device.

Running your app on a device requires a Developer Program membership, which in turn requires an annual fee. You may balk initially, but sooner or later you're going to get over it and accept that this fee is worth paying. (The temporary ability to run your app on a device *without* a paid Developer Program membership is very limited and I'm not going to discuss it.)

Obtaining a Developer Program Membership

To obtain a Developer Program membership, go to the Apple Developer Program web page (*https://developer.apple.com/programs*) and initiate the enrollment process. When you're starting out, the Individual program is sufficient. The Organization program costs no more, but adds the ability to privilege additional team members in various roles; you do *not* need the Organization program merely to distribute your built app to other users for testing.

Your Developer Program membership involves two things:

An Apple ID
> The user ID that identifies you at Apple's site (along with the corresponding password). You'll use your Developer Program Apple ID for all kinds of things. In addition to letting you prepare an app to run on a device, this same Apple ID lets you post on Apple's development forums, download Xcode beta versions, and so forth.

A team name
> You, under a single Apple ID, can belong to more than one *team*. On each team, you will have one or more *roles* dictating your privileges. If you are the head (or sole member) of the team, you are the *team agent*, meaning that you can do everything: you can develop apps, run them on your device, submit apps to the App Store, and receive the money for any paid apps that sell copies there.

Having established your Developer Program Apple ID, you should enter it into the Accounts preference pane in Xcode. Click the Plus button at the bottom left and select Apple ID as the type of account to add. Provide the Apple ID and password. From now on, Xcode will identify you through the team name(s) associated with this Apple ID; you shouldn't need to tell Xcode this password again.

Signing an App

Running an app on a device is a remarkably complicated business. You will need to *sign* the app as you build it. An app that is not properly signed for a device will not run on that device (assuming you haven't jailbroken the device). Signing an app requires two things:

An identity
> An identity represents Apple's permission for a given team to develop, *on this computer*, apps that can run on a device. It consists of two parts:

A private key
> The private key is stored in the keychain on the computer. It identifies a computer where this team can *potentially* develop device-targeted apps.

A certificate
> A certificate is a virtual permission slip from Apple. It contains the public key matching the private key (because you told Apple the public key when you asked for the certificate). With a copy of this certificate, any machine holding the private key can *actually* be used to develop device-targeted apps under the name of this team.

A provisioning profile
> A provisioning profile is a virtual permission slip from Apple, uniting four things:
>
> * An *identity*.
> * An *app*, identified by its bundle identifier.
> * A list of eligible *devices*, identified by their unique device identifiers (UDIDs).
> * A list of *entitlements*. An entitlement is a special privilege that not every app needs, such as the ability to talk to iCloud. You won't concern yourself with entitlements unless you write an app that needs one.

A provisioning profile is therefore sufficient for signing an app as you build it. It says that on *this* computer it is permitted to build *this* app such that it will run on *these* devices.

There are two types of identity, and hence two types of certificate and provisioning profile: *development* and *distribution* (a distribution certificate is also called a *production* certificate). We are concerned here with the development identity, certificate, and profile; I'll talk about the distribution side later.

The only thing that belongs entirely to you is the private key in your computer's keychain. Apple is the ultimate keeper of all other information: your certificates, your provisioning profiles, what apps and what devices you've registered. Your communication with Apple, when you need to verify or obtain a copy of this information, will take place through one of two means:

The developer member center
> A set of web pages at *https://developer.apple.com/account*. Having logged in with your Apple ID, you can click Certificates, Identifiers & Profiles (or go directly to *https://developer.apple.com/account/resources*) to access all features and information to which you are entitled by your membership type and role. (This is the area of Apple's site formerly referred to as the Portal.)

Xcode
> Just about everything you would need to do at the developer member center can be done through Xcode instead. When all goes well, using Xcode is a lot simpler! If there's a problem, you can head for the developer member center to iron it out.

Automatic Signing

Apple provides two distinct ways of obtaining and managing certificates and profiles in connection with a project — automatic signing, and manual signing. For new projects, automatic signing is the default. This is indicated by the fact that the "Automatically manage signing" checkbox is checked in the Signing & Capabilities pane when you edit your project's app target (Figure 9-20).

To see just how automatic Xcode's signing management can be, let's start at a stage where as yet you have neither a development certificate in your computer's keychain nor a development profile for any app. But you do have a Developer Program Apple ID, and you've entered it into Xcode's Accounts preference pane. Then, when you create a new project (File → New → Project), you'll see on the second screen ("Choose options for your new project") a pop-up menu listing all the teams with which your Apple ID is associated. Specify the desired team here.

When you then create the project on disk and the project window opens, *everything happens automatically*. Your computer's keychain creates a private key for a development certificate. The public key is sent to Apple. The actual development certificate is created at the developer member center, and is downloaded and installed into your computer's keychain. With no conscious effort, you've obtained a development identity!

Figure 9-17. Xcode knows of no devices

Figure 9-18. Xcode offers to register a device

If you've never run on any device before, and if you haven't manually registered any devices at the developer member center, that might be as far as Xcode can go for now. If so, you'll see some warnings in the Signing & Capabilities pane, similar to Figure 9-17.

Now connect a device via USB to your computer and select it as the destination, either under Product → Destination or in the Scheme pop-up menu in the project window toolbar. Try to build. This causes a dialog to appear, offering to register the device (Figure 9-18). Click Register Device!

The problem is resolved; the error vanishes. You can switch to the Report navigator to learn what just happened (Figure 9-19).

As the Report navigator tells us, the device has been registered — and a development provisioning profile has been created and downloaded (and has been stored in your *~/Library/MobileDevice/Provisioning Profiles* folder). This is a *universal* iOS Team Provisioning Profile — also known as a *wildcard* or *XC wildcard* profile — and that is all you need in order to run any basic app on any device. Figure 9-20 shows the resulting display in the Signing & Capabilities pane.

Figure 9-19. Xcode has registered a device for us

Figure 9-20. Xcode manages signing credentials automatically

You are now almost ready to run this project on this device. There may, however, be one further step: you might have to disconnect the device from USB and connect it again. This is so that Xcode can recognize the device afresh and prepare for debugging on it. This process is rather time-consuming; a progress indication is shown at the top of the project window, and in the Devices and Simulators window.

The good news is that once you *already* have a development certificate, and once Xcode has *already* generated and downloaded a universal iOS Team Provisioning Profile, and once your device is *already* registered with Apple and prepared by Xcode for debugging, *none* of that will be necessary ever again. When you create a new project, you supply your team name. Xcode now knows everything it needs to know! The development certificate is valid for this computer, the universal iOS Team Provisioning Profile is universal, and the device is registered with Apple and prepared for debugging. Therefore, you should from now on be able to create a project and run it on this device *immediately.*

You can confirm your possession of a universal development provisioning profile by clicking the "i" button at the right of the Provisioning Profile (Figure 9-20): a popover displays information about the provisioning profile, as shown in Figure 9-21.

The asterisk (*) in that popover tells you that this is a universal profile, not restricted to one particular app ID. The universal development profile allows you to run *any* app on the targeted device for testing purposes, provided that the app doesn't require special entitlements (such as using iCloud). If you turn on any entitlements for an app target (which you would do by adding a capability from the Signing & Capabilities pane when you edit the app target), and if you're using automatic signing, Xcode

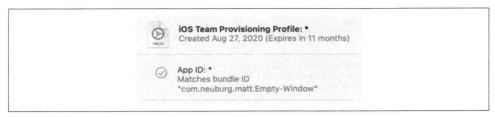

Figure 9-21. A universal development profile

will communicate with the developer member center to attach those entitlements to your registered app; then it will create a new provisioning profile that includes those entitlements, download it, and use it for this project.

Manual Signing

If you don't want a project's signing to be managed automatically by Xcode, simply uncheck the "Automatically manage signing" checkbox. This causes Xcode to take its hands off completely. Xcode won't automatically generate or choose a development certificate or a provisioning profile; you will have to do it all yourself.

If you need to obtain a development certificate manually, there are two possible approaches:

The Accounts preference pane
> In Xcode's Accounts preference pane, select your team name and click Manage Certificates to summon the "Signing certificates" dialog. Click the Plus button at the lower left, and choose Apple Development. Xcode will communicate with the developer member center and a development certificate will be created and installed on your computer.

Keychain Access and the developer member center
> Go to Certificates at the developer member center, click the Plus button, ask for an Apple Development certificate, click Continue, and follow the instructions that the page links to:

> 1. You begin by generating the private key in your computer's keychain. Launch the Keychain Access application and choose Keychain Access → Certificate Assistant → Request a Certificate From a Certificate Authority. Click the "Saved to disk" radio button and save the certificate signing request file onto your computer.

> 2. At the developer member center, upload the certificate signing request file. The actual certificate is generated; download it, and double-click to install it into the keychain. (You can then throw away both the certificate request file and the downloaded certificate.)

Figure 9-22. A valid development certificate

Figure 9-22 shows what a valid development certificate looks like in Keychain Access.

Once you have a development certificate, you can use the developer member center to create a development profile manually, if necessary:

1. The *device* must be registered at the developer member center. Look under Devices to see if it is. If it isn't, click the Plus button and enter a name for this device along with its UDID. You can copy the device's UDID from its listing in Xcode's Devices and Simulators window.

2. The *app* must be registered at the developer member center. Look under Identifiers to see if it is. If it isn't, add it: Click Plus. Choose App IDs. Choose App. Enter a description for this app (such as its name). Ignore the App ID Prefix field. Copy the Bundle Identifier from the Signing & Capabilities pane and paste it into the bundle identifier field, and register the app.

   (If your app uses special entitlements, this step is also where you'd associate those entitlements manually with the app.)

3. Under Profiles, click Plus. Ask for an iOS App Development profile. On the next screen, choose the App ID for this app (presumably the one you just created in the previous step). On the next screen, check your development certificate. On the next screen, select the device(s) you want to run on. On the next screen, give this profile a name, and generate the profile. You are now offered a chance to download the profile, but you don't have to do that, because Xcode can do it for you.

4. In Xcode, in the Signing & Capabilities pane, in the Provisioning Profile pop-up menu, choose Download Profile. The profile you created at the developer member center is listed here! Select it. The profile is downloaded and development provisioning is enabled for this project (Figure 9-23).

Running the App

Once you have a development profile applicable to an app and a device, you can connect the device via USB, choose it as the destination in the Scheme pop-up menu, and build and run the app. (If you're asked for permission to access your keychain, you should grant it.)

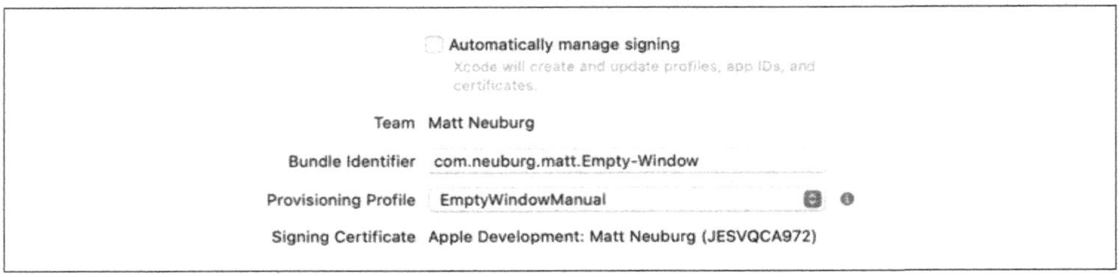

Figure 9-23. Manual code signing

The app is built, loaded onto your device, and launched. As long as you launch the app from Xcode, everything is just as when running in the Simulator. You can run and you can debug. The running app is in communication with Xcode, so that you can stop at breakpoints, read messages in the console, profile your app with Instruments, and so on. The outward difference is that to interact physically with the app, you use the device, not the Simulator.

You can also configure your device to allow Xcode to build and run apps on it *without* a USB connection. To do so, start with the device connected via USB; locate the device in the Devices and Simulators window and check "Connect via network." The device can now be used as a build and run destination *wirelessly*, provided it is connected via WiFi to the local network or to some other network that your computer can access by its IP address. You can build and run from Xcode, pausing at breakpoints and receiving console messages, even though the device is not physically attached to your computer. This would be useful particularly if the app you're testing requires the device to be manipulated in ways that are difficult when the device is tethered by a USB cable.

Managing Development Certificates and Devices

You're allowed to have more than one development certificate, so there should be no problem running your project on a device from another computer. Just do what you did on the first computer! If you're using automatic signing, a new certificate will be generated for you, and it won't conflict with the existing certificate for the first computer.

When a device is attached to the computer, it appears in Xcode's Devices and Simulators window. If this device has never been prepared for development, you can ask Xcode to prepare it for development. You can then build and run onto the device. If the device isn't registered at the member center, a dialog appears offering to let you register it; click Register Device, and now the device *is* registered. Your automatically generated provisioning profile is modified to include this device, and you are now able to build and run on it.

The Devices and Simulators window can be used to communicate in other ways with a connected device. Using the contextual menu, you can copy the device's UDID, and you can view and manage provisioning profiles on the device. In the main part of the window, you can see (and delete) apps that have been installed for development using Xcode, and you can view and download their sandboxes. You can take screenshots. You can view the device's stored logs. You can open the Console application to view the device's console output in real time.

Profiling

Xcode provides tools for probing the internal behavior of your app graphically and numerically, and you should keep an eye on those tools. The gauges in the Debug navigator allow you to monitor key indicators, such as CPU and memory usage, any time you run your app. Memory debugging gives you a graphical view of your app's objects and their ownership chains, and can even reveal memory leaks. And Instruments, a sophisticated and powerful utility application, collects profiling data that can help track down problems and provide the numeric information you need to improve your app's performance and responsiveness.

Gauges

The gauges in the Debug navigator are operating whenever you build and run your app. Click a gauge to see further detail displayed in the editor. The gauges do not provide highly detailed information, but they are extremely lightweight and always active, so they are an easy way to get a general sense of your running app's behavior at any time. If there's a problem, such as a prolonged period of unexpectedly high CPU usage or a relentless unchecked increase in memory usage, you can spot it in the gauges and then use Instruments to help track it down.

There are four basic gauges: CPU, Memory, Disk, and Network. Depending on the circumstances, you may see additional gauges. An Energy Impact gauge appears when running on a device, and for certain devices, a GPU gauge may appear as well.

In Figure 9-24, I've been heavily exercising my app for a few moments, repeating the most calculation- and memory-intensive actions I expect the user to perform. These actions do cause some spikes in energy usage, but that's to be expected; this is a user-initiated action, and the user won't perform it very often. Meanwhile, my app's memory usage remains level. So I don't suspect any issues.

 Note that Figure 9-24 is the result of running *on a device*. Running in the Simulator might give completely different — and misleading — results.

Profiling | 477

Figure 9-24. The Debug gauges

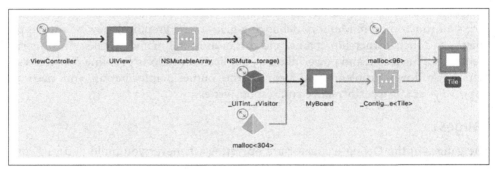

Figure 9-25. A memory graph

Memory Debugging

Memory debugging lets you pause your app and view a graphical display of your object hierarchy at that moment. This is valuable not only for detecting problems but also for understanding your app's object structure.

To use memory debugging, run the app and click the Debug Memory Graph button in the debug bar (Figure 9-25). The app pauses, and you are shown a drawing of your app's objects, linked by their chains of ownership. The Debug navigator lists your objects hierarchically; click an object to see a different part of the graph. Double-click an object in the graph to refocus the graph on that object.

In my app, the root view controller is a ViewController whose view's subviews include a MyBoard view whose `tilesInOrder` property is an array of Tile views. Figure 9-25 displays that situation.

At the cost of some additional overhead, you can enable the malloc stack before running your app: edit the scheme's Run action and under Diagnostics check Malloc Stack Logging with the pop-up menu set to All Allocation and Free History. When you run the app, selecting an object in the memory graph provides a backtrace in the

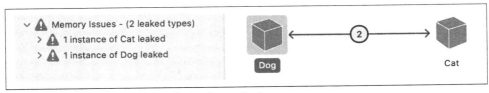

Figure 9-26. The memory graph displays a leak

Memory inspector that tells you *how* each object came into being. If the backtrace is collapsed, hover the mouse over the word Backtrace and click the Expand button that appears. Hover over a line of the backtrace and click the right-arrow button to jump to that line of your code.

Memory debugging also detects memory leaks. Such leaks will cause an error icon to appear, and are listed in the Runtime pane of the Issue navigator. Suppose we run the example from Chapter 5 where I have a Dog class instance and a Cat class instance with strong references to one another and no other references to either instance, so they are both leaking. The leaking Cat and Dog are listed in the Issue navigator, and clicking one them displays a graph of the problem: the Cat and the Dog are retaining one another (Figure 9-26).

Instruments

To get started with Instruments, first set the desired destination in the Scheme pop-up menu in the project window toolbar. The destination should be a device if possible; Instruments on the Simulator does not reflect the reality you're trying to measure. Now choose Product → Profile. Your app builds using the Profile action for your scheme; by default, this uses the Release build configuration, which is what you want. Instruments launches; if your scheme's Instrument pop-up menu for the Profile action is set to Ask on Launch (the default), Instruments presents a dialog where you choose a template.

Alternatively, click Profile In Instruments in a Debug navigator gauge editor; this is convenient when the gauges have suggested a possible problem, and you want to reproduce that problem under the more detailed monitoring of Instruments. Instruments launches, selecting the appropriate template for you. A dialog offers two options: Restart stops your app and relaunches it with Instruments, whereas Profile keeps your app running and hooks Instruments into it.

Once the Instruments main window appears, if you chose Product → Profile, you'll probably have to click the Record button, or choose File → Record Trace, to get your app running. Now you should interact with your app like a user; Instruments will record its statistics.

Figure 9-27 shows me doing much the same thing in Instruments that I did with the Debug navigator gauges in Figure 9-24. I've set the destination to my device. I choose

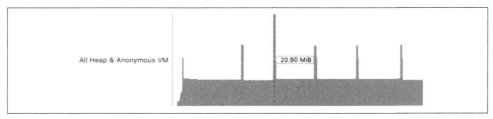

Figure 9-27. Instruments graphs memory usage over time

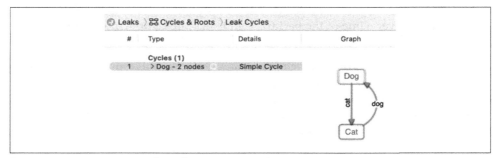

Figure 9-28. Instruments describes a retain cycle

Product → Profile; when Instruments launches, I choose the Allocations template. With my app running under Instruments, I exercise it for a while and then pause Instruments, which meanwhile has charted my memory usage. Examining the chart, I find that there are spikes up to about 21MB, but the app always settles back down to a much lower level (around 6MB). Those are very gentle and steady memory usage figures, so I'm happy.

The Leaks template can help you detect memory leaks (similar to the memory graph leak detection I discussed earlier). In Figure 9-28, I've again run the retain cycle code from Chapter 5, profiling the app using the Leaks template. Instruments has detected the leak, and has diagrammed the issue.

In the next example, I'm curious as to whether I can shorten the time it takes my app to load a photo image. I've set the destination to a device, because that's where speed matters and needs to be measured. I choose Product → Profile. Instruments launches, and I choose the Time Profiler template. When the app launches under Instruments on the device, I load new images repeatedly to exercise this part of my code for about ten seconds.

In Figure 9-29, I've paused Instruments, and am looking at what it's telling me. Opening the disclosure indicators in the lower portion of the window, I can drill down to my own code, indicated by the user icon.

By double-clicking the listing of that line, I can see my own code, time-profiled (Figure 9-30). The profiler is drawing my attention to the call to CGImageSource-

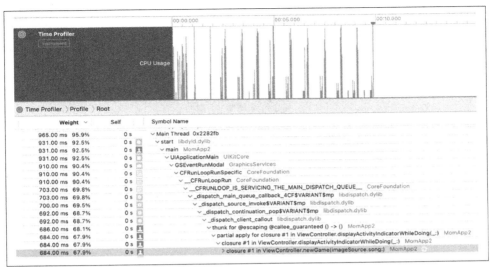

Figure 9-29. Drilling down into the time profile

```
let imref = CGImageSourceCreateThumbnailAtIndex(src, 0, opts as CFDictionary)!   ⊕ 63.97%

// turn it into a UIImage marked with the appropriate scale

let im = UIImage(cgImage: imref, scale: scaleToAskFor, orientation: .up)

self.board.newGame(image: im, song: song)                                        ⊕ 32.36%
```

Figure 9-30. My code, time-profiled

CreateThumbnailAtIndex; this is where we're spending most of our CPU time. That call is in the ImageIO framework; it isn't my code, so I can't make it run any faster. It may be, however, that I could load the image another way; at the expense of some temporary memory usage, perhaps I could load the image at full size and scale it down by redrawing it myself. If I'm concerned about speed here, I could spend a little time experimenting. The point is that now I know *what* the experiment should be. This is just the sort of focused, fact-based numerical analysis at which Instruments excels.

You can inject custom messages into your Instruments graphs in the form of *signposts*. For instance, based on the first Instruments example, I may suspect that my highest memory spikes are taking place within my newGame method. To confirm this, I'll add some signposts. I import os and configure an OSLog object called mylog with a .pointsOfInterest category:

```
let mylog = OSLog(subsystem: "diabelli", category: .pointsOfInterest)
```

Then I instrument the start and end of my newGame method with os_signpost calls:

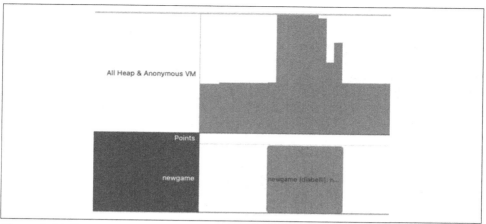

Figure 9-31. Signposts in Instruments

```
private func newGame(imageSource: Any, song: String) {
    os_signpost(.begin, log: mylog, name: "newgame")
    // ...
    os_signpost(.end, log: mylog, name: "newgame")
}
```

To prepare my Instruments template, I start with the Allocations template; then I choose View → Show Library to bring up the instrument chooser, and add the Points of Interest instrument to my template. When I run the app, Instruments displays the `"newgame"` signposts — and sure enough, they surround the memory spikes (Figure 9-31).

Those examples barely scratch the surface. Use of Instruments is an advanced topic; an entire book could be written about Instruments alone. The Instruments application comes with online help that's definitely worth studying. Many WWDC videos from current and prior years are about Instruments; look particularly for sessions with "Instruments" or "Performance" in their names.

Localization

A device or an individual app can be set by the user to prefer a certain language as its primary language. You might like your app's interface to respond to this situation by appearing in that language. This is achieved by *localizing* the app for that language. You will probably want to implement localization relatively late in the development of the app, after the app has achieved its final form, in preparation for distribution.

Localization operates through *localization folders* with an *.lproj* extension in your project folder and in the built app bundle (Figure 6-6). When your app obtains a resource, if it is running on a system whose language corresponds to a localization folder, if that localization folder contains a version of that resource, that's the version that is loaded.

Any type of resource can live in these localization folders; you will be particularly concerned with *text* that is to appear in your interface. Such text must be maintained in specially formatted *.strings* files, with special names:

- To localize your *Info.plist* file, use *InfoPlist.strings*.
- To localize your *Main.storyboard*, use *Main.strings*.
- To localize your code strings, use *Localizable.strings*.

Fortunately, you don't have to create or maintain these files manually! Instead, you work with exported XML files in the standard *.xliff* format. Xcode will generate *.xliff* files automatically, based on the structure and content of your project; it will also read them and will turn them automatically into the various localized *.strings* files.

Creating Localized Content

To experiment with localization, our app needs some localizable content:

1. Edit the target and enter a value in the Display Name text field in the General pane. Our Empty Window app already says "Empty Window" here, but it's in gray, indicating that this is merely an *automatic* display name; enter "Empty Window" explicitly (and press Tab), to make this an *actual* display name. You have now created a "Bundle display name" key (CFBundleDisplayName) in the *Info.plist* file. That key will be localized.

2. Edit *Main.storyboard* and confirm that it contains a button whose title is "Hello." That title will be localized. (It will help the example if you also widen the button to about 100 points.)

3. Edit *ViewController.swift*. The code here contains some string literals, such as "Howdy!":

```
@IBAction func buttonPressed(_ sender: Any) {
    let alert = UIAlertController(
        title: "Howdy!", message: "You tapped me!",
        preferredStyle: .alert)
    alert.addAction(
        UIAlertAction(title: "OK", style: .cancel))
    self.present(alert, animated: true)
}
```

That code *won't* be localized, unless we modify it. Your code needs to call the global NSLocalizedString function; you'll usually supply these parameters:

key *(first parameter, no label)*
    The first parameter is the key into a *.strings* file.

value
> The default string if there's no *.strings* file for the current language.

comment
> An explanatory comment.

So modify our `buttonPressed` method to look like this:

```
@IBAction func buttonPressed(_ sender: Any) {
    let alert = UIAlertController(
        title: NSLocalizedString(
            "Greeting", value:"Howdy!", comment:"Say hello"),
        message: NSLocalizedString(
            "Tapped", value:"You tapped me!",
            comment:"User tapped button"),
        preferredStyle: .alert)
    alert.addAction(UIAlertAction(
        title: NSLocalizedString(
            "Accept", value:"OK", comment:"Dismiss"),
        style: .cancel))
    self.present(alert, animated: true)
}
```

Exporting

Now we're going to give our project an actual localization, and we'll export an editable *.xliff* file expressing the details of that localization. For my localization language, I'll choose French:

1. Edit the project. In the Info pane, under Localizations, click the Plus button. In the pop-up menu that appears, choose French. In the dialog, click Finish.

2. Still editing the project, choose Editor → Export For Localization. In the dialog that appears, check French. You're about to create a folder, so call it something like Empty Window Localization and save it to the desktop.

The result is an *.xcloc* bundle called *fr.xcloc* (for French). It's an ordinary folder containing subfolders, along with a *contents.json* file describing the output (Figure 9-32).

The heart of this output is an XML file called *fr.xliff* (inside the *Localized Contents* subfolder). Examining this file, you'll observe that our app's localizable strings have all been discovered and have been turned into `<file>` elements. Looking at the `original` attribute, you can see what files these represent. The *InfoPlist.strings* file localizes our *Info.plist*; the *Main.storyboard* file localizes our main storyboard; and the *Localizable.strings* file localizes our code.

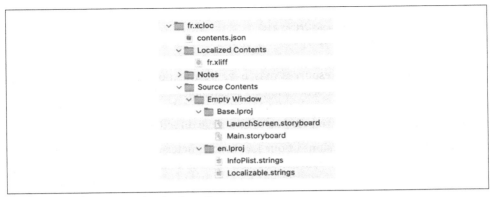

Figure 9-32. An exported xcloc bundle

Editing

Now let's pretend that you are the French translator, tasked with creating the French localization of this app. Your job is to *modify* the *fr.xliff* file by supplying a `<target>` tag for every `<source>` tag that is to be translated into French. Your edited file might contain, at the appropriate places, translations like this (note that the id and Object-ID attributes will be different in your actual *fr.xliff* file):

```
<trans-unit id="RoQ-mP-swT.normalTitle">
  <source>Hello</source>
  <target>Bonjour</target>
  <note>Class="UIButton"; normalTitle="Hello"; ObjectID="RoQ-mP-swT";</note>
</trans-unit>

<trans-unit id="CFBundleDisplayName">
  <source>Empty Window</source>
  <target>Fenêtre Vide</target>
</trans-unit>
<trans-unit id="CFBundleName">
  <source>Empty Window</source>
  <target>Empty Window</target>
</trans-unit>

<trans-unit id="Accept">
  <source>OK</source>
  <target>OK</target>
  <note>Dismiss</note>
</trans-unit>
<trans-unit id="Greeting">
  <source>Howdy!</source>
  <target>Bonjour!</target>
  <note>Say hello</note>
</trans-unit>
<trans-unit id="Tapped">
```

```
        <source>You tapped me!</source>
        <target>Vous m'avez tapé!</target>
        <note>User tapped button</note>
    </trans-unit>
```

Other types of localizable resources may have been exported automatically as well. For example, images in the asset catalog are localizable, and these are exported too (in *Localized Contents*). If an asset catalog was exported for localization, the translator can edit or replace the localized version of an image directly.

In addition, the *original* versions of our localizable material were exported (in *Source Contents*); and your export can include screenshots taken during interface testing (described earlier in this chapter). These can give the translator valuable context as to the usage of the terms to be translated.

Importing

The French translator, having edited the *fr.xliff* file and any exported localizable asset catalog images, returns the *fr.xcloc* folder to us. We proceed to incorporate it back into our project:

1. Edit the project.

2. Choose Editor → Import Localizations; in the dialog, locate and open the *fr.xcloc* folder.

Xcode parses the *.xcloc* folder, locates the *fr.xliff* file inside it, opens and reads it, and creates the corresponding files in the project. In particular, the project folder now contains a *fr.lproj* folder containing *.strings* files in the correct format, namely key-value pairs like this:

```
/* Optional comments are C-style comments */
"key" = "value";
```

The *.strings* files in our *fr.lproj* folder include the following:

- An *InfoPlist.strings* file, localized for French, corresponding to our *Info.plist* file. It reads like this:

```
/* Bundle display name */
"CFBundleDisplayName" = "Fenêtre Vide";

/* Bundle name */
"CFBundleName" = "Empty Window";
```

- A *Main.strings* file, localized for French, corresponding to *Main.storyboard*. It will be similar to this:

```
/* Class="UIButton"; normalTitle="Hello"; ObjectID="RoQ-mP-swT"; */
"RoQ-mP-swT.normalTitle" = "Bonjour";
```

- A *Localizable.strings* file, localized for French, localizing the strings in our code. It looks like this:

```
/* Dismiss */
"Accept" = "OK";

/* Say hello */
"Greeting" = "Bonjour!";

/* User tapped button */
"Tapped" = "Vous m'avez tapé!";
```

If the translator has edited any exported asset catalog images, they will be incorporated into the appropriate slots in our asset catalog.

Testing Localization

Build and run the project in the Simulator. The project runs in English, so the button title is still "Hello," and the alert that it summons when you tap it still contains "Howdy!", "You tapped me!", and "OK." Stop the project in Xcode.

Now we're going to transport ourselves magically to France! Edit the scheme. In the scheme's Run action, under the Options pane, change the Application Language to French. Then build and run again. Presto! The button in the interface has the title Bonjour. When we tap it, the alert contains "Bonjour!", "Vous m'avez tapé!", and "OK."

That doesn't prove, however, that our *Info.plist* localizations are working. To test that, in the Simulator, use the Settings app to change the system language to French (under General → Language and Region). You'll see that, in the Springboard, our app's title has changed to *Fenêtre Vide*.

In real life, preparing your nib files to deal with localization will take some additional work. In particular, you'll want to use autolayout, configuring your interface so that interface objects containing text have room to grow and shrink to compensate for the change in the length of their text in different languages.

To view your interface under different localizations, you can preview your localized nib files within Xcode, without running the app. Edit a *.storyboard* or *.xib* file and choose Editor → Preview (or choose Preview from the Editor Options pop-up menu at the top right of the editor pane). In the preview pane, a pop-up menu at the lower right lists localizations; choose from the menu to switch between them. A "double-length pseudolanguage" stress-tests your interface with really long localized replacement text.

Test plans (discussed earlier in this chapter) let you create multiple configurations, each of which can have a different system language and region. When you run a test, it runs under all of the current test plan's configurations in succession. This provides an automated way to check that your app behaves correctly under all localizations.

Distribution

Distribution means sharing your built app with users (other than members of your team) for running on their devices. There are two primary kinds of distribution:

Ad Hoc distribution

>   You are providing a copy of your app to a limited set of known users so that they can try it on specific devices and report bugs, make suggestions, and so forth.

App Store distribution

>   You are providing the app to the App Store. This could be for one of two reasons:

>   *TestFlight testing*

>>   You are providing access to the app temporarily to certain users for testing through TestFlight.

>   *Sale*

>>   You are providing the app to the App Store to be listed publicly, so that anyone can download it and run it, possibly for a fee.

Making an Archive

To create a copy of your app for distribution, you need first to build an *archive* of your app. An archive is basically a preserved build. It has three main purposes:

Distribution

>   An archive will serve as the basis for subsequent distribution of the app; the distributed app will be *exported* from the archive.

Reproduction

>   Every time you build, conditions can vary, so the resulting app might behave slightly differently. But every distribution from a particular archive contains an identical binary and will behave the same way. If a bug report arrives based on an app distributed from a particular archive, you can distribute that archive to yourself and run it, knowing that you are testing exactly the same app.

Symbolication

>   The archive includes a *.dSYM* file that allows Xcode to accept a crash log and report the crash's location in your code. This helps you to deal with crash reports from users.

Here's how to build an archive of your app:

1. Set the destination in the Scheme pop-up menu in the project window toolbar to Any iOS Device. Until you do this, the Product → Archive menu item will be disabled. You do *not* have to have a device connected; you are not building to run on a *particular* device, but saving an archive that will run on *some* device.

2. If you like, edit the scheme to confirm that the Release build configuration will be used for the Archive action. This is the default, but it does no harm to double-check.

3. Choose Product → Archive. The app is compiled and built. The archive itself is stored in a date folder within your user *~/Library/Developer/Xcode/Archives* folder. Also, it is listed in Xcode's Organizer window (Window → Organizer) under the Empty Window app's Products → Archives entry; this window may open spontaneously to show the archive you've just created. You can add a description here; you can also change the archive's name (this won't affect the name of the app).

You've just signed your archive with a development profile; that's good, because it means you can run the archived build directly on your device. However, a development profile can't be used to make an Ad Hoc or App Store build of your app; therefore, when you export the archive to form an Ad Hoc or App Store build, Xcode will embed the appropriate *distribution* profile instead. So now, in order to export from your archive, you need a distribution certificate and a distribution profile.

The Distribution Certificate

A distribution certificate (sometimes called a *production* certificate) is essential for distributing your app to other users. There are three ways to obtain a distribution certificate, parallel to the three ways of obtaining a development certificate described earlier in this chapter:

Automatic signing
> If you're using automatic signing, and if you have no distribution certificate, then when you first export the archive to the App Store (as I'll describe later in this chapter), Xcode will offer to create and download a distribution certificate for you, automatically, along with a distribution profile.

The Accounts preference pane
> You can request a distribution certificate through Xcode's Accounts preference pane: select your Apple ID, choose your team, click Manage Certificates to show the "Signing certificates" dialog, click the Plus button at the bottom left, and ask for an Apple Distribution certificate.

Keychain Access and the developer member center
You can obtain a distribution certificate manually using the Keychain Access application and the developer member center, exactly as I described earlier for obtaining a development certificate manually.

Once you've obtained a distribution certificate, you'll see it in your keychain. It will look just like Figure 9-22, except that it will say "Distribution" instead of "Development."

There is an important difference between distribution certificates and development certificates: There's a fixed limit on how many distribution certificates a team can have. (For a while, that limit was one, but it may have been raised subsequently to three.) This means that you can run out of distribution certificates — especially if you are trying to distribute from more than one computer.

Let's say your distribution certificate is in the keychain of your first computer. On your second computer, Xcode reports the *existence* of the distribution certificate (in the Accounts preference pane, under Manage Certificates), but tells you that it *isn't* in the keychain of *this* computer. You'd like to install a *copy* of your *existing* distribution certificate. But you can't simply go to the developer member center and download a copy of the existing distribution certificate, because the existing distribution certificate is matched to a private key, and won't work without it — and that private key is still sitting in the keychain of the first computer.

The solution is to return to the first computer, and, in the Accounts preference pane, under Manage Certificates, Control-click that certificate and choose Export Certificate from the contextual menu. You'll be asked to save the resulting file, securing it with a password. The password is needed because this file, a *.p12* file, contains the private key from your keychain. Now copy the *.p12* file to the second computer. (You could email it to yourself.) On that computer, open the exported file, using the password. The private key and the certificate are imported into the keychain of the second computer. You can then throw away all copies of the *.p12* file; it has done its job.

The Distribution Profile

Obtaining a distribution profile is like obtaining a development profile. If you're using automatic signing for this project, Xcode will probably be able to create an appropriate distribution profile for you automatically when you export your archive.

You can also obtain a distribution profile manually, at the developer member center, under Certificates, Identifiers & Profiles. The procedure is similar to obtaining a development profile manually, with a few slight differences:

1. If this is to be an Ad Hoc distribution profile, collect the UDIDs of all the devices where this build is to run, and make sure you've added each of them at the

---

developer member center under Devices. (For an App Store distribution profile, omit this step.)

2. Make sure that the app is registered at the developer member center under Identifiers, as I described earlier in this chapter.

3. Under Profiles, click the Plus button to ask for a new profile. Choose an Ad Hoc or App Store profile. On the next screen, choose your app from the pop-up menu. On the next screen, choose your distribution certificate. On the next screen, for an Ad Hoc profile only, specify the devices you want this app to run on. On the next screen, give the profile a name.

    Be careful about the profile's name, as you might need to be able to recognize it later from within Xcode! My own practice is to assign a name containing the term "AdHoc" or "AppStore" and the name of the app.

4. Click Done. You should subsequently be able to download the profile from within Xcode (and if not, you can click Download at the developer member center).

Distribution for Testing

There are two ways to distribute your app for testing: Ad Hoc distribution and TestFlight distribution. I'll briefly describe each of them.

Ad Hoc distribution

Here are the steps for creating an Ad Hoc distribution file from an archive:

1. In the Organizer window, under Archives, select the archive and click Distribute App at the upper right. A dialog appears. Here, you are to specify a method; choose Ad Hoc. Click Next.

2. In the next screen, you may be offered various options:

    App Thinning
    This means that multiple copies of the app can be created, each containing resources appropriate only to one type of device, simulating what the App Store will do when the user downloads the app to a device. There would normally be no need for this, though it might be interesting to learn the size of your thinned app.

    Rebuild from Bitcode
    Bitcode allows the App Store to regenerate your app to incorporate future optimizations. If you're going to be using bitcode when you upload to the App Store, you might like to use it when you perform your Ad Hoc build. Personally, I avoid bitcode, so I would uncheck this checkbox.

3. In the next screen, you may be offered a choice between automatic and manual signing. An automatically generated Ad Hoc distribution profile will be configured to run on all devices registered for your team at the developer member center. If you choose manual signing, you'll see another screen where you can specify the certificate and choose an Ad Hoc distribution profile, either from the member center or (if you've downloaded the distribution profile already) from your computer.

4. The archive is prepared, and a summary window is displayed. The name of the provisioning profile is shown, so you can tell that the right thing is happening. Click Export.

5. You are shown a dialog for saving a folder. The file will be inside that folder, with the suffix *.ipa* ("iPhone app"), accompanied by property list and log files describing the export process.

6. Locate in the Finder the *.ipa* file you just saved. Provide this file to your users with instructions.

How should a user who has received the *.ipa* file copy it onto a registered device? Starting with macOS 10.15 Catalina, it's ridiculously easy: use the Finder! The user attaches the device to the computer (clicking the various Trust buttons if necessary), selects the device in a Finder window sidebar, and just drags the app right onto the device's window.

If there's any difficulty, another reliable way is to download the Apple Configurator application from the Mac App Store. Attach the device to the computer and launch Apple Configurator. An image of the device's screen appears in the Configurator window. Drag the *.ipa* file from the Finder onto that image, and it will be copied onto the device.

TestFlight distribution

The number of Ad Hoc testers is limited to 100 devices per year per developer (not per app). Devices used for development are counted against this limit. You can work around this limit, and provide your betas more conveniently to testers, by using Test-Flight beta testing instead.

TestFlight has many advantages over Ad Hoc testing. It lifts the limit of 100 devices to a limit of 10000 testers. It is far more convenient for your testers than Ad Hoc distribution, because they download and install prerelease versions of your app directly from the App Store onto their devices, through the TestFlight app. Communication between you and your testers is handled seamlessly: TestFlight emails invitations to testers, allows testers to provide feedback comments, collects crash logs, notifies testers when you update the app, and so forth.

Configuration is performed at the App Store Connect site; a prerelease version uploaded to App Store Connect must be exported as if for App Store distribution (see the discussion of App Store submission later in this chapter). See the "Test a beta version" chapter of Apple's *App Store Connect Help* document (Help → App Store Connect Help).

Prerelease versions of your app intended for distribution to beta testers require review by Apple. Basically, the rule is that if your app's minor version number increases, you can expect a delay while Apple performs the review. On the other hand, *internal* testers (team members who have direct access to your App Store Connect account) can download new versions immediately. That includes you! I often use TestFlight as a way of distributing a build to myself so that I can test on a device under real-world conditions.

Final App Preparations

As the big day approaches when you're thinking of submitting your app to the App Store, don't become so excited by the prospect of huge fame and massive profits that you rush the all-important final stages of app preparation. Apple has a lot of requirements, and failure to meet them can cause your app to be rejected. Take your time. Make a checklist and go through it carefully. See Apple's *App Store Connect Help* and the "Icons and Images" chapter of the *iOS Human Interface Guidelines*.

Icons in the app

The best way to provide your app with icons is to use the asset catalog (Figure 9-33). The image sizes needed are listed in the asset catalog itself. To determine which slots should be displayed, use the checkboxes in the Attributes inspector when you select the icon set. To add an image, drag it from the Finder into the appropriate slot.

An icon file must be a PNG file, without alpha transparency. It should be a full square; the rounding of the corners will be added for you. Apple seems nowadays to prefer simple, cartoony images with a few bright colors and possibly a gentle gradient background.

App icon sizes have changed over the years. If your app is to be backward compatible to earlier systems, you may need additional icons in additional sizes, corresponding to the expectations of those earlier systems. Conversely, new devices can come along, bringing with them new icon size requirements (this happened when the iPad Pro appeared on the scene). Again, this is exactly the sort of thing the asset catalog will help you with.

Optionally, you may elect to include smaller versions of your icon to appear when the user does a search on the device, as well as in the Settings app if you include a settings

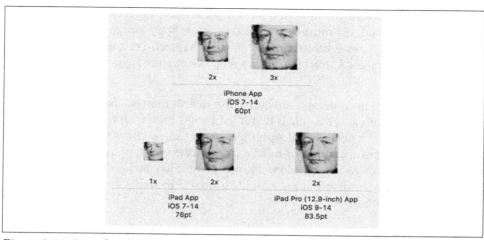

Figure 9-33. Icon slots in the asset catalog

Figure 9-34. Marketing icon slot in the asset catalog

bundle. However, I never include those icons; the system's scaled-down versions of my app icons look fine to me.

Marketing icon

To submit an app to the App Store, you will need to supply a 1024×1024 PNG or high-quality JPEG icon to be displayed at the App Store (the *marketing icon*). Apple's guidelines say that it should not merely be a scaled-up version of your app's icon; but it must not differ perceptibly from your app's icon, either, or your app will be rejected (I know this from bitter experience).

The marketing icon should be included in the asset catalog. There's a slot for it, along with the slots for the real app icons (Figure 9-34).

Launch images

There is a delay between the moment when the user taps your app's icon to launch it and the moment when your app is up and running and displaying its initial window.

To cover this delay and give the user a visible indication that something is happening, a launch image needs to be displayed during that interval.

The launch image needn't be detailed; in fact, it probably should not be. It might be just a blank depiction of the main elements or regions of the interface that will be present when the app has finished launching. In this way, when the app *does* finish launching, those elements or regions appear to be filled in as the launch image fades away to reveal the real app.

To prepare the launch image, you use a *launch nib file* — a *.xib* or *.storyboard* file containing a single view. You construct this view using subviews and autolayout. The view is automatically reconfigured to match the screen size and orientation of the device on which the app is launching, and label and button text can be localized. The launch image will be a snapshot of this view.

By default, a new app project comes with a *LaunchScreen.storyboard* file. This is where you design your launch image. The *Info.plist* points to this file as the value of its "Launch screen interface file base name" key (UILaunchStoryboardName). You can configure the *Info.plist*, if necessary, by editing the target and setting the Launch Screen File field (under App Icons and Launch Images).

Custom fonts included in your app bundle cannot be displayed in a launch nib file. This is because they have not yet been loaded at the time the launch screen needs to be displayed. Also, code cannot run in association with the display of the launch screen; by definition, your app is launching and its code has not yet started to run. None of those limitations should be a concern. Keep the launch screen simple and minimal. Don't try to misuse it as some kind of introductory splash screen. If you want a splash screen, configure a real view controller to display its view when the app has finished launching.

Screenshots and Video Previews

When you submit your app to the App Store, you will be asked for one or more screenshots of your app in action to be displayed at the App Store. These screenshots must demonstrate actual user experience of the app, or your app may be rejected by Apple's review team. You should take them beforehand and be prepared to provide them during the app submission process. You can provide a screenshot corresponding to the screen size and resolution of every device on which your app can run, or you can reuse a larger-size screenshot for smaller sizes.

You can obtain screenshots either from the Simulator or from a device connected to the computer:

Simulator

Run the app in the Simulator with the desired device type as your destination. Choose File → Save Screen. Alternatively, click the Save Screen button above the simulator window. New in Xcode 12, a miniature screenshot window appears; Control-click it to choose an option for disposing of the screenshot. By default, it is saved to the Desktop. You can also generate a screenshot from the command-line. For instance:

```
% xcrun simctl io booted screenshot myscreenshot.png
```

That command saves a screenshot as *myscreenshot.png* in my home directory (because that's where I was in the Terminal when I gave the command).

Device

In Xcode, in the Devices and Simulators window, locate your connected device under Devices and click Take Screenshot. Alternatively, choose Debug → View Debugging → Take Screenshot of [Device].

You can also take a screenshot directly on a device. If the device has a Home button, click the screen lock button and the Home button simultaneously. If not, click the screen lock button and the Volume Up button simultaneously. Now the screenshot is saved in the Photos app, and you can communicate it to your computer in any convenient way (such as by emailing it to yourself).

You probably don't have devices with every size you need in order to submit screenshots to the App Store. The Simulator supplies every needed device size. It may be, however, that your app doesn't run properly on the Simulator, because it uses features that exist only on a device. I frequently solve this problem by supplying artificial data to my app, on the simulator only (as I described earlier, "Build Action" on page 423), so that its interface works sufficiently to let me capture screenshots.

You can also submit to the App Store a video preview showing your app in action; it can be up to 30 seconds long, in H.264 or Apple ProRes format. One way to capture the video preview is with your device and QuickTime Player:

1. Connect the device to the computer and launch QuickTime Player. Choose File → New Movie Recording.

2. If necessary, set the Camera and Microphone to the device, using the pop-up menu next to the Record button that appears when you hover the mouse over the QuickTime Player window.

3. Start recording, and exercise the app on the device. When you're finished, stop recording and save. The resulting movie file can be edited to prepare it for submission to the App Store.

You can also capture a video preview from a simulator, using the command-line. I might say this in the Terminal:

```
% xcrun simctl io booted recordVideo --codec=h264 mymovie.mov
```

The video preview begins recording, and continues until I press Control-C in the Terminal.

For more details, see the "App preview specifications" section of the Reference chapter of Apple's *App Store Connect Help*.

Property List Settings

A number of settings in the *Info.plist* are crucial to the proper behavior of your app. You should peruse Apple's *Information Property List Key Reference* for full information. Most of the required keys are created as part of the template, and are given reasonable default values, but you should check them anyway. The following are particularly worthy of attention:

Bundle display name (`CFBundleDisplayName`)
> The name that appears under your app's icon on the device screen; this name needs to be short in order to avoid truncation. I talked earlier in this chapter about how to localize the display name. You can enter this value directly in the General pane when you edit your app target.

Supported interface orientations (`UISupportedInterfaceOrientations`)
> This key designates the totality of orientations in which the app is ever permitted to appear. I talked earlier in this chapter about the interface for making these settings with checkboxes in the General pane of the target editor, but you get better fine tuning by editing the *Info.plist* directly. For example, it might be necessary to reorder the orientations (because on an iPhone the *first* orientation listed may be the one into which the app will actually launch).

Required device capabilities (`UIRequiredDeviceCapabilities`)
> You should set this key if the app requires capabilities that are not present on all devices. But don't use this key unless it makes no sense for your app to run *at all* on a device lacking the specified capabilities.

Bundle version
> Your app needs a version number. The best place to set it is the General pane of the target editor. Things are a little confusing here because there are two fields:

> *Version*
> > Corresponds in the *Info.plist* to "Bundle versions string, short" (`CFBundle-ShortVersionString`). This is a user-facing string and needs to be a version string, such as `"1.0"`. It will be displayed at the App Store, distinguishing one release from another. Failure to increment the version string when submitting an update will cause the update to be rejected.

Build

Corresponds in the *Info.plist* to "Bundle version" (`CFBundleVersion`). The user never sees this value. I treat it as an independent integer value. It is legal to increment the Build number without incrementing the Version number, and that is what I do when I submit several successive builds of the same prospective release during TestFlight testing.

The interplay between TestFlight versions and App Store versions is a little tricky. If you're satisfied with a TestFlight version, you can submit the very same binary, which is already present at App Store Connect, for distribution by the App Store. But once you have submitted a version to the App Store, the next build that you submit, even if it is just for TestFlight, must have a higher version string; upping the build number is not sufficient.

 Version strings don't work like decimal numbers! Each component of the string is treated as an *integer*. A short version string "1.4" is not "higher" than a version string "1.32" — because 4 is smaller than 32. As usual, I learned this lesson the hard way.

Submission to the App Store

When you're satisfied that your app works well, and you've installed or collected all the necessary resources, you're ready to submit your app to the App Store for distribution. To do so, you'll need to make preparations at the App Store Connect site (*https://appstoreconnect.apple.com*).

 The first time you visit App Store Connect, you should go to the Contracts section and complete submission of your contract. You can't offer any apps for sale until you do, and even free apps require completion of a contractual form.

I'm not going to recite all the steps you have to go through to tell App Store Connect about your app, as these are described thoroughly in Apple's *App Store Connect Help* document, which is the final word on such matters. But here are some of the main pieces of information you will sooner or later have to supply (and see also *https:// developer.apple.com/app-store/product-page*):

Your app's name

This is the name that will appear at the App Store; it need not be identical to the short name that will appear under the app's icon on the device, dictated by the "Bundle display name" setting in your *Info.plist* file. Apple now requires that this name be 30 characters or fewer. You can get a rude shock when you submit your app's information to App Store Connect and discover that the name you wanted is already taken. There is no reliable way to learn this in advance, and such a discovery can necessitate a certain amount of last-minute scrambling on your part. (Can you guess how I know that?)

Subtitle

A description of the app, 30 characters or fewer, that will appear below the name at the App Store.

Description

You must supply a description of fewer than 4,000 characters; Apple recommends fewer than 580 characters, and the first paragraph is the most important, because this may be all that users see at first when they visit the App Store. It must be pure text, with no HTML or character styling.

Promotional text

Optional; 170 characters or fewer. The significance of the promotional text is that you can change it for an existing app, without uploading a new build.

Keywords

A comma-separated list, shorter than 100 characters. These keywords will be used, in addition to your app's name, to help users discover your app through the Search feature of the App Store.

Privacy policy

The URL of a web page describing your privacy policy.

Support

The URL of a web site where users can find more information about your app.

Copyright

Do not include a copyright symbol in this string; it will be added for you at the App Store.

SKU number

This is arbitrary, so don't get nervous about it. It's just an identifier that's unique within the world of your own apps. It's convenient if it has something to do with your app's name. It needn't be a number; it can actually be any string.

Price

You don't get to make up a price. You have to choose from a list of pricing "tiers."

Availability Date

There's an option to make the app available as soon as it is approved, and this will typically be your choice.

 As you submit information, click Save often! If the connection goes down and you haven't explicitly saved, all your work can be lost. (Can you guess how I know that?)

Once your app is initially registered at App Store Connect, and when you have an archived build ready for distribution, you can export and upload it. The export process is similar to what I described earlier for Ad Hoc distribution. Select the archived build in the Organizer and click Distribute App; on the next screen, select App Store Connect. Subsequent options are slightly different from the options for an Ad Hoc distribution: you won't see anything about app thinning, because that depends on how the user obtains the app; you'll see the bitcode checkbox; and there's a checkbox for uploading symbols, which should make it easier to analyze crash reports. Eventually, a screen is displayed summarizing the *.ipa* content, and you can now upload to App Store Connect or save to disk:

Upload to App Store Connect
> The upload is performed within Xcode, and the app will be validated at the far end.

Save to disk
> You can perform the upload later using Transporter, available from the App Store (*https://apps.apple.com/us/app/transporter/id1450874784*).

After uploading the archive, you have one final step to perform. Wait for the binary to be processed at Apple's end. (You should receive an email when processing has completed.) Then return to App Store Connect, where you submitted your app information. You will now be able to select the binary, save, and submit the app for review.

You will subsequently receive notifications from Apple informing you of your app's status as it passes through various stages: "Waiting For Review," "In Review," and finally, if all has gone well, "Ready For Sale" (even if it's a free app). Your app will then appear at the App Store.

Once your app is registered at the App Store, you do *not* need to make further preparations merely to upload a new build. Simply increase the build number or version string, as I described earlier, and upload the build. If this build is for TestFlight, and if this version has already been reviewed for TestFlight, the new build becomes available for testing immediately. If this build is for the App Store, you can upload it first and register the new version at App Store Connect later.

PART III

Cocoa

The Cocoa Touch frameworks provide the general capabilities needed by any iOS application. Buttons can be tapped, text can be read, screens of interface can succeed one another, because Cocoa makes it so. To use the framework, you must learn to let the framework use you. You must put your code in the right place so that it will be called at the right time. You must fulfill certain obligations that Cocoa expects of you. You master Cocoa by being Cocoa's obedient servant. In this part of the book, that's what you'll learn to do.

- Chapter 10 describes how Cocoa is organized and structured through such Objective-C language features as subclassing, categories, and protocols. Then some important built-in Cocoa object types are introduced. The chapter concludes with a description of Cocoa key–value coding and a look at how the root NSObject class is organized.

- Chapter 11 presents Cocoa's event-driven model of activity, along with its major design patterns and event-related features — notifications, delegation, data sources, target–action, the responder chain, and key–value observing. The chapter concludes with some words of wisdom about managing the barrage of events Cocoa will be throwing at you, and how to escape that barrage momentarily with delayed performance.

- Chapter 12 is about Cocoa memory management. I'll explain how memory management of reference types works. Then some special memory management situations are described: autorelease pools, retain cycles, notifications and timers, nib loading, and CFTypeRefs. The chapter concludes with a discussion of Cocoa property memory management, and advice on how to debug memory management issues.

- Chapter 13 discusses the question of how your objects are going to see and communicate with one another within the confines of the Cocoa-based world. It concludes with a look at two new ways of managing object communications, the Combine framework and SwiftUI.

Finally, don't forget to read Appendix A for more detail about how Objective-C and Swift interact and cooperate.

CHAPTER 10

Cocoa Classes

When you program iOS through Foundation and UIKit, you're programming Cocoa. The Cocoa API is written mostly in Objective-C, and Cocoa itself consists mostly of Objective-C classes, derived from the root class, NSObject.

This chapter introduces Cocoa's class structure and explains how Cocoa is conceptually organized, in terms of its underlying Objective-C features, along with a survey of some of the most commonly encountered Cocoa utility classes. The chapter then discusses Objective-C instance properties and Cocoa key–value coding, and concludes with a description of the Cocoa root class and its features, which are inherited by all Cocoa classes.

Subclassing

Cocoa supplies a large repertory of objects that already know how to behave in certain desirable ways. A UIButton knows how to draw itself and how to respond when the user taps it; a UITextField knows how to display editable text, how to summon the keyboard, and how to accept keyboard input. When the default behavior or appearance of an object supplied by Cocoa isn't quite what you're after, you'll want to customize it.

But that does *not* necessarily mean you need to subclass! In fact, subclassing is one of the rarer ways in which your code will relate to Cocoa. Most built-in Cocoa Touch classes will never need subclassing (and some, in their documentation, downright forbid it).

Instead, Cocoa classes are often heavily endowed with methods that you can call and properties that you can set precisely in order to customize an instance, and these will be your first resort. Always study the documentation for a Cocoa class to see whether instances can already be made to do what you want. The UIButton class documentation shows that you can set a button's title, title color, internal image, background image, and many other features and behaviors, without subclassing.

In addition, many built-in classes use delegation (Chapter 11) as the preferred way of letting you customize their behavior. You wouldn't subclass UITextField just in order to respond in some special way when the user types text, because the delegate mechanism and the UITextFieldDelegate protocol provide ways to do that.

Nevertheless, sometimes setting properties and calling methods and using delegation won't suffice to customize an instance the way you want to. In such cases, a Cocoa class may provide methods that are called by the runtime at key moments in the life of the instance, allowing you to customize that class's behavior by subclassing and overriding. In fact, certain Cocoa Touch classes are subclassed routinely, constituting the exception that proves the rule.

A case in point is UIViewController. Every Cocoa app uses view controllers, but a plain vanilla UIViewController, not subclassed, is very rare. A Cocoa iOS app without at least one UIViewController subclass would be practically impossible. Subclassing is how you inject *your* functionality into a view controller. Much of your code will probably revolve around UIViewController subclasses that you have written.

Another case in point is UIView. Cocoa Touch is full of built-in UIView subclasses that behave and draw themselves as needed (UIButton, UITextField, and so on), and you will rarely need to subclass any of them. On the other hand, you might create your *own* UIView subclass, whose job would be to draw itself in some completely new way.

You don't actually draw a UIView; rather, when a UIView needs drawing, its `draw(_:)` method is called so that the view can draw itself. So the way to draw a custom UIView is to subclass UIView and implement `draw(_:)` in the subclass. As the documentation says, "Subclasses that … draw their view's content should override this method and implement their drawing code there." The documentation is saying that you *need* to subclass UIView in order to draw custom content.

Suppose we want our window to contain a horizontal line. There is no horizontal line interface widget built into Cocoa, so we'll just have to roll our own — a UIView that draws itself as a horizontal line. Let's try it:

1. In our Empty Window example project, choose File → New → File and specify iOS → Source → Cocoa Touch Class, and in particular a subclass of UIView. Call the class MyHorizLine. Xcode creates *MyHorizLine.swift*. Make sure it's part of the app target.

2. In *MyHorizLine.swift*, replace the contents of the class declaration with this (without further explanation):

```
    required init?(coder: NSCoder) {
        super.init(coder:coder)
        self.backgroundColor = .clear
    }
    override func draw(_ rect: CGRect) {
        let c = UIGraphicsGetCurrentContext()!
        c.move(to:CGPoint(x: 0, y: 0))
        c.addLine(to:CGPoint(x: self.bounds.size.width, y: 0))
        c.strokePath()
    }
```

3. Edit the storyboard. Find UIView in the Library (it is called simply "View") and drag it into the View object in the canvas. You may resize it to be less tall.

4. Select the UIView that you just dragged into the canvas and use the Identity inspector to change its class to MyHorizLine.

Build and run the app in the Simulator. You'll see a horizontal line corresponding to the location of the top of the MyHorizLine instance in the nib. Our view has drawn itself as a horizontal line, because we subclassed it to do so.

In that example, we started with a bare UIView that had no drawing functionality of its own. But you might also be able to subclass a built-in UIView subclass to modify the way it already draws itself. In the UILabel class documentation, the discussions of both `drawText(in:)` and `textRect(forBounds:limitedToNumberOfLines:)` refer explicitly to overriding these methods. The implication is that these are methods that will be called for us, automatically, by Cocoa, as a label draws itself; we can subclass UILabel and implement these methods in our subclass to modify how a particular label draws itself.

In one of my own apps, I subclass UILabel and override `drawText(in:)` to make a label that draws its own rectangular border and has its content inset somewhat from that border. As the documentation tells us: "In your overridden method, you can configure the current context further and then invoke `super` to do the actual drawing [of the text]." Let's try it:

1. In the Empty Window project, make a new class file, a UILabel subclass; call the class MyBoundedLabel.

2. In *MyBoundedLabel.swift*, insert this code into the body of the class declaration:

```
    override func drawText(in rect: CGRect) {
        let context = UIGraphicsGetCurrentContext()!
        context.stroke(self.bounds.insetBy(dx: 1.0, dy: 1.0))
        super.drawText(in: rect.insetBy(dx: 5.0, dy: 5.0))
    }
```

3. Edit the storyboard, add a UILabel to the interface, and change its class in the Identity inspector to MyBoundedLabel.

Build and run the app. As you can see, the rectangle is drawn and the label's text is inset within it.

Categories and Extensions

A *category* is an Objective-C language feature that allows code to reach right into an existing class and inject additional methods. This is comparable to a Swift extension (Chapter 4), so I'll start by reminding you how extensions are used, and then I'll describe how Cocoa uses categories.

 Objective-C categories have names, and you may see references to these names in the headers, the documentation, and so forth. However, the names are effectively meaningless, so don't worry about them.

How Swift Uses Extensions

In the Swift standard library header, many native object type declarations consist of an initial declaration followed by a series of extensions. After declaring the generic struct `Array<Element>`, the header proceeds to declare some dozen extensions on the Array struct. Some of these add protocol adoptions; all of them add declarations of properties or methods. These extensions are not, for the most part, functionally significant. The header could have declared the Array struct with all of those properties and methods within the body of a single declaration. Instead, it breaks things up into multiple extensions as a way of clumping related functionality together, organizing this object type's members so as to make them easier for human readers to understand.

In the Swift Core Graphics header, on the other hand, extensions *are* functionally significant — and just about everything *is* an extension — because Swift is adapting types that are already defined elsewhere. It adapts Swift numeric types for use with Core Graphics and CGFloat, and it adapts C structs such as CGPoint and CGRect for use as Swift object types.

How You Use Extensions

For the sake of object-oriented encapsulation, you will often want to write a function that you inject, as a method, into an existing object type. To do so, you'll write an extension. Subclassing merely to add a method or two is heavy-handed — and besides, it often wouldn't help you do what you need to do.

Suppose you wanted to add a method to Cocoa's UIView class. You could subclass UIView and declare your method, but then it would be present only in your UIView subclass and in subclasses of that subclass. It would *not* be present in UIButton, UILabel, and all the other built-in UIView subclasses, because they are subclasses of

UIView, not of *your* subclass. An extension solves the problem beautifully: you inject your method into UIView, and it is inherited by all built-in UIView subclasses as well.

For more fine-grained injection of functionality, you can use protocol extensions. Suppose I want UIButton and UIBarButtonItem — which is not a UIView, but does have button-like behavior — to share a certain method. I can declare a protocol with a method, implement that method in a protocol extension, and then use extensions to make UIButton and UIBarButtonItem adopt that protocol and acquire that method:

```
protocol ButtonLike {
    func behaveInButtonLikeWay()
}
extension ButtonLike {
    func behaveInButtonLikeWay() {
        // ...
    }
}
extension UIButton : ButtonLike {}
extension UIBarButtonItem : ButtonLike {}
```

How Cocoa Uses Categories

Cocoa uses categories as an organizational tool much as Swift uses extensions. The declaration of a class will often be divided by functionality into multiple categories; these can even appear in separate header files.

A good example is NSString. NSString is defined as part of the Foundation framework, and its basic methods are declared in *NSString.h*. Here we find that NSString itself, aside from its initializers, has just two members, `length` and `character(at:)`, because these are regarded as the minimum functionality that a string needs in order to be a string.

Additional NSString methods — those that create a string, deal with a string's encoding, split a string, search in a string, and so on — are clumped into categories. These are shown in the Swift translation of the header as extensions. After the declaration for the NSString class itself, we find this in the Swift translation of the header:

```
extension NSString {
    func substring(from: Int) -> String
    func substring(to: Int) -> String
    // ...
}
```

That is actually Swift's translation of this Objective-C code:

```
@interface NSString (NSStringExtensionMethods)
- (NSString *)substringFromIndex:(NSUInteger)from;
- (NSString *)substringToIndex:(NSUInteger)to;
// ...
@end
```

That notation — the keyword @interface, followed by a class name, followed by another name in parentheses — is an Objective-C category.

Moreover, although the declarations for some of Cocoa's NSString categories appear in this same file, *NSString.h*, many of them appear elsewhere:

- A string may serve as a file pathname, so we also find a category on NSString in *NSPathUtilities.h*, where methods and properties such as pathComponents are declared for splitting a pathname string into its constituents and the like.

- In *NSURL.h*, which is devoted primarily to declaring the NSURL class (and *its* categories), there is also another NSString category, declaring methods for dealing with percent encoding in a URL string, such as addingPercent-Encoding(withAllowedCharacters:).

- Off in a completely different framework (UIKit), *NSStringDrawing.h* adds two further NSString categories, with methods like draw(at:withAttributes:) having to do with drawing a string in a graphics context.

This organization means that the NSString methods are not gathered in a single header file. In general, fortunately, this won't matter to you as a programmer, because an NSString is an NSString, no matter how it acquires its methods.

Protocols

Objective-C has protocols, and these are generally comparable to and compatible with Swift protocols (see Chapter 4). Since classes are the only Objective-C object type, all Objective-C protocols are seen by Swift as class protocols. Conversely, Swift protocols marked as @objc are implicitly class protocols and can be seen by Objective-C. Cocoa makes extensive use of protocols.

A case in point is how Cocoa objects are copied. Some objects can be copied; some can't. This has nothing to do with an object's class heritage. Yet we would like a uniform method to which any object that *can* be copied will respond. So Cocoa defines a protocol named NSCopying, which declares just one required method, copyWith-Zone:. Here's how *NSObject.h* declares the NSCopying protocol:

```
@protocol NSCopying
- (id)copyWithZone:(nullable NSZone *)zone;
@end
```

That's translated into Swift:

```
protocol NSCopying {
    func copy(with zone: NSZone? = nil) -> Any
}
```

The NSCopying protocol declaration in *NSObject.h*, however, is not a statement that NSObject *itself* conforms to NSCopying. Indeed, NSObject does *not* conform to NSCopying! This doesn't compile:

```
let obj = NSObject().copy(with:nil) // compile error
```

But this does compile, because NSString *does* conform to NSCopying:

```
let s = ("hello" as NSString).copy(with: nil)
```

Far and away the most pervasive use of protocols in Cocoa is in connection with the delegation pattern. I'll discuss this pattern in detail in Chapter 11, but you can readily see an example in our handy Empty Window project: the AppDelegate class provided by the project template is declared like this:

```
class AppDelegate: UIResponder, UIApplicationDelegate { // ...
```

AppDelegate's chief purpose on earth is to serve as the shared application's delegate. The shared application object is a UIApplication, and UIApplication's `delegate` property is declared like this (I'll explain the `unsafe` modifier in Chapter 12):

```
unowned(unsafe) var delegate: UIApplicationDelegate?
```

The `UIApplicationDelegate` type is a protocol. UIApplication is saying: "I don't care what class my delegate belongs to, but whatever it is, it should conform to the UIApplicationDelegate protocol." Such conformance constitutes a promise that the delegate will implement instance methods declared by the protocol, such as `application(_:didFinishLaunchingWithOptions:)`. The AppDelegate class officially announces its role by explicitly adopting the UIApplicationDelegate protocol.

A Cocoa protocol has its own documentation page. When the UIApplication class documentation tells you that the `delegate` property is typed as UIApplicationDelegate, it's implicitly telling you that if you want to know what messages the application's delegate might receive, you need to look in the UIApplicationDelegate protocol documentation. `application(_:didFinishLaunchingWithOptions:)` isn't mentioned anywhere in the UIApplication class documentation page; it's in the UIApplicationDelegate protocol documentation page.

Optional Members

Objective-C protocols, and Swift protocols marked as `@objc`, can have optional members (see "Optional Protocol Members" on page 197). The UIApplicationDelegate protocol method `application(_:didFinishLaunchingWithOptions:)` is a case in point; it's optional. But how, in practice, is an optional member feasible? We know that if a message is sent to an object and the object can't handle that message, an exception is raised and your app will likely crash. How does Objective-C prevent that from happening?

The answer is that Objective-C is both dynamic and introspective. Objective-C can ask an object whether it can deal with a message without actually sending it that message. The key method here is NSObject's `responds(to:)` method (Objective-C `respondsToSelector:`), which takes a selector parameter (see Chapter 2) and returns a Bool. Thus it is possible to send a message to an object *conditionally* — that is, only if it would be safe to do so.

Demonstrating `responds(to:)` in Swift is generally a little tricky, because Swift, with its strict type checking, doesn't want to let us send an object a message to which it might not respond. In this artificial example, I start by defining, at top level, a class that derives from NSObject, because otherwise we can't send `responds(to:)` to it, along with an `@objc` protocol to declare the message that I want to send conditionally:

```
class MyClass : NSObject {
}
@objc protocol Dummy {
    func woohoo()
}
```

Now I can say this:

```
let mc = MyClass()
if mc.responds(to: #selector(Dummy.woohoo)) {
    (mc as AnyObject).woohoo()
}
```

Note the cast of `mc` to AnyObject. This causes Swift to abandon its strict type checking (see "Suppressing type checking" on page 225); we can now send this object any message that Swift knows about, provided it is susceptible to Objective-C introspection — that's why I marked my protocol declaration as `@objc` to start with. As you know, Swift provides a shorthand for sending a message conditionally: append a question mark to the name of the message. I could have written this:

```
let mc = MyClass()
(mc as AnyObject).woohoo?()
```

Behind the scenes, those two approaches are exactly the same; the latter is syntactic sugar for the former. In response to the question mark, Swift is calling `responds(to:)` for us, and will refrain from sending woohoo to this object if it *doesn't* respond to this selector.

That explains how optional protocol members work. It is no coincidence that Swift treats optional protocol members like AnyObject members. Here's the example I gave in Chapter 4:

```
@objc protocol Flier {
    @objc optional var song : String {get}
    @objc optional func sing()
}
```

When you call sing?() on an object typed as Flier, responds(to:) is called behind the scenes to determine whether this call is safe. That is also why optional protocol members work only on @objc protocols and classes derived from NSObject: Swift is relying here on a purely Objective-C feature.

You wouldn't want to send a message optionally, or call responds(to:) explicitly, before sending just any old message, because it isn't generally necessary except with optional methods, and it slows things down a little. But Cocoa does in fact call responds(to:) on your objects as a matter of course. To see that this is true, implement responds(to:) on the AppDelegate class in our Empty Window project and instrument it with logging:

```
override func responds(to aSelector: Selector) -> Bool {
    print(aSelector)
    return super.responds(to:aSelector)
}
```

The output on my machine, as the Empty Window app launches, includes the following:

```
application:handleOpenURL:
application:openURL:sourceApplication:annotation:
application:openURL:options:
applicationDidReceiveMemoryWarning:
applicationWillTerminate:
applicationSignificantTimeChange:
application:willChangeStatusBarOrientation:duration:
application:didChangeStatusBarOrientation:
application:willChangeStatusBarFrame:
application:didChangeStatusBarFrame:
application:deviceAccelerated:
application:deviceChangedOrientation:
applicationDidBecomeActive:
applicationWillResignActive:
applicationDidEnterBackground:
applicationWillEnterForeground:
applicationWillSuspend:
application:didResumeWithOptions:
application:shouldSaveApplicationState:
application:shouldSaveSecureApplicationState:
application:supportedInterfaceOrientationsForWindow:
application:defaultWhitePointAdaptivityStyleForWindow:
```

```
application:configurationForConnectingSceneSession:options:
application:didDiscardSceneSessions:
application:performFetchWithCompletionHandler:
application:didReceiveRemoteNotification:fetchCompletionHandler:
application:willFinishLaunchingWithOptions:
application:didFinishLaunchingWithOptions:
```

That's Cocoa, checking to see which optional UIApplicationDelegate protocol methods are actually implemented by our AppDelegate instance. Cocoa checks all the optional protocol methods once, when it first meets the object in question, and presumably stores the results; the app is slowed a tiny bit by this one-time initial bombardment of `responds(to:)` calls, but now Cocoa knows all the answers and won't have to perform any of these same checks on the same object later. The entire pattern of a delegate with optional delegate members depends upon this technique.

Informal Protocols

You may occasionally see, online or in the Cocoa documentation, a reference to an *informal protocol*. An informal protocol isn't really a protocol at all; it's just an Objective-C trick for providing the compiler with a knowledge of a method name so that it will allow a message to be sent without complaining.

There are two complementary ways to implement an informal protocol. One is to define a category on NSObject; this makes any object eligible to receive the messages listed in the category. The other is to define a protocol to which no class formally conforms; instead, messages listed in the protocol are sent only to objects typed as id (AnyObject), suppressing any objections from the compiler.

These techniques were widespread in Cocoa before Objective-C protocols could declare methods as optional; now they are largely unnecessary, and are also mildly dangerous. Nowadays, very few informal protocols remain, but they do exist. NSKey-ValueCoding (discussed later in this chapter) is an informal protocol; you may see the term NSKeyValueCoding in the documentation and elsewhere, but there isn't actually any such type — it's a category on NSObject.

Some Foundation Classes

The Foundation classes of Cocoa provide basic data types and utilities that will form the basis of your communication with Cocoa. In this section, I'll survey those that you'll probably want to be aware of initially. For more information, start with Apple's list of the Foundation classes in the Foundation framework documentation page.

In many situations, you can use Foundation classes implicitly by way of Swift classes. That's because of Swift's ability to *bridge* between its own classes and those of Foundation. There are two kinds of bridging to be distinguished here:

Native Swift types

Certain purely native Swift types are bridged to Objective-C types for purposes of interoperability. For instance, String and Array are native Swift types, with an independent existence. String is bridged to NSString (Chapter 3), and Array is bridged to NSArray (Chapter 4), so a String and an NSString can be cast to one another, and an Array and an NSArray can be cast to one another. But in fact you'll rarely need to cast, because wherever the Objective-C API expects you to pass an NSString or an NSArray, these will be typed in the Swift translation of that API as a String or an Array. And when you use String or Array in the presence of Foundation, many NSString and NSArray properties and methods spring to life.

Foundation overlay types

The Swift Foundation overlay puts a native Swift interface in front of many Foundation types. The Swift interface is distinguished by dropping the "NS" prefix that marks Foundation class names. These are not native Swift types; they are façades for Objective-C types, meaning that you cannot use them except in the presence of Cocoa's Foundation framework. For instance, Objective-C NSData is accessed through Swift Data, and Objective-C NSDate is accessed through Swift Date — though you can still use NSData and NSDate directly if you really want to. The Swift and Objective-C types are bridged to one another, and the API shows the Swift type, so casting and passing both work as you would expect. The Swift types provide many conveniences that the Objective-C types do not: they may declare adoption of appropriate Swift protocols such as Equatable, Hashable, and Comparable, and, in some cases, they may be value types (structs) where the Objective-C types are reference types (classes).

NSRange

NSRange is a C struct (see Appendix A). Its components are integers, `location` and `length`. An NSRange whose `location` is 1 starts at the second element of something (because element counting is always zero-based), and if its `length` is 2 it designates this element and the next.

A Swift Range and a Cocoa NSRange are constructed very differently from one another. A Swift Range is defined by two endpoints. A Cocoa NSRange is defined by a starting point and a length. Nevertheless, Swift goes to some lengths (in the Foundation overlay) to help you work with an NSRange:

- NSRange is endowed with Range-like members such as `lowerBound`, `upperBound`, and `contains(_:)`.

- You can coerce a Swift Range whose Bound type (the type of its endpoints) is Int (or any other integer type) to an NSRange.

- You can coerce from an NSRange to a Swift Range — resulting in an Optional wrapping a Range, for reasons I'll explain in a moment.

For example:

```
// Range to NSRange
let r = 2..<4
let nsr = NSRange(r) // (2,2), an NSRange
// NSRange to Range
let nsr2 = NSRange(location: 2, length: 2)
let r2 = Range(nsr2) // Optional wrapping Range 2..<4
```

But what about strings? A Swift String's range Bound type is *not* Int; it is String.Index. Meanwhile, on the Cocoa side, an NSString still uses an NSRange whose components are integers. Not only is there a type mismatch, there's also a value mismatch, because (as I explained in Chapter 3) a String is indexed on its characters, meaning its graphemes, but an NSString is indexed on its Unicode codepoints.

Sometimes, Swift will solve the problem by crossing the bridge for you in both directions; here's an example I've already used:

```
let s = "hello"
let range = s.range(of:"ell") // Optional wrapping Range 1..<4
```

The range(of:) method in that code is actually a Cocoa method. Swift has cast the String s to an NSString for us, called a Foundation method that returns an NSRange, and coerced the NSRange to a Swift Range (wrapped in an Optional), adjusting its value as needed, entirely behind the scenes.

On other occasions, you will want to perform that coercion explicitly. For this purpose, Range has an initializer init(_:in:), taking an NSRange and the String to which the resulting range is to apply:

```
let range = NSRange(location: 1, length: 3)
let r = Range(range, in:"hello") // Optional wrapping 1..<4 of String.Index
```

And NSRange has the converse initializer init(_:in:), taking a Range of String.Index and the String to which it applies:

```
let s = "hello"
let range = NSRange(s.range(of:"ell")!, in: s) // (1,3), an NSRange
```

Sometimes, however, you actively *want* to operate in the Cocoa Foundation world, *without* bridging back to Swift. You can do that by casting:

```
let s = "Hello"
let range = (s as NSString).range(of: "ell") // NSRange
let mas = NSMutableAttributedString(string:s)
mas.addAttributes([.foregroundColor:UIColor.red], range: range)
```

In that code, we cast a String to an NSString so as to be able to call NSString's range(of:) and get an NSRange, because that is what NSMutableAttributedString's `addAttributes(_:range:)` wants as its second parameter. It would be wasteful and time-consuming to call `range(of:)` on a Swift String, which crosses into the Foundation world, gets the range, and brings it back to the Swift world, only to convert it back to an NSRange *again*.

NSNotFound

`NSNotFound` is a constant integer indicating that some requested element was not found. The true numeric value of `NSNotFound` is of no concern; you always compare against `NSNotFound` itself to learn whether a result is meaningful. If you ask for the index of a certain object in an NSArray and the object isn't present, the result is `NSNotFound`:

```
let arr = ["hey"] as NSArray
let ix = arr.index(of:"ho")
if ix == NSNotFound {
    print("it wasn't found")
}
```

Why does Cocoa resort to an integer value with a special meaning in this way? Because it has to. The result could not be `0` to indicate the absence of the object, because `0` would indicate the first element of the array. Nor could it be `-1`, because an NSArray index value is always positive. Nor could it be `nil`, because Objective-C can't return `nil` when an integer is expected (and even if it could, it would be seen as another way of saying `0`). Contrast Swift, whose Array `firstIndex(of:)` method returns an Int wrapped in an Optional, precisely so that it *can* return `nil` to indicate that the target object wasn't found.

If a search returns an NSRange and the thing sought is not present, the `location` component of the result will be `NSNotFound`. This means that, when you turn an NSRange into a Swift Range, the NSRange's `location` might be `NSNotFound`, and Swift needs to be able to express that as a `nil` Range. That's why the initializers for coercing an NSRange to a Range are failable. It is also why, when you call NSString's `range(of:)` method on a Swift String, the result is an Optional:

```
let s = "hello"
let r = s.range(of:"ha") // nil; an Optional wrapping a Swift Range
```

NSString and Friends

NSString is the Cocoa object version of a string. NSString and Swift String are bridged to one another, and you will often move between them without thinking, passing a Swift String to Cocoa, calling Cocoa NSString methods on a Swift String, and so forth:

```
let s = "hello"
let s2 = s.capitalized
```

In that code, s is a Swift String and s2 is a Swift String, but the `capitalized` property actually belongs to Cocoa. In the course of that code, a Swift String has been bridged to NSString and passed to Cocoa, which has processed it to get the capitalized string; the capitalized string is an NSString, but it has been bridged back to a Swift String. In all likelihood, you are not conscious of the bridging; `capitalized` feels like a native String property, but it isn't — as you can readily prove by trying to use it in an environment where Foundation is not imported.

In some cases, Swift may fail to cross the bridge implicitly for you, and you will need to cast explicitly. If s is a Swift string, you can't call `appendingPathExtension` on it directly:

```
let s = "MyFile"
let s2 = s.appendingPathExtension("txt") // compile error
```

You have to cast explicitly to NSString:

```
let s2 = (s as NSString).appendingPathExtension("txt")
```

Similarly, to use NSString's `substring(to:)`, you must cast the String to an NSString beforehand:

```
let s2 = (s as NSString).substring(to:4)
```

In this situation, however, we can stay entirely within the Swift world by calling `prefix`, which is a native Swift method, not a Foundation method; delightfully, it takes an Int, not a String.Index:

```
let s2 = s.prefix(4)
```

However, those two calls are not equivalent: they can give different answers! The reason is that String and NSString have fundamentally different notions of what constitutes an element of a string (see "The String–NSString Element Mismatch" on page 97). A String must resolve its elements into characters, which means that it must walk the string, coalescing any combining codepoints; an NSString behaves as if it were an array of UTF-16 codepoints. On the Swift side, each increment in a String.Index corresponds to a true character, but access by index or range requires walking the string; on the Cocoa side, access by index or range is extremely fast, but might not correspond to character boundaries. (See the "Characters and Grapheme Clusters" chapter of Apple's *String Programming Guide* in the documentation archive.)

Another important difference between a Swift String and a Cocoa NSString is that an NSString is immutable. This means that, with NSString, you can do things such as obtain a new string based on the first — as `capitalized` and `substring(to:)` do — but you can't change the string *in place*. To do that, you need another class, a subclass of NSString, NSMutableString. Swift String isn't bridged to NSMutableString, so you can't get from String to NSMutableString merely by casting. To obtain an NSMutableString, you'll have to make one. The simplest way to do that is with

NSMutableString's initializer `init(string:)`, which expects an NSString — meaning that you can pass a Swift String. Coming back the other way, you can cast all the way from NSMutableString to a Swift String in one move, because an NSMutableString is an NSString:

```
let s = "hello"
let ms = NSMutableString(string:s)
ms.deleteCharacters(in:NSRange(location: ms.length-1, length:1))
let s2 = (ms as String) + "ion" // now s2 is a Swift String, "hellion"
```

As I said in Chapter 3, native Swift String methods are thin on the ground. All the real string-processing power lives over on the Cocoa side of the bridge. So you're going to be crossing that bridge a lot! And this will not be only for the power of the NSString and NSMutableString classes. Many other useful classes are associated with them. Suppose you want to search a string for some substring; all the best ways come from Cocoa:

- An NSString can be searched using various `range` methods, with numerous options such as ignoring diacriticals, ignoring case, and searching backward.

- Perhaps you don't know exactly what you're looking for: you need to describe it structurally. A Scanner (Objective-C NSScanner) lets you walk through a string looking for pieces that fit certain criteria; for example, with Scanner (and CharacterSet, Objective-C NSCharacterSet) you can skip past everything in a string that precedes a number and then extract the number.

- By specifying the `.regularExpression` search option, you can search using a regular expression. Regular expressions are also supported as a separate class, NSRegularExpression, which in turn uses NSTextCheckingResult to describe match results.

- More sophisticated automated textual analysis is supported by some additional classes, such as NSDataDetector, an NSRegularExpression subclass that efficiently finds certain types of string expression such as a URL or a phone number.

In this example, our goal is to replace all occurrences of the word "hell" with the word "heaven." We don't want to replace mere occurrences of the *substring* "hell" — the word "hello" should be left intact. Clearly our search needs some intelligence as to what constitutes a word boundary. That sounds like a job for a regular expression. Swift doesn't have regular expressions, so the work has to be done by Cocoa:

```
var s = "hello world, go to hell"
let r = try! NSRegularExpression(
    pattern: #"\bhell\b"#,
    options: .caseInsensitive)
s = r.stringByReplacingMatches(
```

```
        in: s,
        range: NSRange(s.startIndex..., in:s),
        withTemplate: "heaven")
    // s is "hello world, go to heaven"
```

NSString also has convenience utilities for working with a file path string, and is often used in conjunction with URL (Objective-C NSURL), which is another Foundation type worth looking into, along with its companion types, URLComponents (Objective-C NSURLComponents) and URLQueryItem (Objective-C NSURLQueryItem). In addition, NSString — like some other classes discussed in this section — provides methods for writing out to a file's contents or reading in a file's contents; the file can be specified either as a string file path or as a URL.

An NSString carries no font and size information. Interface objects that display strings (such as UILabel) have a `font` property that is a UIFont; but this determines the *single* font and size in which the string will display. If you want styled text — where different runs of text have different style attributes (size, font, color, and so forth) — you need to use NSAttributedString, along with its supporting classes NSMutableAttributedString, NSParagraphStyle, and NSMutableParagraphStyle. These allow you to style text and paragraphs easily in sophisticated ways. The built-in interface objects that display text can display an attributed string.

String drawing in a graphics context can be performed with methods provided through the NSStringDrawing category on NSString and on NSAttributedString.

NSDate and Friends

A Date (Objective-C NSDate) is a date and time, represented internally as a number of seconds since some reference date. Calling Date's initializer `init()` — that is, saying `Date()` — gives you a Date object for the current date and time. Many date operations will also involve the use of DateComponents (Objective-C NSDateComponents), and conversions between Date and DateComponents require use of a Calendar (Objective-C NSCalendar). Here's an example of constructing a date based on its calendrical values:

```
let greg = Calendar(identifier:.gregorian)
let comp = DateComponents(calendar: greg,
    year: 2020, month: 8, day: 10, hour: 15)
let d = comp.date // Optional wrapping Date
```

Similarly, DateComponents provides the correct way to do date arithmetic. Here's how to add one month to a given date:

```
let d = Date() // or whatever
let comp = DateComponents(month:1)
let greg = Calendar(identifier:.gregorian)
let d2 = greg.date(byAdding: comp, to:d) // Optional wrapping Date
```

Because a Date is essentially a wrapper for a TimeInterval (a Double), Swift can overload the arithmetic operators so that you can do arithmetic directly on a Date:

```
let d = Date()
let d2 = d + 4 // 4 seconds later
```

You can express the range between two dates as a DateInterval (Objective-C NSDate-Interval). DateIntervals can be compared, intersected, and checked for containment:

```
let greg = Calendar(identifier:.gregorian)
let d1 = DateComponents(calendar: greg,
    year: 2020, month: 1, day: 1, hour: 0).date!
let d2 = DateComponents(calendar: greg,
    year: 2020, month: 8, day: 10, hour: 15).date!
let di = DateInterval(start: d1, end: d2)
if di.contains(Date()) { // are we currently between those two dates?
```

You will also likely be concerned with dates represented as strings. If you don't take explicit charge of a date's string representation, it is represented by a string whose format may surprise you. If you simply print a Date, you are shown the date in the GMT timezone, which can be confusing if that isn't where you live. A simple solution when you're just logging to the console is to call description(with:), whose parameter is a Locale (Objective-C NSLocale) comprising the user's current time zone, language, region format, and calendar settings:

```
print(d)
// 2020-08-10 22:00:00 +0000
print(d.description(with:Locale.current))
// Monday, August 10, 2020 at 3:00:00 PM Pacific Daylight Time
```

For full control over date strings, especially when presenting them to the user, use DateFormatter (Objective-C NSDateFormatter), which takes a format string describing how the date string is laid out:

```
let df = DateFormatter()
df.dateFormat = "M/d/y"
let s = df.string(from: Date())
// 7/6/2020
```

For the date format string notation, see Appendix F of *Unicode Technical Report 35*.

DateFormatter knows how to make a date string that conforms to the user's local conventions. In this example, we call the class method dateFormat(from-Template:options:locale:) with the current locale as configured on the user's device. The template: is a string listing the date components to be used, but their order, punctuation, and language are left up to the locale:

```
let df = DateFormatter()
let format = DateFormatter.dateFormat(
    fromTemplate:"dMMMMyyyyhmmaz", options:0,
    locale:Locale.current)
df.dateFormat = format
let s = df.string(from:Date())
```

The result is that the date is shown in the user's time zone and language, using the correct linguistic conventions. That involves a combination of region format and language, which are two separate settings:

- On my device, the result might be "July 9, 2020, 12:34 PM PDT."
- If I change my device's *region* to France, it might be "9 July 2020 at 12:34 pm GMT-7."
- If I also change my device's *language* to French, and if my app is localized for French, it might be "9 juillet 2020 à 12:34 PM UTC–7."

DateFormatter can also parse a date string into a Date — but be sure that the date format is correct. This attempt to parse a string will fail, because the date format doesn't match the way the string is constructed:

```
let df = DateFormatter()
df.locale = Locale(identifier: "en_US_POSIX")
df.dateFormat = "M/d/y"
let d = df.date(from: "14/7/2020") // nil; should have been "d/M/y"
```

 Setting the Locale to "en_US_POSIX" guarantees that we will override the device's settings. Forgetting to do this, and then wondering why parsing a string into a Date fails on some devices, is a common beginner error, particularly when you were expecting 12-hour vs. 24-hour time formatting.

NSNumber

An NSNumber is an object that wraps a numeric value. The wrapped value can be any standard Objective-C numeric type (including BOOL, the Objective-C equivalent of Swift Bool). In Swift, everything is an object — a number is a Struct instance — so it comes as a surprise to Swift users that NSNumber is needed. But an ordinary number in Objective-C is a scalar, not an object, so it cannot be used where an object is expected; and an object cannot be used where a number is expected. Thus, NSNumber solves an important problem for Objective-C, converting a number into an object and back again.

Swift does its best to shield you from having to deal directly with NSNumber. It bridges Swift numeric types to Objective-C in two different ways:

As a scalar

   If Objective-C expects an ordinary number, a Swift number is bridged to an ordinary number (a scalar):

```
UIView.animate(withDuration: 1,
    animations: whatToAnimate, completion: whatToDoLater)
```

Objective-C `animateWithDuration:animations:completion:` takes a C double as its first parameter. The Swift numeric object that you supply as the first argument to `animate(withDuration:animations:completion:)` becomes a C double.

As an NSNumber

If Objective-C expects an object, a Swift numeric type is bridged to an NSNumber (including Bool, because NSNumber can wrap an Objective-C BOOL):

```
UserDefaults.standard.set(1, forKey:"Score")
```

Objective-C `setObject:forKey:` takes an Objective-C object as its first parameter. The Swift numeric object that you supply as the first argument to `set(_:forKey:)` becomes an NSNumber.

Naturally, if you need to cross the bridge explicitly, you can. You can cast a Swift number to an NSNumber:

```
let n = 1 as NSNumber
```

Coming back from Objective-C to Swift, an NSNumber (or an Any that is actually an NSNumber) can be unwrapped by casting it down to a numeric type — provided the wrapped numeric value matches the type. To illustrate, I'll fetch the NSNumber that I created in UserDefaults by bridging a moment ago:

```
let n = UserDefaults.standard.value(forKey:"Score")
// n is an Optional<Any> containing an NSNumber
let i = n as! Int // legal
let d = n as! Double // legal
```

An NSNumber object is just a wrapper and no more. It can't be used directly for numeric calculations; it isn't a number. It *wraps* a number. One way or another, if you want a number, you have to extract it from the NSNumber.

An NSNumber subclass, NSDecimalNumber, on the other hand, *can* be used in calculations, thanks to a bunch of arithmetic methods:

```
let dec1 = 4.0 as NSDecimalNumber
let dec2 = 5.0 as NSDecimalNumber
let sum = dec1.adding(dec2) // 9.0
```

Underlying NSDecimalNumber is the Decimal struct (Objective-C NSDecimal); it is an NSDecimalNumber's `decimalValue`. In Objective-C, NSDecimal comes with C functions that are faster than NSDecimalNumber methods. In Swift, things are even better, because the arithmetic operators are overloaded to allow you to do Decimal arithmetic; you are likely to prefer working with Decimal rather than NSDecimal-Number:

```
let dec1 = Decimal(4.0)
let dec2 = Decimal(5.0)
let sum = dec1 + dec2
```

Why does Decimal exist? Well, a computer thinks in binary, and native numeric types are stored in a base-2 representation. When there are digits after the decimal point, the results of an arithmetic operation may not appear quite as you would expect:

```
let d1 = 0.2222
let d2 = 0.2221
let diff = d1 - d2 // 0.0001000000000000167
```

(The reasons for that kind of result are explained in a classic exposition entitled *What Every Computer Scientist Should Know About Floating-Point Arithmetic*.)

Decimal, on the other hand, represents base-10 numbers, and its operations are base-10 operations:

```
let dec1 = Decimal(d1) // 0.2222
let dec2 = Decimal(d2) // 0.2221
let decDiff = dec1 - dec2 // 0.0001
let diff = NSDecimalNumber(decimal: decDiff).doubleValue // 0.0001
```

But of course Decimal operations are much slower than normal arithmetic operations! So you'll use them only when you have to.

NSValue

NSValue is NSNumber's superclass. It is used for wrapping nonnumeric C values, such as C structs, where an object is expected. The problem being solved here is parallel to the problem solved by NSNumber: a Swift struct is an object, but a C struct is not, so a struct cannot be used in Objective-C where an object is expected, and *vice versa*.

Convenience methods provided through the NSValueUIGeometryExtensions category on NSValue allow easy wrapping and unwrapping of such common structs as CGPoint, CGSize, CGRect, CGAffineTransform, UIEdgeInsets, and UIOffset:

```
let pt = self.oldButtonCenter // a CGPoint
let val = NSValue(cgPoint:pt)
```

Additional categories allow easy wrapping and unwrapping of NSRange, CATransform3D, CMTime, CMTimeMapping, CMTimeRange, MKCoordinate, and MKCoordinateSpan (and you are unlikely to need to store any other kind of C value in an NSValue, but if you do need to, you can).

But you will rarely need to deal with NSValue explicitly, because Swift will wrap any of those common structs in an NSValue for you as it crosses the bridge from Swift to Objective-C. Here's an example from my own real-life code:

```
let pt = CGPoint(
    x: screenbounds.midX + r * cos(rads),
    y: screenbounds.midY + r * sin(rads)
)
// apply an animation of ourself to that point
let anim = CABasicAnimation(keyPath:"position")
anim.fromValue = self.position
anim.toValue = pt
```

In that code, `self.position` and `pt` are both CGPoints. The CABasicAnimation properties `fromValue` and `toValue` need to be Objective-C objects (that is, class instances) so that Cocoa can obey them to perform the animation. It is therefore necessary to wrap `self.position` and `pt` as NSValue objects. But *you* don't have to do that; Swift wraps those CGPoints as NSValue objects for you, Cocoa is able to interpret and obey them, and the animation works correctly.

The same thing is true of an array of common structs. Again, animation is a case in point. If you assign an array of CGPoint to a CAKeyframeAnimation's `values` property, the animation will work properly, without your having to map the CGPoints to NSValues first. That's because Swift maps them for you as the array crosses the bridge.

NSData

Data (Objective-C NSData) is a general sequence of bytes (UInt8); basically, it's just a buffer, a chunk of memory. In Objective-C, NSData is immutable; the mutable version is its subclass NSMutableData. In Swift, however, where Data is a bridged value type imposed in front of NSData, a Data object is mutable if it was declared with `var`, just like any other value type. Moreover, because a Data object represents a byte sequence, Swift makes it a Collection (and therefore a Sequence), causing Swift features such as enumeration with `for...in`, subscripting, and `append(_:)` to spring to life. Thus, although you can work with NSData and NSMutableData if you want to (by casting to cross the bridge), you are much more likely to prefer Data.

In practice, Data tends to arise in two main ways:

When downloading from the internet
    URLSession (Objective-C NSURLSession) supplies whatever it retrieves from the internet as Data. Transforming it from there into (let's say) a string, specifying the correct encoding, would then be up to you.

When serializing an object
    A typical use case is that you're storing an object as a file or in user preferences (UserDefaults). You can't store a UIColor value directly into user preferences. So if the user has made a color choice and you need to save it, you transform the UIColor into a Data object (using NSKeyedArchiver) and save that:

```
let ud = UserDefaults.standard
let c = UIColor.blue
let cdata = try! NSKeyedArchiver.archivedData(
    withRootObject: c, requiringSecureCoding: true)
ud.set(cdata, forKey: "myColor")
```

NSMeasurement and Friends

The Measurement type (Objective-C NSMeasurement) embodies the notion of a measurement by some unit (Unit, Objective-C NSUnit). A unit may be along some dimension that can be expressed in different units convertible to one another; by reducing values in different units of the same dimension to a base unit, a Measurement permits you to perform arithmetic operations and conversions.

The dimensions, which are all subclasses of the (abstract) Dimension class (Objective-C NSDimension, an NSUnit subclass), have names like UnitAngle and UnitLength (Objective-C NSUnitAngle, NSUnitLength), and have class properties vending an instance corresponding to a particular unit type; UnitAngle has class properties `degrees` and `radians` and others, UnitLength has class properties `miles` and `kilometers`, and so on.

To illustrate, I'll add 5 miles to 6 kilometers:

```
let m1 = Measurement(value:5, unit: UnitLength.miles)
let m2 = Measurement(value:6, unit: UnitLength.kilometers)
let total = m1 + m2
```

The answer, `total`, is 14046.7 meters under the hood, because meters are the base unit of length. But it can be converted to any length unit:

```
let totalFeet = total.converted(to: .feet).value // 46084.9737532808
```

If your goal is to output a measurement as a user-facing string, use a Measurement-Formatter (Objective-C NSMeasurementFormatter). Its behavior is locale-dependent by default, expressing the value and the units as the user would expect:

```
let mf = MeasurementFormatter()
let s = mf.string(from:total) // "8.728 mi"
```

My code says nothing about miles, but the MeasurementFormatter outputs `"8.728 mi"` because my device is set to United States (region) and English (language). If my device is set to France (region) and French (language), the very same code outputs `"14,047 km"` — using the French decimal point notation and the French preferred unit of distance measurement.

Equality, Hashability, and Comparison

In Swift, the equality and comparison operators can be overridden for an object type that adopts Equatable and Comparable ("Operators" on page 299). But Objective-C operators are applicable only to scalars. Objective-C therefore performs comparison of object instances in a special way, and it can be useful to know about this when working with Cocoa classes.

To permit determination of whether two objects are "equal" — whatever that may mean for this object type — an Objective-C class must implement isEqual(_:), which is inherited from NSObject. Swift will help out by treating NSObject as Equatable and by permitting the use of the == operator, implicitly converting it to an isEqual(_:) call. Thus, if a class derived from NSObject implements isEqual(_:), ordinary Swift comparison will work. If an NSObject subclass *doesn't* implement isEqual(_:), it inherits NSObject's implementation, which compares the two objects for identity (like Swift's === operator).

These two Dog objects can be compared with the == operator, even though Dog does not adopt Equatable, because they derive from NSObject. Dog doesn't implement isEqual(_:), so == defaults to using NSObject's identity comparison:

```
class Dog : NSObject {
    var name : String
    var license : Int
    init(name:String, license:Int) {
        self.name = name
        self.license = license
    }
}
let d1 = Dog(name:"Fido", license:1)
let d2 = Dog(name:"Fido", license:1)
let ok = d1 == d2 // false
```

If we wanted two Dogs with the same name and license to be considered equal, we'd need to implement isEqual(_:), like this:

```
class Dog : NSObject {
    var name : String
    var license : Int
    init(name:String, license:Int) {
        self.name = name
        self.license = license
    }
    override func isEqual(_ object: Any?) -> Bool {
        if let otherdog = object as? Dog {
            return (otherdog.name == self.name &&
                otherdog.license == self.license)
        }
        return false
    }
}
let d1 = Dog(name:"Fido", license:1)
let d2 = Dog(name:"Fido", license:1)
let ok = d1 == d2 // true
```

At this point, you might be saying (thinking of "Synthesized Protocol Implementations" on page 313): "But wait, why don't you just declare Dog to adopt Equatable and get autosynthesis of equatability based on its properties?" But you can't do that. Autosynthesis of Equatable conformance doesn't work for classes, and in any case Dog is *already* Equatable by virtue of being an NSObject subclass. Besides, Equatable is about how to implement ==, whereas what we need to implement here is isEqual:.

Foundation types implement isEqual(_:) in a sensible way, so Swift equatability works as you would expect. NSNumber implements isEqual(_:) by comparing the underlying numbers; thus, you can use NSNumber where a Swift Equatable is expected, and, because a Swift number will be cast automatically to an NSNumber if needed, you can even compare an NSNumber to a Swift number:

```
let n1 = 1 as NSNumber
let n2 = 2 as NSNumber
let n3 = 3 as NSNumber
let ok = n2 == 2 // true
let ix = [n1,n2,n3].firstIndex(of:2) // Optional wrapping 1
```

By the same token, for an NSObject subclass to work properly where hashability is required — as a dictionary key or a set member, even if this is a Swift Dictionary or Set — it must conform to the NSObject notion of hashability, namely, an implementation of isEqual(_:) plus a corresponding override of the NSObject hash property, meaning that two equal objects should have equal hash values. If we wanted our Dog from the previous code to be usable in a Set, we'd need to override hash; that would be tricky to implement on our own, but fortunately the Hasher struct (introduced in Swift 4.2) makes it easy:

```
class Dog : NSObject {
    var name : String
    var license : Int
    init(name:String, license:Int) {
        self.name = name
        self.license = license
    }
    override func isEqual(_ object: Any?) -> Bool {
        if let otherdog = object as? Dog {
            return (otherdog.name == self.name &&
                otherdog.license == self.license)
        }
        return false
    }
    override var hash: Int {
        var h = Hasher()
        h.combine(self.name)
        h.combine(self.license)
        return h.finalize()
    }
}
```

```
var set = Set<Dog>()
set.insert(Dog(name:"Fido", license:1))
set.insert(Dog(name:"Fido", license:1))
print(set.count) // 1
```

Foundation types come with a built-in `hash` implementation (and the Swift overlay types are all both Equatable and Hashable as well).

In Objective-C it is also up to individual classes to supply ordered comparison methods. The standard method is `compare(_:)`, which returns one of three cases of ComparisonResult (Objective-C NSComparisonResult):

`.orderedAscending`
> The receiver is less than the argument.

`.orderedSame`
> The receiver is equal to the argument.

`.orderedDescending`
> The receiver is greater than the argument.

Swift comparison operators (< and so forth) do *not* magically call `compare(_:)` for you. You can't compare two NSNumber values directly:

```
let n1 = 1 as NSNumber
let n2 = 2 as NSNumber
let ok = n1 < n2 // compile error
```

You will typically fall back on calling `compare(_:)` yourself:

```
let n1 = 1 as NSNumber
let n2 = 2 as NSNumber
let ok = n1.compare(n2) == .orderedAscending // true
```

On the other hand, a Swift Foundation overlay type *can* adopt Comparable, and in that case comparison operators *do* work. You can't use the < operator to compare two NSDate values, but you *can* use it to compare two Date values.

NSArray and NSMutableArray

NSArray is Objective-C's array object type. It is fundamentally similar to Swift Array, and they are bridged to one another; but NSArray elements must be objects (classes and class instances), and they don't have to be of a single type. For a full discussion of how to bridge back and forth between Swift Array and Objective-C NSArray, implicitly and by casting, see "Swift Array and Objective-C NSArray" on page 243.

An NSArray's length is its `count`, and an element can be obtained by index number using `object(at:)`. The index of the first element, as with a Swift Array, is zero, so the index of the last element is `count` minus one.

Instead of calling `object(at:)`, you can use subscripting with an NSArray. This is not because NSArray is bridged to Swift Array, but because NSArray implements an Objective-C method, `objectAtIndexedSubscript:`, which is the Objective-C equivalent of a Swift `subscript` getter. In fact, when you examine the NSArray header file translated into Swift, that method is shown as a `subscript` declaration!

You can seek an object within an array with `index(of:)` or `indexOfObject-Identical(to:)`; the former's idea of equality is to call `isEqual(_:)`, whereas the latter uses object identity (like Swift's `===`). If the object is not found in the array, the result is `NSNotFound`.

Like an Objective-C NSString, an NSArray is immutable. This doesn't mean you can't mutate any of the objects it contains; it means that once the NSArray is formed you can't remove an object from it, insert an object into it, or replace an object at a given index. To do those things while staying in the Objective-C world, you can derive a new array consisting of the original array plus or minus some objects, or use NSArray's subclass, NSMutableArray.

Swift Array is not bridged to NSMutableArray; if you want an NSMutableArray, you must create it. The simplest way is with the NSMutableArray initializers, `init()` or `init(array:)`. Once you have an NSMutableArray, you can call methods such as `insert(_:at:)` and `replaceObject(at:with:)`. You can also assign into an NSMutableArray using subscripting. Again, this is because NSMutableArray implements a special Objective-C method, `setObject:atIndexedSubscript:`; Swift recognizes this as equivalent to a `subscript` setter.

Coming back the other way, you can cast an NSMutableArray down to a Swift array:

```
let marr = NSMutableArray()
marr.add(1) // an NSNumber
marr.add(2) // an NSNumber
let arr = marr as NSArray as! [Int]
```

Cocoa provides ways to sort an array, as well as to search or filter an array by passing a function. You might prefer to perform those kinds of operation in the Swift Array world, but it can be useful to know how to do them the Cocoa way:

```
let pep = ["Manny", "Moe", "Jack"] as NSArray
let ems = pep.objects(
    at: pep.indexesOfObjects { obj, idx, stop -> Bool in
        return (obj as! NSString).range(
            of: "m", options:.caseInsensitive
            ).location == 0
    }
) // ["Manny", "Moe"]
```

NSDictionary and NSMutableDictionary

NSDictionary is Objective-C's dictionary object type. It is fundamentally similar to Swift Dictionary, and they are bridged to one another. But NSDictionary keys and values must be objects (classes and class instances), and they don't have to be of a single type; the keys must conform to NSCopying and must be hashable. See "Swift Dictionary and Objective-C NSDictionary" on page 251 for a full discussion of how to bridge back and forth between Swift Dictionary and Objective-C NSDictionary, including casting.

An NSDictionary is immutable; its mutable subclass is NSMutableDictionary. Swift Dictionary is not bridged to NSMutableDictionary; you can most easily make an NSMutableDictionary with an initializer, `init()` or `init(dictionary:)`, and you can cast an NSMutableDictionary down to a Swift Dictionary type.

The keys of an NSDictionary are distinct (using `isEqual(_:)` for comparison). If you add a key–value pair to an NSMutableDictionary, then if that key is not already present, the pair is simply added, but if the key is already present, then the corresponding value is replaced. This is parallel to the behavior of Swift Dictionary.

The fundamental use of an NSDictionary is to request an entry's value by key (using `object(forKey:)`); if no such key exists, the result is `nil`. In Objective-C, `nil` is not an object and cannot be a value in an NSDictionary, so the meaning of this response is unambiguous. Swift handles this by treating the result of `object(forKey:)` as an Optional wrapping an Any.

Subscripting is possible on an NSDictionary or an NSMutableDictionary, for similar reasons to an NSArray or an NSMutableArray. NSDictionary implements `objectForKeyedSubscript:`, and Swift understands this as equivalent to a `subscript` getter. In addition, NSMutableDictionary implements `setObject:forKeyedSubscript:`, and Swift understands this as equivalent to a `subscript` setter.

Like a Swift Dictionary, an NSDictionary is unordered. You can get from an NSDictionary a list of keys (`allKeys`), a list of values (`allValues`), or a list of keys sorted by value. You can also walk through the key–value pairs, and you can even filter an NSDictionary by a test against its values.

NSSet and Friends

An NSSet is an unordered collection of distinct objects. Swift Set is bridged to NSSet, and the Swift Foundation overlay even allows you to initialize an NSSet from a Swift array literal. But NSSet elements must be objects (classes and class instances), and they don't have to be of a single type. For details, see "Swift Set and Objective-C NSSet" on page 257.

"Distinct" for an NSSet means that no two objects in a set can return `true` when they are compared using `isEqual(_:)`. Learning whether an object is present in a set is much more efficient than seeking it in an array (because a set's elements are hashable), and you can ask whether one set is a subset of, or intersects, another set. You can walk through (enumerate) a set with the `for...in` construct, though the order is of course undefined. You can filter a set, as you can an NSArray. Indeed, much of what you can do with a set is parallel to what you can do with an array, except that you can't do anything with a set that involves the notion of ordering.

To transcend that restriction, you can use an *ordered set*. An ordered set (NSOrderedSet) is very like an array, and the methods for working with it are similar to the methods for working with an array — you can even fetch an element by subscripting (because it implements `objectAtIndexedSubscript:`). But an ordered set's elements must be distinct. An ordered set provides many of the advantages of sets: as with an NSSet, learning whether an object is present in an ordered set is much more efficient than for an array, and you can readily take the union, intersection, or difference with another set. Since the distinctness restriction will often prove no restriction at all (because the elements were going to be distinct anyway), it can be worthwhile to use NSOrderedSet instead of NSArray where possible.

An NSSet is immutable. You can derive one NSSet from another by adding or removing elements, or you can use its subclass, NSMutableSet. Similarly, NSOrderedSet has its mutable counterpart, NSMutableOrderedSet (which you can insert into by subscripting, because it implements `setObject:atIndexedSubscript:`). There is no penalty for adding to a set an object that the set already contains; nothing is added (and so the distinctness rule is enforced), but there's no error.

NSCountedSet, a subclass of NSMutableSet, is a mutable unordered collection of objects that are *not* necessarily distinct (this concept is often referred to as a *bag*). It is implemented as a set plus a count of how many times each element has been added.

NSMutableSet, NSCountedSet, NSOrderedSet, and NSMutableOrderedSet are easily formed from a set or an array using an initializer. Coming back the other way, you can cast an NSMutableSet or NSCountedSet down to a Swift Set. Because of their special behaviors, however, you are much more likely to leave an NSCountedSet or NSOrderedSet in its Objective-C form for as long as you're working with it.

NSIndexSet

IndexSet (Objective-C NSIndexSet) represents a collection of unique whole numbers; its purpose is to express element numbers of an ordered collection, such as an array. For instance, to retrieve multiple elements simultaneously from an NSArray, you specify the desired indexes as an IndexSet. It is also used with other things that are array-like; for example, you pass an IndexSet to a UITableView to indicate what sections to insert or delete.

NSIndexSet is immutable; it has a mutable subclass, NSMutableIndexSet. But Index-Set is a value type, so it is mutable if the declaration uses `var`. And, as with other Swift types imposed in front of Foundation types, IndexSet gets to do all sorts of convenient Swift magic. Comparison and arithmetic operators work directly with IndexSet values. Even more important, an IndexSet acts like a Set: it adopts the SetAlgebra protocol, and methods like `contains(_:)` and `intersection(_:)` spring to life. You probably won't need NSMutableIndexSet at all.

To take a specific example, let's say you want to speak of the elements at indexes 1, 2, 3, 4, 8, 9, and 10 of an array. IndexSet expresses this notion in some compact implementation that can be readily queried. The actual implementation is opaque, but you can imagine that this IndexSet might consist of two Ranges, `1...4` and `8...10`, and IndexSet's methods actually invite you to think of it as a Set of Ranges:

```
let arr = ["zero", "one", "two", "three", "four", "five",
    "six", "seven", "eight", "nine", "ten"]
var ixs = IndexSet()
ixs.insert(integersIn: 1...4)
ixs.insert(integersIn: 8...10)
let arr2 = (arr as NSArray).objects(at:ixs)
// ["one", "two", "three", "four", "eight", "nine", "ten"]
```

To walk through (enumerate) the index values specified by an IndexSet, you can use `for...in`; alternatively, you can walk through an IndexSet's indexes or ranges by calling various `enumerate` methods that let you pass a function returning a Bool.

 A Swift Array cannot access elements by way of IndexSet; IndexSet is ultimately a façade for NSIndexSet, and applies only to NSArray. As of this writing, though, there's a Swift Evolution proposal for adding a true native Swift type, RangeSet, that will allow subscripting into a native Swift collection. You can try it out by way of the Standard Library Preview package, *https://github.com/apple/swift-standard-library-preview*.

NSNull

The NSNull class does nothing but supply a pointer to a singleton object, `NSNull()`. This singleton object is used to stand for `nil` in situations where an actual Objective-C object is required and `nil` is not permitted. You can't use `nil` as the value of an element of an Objective-C collection (such as NSArray, NSDictionary, or NSSet), so you'd use `NSNull()` instead.

`NSNull()` makes it possible for a Swift Array of Optional to be handed to Objective-C. The Swift Array might contain `nil`, which is illegal in Objective-C. But Swift will bridge the Array of Optional for you, as it crosses into Objective-C, by substituting `NSNull()` for any `nil` elements. And, coming back the other way, Swift will perform the inverse operation when you cast an NSArray down to an Array of Optional, substituting nil for any NSNull() elements.

You can test an object for equality against NSNull() using the ordinary equality operator (==), because it falls back on NSObject's isEqual(_:), which is identity comparison. This is a singleton instance, and therefore identity comparison works.

Immutable and Mutable

Cocoa Foundation has a pattern of class pairs where the superclass is immutable and the subclass is mutable; I've given many examples already, such as NSString and NSMutableString, or NSArray and NSMutableArray. This is similar to the Swift distinction between a constant (let) and a true variable (var). An NSArray being immutable means that you can't append or insert into this array, or replace or delete an element of this array; but if its elements are reference types — and of course, for an NSArray, they *are* reference types — you can mutate an element in place. That's just like the behavior of a Swift Array referred to with let.

The reason why Cocoa needs these immutable/mutable pairs is to prevent unauthorized mutation. An NSString object, say, is an ordinary class instance — a reference type. If NSString were mutable, an NSString property of a class could be mutated by some other object, behind this class's back. To prevent that from happening, a class will work internally and temporarily with a mutable instance, but then store and vend to other classes an immutable instance, protecting the value from being changed by anyone else. Swift doesn't face the same issue, because its fundamental built-in object types such as String, Array, and Dictionary are structs, and therefore are value types, which cannot be mutated in place; they can be changed only by being replaced, and that is something that can be guarded against, or detected through a setter observer. NSString isn't a value *type*, but as far as mutability is concerned, it displays value *semantics* ("Value Types and Reference Types" on page 153).

The documentation may not make it completely obvious that the mutable classes obey and, if appropriate, override the methods of their immutable superclasses. Dozens of NSMutableArray methods are not listed on NSMutableArray's class documentation page, because they are inherited from NSArray. And when such methods are inherited by the mutable subclass, they may be overridden to fit the mutable subclass. NSArray's init(array:) generates an immutable array, but NSMutableArray's init(array:) — which isn't even listed on the NSMutableArray documentation page, because it is inherited from NSArray — generates a mutable array.

That fact also answers the question of how to make an immutable array mutable, and *vice versa*. This single method, init(array:), can transform an array between immutable and mutable in either direction. You can also use copy (produces an immutable copy) and mutableCopy (produces a mutable copy), both inherited from

NSObject; but these are not as convenient because they yield an Any which must then be cast.

 These immutable/mutable class pairs are all implemented as *class clusters*, which means that Cocoa uses a secret class, different from the documented class you work with. You may discover this by peeking under the hood; an NSString, for instance, might be characterized as an NSTaggedPointerString or an NSCFString. You should not spend any time wondering about this secret class. It's a mere implementation detail, and is subject to change without notice; you should never have looked at it in the first place.

Property Lists

A *property list* is a string (XML) representation of data. The Foundation classes NSString, NSData, NSArray, and NSDictionary are the only Cocoa classes that can be expressed directly in a property list. Moreover, an NSArray or NSDictionary can be expressed in a property list only if its elements are instances of those classes, along with NSDate and NSNumber. Those are the *property list types*.

(That is why, as I mentioned earlier, you must convert a UIColor into a Data object in order to store it in user defaults; the user defaults storage *is* a property list, and UIColor is not a property list type. But Data *is* a property list type, because it is bridged to NSData.)

The primary use of a property list is as a way of *serializing* a value — saving it to disk in a form from which it can be reconstructed. NSArray and NSDictionary provide write methods that generate property list files; conversely, they also provide initializers that create an NSArray object or an NSDictionary object based on the property list contents of a given file. (The NSString and NSData write methods just write the data out as a file directly, not as a property list.)

Here I'll create an array of strings and write it out to disk as a property list file:

```
let arr = ["Manny", "Moe", "Jack"]
let fm = FileManager.default
let temp = fm.temporaryDirectory
let f = temp.appendingPathComponent("pep.plist")
try! (arr as NSArray).write(to: f)
```

The result is a file that looks like this:

```
<?xml version="1.0" encoding="UTF-8"?>
<!DOCTYPE plist PUBLIC "-//Apple//DTD PLIST 1.0//EN"
    "http://www.apple.com/DTDs/PropertyList-1.0.dtd">
<plist version="1.0">
<array>
    <string>Manny</string>
```

```
    <string>Moe</string>
    <string>Jack</string>
</array>
</plist>
```

When you reconstruct an NSArray or NSDictionary object from a property list file in this way, the collections, string objects, and data objects in the collection are all immutable. If you want them to be mutable, or if you want to convert an instance of one of the other property list classes to a property list, you'll use the PropertyList-Serialization class (Objective-C NSPropertyListSerialization; see the *Property List Programming Guide* in the documentation archive).

Codable

Property lists are a Cocoa Objective-C construct, useful for serializing objects. But in Swift you can serialize an object without crossing the bridge into the Objective-C world, provided it adopts the Codable protocol. In effect, every native Swift type and every Foundation overlay type *does* adopt the Codable protocol! This means, among other things, that enums and structs can easily be serialized.

There are three main use cases, involving three pairs of classes to serialize the object and extract it again later; what you're encoding to and decoding from is a Data object:

Property lists
    Use PropertyListEncoder and PropertyListDecoder.

JSON
    Use JSONEncoder and JSONDecoder.

NSCoder
    Use NSKeyedArchiver and NSKeyedUnarchiver.

To illustrate, let's rewrite the previous example, serializing an array of strings to a property list, without casting it to an NSArray. This works because both Swift Array and Swift String adopt Codable; indeed, thanks to conditional conformance (Chapter 4), an Array is Codable only just in case its element type is Codable:

```
let arr = ["Manny", "Moe", "Jack"]
let fm = FileManager.default
let temp = fm.temporaryDirectory
let f = temp.appendingPathComponent("pep.plist")
let penc = PropertyListEncoder()
penc.outputFormat = .xml
let d = try! penc.encode(arr)
try! d.write(to: f)
```

The resulting file looks like this:

```
<?xml version="1.0" encoding="UTF-8"?>
<!DOCTYPE plist PUBLIC "-//Apple//DTD PLIST 1.0//EN"
    "http://www.apple.com/DTDs/PropertyList-1.0.dtd">
<plist version="1.0">
<array>
    <string>Manny</string>
    <string>Moe</string>
    <string>Jack</string>
</array>
</plist>
```

That example doesn't do anything that we couldn't have done with NSArray. But now consider, for instance, an index set. You can't write an NSIndexSet directly into a property list using Objective-C, because NSIndexSet is not a property list type. But the Swift Foundation overlay type, IndexSet, is Codable:

```
let penc = PropertyListEncoder()
penc.outputFormat = .xml
let d = try! penc.encode(IndexSet([1,2,3]))
```

And here's the result:

```
<?xml version="1.0" encoding="UTF-8"?>
<!DOCTYPE plist PUBLIC "-//Apple//DTD PLIST 1.0//EN"
    "http://www.apple.com/DTDs/PropertyList-1.0.dtd">
<plist version="1.0">
<dict>
    <key>indexes</key>
    <array>
        <dict>
            <key>length</key>
            <integer>3</integer>
            <key>location</key>
            <integer>1</integer>
        </dict>
    </array>
</dict>
</plist>
```

Notice how cleverly Swift has encoded this object. You can't put an IndexSet into a property list — but this property list doesn't contain any IndexSet! It is composed entirely of legal property list types — a dictionary containing an array of dictionaries whose values are numbers. And Swift can extract the encoded object from the property list:

```
let ix = try! PropertyListDecoder().decode(IndexSet.self, from: d)
// [1,2,3]
```

Your own custom types can adopt Codable and make themselves encodable in the same way. In fact, in the simplest case, adopting Codable is *all* you have to do! If the type's properties are themselves Codable, the right thing will happen automatically. The Codable protocol has two required methods, but we don't have to implement them because default implementations are synthesized (see "Synthesized Protocol Implementations" on page 313) — though we *could* implement them if we wanted to customize the details of encoding and decoding.

Here's a simple Person struct:

```
struct Person : Codable {
    let firstName : String
    let lastName : String
}
```

Person adopts Codable, so with no further effort we can turn a Person into a property list:

```
let p = Person(firstName: "Matt", lastName: "Neuburg")
let penc = PropertyListEncoder()
penc.outputFormat = .xml
let d = try! penc.encode(p)
```

Here's our encoded Person:

```
<?xml version="1.0" encoding="UTF-8"?>
<!DOCTYPE plist PUBLIC "-//Apple//DTD PLIST 1.0//EN"
    "http://www.apple.com/DTDs/PropertyList-1.0.dtd">
<plist version="1.0">
<dict>
    <key>firstName</key>
    <string>Matt</string>
    <key>lastName</key>
    <string>Neuburg</string>
</dict>
</plist>
```

Observe that this would work just as well for, say, an array of Person, or a dictionary with Person values, or any Codable struct with a Person property.

UserDefaults is a property list, so an object that isn't a property list type must be archived to a Data object in order to store it in UserDefaults. A PropertyListEncoder creates a Data object, so we can use it to store a Person object in UserDefaults:

```
let ud = UserDefaults.standard
let p = Person(firstName: "Matt", lastName: "Neuburg")
let pdata = try! PropertyListEncoder().encode(p)
ud.set(pdata, forKey: "person")
```

Encoding as JSON is similar to encoding as a property list:

```
let p = Person(firstName: "Matt", lastName: "Neuburg")
let jenc = JSONEncoder()
jenc.outputFormatting = .prettyPrinted
let d = try! jenc.encode(p)
print(String(data:d, encoding:.utf8)!)
/*
{
```

```
        "firstName" : "Matt",
        "lastName" : "Neuburg"
    }
*/
```

The final use case is encoding or decoding through an NSCoder. There are various situations where Cocoa lends you an NSCoder object and invites you to put some data into it or pull some data out of it. The NSCoder in question will be either an NSKeyedArchiver, when you're encoding, or an NSKeyedUnarchiver, when you're decoding. These subclasses, respectively, provide methods encodeEncodable(_:for-Key:), which takes a Codable object, and decodeDecodable(_:forKey:), which produces a Codable object. Thus, your Codable adopters can pass into and out of an archive by way of NSCoder.

As I mentioned earlier, your Codable adopter can take more control of the encoding and decoding process. You can map between your object's property names and the encoded key names by adding a CodingKeys enum, and you can provide an explicit implementation of the encode(to:) and decode(from:) methods instead of letting them be synthesized for you. For more information, consult the help document "Encoding and Decoding Custom Types."

Accessors, Properties, and Key–Value Coding

An Objective-C instance variable is structurally similar to a Swift instance property: it's a variable that accompanies each instance of a class, with a lifetime and value associated with that particular instance. An Objective-C instance variable, however, is usually private, in the sense that instances of other classes can't see it (and Swift can't see it). If an instance variable is to be made public, an Objective-C class will typically implement *accessor methods*: a getter method and (if this instance variable is to be publicly writable) a setter method. This is such a common thing to do that there are naming conventions:

The getter method
> A getter should have the same name as the instance variable (without an initial underscore if the instance variable has one). If the instance variable is named myVar (or _myVar), the getter method should be named myVar.

The setter method
> A setter method's name should start with set, followed by a capitalized version of the instance variable's name (without an initial underscore if the instance variable has one). The setter should take one parameter — the new value to be assigned to the instance variable. If the instance variable is named myVar (or _myVar), the setter should be named setMyVar:.

This pattern — a getter method, possibly accompanied by an appropriately named setter method — is so common that the Objective-C language provides a shorthand: a class can declare a *property*, using the keyword `@property` and a name. Here's a line from the UIView class declaration in Objective-C (ignore the material in the parentheses):

```
@property(nonatomic) CGRect frame;
```

This declaration constitutes a promise that there is a getter accessor method `frame` returning a CGRect, along with a setter accessor method `setFrame:` that takes a CGRect parameter.

When Objective-C formally declares a `@property` in this way, *Swift sees it as a Swift property*. UIView's `frame` property declaration is translated directly into a Swift declaration of an instance property `frame` of type CGRect:

```
var frame: CGRect
```

An Objective-C property name, however, is mere syntactic sugar; Objective-C objects do not really "have" properties. When you apparently set a UIView's `frame` property, you are actually calling its `setFrame:` setter method, and when you apparently get a UIView's `frame` property, you are actually calling its `frame` getter method. In Objective-C, use of the property is optional; Objective-C code can, and often does, call the `setFrame:` and `frame` methods *directly*. But you can't do that in Swift! If an Objective-C class has a formal `@property` declaration, *the accessor methods are hidden from Swift*.

An Objective-C property declaration can include the word `readonly` in the parentheses. This indicates that there is a getter but no setter:

```
@property(nonatomic,readonly,strong) CALayer *layer;
```

(Ignore the other material in the parentheses.) Swift will reflect this restriction with `{get}` after the declaration, as if this were a computed read-only property; the compiler will not permit you to assign to such a property:

```
var layer: CALayer { get }
```

Although Objective-C accessor methods may literally be ways of accessing an invisible instance variable, they don't have to be. When you set a UIView's `frame` property and the `setFrame:` accessor method is called, you have no way of knowing what that method is really doing: it might be setting an instance variable called `frame` or `_frame`, but who knows? In this sense, accessors and properties are a façade, hiding the underlying implementation. This is similar to how, within Swift, you can set a variable without knowing or caring whether it is a stored variable or a computed variable (and, if it is a computed variable, without knowing what its getter and setter functions really do).

Swift Accessors

Just as Objective-C properties are actually a shorthand for accessor methods, so Objective-C treats Swift properties as a shorthand for accessor methods — even though no such methods are formally present. If you, in Swift, declare that a class has a property prop, Objective-C can call a prop method to get its value or a setProp: method to set its value, *even though you have not implemented such methods*. Those calls are routed to your property through *implicit* accessor methods.

In Swift, you should *not* write *explicit* accessor methods for a property; the compiler will stop you if you attempt to do so. If you need to implement an accessor method explicitly and formally, use a computed property. Here I'll add to my UIView-Controller subclass a computed color property with a getter and a setter:

```
class ViewController: UIViewController {
    @objc var color : UIColor {
        get {
            print("someone called the getter")
            return .red
        }
        set {
            print("someone called the setter")
        }
    }
}
```

Objective-C code can now call explicitly the implicit setColor: and color accessor methods — and when it does, the computed property's setter and getter methods are in fact called:

```
ViewController* vc = [ViewController new];
[vc setColor:[UIColor redColor]]; // "someone called the setter"
UIColor* c = [vc color]; // "someone called the getter"
```

This proves that, in Objective-C's mind, you *have* provided setColor: and color accessor methods.

You can even *change* the Objective-C names of accessor methods! To do so, follow the @objc attribute with the Objective-C name in parentheses. You can add it to a computed property's setter and getter methods, or you can add it to a property itself:

```
@objc(hue) var color : UIColor?
```

Objective-C code can now call hue and setHue: accessor methods directly.

If, in speaking to Objective-C, you need to pass a selector for an accessor method, precede the contents of the #selector expression with getter: or setter:. For example, #selector(setter:color) is "setHue:" if we have modified our color property's Objective-C name with @objc(hue) (or "setColor:" if we have not).

If all you want to do is add functionality to the setter, use a setter observer. To add functionality to the Objective-C setFrame: method in your UIView subclass, you can override the frame property and write a didSet observer:

```
class MyView: UIView {
    override var frame : CGRect {
        didSet {
            print("the frame setter was called: \(super.frame)")
        }
    }
}
```

Key–Value Coding

Cocoa can dynamically call an accessor method, or access an instance variable, based on a string name specified at runtime, through a mechanism called *key–value coding* (KVC). The string name is the *key*; what is passed or returned is the *value*. The basis for key–value coding is the NSKeyValueCoding protocol, an informal protocol; it is actually a category injected into NSObject. A Swift class, to be susceptible to key–value coding, must therefore be derived from NSObject.

The fundamental Cocoa key–value coding methods are setValue(_:forKey:) and value(forKey:). When one of these methods is called on an object, the object is introspected. In simplified terms, first the appropriate accessor method is sought; if it doesn't exist, the instance variable is accessed directly. The value can be an Objective-C object of any type, so its Objective-C type is id; therefore it is typed in Swift as Any. Whatever you pass into setValue(_:forKey:) will cross the bridge from Swift to Objective-C. Coming back the other way, when calling value(for-Key:), you'll receive an Optional wrapping an Any; you'll want to cast this down safely to its expected type.

A class is *key–value coding compliant* (or *KVC compliant*) on a given key if it provides the accessor methods, or possesses the instance variable, required for access through that key. An attempt to access a key for which a class is *not* key–value coding compliant will likely cause a crash at runtime. It is useful to be familiar with the message you'll get when such a crash occurs, so let's cause it deliberately:

```
let obj = NSObject()
obj.setValue("hello", forKey:"keyName") // crash
```

The console says: "This class is not key value coding-compliant for the key key-Name." The last word in that error message is the key string that caused the trouble.

What would it take for that method call *not* to crash? The class of the object to which it is sent would need to have a setKeyName: setter method, or a keyName or _keyName instance variable. In Swift, as I demonstrated in the previous section, an instance property implies the existence of accessor methods. So we can use Cocoa key–value coding on an instance of any NSObject subclass that has a declared property, provided the key string is the string name of that property. Let's try it! Here is such a class:

```
class Dog : NSObject {
    @objc var name : String = ""
}
```

And here's our test:

```
let d = Dog()
d.setValue("Fido", forKey:"name") // no crash!
print(d.name) // "Fido" - it worked!
```

How Outlets Work

Key–value coding lies at the heart of how outlet connections work (Chapter 7). Suppose that you have a class Dog with an @IBOutlet property master typed as Person, and you've drawn a "master" outlet from a Dog object in the nib to a Person object in the nib. The name of that outlet, "master", is just a string. When the nib loads, the outlet name "master" is translated *through key–value coding* to the accessor method name setMaster:, and your Dog instance's setMaster: implicit accessor method is called with the Person instance as its parameter, setting the value of your Dog instance's master property to the Person instance (Figure 7-8).

If something goes wrong with the match between the outlet name in the nib and the name of the property in the class, then at runtime, when the nib loads, Cocoa's attempt to use key–value coding to set a value in your object based on the name of the outlet will fail, and your app will crash — with an error message complaining (you guessed it) that the class is not key–value coding compliant for the key. (The key here is the outlet name.) A likely way for this to happen is that you formed the outlet correctly but then later changed the name of (or deleted) the property in the class; see "Misconfigured Outlets" on page 393.

Cocoa Key Paths

A Cocoa *key path* allows you to chain keys in a single expression. If an object is key–value coding compliant for a certain key, and if the value of that key is itself an object that is key–value coding compliant for another key, you can chain those keys by calling value(forKeyPath:) and setValue(_:forKeyPath:).

A key path string looks like a succession of key names joined using dot-notation. valueForKeyPath("key1.key2") effectively calls value(forKey:) on the message receiver, with "key1" as the key, and then takes the object returned from that call and calls value(forKey:) on that object, with "key2" as the key.

To illustrate, here are two classes that form a chain of properties — a DogOwner that has a dog property which is a Dog that has a name property:

```
class Dog : NSObject {
    @objc var name : String = ""
}
class DogOwner : NSObject {
    @objc var dog : Dog?
}
```

Now let's configure an actual chain:

```
let owner = DogOwner()
let dog = Dog()
dog.name = "Fido"
owner.dog = dog
```

Now we can use key–value coding with a key path to work our way down the chain:

```
if let name = owner.value(forKeyPath:"dog.name") as? String {
```

We retrieve the value as an Optional wrapping an Any which is actually a string, and we cast down safely to retrieve the real value, "Fido".

Uses of Key–Value Coding

Cocoa key–value coding allows you, in effect, to decide at runtime, based on a string, what accessor to call. In the simplest case, you're using a string to access a dynamically specified property. That's useful in Objective-C code; but such unfettered introspective dynamism is contrary to the spirit of Swift, and in translating my own Objective-C code into Swift I have generally found myself accomplishing the same ends by other means.

Nevertheless, key–value coding remains useful in programming iOS, especially because a number of built-in Cocoa classes permit you to use it in special ways:

- If you send value(forKey:) to an NSArray, it sends value(forKey:) to each of its elements and returns a new array consisting of the results, an elegant shorthand. NSSet behaves similarly.

- NSDictionary implements value(forKey:) as an alternative to object(forKey:) (useful particularly if you have an NSArray of dictionaries). Similarly, NSMutableDictionary treats setValue(_:forKey:) as a synonym for set(_:forKey:), except that the first parameter can be nil, in which case removeObject(forKey:) is called.

- NSSortDescriptor sorts an NSArray by sending value(forKey:) to each of its elements. This makes it easy to sort an array of dictionaries on the value of a particular dictionary key, or an array of objects on the value of a particular property.

- NSManagedObject, used in conjunction with Core Data, is guaranteed to be key–value coding compliant for attributes you've configured in the entity model. It's common to access those attributes with `value(forKey:)` and `setValue(_:forKey:)`.

- CALayer and CAAnimation permit you to use key–value coding to define and retrieve the values for *arbitrary* keys, as if they were a kind of dictionary; they are, in effect, key–value coding compliant for *every key*. This is extremely helpful for attaching extra information to an instance of one of these classes.

Also, many Cocoa APIs use key–value coding indirectly: you supply a key string, and Cocoa applies it for you. For example, a CABasicAnimation must be initialized with a `keyPath` string parameter:

```
let anim = CABasicAnimation(keyPath:"transform")
```

What you're really doing here is telling the animation that you're going to want to animate a CALayer's `transform` property. Similarly, the AV Foundation framework, used in conjunction with videos, takes string keys to specify properties whose value you're going to be interested in:

```
let url = Bundle.main.url(forResource:"ElMirage", withExtension:"mp4")!
let asset = AVURLAsset(url:url)
asset.loadValuesAsynchronously(forKeys:["tracks"]) {
```

That works because an AVURLAsset has a `tracks` property.

KeyPath Notation

Using key–value coding can be dangerous, because you risk using a key for which the target object is not key–value coding compliant. But Swift can often provide some measure of safety. Instead of forming the key string yourself, you ask the Swift compiler to form it for you. To do so, use `#keyPath` notation.

`#keyPath` notation is similar to `#selector` syntax (Chapter 2): you're asking the Swift compiler to form the key string for you, and it will refuse if it can't confirm that the key in question is legal. We crashed by saying this:

```
let obj = NSObject()
obj.setValue("hello", forKey:"keyName") // crash
```

But if we had used `#keyPath` notation, our code wouldn't have crashed — because it wouldn't even have compiled:

```
let obj = NSObject()
obj.setValue("howdy", forKey: #keyPath(NSObject.keyName)) // compile error
```

Now return to our Dog with a `name` property:

```
class Dog : NSObject {
    @objc var name : String = ""
}
```

This compiles, because Swift *knows* that Dog has a `name` property:

```
let d = Dog()
d.setValue("Fido", forKey:#keyPath(Dog.name))
```

But that code will *not* compile if Dog is not an NSObject subclass, or if its `name` property is not exposed to Objective-C. Thus the Swift compiler can often help to save us from ourselves. Some of my earlier examples can be rewritten more safely using `#key-Path` notation, and in real life, this is how I would write them:

```
let anim = CABasicAnimation(keyPath: #keyPath(CALayer.transform))
```

And:

```
let url = Bundle.main.url(forResource:"ElMirage", withExtension:"mp4")!
let asset = AVURLAsset(url:url)
let tracks = #keyPath(AVURLAsset.tracks)
asset.loadValuesAsynchronously(forKeys:[tracks]) {
```

But the compiler can't *always* save us from ourselves. There are situations where you can't form a string indirectly using `#keyPath` notation, and you'll just have to hand Cocoa a string that you form yourself. For example (`self` is a CALayer):

```
self.rotationLayer.setValue(.pi/4.0, forKeyPath:"transform.rotation.y")
```

You can't rewrite that using `#keyPath(CALayer.transform.rotation.y)`, because the compiler won't let you form that key path. The problem is that the compiler is unaware of any `rotation` property of a CALayer `transform` — because there is no such property. That sort of key path works by a special dispensation within Cocoa: CATransform3D (the type of a CALayer's `transform`) is key–value coding compliant for a repertoire of keys and key paths that don't correspond to any actual properties, and Swift has no way of knowing that.

You may be wondering how all of this relates to Swift's own key path mechanism (Chapter 5). If a Dog has a `name` property, you can say:

```
let d = Dog()
d[keyPath:\.name] = "Rover"
```

That is a completely different mechanism! You'll surely prefer to use the Swift mechanism where possible. It provides complete safety, along with type information; a Swift KeyPath object is strongly typed, because it is a generic, specified to the type of the corresponding property. But that won't help you when you're talking to Cocoa. Objective-C key–value coding uses string keys, and a Swift KeyPath object cannot be magically transformed into a string key.

Cocoa key–value coding is a powerful technology with many ramifications beyond what I've described here; see Apple's *Key-Value Coding Programming Guide* in the documentation archive for full information.

The Secret Life of NSObject

Every Objective-C class inherits from NSObject, which is constructed in a rather elaborate way:

- It defines some native class methods and instance methods having mostly to do with the basics of instantiation and of method sending and resolution.

- It adopts the NSObject protocol. This protocol declares instance methods having mostly to do with memory management, the relationship between an instance and its class, and introspection. Because all the NSObject protocol methods are required, the NSObject class implements them all. In Swift, the NSObject protocol is called NSObjectProtocol, to avoid name clash.

- It implements convenience methods related to the NSCopying, NSMutableCopying, and NSCoding protocols, without formally adopting those protocols. NSObject intentionally doesn't adopt these protocols because this would cause all other classes to adopt them, which would be wrong. But thanks to this architecture, if a class *does* adopt one of these protocols, you can call the corresponding convenience method. For instance, NSObject implements the copy instance method, so you can call copy on any instance, but you'll crash unless the instance's class also adopts the NSCopying protocol and implements copy(with:).

- A large number of methods are injected into NSObject by more than two dozen categories on NSObject, scattered among various header files. For example, awakeFromNib (see Chapter 7) comes from the UINibLoadingAdditions category on NSObject, declared in *UINibLoading.h*.

- A class object is an object. Therefore all Objective-C classes, which are objects of type Class, inherit from NSObject. Therefore, *any instance method of NSObject can be called on a class object as a class method!* For example, responds(to:) is defined as an instance method by the NSObject protocol, but it can (therefore) be treated also as a class method and sent to a class object.

Taken as a whole, the NSObject methods may be roughly classified as follows:

Creation, destruction, and memory management
Methods for creating an instance, such as alloc and copy, along with methods for learning when something is happening in the lifetime of an object, such as initialize and dealloc, plus methods that manage memory.

Class relationships

Methods for learning an object's class and inheritance, such as `superclass`, `isKind(of:)`, and `isMember(of:)`.

Object introspection and comparison

Methods for asking what would happen if an object were sent a certain message, such as `responds(to:)`, for representing an object as a string (`description`), and for comparing objects (`isEqual(_:)`).

Message response

Methods for meddling with what *does* happen when an object is sent a certain message, such as `doesNotRecognizeSelector(_:)`. If you're curious, see the *Objective-C Runtime Programming Guide* in the documentation archive.

Message sending

Methods for sending a message dynamically. For example, `perform(_:)` takes a selector as parameter, and sending it to an object tells that object to perform that selector. This might seem identical to just sending that message to that object, but what if you don't know what message to send until runtime? Moreover, variants on `perform` allow you to send a message on a specified thread, or to send a message after a certain amount of time has passed (`perform(_:with:after-Delay:)` and similar).

CHAPTER 11

Cocoa Events

All of your app's executable code lies in its functions. The impetus for a function being called must come from somewhere. One of your functions may call another, but who will call the first function in the first place? How, ultimately, will *any* of your code *ever* run?

After your app has completely finished launching, *none* of your code runs. UIApplicationMain (see "How an App Gets Going" on page 370) just sits and loops — the *event loop* — waiting for something to happen. In general, the user needs to *do* something, such as touching the screen, or switching away from your app. When something does happen, the runtime detects it and informs your app, and Cocoa can call your code.

But Cocoa can call your code only if your code is there to be called. Your code is like a panel of buttons, ready for Cocoa to press one. If something happens that Cocoa feels your code needs to know about and respond to, it presses the right button — if the right button is there. Cocoa wants to send your code a message, but your code must have ears to hear.

The art of Cocoa programming lies in knowing *what* messages Cocoa would like to send your app. You organize your code, right from the start, with those messages in mind. Cocoa makes certain promises about how and when it will dispatch messages to your code. These are Cocoa's *events*. Your job is to know what those events are and how they will arrive; armed with that knowledge, you can arrange for your code to respond to them.

Reasons for Events

Broadly speaking, the reasons you might receive an event may be divided informally into four categories. These categories are not official; I made them up. Often it isn't completely clear which of these categories an event fits into. But they are still generally useful for visualizing how and why Cocoa interacts with your code:

User events

The user does something interactive, and an event is triggered directly. Obvious examples are events that you get when the user taps or swipes the screen, or types a key on the keyboard.

Lifetime events

These are events notifying you of the arrival of a stage in the life of the app, such as the fact that the app is starting up or is about to go into the background, or of a component of the app, such as the fact that a UIViewController's view has just loaded or is about to be removed from the screen.

Functional events

Cocoa is about to do something by calling its own code, and is willing to let you subclass and override that code so as to modify its behavior. I would put into this category UIView's draw(_:) (your chance to have a view draw itself), with which we experimented in Chapter 10.

Query events

Cocoa turns to you to ask a question; its behavior will depend upon your answer. The way data appears in a table (a UITableView) is that Cocoa asks you how many rows the table should have, and then, for each row, asks you for the corresponding cell.

Subclassing

A built-in Cocoa class may define methods that Cocoa itself will call if you override them in a subclass, so that your custom behavior, and not (merely) the default behavior, will take place. As I explained in Chapter 10, this is not a commonly used architecture in Cocoa, but for many classes it's there if you need it, and for certain classes it is downright essential. UIView and UIViewController are the best examples.

UIView's draw(_:) is what I call a functional event. By default it does nothing, but by overriding it in a UIView subclass, you dictate how a view draws itself. You don't know exactly when this method will be called, and you don't care; when it is, you draw, and this guarantees that the view will always appear the way you want it to.

UIViewController is a class meant for subclassing, and is probably the only Cocoa class that you will *regularly* subclass. Of the methods listed in the UIViewController class documentation, just about all are methods you might have reason to override. If you create a UIViewController subclass in Xcode, you'll see that the template already includes some method overrides to get you started. viewDidLoad is called to let you know that your view controller has obtained its main view (its view), so that you can perform initializations; it's an obvious example of a lifetime event. And UIView-Controller has many other lifetime events that you can and will override in order to get fine control over what happens when.

Not only methods but also properties may be overridden in order to get an event. A case in point is UIViewController's `supportedInterfaceOrientations`. You'll override this property as a computed variable in order to receive what I call a query event. Whenever Cocoa wants to know what orientations your view can appear in, it fetches the value of this property; your getter is a function that is called at that moment, and its job is to return a bitmask ("Option sets" on page 255) providing the answer to that question. You trust Cocoa to trigger this call at the appropriate moments, so that if the user rotates the device, your app's interface will or won't be rotated to compensate, depending on what value you return.

When you're looking for events that you can receive through subclassing, be sure to look upward though the inheritance hierarchy. If you're wondering how to get an event when your custom UILabel subclass is embedded into another view, you won't find the answer in the UILabel class documentation; a UILabel receives the appropriate event by virtue of being a UIView. In the UIView class documentation, you'll learn that you can override `didMoveToSuperview` to be informed when this happens.

By the same token, look upward through adopted protocols as well. If you're wondering how to get an event when your view controller's view is about to undergo app rotation, you won't find out by looking in the UIViewController class documentation; a UIViewController receives the appropriate event by virtue of adopting the UIContentContainer protocol. In the UIContentContainer protocol documentation, you'll learn that you can override `viewWillTransition(to:with:)`.

Notifications

Cocoa provides your app with a single NotificationCenter instance (Objective-C NSNotificationCenter), available as `NotificationCenter.default`. This instance, the *notification center*, is the basis of a mechanism for sending and receiving messages called *notifications*. A notification is a Notification instance (Objective-C NSNotification).

Think of a notification as having a topic and a sender. The topic is some subject matter that might be of interest to others; the sender is some object that others might be interested in hearing from. The notification center functions as a kind of broker for message transmission:

1. A potential recipient of messages can *register* with the notification center, saying: "Hey, if any messages on this topic or from this sender arrive, please pass them on to me."

2. A sender does in fact hand the notification center a message to send out; this is called *posting* a notification.

3. When the notification center receives a posting on a certain topic or from a certain sender, it looks through its list of registered recipients and passes along the message to any recipients that match.

More than one recipient can register for messages with the same topic or sender. The notification mechanism is well described as a dispatching or broadcasting mechanism. It lets the poster send a message without knowing or caring whether there are recipients or, if there are, who or how many they may be. And it lets the recipient arrange to receive the message without being in direct contact with the sender (possibly without even knowing who the sender is).

Who can post a notification? Anyone who cares to! There are two main posters of notifications to consider — Cocoa and you:

Cocoa

Cocoa posts notifications through the notification center, and your code can register to receive them. Notifications are a way for your code to receive events from Cocoa. You'll find a separate Notifications section in the documentation for a class that provides them.

You

You can post notifications yourself as a way of communicating with your own code. This relieves your app's architecture from the formal responsibility of somehow hooking up instances just so a message can pass from one to the other (which can sometimes be quite tricky or onerous, as I'll discuss in Chapter 13). When objects are conceptually "distant" from one another, notifications can be a fairly lightweight way of permitting one to message the other.

A Notification instance has three pieces of information associated with it, which can be retrieved through properties:

name

The *topic* of the notification. It's a string, but it has been wrapped up in a Notification.Name, a struct adopting RawRepresentable with a String rawValue. Built-in Cocoa notification names are vended as static/class Notification.Name properties, either of Notification.Name itself or of the class that sends them.

object

An instance associated with the notification; typically, the *sender* who posted it.

userInfo

An Optional dictionary; if not nil, it contains additional information associated with the notification. What information it will contain, and under what keys, depends on the particular notification; you have to consult the documentation.

When you post a notification yourself, you can put anything you like into the `userInfo` for the notification's recipient(s) to retrieve. Do *not* misuse a notification's `object` as a way of passing along a value. That's what the `userInfo` is for.

Receiving a Notification

To register to receive notifications, you send one of two messages to the notification center.

Selector-based registration

One way to register for notifications is to call the notification center's `add-Observer(_:selector:name:object:)`. The parameters are:

`observer:`
> The first parameter is the instance to which the notification is to be sent. This will typically be `self`; it would be quite unusual for one instance to register a different instance as the receiver of a notification.

`selector:`
> The message to be sent to the observer instance when the notification occurs. The designated method should take one parameter, which will be the Notification instance. The selector must specify correctly a method that is exposed to Objective-C; Swift's `#selector` syntax will help you with that (see Chapter 2).

`name:`
> The `name` (topic) of the notification you'd like to receive. If this is `nil`, you're asking to receive *all* notifications associated with the object designated in the `object:` parameter.

`object:`
> The `object` (sender) of the notification you're interested in. If this is `nil`, you're asking to receive *all* notifications with the name designated in the `name:` parameter. (If both the `name:` and `object:` parameters are `nil`, you're asking to receive all notifications!)

Here's a real-life example. There is a music player belonging to the MPMusicPlayerController class; this class promises to post a notification whenever the music player starts playing a different song. (To find this out, I look under Notifications in the MPMusicPlayerController class documentation; the notification in question is called `MPMusicPlayerControllerNowPlayingItemDidChange`.) In my app, I want to receive that notification and change my interface accordingly.

Here's how I register myself to receive the desired playback notification:

```
NotificationCenter.default.addObserver(self,
    selector: #selector(nowPlayingItemChanged),
    name: .MPMusicPlayerControllerNowPlayingItemDidChange,
    object: nil)
```

As a result, whenever an .MPMusicPlayerControllerNowPlayingItemDidChange notification is posted, my nowPlayingItemChanged method will be called. Note that this method must be marked @objc so that Objective-C can see it (the Swift compiler will help out by ensuring this when you use #selector syntax):

```
@objc func nowPlayingItemChanged (_ n:Notification) {
    self.updateNowPlayingItem()
    // ... and so on ...
}
```

Function-based registration

Heavy use of addObserver(_:selector:name:object:) means that your code ends up peppered with methods that exist solely in order to be called by the notification center. There is nothing about these methods that tells you what they are for — you may want to use explicit comments to remind yourself — and the methods are separate from the registration call, which can make your code rather confusing.

One way to solve that problem is to use the *other* way of registering to receive a notification, addObserver(forName:object:queue:using:). The parameters are:

- The name: and object: parameters are just like those of the addObserver(_:selector:name:object:) method.

- Instead of providing an observer and a selector, you provide (as the using: parameter) a *function* consisting of the actual code to be executed when the notification arrives. This function should take one parameter — the Notification itself. You can use an anonymous function, and typically you will.

- The queue: is the OperationQueue on which your using: function will be called. It will usually be nil. (Explaining what a non-nil queue would mean is outside the scope of this book.)

- This method also returns a value, which is in fact the observer that has been registered with the notification center. I'll talk more about that in a moment.

The outcome is that your registration for a notification and your response when the notification arrives are encapsulated in a single call:

```
let ob = NotificationCenter.default.addObserver(
    forName: .MPMusicPlayerControllerNowPlayingItemDidChange,
    object: nil, queue: nil) { _ in
        self.updateNowPlayingItem()
        // ... and so on ...
    }
```

That can be a much cleaner way of dealing with notifications. Unfortunately, using `addObserver(forName:...)` correctly is a little more complicated than that, because you still need to unregister the observer, as I'll discuss in the next section.

Unregistering

To unregister an object as a recipient of notifications, call the notification center's `removeObserver(_:)` method. Alternatively, you can unregister an object for just a specific set of notifications with `removeObserver(_:name:object:)`. The object passed as the first argument is the object that is no longer to receive notifications. What object that is depends on how you registered it in the first place:

You called `addObserver(_:selector:name:object:)`
> You *supplied* an observer originally, as the first argument; that is the observer you will now unregister. This will typically be `self`.

You called `addObserver(forName:object:queue:using:)`
> The call *returned* an observer token object typed as an NSObjectProtocol (its real class and nature are undocumented); that is the observer you will now unregister.

In the old days, if you failed to unregister an object as a notification recipient and that object went out of existence, your app would crash the next time the notification was sent — because the runtime was trying to send a message to an object that was now missing in action. But in iOS 9, Apple introduced a safety check. Nowadays, if the notification center tries to send a message to a nonexistent object, there is no crash, and the notification center helpfully unregisters the object for you.

What you need to do as you go out of existence depends, once again, on how you registered in the first place:

You called `addObserver(_:selector:name:object:)`
> You probably don't need to unregister the object passed as the first argument. If that object goes out of existence, and if the notification is posted subsequently, there won't be any crash.

You called `addObserver(forName:object:queue:using:)`
> You *do* need to unregister the observer, because otherwise the notification center *keeps it alive* and can continue to send notifications to it (which means that the attached function will continue to be called).

So the question now boils down to how you're going to unregister the observer returned by a call to `addObserver(forName:object:queue:using:)`. If you only need to receive a notification *once,* you can unregister from within the anonymous function that runs when the notification is received (because the observer is in scope within the anonymous function). Otherwise, you'll have to keep a separate persistent reference to the observer object so that you can unregister it later.

What's a good way to do that? Let's assume you're going to be calling add-Observer(forName:object:queue:using:) many times from within the same class. Then you're going to end up receiving many observer tokens, and you'll need to preserve a reference to all of them. One obvious approach is to store the observers in an instance property that is a mutable collection. My favored approach is a Set property:

```
var observers = Set<NSObject>()
```

So now, each time I register for a notification by calling addObserver(forName:object:queue:using:), I capture the result and add it to the set:

```
let ob = NotificationCenter.default.addObserver(
    forName: .MPMusicPlayerControllerNowPlayingItemDidChange,
    object: nil, queue: nil) { _ in
        self.updateNowPlayingItem()
        // ... and so on ...
    }
self.observers.insert(ob as! NSObject)
```

When it's time to unregister all observers, I enumerate the set and empty it:

```
for ob in self.observers {
    NotificationCenter.default.removeObserver(ob)
}
self.observers.removeAll()
```

 Use of addObserver(forName:...) can also involve you in some memory management complications that I'll talk about in Chapter 12.

Posting a Notification

Notifications can be a way of communicating between your own objects. You post a notification yourself (in one object) and receive it yourself (in another object). This is probably not a good way to compensate for a failure to devise proper lines of communication between objects, but it can be appropriate when the objects are conceptually distant or independent from one another, or when you need the flexibility of broadcasting to multiple recipients.

To post a notification, send post(name:object:userInfo:) to the notification center. For the name:, you'll have to coerce a string into a Notification.Name. There are two main places to do this:

In the name: *argument*

You perform the coercion directly in the method call; for example, you might say Notification.Name("someName"). That's simple but error-prone: you'll need to perform the same coercion twice (to post the notification and to register to receive it), and the repeated string literal is an invitation to make a typing mistake and have things mysteriously go wrong.

As a globally available constant

You define a namespaced constant beforehand, and use it both when posting the notification and when registering for it. This approach localizes the coercion in a single place; it's a little more work than the first approach, but it's more correct and you should use it.

For example, one of my apps is a simple card game. The game needs to know when a card is tapped. But a card knows nothing about the game; when it is tapped, it simply emits a virtual shriek by posting a notification. I've defined my notification name by extending my Card class:

```
extension Card {
    static let tappedNotification = Notification.Name("cardTapped")
}
```

When a card is tapped, it responds like this:

```
NotificationCenter.default.post(name: Self.tappedNotification, object: self)
```

The game object has registered for `Card.tappedNotification`, so it hears about this and retrieves the notification's `object`; now it knows what card was tapped and can proceed appropriately.

The notification center has no API for introspecting it in code, but you can introspect it while paused in the debugger; enter `po Notification-Center.default` to see a list of registered notifications, with the name, object, recipient, and options for each. The object and recipient are listed as memory addresses, but you can learn more from such an address by entering `expr -l objc -O --` followed by the address.

Timer

A Timer (Objective-C NSTimer) is not a notification, but it behaves quite similarly. It gives off a signal (*fires*) after the lapse of a certain time interval. Thus you can arrange to get an event when a certain time has elapsed. The timing is not perfectly accurate, nor is it intended to be, but it's good enough for most purposes.

A timer that is actively watching the clock is said to be *scheduled*. A timer may fire once, or it may be a *repeating* timer. To stop a timer, it must be *invalidated*. A timer that is set to fire once is invalidated automatically after it fires; a repeating timer repeats until *you* invalidate it by sending it the `invalidate` message. An invalidated timer should be regarded as dead: you cannot revive it or use it for anything further, and you should probably not send any messages to it.

For example, one of my apps is a game with a score; I want to penalize the user by diminishing the score for every ten seconds that elapses after each move without the user making a further move. So I create and schedule a repeating timer whose time interval is ten seconds. Whenever the timer fires, I diminish the score. Whenever the user moves, I invalidate the existing timer and start over with a new repeating timer.

The simplest way to create a timer is with a class method that also schedules the timer, so that it begins watching the clock immediately:

`scheduledTimer(timeInterval:target:selector:userInfo:repeats:)`
> The `target:` and `selector:` determine what message will be sent to what object when the timer fires; the method in question should take one parameter, which will be a reference to the timer. The `userInfo:` is just like the `userInfo:` of a notification.

`scheduledTimer(withTimeInterval:repeats:block:)`
> You provide a function to be called when the timer fires; the function should take one parameter, which will be a reference to the timer.

A repeating Timer is often maintained as an instance property, so that you can invalidate it later on. But be careful! There is a temptation to call `scheduledTimer(timeInterval:target:selector:userInfo:repeats:)` directly as the initializer in your declaration of a Timer instance property, like this:

```
class ViewController : UIViewController {
    var timer = Timer.scheduledTimer(timeInterval: 1, target: self,
        selector: #selector(timerFired), userInfo: nil, repeats: true)
```

If the `target` is `self`, that won't work, because `self` doesn't exist yet at the time you're initializing the instance property. (In my opinion, Swift should warn you about this, and I regard its failure to do so as a bug.) Use deferred initialization instead ("Deferred initialization of properties" on page 126):

```
class ViewController: UIViewController {
    var timer : Timer!
    override func viewDidLoad() {
        super.viewDidLoad()
        self.timer = Timer.scheduledTimer(timeInterval: 1, target: self,
            selector: #selector(timerFired), userInfo: nil, repeats: true)
    }
```

 Timers have some memory management implications that I'll be discussing in Chapter 12.

Delegation

Delegation is an object-oriented design pattern, a relationship between two objects in which a primary object's behavior is customized or assisted by a secondary object. The secondary object is the primary object's *delegate*. No subclassing is involved, and indeed the primary object is agnostic about the delegate's class.

The class of the primary object can be Cocoa's class or your class. As with notifications, you'll want to understand Cocoa's delegation pattern because it's an important way of getting events from Cocoa; plus, you might want to implement the pattern yourself as a useful way of communicating between your own objects.

Cocoa Delegation

As implemented by Cocoa, here's how delegation works:

1. A built-in Cocoa class has an instance property, usually called `delegate` (it will certainly have `delegate` in its name).

2. The Cocoa class promises that at certain moments it will turn to its delegate for instructions by sending it a certain message.

3. One of those moments arrives! If the Cocoa instance finds that its delegate is not `nil`, and that its delegate is prepared to receive that message, the Cocoa instance sends the message to the delegate.

Delegation is one of Cocoa's main uses of protocols (Chapter 10). In the old days, delegate methods were listed in the Cocoa class's documentation, and their names were made known to the compiler through an informal protocol (a category on NSObject). Nowadays, a class's delegate methods are usually listed in a genuine protocol with its own documentation. There are over 70 Cocoa delegate protocols; that shows how heavily Cocoa relies on delegation. Most delegate methods are optional, but in a few cases you'll discover some that are required.

To take advantage of Cocoa delegation, you'll have one of *your* classes adopt a Cocoa delegate protocol, and you'll set some Cocoa object's `delegate` (typed as that protocol) to an instance of your class. You might form the connection in code; alternatively, you might do it in a nib by connecting an object's `delegate` outlet to an appropriate object within the nib. Now *you* are the delegate, and you get to help determine the Cocoa object's behavior.

Your delegate class will probably do other things besides serving as this instance's delegate. Indeed, one of the nice things about delegation is that it leaves you free to slot delegate code into your class architecture however you like; the delegate type is a protocol, so the actual delegate can be an instance of *any* class.

Here's a typical example. I want to ensure that my app's root view controller, a UINavigationController, should appear only in portrait orientation when this view controller is in charge. But UINavigationController isn't my class; my class is a *different* view controller, a UIViewController subclass, which acts as the UINavigationController's child. How can the child tell the parent how to rotate?

Delegation to the rescue! UINavigationController has a `delegate` property, typed as UINavigationControllerDelegate (a protocol). It promises to send this delegate the `navigationControllerSupportedInterfaceOrientations(_:)` message when it needs to know how to rotate. So my view controller, very early in its lifetime, sets itself as the UINavigationController's delegate. It also implements the `navigation-ControllerSupportedInterfaceOrientations(_:)` method. Presto, the problem is solved:

```
class ViewController : UIViewController, UINavigationControllerDelegate {
    override func viewDidLoad() {
        super.viewDidLoad()
        self.navigationController?.delegate = self
    }
    func navigationControllerSupportedInterfaceOrientations(
        _ nav: UINavigationController) -> UIInterfaceOrientationMask {
            return .portrait
    }
}
```

When you're searching the documentation for how you can be notified of a certain event, be sure to consult the corresponding delegate protocol, if there is one. Suppose you'd like to know when the user taps in a UITextField to start editing it. You won't find anything relevant in the UITextField class documentation; what you're after is `textFieldDidBeginEditing(_:)` in the UITextFieldDelegate protocol.

 You might be tempted to try to inject a method into a class that adopts a Cocoa delegate protocol by extending the protocol and implementing the delegate method in the protocol extension. That isn't going to work, because Objective-C can't see Swift protocol extensions (see Appendix A). You can call such a method from Swift, but Cocoa is *never* going to call it, because it doesn't know that the method implementation exists.

Implementing Delegation

The Cocoa protocol-and-delegate pattern is very useful, and you'll probably want to adopt it in your own code. Setting up the pattern takes some practice, and can be a little time-consuming. But it's a clean solution to the problem of apportioning knowledge and responsibilities among your objects. I'll demonstrate with an example from one of my apps.

The app declares a view controller, a UIViewController subclass called ColorPicker-Controller; its view contains three sliders that the user can move to choose a color. Some other view controller will create and present the ColorPickerController instance, displaying its view. When the user taps Done or Cancel, the view should be dismissed and the ColorPickerController instance can go out of existence; but first, I need to send a message from the ColorPickerController instance *back to the view controller that presented it*, reporting what color the user chose.

Here's the declaration for the message that I want the ColorPickerController to send before it goes out of existence:

```
func colorPicker(_ picker:ColorPickerController,
    didSetColorNamed theName:String?,
    to theColor:UIColor?)
```

The question is: where and how should this method be declared?

Now, it happens that in my app I know the class of the instance that will in fact present the ColorPickerController: it is a SettingsController. So I could simply declare this method in SettingsController and stop. But that would mean that the ColorPickerController, in order to send this message to the SettingsController, must *know* that the instance that presented it *is* a SettingsController. That's wrong. Surely it is a mere *contingent* fact that the instance being sent this message is a Settings-Controller; it should be open to *any* class to present and dismiss a ColorPicker-Controller.

Therefore we want ColorPickerController *itself* to declare the method that *it itself is going to call*; and we want it to send that message blindly to some receiver, without regard to the class of that receiver. That's what a protocol is for!

The solution, then, is for ColorPickerController to define a protocol, with this method as part of that protocol, and for the class that presents a ColorPicker-Controller to conform to that protocol. ColorPickerController will also need an appropriately typed `delegate` instance property; this provides the channel of communication, and tells the compiler that sending this message is legal:

```
protocol ColorPickerDelegate : AnyObject {
    // color == nil on cancel
    func colorPicker(_ picker:ColorPickerController,
        didSetColorNamed theName:String?,
        to theColor:UIColor?)
}
class ColorPickerController : UIViewController {
    weak var delegate: ColorPickerDelegate?
    // ...
}
```

(For the `weak` attribute and the `AnyObject` designation, see Chapter 5.) When my SettingsController instance creates and configures and presents a ColorPicker-Controller instance, it also sets itself as that ColorPickerController's `delegate` — which it can do, because it adopts the protocol:

```
extension SettingsController : ColorPickerDelegate {
    func showColorPicker() {
        let colorName = // ...
        let c = // ...
        let cpc = ColorPickerController(colorName:colorName, color:c)
        cpc.delegate = self
```

```
        self.present(cpc, animated: true)
    }
    func colorPicker(_ picker:ColorPickerController,
        didSetColorNamed theName:String?,
        to theColor:UIColor?) {
            // ...
    }
}
```

When the user picks a color, the ColorPickerController *knows* to whom it should send `colorPicker(_:didSetColorNamed:to:)` — namely, its delegate! And the compiler allows this, because the delegate has adopted the ColorPickerDelegate protocol:

```
@IBAction func dismissColorPicker(_ sender : Any?) { // user tapped Done
    let c : UIColor? = self.color
    self.delegate?.colorPicker(self, didSetColorNamed: self.colorName, to: c)
}
```

Data Sources

A *data source* is like a delegate, except that its methods supply the data for another object to display. The chief Cocoa classes with data sources are UITableView, UICollectionView, UIPickerView, and UIPageViewController. In each case, the data source must formally adopt a data source protocol with required methods.

It comes as a surprise to some beginners that a data source is necessary at all. Why isn't a table's data just a property of the table? The reason is that such an architecture would violate generality. A view displays data; the structure and management of that data is a separate matter, and is up to the data source. The only requirement is that the data source must be able to supply information quickly, because it will be asked for it in real time when the data needs displaying.

Another surprise is that the data source is different from the delegate. But this again is only for generality; it's an option, not a requirement. There is no reason why the data source and the delegate should not be the same object, and most of the time they probably will be.

In this example from one of my apps, I implement a UIPickerView that allows the user to configure a game by saying how many stages it should consist of ("1 Stage," "2 Stages," and so on). The first two methods are UIPickerView data source methods; the third method is a UIPickerView delegate method. It takes all three methods to supply the picker view's content:

```
extension NewGameController: UIPickerViewDataSource, UIPickerViewDelegate {
    func numberOfComponents(in pickerView: UIPickerView) -> Int {
        return 1
    }
    func pickerView(_ pickerView: UIPickerView,
        numberOfRowsInComponent component: Int) -> Int {
```

```
            return 9
    }
    func pickerView(_ pickerView: UIPickerView,
        titleForRow row: Int, forComponent component: Int) -> String? {
            return "\(row+1) Stage" + ( row > 0 ? "s" : "")
    }
}
```

Actions

An *action* is a message emitted by an instance of a UIControl subclass (a *control*) reporting a significant user event taking place in that control. The UIControl subclasses are all simple interface objects that the user can interact with directly, such as a button (UIButton) or a segmented control (UISegmentedControl).

The significant user events (*control events*) are listed under UIControl.Event in the Constants section of the UIControl class documentation. Different controls implement different control events: a segmented control's Value Changed event signifies that the user has tapped a segment, but a button's Touch Up Inside event signifies that the user has tapped the button. Of itself, a control event has no external effect; the control responds visually (a tapped button looks tapped), but it doesn't automatically share the information that the event has taken place. If you want to know when a control event takes place, so that you can respond to it in your code, *you* must arrange for that control event to trigger an *action message*.

Here's how it works. A control maintains an internal dispatch table: for each control event, there can be any number of target–action pairs, in each of which the *action* is a selector designating the name of a method, and the *target* is an object on which that method is to be called. When a control event occurs, the control consults its dispatch table, finds all the target–action pairs associated with that control event, and sends each action message to the corresponding target (Figure 11-1).

There are two ways to manipulate a control's action dispatch table:

Action connection
> You can configure an action connection in a nib. I described in Chapter 7 how to do this, but I didn't completely explain the underlying mechanism. Now all is revealed: an action connection formed in the nib editor is a visual way of configuring a control's action dispatch table.

Code
> Your code can directly configure the control's action dispatch table. The key method here is the UIControl instance method `addTarget(_:action:for:)`, where the `target:` is an object, the `action:` is a selector, and the `for:` parameter is a UIControl.Event bitmask ("Option sets" on page 255).

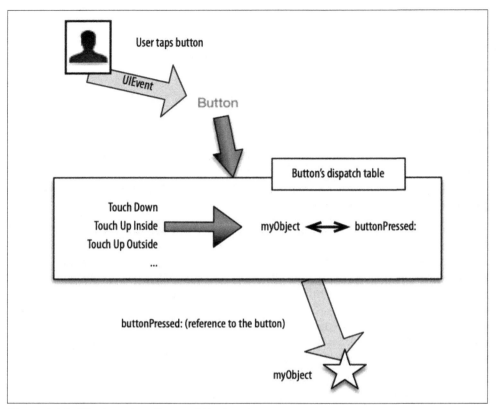

Figure 11-1. The target–action architecture

Recall the example of a control and its action from Chapter 7. We have a button-Pressed(_:) method:

```
@IBAction func buttonPressed(_ sender: Any) {
    let alert = UIAlertController(
        title: "Howdy!", message: "You tapped me!", preferredStyle: .alert)
    alert.addAction(
        UIAlertAction(title: "OK", style: .cancel))
    self.present(alert, animated: true)
}
```

That sort of method is an *action handler*. Its purpose is to be called when the user taps a certain button in the interface. In Chapter 7, we arranged for that to happen by setting up an action connection in the nib: we connected the button's Touch Up Inside event to the ViewController buttonPressed(_:) method. In reality, we were forming a target–action pair and adding that target–action pair to the button's dispatch table for the Touch Up Inside control event.

Instead of making that arrangement in the nib, we could have done the same thing in code. Suppose we had *never* drawn that action connection. And suppose that, instead, we have an outlet connection from the view controller to the button, called `self.button`. Then the view controller, after the nib loads, can configure the button's dispatch table like this:

```
self.button.addTarget(self,
    action: #selector(buttonPressed),
    for: .touchUpInside)
```

The signature for the action selector can be in any of three forms:

- The fullest form takes two parameters:
  - The control.
  - The UIEvent that generated the control event. This will rarely be needed. (I'll talk more about UIEvents in the next section.)
- A shorter form, the one most commonly used, omits the second parameter. `buttonPressed(_:)` is an example; it takes one parameter. When `button-Pressed(_:)` is called through an action message emanating from the button, its parameter will be a reference to the button.
- There is a still shorter form that omits both parameters.

Curiously, none of the action selector parameters provide any way to learn *which* control event triggered the current action selector call! To distinguish a Touch Up Inside control event from a Touch Up Outside control event, their corresponding target–action pairs must specify two different action handlers; if you dispatch them to the same action handler, that handler cannot discover which control event occurred.

New in iOS 14, a UIControl's target and action can be expressed by attaching to the UIControl a UIAction instance encapsulating the action as a function — probably an anonymous function. In this way, there is no explicit target and no separate action method. This is a very nice notation, but behind the scenes it is still the target–action architecture.

 A control event can have multiple target–action pairs. You might configure it this way intentionally, but it is also possible to do so accidentally. Unintentionally giving a control event a target–action pair without removing its *existing* target-action pair is an easy mistake to make, and can cause some very mysterious behavior. If you form an action connection in the nib *and* configure the dispatch table in code, a tap on the button will cause the action handler method to be called *twice*.

The Responder Chain

Whenever the user does something with a finger (sets it down on the screen, moves it, raises it from the screen), a touch object (UITouch) is used to represent that finger. UIEvents are the lowest-level objects charged with communication of touch objects to your app; a UIEvent is basically a timestamp (a Double) along with a collection (Set) of touch objects. As I said in the previous section, you can receive a UIEvent along with a control event, but you will rarely need to do so.

A *responder* is an object that knows how to receive UIEvents directly. It is an instance of UIResponder or a UIResponder subclass. If you examine the Cocoa class hierarchy, you'll find that just about any class that has anything to do with display on the screen is a responder. A UIView is a responder. A UIWindow is a responder. A UIViewController is a responder. Even a UIApplication is a responder. Even the app delegate is a responder!

A UIResponder has four low-level methods for receiving touch-related UIEvents:

- touchesBegan(_:with:)
- touchesMoved(_:with:)
- touchesEnded(_:with:)
- touchesCancelled(_:with:)

These methods — the *touch methods* — are called to notify a responder that a touch event has occurred: the user has placed, moved, or lifted a finger from the screen. No matter how your code ultimately hears about a user-related touch event — indeed, even if your code *never* hears about a touch event directly — the touch was initially communicated to a responder through one of the touch methods.

The mechanism for this communication starts by deciding which responder the user touched. The UIView methods hitTest(_:with:) and point(inside:with:) are called until the correct view (the *hit-test view*) is located. Then UIApplication's sendEvent(_:) method is called, which calls UIWindow's sendEvent(_:), which now wants to call the correct touch method in some responder.

So now the runtime starts looking for a responder that *implements* the correct touch method, so that the touch event can be reported by calling it. That responder need not be the hit-test view! The hit-test view is just the starting place for the search. The search depends upon the fact that your app's responders participate in a *responder chain*, which essentially links them up through the view hierarchy.

The responder chain, from bottom to top, looks roughly like this:

1. The UIView that we start with (here, the hit-test view).
2. If this UIView is a UIViewController's view, that UIViewController.

---

3. The UIView's superview.

4. Go back to step 2 and repeat! Keep repeating until we reach…

5. The UIWindow (and the UIWindowScene).

6. The UIApplication.

7. The UIApplication's delegate.

The next responder up the responder chain is a responder's *next responder*, which is obtained from a responder through its `next` property (which returns an Optional wrapping a UIResponder). Thus the responder chain can be walked upward from any responder to the top of the chain.

Nil-Targeted Actions

A *nil-targeted* action is a UIControl target–action pair in which the target is `nil`. There is no designated target object, so the following rule is used: starting with the hit-test view (the view with which the user is interacting), Cocoa walks up the responder chain looking for an object that can respond to the action message:

- If a responder is found that handles this message, that method is called on that responder, and that's the end.

- If we get all the way to the top of the responder chain without finding a responder to handle this message, nothing happens; the message goes unhandled, with no penalty.

Here's a UIButton subclass that configures itself to call a nil-targeted action when tapped:

```
override func awakeFromNib() {
    super.awakeFromNib()
    class Dummy {
        @objc func buttonPressed(_:Any) {}
    }
    self.addTarget(nil, // nil-targeted
        action: #selector(Dummy.buttonPressed),
        for: .touchUpInside)
}
```

That's a nil-targeted action. So what happens when the user taps the button? First, Cocoa looks in the UIButton itself to see whether it responds to `buttonPressed`. If not, it looks in the UIView that is its superview. And so on, up the responder chain. There is surely a view controller that owns the view that contains the button; if the view controller is the first responder encountered in the search whose class implements `buttonPressed`, tapping the button will cause the view controller's `buttonPressed` to be called — even though the view controller is not the target!

The declaration for your action handler method (such as buttonPressed) must be marked @objc (or @IBAction). Otherwise, Cocoa won't be able to find it as it walks up the responder chain.

It's obvious how to construct a nil-targeted action in code: you set up a target–action pair where the target is nil, as in the preceding example. But how do you construct a nil-targeted action in a nib? The answer is: you form a connection to the First Responder proxy object (in the dock). That's what the First Responder proxy object is for! The First Responder isn't a real object with a known class, so before you can connect an action to it, you have to define the action message within the First Responder proxy object, like this:

1. Select the First Responder proxy in the nib, and switch to the Attributes inspector.

2. You'll see a table (probably empty) of user-defined nil-targeted First Responder actions. Click the Plus button and give the new action a name; it must take a single parameter (so that its name will end with a colon).

3. Now you can Control-drag from a control, such as a UIButton, to the First Responder proxy to specify a nil-targeted action with the name you specified.

Key–Value Observing

Key–value observing, or *KVO*, is rather like a target–action mechanism that works between *any* two objects. One object (the observer) registers directly with another object (the observed) so as to be notified *when a value in the observed object changes*. The observed object doesn't actually have to *do* anything; when the value in the observed object changes, the observer is *automatically* notified.

The process of using KVO may be broken down into stages:

Registration
> The observer — that is, the object that desires to hear about future changes in a value belonging to the observed object — must register with that observed object.

Change
> A change takes place in the value belonging to the observed object, and it must take place in a special way — a KVO compliant way. Typically, this means using a key–value coding compliant accessor to make the change. Setting a property passes through a key–value coding compliant accessor.

Notification
> The observer is automatically notified that the value in the observed object has changed.

Unregistration

   The observer eventually unregisters to prevent the arrival of further notifications about the observed value of the observed object.

As with notifications and delegation, you can use KVO with Cocoa objects or you can implement it as a form of communication between your own objects. When you use KVO with Cocoa:

- The observer will be *your* object; you will write the code that will respond when the observer is notified of the change for which it has registered.

- The observed object will be *Cocoa's* object. Many Cocoa objects promise to behave in a KVO compliant way. Certain frameworks, such as the AVFoundation framework, don't implement delegation or notifications very much; instead, they expect you to use KVO to hear about what they are doing. Thus, KVO can be an important form of Cocoa event.

When you use KVO with your own observed object, you have to configure that object to be KVO compliant for one or more values. I'll explain later how to do that.

Registration and Notification

There are two different ways to configure KVO registration and notification. The first way is the Cocoa way; it basically just translates the Objective-C API directly into Swift. The second way is provided by Swift; it uses the Cocoa way under the hood, but it shields you from some of the messy details.

I'll first describe the Cocoa way, just so that you understand the mess that the Swift way shields you from:

1. In the Cocoa way, you call `addObserver(_:forKeyPath:options:context:)` on the object whose property you want to observe, using a Cocoa key path (Chapter 10).

2. Subsequently, the observer's `observeValue(forKeyPath:of:change:context:)` is called for every change for which this observer has been registered.

There are two problems here. First, step 1 and step 2 happen in two different places; there's a disconnect between the two steps. And second, this observer might be observing more than one property, possibly in more than one observed object, so there can be many repetitions of step 1; but no matter how many times step 1 happens, *there is only one step 2*. There is just one single observer method, through which all observation calls must flow — which constitutes a nasty bottleneck. That's what the Swift way protects you from.

Here's how the Swift way works. You register by calling `observe(_:options:change-Handler:)` on the object whose property you want to observe, with these parameters:

`keyPath:`
> The first parameter is a Swift key path (Chapter 5), not a Cocoa key path.

`options:`
> An NSKeyValueObservingOptions bitmask (an option set) specifying such things as when you want to be notified (only when the observed value changes, or now as well) and what information you want included in the notification (the old value, the new value, or both).

`changeHandler:`
> A function to be called as a way of sending the notification. It will typically be an anonymous function, making it part of the registration. It should take two parameters:
>
> *The object*
> > This will be the observed object with which we are registered.
>
> *The change*
> > An NSKeyValueObservedChange object. Its properties give you information such as the old value and the new value if you requested them in the `options:` argument.

The call to `observe(_:options:changeHandler:)` also returns a value, an NSKey-ValueObservation instance. *That* is the registered observer.

The Swift key–value observing API is a *language* feature, not an SDK feature. It puts a convenient mechanism in front of the Cocoa API, but it still *uses* the Cocoa API. When you call `observe(_:options:changeHandler:)`, Swift calls `addObserver(_:forKeyPath:options:context:)` to register the observer with the observed object. And the NSKeyValueObservation object implements the bottleneck method `observeValue(forKeyPath:of:change:context:)` to receive notification messages, which it passes on to you.

Unregistering

Unregistration is performed through a message to the observed object, namely `removeObserver(_:forKeyPath:context:)`. If the observer goes out of existence without unregistering, the observed object might later try to send a message to a nonexistent observer, resulting in a crash. So the observer needs to maintain a reference to the observed object and, at the latest, must unregister itself when going out of existence.

That can be a daunting responsibility — and is yet another thing that the Swift API helps you with. The NSKeyValueObservation object returned from the call to `observe(_:options:changeHandler:)` maintains a reference to the observed object, so you don't have to; and it will unregister itself, by calling `removeObserver(_:for-KeyPath:context:)` on the observed object, either if you send it the `invalidate` message or *automatically* when it itself is about to go out of existence.

Your job is to capture the NSKeyValueObservation object and maintain it, probably in an instance property of the observer. That's all, because this means it will go out of existence, at the latest, when the observer does — and at that moment will unregister itself in good order. But you *must* capture and maintain that object somehow! If you don't, it will go out of existence and unregister itself *immediately* — before a notification is ever sent — and you'll never get any notifications in the first place.

Another problem is what happens if *the observed object* goes out of existence when observers are still registered on it. There are two cases:

In iOS 10 and before
> Your app will crash immediately. To prevent that, if the observed object is about to go out of existence while the observer continues to exist, you must unregister the NSKeyValueObservation object explicitly, yourself, by sending it the `invalidate` message.

In iOS 11 and later
> There are no bad consequences. There is no crash, and the NSKeyValueObservation object sends itself the `invalidate` message.

Key–Value Observing Example

To demonstrate KVO, I'll declare classes to play both roles, the observer and the observed.

First, the observed. My Observed class has a `value` instance property that we want other objects to be able to observe:

```
class Observed : NSObject { ❶
    @objc dynamic var value : Bool = false ❷
}
```

❶ The observed object's class must derive from NSObject; otherwise, you won't be able to call `observe(_:options:changeHandler:)` on it. That's because the mechanism for being observed is a feature of NSObject.

❷ The property to be observed must be declared `@objc` in order to expose it to Objective-C — and it must also be declared `dynamic`. That's because KVO works by *swizzling* the accessor methods; Cocoa needs to be able to reach right in and change this object's code, and it can't do that unless the property is `dynamic`.

The Observer class contains code that registers with an Observed to hear about changes in its `value` property:

```
class Observer {
    var obs = Set<NSKeyValueObservation>() ❶
    func register(with observed:Observed) {
        let opts : NSKeyValueObservingOptions = [.old, .new]
        let ob = observed.observe(\.value, options: opts) { obj,change in ❷
            if let oldValue = change.oldValue {
                print("old value was \(oldValue)")
            }
            if let newValue = change.newValue {
                print("new value is \(newValue)")
            }
        }
        obs.insert(ob) ❸
    }
}
```

❶ Observer has an instance property for maintaining NSKeyValueObservation objects. As with Notification observer tokens (discussed earlier in this chapter), I like to use a Set for this purpose.

❷ Observer (in its register(with:) method) will register with an Observed instance by calling observe(_:options:changeHandler:), using a Swift key path to specify the value property. I've illustrated the use of NSKeyValueObserving-Options by asking for both the old and new values of the observed property when a notification arrives. That information will arrive into the notification function inside an NSKeyValueObservedChange object.

❸ The call to observe(_:options:changeHandler:) returns an NSKeyValueOb-servation object. It is *crucial* to ensure the continued existence of this object; otherwise, it will go out of existence and unregister itself before the notification can ever arrive. Therefore, I immediately store it in the Set instance property that was declared for this purpose.

Presume now that we have a persistent Observer instance, observer, and that its register(with:) has been called with argument observed, an Observed instance that is also persistent:

```
observer.register(with: observed)
```

So much for registration!

Now let's talk about change and notification. Somehow, someone sets observed's value property to true. That changes it in a KVO compliant way. So, at that moment, the notification is sent and the anonymous function is called! The following appears in the console:

```
old value was false
new value is true
```

Finally, let's talk about unregistering. As long as we are running in iOS 11 or later, there is nothing to talk about! It doesn't matter whether observed or observer goes out of existence first; everything happens automatically and in good order:

- If observed goes out of existence first, there is no crash and there will be no further notifications.
- When observer goes out of existence, the obs property is destroyed, and so the NSKeyValueObservation object is destroyed — and at that moment, if observed still exists, the NSKeyValueObservation object unregisters itself (and if observed no longer exists, nothing bad happens).

In general your real-life use of KVO in programming iOS will likely be as simple as that. Cocoa key–value observing, however, is a deep and complex mechanism; consult Apple's *Key-Value Observing Programming Guide* in the documentation archive for full information.

Swamped by Events

Cocoa has the potential to send *lots* of events, telling you what the user has done, informing you of each stage in the lifetime of your app and its objects, asking for your input on how to proceed. To receive the events that you need to hear about, your code is peppered with *entry points* — methods that you have written with just the right name and in just the right class so that they can be called as Cocoa events. In fact, it is easy to imagine that in many cases your code for a class will consist almost entirely of entry points.

Arranging all those entry points is one of your primary challenges as a Cocoa programmer. You know what you want to do, but you don't get to "just do it." You have to divide up your app's functionality and allocate it in accordance with when and how Cocoa is going to call into your code. You know the events that Cocoa is going to want to send you, and you need to be prepared to receive them. Before you've written a single line of your own code, the skeleton structure of a class is likely to have been largely mapped out for you.

Suppose that your iPhone app presents an interface consisting of a table view. You'll probably subclass UITableViewController (a built-in UIViewController subclass); an instance of your subclass will own and control the table view, and you'll probably use it as the table view's data source and delegate as well. In this single class, then, you're likely to want to implement *at a minimum* the following methods:

init(coder:) *or* init(nibName:bundle:)
    UIViewController lifetime method, where you perform instance initializations.

`viewDidLoad`
> UIViewController lifetime method, where you perform view-related initializations and deferred initializations.

`viewDidAppear`
> UIViewController lifetime method, where you set up states that need to apply only while your view is onscreen. If you're going to register for a notification or set up a timer, this is a likely place to do it.

`viewDidDisappear`
> UIViewController lifetime method, where you reverse what you did in `viewDidAppear`. This would be a likely place to unregister for a notification or invalidate a repeating timer that you set up in `viewDidAppear`.

`supportedInterfaceOrientations`
> UIViewController query method, where you specify what device orientations are allowed for this view controller's main view.

`numberOfSections(in:)`
`tableView(_:numberOfRowsInSection:)`
`tableView(_:cellForRowAt:)`
> UITableView data source query methods, where you specify the contents of the table.

`tableView(_:didSelectRowAt:)`
> UITableView delegate user action method, where you respond when the user taps a row of the table.

`deinit`
> Swift class instance lifetime method, where you perform end-of-life cleanup.

Suppose, further, that you do in fact use `viewDidAppear` to register for a notification and to set up a timer, using the target–selector architecture; then you must also implement the methods specified by those selectors.

We already have, then, about a dozen methods whose presence is effectively boilerplate. These are not *your* methods; *you* are never going to call them. They are *Cocoa's* methods, which you have placed here so that each can be called at the appropriate moment in the life story of your app.

A Cocoa program consists of numerous disconnected entry points, each with its own meaning, each called at its own set moment. The logic of such a program is far from obvious; a Cocoa program, even *your* program, even while you're writing it, is hard to read and hard to understand. To figure out what our hypothetical class does, you have to know *already* such things as when `viewDidAppear` is called and how it is typically used; otherwise, you don't know what this method is for. Moreover, because of your code's object-oriented structure, multiple methods in this class (and perhaps others) will be managing the same instance properties; your program's logic is divided between methods and even across different classes.

Your challenges are compounded by surprises involving the *order* of events. Beginners (and even experienced programmers) are often mystified when their program doesn't work as expected, because they have wrong expectations about *when* an entry point will be called, or what the state of an instance will be when it *is* called. To make matters worse, the order of events isn't even reliable; my apps often break when I upgrade them from one iOS version to the next, because the new version of iOS is sending certain events in a different order from the old version.

How will you find your way through the swamp of events that a Cocoa program consists of? There's no easy solution, but here's some simple advice:

Write comments
> Comment every method, quite heavily if need be, saying what that method does and under what circumstances you expect it to be called — especially if it is an entry point, where it is Cocoa itself that will do the calling.

Debug
> Instrument your code heavily during development with caveman debugging (see Chapter 9). As you test your code, keep an eye on the console output and check whether the messages make sense. You may be surprised at what you discover. If things don't work as expected, add breakpoints and run the app again so you can see the order of execution and watch the variables and properties as they change.

Perhaps the most common kind of mistake in writing a Cocoa app is not that there's a bug in your code itself, but that you've put the code *in the wrong place*. Your code isn't running, or it's running at the wrong time, or the pieces are running in the wrong order. I see questions about this sort of thing all the time on the various online user forums (these are all actual examples that appeared over the course of just two days):

- *There's a delay between the time when my view appears and when my button takes on its correct title.*

  That's because you put the code that sets the button's title in `viewDidAppear`. That's *too late*; your code needs to run earlier, perhaps in `viewWillAppear`.

- *My subviews are positioned in code and they're turning out all wrong.*

  That's because you put the code that positions your subviews in `viewDidLoad`. That's *too early*; your code needs to run later, when your view's dimensions have been determined.

- *My view is rotating even though my view controller's `supportedInterface-Orientations` says not to.*

  That's because you implemented `supportedInterfaceOrientations` in the *wrong class*. Only the topmost view controller in the view controller hierarchy is consulted through this property.

- *I set up an action connection for Value Changed on a text field, but my code isn't being called when the user edits.*

  That's because you connected the *wrong control event*; a text field emits Editing Changed, not Value Changed.

Delayed Performance

Your code is executed in response to some event; but your code in turn may trigger a new event or chain of events. Sometimes this causes bad things to happen: there might be a crash, or Cocoa might appear not to have done what you said to do. To solve this problem, perhaps you just need to step outside Cocoa's own chain of events for a moment and wait for everything to settle down before proceeding.

The technique for doing this is called *delayed performance*. You tell Cocoa to do something, not right this moment, but in a little while, when things have settled down. Perhaps you need only a very short delay, just to let Cocoa finish doing something, such as laying out the interface. Technically, you're allowing the current run loop to finish, completing and unwinding the entire current call stack, before proceeding further with your own code.

When you program Cocoa, you're likely to be using delayed performance a lot more than you might expect. With experience, you'll develop a kind of sixth sense for when delayed performance might be the solution to your difficulties.

The main way to get delayed performance is by calling DispatchQueue's `after(when:execute:)` method. It takes a function stating what should happen after the specified time has passed. Here's a utility function that encapsulates the call:

```
func delay(_ delay:Double, closure:@escaping () -> ()) {
    let when = DispatchTime.now() + delay
    DispatchQueue.main.asyncAfter(deadline: when, execute: closure)
}
```

That utility function is so important that I routinely paste it at the top level of the AppDelegate class file in every app I write. To use it, I call `delay` with a delay time (usually a very small number of seconds such as `0.1`) and an anonymous function saying what to do after the delay. Note that what you propose to do in this anonymous function will be done later on; you're deliberately breaking out of your own code's line-by-line sequence of execution. So a delayed performance call will typically be the last call in its own surrounding function, and cannot return any value.

In this example from one of my own apps, the user has tapped a row of a table, and my code responds by creating and showing a new view controller:

```
override func tableView(_ tableView: UITableView,
    didSelectRowAt indexPath: IndexPath) {
        let t = TracksViewController(
            mediaItemCollection: self.albums[indexPath.row])
        self.navigationController?.pushViewController(t, animated: true)
}
```

Unfortunately, the innocent-looking call to my TracksViewController initializer init(mediaItemCollection:) can take a moment to complete, so the app comes to a stop with the table row highlighted — very briefly, but just long enough to startle the user. To cover this delay with a sense of activity, I've rigged my UITableViewCell subclass to show a spinning activity indicator when it's selected:

```
override func setSelected(_ selected: Bool, animated: Bool) {
    if selected {
        self.activityIndicator.startAnimating()
    } else {
        self.activityIndicator.stopAnimating()
    }
    super.setSelected(selected, animated: animated)
}
```

But there's a problem: the spinning activity indicator never appears and never spins. The reason is that the events are stumbling over one another here. UITableViewCell's setSelected(_:animated:) isn't called until the UITableView delegate method tableView(_:didSelectRowAt:) has finished. But the delay we're trying to paper over is *during* tableView(_:didSelectRowAt:); the whole problem is that it *doesn't* finish fast enough.

Delayed performance to the rescue! I'll rewrite tableView(_:didSelectRowAt:) so that it finishes immediately — triggering setSelected(_:animated:) immediately and causing the activity indicator to appear and spin — and I'll use delayed performance to call init(mediaItemCollection:) later on, when the interface has ironed itself out:

```
override func tableView(_ tableView: UITableView,
    didSelectRowAt indexPath: IndexPath) {
        delay(0.1) {
            let t = TracksViewController(
                mediaItemCollection: self.albums[indexPath.row])
            self.navigationController?.pushViewController(t, animated: true)
        }
}
```

CHAPTER 12

Memory Management

Classes, both in Swift and in Objective-C, are *reference types* (see "Value Types and Reference Types" on page 153). Behind the scenes, Swift and Objective-C memory management for reference types works essentially the same way. Such memory management, as I pointed out in Chapter 5, can be a tricky business.

Fortunately, Swift uses ARC (automatic reference counting), so you don't have to manage the memory for every reference type object explicitly and individually, as was once necessary in Objective-C. Thanks to ARC, you are far less likely to make a memory management mistake, and more of your time is liberated to concentrate on what your app actually does instead of dealing with memory management concerns.

Still, even in Swift, and even with ARC, it is possible to make a memory management mistake, or to be caught unawares by Cocoa's memory management behavior. A memory management mistake can lead to runaway excessive memory usage, crashes, or mysterious misbehavior of your app. Cocoa memory management can be surprising in individual cases, and can mislead you into making a memory management mistake; so you need to understand, and prepare for, what Cocoa is going to do.

Principles of Cocoa Memory Management

The reason why reference type memory must be managed at all is that references to reference type objects are merely pointers to the actual object, and there can be multiple references (pointers) to the very same object. This means that every reference must deal carefully with that object, out of consideration for the needs of other possible references. At the very latest, the object *should* go out of existence when there are *no* pointers to it. But so long as there are *any* pointers to it, the object must *not* go out of existence.

To illustrate, imagine three objects, Manny, Moe, and Jack, where both Manny and Moe have references to Jack. Jack is the object whose memory we are concerned to manage:

The object must not go out of existence too late

> If both Manny and Moe go out of existence, and if no other object has a reference to Jack, Jack should go out of existence too. An object without a pointer to it is useless; it is occupying memory, but no other object has, or can ever get, a reference to it. This is a *memory leak*.

The object must not go out of existence too soon

> If both Manny and Moe have a pointer to Jack, and if Manny somehow causes Jack to go out of existence, poor old Moe is left with a pointer to nothing (or worse, to garbage). A pointer whose object has been destroyed behind the pointer's back is a *dangling pointer*. If Moe subsequently uses that dangling pointer to send a message to the object that he thinks is there, the app will crash.

To prevent both memory leakage and dangling pointers, there is a policy of manual memory management based on a number, maintained by every reference type object, called its *retain count*. The rule is that other objects can increment or decrement an object's retain count — and that's all they are allowed to do. As long as an object's retain count is positive, the object will persist. No object has the direct power to tell another object to be destroyed; rather, as soon as an object's retain count is decremented to zero, it is destroyed automatically.

By this policy, every object that needs Jack to persist should increment Jack's retain count, and should decrement it once again when it no longer needs Jack to persist. As long as all objects are well-behaved in accordance with this policy, the problem of manual memory management is effectively solved:

- There cannot be any dangling pointers, because any object that has a pointer to Jack has incremented Jack's retain count, ensuring that Jack persists.

- There cannot be any memory leaks, because any object that no longer needs Jack decrements Jack's retain count. If every object that doesn't need Jack any longer behaves this way, then when *no* object needs Jack any longer, Jack's retain count will reach zero and Jack will go out of existence.

Rules of Cocoa Memory Management

An object is well-behaved with respect to memory management as long as it adheres to certain very simple, well-defined rules in conformity with the basic concepts of memory management. The underlying ethic is that *each* object that has a reference to a reference type object is responsible solely for *its own* memory management of that object, in accordance with these rules. If *all* objects that ever get a reference to this reference type object behave correctly with respect to these rules, the object's memory will be managed correctly and it will go out of existence exactly when it is no longer needed:

- If Manny or Moe *explicitly instantiates* Jack — by directly calling an initializer — then the initializer *increments* Jack's retain count.

- If Manny or Moe *makes a copy* of Jack — by calling `copy` or `mutableCopy` or any other method with `copy` in its name — then the copy method *increments* the retain count of this new, duplicate Jack.

- If Manny or Moe *acquires* a reference to Jack (not through explicit instantiation or copying), and needs Jack to *persist* — long enough to work with Jack in code, or long enough to be the value of an instance property — then he himself *increments* Jack's retain count. (This is called *retaining* Jack.)

- If and only if Manny or Moe has done any of those things — that is, if Manny or Moe has ever directly or indirectly caused Jack's retain count to be incremented — then when he himself no longer needs his reference to Jack, before letting go of that reference, he *decrements* Jack's retain count to balance exactly all previous increments that he himself has performed. (This is called *releasing* Jack.) Having released Jack, Manny or Moe should then assume that Jack no longer exists, because if this causes Jack's retain count to drop to zero, Jack *will* no longer exist. This is the *golden rule of memory management* — the rule that makes memory management work coherently and correctly.

A general way to understand the golden rule of memory management is in terms of *ownership*. If Manny has created, copied, or retained Jack — that is, if Manny has ever incremented Jack's retain count — Manny has asserted ownership of Jack. Both Manny and Moe can own Jack at the same time, but each is responsible only for managing his own ownership of Jack correctly. It is the responsibility of an owner of Jack eventually to decrement Jack's retain count — to release Jack, resigning ownership of Jack. The owner says: "Jack may or may not persist after this, but as for me, I'm done with Jack, and Jack can go out of existence as far as I'm concerned." At the same time, a nonowner of Jack must *never* release Jack. As long as all objects behave this way with respect to Jack, Jack will not leak nor will any pointer to Jack be left dangling.

What ARC Is and What It Does

Once upon a time, retaining and releasing an object was a matter of you, the programmer, literally sending `retain` and `release` messages to it. NSObject still implements `retain` and `release`, but under ARC (and in Swift) you can't call them. That's because ARC is calling them for you! That's ARC's job — to do for you what you would have had to do if memory management were still up to the programmer.

ARC is implemented as part of the compiler. The compiler is literally modifying your code by inserting `retain` and `release` calls behind the scenes. When you receive a reference type object by calling some method, ARC immediately retains it so that it will persist for as long as this same code continues to run; then ARC releases it when the code comes to an end. Similarly, when you create or copy a reference type object, ARC knows that its retain count has been incremented, and releases it when the code comes to an end.

ARC is very conservative, but also very accurate. In effect, ARC retains at every juncture that might have the slightest implications for memory management: it retains when an object is received as an argument, it retains when an object is assigned to a variable, and so forth. It may even insert temporary variables, behind the scenes, to enable it to refer sufficiently early to an object so that it can retain it. But of course it eventually also releases to match.

How Cocoa Objects Manage Memory

Built-in Cocoa objects will take ownership of objects that you hand to them, by retaining them, if it makes sense for them to do so, and will of course then balance that retain with a release later. Indeed, this is so generally true that if a Cocoa object is *not* going to retain an object you hand it, there will be a note to that effect in the documentation.

A collection, such as an array or dictionary, is a particularly obvious case in point. An object can hardly be an element of a collection if that object can go out of existence at any time; so when you add an element to a collection, the collection asserts ownership of the object by retaining it. Thereafter, the collection acts as a well-behaved owner. If this is a mutable collection, then if an element is removed from it, the collection releases that element. If the collection object goes out of existence, it releases all its elements.

Prior to ARC, removing an object from a mutable collection constituted a potential trap. Consider the following Objective-C code:

```
id obj = myMutableArray[0]; // an NSMutableArray
[myMutableArray removeObjectAtIndex: 0]; // bad idea in non-ARC code!
// ... could crash here by referring to obj ...
```

As I just said, when you remove an object from a mutable collection, the collection releases it. So, without ARC, the second line of that code involves an implicit release of the object that used to be the first element of `myMutableArray`. If this reduces the object's retain count to zero, it will be destroyed. The pointer `obj` will then be a dangling pointer, and a crash may be in our future when we try to use it as if it were a real object.

With ARC, however, that sort of danger doesn't exist. Assigning a reference type object to a variable retains it! But we *did* assign this object to a variable, obj, *before* we removed it from the collection. Therefore, that code is perfectly safe, and so is its Swift equivalent:

```
let obj = myMutableArray[0] // retain
myMutableArray.removeObject(at:0) // release
// ... safe to refer to obj ...
```

The first line retains the object. The second line releases the object, but that release balances the retain that was placed on the object when the object was placed in the collection originally. The object's retain count is still more than zero, and it continues to exist for the duration of this code.

Autorelease Pool

When a method creates an instance and returns that instance, some memory management hanky-panky has to take place. Consider this simple code:

```
func makeImage() -> UIImage? {
    if let im = UIImage(named:"myImage") {
        return im
    }
    return nil
}
```

Think about the retain count of im, the UIImage we are returning. This retain count has been incremented by our call to the UIImage initializer UIImage(named:). According to the golden rule of memory management, as we pass im out of our own control by returning it, we should decrement the retain count of im, balancing the increment and surrendering ownership. But when can we possibly do that? If we do it *before* the line return im, the retain count of im will be zero and it will vanish in a puff of smoke; we will be returning a dangling pointer. But we can't do it *after* the line return im, because when that line is executed, our code comes to an end.

Clearly, we need a way to vend this object without decrementing its retain count *now* — so that it stays in existence long enough for the caller to receive and work with it — while ensuring that at some future time we *will* decrement its retain count, so as to balance our init(named:) call and fulfill our own management of this object's memory. The solution is something midway between releasing the object and not releasing it — *autoreleasing* it.

Here's how autoreleasing works. Your code runs in the presence of something called an *autorelease pool*. When ARC autoreleases an object, that object is placed in the autorelease pool, and a number is incremented saying how many times this object has been placed in this autorelease pool. From time to time, when nothing else is going on, the autorelease pool is automatically *drained*. This means that the

33.79 MB

Figure 12-1. Memory usage grows during a loop

autorelease pool releases each of its objects, the same number of times as that object was placed in this autorelease pool, and empties itself of all objects. If that causes an object's retain count to be zero, so be it; the object is destroyed in the usual way. So autoreleasing an object is just like releasing it, but with a proviso, "later, not right this second."

In general, autoreleasing and the autorelease pool are merely an implementation detail. You can't see them; they are just part of how ARC works. But sometimes, on very rare occasions, you might want to drain the autorelease pool yourself. Consider the following code (it's slightly artificial, but that's because demonstrating the need to drain the autorelease pool isn't easy):

```
func test() {
    let path = Bundle.main.path(forResource:"001", ofType: "png")!
    for j in 0 ..< 50 {
        for i in 0 ..< 100 {
            let im = UIImage(contentsOfFile: path)
        }
    }
}
```

That method does something that looks utterly innocuous; it loads an image. But it loads it repeatedly in a loop. As the loop runs, memory climbs constantly (Figure 12-1); by the time our method comes to an end, our app's memory usage has reached almost 34MB. This is not because the images aren't being released each time through the loop; it's because a lot of *intermediate* objects — things you've never even heard of, such as NSPathStore2 objects — are secondarily generated by our call to init(contentsOfFile:) *and are autoreleased.* As we keep looping, those objects are all sitting there, piling up in the autorelease pool by the tens of thousands, waiting for the pool to be drained. When our code finally comes to an end, the autorelease pool *is* drained, and our memory usage drops precipitately back down to almost nothing.

Granted, 34MB isn't exactly a massive amount of memory. But you may imagine that a more elaborate inner loop might generate more and larger autoreleased objects, and that our memory usage could potentially rise quite significantly. It would be nice to have a way to drain the autorelease pool *manually* now and then during the course of a loop with many iterations. Swift provides such a way — the global autoreleasepool function, which takes a single argument that you'll supply as an anonymous function using trailing closure syntax. Before the anonymous function is called, a special temporary autorelease pool is created, and is used for all autoreleased

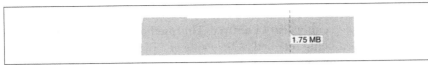

1.75 MB

Figure 12-2. Memory usage holds steady with an autorelease pool

objects thereafter. After the anonymous function exits, the temporary autorelease pool is drained and goes out of existence. Here's the same method with an `autoreleasepool` call wrapping the inner loop:

```
func test() {
    let path = Bundle.main.path(forResource:"001", ofType: "png")!
    for j in 0 ..< 50 {
        autoreleasepool {
            for i in 0 ..< 100 {
                let im = UIImage(contentsOfFile: path)
            }
        }
    }
}
```

The difference in memory usage is dramatic: memory holds roughly steady at less than 2MB (Figure 12-2). Setting up and draining the temporary autorelease pool probably involves some overhead, so if possible you may want to divide your loop into an outer and an inner loop, as shown in the example, so that the autorelease pool is not set up and torn down on every iteration.

Memory Management of Instance Properties

Before ARC, managing memory for instance properties (Objective-C instance variables, Chapter 10) was one of the trickiest parts of Cocoa programming. The correct behavior is to retain a reference type object when you assign it to a property, and then release it when either of these things happens:

- You assign a different value to the same property.
- The instance whose instance property this is goes out of existence.

Memory management for a property therefore had to be distributed in two places:

The setter method for the property
> The setter must release whatever object is currently the value of the property, and must retain whatever object is being assigned to that property. The exact details can be quite tricky (what if they are the same object?), and before ARC it was easy for programmers to get them wrong.

The owner's `dealloc` *method*

> This is the Objective-C equivalent of `deinit`. This method must be implemented to release every object being retained as the value of a property, or the object will leak when the owner goes out of existence.

Fortunately, ARC understands all that, and in Swift the memory of instance properties, like the memory of all variables, is managed correctly for you.

That fact also gives us a clue as to how to *release an object on demand* when you are holding it in an instance property. This is a valuable thing to be able to do, because an object may be using a lot of memory. You don't want to put too great a strain on the device's memory, so you want to release the object as soon as you're done with it. Also, when your app goes into the background and is suspended, the Watchdog process will terminate it in the background if it is found to be using too much memory; so you might want to release this object when you are notified that the app is about to be backgrounded.

You can't call `release` explicitly, so you need another way to do it, some way that is consonant with the design and behavior of ARC. The solution is to *assign something else* — something small — to this property. That causes the object that was previously the value of this property to be released. A commonly used approach is to type this property as an Optional. This means that `nil` can be assigned to it, purely as a way of replacing the object that is the instance property's current value and releasing it.

Retain Cycles and Weak References

As I explained in Chapter 5, you can get yourself into a retain cycle where two reference type objects have references to one another: for example, each is the value of the other's instance property. If such a situation is allowed to persist until no other objects have a reference to either of these objects, then neither can go out of existence, because each has a retain count greater than zero and neither will "go first" and release the other. Since these two objects, *ex hypothesi*, can no longer be referred to by any object except one another, this situation can now never be remedied — these objects are leaking.

The solution is to step in and modify how the memory is managed for one of these references. By default, a reference is a strong reference: assigning to it retains the assigned value. In Swift, you can declare a reference type variable as `weak` or as `unowned` to change the way its memory is managed:

`weak`

> When a reference is `weak`, ARC does *not* retain the object assigned to it. This seems dangerous, because it means that the object might go out of existence behind our backs, leaving us with a dangling pointer and leading to a potential

crash later on. But ARC is very clever about this. A reference marked as weak *must be a var reference to an Optional.* ARC keeps track of all weak references and all objects assigned to them. When such an object's retain count drops to zero and the object is about to be destroyed, just before the object's deinit is called, ARC sneaks in and assigns nil to the reference. Provided you handle the Optional coherently (by coping with the fact that it might suddenly be nil), nothing bad can happen.

unowned

An unowned reference is a different kettle of fish. When you mark a reference as unowned, you're telling ARC to take its hands off completely: it does no memory management at all when something is assigned to this reference. This really *is* dangerous — if the object referred to goes out of existence, you really *can* be left with a dangling pointer and you really *can* crash. That is why you must never use unowned unless you know that the object referred to will *not* go out of existence: unowned is safe, provided the object referred to will outlive the object that refers to it. So an unowned reference should point at all times to some single independent object, retained in some other way, without which the referrer cannot exist at all.

A weak reference is commonly used to connect an object to its delegate (Chapter 11):

```
class ColorPickerController : UIViewController {
    weak var delegate: ColorPickerDelegate?
    // ...
}
```

A delegate is an independent entity; there is usually no reason why an object needs to claim ownership of its delegate. Indeed, an object is usually its delegate's servant, not its owner, and ownership, if there is any, runs the other way; Object A might create *and retain* Object B, and make itself Object B's delegate:

```
let cpc = ColorPickerController(colorName:colorName, color:c)
cpc.delegate = self
self.present(cpc, animated: true) // retains cpc
```

There's no danger of a retain cycle in that code, because the delegate property is weak. This view controller (self) is not somehow retaining itself.

Very rarely, you may encounter properties of built-in Cocoa classes that keep weak references as *non-ARC* weak references (because they are old and backward compatible, whereas ARC is new). Such properties are declared in Objective-C using the keyword assign. NSCache's delegate property is declared like this:

```
@property (nullable, assign) id<NSCacheDelegate> delegate;
```

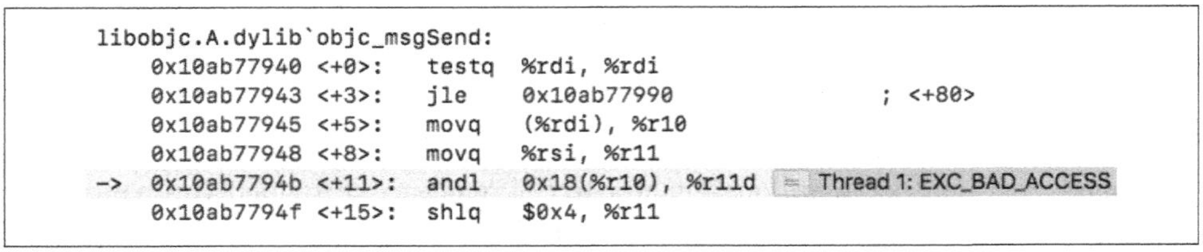

```
libobjc.A.dylib`objc_msgSend:
    0x10ab77940 <+0>:    testq  %rdi, %rdi
    0x10ab77943 <+3>:    jle    0x10ab77990            ; <+80>
    0x10ab77945 <+5>:    movq   (%rdi), %r10
    0x10ab77948 <+8>:    movq   %rsi, %r11
->  0x10ab7794b <+11>:   andl   0x18(%r10), %r11d  =  Thread 1: EXC_BAD_ACCESS
    0x10ab7794f <+15>:   shlq   $0x4, %r11
```

Figure 12-3. A crash from messaging a dangling pointer

In Swift, that declaration is translated like this:

```
unowned(unsafe) var delegate: NSCacheDelegate?
```

The Swift term unowned and the Objective-C term `assign` are synonyms; they tell you that there's no ARC memory management here. The unsafe designation is a further warning inserted by Swift; unlike your own code, where you won't use unowned unless it is safe, Cocoa's unowned is potentially dangerous and you need to exercise caution.

A reference such as an NSCache's `delegate` can end up as a dangling pointer, pointing at garbage, if the object to which that reference was pointing has gone out of existence. If anyone tries to send a message by way of such a reference, the app will then crash. This is the delegate, so what usually happens is that Cocoa tries to send it a delegate message. The tell-tale sign of such a crash is that EXC_BAD_ACCESS is reported somewhere in objc_msgSend (Figure 12-3).

Figuring out the cause of a crash like that can be quite difficult, especially since the crash itself typically takes place long after the point where the real mistake occurred, namely that some object went out of existence while a reference to it continued to exist. You might not even know *what* object went out of existence. (This is the sort of situation in which you might need to "turn on zombies" in order to debug, as I'll describe at the end of this chapter.)

Non-ARC weak references of this kind are few and far between in Cocoa nowadays; but they were once relatively common, so the earlier the iOS version on which you're running, the more likely you are to encounter one. Fortunately, it's easy to avoid a dangling pointer by making sure there is always something to point to. With an NSCache's `delegate`, if the delegate object is about to go out of existence at a time when the NSCache instance still exists, we would assign nil (or some other object) to the `delegate` property, rendering it harmless.

Unusual Memory Management Situations

This section discusses some situations that call for some special memory management handling on your part.

Notification Observers

Recall the example I gave in Chapter 11, where you register with the notification center by calling addObserver(forName:object:queue:using:), like this:

```
let ob = NotificationCenter.default.addObserver(
    forName: .MPMusicPlayerControllerNowPlayingItemDidChange,
    object: nil, queue: nil) { _ in
        self.updateNowPlayingItem()
        // ... and so on ...
    }
self.observers.insert(ob as! NSObject)
```

I didn't tell you at the time, but that code has the potential to cause a serious memory leak. The reason is that the observer token object (ob) returned from the registration call is *retained by the notification center* until you unregister it. (I regard this as something of a dirty trick on the notification center's part; I think I understand Apple's reasoning in designing things this way, but I also think they reasoned incorrectly.)

So the observer token object is likely to leak — but that isn't the serious part. The serious part is that the observer token object is *also* retaining *the view controller* (self) through the anonymous function. The reason is that functions are closures, and this function refers to self. So the view controller is leaking along with the observer token. That's bad. A view controller together with its properties, including its view, constitutes a heavyweight object and needs to go out existence when it is no longer needed. You cannot solve the problem merely by unregistering the observer in the view controller's deinit, because *ex hypothesi* deinit isn't going to be called; that is what leaking *means*.

The solution to the leakage of self is to mark self as weak or (preferably) unowned in the anonymous function. Now deinit will be called and the view controller can go out of existence in good order. But we must *still* remember to unregister the observer token object, because otherwise the observer token itself will still leak, and its function can be called again even though self no longer exists (and if we marked self as unowned, the app will crash at that moment with a dangling pointer). A complete solution looks something like this:

```
var observers = Set<NSObject>()
override func viewDidLoad() {
    super.viewDidLoad()
    let ob = NotificationCenter.default.addObserver(
        forName: .MPMusicPlayerControllerNowPlayingItemDidChange,
        object: nil, queue: nil) { [unowned self] _ in ❶
            self.updateNowPlayingItem()
            // ... and so on ...
        }
    self.observers.insert(ob as! NSObject)
}
```

```
deinit {
    for ob in self.observers {
        NotificationCenter.default.removeObserver(ob) ❷
    }
}
```

❶ If you omit unowned self, then self will leak (and deinit will never be called).

❷ If you omit removeObserver, then any observers will leak, and we can crash if the notification center later sends a notification to an observer with an unowned reference to a self that no longer exists.

KVO Observers

The NSKeyValueObservation observer object that you get when you call observe(_:options:changeHandler:) (Chapter 11) is quite similar to the observer token object you get from the notification center. You maintain a reference to the observer object, because otherwise the notification message won't arrive. And you'll probably want to let the observer object just go out of existence when you yourself go out of existence, because it will then unregister itself automatically, which is exactly what you want.

The problem is that if your notification function refers to self, that's a retain cycle, because you are retaining an observer whose function is also retaining you. Therefore you *won't* go out of existence, so the observer won't go out of existence either and won't be automatically unregistered. The solution, once again, is to mark self as unowned in the notification function:

```
var obs = Set<NSKeyValueObservation>()
func registerWith(_ mc:MyClass1) {
    let opts : NSKeyValueObservingOptions = [.old, .new]
    let ob = mc.observe(\.value, options: opts) {
        [unowned self] obj, change in
        print(self) // potential leak
    }
    obs.insert(ob)
}
```

Timers

The class documentation for Timer (Chapter 10) says that "run loops maintain strong references to their timers"; it then says of scheduledTimer(timeInterval:target:selector:userInfo:repeats:) that "The timer maintains a strong reference to target until it (the timer) is invalidated." This should set off alarm bells in your head: "Danger, Will Robinson, danger!" The documentation is warning you that as long as a repeating timer has not been invalidated, the target is being retained by the run loop; the only way to stop this is to send the invalidate message to the timer. (With a non-repeating timer, the problem arises less starkly, because the timer invalidates itself immediately after firing.)

Moreover, the `target:` argument is probably `self`. This means that you (`self`) are being retained, and cannot go out of existence until you invalidate the timer. So when will you that? You can't do it in your `deinit` implementation, because as long as the timer is repeating and has not been sent the `invalidate` message, `deinit` won't be called. You therefore need to find another appropriate moment for sending `invalidate` to the timer, such as `viewDidDisappear`:

```swift
var timer : Timer!
override func viewWillAppear(_ animated: Bool) {
    super.viewWillAppear(animated)
    self.timer = Timer.scheduledTimer(timeInterval: 1, target: self,
        selector: #selector(fired), userInfo: nil, repeats: true)
    self.timer.tolerance = 0.1
}
@objc func fired(_ t:Timer) {
    print("timer fired")
}
override func viewDidDisappear(_ animated: Bool) {
    super.viewDidDisappear(animated)
    self.timer.invalidate()
}
```

Instead, a more flexible approach is to call the `scheduledTimer(withTime-Interval:repeats:block:)` class method. Now there is no retained `target:` — but there is a retained function. If the timer is a repeating timer, you are retaining it so that you can invalidate it later, but the timer is retaining the function, and if that function involves a reference to `self`, it will retain `self`, causing a retain cycle. But we know what to do about that! Mark `self` as `weak` or `unowned` in the function. Now you *can* invalidate the timer in `deinit`. This is similar to the two-part solution I described earlier for notification observer token objects:

```swift
var timer : Timer!
override func viewDidLoad() {
    super.viewDidLoad()
    self.timer = Timer.scheduledTimer(withTimeInterval: 1, repeats: true) {
        [unowned self] t in // *
        self.fired(t)
    }
}
func fired(_ t:Timer) {
    print("timer fired")
}
deinit {
    self.timer.invalidate() // *
}
```

Other Unusual Situations

Other Cocoa objects with unusual memory management behavior will usually be called out clearly in the documentation. A CAAnimation object *retains its delegate*; this is exceptional and can cause serious trouble if you're not conscious of it (as usual, I speak from bitter experience). There are also situations where the documentation fails to warn of any special memory management considerations, but you can wind up with a retain cycle anyway. Discovering the problem can be tricky. Areas of Cocoa that have given me trouble include UIKit Dynamics (a UIDynamicBehavior's `action` handler) and WebKit (a WKWebKit's WKScriptMessageHandler).

Three Foundation collection classes — NSPointerArray, NSHashTable, and NSMap-Table — are similar respectively to NSMutableArray, NSMutableSet, and NSMutableDictionary, except that (among other things) their memory management policy is up to you. An NSHashTable created with the `weakObjects` class method maintains ARC-weak references to its elements, meaning that they are replaced by `nil` if the retain count of the object to which they were pointing has dropped to zero. You may find uses for these classes as a way of avoiding retain cycles.

Nib Loading and Memory Management

When a nib loads, it instantiates its nib objects (Chapter 7). What happens to these instantiated objects? A view retains its subviews, but what about the top-level objects, which are not subviews of any view? They do *not* have elevated retain counts; if someone doesn't immediately retain them, they'll simply vanish in a puff of smoke.

If you don't want that to happen — and if you did, why would you be loading this nib in the first place? — you need to capture a reference to the top-level objects instantiated from the nib. There are two ways of doing that.

The first approach is to capture the result of the nib-loading code. When a nib is loaded by calling Bundle's `loadNibNamed(_:owner:options:)` or UINib's `instantiate(withOwner:options:)`, an array is returned consisting of the top-level objects instantiated by the nib-loading mechanism. So it's sufficient to retain this array, or the objects in it. We did that in Chapter 7 when we loaded a nib and assigned the result to a variable, like this:

```
let arr = Bundle.main.loadNibNamed("View", owner: nil)!
let v = arr[0] as! UIView
self.view.addSubview(v)
```

The other possibility is to configure the nib owner with outlets that will retain the nib's top-level objects when they are instantiated. We did that in Chapter 7 when we set up an outlet like this:

```
class ViewController: UIViewController {
    @IBOutlet var coolview : UIView!
```

We then loaded the nib with this view controller as owner:

```
Bundle.main.loadNibNamed("View", owner: self)
self.view.addSubview(self.coolview)
```

In the first line, the nib-loading mechanism instantiates the top-level view from the nib and assigns it to `self.coolview`. Since `self.coolview` is a strong reference, it retains the view, and the view is still there when we insert it into the interface in the second line.

In real life, `@IBOutlet` properties that will be set by the loading of a nib are usually marked weak. Such outlet properties work properly as long as the object referred to will be retained by someone else — for instance, because it's already a subview of your view controller's main view. A view controller retains its main view, and a view is retained by its superview, so the nib-loading process will cause this view to be retained, and there is no need for your `@IBOutlet` property to retain it as well.

Memory Management of CFTypeRefs

A CFTypeRef is a pure C analog to an Objective-C object. In Objective-C, CFTypeRef types are distinguished by the suffix `Ref` at the end of their name; in Swift, this `Ref` suffix is dropped. For instance, a CGContextRef is a CFTypeRef, and is known in Swift as a CGContext.

A CFTypeRef is a pointer to an opaque C struct (see Appendix A), where "opaque" means that the struct has no directly accessible components. This struct acts as a pseudo-object; a CFTypeRef is analogous to an object type. In Objective-C, the fact that this thing is not an object is particularly obvious, because the code that operates upon a CFTypeRef is not object-oriented. A CFTypeRef has no properties or methods, and you do not send any messages to it; you work with CFTypeRefs entirely through global C functions. In Swift's Core Graphics overlay, however, those global C functions are hand-tweaked to *look* like methods; for instance, the `CGContextDraw-LinearGradient` C function is called, in Swift, by sending `drawLinear-Gradient(_:start:end:options:)` to a CGContext pseudo-object, just as if a CGContext were an object and `drawLinearGradient` were an instance method.

Here's some actual Swift code for drawing a gradient; `con` is a CGContext, `sp` is a CGColorSpace, and `grad` is a CGGradient (all of them being CFTypeRefs):

```
let con = UIGraphicsGetCurrentContext()!
let locs : [CGFloat] = [ 0.0, 0.5, 1.0 ]
let colors : [CGFloat] = [
    0.8, 0.4, // starting color, transparent light gray
    0.1, 0.5, // intermediate color, darker less transparent gray
```

```
    0.8, 0.4, // ending color, transparent light gray
]
let sp = CGColorSpaceCreateDeviceGray()
let grad = CGGradient(colorSpace: sp,
    colorComponents: colors, locations: locs, count: 3)!
con.drawLinearGradient(grad,
    start: CGPoint(x:89,y:0), end: CGPoint(x:111,y:0), options:[])
```

Despite being only a pseudo-object, a CFTypeRef is a reference type, and its memory must be managed in just the same way as that of a real object. Therefore, a CFType-Ref pseudo-object has a retain count! And this retain count works exactly as for a true object, in accordance with the golden rule of memory management. A CFType-Ref must be retained when it comes within the sphere of influence of an owner who wants it to persist, and it must be released when that owner no longer needs it.

In Objective-C, the golden rule, as applied to CFTypeRefs, is that if you obtained a CFTypeRef object through a function whose name contains the word Create or Copy, its retain count has been incremented. In addition, if you are worried about the object persisting, you'll retain it explicitly by calling the CFRetain function to increment its retain count. To balance your Create, Copy, or CFRetain call, you must eventually release the object. By default, you'll do that by calling the CFRelease function; some CFTypeRefs, however, have their own dedicated object release functions — for CGPath, for instance, there's a dedicated CGPathRelease function. There's no ARC management of CFTypeRefs in Objective-C, so you have to do all of this yourself, explicitly.

In Swift, however, you will *never* need to call CFRetain, or any form of CFRelease; indeed, you cannot. Swift will do it for you, behind the scenes, automatically.

Think of CFTypeRefs as living in two worlds: the CFTypeRef world of pure C, and the memory-managed object-oriented world of Swift. When you obtain a CFTypeRef pseudo-object, it *crosses the bridge* from the CFTypeRef world into the Swift world. From that moment on, until you are done with it, it needs memory management. Swift is aware of this, and for the most part, Swift itself will use the golden rule and will apply correct memory management. The code I showed earlier for drawing a gradient is in fact memory-management complete. In Objective-C, we would have to release sp and grad, because they arrived into our world through Create calls; if we failed to do this, they would leak. In Swift, however, there is no need, because Swift will do it for us. (See Appendix A for more about how objects move between the CFTypeRef world and the memory-managed object world.)

Working with CFTypeRefs in Swift, then, is much easier than in Objective-C. In Swift, you can treat CFTypeRef pseudo-objects as actual objects! You can assign a CFTypeRef to a property in Swift, or pass it as an argument to a Swift function, and its memory will be managed correctly; in Objective-C, those are tricky things to do.

It is still possible, though, to receive a CFTypeRef through some API that lacks memory management information. Such a value will come forcibly to your attention, because it will arrive into Swift, not as a CFTypeRef, but as an Unmanaged generic wrapping the actual CFTypeRef. That situation alerts you to the fact that Swift does not know how to proceed with the memory management of this pseudo-object. You will be unable to use the CFTypeRef until you extract it by calling the Unmanaged object's `takeRetainedValue` or `takeUnretainedValue` method. You will call whichever method tells Swift how to manage the memory for this object correctly. For a CFTypeRef with an incremented retain count (usually acquired through a function with `Create` or `Copy` in its name), call `takeRetainedValue`; otherwise, call `takeUnretainedValue`.

Property Memory Management Policies

In Objective-C, a `@property` declaration (see Chapter 10) includes a statement of the memory management policy implemented by the corresponding setter accessor method. It is useful to be aware of this and to know how such policy statements are translated into Swift.

Earlier I said that a UIViewController retains its `view` (its main view). How do I know this? Because the `@property` declaration tells me so:

```
@property(null_resettable, nonatomic, strong) UIView *view;
```

The term `strong` means that the setter retains the incoming UIView object. The Swift translation of this declaration doesn't add any attribute to the variable:

```
var view: UIView!
```

The default in Swift is that a variable referring to a reference object type *is* a strong reference. This means that it retains the object. You can safely conclude from this declaration that a UIViewController retains its `view`.

The possible memory management policies for a Cocoa property are:

`strong`, `retain` *(no Swift equivalent term)*
> The default. The two terms are pure synonyms; `retain` is the term inherited from pre-ARC days. Assignment to this property releases the existing value (if any) and retains the incoming value.

`copy` *(Swift* `@NSCopying`*)*
> The same as `strong` or `retain`, except that the setter copies the incoming value by sending `copy` to it; the incoming value must be an object of a type that adopts NSCopying, to ensure that this is possible. The copy, which has an increased retain count already, becomes the new value.

weak *(Swift* weak*)*

An ARC-weak reference. The incoming object value is not retained, but if it goes out of existence behind our back, ARC will magically substitute nil as the value of this property, which must be typed as an Optional declared with var.

assign *(Swift* unowned(unsafe)*)*

No memory management. This policy is inherited from pre-ARC days, and is inherently unsafe (hence the additional unsafe warning in the Swift translation of the name): if the object referred to goes out of existence, this reference will become a dangling pointer and can cause a crash if you subsequently try to use it.

The copy policy is used by Cocoa particularly when an immutable class has a mutable subclass (such as NSString and NSMutableString, or NSArray and NSMutableArray; see Chapter 10). The idea is to deal with the danger of the setter's caller passing an object of the mutable subclass. This is possible because, in accordance with the substitution principle of polymorphism (Chapter 4), wherever an instance of a class is expected, an instance of its subclass can be used instead. It would be bad if this were to happen, because now the caller might keep a reference to the incoming value and, since it is in fact mutable, could later mutate it behind our back. To prevent this, the setter calls copy on the incoming object; this creates a new instance, separate from the object provided — and belonging to the immutable class.

In Swift, this problem is unlikely to arise with strings and arrays, because on the Swift side these are value types (structs) and are effectively copied when assigned, passed as an argument, or received as a return value. Cocoa's NSString and NSArray property declarations, when translated into Swift as String and Array property declarations, don't show any special marking corresponding to Objective-C copy. But Cocoa types that are *not* bridged to Swift value types *do* show a marking: @NSCopying. The declaration of the attributedText property of a UILabel appears like this in Swift:

```
@NSCopying var attributedText: NSAttributedString?
```

NSAttributedString has a mutable subclass, NSMutableAttributedString. You've probably configured this attributed string as an NSMutableAttributedString, and now you're assigning it as a UILabel's attributedText. The UILabel doesn't want you keeping a reference to this mutable string and mutating it in place, since that would change the value of the property without passing through the setter. It copies the incoming value to ensure that what it has is a separate immutable NSAttributed-String.

You'll want to do the same thing in your own code, and you can. Simply mark your property with the @NSCopying attribute; Swift will enforce the copy policy and will take care of the actual copying for you whenever this property is assigned to:

```
class StringDrawer {
    @NSCopying var attributedString : NSAttributedString!
    // ...
}
```

If, as is sometimes the case, your own class wants the internal ability to mutate the value of this property while preventing a mutable value from arriving from outside, put a private computed property façade in front of it whose getter transforms it to the corresponding mutable type:

```
class StringDrawer {
    @NSCopying var attributedString : NSAttributedString!
    private var mutableAttributedString : NSMutableAttributedString! {
        get {
            if self.attributedString == nil {return nil}
            return NSMutableAttributedString(
                attributedString:self.attributedString)
        }
        set {
            self.attributedString = newValue
        }
    }
    // ...
}
```

@NSCopying can be used *only* for instance properties of classes, not of structs or enums — and only in the presence of Foundation, because that is where the NSCopying protocol is defined, which the type of a variable marked as @NSCopying must adopt.

Debugging Memory Management Mistakes

Though far less likely to occur under ARC (and Swift), memory management mistakes *can* still occur, especially because a programmer is apt to assume that they can't. Experience suggests that you should use every tool at your disposal to ferret out possible mistakes. Here are some of those tools (and see Chapter 9):

- The memory gauge in the Debug navigator charts memory usage whenever your app runs, allowing you to observe possible memory leakage or other unwarranted heavy memory use. Note that memory management in the Simulator is not necessarily indicative of reality! Always observe the memory gauge with the app running on a device before making a judgment.

- Instruments (Product → Profile) has excellent tools for discerning leaks and tracking memory management of individual objects (Leaks, Allocations).

- Good old caveman debugging can help confirm that your objects are behaving as you want them to. Implement `deinit` with a `print` call. If it isn't called, your object is not going out of existence. This technique can reveal problems that even Instruments will not directly expose.

- Memory graphing ("Memory Debugging" on page 478) will draw you a picture of the ownership relations between your objects; circular references are usually easy to spot. In conjunction with Malloc Stack Logging, you can trace object ownership through the actual retain calls.

- Dangling pointers are particularly difficult to track down, but they can often be located by "turning on zombies." This is easy in Instruments with the Zombies template (on a device). Alternatively, edit the Run action in your scheme, switch to the Diagnostics tab, and check Enable Zombie Objects. The result is that an object that goes out of existence is replaced by a "zombie" that will report to the console if a message is sent to it ("message sent to deallocated instance"). Moreover, the zombie knows what *kind* of object it replaces, so you can learn *what* got deallocated. Be sure to turn zombies back off when you've finished tracking down your dangling pointers. Don't use zombies with the Leaks instrument: zombies *are* leaks.

- The Address Sanitizer (also in the scheme's Run action's Diagnostics tab) lets you debug even more subtle forms of memory misuse. Here we're doing a Very Bad Thing, writing directly into memory that doesn't belong to us:

```
let b = UnsafeMutablePointer<CGFloat>.allocate(capacity:3)
b.initializeFrom([0.1, 0.2, 0.3])
b[4] = 0.4
```

That code probably won't crash; it corrupts memory silently, which is even worse. But if we run our app under Address Sanitizer, it detects the problem and reports a heap buffer overflow.

CHAPTER 13

Communication Between Objects

As soon as an app grows to more than a few objects, puzzling questions can arise about how to send a message or communicate data between one object and another. It may require some planning to construct your code so that all the pieces fit together and information can be shared as needed at the right moment. This chapter presents some organizational considerations that will help you arrange for coherent communication between objects.

Visibility Through an Instance Property

One object's ability to communicate with another often comes down to one object being able to *see* another. If the object Manny needs to be able to find the object Jack repeatedly and reliably over the long term so as to be able to send Jack messages, Manny will presumably need a way of seeing Jack in the first place.

One obvious solution is an instance property of Manny whose value *is* Jack. An instance property is appropriate particularly when Manny and Jack share certain responsibilities or supplement one another's functionality. Here are some commonly occurring cases where one object needs to have an instance property pointing at another:

- The application object and its delegate
- A table view and its data source
- A view controller and the view that it controls

Manny may have an instance property pointing to Jack, but this does not necessarily imply that Manny needs to assert *ownership* of Jack as a matter of memory management policy (see Chapter 12). Here are some common situations in which one object has a property pointing to another object, but does not retain that object:

- An object does not typically retain its delegate or its data source.
- An object that implements the target–action pattern, such as a UIControl, does not retain its target.

By using a weak reference and typing the property as an Optional, and then treating the Optional coherently and safely, Manny can keep a reference to Jack without owning Jack (while coping with the possibility that his supposed reference to Jack will turn out to be `nil`). On the other hand, sometimes ownership is appropriate and crucial. A view controller is useless without a view to control, and its view truly belongs to the view controller and to no one else; once a view controller has a view, it will retain it, releasing it only when it itself goes out of existence.

Objects can perform two-way communication without both of them holding references to one another. It may be sufficient for *one* of them to have a reference to the other — because the former, as part of a message to the latter, can include a reference to himself. Manny might send a message to Jack where one of the parameters is a reference to Manny; this might merely constitute a form of identification, or an invitation to Jack to send a message back to Manny if Jack needs further information while doing whatever this method does. Manny makes himself, as it were, momentarily visible to Jack; Jack should not wantonly retain Manny (especially since there's an obvious risk of a retain cycle). Again, this is a common pattern:

- The parameter of the delegate message `textFieldShouldBeginEditing(_:)` is a reference to the UITextField that sent the message.
- The first parameter of a target–action message is a reference to the control that sent the message.

Visibility by Instantiation

Every instance comes from somewhere and at someone's behest: some object sent a message commanding this instance to come into existence in the first place. The commanding object therefore has a reference to the new instance at the moment of instantiation. When Manny creates Jack, Manny has a reference to Jack.

That simple fact can serve as the starting point for establishing future communication. If Manny creates Jack and knows that he (Manny) will need a reference to Jack later on, Manny can keep the reference that he obtained by creating Jack in the first place.

Or it might be the other way around: Manny creates Jack and knows that Jack will need a reference to Manny later on, so Manny can supply that reference immediately after creating Jack, and Jack will then keep it. Delegation is a case in point. Manny may create Jack and immediately make himself Jack's delegate, as in my example code in Chapter 11:

```
let cpc = ColorPickerController(colorName:colorName, color:c)
cpc.delegate = self
```

When Manny creates Jack, it might not be a reference to Manny himself that Jack needs, but to something that Manny knows or has. You will presumably endow Jack with a method or property so that Manny can hand over that information. In fact, if Jack simply cannot live without the information, it might be reasonable to endow Jack with an initializer that *requires* this information as part of the very act of creation.

This example (Chapter 11) comes from a table view controller. The user has tapped a row of the table. In response, we create a secondary table view controller, a Tracks-ViewController instance; we hand it the data it will need, and display the secondary table view:

```
override func tableView(_ tableView: UITableView,
    didSelectRowAt indexPath: IndexPath) {
        delay(0.1) {
            let t = TracksViewController(
                mediaItemCollection: self.albums[indexPath.row])
            self.navigationController?.pushViewController(t, animated: true)
        }
    }
```

In that code, I instantiate the TracksViewController by calling its initializer, `init(mediaItemCollection:)`, which requires me to hand over the media item collection that the view controller will need as the basis of its table view. And where did this initializer come from? I made it up! I have deliberately devised TracksViewController to have a designated initializer `init(mediaItemCollection:)`, making it virtually obligatory for a TracksViewController to have access, from the moment it comes into existence, to the data it needs.

A similar situation is when a segue in a storyboard is triggered. There are two view controllers that may need to meet — the view controllers at the two ends of the segue, the source view controller and the destination view controller. This is parallel to the situation where one view controller creates another view controller and presents it, but there's an important difference: with a triggered segue, the source view controller *doesn't* create the destination view controller. But it probably still needs a reference to the destination view controller, very early in the life of the latter, so that it can hand over any needed information. How will it get that reference?

At the moment the segue is triggered, the source view controller already exists, and the segue knows what view controller it is; and the segue itself instantiates the destination view controller. So the segue immediately turns to the source view controller and *hands* it a reference to the destination view controller — for example, by calling the source view controller's `prepare(for:sender:)` method. This is the source view controller's chance to obtain a reference to the newly instantiated destination view controller — and to make itself the destination view controller's delegate, or hand it any needed information, and so forth.

In the first situation, one view controller *creates* another view controller instance. In the second situation, the source view controller of a segue is brought together with the destination view controller by the `prepare(for:sender:)` event. In each case, the first view controller, for one brief shining moment, has a reference to the second view controller. Therefore it takes advantage of that moment to hand the second view controller instance the information it needs. There will be no better moment to do this. Knowing the moment, and taking care not to miss it, is part of the art of data communication.

Getting a Reference

So much for what happens when another object *first* comes into existence. But sometimes you know that another object *already* exists somewhere out there, but you don't know how to refer to it. That kind of situation can be a particular source of frustration.

Let's say you're a view controller and there's some other view controller you need to talk to. But you didn't instantiate the other view controller, and you are not the source view controller for the segue that instantiated the other view controller. You may know a lot about this other view controller — you know what its class is, and you can probably see its view sitting there in the interface when you run the app — but you cannot get hold of it in code.

Here's what *not* to do in that situation: You know the class of the view controller you're looking for, so you *make* an instance of that class. That won't do you any good! The instance you want to talk to is a particular instance that *already* exists. There's no point making *another* instance. If you lose your car in a parking lot, the solution is not to build *another* car of the same model; the solution is to find *your* car.

For example, in a real-life iOS app, you will have a root view controller, which will be an instance of some type of UIViewController. Let's say it's an instance of the View-Controller class. Once your app is up and running, this instance already exists. Now suppose we are in some other view controller, and we want to talk to the View-Controller instance that is serving as the root view controller of the app. It would be counterproductive to try to speak to the root view controller by *instantiating* the ViewController class:

```
let theVC = ViewController() // legal but pointless
```

All that does is to make a *second, different* instance of the ViewController class, and your messages to that instance will be wasted, as it is not the instance of View-Controller that you wanted to talk to. That particular instance *already exists;* what you want is to *get a reference* to that already existing instance. But how? Here are some considerations that will help you.

Visibility by Relationship

It is not the *class* of an already existing object that will get you a reference to that object, but rather the *relationship* between you and that object. Objects may acquire the ability to see one another automatically by virtue of their position in a containing structure. Before worrying about how to supply one object with a reference to another, consider whether there may *already* be a chain of references leading from one to the other.

A subview can see its superview, through its `superview` property. A superview can see all its subviews, through its `subviews` property, and can pick out a specific subview through that subview's `tag` property, by calling the `viewWithTag(_:)` method. A subview in a window can see its window, through its `window` property. Working your way up or down the view hierarchy by means of these properties, it may be possible to obtain the desired reference.

A view controller can see its view through its `view` property, and from there can work its way down to subviews to which it may not have an outlet. What about going in the other direction? A responder (Chapter 11) can see the next object up the responder chain, through the `next` property — which also means, because of the structure of the responder chain, that a view controller's main view can see the view controller.

View controllers are themselves part of a hierarchy and therefore can see one another. If a view controller is currently presenting a view through a second view controller, the latter is the former's `presentedViewController`, and the former is the latter's `presentingViewController`. If a view controller is the child of a UINavigationController, the latter is its `navigationController`. A UINavigation-Controller's visible view is controlled by its `visibleViewController`. And so forth.

Global Visibility

Some objects are globally visible — that is, they are visible to all other objects. Object types themselves are an important example. As I pointed out in Chapter 4, it is perfectly reasonable to use a Swift struct with static members as a way of providing globally available namespaced constants ("Struct as Namespace" on page 152).

Classes sometimes have class methods or properties that vend singleton instances. Some of these singletons, in turn, have properties pointing to other objects, making those other objects likewise globally visible. Any object can see the singleton UIApplication instance as `UIApplication.shared`. So any object can also see the app's primary window, because that is the first element of the singleton UIApplication instance's `windows` property. And any object can see the app delegate, because that is the application's `delegate` property. And the chain continues: any object can see the app's root view controller, because that is the primary window's `rootView-Controller` — and from there, as I said in the previous section, we can navigate the view controller hierarchy and the view hierarchy.

So now we know how to solve the problem I posed earlier of getting a reference to the app's root view controller. We start with the globally visible shared application instance:

```
let app = UIApplication.shared
```

From there we can get the window:

```
let window = app.windows.first
```

That window owns the root view controller, and will hand us a reference to it through its `rootViewController` property:

```
let vc = window?.rootViewController
```

And voilà — a reference to our app's root view controller. To obtain the reference to this persistent instance, we have created, in effect, a chain leading from the known to the unknown, from a globally available class to the particular desired instance.

You can make your own objects globally visible by attaching them to a globally visible object. For example, a public property of the app delegate, which you are free to create, is globally visible by virtue of the app delegate being globally visible (by virtue of the shared application being globally visible).

Another globally visible object is the shared defaults object obtained as `User-Defaults.standard`. This object is the gateway to storage and retrieval of user defaults, which is similar to a dictionary (a collection of values named by keys). The user defaults are automatically saved when your application quits and are automatically available when your application is launched again later, so they are one of the ways in which your app maintains information between launches. But, being globally visible, they are also a conduit for communicating values within your app.

In one of my apps there's a preference setting I call `Default.hazyStripy`. This determines whether a certain visible interface object (a card in a game) is drawn with a hazy fill or a stripy fill. This is a setting that the user can change, so there is a preferences interface allowing the user to make this change. When the user displays this preferences interface, I examine the `Default.hazyStripy` setting in the user defaults to configure the preferences interface to reflect it in a segmented control (called `self.hazyStripy`):

```
func setHazyStripy () {
    let hs = UserDefaults.standard
        .object(forKey:Default.hazyStripy) as! Int
    self.hazyStripy.selectedSegmentIndex = hs
}
```

Conversely, if the user interacts with the preferences interface, tapping the `hazy-Stripy` segmented control to change its setting, I respond by changing the actual `Default.hazyStripy` setting in the user defaults:

```
@IBAction func hazyStripyChange(_ sender: Any) {
    let hs = self.hazyStripy.selectedSegmentIndex
    UserDefaults.standard.set(hs, forKey: Default.hazyStripy)
}
```

But here's the really interesting part. The preferences interface is not the only object that uses the `Default.hazyStripy` setting in the user defaults; the drawing code that actually draws the hazy-or-stripy-filled card also uses it, so as to know how the card should draw itself! When the user leaves the preferences interface and the card game reappears, the cards are redrawn — consulting the `Default.hazyStripy` setting in UserDefaults in order to do so:

```
override func draw(_ rect: CGRect) {
    let hazy : Bool = UserDefaults.standard
        .integer(forKey:Default.hazyStripy) == HazyStripy.hazy.rawValue
    CardPainter.shared.drawCard(self.card, hazy:hazy)
}
```

There is no need for the card object and the view controller object that manages the preferences interface to be able to see one another, because they can both see this common object, the `Default.hazyStripy` user default. UserDefaults becomes, in itself, a global conduit for communicating information from one part of my app to another.

Notifications and Key–Value Observing

Notifications (Chapter 11) can be a way to communicate between objects that are conceptually distant from one another without bothering to provide *any* way for one to see the other. All they really need to have in common is a knowledge of the name of the notification. Every object can see the notification center — it is a globally visible object — so every object can arrange to post or receive a notification.

Using a notification in this way may seem lazy, an evasion of your responsibility to architect your objects sensibly. But sometimes one object doesn't need to know, and indeed shouldn't know, what object (or objects) it is sending a message to.

Recall the example I gave in Chapter 11. In a simple card game app, the game needs to know when a card is tapped. A card, when it is tapped, knowing nothing about the game, simply emits a virtual shriek by posting a notification; the game object has registered for this notification and takes over from there:

```
NotificationCenter.default.post(name: Self.tappedNotification, object: self)
```

Here's another example, taking advantage of the fact that notifications are a broadcast mechanism. In one of my apps, the app delegate may detect a need to tear down the interface and build it back up again from scratch. If this is to happen without causing memory leaks (and all sorts of other havoc), every view controller that is currently running a repeating Timer needs to invalidate that timer (Chapter 12). Rather than my having to work out what view controllers those might be, and endowing every view controller with a method that can be called, I simply have the app delegate shout "Everybody stop timers!" by posting a notification. All my view controllers that run timers have registered for this notification, and they know what to do when they receive it.

By the same token, Cocoa itself provides notification versions of many delegate and action messages. The app delegate has a method for being told when the app goes into the background, but other objects might need to know this too; those objects can register for the corresponding notification.

Similarly, key–value observing can be used to keep two conceptually distant objects synchronized with one another: a property of one object changes, and the other object hears about the change. As I said in Chapter 11, entire areas of Cocoa routinely expect you to use KVO when you want to be notified of a change in an object property. You can configure the same sort of thing with your own objects.

The Combine Framework

There is some commonality between mechanisms such as the notification center and key–value observing. In both cases, you register with some other object to receive a certain message whenever that other object cares to send it. Basically, you're opening and configuring a pipeline of communication, and leaving it in place until you no longer need it. Looked at in that way, notifications and key–value observing seem closely related to one another. In fact, the target–action mechanism of reporting control events seems related as well. So does a Timer. So does delayed performance.

The Combine framework, introduced in Swift 5.1 and iOS 13, offers to unify these architectures (and others) under a single head. At its heart, Combine depends upon an abstract notion of publish-and-subscribe, and reifies that abstraction with two protocols, Publisher and Subscriber:

Publisher
A publisher promises to provide a certain kind of a value, perhaps repeatedly, at some time in the future.

Subscriber

> A Subscriber registers itself with (subscribes to) a Publisher to receive its value whenever that value may come along.

When a Subscriber subscribes to a Publisher, here's what happens:

1. The Publisher responds by handing the Subscriber a Subscription (yet another protocol).

2. The Subscriber can then use the Subscription to ask the Publisher for a value.

3. The Publisher can respond by sending, whenever it cares to, a value to the Subscriber. It can do this as many times as it likes.

4. In some situations, the entire connection can be cancelled when the Subscriber no longer wishes to receive values.

That's a rather elaborate-sounding dance, but in most cases you won't experience it that way. You won't experience the dance at all! Instead, you'll just hook up a built-in subscriber directly to a built-in publisher and all the right things will happen.

To illustrate, I'll start with a trivial example. One of the simplest forms of publisher is a Subject. Every time you call `send(_:)` on a Subject, handing it a value, it sends that value to its subscribers. There are just two kinds of Subject:

PassthroughSubject

> Produces the value sent to it with `send`.

CurrentValueSubject

> Like a PassthroughSubject, except that it has a value at the outset, and produces it to any new subscriber.

Let's make a Subject:

```
let pass = PassthroughSubject<String,Never>()
pass.send("howdy")
```

That compiles and runs, but we don't know that anything happened because we have no subscriber. There are just two built-in independent subscribers, and each can be created with a convenience method sent to a publisher; the method subscribes the subscriber to the publisher and returns it:

`sink`

> Takes a function to be called whenever a value is received. The function takes a single parameter, namely the value.

`assign`

> Takes a Swift key path and an object. Whenever a value is received, assigns that value to the property of that object designated by the key path.

So here's a complete publish-and-subscribe example:

```
let pass = PassthroughSubject<String,Never>()
let sink = pass.sink {
    print($0)
}
pass.send("howdy") // howdy
```

That works, in the sense that `"howdy"` appears in the console; but it still isn't a very realistic example. In real life, we're never going to make a publisher, subscribe to it, and make it publish, all within the immediate local scope of a single series of commands. In a realistic scenario:

- The publisher belongs to, and is vended by, one object.
- The subscriber is created and attached to the publisher by a different object.
- If the publisher publishes at all, that will happen at some unknown future time. Therefore the subscriber needs to *persist* long enough to wait for the publisher to publish.

To simulate that, let's store our publisher and subscriber in instance properties, and let's make the publisher publish only after a delay:

```
let pass = PassthroughSubject<String,Never>()
var storage = Set<AnyCancellable>()
override func viewDidLoad() {
    super.viewDidLoad()
    let sink = self.pass.sink {
        print($0)
    }
    sink.store(in: &self.storage)
    delay(1) {
        self.pass.send("howdy") // howdy
    }
}
```

In that code, the Subject publisher persists long enough for us to make it publish one second later, because it is assigned to an instance property. And the `sink` subscriber is *also* assigned to an instance property; in particular, it is added to a Set of AnyCancellable, using the `store(in:)` method. The result is that when we come along one second later and tell the Subject publisher to publish, the `sink` subscriber still exists, inside the `storage` Set, and receives the published value and prints it.

To help you take advantage of the Combine framework in your Cocoa code, a number of Foundation and Cocoa types vend Combine publishers, such as:

- The notification center
- A KVO compliant property
- A computed property declared with the `@Published` property wrapper
- The Timer class

- A Scheduler (used for delayed performance; DispatchQueue, OperationQueue, and RunLoop are all Schedulers)
- A URLSession (for obtaining a value via the network)

Besides publishers and subscribers, there are also *operators*. An operator is a publisher that is somewhat like a subscriber, in that it can be attached to another publisher. The real power of the Combine framework lies in the operators. By *chaining* operators, you construct a *pipeline* that passes along only the information you're really interested in; the logic of analyzing, filtering, and transforming that information is pushed up into the pipeline itself.

To illustrate, I'll use the notification center as my source of data. Let's go back to my example of a Card view that emits a virtual shriek when it is tapped by posting a notification:

```
static let tapped = Notification.Name("tapped")
@objc func tapped() {
    NotificationCenter.default.post(name: Self.tapped, object: self)
}
```

Now let's say, for purposes of the example, that what the game is interested in when it receives one of these notifications is the string value of the name property of the Card that posted the notification. Getting that information is a two-stage process. First, we have to register to receive notifications at all:

```
NotificationCenter.default.addObserver(self,
    selector: #selector(cardTapped), name: Card.tapped, object: nil)
```

Then, when we receive a notification, we have to look to see that its object really is a Card, and if it is, fetch its name property and do something with it:

```
@objc func cardTapped(_ n:Notification) {
    if let card = n.object as? Card {
        let name = card.name
        print(name) // or something
    }
}
```

Now let's do the same thing using the Combine framework. We obtain a publisher from the notification center by calling its publisher method. But we don't stop there. We don't want to receive a notification if the object isn't a Card, so we use the compactMap operator to cast it safely to Card — and if it isn't a Card, the pipeline just stops as if nothing had happened. And we only want the Card's name, so we use the map operator to get it. Here's the result:

```
let cardTappedCardNamePublisher =
    NotificationCenter.default.publisher(for: Card.tapped)
        .compactMap {$0.object as? Card}
        .map {$0.name}
```

Let's say that `cardTappedCardNamePublisher` is an instance property of our view controller. Then what we now have in this instance property is a publisher that publishes the string name of a Card if that Card posts the `tapped` notification, and otherwise does nothing. Do you see what I mean when I say that the logic is pushed up into the pipeline?

Finally, let's arrange to receive that string, by subscribing to the publisher:

```
let sink = self.cardTappedCardNamePublisher.sink {
    print($0)
}
sink.store(in: &self.storage)
```

Here's another example. You may have noticed that I didn't list controls (UIControl) among the built-in publishers. This means we can't automatically replace the control target–action mechanism using the Combine framework. However, with just a little modification, we can turn a control into a publisher. I'll demonstrate with a switch control (UISwitch). It has an `isOn` property, which is changed when the user toggles the switch on or off. The target–action way to learn that this has happened is through the switch's `.valueChanged` control event. Let's write a UISwitch subclass where we vend a publisher and funnel the `isOn` value through it (I'll use the new iOS 14 UIAction notation):

```
class MySwitch : UISwitch {
    @Published var isOnPublisher = false
    required init?(coder: NSCoder) {
        super.init(coder:coder)
        self.isOnPublisher = self.isOn
        let action = UIAction {[unowned self] _ in
            self.isOnPublisher = self.isOn
        }
        self.addAction(action, for: .valueChanged)
    }
}
```

That code illustrates the `@Published` property wrapper. This creates a publisher behind the scenes, and vends it through the property wrapper's dollar-sign `projectedValue` ("Property Wrappers" on page 322). With our subclass, the way to be kept informed about changes to the switch's `isOn` property is to subscribe to its publisher, namely `$isOnPublisher`.

So let's subscribe to it! Suppose we are the view controller that ultimately owns this switch. And suppose we have an outlet to the switch:

```
@IBOutlet var mySwitch : MySwitch!
```

Then we, the view controller, can subscribe to that publisher:

```
let sink = self.mySwitch.$isOnPublisher.sink {
    print($0)
}
sink.store(in: &self.storage)
```

But wait — doesn't that look awfully familiar? Yes, it does — and that's the point. Using Combine, we've effectively reduced the notification center mechanism and the control target–action mechanism to the *same mechanism.*

Even more of the power of the Combine framework emerges when we build complex pipelines. To illustrate, let's combine (sorry about that) the notification center pipeline and the switch pipeline. Imagine that our interface consists of Cards along with a switch. When the switch is on, the cards are interactive: the user can tap one, and we hear about it. When the switch is off, the user's taps do nothing.

To implement this, we can put the notification center publisher and the switch publisher together into a single pipeline. The Combine publisher that does that is CombineLatest:

```
lazy var combination =
    Publishers.CombineLatest(
        self.cardTappedCardNamePublisher,
        self.mySwitch.$isOnPublisher
    )
```

What we now have is a publisher that channels the pipelines from our other two publishers into one. It remembers every value that last arrived from either source, and when it gets a new value, it emits a tuple consisting of both values. In our case, that's a (String,Bool).

However, that's not what we actually want to have coming down the pipeline at us. We still want just the string name of the tapped card. So we'll use the map operator to extract it:

```
lazy var combination =
    Publishers.CombineLatest(
        self.cardTappedCardNamePublisher,
        self.mySwitch.$isOnPublisher
    )
    .map { $0.0 }
```

Now we're getting just the string name, but we're getting *too many* string names; the switch isn't having any effect. The pipeline is emitting values in response to user taps even when the switch is off! The whole idea of combining these two publishers was to *eliminate* any output when the switch is off. So we'll interpose the filter operator to block any tuples whose Bool is false:

```
lazy var combination =
    Publishers.CombineLatest(
        self.cardTappedCardNamePublisher,
        self.mySwitch.$isOnPublisher
    )
    .filter { $0.1 }
    .map { $0.0 }
```

This is looking much better. If the user taps while the switch is on, we get the card name. If the user taps while the switch is off, nothing happens. But there's still one little problem. The CombineLatest publisher publishes if it gets a value from *either* of its source publishers. That means we don't just get a value when the user taps a Card; we also get a value when the user toggles the switch. We don't want that value to come out the end of the pipeline; we just want to use it to allow or prevent the arrival of the Card name.

What we want to do here is compare *two* values: the new tuple coming down the pipeline, and the *previous* tuple that came down the pipeline most recently. If the difference between the new tuple and the old tuple is merely that the Bool changed, we don't want to emit a value from the pipeline. The way to obtain both the current value and the previous value is with the `scan` operator. I'll use that operator to pass both the old switch value and the new switch value down the pipeline. Then, in the `filter` operator, I'll block any value unless *both* the old switch value *and* the new switch value are `true`:

```
lazy var combination =
    Publishers.CombineLatest(
        self.cardTappedCardNamePublisher,
        self.mySwitch.$isOnPublisher
    )
    .scan(("",true,true)) { ($1.0, $0.2, $1.1) }
    .filter { $0.1 && $0.2 }
    .map { $0.0 }
```

Our goal is accomplished. If the user taps a Card while the switch is on, the pipeline produces its name. If the user taps a Card while the switch is off, or toggles the switch, nothing happens.

These examples have only scratched the surface of what the Combine framework can do; but they demonstrate its spirit. And the potential benefits are profound. In Chapter 11 I complained that the event-driven nature of the Cocoa framework means that you're bombarded with events through different entry points at different times, so that state has to be maintained in shared instance properties, and understanding the implications of any single entry point method call can be difficult. The Combine framework offers the potential of funneling events into pipelines whose logic can be manipulated internally, so that what comes out is just the information you need when you need it.

There isn't room in this book for a full discussion of the Combine framework; for more, see *https://www.apeth.com/UnderstandingCombine/*, where I've written an online tutorial about Combine.

Alternative Architectures

In real life, one way to improve communication between objects in an app of any complexity is to plan the internal architecture of the app appropriately. My goal in this section is not to recommend this or that alternative architecture, but rather to make you aware of some of the possibilities and how they can ease the pain of communicating between objects in your app.

Model–View–Controller

The naïve standard architecture implied by Cocoa's classes is called *Model–View–Controller* (MVC). In this terminology, *model* is the data; *view* is what the user sees and interacts with; and *controller* is the code that mediates between them, deciding what data to display to the user and how, and responding to the user's actions by modifying the data.

The name *view controller* implies that a UIViewController is a controller. Each scene of the app corresponds to one view controller, and the view controllers do all the work of moving data around the app. If one view controller pushes or presents another, it hands the needed data "forward" to that view controller. When a pushed or presented view controller goes out of existence, it hands the needed data "back" to the view controller that pushed or presented it.

Simple MVC, on its own, has some unfortunate consequences. As soon as an app consists of more than one or two view controllers, or if there is a need to access data that cannot easily be handed back and forth in this way, we get into the sort of difficulties that I've been describing in this chapter. Moreover, this architecture has a tendency to lead to very large view controller classes, which can make the code hard to read — because functionality is hard to find and trace and understand — and hard to maintain. It can also make the code hard to test.

Router and Data Space

The fact is that view controllers exist; we're stuck with them (unless you opt to drop UIKit programming altogether and go with SwiftUI, as I'll describe in the next section). One key step towards making view controllers tractable is to get the business of navigation from one view controller to another out of the hands of the view controllers themselves. The idea here is that no view controller should know about the existence of any other view controller. Such knowledge constitutes a leakage of responsibility. Instead, we need some centralized mechanism to which we can turn and ask to go to a different scene, whatever that may turn out to mean. This mechanism is usually called the *router;* some architectures refer to it as the *coordinator,* or *flow coordinator.* (For a basic example, take a look at URLNavigator on GitHub.)

Using a router means you're almost certainly going to have to abandon storyboard segues, or at least automatic segues. That may be disappointing, but such is the price that must be paid for separation of responsibilities. The whole idea is that all navigation must be performed by way of the central mechanism; an automatically triggered segue would go behind the router's back. Indeed, a complication arises because UIKit wants to perform "back" navigation automatically. Both a navigation controller's Back button and dismissal of a presented view controller threaten to take place without consulting our code at all; you might have to take definite steps to make sure that that doesn't happen.

When a view controller doesn't know anything about other view controllers, it doesn't know what data the next view controller needs. The router therefore also has the responsibility for communicating any needed data to the next view controller. We can imagine the router turning to the first view controller and asking it for the data and passing it along to the next view controller; but at that point we may start to wonder why a view controller is maintaining any real data in the first place. Why isn't there just *the data* belonging to the app as a whole?

The idea here is that perhaps we could put the data in some centralized global location, where anyone can access it. I call this centralized location the *data space.* The Combine framework is a great way to organize access to the data space. The data space can use Combine pipelines to vend an automatic messaging mechanism. If something changes the data, all subscribers hear about it instantly, and the state of the app remains synchronized everywhere.

Model–View–Presenter

A further key insight is the realization that, in the Model–View–Controller division of responsibilities, a view controller should perhaps be considered View, not Controller. (Your eyes will be opened to this notion if you watch a wonderful YouTube video by Dave DeLong.) On this basis, all the logic for deciding what to show the user and how to respond to user actions can be moved out of the view controller into another class, which we may call the Presenter. The Presenter knows nothing of the details of the visible interface, and the view controller knows nothing of the Model. The Presenter is the one that knows about and talks to the Model; at the same time, the Presenter and the view controller communicate with one another solely in terms of *intent.*

For example, let's say the data represents a bank account. The Presenter might consult the Model and then say to the view controller: "Here is a number. Display it to the user, as being the user's current balance." The Presenter knows nothing of *how* the view controller will do that. The view controller, meanwhile, is responsible for making that number visible to the user, and no more. The view controller knows that the interface has a UILabel for this purpose, and it formats the number and displays it in the label. It knows nothing of where the number came from.

Going the other way, when the user does something, such as tapping a button, the view controller will interpret that button in terms of intent, and will say to the Presenter: "Here is what the user wants to do." The Presenter is then responsible for the action logic of deciding how to proceed, which might involve consulting or changing the Model.

This approach has many advantages. The view controller is pared down to the status of an intermediary; it musters the visible interface and communicates with the Presenter, and that's *all* it does. So view controllers are smaller and simpler. It is now far easier for you to find your code, because it will be readily evident what are view controller concerns and what are Presenter concerns. Moreover, the Presenter is testable: given a certain intent as input, does it respond correctly as output? Your unit tests can ask questions like that, without involving the any interface.

Another sign of the Presenter's power is that, when used in conjunction with a router, the Presenter usually doesn't have to import UIKit. It knows nothing of views or view controllers! It embodies the pure logic of a scene's behavior without reference to anything extraneous.

However, the app *as a whole* has now become more elaborate. Every scene consists of a little cluster of instances. In addition to the view controller, there is a corresponding Presenter. Every time the router creates and configures a new view controller, it must also create the corresponding Presenter and hook the two together correctly. The need for this *assembly* step is part of the price that must be paid for the resulting simplicity and testability.

Protocols and Reactive Programming

In my discussion of Model–View–Presenter, I have avoided specifying the exact mechanism by which the View (meaning the view controller) and the corresponding Presenter will communicate with one another. The most obvious approach is that each of them has methods that the other is allowed to call. To make this contract explicit, as well as to facilitate testing, it's probably a good idea to express these public interfaces as protocols — one stating what the view controller is allowed to say to the Presenter, and another stating what the Presenter is allowed to say to the view controller.

It might also be nice to make this communication more automatic. For instance, we could put a setter observer on some property of the view controller, so that when a user action changes that property, the change is relayed directly to the Presenter.

Similarly, a change in some property of the Presenter could be relayed directly to the view controller.

One can then imagine going even further and replacing the property observers with a "reactive" mechanism. Before iOS 13, this mechanism typically comes from some third-party library; nowadays, we can use the Combine framework. If we make the same sort of connection between the Presenter and the data, we end up with a kind of automatic data flow throughout the app. Ideally, the interface should depend directly on the data.

VIPER

An even more extreme separation of responsibilities is the VIPER architecture, which stands for View–Interactor–Presenter–Entity–Router. Despite the alphabet soup, this architecture is really just a separation of the Presenter into multiple objects. The Presenter itself communicates with the view controller and maintains local state; it does no "real work." The Interactor is the Presenter's conduit to the data, and there is a *wireframe* that is the Presenter's conduit to the router.

VIPER is arguably too much of a good thing, and in my experience it is more a religious aspiration than a practical tool. Still, used correctly, it makes finding your code dead easy. For a good introduction to VIPER, see *https://github.com/infinum/iOS-VIPER-Xcode-Templates*.

SwiftUI

The SwiftUI framework is a wholesale alternative to Cocoa. It operates on a programming paradigm that's completely different from Cocoa's, and offers the promise of writing iOS apps in a totally different way — not to mention that the same code might be reusable on Apple TV, Apple Watch, and desktop Macs. SwiftUI as a whole is outside the scope of this book; it needs a book of its own. The subject here is how objects see and communicate with one another.

To illustrate how SwiftUI deals with communication, let's start with the prototypical "Hello World" app:

```
struct ContentView : View {
    var body: some View {
        Text("Hello World")
    }
}
```

That code puts the text "Hello World" in the middle of the screen. But how? It doesn't seem to contain any runnable code. Well, actually it does: body is a computed property, and the curly braces that surround Text("Hello World") are its getter (with return omitted). The interface is constructed in code and returned. But that's not quite accurate; it isn't the *interface* that's returned — it's a *description* of the interface.

In SwiftUI, there is no storyboard; there are no nibs; there are no outlets. There is no UIViewController; there isn't even a UIView. Text is a mere struct, and View is just a protocol. A SwiftUI View is extremely lightweight, and is barely persistent. There are no entry points other than the body property getter, which is merely the answer to an occasional question, "What should this view look like at this moment?"

The most pervasive object-oriented pattern in SwiftUI is that one View instantiates another View. Our simple "Hello World" app consists entirely of our ContentView instantiating a Text object in its body getter. This is the same pattern of visibility by instantiation that I discussed at the start of this chapter: when Manny creates Jack, Manny has a reference to Jack and can hand Jack any information that Jack needs in order to do his job. We do not have to get a reference to something in order to customize its appearance; we customize its appearance as part of its initialization. There is no need for the ContentView to get a reference to the Text in order to tell it what its visible content ("Hello World") should be; the ContentView creates the Text *with* that content.

Function Builders and Modifiers

SwiftUI's syntax for constructing interfaces is declarative and functional rather than imperative and sequential. To illustrate, I'll add a button to the interface. I'll declare the button without giving it any functionality:

```
struct ContentView : View {
    var body: some View {
        HStack {
            Text("Hello World")
            Spacer()
            Button("Tap Me") {
                // does nothing
            }
        }.frame(width: 200)
    }
}
```

The Text object returned by the body getter has been replaced by an HStack, which lines up views horizontally. Inside the HStack's curly braces are three objects in series: a Text, a Spacer, and a Button. That seems impossible syntactically. What's happening? The curly braces after HStack are the body of an anonymous function, supplied using trailing closure syntax as a parameter to HStack's initializer. That initializer is allowed to "list" three objects because it is fed to a ViewBuilder, which is a function builder ("Function Builders" on page 329); the ViewBuilder wraps up those objects in a TupleView, and that is what is returned from the anonymous function.

The `frame` method being called on the HStack determines the width of the HStack on the screen. What's interesting about it is that it *is* a method. Instead of getting a reference to the HStack object and setting a property *of* that object, we apply a method directly *to* that object. This sort of method is called a *modifier,* and it returns in effect the very same instance to which it was sent. The modified instance is of a more complex type, but this complexity is hidden from us by type erasure and ultimately by the body reverse generic return type `some View` (see "Reverse Generics" on page 327). And modifiers can be chained, just like operators in the Combine framework; the effect is that we describe the object in more and more detail. If we wanted our text-and-button HStack to have a yellow background with 20-pixel margins, we could write:

```
HStack {
    Text("Hello World")
    Spacer()
    Button("Tap Me") {
        // does nothing
    }
}.frame(width: 200)
.padding(20)
.background(Color.yellow)
```

State Properties

At this point, you may be saying: "Fine, I see how visibility by instantiation is sufficient when all you want to do is create the app's *initial* interface; you configure a view's initial appearance in its initializer. But what about when the interface needs to *change* over the course of the app's lifetime?" Amazingly, the answer is the same: SwiftUI *still* handles everything through a view's initializer. But how can that be?

To demonstrate, let's give our button some functionality. In particular, the user should be able to tap the button to toggle the text between "Hello World" and "Goodbye World." Here's how to do that:

```
struct ContentView : View {
    @State var isHello = true ❶
    var greeting : String {
        self.isHello ? "Hello" : "Goodbye" ❷
    }
    var body: some View {
        HStack {
            Text(self.greeting + " World")
            Spacer()
            Button("Tap Me") {
                self.isHello.toggle() ❸
            }
        }.frame(width: 200)
```

```
            .padding(20)
            .background(Color.yellow)
        }
    }
```

❶ We have declared an isHello instance property on which the interface depends — in this case, whether the text should read "Hello World" or "Goodbye World." Crucially, this instance property is declared with the @State property wrapper. This means that if the value of isHello changes, whatever depends upon it will be recalculated. So in our code, whenever isHello changes, *the body getter will be called again.*

❷ For simplicity and clarity, we also declare a computed instance property greeting that translates the Bool of the @State property isHello into a corresponding string.

❸ The button's action — what it should do when tapped — is supplied as an anonymous function, using trailing closure syntax, as part of its initializer. That action changes the value of the @State property isHello. When the @State property isHello changes in response to the tapping of the button, the body getter is called *again* — and the Text content is freshly calculated and takes on its new value. The new result is returned and displayed, and so we have achieved what we set out to accomplish: tapping the button changes the text displayed on the screen.

Notice what did *not* happen in that example:

- The button did not use a target–action architecture: there is no separate target to send a message to, and there is no separate action function. Instead, the action function is part of the button.

- The action function did not talk to the Text to change what it displays; it talked only to the @State property.

- The @State property has no setter observer that talks to the Text. Instead, the change in the @State property effectively flows "downhill" to the body of the View, *automatically.*

In that code, there are no event handlers, no events, and no action handlers. And there are no references from one object to another! There is no problem of communicating data from one object to another, because objects don't try to communicate with one another. There is just a View and its state at any given moment.

Moreover, view state in SwiftUI can be maintained *only* through @State properties. A View stored property can't be settable; a view is a struct and isn't mutable. A @State property, on the other hand, is a computed property backed by a property wrapper whose underlying State struct *is* mutable. In this way, SwiftUI forces you to clarify the locus of state throughout your app.

Another important lesson of our code is that View objects are ephemeral. A View's body getter can be called at any time; it generates some Views, like our Text, that describe the interface and are then thrown away. You never know how often a View's body may be called; you never know how often a View struct like our ContentView will be created anew. And you don't need to know! All that matters is that you can instantly describe the interface based on the state.

Bindings

Some views have even tighter coupling with a @State. To illustrate, I'll replace the Button in our example with a Toggle:

```
struct ContentView : View {
    @State var isHello = true
    var greeting : String {
        self.isHello ? "Hello" : "Goodbye"
    }
    var body: some View {
        VStack {
            Text(self.greeting + " World")
            Spacer()
            Toggle("Friendly", isOn: $isHello) // *
        }.frame(width: 150, height: 100)
        .padding(20)
        .background(Color.yellow)
    }
}
```

A Toggle is drawn as a labeled UISwitch. When the user changes the switch, the Text changes in the interface. But how?

A Toggle takes a Binding in its initializer. The State property wrapper vends a Binding property as its dollar-sign projectedValue. Our @State property is isHello, so its binding is $isHello. We handed that binding to the Toggle when we initialized it. When the user changes the UISwitch value, that binding's value is toggled. That change takes place in the @State property, and so, once again, the Text changes accordingly.

That is somewhat similar to what we did in the earlier discussion of the Combine framework, where we modified a UISwitch to vend a Publisher of its own isOn value — except that in SwiftUI, the communication between the @State property and the Toggle is two-way and automatic by way of the binding. Our Toggle has no action function, and doesn't need one, because it is tightly integrated with a Bool property through a binding.

Passing Data Downhill

So far, the only objects our ContentView has created are instances of built-in types — Text, Button, Spacer, Toggle. But what if you wanted to create an instance of a *custom* type? How would you pass data from the View that does the creating to the View that is created? In exactly the same way that we've been doing it up to now! You give your custom type a property, and you set that property as part of the custom type's initialization.

That is legal, even though a View is an immutable struct whose stored properties cannot be set, because we are *not* mutating the struct; we are *initializing* it. It is also easy, because a View is just a struct. Typically, you won't even bother to write an initializer for your custom View; the implicit memberwise initializer will be sufficient.

In this example, we present modally a secondary view, an instance of a Greeting struct that we ourselves have defined:

```
struct ContentView : View {
    @State var isHello = true
    var greeting : String {
        self.isHello ? "Hello" : "Goodbye"
    }
    @State var showSheet = false
    var body: some View {
        VStack {
            Button("Show Message") {
                self.showSheet.toggle()
            }.sheet(isPresented: $showSheet) {
                Greeting(greeting: self.greeting) // *
            }
            Spacer()
            Toggle("Friendly", isOn: $isHello)
        }.frame(width: 150, height: 100)
        .padding(20)
        .background(Color.yellow)
    }
}
struct Greeting : View {
    let greeting : String
    var body: some View {
        Text(greeting + " World")
    }
}
```

The sheet modifier is the SwiftUI equivalent of a Cocoa presented view controller. It describes a view that we intend to present modally. Whether it is actively presenting that view modally depends upon a binding to a Bool, which we have supplied by adding a @State property called showSheet. The Button toggles showSheet to true, and the binding $showSheet toggles to true in response, and causes the view to be presented.

The view we want to present is a wrapper for a Text that will display the "Hello World" or "Goodbye World" greeting; we have named that wrapper view Greeting, and we instantiate it in an anonymous function that we supply as the last parameter to the sheet modifier, using trailing closure syntax. When we instantiate Greeting, we must also *configure* the Greeting instance we are creating. We do that through the Greeting initializer. The Greeting struct belongs to us, so we're free to give it a greeting property, and Swift synthesizes the memberwise initializer with a greeting: parameter. All we have to do is set that property as we create the Greeting. Once again, the data flows "downhill."

Passing Data Uphill

What about when the data needs to flow "uphill" out of the secondary view back to the view that presented it? This is the sort of problem that you'd solve in Cocoa programming using the protocol-and-delegate pattern ("Implementing Delegation" on page 558). In SwiftUI, you simply "lend" the secondary view the binding from a @State property.

Suppose our Greeting view is to contain a text field (SwiftUI TextField) in which is to be entered the user's name, and that this information is to be communicated back to our ContentView. Then ContentView would contain another @State property:

```
@State var name = ""
```

And Greeting would contain a @Binding property:

```
@Binding var username : String
```

When ContentView initializes Greeting, the memberwise initializer now has a username: parameter that takes a string Binding; we hand it the binding from the @State property:

```
Button("Show Message") {
    self.showSheet.toggle()
}.sheet(isPresented: $showSheet) {
    Greeting(greeting: self.greeting,
             username: self.$name)
}
```

And Greeting's TextField is initialized with that binding:

```
TextField("Your Name", text:$username)
    .frame(width:200)
    .textFieldStyle(RoundedBorderTextFieldStyle())
```

Whatever the user types in this text field in the Greeting view flows "uphill" through the username binding, which is the @State property name binding, and changes the value of the @State property name back in the ContentView. And now the data flows "downhill" once more: the ContentView body getter will be called again, and all views that depend upon this @State property will change to match.

Once again, what's most significant in that example is what we *didn't* do. We didn't get a reference from the Greeting back to the ContentView. The Greeting didn't call any method of the ContentView. It didn't set a property of the ContentView. It set its *own* property, username. Communication between objects takes place through bindings in SwiftUI. They are like little pipelines from one object to another — and the object at one end (our Greeting) doesn't have to know anything about what's at the other end.

Custom State Objects

You can construct your own state object by writing a custom class that conforms to the ObservableObject protocol. For example, your app's data might reside in, or be accessed through, an ObservableObject. To use it, you can assign an instance of your class into a @StateObject property. Then you can access its properties directly. Any properties of an ObservableObject that are marked with the @Published attribute will behave like @State properties: when a @Published property changes, your body getter that references it is called again, and you can access an associated binding through the dollar-sign projectedValue of the underlying StateObject property wrapper struct.

To illustrate, suppose we want the name entered into the text field by the user to persist between launches. We can implement that functionality using an ObservableObject. To get started, I'll write a simple NameSaver class with a username property:

```
class NameSaver : ObservableObject {
    @Published var username: String = ""
    // ...
}
```

An ObservableObject has an objectWillChange property that is a Publisher; in fact, it is a Subject, as I described in the earlier discussion of the Combine framework. The objectWillChange property is synthesized automatically, so we don't have to declare it (though we can if we want to). Being a Subject, it notifies its subscribers whenever its send method is called. A @Published property of an ObservableObject automatically calls that send method. It is also itself a Publisher — or rather, its dollar-sign projectedValue is a Publisher. So if our Views refer to a NameSaver instance in a @StateObject property, they will automatically be updated when the NameSaver's username changes. Our NameSaver will be the ultimate "source of truth" for the username.

In our ContentView, there is no longer a @State String property called name; it is replaced by a @StateObject NameSaver property called nameSaver, which is the new "source of truth":

```
@StateObject var nameSaver = NameSaver()
```

When we need to access the value of the NameSaver username property, we do so directly:

```
Text(self.nameSaver.username.isEmpty ? "" :
    greeting + ", " + self.nameSaver.username)
```

When we need a binding to the NameSaver username property, we pass through the binding from nameSaver, namely $nameSaver:

```
Button("Show Message") {
    self.showSheet.toggle()
}.sheet(isPresented: $showSheet) {
    Greeting(greeting: self.greeting,
             username: self.$nameSaver.username)
}
```

The app now works exactly as it did before. But if that was all we wanted, why did we create NameSaver in the first place? We did it so that we can give NameSaver further functionality — namely, to save the username to disk. Let's add that functionality to NameSaver now.

The idea here is to back the username property with a file on disk. When a Name-Saver is initialized, I'll have it read the username value from disk. And when the username value changes, I want it to be written to disk. To ensure that, I'll construct a Combine pipeline that subscribes to the username publisher and responds to changes by saving the new value.

Here's a slightly simplified version of the resulting code:

```
var storage = Set<AnyCancellable>()
var fileURL : URL? { /* return URL of text file on disk */ }
init() {
    self.username = self.read() ?? ""
    self.$username
        .sink { self.save($0) }
        .store(in: &self.storage)
}
func read() -> String? {
    if let url = self.fileURL {
        return try? String(contentsOf: url, encoding: .utf8)
    }
    return nil
}
```

```
func save(_ newName: String) {
    if let url = self.fileURL {
        try? newName.write(to: url, atomically: true, encoding: .utf8)
    }
}
```

Presto! The username that the user types in the TextField is now saved to disk and persists between launches.

C, Objective-C, and Swift

The APIs for Cocoa and its associated frameworks are written in Objective-C or its underlying base language, C. Messages that you send to Cocoa using Swift are being translated for you into Objective-C. Objects that you send and receive back and forth across the Swift/Objective-C bridge are Objective-C objects. Some objects that you send from Swift to Objective-C are even being translated for you into other object types, or into nonobject types.

This appendix summarizes the relevant linguistic features of C and Objective-C, and describes how Swift interfaces with those features. I do not explain here how to write Objective-C! For example, I'll talk about Objective-C methods and method declarations, because you need to know how to call an Objective-C method from Swift; but I'm not going to explain how to call an Objective-C method using Objective-C.

The C Language

Objective-C is a superset of C; to put it another way, C provides the linguistic underpinnings of Objective-C. Everything that is true of C is true also of Objective-C. It is possible, and often necessary, to write long stretches of Objective-C code that are, in effect, pure C. Some of the Cocoa APIs are written in C. Therefore, in order to know about Objective-C, it is necessary to know about C.

The C language was evolved during the early 1970s at Bell Labs in conjunction with the creation of Unix. The reference manual, *The C Language* by Brian Kernighan and Dennis M. Ritchie, was published in 1978, and remains one of the best computer books ever written.

C statements, including declarations, must end in a semicolon. Variables must be declared before use. A variable declaration consists of a data type name followed by the variable name, optionally followed by assignment of an initial value:

```
int i;
double d = 3.14159;
```

The C `typedef` statement starts with an existing type name and defines a new synonym for it:

```
typedef double NSTimeInterval;
```

C Data Types

C is not an object-oriented language; its data types are not objects (they are *scalars*). The basic built-in C data types are all numeric: char (one byte), int (four bytes), float and double (floating-point numbers), and varieties such as short (short integer), long (long integer), unsigned short, and so on. Objective-C adds NSInteger, NSUInteger (unsigned), and CGFloat. The C bool type is actually a numeric, with zero representing false; Objective-C adds BOOL, which is also a numeric. Even the C native text type (string) is actually a null-terminated array of char, and I'll discuss it later.

Swift supplies numeric types that interface directly with C numeric types, even though Swift's types are objects and C's types are not. Swift type aliases provide names that correspond to the C type names: a Swift CBool (Bool) is a C bool, a Swift CChar (Int8) is a C char, a Swift CInt (Int32) is a C int, a Swift CFloat (Float) is a C float, and so on. Swift Int interchanges with NSInteger; Swift UInt interchanges with NSUInteger. CGFloat is adopted as a Swift type name. Swift ObjCBool represents Objective-C BOOL, but it is not a Bool; to derive the Bool, take its `boolValue`. (You can, however, assign a Swift Bool *literal* where an ObjCBool is expected, because ObjCBool adopts ExpressibleByBooleanLiteral.)

A major difference between C and Swift is that C (and therefore Objective-C) implicitly coerces when values of different numeric types are assigned, passed, compared to, or combined with one another; Swift doesn't, so you must coerce explicitly to make types match exactly, as I described in Chapter 3.

C Enums

A C enum is numeric; values are some sort of integer, and can be implicit (starting from 0) or explicit. Enums arrive in various forms into Swift, depending on how they are declared.

Old-fashioned C enum

This is the simplest and oldest form:

```
enum State {
    kDead,
    kAlive
};
typedef enum State State;
```

(The `typedef` in the last line merely allows C programs to use the term `State` as the name of this type instead of the more verbose `enum State`.) In C, the enumerand names `kDead` and `kAlive` are not "cases" of anything; they are not namespaced. They are constants, and as they are not explicitly initialized, they represent 0 and 1 respectively. An enum declaration can specify the integer type further; this one doesn't, so the values are typed in Swift as UInt32.

This old-fashioned sort of C enum arrives as a Swift struct adopting the RawRepresentable protocol, and its enumerands (here, `kDead` and `kAlive`) arrive into Swift as synonyms for instances of the State struct with an appropriate `rawValue` (here, 0 and 1 respectively). The result is that you can use the enumerand names as a medium of interchange wherever a State enum arrives from or is expected by C. If a C function `setState` takes a State enum parameter, you can call it with one of the State enumerand names:

```
setState(kDead)
```

Observe that there are no namespaces in this story! The enumerands are bare names, not members of the State struct; you say `kDead`, not `State.kDead`. If you are curious about what integer is represented by the name `kDead`, you have to take its `rawValue`. You can also create an arbitrary State value by calling its `init(rawValue:)` initializer — there is no check to see whether this value is one of the defined constants. But you aren't expected to do either of those things.

NS_ENUM

Starting back in Xcode 4.4, a C enum notation was introduced that uses the NS_ENUM macro:

```
typedef NS_ENUM(NSInteger, UIStatusBarAnimation) {
    UIStatusBarAnimationNone,
    UIStatusBarAnimationFade,
    UIStatusBarAnimationSlide,
};
```

That notation both specifies the integer type and associates a type name with this enum as a whole. Swift imports an enum declared this way *as a Swift enum* with the name and raw value type intact; the enumerand names become namespaced case names, with the common prefix subtracted:

```
enum UIStatusBarAnimation : Int {
    case none
    case fade
    case slide
}
```

Going the other way, a Swift enum with an Int raw value type can be exposed to Objective-C using the `@objc` attribute:

```
@objc enum Star : Int {
    case blue
    case white
    case yellow
    case red
}
```

Objective-C sees that as an enum with type NSInteger and enumerand names `Star-Blue`, `StarWhite`, and so on.

In the special case where the `NS_ENUM` type name ends in `Error`, it arrives into Swift as a struct conforming to Error. Here's the start of an enum declaration from the Core Location framework:

```
typedef NS_ENUM(NSInteger, CLError) {
    kCLErrorLocationUnknown = 0,
    kCLErrorDenied,
    kCLErrorNetwork,
    // ...
};
```

The result is that when Objective-C throws an NSError whose domain is `kCLError-Domain` and whose code is `kCLErrorLocationUnknown`, Swift can catch it by saying `catch CLError.locationUnknown`.

A knotty problem arises when you write a Swift switch statement that exhausts a C enum tag's cases. What if, in a future release, the C code is changed to add a case to this enum? If that happens, and if your "exhaustive" switch receives an unknown case, you'll crash. But Swift is ready with a solution:

- When you compile your code, you'll be warned by the compiler that this enum "may have additional unknown values." To remove the warning, you add a `default` case. Normally, the compiler would warn you that your `default` case will never be executed, because your switch is exhaustive; but in this situation, your switch might *not* be exhaustive some day, so that warning doesn't appear.

- In addition, you mark the `default` case with the `@unknown` attribute. This tells the compiler that you *think* your switch is exhaustive (without the `default`), and you'd like to be warned if it isn't. If your switch isn't exhaustive, you'll get the warning now; if some day a new case is added to the enum, you'll get the warning then, and you can silence it by adding the new case to your switch.

Let's demonstrate. Here's a C enum:

```
typedef NS_ENUM(NSInteger, TestEnum) {
    TestEnumOne
    TestEnumTwo
};
```

This arrives into Swift as an enum called TestEnum. Here's an exhaustive switch over a TestEnum:

```
switch test { // test is a TestEnum
case .one : break
case .two : break
} // compiler warns
```

We get a warning from the compiler. Our switch looks exhaustive, but in the future it might not be. So we add an @unknown default case, and the warning goes away:

```
switch test { // test is a TestEnum
case .one : break
case .two : break
@unknown default: break
}
```

Suppose the C enum later acquires another case (case .three). No problem! Our Swift switch is crash-proof, because there's a default case. Even better, when we compile against the C code, our Swift switch will get another warning, telling us that the switch is no longer exhaustive.

If the Objective-C code is our own, and if we're sure that the C enum will never acquire a new case, we can mark it with NS_CLOSED_ENUM instead of NS_ENUM; this will cause Swift to treat TestEnum like an ordinary Swift enum.

 Some enums in the Swift standard library and Foundation overlays are marked as open to future additional cases in the same way as NS_ENUM.

NS_OPTIONS

Another variant of C enum notation, using the NS_OPTIONS macro, is suitable for bitmasks:

```
typedef NS_OPTIONS(NSUInteger, UIViewAutoresizing) {
    UIViewAutoresizingNone              = 0,
    UIViewAutoresizingFlexibleLeftMargin   = 1 << 0,
    UIViewAutoresizingFlexibleWidth        = 1 << 1,
    UIViewAutoresizingFlexibleRightMargin  = 1 << 2,
    UIViewAutoresizingFlexibleTopMargin    = 1 << 3,
    UIViewAutoresizingFlexibleHeight       = 1 << 4,
    UIViewAutoresizingFlexibleBottomMargin = 1 << 5
};
```

An enum declared like that arrives into Swift as a struct adopting the OptionSet protocol. The OptionSet protocol adopts the RawRepresentable protocol, so this is a struct with a rawValue instance property holding the underlying integer. The C enum case names are represented by static properties, each of whose values is an instance of this struct; the names of these static properties are imported with the common prefix subtracted. In Swift, this struct is namespaced by nesting it into the UIView class as UIView.AutoresizingMask:

```
struct AutoresizingMask : OptionSet {
    init(rawValue: UInt)
    static var flexibleLeftMargin: UIView.AutoresizingMask { get }
    static var flexibleWidth: UIView.AutoresizingMask { get }
    static var flexibleRightMargin: UIView.AutoresizingMask { get }
    static var flexibleTopMargin: UIView.AutoresizingMask { get }
    static var flexibleHeight: UIView.AutoresizingMask { get }
    static var flexibleBottomMargin: UIView.AutoresizingMask { get }
}
```

When you say something like `UIView.AutoresizingMask.flexibleLeftMargin`, it *looks* as if you are initializing a case of a Swift enum, but in fact this is an instance of the UIView.AutoresizingMask struct, whose `rawValue` property has been set to the value declared by the original C enum — which, for `.flexibleLeftMargin`, is `1<<0`. Because a static property of this struct is an instance of the same struct, you can, as I explained in "Inference of Type Name with Static/Class Members" on page 141, omit the struct name when supplying a static property name where the struct is expected:

```
self.view.autoresizingMask = .flexibleWidth
```

Because this is an OptionSet struct, you can represent and manipulate the bitmask as if it were a Set:

```
self.view.autoresizingMask = [.flexibleWidth, .flexibleHeight]
```

 In Objective-C, where an `NS_OPTIONS` enum is expected, you pass `0` to indicate that no options are provided. In Swift, where a corresponding struct is expected, you pass `[]` (an empty set) or omit the `options:` parameter entirely. Some `NS_OPTIONS` enums have an explicit option that *means* `0`; Swift sometimes won't bother to import its name, because passing `[]` means the same thing. To set a UIView.AutoresizingMask value to `UIViewAutoresizingNone` in Swift, set it to `[]` (not `.none`).

Global string constants

The names of many Objective-C global string constants (referred to jokingly by Apple as *stringly typed*) are namespaced by importing them into Swift as static struct properties. This is accomplished by means of the `NS_STRING_ENUM` and `NS_EXTENSIBLE_STRING_ENUM` Objective-C macros. For example, the names of the NSAttributedString attribute keys used to be simple global string constants (type `NSString*`):

```
NSString* const NSFontAttributeName;
NSString* const NSParagraphStyleAttributeName;
NSString* const NSForegroundColorAttributeName;
// ... and so on ...
```

This meant that they were global string constants in Swift as well. Now, however, they are typed as NSAttributedStringKey values:

```
NSAttributedStringKey const NSFontAttributeName;
NSAttributedStringKey const NSParagraphStyleAttributeName;
NSAttributedStringKey const NSForegroundColorAttributeName;
// ... and so on ...
```

NSAttributedStringKey, in Objective-C, is just a synonym for NSString, but it is marked with the NS_EXTENSIBLE_STRING_ENUM macro:

```
typedef NSString * NSAttributedStringKey NS_EXTENSIBLE_STRING_ENUM;
```

The result is that these names are imported into Swift as namespaced static properties of an NSAttributedString.Key struct with names like .name, .paragraphStyle, and so on. Moreover, a dictionary that expects these keys has a key type of NSAttributed-String.Key, so you can write compact code like this:

```
self.navigationController?.navigationBar.titleTextAttributes = [
    .font: UIFont(name: "ChalkboardSE-Bold", size: 20)!,
    .foregroundColor: UIColor.darkText
]
```

C Structs

A C struct is a compound type whose elements can be accessed by name using dot-notation after a reference to the struct:

```
struct CGPoint {
    CGFloat x;
    CGFloat y;
};
typedef struct CGPoint CGPoint;
```

After that declaration, it becomes possible to talk like this in C:

```
CGPoint p;
p.x = 100;
p.y = 200;
```

A C struct arrives wholesale into Swift as a Swift struct, which is thereupon endowed with Swift struct features. CGPoint in Swift has CGFloat instance properties x and y, but it also magically acquires the implicit memberwise initializer! In addition, a zeroing initializer with no parameters is injected; saying CGPoint() makes a CGPoint whose x and y are both 0. Extensions can supply additional features, and the Swift CoreGraphics header adds a few to CGPoint:

```
extension CGPoint {
    static var zero: CGPoint { get }
    init(x: Int, y: Int)
    init(x: Double, y: Double)
}
```

As you can see, a Swift CGPoint has additional initializers accepting Int or Double arguments, along with another way of making a zero CGPoint, `CGPoint.zero`. CGSize is treated similarly. CGRect is particularly well endowed with added methods and properties in Swift.

The fact that a Swift struct is an object, while a C struct is not, does not pose any problems of communication. You can assign or pass a Swift CGPoint where a C CGPoint is expected, because CGPoint came from C in the first place. The fact that Swift has endowed CGPoint with object methods and properties doesn't matter; C doesn't see them. All C cares about are the x and y elements of this CGPoint, which are communicated from Swift to C without difficulty.

C Pointers

A C pointer is an integer designating the location in memory (the *address*) where the real data resides. Allocating and disposing of that memory is a separate matter. The declaration for a pointer to a data type is written with an asterisk after the data type name; a space can appear on either or both sides of the asterisk. These are equivalent declarations of a pointer-to-int:

```
int *intPtr1;
int* intPtr2;
int * intPtr3;
```

The type name itself is `int*` (or, with a space, `int *`). Objective-C, for reasons that I'll explain later, uses C pointers heavily, so you're going to be seeing that asterisk a lot if you look at any Objective-C.

A C pointer arrives into Swift as an UnsafePointer or, if writable, an UnsafeMutablePointer; this is a generic, and is specified to the actual type of data pointed to. (A pointer is "unsafe" because Swift isn't managing the memory for, and can't even guarantee the integrity of, what is pointed to.)

To illustrate, here's an Objective-C UIColor method declaration; I haven't discussed this syntax yet, but just concentrate on the types in parentheses:

```
- (BOOL) getRed: (CGFloat *) red
    green: (CGFloat *) green
    blue: (CGFloat *) blue
    alpha: (CGFloat *) alpha;
```

CGFloat is a basic numeric type. The type `CGFloat *` states (despite the space) that these parameters are all `CGFloat*` — that is, pointer-to-CGFloat.

The Swift translation of that declaration looks, in effect, like this:

```
func getRed(_ red: UnsafeMutablePointer<CGFloat>,
    green: UnsafeMutablePointer<CGFloat>,
    blue: UnsafeMutablePointer<CGFloat>,
    alpha: UnsafeMutablePointer<CGFloat>) -> Bool
```

UnsafeMutablePointer in this context is used like a Swift inout parameter: you declare and initialize a var of the appropriate type beforehand, and then pass its address as argument by way of the & prefix operator. When you pass the address of a reference in this way, you are in fact creating and passing a pointer:

```
var r : CGFloat = 0
var g : CGFloat = 0
var b : CGFloat = 0
var a : CGFloat = 0
c.getRed(&r, green: &g, blue: &b, alpha: &a)
```

It's fine to take the address of a variable reference and hand it to a C function that returns immediately, as we are doing here; but do not *persist* such an address yourself. If r is a CGFloat, saying let rPtr = &r would be a really bad idea; the compiler will warn, and in future this warning is slated to be promoted to be an error. If you need to do that sort of thing, call some form of withUnsafePointer, which takes an anonymous function within which the pointer is valid.

In C, to access the memory pointed to by a pointer, you use an asterisk before the pointer's name: *intPtr is "the thing pointed to by the pointer intPtr." In Swift, you use the pointer's pointee property. In this example, we receive a stop parameter typed originally as a BOOL*, a pointer-to-BOOL; in Swift, it's an UnsafeMutable-Pointer<ObjCBool>. To set the BOOL at the far end of this pointer, we set the pointer's pointee:

```
// mas is an NSMutableAttributedString, r is an NSRange, f is a UIFont
mas.enumerateAttribute(.font, in: r) { value, r, stop in
    if let value = value as? UIFont, value == f {
        // ...
        stop.pointee = true
    }
}
```

The most general type of C pointer is pointer-to-void (void*), also known as the *generic pointer*. The term void here means that no type is specified; it is legal in C to use a generic pointer wherever a specific type of pointer is expected, and *vice versa*. In effect, pointer-to-void casts away type checking as to what's at the far end of the pointer. This will appear in Swift as a "raw" pointer, either UnsafeRawPointer or UnsafeMutableRawPointer.

Raw pointers are even more unsafe than normal pointers; not only the lifetime and extent of the memory pointed to, but also the *type* of what's in that memory, is now your responsibility. As far as the pointer is concerned, what the memory contains is just bytes. You can cast a typed unsafe pointer to a raw unsafe pointer, but not the other way. Instead, starting with a raw pointer, you can `load` an object from an address within the memory, or you can *bind* the memory to derive a typed pointer to the same memory:

```
// buff is a CVImageBuffer
if let baseAddress = CVPixelBufferGetBaseAddress(buff) {
    // baseAddress is an UnsafeMutableRawPointer
    let addrptr = baseAddress.assumingMemoryBound(to: UInt8.self) // *
    // addrptr is an UnsafeMutablePointer<UInt8>
    // ...
}
```

C Arrays

A C array contains a fixed number of elements of a single data type. Under the hood, it is a contiguous block of memory sized to accommodate this number of elements of this data type. For this reason, the name of an array in C is the name of a pointer to the first element of the array. If `arr` has been declared as an array of int, the term `arr` can be used wherever a value of type `int*` (a pointer-to-int) is expected. The C language will indicate an array type either by appending square brackets to a reference or as a pointer.

For example, the C function `CGContextStrokeLineSegments` is declared like this:

```
void CGContextStrokeLineSegments(CGContextRef c,
    const CGPoint points[],
    size_t count
);
```

The square brackets in the second line tell you that the second parameter is a C array of CGPoints. A C array carries no information about how many elements it contains, so to pass this C array to this function, you must also *tell* the function how many elements the array contains; that's what the third parameter is for. A C array of CGPoint is a pointer to a CGPoint, so this function's declaration is translated into Swift like this:

```
func __strokeLineSegments(
    between points: UnsafePointer<CGPoint>?,
    count: Int)
```

Now, you're not really expected to call that function. The CGContext Swift overlay provides a pure Swift version, `strokeLineSegments`, which takes a Swift array of CGPoint with no need to provide a `count`; and the original `CGContextStrokeLine-Segments` has been marked `NS_REFINED_FOR_SWIFT` to generate the two underscores and hide it from you. But let's say you wanted to call `__strokeLineSegments` anyway. How would you do it?

To call __strokeLineSegments and pass it a C array of CGPoints, it would appear that you need to *make* a C array of CGPoints. A C array is not, by any stretch of the imagination, a Swift array; so how on earth will you do this? Surprise! You don't have to. Even though a Swift array is not a C array, you can pass a pointer to a Swift array here. In this example, you don't even need to pass a pointer; you can pass a reference to a Swift array *itself*. And since this is not a mutable pointer, you can declare the array with let; indeed, you can even pass a Swift array literal! No matter which approach you choose, Swift will convert to a C array for you as the argument crosses the bridge from Swift to C:

```
let c = UIGraphicsGetCurrentContext()!
let arr = [
    CGPoint(x:0,y:0),
    CGPoint(x:50,y:50),
    CGPoint(x:50,y:50),
    CGPoint(x:0,y:100),
]
c.__strokeLineSegments(between: arr, count: arr.count)
```

However, you *can* form a C array if you really want to. This is where the "Unsafe" in an unsafe pointer really comes into play: you must manage the memory yourself, explicitly, and getting it right is entirely up to you. First, you set aside the block of memory by declaring an UnsafeMutablePointer of the desired type and calling the class method allocate(capacity:) with the desired number of elements. Then you populate (technically, *initialize*) that memory. You will also be responsible for undoing all of that later; you deinitialize the memory and deallocate it. The best way to ensure that is to configure the block of memory and then immediately complete the memory management in a defer block:

```
let ptr = UnsafeMutablePointer<CGPoint>.allocate(capacity:4)
ptr.initialize(repeating: .zero, count: 4)
defer {
    ptr.deinitialize(count:4)
    ptr.deallocate()
}
```

Now that memory management is configured, you can manipulate the element values. In this instance, we want to write real CGPoint values into the memory block. You could do this by manipulating the pointee, but you can also use subscripting, which might be a lot more convenient. Be careful to stay within the block of memory you have configured! There's no range checking, and writing outside memory you own can mysteriously wreck your program later:

```
ptr[0] = CGPoint(x:0,y:0)
ptr[1] = CGPoint(x:50,y:50)
ptr[2] = CGPoint(x:50,y:50)
ptr[3] = CGPoint(x:0,y:100)
```

Finally, since the UnsafeMutablePointer *is* a pointer, you pass *it*, not a pointer to it, as argument:

```
let c = UIGraphicsGetCurrentContext()!
c.__strokeLineSegments(between: ptr, count: 4)
```

The same convenient subscripting is available when you receive a C array. In this example, col is a UIColor; comp is typed as an UnsafePointer to CGFloat. That is really a C array of CGFloat, and so you can access its elements by subscripting:

```
if let comp = col.cgColor.__unsafeComponents,
    let sp = col.cgColor.colorSpace,
    sp.model == .rgb {
        let red = comp[0]
        let green = comp[1]
        let blue = comp[2]
        let alpha = comp[3]
        // ...
}
```

C Strings

The native C string type is not a distinct type; it is a null-terminated array of char. Therefore it may be typed in Swift as [Int8] or [CChar], because CChar is Int8, or as UnsafePointer<Int8> or UnsafePointer<CChar>, because a C array is a pointer to the first element of the array. These representations are effectively interchangeable.

A C string can't be formed as a literal in Swift, but you can pass a Swift String where a C string is expected; in this example, takeCString is a C function that takes a C string:

```
let s = "hello"
takeCString("hello") // fine
takeCString(s) // fine too
```

If you have to, you can form a real C string in Swift. The Swift Foundation overlay provides the cString(using:) method:

```
let arrayOfCChar : [CChar]? = s.cString(using: .utf8)
takeCString(arrayOfCChar!)
```

Swift String provides the utf8CString property, a ContiguousArray<CChar>; you can turn that into a pointer with the withUnsafeBufferPointer method:

```
let contiguousArrayOfCChar : ContiguousArray<CChar> = s.utf8CString
contiguousArrayOfCChar.withUnsafeBufferPointer { ptr -> Void in
    takeCString(ptr.baseAddress!)
}
```

More simply, you can call the String withCString method:

```
s.withCString { ptr -> Void in
    takeCString(ptr)
}
```

In the other direction, a UTF-8 C string can be rendered into a Swift String by way of a Swift String initializer such as `init(cString:)` or `init?(validatingUTF8:)`. To specify some other encoding, call the static method `decodeCString(_:as:)`. In this example, `returnCString` is a C function that returns a C string:

```
let result : UnsafePointer<Int8> = returnCString()
let resultString : String = String(cString: result)
```

C Functions

A C function declaration starts with the return type (which might be void, meaning no returned value), followed by the function name, followed by a parameter list — parentheses containing comma-separated pairs consisting of the type followed by the parameter name. The parameter names are purely internal. C functions are global, and Swift can call them directly.

Here's the C declaration for an Audio Services function:

```
OSStatus AudioServicesCreateSystemSoundID(
    CFURLRef inFileURL,
    SystemSoundID* outSystemSoundID)
```

An OSStatus is basically an Int32. A CFURLRef is a CFTypeRef ("Memory Management of CFTypeRefs" on page 591) and is called CFURL in Swift. A SystemSoundID is a UInt32, and the * makes this a C pointer, as we already know. The whole thing translates directly into Swift:

```
func AudioServicesCreateSystemSoundID(
    _ inFileURL: CFURL,
    _ outSystemSoundID: UnsafeMutablePointer<SystemSoundID>) -> OSStatus
```

CFURL is (for reasons that I'll explain later) interchangeable with NSURL and Swift URL; so here we are, calling this C function in Swift:

```
let sndurl = Bundle.main.url(forResource: "test", withExtension: "aif")!
var snd : SystemSoundID = 0
AudioServicesCreateSystemSoundID(sndurl as CFURL, &snd)
```

Struct functions

Most of the commonly used C global functions in Cocoa operate on a struct; they have the name of that struct as the first element of their name, and have that struct itself as their first parameter. In Swift, where structs are objects, these functions are often transformed into methods on the struct.

For example, in Objective-C, the way to construct a CGRect from scratch is with the `CGRectMake` function, and the way to divide a CGRect is with the `CGRectDivide` function:

```
CGRect rect = CGRectMake(10,10,100,100);
CGRect arrow;
CGRect body;
CGRectDivide(rect, &arrow, &body, arrowHeight, CGRectMinYEdge);
```

In Swift, `CGRectMake` is overshadowed by the CGRect struct initializer `init(x:y:width:height:)`, and `CGRectDivide` is overshadowed by the CGRect divided method:

```
let rect = CGRect(x: 10, y: 10, width: 100, height: 100)
let (arrow, body) = rect.divided(atDistance: arrowHeight, from: .minYEdge)
```

Pointer-to-function

In C, a function has a type based on its signature, and the name of a function is a reference to the function, and so it is possible to pass a function — sometimes termed a *pointer-to-function* — by using the function's name where a function of that type is expected.

Here's the declaration for a C function from the Audio Toolbox framework:

```
OSStatus AudioServicesAddSystemSoundCompletion(SystemSoundID inSystemSoundID,
    CFRunLoopRef __nullable inRunLoop,
    CFStringRef __nullable inRunLoopMode,
    AudioServicesSystemSoundCompletionProc inCompletionRoutine,
    void * __nullable inClientData)
```

(I'll explain the term __nullable later.) What's an AudioServicesSystemSoundCompletionProc? Here's how it's declared:

```
typedef void (*AudioServicesSystemSoundCompletionProc)(
    SystemSoundID ssID,
    void* __nullable clientData);
```

In the first line, the asterisk and name in parentheses means that this is the name of a pointer-to-function. A SystemSoundID is a UInt32. So this declaration means that an AudioServicesSystemSoundCompletionProc is a pointer to a function taking two parameters (typed UInt32 and pointer-to-void) and returning no result.

Amazingly, you can pass a Swift function where a C pointer-to-function is expected! As always when passing a function, you can define the function separately and pass its name, or you can form the function inline as an anonymous function. If you're going to define the function separately, it cannot be a method. A function defined at the top level of a file is fine; so is a function defined locally within a function.

So here's my AudioServicesSystemSoundCompletionProc, declared at the top level of a file:

```
func soundFinished(_ snd:UInt32, _ c:UnsafeMutableRawPointer?) {
    AudioServicesRemoveSystemSoundCompletion(snd)
    AudioServicesDisposeSystemSoundID(snd)
}
```

And here's my code for playing a sound file as a system sound, including a call to `AudioServicesAddSystemSoundCompletion`:

```
let sndurl = Bundle.main.url(forResource: "test", withExtension: "aif")!
var snd : SystemSoundID = 0
AudioServicesCreateSystemSoundID(sndurl as CFURL, &snd)
AudioServicesAddSystemSoundCompletion(snd, nil, nil, soundFinished, nil)
AudioServicesPlaySystemSound(snd)
```

Objective-C

Objective-C is built on top of C. It adds some syntax and features, but it continues at the same time to use C syntax and data types, and remains C under the hood.

The Objective-C language was created by Brad Cox and Tom Love in the early 1980s to furnish C with the object-oriented capabilities of Smalltalk. Its adoption by NeXT, under the leadership of Steve Jobs, drove the evolution toward the mature form of the language during the late 1980s, spearheaded by Steve Naroff. In 1997, when Jobs had returned to Apple and Apple acquired NeXT, Objective-C became the language of Mac OS X Cocoa. Cocoa Touch, created for the iPhone a decade later, still uses Objective-C; that's why your use of Swift in programming iOS and UIKit depends upon Swift's interoperability with Objective-C.

Unlike Swift, Objective-C has no namespaces. For this reason, different frameworks distinguish their contents by starting the names of types, functions, and constants with distinct prefixes. The "CG" in "CGFloat" stands for Core Graphics, because it is declared in the Core Graphics framework. The "NS" in "NSString" stands for NeXT-Step, the framework that later became Cocoa.

Objective-C Objects and C Pointers

All the data types and syntax of C are part of Objective-C. But Objective-C is object-oriented, so it needs a way of adding objects to C. It does this by taking advantage of C pointers. C pointers accommodate having anything at all at the far end of the pointer; management of whatever is pointed to is a separate matter, and that's just what Objective-C takes care of. Objective-C object types are expressed using C pointer syntax.

Here's the Objective-C declaration for the `addSubview:` method:

```
- (void)addSubview:(UIView *)view;
```

I haven't discussed Objective-C method declaration syntax yet, but focus on the type declaration for the `view` parameter, in parentheses: it is `UIView*`. This appears to mean "a pointer to a UIView." It does mean that — and it doesn't. What's at the far end of the pointer is certainly a UIView instance. But *all* Objective-C object references are pointers. The fact that this is a pointer is merely a consequence of the fact that it's an object.

The Swift translation of this method declaration doesn't appear to involve any pointers:

```
func addSubview(_ view: UIView)
```

In general, in Swift, you will simply pass a reference to a class instance where Objective-C expects a class instance; the asterisk used in Objective-C to express the fact that this is an object won't matter. What you pass as argument when calling `addSubview(_:)` from Swift is a UIView instance — which is exactly what Objective-C expects. There is, of course, a sense in which you *are* passing a pointer when you pass a class instance — because classes are reference types! A class instance is actually seen the same way by both Swift and Objective-C; the difference is that Swift doesn't use pointer *notation*.

Objective-C's `id` type is a general pointer to an object — the object equivalent of C pointer-to-void. Any object type can be assigned or cast to or from an `id`. Because `id` is itself a pointer, a reference declared as `id` doesn't use an asterisk; it is rare (though not impossible) to encounter an `id*`.

Objective-C Objects and Swift Objects

Objective-C objects are classes and instances of classes. They arrive into Swift more or less intact. You won't have any trouble subclassing Objective-C classes or working with instances of Objective-C classes. (For how Swift sees Objective-C properties and accessors, see Chapter 10.)

Going the other way, when Objective-C expects an object, it expects a class or an instance of a class, and Swift can provide it. But what Objective-C means by a class, in general, is a subclass of NSObject. Every other kind of object known to Swift has to be bridged or boxed in order to survive the journey into Objective-C's world. Moreover, many features of Swift are meaningless to Objective-C, and those features are invisible to Objective-C. Objective-C can't see any of the following:

- Swift enums, except for an `@objc` enum with an Int raw value
- Swift structs, except for structs that come ultimately from C or that are bridged to Objective-C classes
- Swift classes not derived from NSObject
- Swift protocols not marked `@objc`

- Protocol extensions
- Generics
- Tuples
- Nested types

Nothing in that list can be directly exposed to Objective-C — and, by implication, nothing that *involves* anything in that list can be exposed to Objective-C. Suppose we have a class MyClass not derived from NSObject. Then if your UIViewController subclass has a property typed as MyClass, that property cannot be exposed to Objective-C; and if your UIViewController subclass has a method that receives or returns a value typed as MyClass, that method cannot be exposed to Objective-C.

Nevertheless, you are perfectly free to use such properties and methods, even in a class (such as a UIViewController subclass) that *is* exposed to Objective-C. Objective-C simply won't be able to see those aspects of the class that would be meaningless to it.

Exposure of Swift to Objective-C

Since Swift 4, invisibility of Swift code to Objective-C *is the norm*. With a few exceptions, even if Objective-C *can* theoretically see a thing, it *won't* see it unless you explicitly expose it to Objective-C. You do that with the @objc attribute.

Let's talk first about the exceptions. These are things in your Swift code that Objective-C will be able to see automatically, *without* an explicit @objc attribute:

- A class derived from NSObject. Such a class will be declared in Swift either as subclassing NSObject itself or as subclassing some NSObject subclass, typically a class defined by Cocoa (such as UIViewController).

- Within such a class, an override of a method defined in Objective-C (such as UIViewController's viewDidLoad) or defined in Swift but marked @objc.

- Within such a class, an implementation of a member of a protocol adopted by the class, if the protocol is defined in Objective-C (such as NSCoding's init(coder:)) or defined in Swift but marked @objc.

- Within such a class, an instance property marked @IBOutlet or @IBInspectable or @NSManaged, or a method marked @IBAction (see Chapter 7).

Otherwise, to expose to Objective-C a property, method, or protocol, mark it with @objc. The compiler will stop you if you try to expose to Objective-C something that it is unable to see (such as a property whose type Objective-C cannot see or cannot understand). A protocol marked as @objc automatically becomes a class protocol.

A useful trick, if you have several methods that you need to expose explicitly to Objective-C, is to clump them into an extension that is itself marked @objc; there is then no need to mark those methods individually with @objc. If most or all of a class's members are to be exposed to Objective-C, you can mark the class @objc-Members; again, there is then no need to mark those members individually with @objc. Conversely, if a class member would be exposed to Objective-C and you want to prevent this, you can mark it @nonobjc.

There are two additional uses of @objc:

Expose a member of a nonObjective-C class
Even if a class is not exposed to Objective-C, it can be useful to mark a member of that class with @objc so that your Swift code can take advantage of Objective-C language features with regard to that member. A Timer using the target–action pattern (Chapter 11) can have a method of a nonObjective-C class as its action, but only if that method is marked @objc, because the method is specified with a selector (Chapter 2) and selectors are an Objective-C feature.

Change the Objective-C name of something
When you mark something with @objc, you can add parentheses containing the name by which you want Objective-C to see this thing. You are free to do this even for a class or a class member that Objective-C can see already. An example appeared in Chapter 10 when I changed the name by which Objective-C sees a property accessor. When using this feature, you bypass Swift's behind-the-scenes *name mangling* designed to prevent clashes with any existing Objective-C names, so you must take responsibility for avoiding such a clash yourself.

 Class members marked @objc, @IBAction, and @IBOutlet can be marked private to speed up compilation and reduce the footprint of the class's exposure to Objective-C. However, as I mentioned in Chapter 5, you shouldn't do that with an implementation of an optional member of an adopted Objective-C protocol.

Bridged Types and Boxed Types

Swift will convert certain native nonclass types to their Objective-C class equivalents for you. The following native Swift structs are bridged to Objective-C class types:

- String to NSString
- Numbers (and Bool) to NSNumber
- Array to NSArray
- Dictionary to NSDictionary
- Set to NSSet

Bridging has two immediate practical consequences for your code:

Parameter passing

You can pass an instance of the Swift struct where the Objective-C class is expected. In fact, in general you'll rarely even encounter the Objective-C class, because the Swift rendering of the API will display it as the Swift struct: if an Objective-C method takes an NSString, you'll see it in Swift as taking a String, and so on.

Casting

You can cast between the Swift struct and the Objective-C class. When casting from Swift to Objective-C, this is not a downcast, so the bare `as` operator is all you need. But casting from Objective-C to Swift, except for NSString to String, involves adding type information — NSNumber wraps some specific numeric type, and the collection types contain elements of some specific type — so you might need to cast down with `as!` or `as?` in order to specify that type.

Also, certain common Objective-C structs that can easily be wrapped by NSValue in Objective-C are bridged to NSValue in Swift. The common structs are CGPoint, CGSize, CGRect, CGAffineTransform, UIEdgeInsets, UIOffset, NSRange, CATransform3D, CMTime, CMTimeMapping, CMTimeRange, MKCoordinate, and MKCoordinateSpan.

In addition, various Cocoa Foundation classes are overlaid by Swift types whose names are the same but without the "NS" prefix. Often, extra functionality is injected to make the type behave in a more Swift-like way; and, where appropriate, the Swift type may be a struct, allowing you to take advantage of Swift value type semantics. NSMutableData, for instance, becomes otiose, because Data, the overlay for Objective-C NSData, is a struct with mutating methods and can be declared with `let` or `var`. And Date, the overlay for Objective-C NSDate, adopts Equatable and Comparable, so that an NSDate method like `earlierDate:` can be replaced by the `min` function.

The Swift overlay types are all bridged to their Foundation counterparts. The Swift rendering of an Objective-C API will show you the Swift overlay type rather than the Objective-C type: a Cocoa method that takes or returns an NSDate in Objective-C will take or return a Date in Swift, and so on. If necessary, you can cast between bridged types; for example, you can turn a Date into an NSDate with `as`.

Objective-C `id` is rendered as Any in Swift. This means that wherever an Objective-C API accepts an `id` parameter, that parameter is typed in Swift as Any and can be passed any Swift value whatever. If that value is of a bridged type, *the bridge is crossed automatically*, just as if you had cast explicitly with `as`. A String becomes an NSString, an Array becomes an NSArray, a number is wrapped in an NSNumber, a CGPoint or other common struct is wrapped in an NSValue, a Data becomes an NSData, and so forth.

The same rule applies when you pass a Swift collection to Objective-C, with regard to the collection's elements. If an element is of a bridged type, *the bridge is crossed automatically*. The typical case in point is when you pass a Swift array to Objective-C: an array of Int becomes an NSArray of NSNumbers; an array of CGPoint becomes an NSArray of NSValues; for an array with an Optional element type, any nil elements become NSNull instances (Chapter 10).

What happens when an object tries to cross the bridge from Swift to Objective-C, but that instance is *not* of a bridged type? (Such an object might be an enum, a struct of a nonbridged type, or a class that doesn't derive from NSObject.) On the one hand, Objective-C can't do anything with this object. On the other hand, the object needs to be allowed to cross the bridge somehow, especially because you, on the Swift side, might ask for the object back again later, and it needs to be returned to you intact.

To illustrate, suppose Person is a struct with a firstName and a lastName property. Then you might need to be able to do something like this:

```
// lay is a CALayer
let p = Person(firstName: "Matt", lastName: "Neuburg")
lay.setValue(p, forKey: "person")
// ... time passes ...
if let p2 = lay.value(forKey: "person") as? Person {
    print(p2.firstName, p2.lastName) // Matt Neuburg
}
```

Amazingly, this works. How? The answer, in a nutshell, is that Swift *boxes* this object into something that Objective-C can see *as* an object, even though Objective-C can't *do* anything with that object other than store and retrieve it. How Swift does this is irrelevant; it's an implementation detail, and none of your business. It happens that in this case the Person object is wrapped up in a _SwiftValue, but that name is unimportant; what's important is that it is an Objective-C object, wrapping the value we provided. In this way, Objective-C is able to store the object for us, in its box, and hand it back to us intact upon request. Like Pandora, Objective-C will cope perfectly well as long as it doesn't look in the box!

Objective-C Methods

In Objective-C, method parameters can (and nearly always do) have external names, and the name of a method as a whole is not distinct from the external names of the parameters: the parameter names are *part* of the method name, with a colon appearing where each parameter would need to go. Here's a typical Objective-C method declaration from Cocoa's NSString class:

```
- (NSString *)stringByReplacingOccurrencesOfString:(NSString *)target
                            withString:(NSString *)replacement
```

The Objective-C name of that method is:

```
stringByReplacingOccurrencesOfString:withString:
```

A declaration for an Objective-C method has three parts:

- Either + or -, meaning that the method is a class method or an instance method, respectively.
- The data type of the return value, in parentheses. It might be void, meaning no returned value.
- The name of the method, split after each colon so as to make room for the parameters. Following each colon is the data type of the parameter, in parentheses, followed by a placeholder (internal) name for the parameter.

Renamification

When Swift calls an Objective-C method, there's an obvious mismatch between the rules and conventions of the two languages:

Swift method names
> A Swift method is a function; the base name of the function is followed by parentheses, and if the function's parameters have external names (labels), they appear inside the parentheses, like this: swiftFunction(parameter:).

Objective-C method names
> An Objective-C method name involves *no* parentheses and has *no* separate base name. If the method takes parameters, the parameter names, each followed by a colon, constitute the name of the method; the first thing in the name is just the name of the first parameter, like this: objCMethodWithParameter:. (If it takes no parameters, its name is just its name with no colon.)

To cope with this mismatch, Swift renders the Objective-C method's name more Swift-like by a process called *renamification*, which is performed by a component called the *Clang importer*, mediating between the two languages. The renamification rules are rather elaborate, but you don't need to know the details; you can get a general sense of how they behave from an example. Here's how the renamification rules transform the stringByReplacingOccurrencesOfString:withString: method into a Swift function:

1. Swift prunes *redundant initial type names*. We're starting with a string, and it's obvious from the return type that a string is returned, so there's no point saying string at the start. We are left with byReplacingOccurrencesOfString:withString:.

2. Swift prunes *initial by*. That's a common Cocoa locution, but Swift finds it merely verbose. Now we're down to `replacingOccurrencesOfString:withString:`.

3. Swift prunes *redundant final type names*. It's obvious that the parameters are strings, so there's no point saying `string` at the end of the parameter names. That leaves `replacingOccurrencesOf:with:`.

4. Finally, Swift decides *where to split* the first parameter name into the Swift base name and the external first parameter name. Here, Swift sees that the first parameter name now ends with a known preposition, `of`, so it splits before that preposition.

Here's the resulting renamification of that method:

```
func replacingOccurrences(of target:String, with replacement:String)
```

And here's an actual example of calling it:

```
let s = "hello"
let s2 = s.replacingOccurrences(of: "ell", with:"ipp")
// s2 is now "hippo"
```

If the Objective-C method being renamified belongs to you, you can intervene manually and *tell* Swift how to renamify this method, by appending `NS_SWIFT_NAME(...)` to the declaration (before the semicolon), where what's inside the parentheses is a Swift function reference. Here's an example:

```
- (void) triumphOverThing: (Thing*) otherThing NS_SWIFT_NAME(triumph(over:));
```

The Clang importer would normally renamify that in Swift as:

```
func triumphOverThing(_ otherThing: Thing)
```

Presumably that's because the importer doesn't understand `over` as a preposition. But by intervening manually, we've told it to use this instead:

```
func triumph(over otherThing: Thing)
```

Internal parameter names

When you *call* an Objective-C method from Swift, Objective-C's internal names for the parameters don't matter; you don't use them, and you don't need to know or care what they are. The internal names do *appear* in the Swift declaration of the method, and they might even help you understand what the method does; but they are not involved in the call. This is the Objective-C declaration of a method:

```
- (NSString *)stringByReplacingOccurrencesOfString:(NSString *)target
                            withString:(NSString *)replacement
```

And this is the Swift translation of that declaration:

```
func replacingOccurrences(of target:String, with replacement:String)
```

But the call site looks like this:

```
let s2 = s.replacingOccurrences(of: "ell", with: "ipp")
```

When you *override* an Objective-C method in Swift, code completion will suggest internal names corresponding to the Objective-C internal names, but you are free to change them. Here's the Objective-C declaration of the UIViewController prepare-ForSegue:sender: instance method:

```
- (void)prepareForSegue:(UIStoryboardSegue *)segue sender:(nullable id)sender;
```

When you override that method in your UIViewController subclass, the suggested template, in accordance with the renamification rules, looks like this:

```
override func prepare(for segue: UIStoryboardSegue, sender: Any?) {
    // ...
}
```

But the internal names are local variable names for your use inside the function body, and Objective-C doesn't care about them; so you can change them. This is a valid (but weird) override of prepareForSegue:sender: in Swift:

```
override func prepare(for war: UIStoryboardSegue, sender bow: Any?) {
    // ...
}
```

Reverse renamification

Now let's talk about what happens going the other way: How does Objective-C see methods declared in Swift? The simplest case is when the first parameter has no external name. Here's a Swift method intended as the action method of a button in the interface:

```
@IBAction func doButton(_ sender: Any?) {
    // ...
}
```

That method is seen by Objective-C as doButton:. That is the canonical form for an action method with one parameter, and for that reason I like to declare my action methods along those lines.

If a Swift method's first parameter does have an external name, then, as seen by Objective-C, that external name is appended to the Swift base name following an inserted preposition with. Here's a Swift method:

```
func makeHash(ingredients stuff:[String]) {
    // ...
}
```

That method is seen by Objective-C as makeHashWithIngredients:.

But if the external name of the first parameter is a preposition, then it is appended directly to the Swift base name. Here's another Swift method:

```
func makeHash(of stuff:[String]) {
    // ...
}
```

That method is seen by Objective-C as makeHashOf:.

Overloading

Unlike Swift, Objective-C does not permit overloading of methods. Two View-Controller instance methods called myMethod: returning no result, one taking a CGFloat parameter and one taking an NSString parameter, would be illegal in Objective-C. Therefore, two such Swift methods, though legal as far as Swift is concerned, would be illegal if they were both visible to Objective-C.

So if methods are overloads of one another in Swift, don't expose *more than one* of those methods to Objective-C.

Variadics

Objective-C has its own version of a variadic parameter. The NSArray instance method arrayWithObjects: is declared like this:

```
+ (id)arrayWithObjects:(id)firstObj, ... ;
```

Unlike Swift, such methods in Objective-C must somehow be told explicitly how many arguments are being supplied. Many such methods, including arrayWith-Objects:, use a nil terminator; that is, the caller supplies nil after the last argument, and the callee knows when it has reached the last argument because it encounters nil. A call to arrayWithObjects: in Objective-C would look something like this:

```
NSArray* pep = [NSArray arrayWithObjects: manny, moe, jack, nil];
```

Objective-C cannot call (or see) a Swift method that takes a variadic parameter. Swift, however, *can* call an Objective-C method that takes a variadic parameter, provided it is marked NS_REQUIRES_NIL_TERMINATION. And in fact, arrayWithObjects: *is* marked in this way, so you can say NSArray(objects:1, 2, 3) and Swift will supply the missing nil terminator.

Initializers and factories

Objective-C initializer methods are instance methods; actual instantiation is performed using the NSObject class method alloc, for which Swift has no equivalent (and doesn't need one), and the initializer message is sent to the instance that results. Here's how you create a UIColor instance by supplying red, green, blue, and alpha values in Objective-C:

```
UIColor* col = [[UIColor alloc] initWithRed:0.5 green:0.6 blue:0.7 alpha:1];
```

The name of that initializer, in Objective-C, is `initWithRed:green:blue:alpha:`. It's declared like this:

```
- (UIColor *)initWithRed:(CGFloat)red green:(CGFloat)green
    blue:(CGFloat)blue alpha:(CGFloat)alpha;
```

In short, an initializer method, to all outward appearances, is just an instance method like any other in Objective-C.

Swift, nevertheless, is able to detect that an Objective-C initializer *is* an initializer, because the name is special — it starts with `init`! Therefore, Swift is able to translate an Objective-C initializer into a Swift initializer. The word `init` is stripped from the start of the method name, and the preposition `with`, if it appears, is stripped as well. What's left is the external name of the first parameter.

So Swift translates the initializer `initWithRed:green:blue:alpha:` from Objective-C into the Swift initializer `init(red:green:blue:alpha:)`, which is declared like this:

```
init(red: CGFloat, green: CGFloat, blue: CGFloat, alpha: CGFloat)
```

And you'd call it like this:

```
let col = UIColor(red: 0.5, green: 0.6, blue: 0.7, alpha: 1.0)
```

The same principle operates in reverse: a Swift initializer `init(value:)` is visible to and callable by Objective-C under the name `initWithValue:`.

 If you're in charge of the Objective-C header being imported into Swift, be sure to mark your designated initializers as `NS_DESIGNATED_INITIALIZER` so that Swift can distinguish them. To block an initializer explicitly from being imported into Swift, mark it `NS_UNAVAILABLE`.

There is a second way to create an instance in Objective-C. Very commonly, a class will supply a *class* method that is a *factory* for instances. For example, the UIColor class has a class factory method `colorWithRed:green:blue:alpha:`, declared as follows:

```
+ (UIColor*) colorWithRed: (CGFloat) red green: (CGFloat) green
                blue: (CGFloat) blue alpha: (CGFloat) alpha;
```

Swift detects a factory method of this kind by some pattern-matching rules — a class method that returns an instance of the class, and whose name begins with the name of the class, stripped of its prefix — and translates it *as an initializer*, stripping the class name (and the `with`) from the start of the first parameter name. If the resulting initializer exists already, as it does in this example, then Swift treats the factory method as superfluous and suppresses it completely! The Objective-C class method `colorWithRed:green:blue:alpha:` isn't callable from Swift, because it would be identical to `init(red:green:blue:alpha:)` which already exists.

Error pointers

There's a specialized pattern in Objective-C where a method returning a BOOL or an object takes an NSErrorPointer parameter — that is, an `NSError**`, the Objective-C equivalent of an `inout` Error. The idea is that if there's an exception, the method returns `false` or `nil` respectively, and sets the NSError parameter by indirection. This is Objective-C's way of solving the problem that it can return only one value (there are no tuples).

For example, NSString has an initializer declared in Objective-C like this:

```
- (instancetype)initWithContentsOfFile:(NSString *)path
                               encoding:(NSStringEncoding)enc
                                  error:(NSError **)error;
```

And here is some Objective-C code that calls that initializer:

```
NSError* err;
NSString* s = [[NSString alloc] initWithContentsOfFile:f
                   encoding:NSUTF8StringEncoding
                   error:&err];
if (s == nil) {
    NSLog(@"%@", err);
}
```

As you can see, the whole procedure really is a lot like using a Swift `inout` parameter. An NSError variable is prepared beforehand, and its address is passed to the initializer as the `error:` argument. After the call, we test the initializer's result for `nil` explicitly, to see whether the initialization succeeded; if it didn't, we can examine the NSError variable to see what the error was. This is an annoyingly elaborate but necessary dance in Objective-C.

In Swift, an Objective-C method that takes an `NSError**` and returns a nullable object or a BOOL is automatically recast to take advantage of the error mechanism. The `error:` parameter is stripped from the Swift translation of the declaration, and is replaced by a `throws` marker:

```
init(contentsOfFile path: String, encoding enc: String.Encoding) throws
```

If there are no other parameters besides the `NSError**` and the parameter name ends `withError:`, those words are stripped to form the base name of the Swift method, which takes no parameters.

If you call a `throws` method that belongs to Objective-C and the Objective-C method returns `nil` or `false`, Swift sees that as a `throw` and throws the error that the Objective-C method returned by indirection. If the Objective-C method gets the pattern wrong and returns `nil` or `false` but forgets to set the NSError, Swift just makes up an error (`_GenericObjCError.nilError`) and throws it anyway. If the Objective-C

---

method returns a BOOL, Swift portrays it as returning no result, as the presence or absence of an error is dispositive.

The same method bridging works also in reverse: a Swift `throws` method that is exposed to Objective-C is seen as taking an `NSError**` parameter.

Selectors

A Cocoa Objective-C method will sometimes expect as parameter the name of a method that Cocoa is to call later. Such a name is called a *selector*. For example, the Objective-C UIControl `addTarget:action:forControlEvents:` method can be called as a way of telling a button in the interface, "From now on, whenever you are tapped, send this message to this object." The object is the `target:` parameter. The message, the `action:` parameter, is a selector. The target object *implements* this method; Cocoa will *call* this method on the target object.

You may imagine that, if this were a Swift method, you'd be passing a function here. But a selector is not the same as a function. It's just a name. Objective-C, unlike Swift, is so dynamic that it is able at runtime to construct and send an arbitrary message to an arbitrary object based on the name alone. Still, a selector is not exactly a string, either; it's a separate object type, designated in Objective-C declarations as SEL and in Swift declarations as Selector.

You can create a Selector by calling the Selector initializer, which takes a string. In the following examples, b is a UIButton:

```
b.addTarget(self, action: Selector("doNewGame:"), for: .touchUpInside)
```

As a shorthand, you can even pass a string literal where a Selector is expected, even though a Selector is not a string:

```
b.addTarget(self, action: "doNewGame:", for: .touchUpInside)
```

But don't do either of those things! Forming a literal selector string by hand is an invitation to form the string incorrectly, resulting in a selector that at best will fail to work, and at worst will cause your app to crash. Swift solves this problem by providing `#selector` syntax (described in Chapter 2):

```
b.addTarget(self, action: #selector(doNewGame), for: .touchUpInside)
```

The use of `#selector` syntax has numerous advantages. In addition to translating the method name to a selector for you, the compiler can check for the existence of the method in question, and can stop you from telling Objective-C to use a selector to call a method that isn't exposed to Objective-C (which would cause a crash at runtime).

Indeed, `#selector` syntax means that you will probably *never* need to form a selector from a string! Nevertheless, you can do so if you really want to. The rules for deriving an Objective-C name string from a Swift method name are completely mechanical:

1. The string starts with everything that precedes the left parenthesis in the method name (the base name).
2. If the method takes *no parameters*, stop. That's the end of the string.
3. If the method's first parameter has an external parameter name, append `With` and a capitalized version of that name, unless it is a preposition, in which case append a capitalized version of it directly.
4. Add a colon.
5. If the method takes exactly *one parameter*, stop. That's the end of the string.
6. If the method takes more than one parameter, add the external names of all remaining parameters, with a colon after each external parameter name.

Observe that this means that if the method takes any parameters, its Objective-C name string will end with a colon. Capitalization counts, and the name should contain no spaces or other punctuation except for the colons.

To illustrate, here are some Swift method declarations, with their Objective-C name strings given in a comment:

```
func sayHello() -> String       // "sayHello"
func say(_ s:String)            // "say:"
func say(string s:String)       // "sayWithString:"
func say(of s:String)           // "sayOf:"
func say(_ s:String, times n:Int) // "say:times:"
```

CFTypeRefs

A CFTypeRef is a pointer to an opaque struct that acts as a pseudo-object. (I talked about CFTypeRef pseudo-objects and their memory management in Chapter 12.) CFTypeRef functions are global C functions. Swift can call C functions, and before Swift 3 introduced renamification, CFTypeRef code looked almost as if Swift were C:

```
// before Swift 3:
let con = UIGraphicsGetCurrentContext()!
let sp = CGColorSpaceCreateDeviceGray() ❶
// ... colors and locs are arrays of CGFloat ...
let grad = CGGradientCreateWithColorComponents (sp, colors, locs, 3) ❷
CGContextDrawLinearGradient ( ❸
    con, grad, CGPointMake(89,0), CGPointMake(111,0), [])
```

Notice that the "subject" of each function call appears at the start of the name:

❶ `CGColorSpaceCreateDeviceGray` creates a CGColorSpace pseudo-object.

❷ `CGGradientCreateWithColorComponents` creates a CGGradient pseudo-object; the first parameter is the CGColorSpace pseudo-object.

❸ `CGContextDrawLinearGradient` draws a gradient in a CGContext pseudo-object; the first parameter is the CGContext pseudo-object, and the second parameter is the CGGradient pseudo-object.

Nowadays, as part of renamification, many commonly used CFTypeRef functions, especially in the Core Graphics framework, are recast as if the "subject" CFTypeRef objects were genuine class instances, with the functions themselves as initializers and instance methods. Those lines are recast in Swift like this (thanks to the mighty power of `NS_SWIFT_NAME`):

```
let con = UIGraphicsGetCurrentContext()!
let sp = CGColorSpaceCreateDeviceGray() ❶
// ... colors and locs are arrays of CGFloat ...
let grad = CGGradient(colorSpace: sp, ❷
    colorComponents: colors, locations: locs, count: 3)
con.drawLinearGradient(grad, ❸
    start: CGPoint(x:89,y:0), end: CGPoint(x:111,y:0), options:[])
```

In that code:

❶ `CGColorSpaceCreateDeviceGray` is unchanged.

❷ `CGGradientCreateWithColorComponents` is turned into a CGGradient pseudo-object initializer, with external parameter names.

❸ `CGContextDrawLinearGradient` is turned into an instance property of a CGContext pseudo-object, with external parameter names.

Many CFTypeRefs are *toll-free bridged* to corresponding Objective-C object types. CFString and NSString, CFNumber and NSNumber, CFArray and NSArray, CFDictionary and NSDictionary are all toll-free bridged (and there are many others). Such pairs are interchangeable by casting. This is much easier in Swift than in Objective-C. In Objective-C, ARC memory management doesn't apply to CFTypeRefs; therefore you must perform a *bridging cast*, to tell Objective-C how to manage this object's memory as it crosses between the memory-managed world of Objective-C objects and the unmanaged world of C and CFTypeRefs. But in Swift, CFTypeRefs *are* memory-managed, and so there is no need for a bridging cast; you can just cast, plain and simple.

In this code from one of my apps, I'm using the ImageIO framework. This framework has a C API (which has not been renamified) and uses CFTypeRefs. `CGImageSourceCopyPropertiesAtIndex` returns a CFDictionary whose keys are CFStrings. The easiest way to obtain a value from a dictionary is by subscripting, but you can't do that with a CFDictionary, because it isn't an object — so I cast it to a Swift dictionary. The key `kCGImagePropertyPixelWidth` is a CFString, and yet when I try to use it directly in a subscript, Swift allows me to do so:

```
let d = CGImageSourceCopyPropertiesAtIndex(src, 0, nil) as! [AnyHashable:Any]
let width = d[kCGImagePropertyPixelWidth] as! CGFloat
```

Similarly, in this code, I form a dictionary d using CFString keys — and then I pass it to the `CGImageSourceCreateThumbnailAtIndex` function where a CFDictionary is expected:

```
let d : [AnyHashable:Any] = [
    kCGImageSourceShouldAllowFloat : true,
    kCGImageSourceCreateThumbnailWithTransform : true,
    kCGImageSourceCreateThumbnailFromImageAlways : true,
    kCGImageSourceThumbnailMaxPixelSize : w
]
let imref = CGImageSourceCreateThumbnailAtIndex(src, 0, d as CFDictionary)!
```

A CFTypeRef is a pointer (to a pseudo-object), so it is interchangeable with C pointer-to-void. This can result in a perplexing situation in Swift. If a C API casts a CFTypeRef as a pointer-to-void, Swift will see it as an UnsafeRawPointer. How can you cast between this and the actual CFTypeRef? You cannot use the memory binding technique that I used earlier to turn an UnsafeRawPointer into an UnsafePointer generic, because the CFTypeRef does not lie at the far end of the pointer; it *is* the pointer.

We might simply call the global `unsafeBitCast` function, but that's dangerous (as the name suggests), because it gives the resulting CFTypeRef no memory management. The correct approach is to pass through an Unmanaged generic to apply memory management; its `fromOpaque` static method takes an UnsafeRawPointer, and its `toOpaque` instance method yields an UnsafeMutableRawPointer. (I owe this technique to Martin R.; see *http://stackoverflow.com/a/33310021/1187415*.)

To illustrate, I'll repeat the earlier example where I called `CGImageSourceCopyPropertiesAtIndex`, but this time I won't cast to a Swift dictionary; I'll work with the result as a CFDictionary to extract the value of its `kCGImagePropertyPixelWidth` key. To do so, I'll call `CFDictionaryGetValue`, which takes an UnsafeRawPointer parameter and returns an UnsafeRawPointer result. To form the parameter, I'll cast a CFString to an UnsafeMutableRawPointer; to work with the result, I'll cast an Unsafe-RawPointer to a CFNumber. No one in his right mind would ever write this code, but it does work:

```
let result = CGImageSourceCopyPropertiesAtIndex(src, 0, nil)!
let key = kCGImagePropertyPixelWidth // CFString
let p1 = Unmanaged.passUnretained(key).toOpaque() // UnsafeMutableRawPointer
let p2 = CFDictionaryGetValue(result, p1) // UnsafeRawPointer
let n = Unmanaged<CFNumber>.fromOpaque(p2!).takeUnretainedValue() // CFNumber
var width : CGFloat = 0
CFNumberGetValue(n, .cgFloatType, &width) // width is now 640.0
```

Blocks

A *block* is a C language feature introduced by Apple starting in iOS 4. It is very like a C function, but it behaves as a closure and can be passed around as a reference type. A block, in fact, is parallel to a Swift function, and the two are interchangeable: you can pass a Swift function where a block is expected, and when a block is handed to you by Cocoa it appears as a function.

In C and Objective-C, a block declaration is signified by the caret character (^), which appears where an asterisk would appear in a C pointer-to-function declaration. The NSArray instance method `sortedArrayUsingComparator:` takes an NSComparator parameter, which is defined through a `typedef` like this:

```
typedef NSComparisonResult (^NSComparator)(id obj1, id obj2);
```

That says: "An NSComparator is a block taking two `id` parameters and returning an NSComparisonResult." In Swift, therefore, that `typedef` is translated as the function signature (Any, Any) -> ComparisonResult. It is then trivial to supply a function of the required type as argument when you call `sortedArray(comparator:)` in Swift:

```
let arr = ["Mannyz", "Moey", "Jackx"]
let arr2 = (arr as NSArray).sortedArray { s1, s2 in
    let c1 = String((s1 as! String).last!)
    let c2 = String((s2 as! String).last!)
    return c1.compare(c2)
} // [Jackx, Moey, Mannyz]
```

In many cases, there won't be a `typedef`, and the type of the block will appear directly in a method declaration. Here's the Objective-C declaration for a UIView class method that takes two block parameters:

```
+ (void)animateWithDuration:(NSTimeInterval)duration
    animations:(void (^)(void))animations
    completion:(void (^ __nullable)(BOOL finished))completion;
```

In that declaration, `animations:` is a block taking no parameters (void) and returning no value, and `completion:` is a block taking one BOOL parameter and returning no value. Here's the Swift translation:

```
class func animate(withDuration duration: TimeInterval,
    animations: @escaping () -> Void,
    completion: ((Bool) -> Void)? = nil)
```

That's a method that you would *call*, passing a function as argument where a block parameter is expected (and see Chapter 2 for an example of actually doing so). Here's a method that you would *implement*, where a function is passed *to you*. This is the Objective-C declaration:

```
- (void)webView:(WKWebView *)webView
    decidePolicyForNavigationAction:(WKNavigationAction *)navigationAction
    decisionHandler:(void (^)(WKNavigationActionPolicy))decisionHandler;
```

You implement this method, and it is called when the user taps a link in a web view, so that you can decide how to respond. The third parameter is a block that takes one parameter — a WKNavigationActionPolicy, which is an enum — and returns no value. The block is passed to you as a Swift function, and you respond by *calling* the function to report your decision:

```
func webView(_ webView: WKWebView,
    decidePolicyFor navigationAction: WKNavigationAction,
    decisionHandler: @escaping (WKNavigationActionPolicy) -> Void) {
        // ...
        decisionHandler(.allow)
}
```

A C function is not a block, but you can also use a Swift function where a C function is expected, as I demonstrated earlier. Going in the other direction, to declare a type as a C pointer-to-function, mark the type as @convention(c). Here are two Swift method declarations:

```
func blockTaker(_ f:() -> ()) {}
func functionTaker(_ f:@convention(c)() -> ()) {}
```

Objective-C sees the first as taking a block, and the second as taking a pointer-to-function.

API Markup

In the early days of Swift, its static strict typing was a poor match for Objective-C's dynamic loose typing, and this made the Swift versions of Objective-C methods ugly and unpleasant:

Too many Optionals

In Objective-C, any object instance reference can be nil. But in Swift, only an Optional can be nil. The default solution was to use implicitly unwrapped Optionals as the medium of object interchange between Objective-C and Swift. But this was ugly, and a blunt instrument, especially because most objects arriving from Objective-C were never *in fact* going to be nil.

Too many umbrella collections

In Objective-C, a collection type such as NSArray can contain elements of multiple object types, and the collection itself is agnostic as to what types of elements it contains. But a Swift collection type can contain elements of just one type, and is itself typed according to that element type. The default solution was for every collection to arrive from Objective-C typed as having AnyObject elements; it then had to be cast down explicitly on the Swift side. This was infuriating.

You would ask for a view's `subviews` and get back an Array of AnyObject, which then had to be cast down to an Array of UIView — when nothing could be more obvious than that a view's subviews would in fact all be UIView objects.

These problems were subsequently solved by modifying the Objective-C language to permit *markup* of declarations in such a way as to communicate to Swift a more specific knowledge of what to expect.

Nullability

An Objective-C object type can be marked as `nullable` or `nonnull`, to specify, respectively, that it might or will never be `nil`. In the same way, C pointer types can be marked `__nullable` or `__nonnull`. Using these markers generally obviates the need for implicitly unwrapped Optionals as a medium of interchange; every type can be either a normal type or a simple Optional, and if it's an Optional, there's a good reason for it. Implicitly unwrapped Optionals are a rare sight in the Cocoa APIs nowadays.

If you're writing an Objective-C header file and you don't mark up any of it as to nullability, you'll return to the bad old days: Swift will see your types as implicitly unwrapped Optionals. Here's an Objective-C method declaration:

```
- (NSString*) badMethod: (NSString*) s;
```

In the absence of markup, Swift sees that as:

```
func badMethod(_ s: String!) -> String!
```

Clearly our Objective-C needs some markup! As soon as your header file contains any markup, the Objective-C compiler will complain until it is *completely* marked up. As a shortcut, you can mark an entire stretch of your header file with a default `nonnull` setting, so that only the exceptional `nullable` types will need explicit markup, like this:

```
NS_ASSUME_NONNULL_BEGIN
- (NSString*) badMethod: (NSString*) s;
- (nullable NSString*) goodMethod: (NSString*) s;
NS_ASSUME_NONNULL_END
```

Swift sees that with no implicitly unwrapped Optionals:

```
func badMethod(_ s: String) -> String
func goodMethod(_ s: String) -> String?
```

You can use the Clang analyzer (Product → Analyze) to help audit the correctness of your nullability markup, but in the end it's your responsibility to tell the truth. If you still want a type to appear as an implicitly unwrapped Optional (perhaps because you're just not sure what the truth is), mark it `null_unspecified`.

Lightweight generics

To mark an Objective-C collection type as containing a certain type of element, the element type can appear in angle brackets (<>) between the name of the collection type and the asterisk. Here's an Objective-C method that returns an array of strings:

```
- (NSArray<NSString*>*) pepBoys;
```

Swift sees the return type of that method as [String], and there will be no need to cast it down.

In the declaration of an actual Objective-C collection type, a placeholder name stands for the type in angle brackets. The declaration for NSArray starts like this:

```
@interface NSArray<ObjectType>
- (NSArray<ObjectType> *)arrayByAddingObject:(ObjectType)anObject;
// ...
```

The first line says that we're going to use ObjectType as the placeholder name for the element type. The second line says that the arrayByAddingObject: method takes an object of the element type and returns an array of the element type. If a particular array is declared as NSArray<NSString*>*, the ObjectType placeholder would be resolved to NSString*. Apple refers to this sort of markup as a *lightweight generic*, and you can readily see why.

In Swift, classes marked up as lightweight generics are imported into Swift as actual generics even if they are not bridged collection types. Suppose I declare my own Objective-C class, parallel to NSArray:

```
@interface Thing<ObjectType> : NSObject
- (void) giveMeAThing:(nonnull ObjectType)anObject;
@end
```

The Thing class arrives into Swift declared as a generic:

```
class Thing<ObjectType> : NSObject where ObjectType : AnyObject {
```

Thing has to be instantiated by resolving the generic somehow. Often, it will be resolved explicitly:

```
let t = Thing<NSString>()
t.giveMeAThing("howdy") // an Int would be illegal here
```

Bilingual Targets

It is legal for a target to be a *bilingual target* — one that contains both Swift files and Objective-C files. A bilingual target can be useful for various reasons:

- You might want to take advantage of Objective-C language features.
- You might want to incorporate third-party code written in Objective-C.

- You might want to incorporate your own existing code written in Objective-C.
- Your app itself may have been written in Objective-C originally, and now you want to migrate part of it (or all of it, in stages) into Swift.

The key question is how, within a single target, Swift and Objective-C hear about one another's code in the first place.

Objective-C, unlike Swift, has a visibility problem already: Objective-C files cannot automatically see one another. Instead, each Objective-C file that needs to see another Objective-C file must be instructed explicitly to see that file, usually with an #import directive at the top of the first file:

- In order to prevent unwanted exposure of private information, an Objective-C class declaration is conventionally spread over *two* files: a header file (*.h*) containing the @interface section, and a code file (*.m*) containing the @implementation section.
- Also conventionally, only *.h* files are ever imported. If declarations of class members, constants, and so forth are to be public, they are placed in a *.h* file.

Visibility of Swift and Objective-C to one another depends upon those conventions: it works through *.h* files. There are two directions of visibility, and they operate separately through two special Objective-C header files:

How Swift sees Objective-C

When you add a Swift file to an Objective-C target, or an Objective-C file to a Swift target, Xcode offers to create a *bridging header*. This is a *.h* file *in the project*. Its default name is derived from the target name — such as *MyCoolApp-Bridging-Header.h* — but the name is arbitrary and can be changed, provided you change the target's Objective-C Bridging Header build setting to match. (Similarly, if you decline the bridging header and you decide later that you want one, create a *.h* file manually and point to it in the target's Objective-C Bridging Header build setting.) An Objective-C *.h* file will then be visible to Swift if you #import it in this bridging header.

How Objective-C sees Swift

When you build your target, the appropriate top-level declarations of *all* your Swift files are *automatically* translated into Objective-C and are used to construct a *generated interface header* within the *Intermediates* build folder for this target, deep inside your *DerivedData* folder. For a target called MyCoolApp, the generated interface header is called *MyCoolApp-Swift.h*. The name may involve some transformation; a space in the target name is translated into an underscore. You can examine or change the header name with the target's Objective-C Generated Interface Header Name build setting. The generated interface header is how your Swift code is exposed to Objective-C in general (even in a single-language Swift project); your own Objective-C files will be able to see your Swift declarations if you #import the generated interface header into each Objective-C file that needs to see them.

To sum up:

- The *bridging header* is visible in your project navigator; you write an #import statement here to make your Objective-C declarations visible to Swift.

- The *generated interface header* is squirreled away in the DerivedData folder; you #import it to make your Swift declarations visible to your Objective-C code.

Here's an actual example. Let's say that I've added to my Swift target, called MyCool-App, a Thing class written in Objective-C. It is distributed over two files, *Thing.h* and *Thing.m*. Then:

- For Swift code to see the Thing class, I need to #import "Thing.h" in the *bridging* header (*MyCoolApp-Bridging-Header.h*).

- For Thing class code to see my Swift declarations, I need to #import "MyCool-App-Swift.h" (the generated bridging header) at the top of *Thing.m*.

That's how Objective-C and Swift are *able* to see one another; but *what* do Objective-C and Swift see when they see one another? Xcode makes it easy to find out, using the code editor's Related Items menu (Control-1). It contains a Generated Interface hierarchical menu:

- In an Objective-C header file (such as *Thing.h*), the Generated Interface menu lists the Swift interface. Choose it to see how these Objective-C declarations are translated into Swift.

- In a Swift file, the Generated Interface menu lists the Objective-C generated interface header. Choose it to see how your target's Swift declarations are translated into Objective-C.

Before Swift existed, all my iOS apps were written in Objective-C. When Swift came along, I translated those apps into Swift. I quickly developed a step-by-step procedure for doing that; here it is:

1. Pick a *.m* file to be translated into Swift. Objective-C cannot subclass a Swift class, so if you have defined both a class and its subclass in Objective-C, start with the subclass. (Leave the app delegate class for last.)

2. Remove that *.m* file from the target. To do so, select the *.m* file and use the File inspector.

3. In every Objective-C file that #imports the corresponding *.h* file, remove that #import statement and import in its place the generated interface header (if you aren't importing it in this file already).

4. If you were importing the corresponding *.h* file in the bridging header, remove the #import statement.

5. Create the *.swift* file for this class. Make sure it is added to the target.

6. In the *.swift* file, declare the class and provide stub declarations for all members that were being made public in the *.h* file. If this class needs to adopt Cocoa protocols, adopt them; you may have to provide stub declarations of required protocol methods as well. If this file needs to refer to any other classes that your target still declares in Objective-C, import their *.h* files in the bridging header.

7. The project should now compile! It doesn't work, of course, because you have not written any real code in the *.swift* file. But who cares about that? Time for a beer!

8. Now fill out the code in the *.swift* file. My technique is to translate more or less line-by-line from the original Objective-C code at first, even though the outcome is not particularly idiomatic or Swifty.

9. When the code for this *.m* file is completely translated into Swift, build and run and test. If the runtime complains (probably accompanied by crashing) that it can't find this class, find all references to it in the nib editor and reenter the class's name in the Identity inspector (and press Tab to set the change). Save and try again.

10. On to the next *.m* file! Repeat all of the above steps.

11. When all of the other files have been translated, translate the app delegate class. At this point, if there are no Objective-C files left in the target, you can delete the *main.m* file (replacing it with a `@main` attribute in the app delegate class declaration) and the *.pch* (precompiled header) file.

Your app should now run, and is rewritten in pure Swift (or is, at least, as pure as you intend to make it). Now go back and think about the code, making it more Swifty and idiomatic. You may well find that things that were clumsy or tricky in Objective-C can be made much neater and clearer in Swift.

You can also do a *partial* conversion of an Objective-C class by *extending* it in Swift. That can be useful as a stage along the path to total conversion, or you might quite reasonably write only one or two methods of an Objective-C class in Swift, just because Swift makes it so much easier to say or understand certain kinds of thing. However, Swift cannot see the Objective-C class's members unless they are made public, so methods and properties that you were previously keeping private in the Objective-C class's *.m* file may have to be declared in its *.h* file.

Index

comparison operators, 91
ComparisonResult, 527
compatibility, backward, 425
compilation, conditional, 422
compile error, 4
    (see also errors, compiler)
Compile Sources build phase, 352
compiler, 4
completion
    code, 435
    type-over, 433
compliant, key–value coding, 540
Components preferences, 358
composition of protocols, 195
compound assignment operators, 90
computed
    properties, 75
    property wrappers, 77, 322
    variable initialization, 73
    variables, 74
concatenating
    arrays, 236
    strings, 94
condition list, 262
conditional
    assignment, 271
    binding, 261, 273, 293
    compilation, 422
    conformance, 222
    evaluation, 270
    initialization, 71
conditions, 82, 259
configurations, 354
conform to a protocol, 190
connections, 387
    action, 399
    between nibs, 404
    creating, 390, 396, 401
    deleting, 395
    outlet, 388, 541
Connections inspector, 345, 393, 396
console, 343, 445
Console application, 447
constants, 7, 69, 152
    global string, 630
constraints, type, 207
    extensions, 221
    multiple, 214
contains, 99, 102, 235

continue, 279
control events, 399, 561
control flow (see flow control)
convenience initializers, 164
convention(c), 656
Copy Bundle Resources build phase, 352
copying instances, 156
count, 96, 233, 252
covariant, 177, 211
coverage, code, 461
crash
    class not key–value coding compliant, 394,
        540, 541
    could not cast value, 179
    deallocated object, 586
    loaded nib but view outlet was not set, 395
    not enough bits, 88
    simultaneous accesses, 312
    unexpectedly found nil, 112, 395
    unrecognized selector, 65, 403
creating
    action connection, 401
    enum, 138
    instance, 15, 35, 123
    outlet, 396
curly braces, 4, 26, 44, 74, 78, 92, 121, 123, 136,
    172, 194, 217, 260
currying, 60
custom attributes, 77
CustomNSError, 287
CustomReflectable, 299
CustomStringConvertible, 192
cycle through a sequence, 274

D

dance, weak–strong, 308
dangling pointers, 578
Data, 523
data sources, 560
data tips, 453
Date, 518
DateComponents, 518
DateFormatter, 519
DateInterval, 519
dates, 518
debug bar, 343
Debug navigator, 342, 452, 477
Debug pane, 343, 452
debugger, Xcode, 449

return type, 26
returned from function, 54
signature, 30
throws, 284
    calling, 285
trailing closures, 47
type, 40
values, 40
variadic parameters, 34
where clauses, 222

G
garbage collection, 303
gauges, 343, 477
generated interface, 345
    header, 660
generic pointer, 634
generics, 201-216
    adopting protocol conditionally, 222
    associated type chains, 212
    classes, subclassing, 210
    declaration, 204
    explicit specialization, 209
    extensions, 221
    functions, 205
    object types, 205
    polymorphism, 211
    protocols, 204
        constraining associated type, 215
    resolution, 203
        contradictory, 206
        explicit, 209
    reverse, 327
    specialization, 203
        (see also generics, resolution)
    type constraints, 207
        extensions, 221
        multiple, 214
    type, telling compiler, 208
    where clauses, 214
        extensions, 221
        methods, 222
getter, 74
    Objective-C, 537, 539
Git, 429
GitHub, 368, 432
GitLab, 432
global
    constants, 152

functions, 9, 15
    C, overshadowed, 637
    class method instead, 218
variables, 9, 67
    initialization, 80
globally visible instances, 602
golden rule of memory management, 579
groups, 339, 350
    blue, 363
    folder-linked, 350
    renaming, 374
guard, 292
guard case, 294
guard let, 293

H
hand-tweaking the APIs, 118, 129, 657
handlers, 44
    (see also functions)
hash, 526
hash character, 92
hashability
    Objective-C objects, 526
    Swift objects, 315
Hashable, 244, 252
    synthesizing, 315
Hasher, 315, 526
hashValue, 245, 315
hasPrefix, 95
hasSuffix, 95
header files, 417
    bridging, 659
    Core Graphics, 506
    generated interface, 660
    jumping to, 417
    Objective-C, 659
    Swift, 15, 418
heads-up display, 391
hexadecimal number, 84
hierarchy
    class, 159
    view, 378
History inspector, 344, 431
HUD, 391

I
IBAction, 400
IBInspectable, 406
IBOutlet, 390

proxy objects, 379, 389
public, 295
Published, 608
Publisher, 604
pyramid of doom, 262

Q

query events, 548
question mark, 107, 115, 180, 198, 265, 271
Quick Help, 344, 414
Quick Look a variable, 453
quotes, 92

R

random, 91
randomElement, 238
Range, 102
ranges, 102
    coercion to NSRange, 514
    indexing with, 103, 232
    iterating in reverse, 302
    partial, 103, 233, 234, 246, 265
    string, 97, 217, 514
raw pointer, 634
raw value, 139
RawRepresentable, 140
read-only variables, 75
Real, 90
recursion, 40
recursive
    initializers, 128
    references, 158
reduce, 242
refactoring, 437
reference types, 153
    memory management, 303
references, 6, 67
    functions, 61
    getting, 600
    object types, 183
        Objective-C, 639
    persisting, 304
    recursive, 158
    same object, 156, 227
    strong, 304
    unowned, 306, 585
    unsafe, 586
    weak, 305, 585
registering

app, 475
    device, 472, 475
    for a notification, 551
    for key–value observing, 567
regular expressions, 517
Related Items menu, 345
release, 579
releasing a property, 584
remove, 101, 236
removeFirst, 236
removeLast, 236
removeSubrange, 103
removeValue, 248
renamification, 645
renaming a project, 373
replaceSubrange, 103
replacing, 442
Report navigator, 343, 461
required initializers, 171, 185, 199
reserved words, 22
resolution, screen, 427
resolving a generic, 203, 209
resources, 362
    app bundle, 362
    asset catalog, 363
    dependent on build type, 424
    dependent on device type, 427
    Swift package, 367
responder, 564
    chain, 564
responds, 510
Result, 329
result of a function, 25
    ignoring, 28
retain, 579
retain count, 578
retain cycles, 303, 584
    anonymous functions, 307
    key–value observing, 588
    notifications, 587
    timers, 589
retains, unusual, 590
rethrows, 286
return, 26
    function from function, 54
    omitting, 27, 48
    type
        anonymous function, 44
        function, 26

UIApplicationMain, 371
UIBackgroundTaskIdentifier, 72
UIControl, 399, 561
UILabel, 505
UIPickerView, 560
UIResponder, 564
UISceneSession, 371, 426
UIView, 504, 548
    (see also views)
UIViewController, 504, 549
    (see also view controller)
UIWindowScene, 371
umbrella types, 223
underflow, 89
underscore
    argument label, 31
    assignment to, 28, 104
    mop-up switch case, 264
    parameter name, 34, 62
        anonymous function, 47
        property wrapper instance, 324
Unicode, 92
UnicodeScalar, 96
unique an array, 253
Unit, 524
unit tests, 456
universal app, 424
universal provisioning profile, 473
unknown default, 628
Unmanaged, 593
unowned references, 306, 585
unregistering
    for a notification, 553, 587
    for key–value observing, 568, 588
unsafe references, 586
UnsafeMutablePointer, 37, 632
UnsafeMutableRawPointer, 633
UnsafePointer, 632
    memory management, 635
UnsafeRawPointer, 633
    casting to CFTypeRef, 654
unwrapping an Optional, 108
updateValue, 248
uppercased, 95
URL, 518
User Defined Runtime Attributes, 406
user events, 548
UserDefaults, 152, 602
    nonproperty-list types in, 536

UTF-8, UTF-16, UTF-32, 96

V

value types, 153
    memory management, 311
values (dictionary), 244
var, 7, 69, 154
variables, 6, 67-82
    coercion, 86
    computed, 74
    declaration, 7, 69
        initialization, 69
        initialization, computed, 73
    façade, 76
    functions as value of, 40
    global, 9, 67
        initialization, 80
    initialization, 7
        Optional, 111
    lazy, 79
    lifetime, 8, 67
    local, 69
    read-only, 75
    scope, 67
    setter observers, 78
    stored, 74
    swapping, 104
    type, 7, 70
        vs. instance type, 175
variables list, 343, 452
variadic parameters, 34
    Objective-C, 648
version control, 429
version string, 497
video previews, 496
view controller, 378, 384
    initial, 371, 379, 384
view debugging, 454
views, 375
    drawing, 504
VIPER, 614
visibility, 12
    (see also scope)
    by instantiation, 598
    by relationship, 601
    through instance property, 597
Void, 29, 106
void, 634

About the Author

Matt Neuburg started programming computers in 1968, when he was 14 years old, as a member of a literally underground high school club, which met once a week to do timesharing on a bank of PDP-10s by way of primitive teletype machines. He also occasionally used Princeton University's IBM-360/67, but gave it up in frustration when one day he dropped his punch cards. He majored in Greek at Swarthmore College, and received his PhD from Cornell University in 1981, writing his doctoral dissertation (about Aeschylus) on a mainframe. He proceeded to teach Classical languages, literature, and culture at many well-known institutions of higher learning, most of which now disavow knowledge of his existence, and to publish numerous scholarly articles unlikely to interest anyone. Meanwhile he obtained an Apple IIc and became hopelessly hooked on computers again, migrating to a Macintosh in 1990. He wrote some educational and utility freeware, became an early regular contributor to the online journal *TidBITS*, and in 1995 left academe to edit *MacTech* magazine. In August 1996 he became a freelancer, which means he has been looking for work ever since. He is the author of *Frontier: The Definitive Guide*, *REALbasic: The Definitive Guide*, and *AppleScript: The Definitive Guide*, as well as *Programming iOS 14* (all for O'Reilly Media).

Colophon

The animal on the cover of *iOS 14 Programming Fundamentals with Swift* is a harp seal (*Pagophilus groenlandicus*), a scientific name that translates to "ice-lover from Greenland." These animals are native to the northern Atlantic and Arctic Oceans, and spend most of their time in the water, only going onto ice packs to give birth and molt. As earless ("true") seals, their streamlined bodies and energy-efficient swimming style make them well-equipped for aquatic life. While eared seal species like sea lions are powerful swimmers, they are considered semiaquatic because they mate and rest on land.

The harp seal has silvery-gray fur, with a large black marking on its back that resembles a harp or wishbone. They grow to be 5–6 feet long, and weigh 300–400 pounds as adults. Due to their cold habitat, they have a thick coat of blubber for insulation. A harp seal's diet is very varied, including several species of fish and crustaceans. They can remain underwater for an average of 16 minutes to hunt for food and are able to dive several hundred feet.

Harp seal pups are born without any protective fat, but are kept warm by their white coat, which absorbs heat from the sun. After nursing for 12 days, the seal pups are abandoned, having tripled their weight due to their mother's high-fat milk. In the subsequent weeks until they are able to swim off the ice, the pups are very vulnerable to predators and will lose nearly half of their weight. Those that survive reach maturity after 4–8 years (depending on their sex) and have an average lifespan of 35 years.

Harp seals are hunted commercially off the coasts of Canada, Norway, Russia, and Greenland for their meat, oil, and fur. Though some of these governments have regulations and enforce hunting quotas, it is believed that the number of animals killed every year is underreported. Public outcry and efforts by conservationists have resulted in a decline in market demand for seal pelts and other products, however.

Many of the animals on O'Reilly covers are endangered; all of them are important to the world.

The cover illustration is by Karen Montgomery, based on a black and white engraving from Wood's *Animate Creation*. The cover fonts are Gilroy Semibold and Guardian Sans. The text font is Adobe Minion Pro; the heading font is Adobe Myriad Condensed; and the code font is Dalton Maag's Ubuntu Mono.

O'REILLY®

There's much more where this came from.

Experience books, videos, live online training courses, and more from O'Reilly and our 200+ partners—all in one place.

Learn more at oreilly.com/online-learning